The Democratic Civilization

THE DEMOCRATIC
CIVILIZATION

LESLIE LIPSON

Professor of Political Science
University of California, Berkeley

New York   OXFORD UNIVERSITY PRESS   1964

Printed in the United States of America

To Davida and David

Preface

This is a book about a special variety of politics, the democratic, which could not have been written and published anywhere else than in a democracy. The first of my obligations, therefore, is to the principles of the political system under which I have the good fortune to live.

The research, planning, and composition have extended over many years. For the opportunity to visit and study in different democracies, and for the time required in the subsequent writing, I am deeply indebted to the officers of the Rockefeller Foundation. Without their continuing support and encouragement, this book could never have been done. To the University of California, which granted me the leave for research, and to the members of its Rockefeller Grant Committee in former years, I offer my thanks.

Portions of the research which are now combined here were published earlier in article form. For permission to use and reprint that material I thank the Editors of *The American Political Science Review*, *Political Studies*, and *La Revue Française de Science Politique*.

Several friends, all of them busy persons, were kind enough to take the trouble to read earlier drafts of certain chapters and give me the benefit of their knowledge and criticism. May I record my warm gratitude to Charles Aikin, Thomas C. Blaisdell, Lawrence Kegan, Adrienne Koch, Peter H. Odegard, Najdan Pasic, and Stefan Riesenfeld.

The academic life obliterates the distinction between one's professional commitment and what used to be called "spare time." A professor's occupation is also his constant preoccupation—a fact to which none can testify better than his immediate family. The brunt of such a *longum opus* was borne by my wife and son, to whom in a special sense the results belong. To them, therefore, I dedicate *The Democratic Civilization*.

Berkeley, California   L.L.
June 1964

Contents

PART II

The Democratic Society

dustrial Economies and Maturing Democracy — Class Relations in Nineteenth-Century Britain — Diagnoses by Disraeli, Marx, and Mill — Agrarian Roots of American Democracy — The Merger of Jefferson and Hamilton — Industrial Expansion of the United States — Big Government for Big Business — The Experience of Continental Europe — The Middle Class in France and Italy — Unifying the Germans: The Liberals or Bismarck — Weimar or Nazism — Pivotal Role of the Middle Class

9. Modern Economic Policies 230

Economic Factors Connected with Democracy — Democracy Under Agrarian Conditions — (1) The Case of Denmark — (2) The New Zealand Parallel — Is Democracy the Luxury of the Rich? — High Living Standards and Democratic States — A Warning About Causal Inferences — Capitalism, Socialism, and Democratic Government — The Dilemma of Liberalism — The Modern Mixed Economies — Public Ownership — The Social Services — Planning and Regulation — The American Economy and State Control — Contrasts in the Affluent Society — The Prestige of the Businessman — Future Responsibilities of Government

PART III

The Politics and Government of Democracy

10. The Sovereign Voters 273

Political Dynamics and Democratic Institutions — Participation by the People — Removal of Obstacles to Universal Suffrage — The Use of the Right To Vote — Reasons for Voting and Non-Voting — Effects of the Electoral System — Voting in New Zealand, A Special Case — Influence on the Vote of Parties and Campaigning — Political Implications of Mass Voting — The Education of the Public — The Frequency of Elections — The Popular Initiative and Referendum — Distrust of the Legislature

11. The Two-Party System 306

The Ancestors of Parties — Why Parties Are Essential to Democratic Government — The Causes of the Party System — The Classic Two-Party Model: Great Britain — Institutional Explanations of British Parties — (1) The Cabinet and the Power To Dissolve — (2) The Electoral System — The Social Roots of British Politics — Dualism, Religious and Economic — Response of the Parties to Industrialism — The Model Exported to Canada, New Zealand, Australia, and South Africa — Institutional Patterns of the Four Countries — Their Social Structures, from Simple to Complex — Summary of Experience in the Older Commonwealth — The Two Party-Systems of the United States — Alignments in Modern American Politics

12. Politics with Many Parties 350

Characteristics of Multipartism — Reasons for the Swiss Party System — Formation of the Parties Before World War I — How the Electoral System Originally Operated —

PART IV

The Democratic Values

The Democratic Civilization

1

Introduction

The strenuous times in which we live confront the human race with more than an ordinary challenge. While mankind is still divided by profound contrasts in material advancement and technical skill, in political system and quality of civilization, we are rapidly extending our physical knowledge—and thereby our mastery—of the planet that is our home. Long before we have learned to inhabit it sociably, with ever lengthening reach we probe the limits of the Earth's atmosphere and have begun to voyage in the vastness of the space beyond. As the crossing of oceans in the sixteenth century projected dynasties and empires into rivalry on fresh continents, so now does disunited humanity brandish its several torches in this, the relay race of the universe. Already Man's newest machines have propelled him into the measureless void, hurtling at a speed whose only bounds are set by the capacities of his intellect and the energy of the atom, to begin a journey whose end no eye can see nor mind foretell.

New Conditions and Old Notions

So spectacular are these events and possibilities that the student of social affairs who witnesses them cannot fail to bestir himself anew with the problems of his own domain. It is evident that the progress of science is already requiring major readjustments in many of our inherited institutions, social relationships, and accepted beliefs. The nation-state, for instance, continues to provide the structural form through which the contacts between governments and the political sentiments of entire peoples are made. Yet, a generation which remembers the two world wars and the world depression has evidence enough that no nation-state, not even the mightiest, is adequate by itself to guarantee for its citizens the economic well being and physical security which are the twin aims of foreign policy. Functioning as the primary unit of political organization, the nation-state has become as ill-adapted to modern needs, and therefore as surely doomed to disappear, as the *Polis* of the Greeks to the age of Philip and Alexander. The concept of sovereignty once served as a convenient tool for the strong monarchs who simultaneously repressed the parochial nobility within their borders and resisted the Papacy and Holy Roman Empire without. It has little relevance for a century in which interdependence, not independence, is the condition of survival and progress. The political cartography of frontiers, military doctrines about bases for defense and offense, such legal formulae as that of territorial waters inside a three-mile limit—these, if never perfectly clarified, could receive in an earlier age enough precision to be useful workaday guides for policy. But how can they be made to embrace the hydrogen bomb, intercontinental rocket, and space satellite? Notions about the individual and his enterprise made more sense in a former stage of development when practically all organization was small, the state as well as business. But they are incongruous with the modern Leviathans —corporate, trade-union, and governmental. The simple theory of the relation between a representative and his constituents has never been harmonized with the growth of disciplined parties; just as the ideal picture of the informed adult making intelligent choices is belied by propagandists at every election and is daily mocked by the advertisers of commercial products. The world's religions summon people to worship their gods and prophet of many names. The priesthoods expound the sacred books, repeat ancestral liturgies, and preach their credos. Yet, though countless individuals thereby obtain emotional satisfaction or self-abandonment or security, religion has never proved its indispensable assumption—that a deity exists—or reconciled the tenets of faith with the data of reason. The discoveries of medical research have so far outstripped the traditional structure of the medical profession that in many countries health, nay even life, may prove too costly for families to buy. Meanwhile, the educational systems that were framed for the aristocrats or middle classes or were planned under ecclesiastical control have been extended by public means to all children in areas that cherish an equalitarian ideal and tax themselves to apply it. How different abilities should be differently trained, however, and how the curricula should be varied to prepare for adult life in our complex society are problems still unsolved.

These and similar instances can be cited of the familiar lag between an altered reality and the necessary social adaptation of deed and dogma. But it would be wrong to imply that all the forward movement is scientific and technical, while everything social drags lamely behind. On the contrary, some impressive gains have been recorded on the social side of our civilization; and, though certain of these undoubtedly are linked to the onrush of science, many were independently inspired and others again have provided the stimulus for exertions by the scientists. Thus, the mass electorate of the modern democracy, endowed with universal adult suffrage, has no precedent in the previous history of mankind. The process of liquidating colonial empires, although its success creates new difficulties, makes it possible that peoples of varied race and culture may eventually consort together in dignity and equality. In scores of communities a humane regard for welfare has reduced for millions the prospect of prolonged poverty or premature death. Thanks to the attack on illiteracy and the steady raising of the school-leaving age, thanks also to the opportunities which the mass media of communication afford, the cultural treasures of the human race can be diffused for wider enjoyment than ever before. Likewise, new institutions have been invented or ancient ones drastically remodeled to enable the state to discharge its heavier responsibilities. A few examples are: the device of federal union, whereby larger groupings and regions may combine under the framework of a single government; the development of international organization; the permanent civil service, recruited by merit and offering its members a life's career; the collection of revenue by equitable tax procedures; and the use of regularly gathered statistical data as a basis for public policy.

What This Book Is About

If one holds, with Bacon, that the function of learning is "the relief of man's estate," then the scholar's duty at this moment in the passage of history is plain. He should do the one thing he can do well, and what he alone is equipped to do. He must study the past, observe the present, estimate the future, reflect, analyze, systematize, and counsel. Thought by itself, as Aristotle observed, moves nothing. But thought is the necessary prelude to choice and decision. Should it succeed in arousing the imagination and evoking enough feeling, it will lead to practical results. The dichotomy, so often bruited, between thought and action, between theory and practice, is a false one. Thinking is a form of action; and action of any kind presupposes or implies a thought. Theory is the generalization of concrete practices; while every practice, indeed anything that works, embodies its latent principle.

In writing this book, I have two principal themes. These are: to examine the democratic form of government and appraise it, and, along with this, to suggest a general theory of the political process. The method employed will be comparative throughout.

The Democratic Record

Its antiquity and modernity alike make democracy a worthy subject for restudy. Organized, and first explicitly discussed, in the Athenian *Polis* of the fifth century B.C., democracy has passed through many phases and vicissitudes and has appeared in several guises. Some have seen in it a revolutionary challenge to constituted authority and vested interest; a symbol of defiance, protest, and liberation; an onslaught upon privilege and class. Others have taken it for granted, accepting its existence as a part of the established order into which they were born and which a placid conservatism sustained. In certain periods, democracy was a rare and curious freak to be noted and described by its contemporaries largely because it was exceptional. In others it lived on only as a literary memory, recorded in the pages of historians, dramatists, and philosophers, who were mostly its critics. Democratic institutions and ideals have known both triumph and setback. After a long obsolescence, they received a second birth in the seventeenth and eighteenth centuries, throve vigorously and on the whole victoriously in the nineteenth, and in the twentieth emerged (though not unscathed) on the winning side of the two global wars in which the democratic ideal was among the issues of combat. Its opponents have included the aristocrats and oligarchs of the ancient world, the medieval nobility and its latter-day descendants, the absolute monarchs of the sixteenth and seventeenth centuries, the merchant-princes of virtually all eras since the power of the people threatened their riches, the majority of the heads of organized religions, the commanders of practically every army in the past and of most of them in the present, and the twentieth-century species of dictator, both fascist and communist. Democracy has been associated with various economies, agrarian no less than industrial, primitive no less than advanced, abundant no less than poor. It has been adapted to countries as small as Iceland, Norway, or New Zealand; or to Great Britain at the height of her power and pomp; or to a population and terrain as vast as the present-day United States. Militarily, it has been founded among both the potent and the weak. Culturally, it has flourished in communities as homogeneous in language and religion as the Danes or Swedes and among those as diversified as the Canadians and the Swiss.

When one considers how great has been the range of democracy in space and time and culture, the truth is readily apparent that no two democracies are cut to precisely the same pattern. The dissimilarities of democratic systems constitute one of the fundamental facts for analysis. As the ensuing chapters will reveal, there is a host of contrasted institutions and procedures all of which with equal validity may be labelled democratic. The framework of the governmental structure, the processes of the party system, the meaning and priorities assigned to the different "operative ideals,"[1] relations between the citizens and their officials, the character of the social order with which the political order is intertwined —on each of these major matters the democracies are markedly at variance. For instance, the democratic states include both the unitary and federal. Some have the presidential executive, some the collegial, others the cabinet type. The party systems may comprise the minimum number of two, or extend to six and even more. Electoral methods can differ as greatly as do proportional representation, preferential voting, and single-member districts with victory by a bare plurality. Democracy can be combined with highly socialized economies, which have a considerable volume of public ownership, state planning and regulation, and social services, or with an economy that retains a larger amount of unregulated capitalism and leaves a wider sphere to the private profit-seeker. The philosophies which democrats propound may place their stress on liberty, while others may emphasize equality. Some have identified democracy with individualism, others with the public interest; with minority rights, or with majority rule. Hence one learns about the nature of democracy by observing and evaluating the numerous constructions that may be placed upon a democratic philosophy, and the equally plentiful blueprints from which the machinery of a democratic state may be constructed. Comparisons must therefore be drawn not only between democratic and non-democratic systems, but also among the democracies themselves. In this way one will discover how much democracy has changed in the course of its evolution and how much it exhibits of continuity and consistency; how much may be altered without sacrifice of essentials, and just what these essentials are.

A form of government which in the course of twenty-four centuries has been practiced in so many states, which has contributed so much to the political development of mankind, and which therefore incorporates so large a segment of human history, possesses intrinsic importance to merit re-examination without further argument or justification. But a writer owes it also to his readers that he state in candor, what indeed the follow-

1. This is the phrase of A. D. Lindsay in *The Modern Democratic State* (Oxford University Press, 1943), Chap. 1.

ing pages will show, that no such study is wholly objective and that his own preferences cannot be altogether excluded from the analysis. I write about democracy because I believe in it; because I think it at its best the noblest of the political systems that men have thus far devised; because even when corrupted—as corrupted it can be—its defects are less grievous and less painfully cured than are the evils of opposite systems; because it has survived through revolution and reaction and has withstood the perils of prosperity and depression, of peace and of war; because from Plato to Hitler, from Aristophanes to Stalin, it has met and confounded its foes, because it continues in our era to confront the fresh challenges of being applied to Asian and African environments and to international organization; because, in a word, it is rich in achievement and pregnant yet with hope.

The General Nature of Politics

The subject of democracy, however, requires discussion of the broad topic to which it is inseparably bound. There are numerous systems of government; there are various philosophies of the state. Democracy is one among several. It never was, and even now is not, the form of government that reigns over the majority of mankind. Whatever one's wishes may be, the truth is that democracy, surveyed historically and internationally, is far from embracing the whole of politics. It is a type or class within a broader category. In this category—the political—every species has distinguishing features which mark it out for what it is and demarcate it from others. But a species also shares in the characteristics of its genus. Thus, whatever is true of politics in general must necessarily apply to any of its particular manifestations. Expressed in other terms, this means that it is impossible to interpret democracy and not to presuppose a general theory of politics; and since to make implications explicit is an aid to intellectual clarity, a basic analysis of politics must be attempted here.

The theory of politics around which this book is written can be briefly summarized. Every state consists of the mingling of three elements: the social context, its politics and institutional framework, and philosophical ideals.

The Social Materials

The first of these recognizes the truth that the state is an integral part of society in the largest sense. To study it in abstract strips away much of the meaning. To divorce it from its surrounding environment distorts the realities which condition its character. What is then seen is not the state, but something else—utopia, perhaps, or a caricature, or a set of algebraic symbols. One can never insist too often on the point that the political process always functions within a social process, affected by it and, of course, acting upon it. Except it be projected, therefore, onto a screen wide enough to include its intimate connections, the state cannot be understood at all. Hence, a student of politics must, first and foremost, be a student of society. How then does society impinge upon the state? The answer is that it does so through any or all of its component factors, interacting with the political system both severally and together. Society is the name for the sum-total of human relationships, associations, and institutions. All these originate in needs whose fulfillment requires union and whose continued satisfaction creates interests. For such interests to be mobilized and to endure, there must be a recognizable point of reference around which a group can cluster and cohere. In this way, corresponding to the needs from which they spring and the interests they generate, there develop the many groupings with which the social order is interlaced.

Swift tells in *Gulliver's Travels* about the political affairs of the state of Lilliput, where the citizens had organized themselves into two factions. The principle over which they disagreed concerned the way to shell a boiled egg. One faction cracked its eggs at the larger end; its opponents, at the smaller. (Lilliput apparently contained no "middle-of-the-shellers," or, if it did, Swift forgot to mention them.) Feeling between Big-Endians and Little-Endians mounted so high that neither could tolerate the other. Civil war ensued and the defeated side was driven into exile. There, dissected down to its hard skeleton, is the anatomy of the political process. Anything social can constitute a starting-point for politics and be relevant to the governance of the state, when it is identifiable, when it is organized, and when it arouses sufficient feeling. Thus, the nature of politics will be influenced, more or less directly, by the patterns of kinship, be they built around the household, family, or clan; by the material resources available for human use, the organization of labor in their production, and the distribution of its fruits; by the geography of Man's habitat, the dictates of its climate, soil, and water, and its relation with areas remote and near; by the languages that people speak, the religions whose deities they worship, the racial stock they inherited; by the education which has molded their minds, informed their intellects, and imparted their beliefs. To none of these can politics be ever alien.

Creative Government

Originating within the matrix of society, it is these issues, needs, and groupings whose harmony or conflict, whose fluidity or solidity, gives the political process its core and substance. But if society breeds the situations which politics seeks to regulate, the latter serves in its turn as the generator of the institutions and procedures of the state. Government itself belongs among our primary social needs. It is no less fundamental than wealth, land, kin, and the rest. Mankind cannot abide in anarchy. Some structure, some order, some system, must be given to our relationships; and this, however we describe the institution that organizes and enforces it, is central to the functions of government. How this occurs can be illustrated with the analogy of a dam. A dam is constructed on a river to control the speed and volume of the onward flow. Instead of being wastefully dissipated or uselessly concentrated, the life-giving water can be distributed by irrigation pipes and canals to the areas where it is most needed. But not only that. A dam can be so built as to harness the energy that passes through it and turn this into electric power. Conservation, conversion, and creation are the products of a single act. With its spillways and turbines, the dam is not merely the recipient of a dynamic which other forces have produced. By governing, it creates. And the very design of the machinery bears directly upon the result. Floods can be prevented, power can be produced, with an efficiency channeled into socially useful purposes. Or alternatively, the structure may be badly designed and the system poorly run, with consequences that are dangerous and even destructive.

Similar to this are the workings of the state. In its relation to the rest of society, the state serves as a conduit through which other forces flow. Family and language, race and religion, economy and ecology—these are tributaries whose currents converge within the stream of politics and then pass into the power-complex of the state. At this point, the state adds the further force which its own functions supply—evolving, as these do, from protection into order and justice and thence to welfare and civilization. For governing is a creative act. From its own power and purposes, it generates a dynamic and produces relationships which were not there before and would not otherwise exist. The institutions through which governments operate and the policies they pursue are a response to the social complex in which they are situated. (Whenever they cease to correspond and the disharmony becomes excessive, a revolution occurs in some fashion or other.) But it is also the nature of these institutions that they develop an inner life of their own, conforming to the requirements of their structure. The players in a game of golf or chess or bridge will estimate the contours of the course, or the relation of the pieces, or the distribution of the cards; and then, obedient to the limitations of the rules, will calculate the probabilities and employ the strategy that seems to their best advantage. Likewise, the patterns of political behavior are shaped into governmental forms that derive, first, from the social content on which politics feeds and, second, from the design of the institutions and the character of the instruments and materials at hand.

Ideal Goals

Into the political process, however, there enters—besides the social context and governmental framework—a third ingredient. This consists of the philosophical principles which are formulated in general terms, though with reference to specific situations. The state, as it exists subjectively in the mental and emotional consciousness of its citizens, is more than a system of institutions and services, or an elite of power-seeking politicians, or a mass of voting statistics. It is also a set of ideas and ideals. *Homo politicus* has the intellectual need to interpret the structures he builds in terms that satisfy his reason, as well as the moral need to justify them to his conscience. The role that a philosophy plays in politics is immediate and important; and the philosopher, though frequently criticized for keeping his head in the clouds, actually has his feet more firmly planted on the ground than is usually recognized.

Perhaps an example will explain the proximity of *Cloudcuckooland* to *Terra Firma*. A government, let us say, indulges in practices which touch directly on the lives and interests of its citizens. It quarters troops on a town and billets the soldiers in private homes. It collects revenue by a method it has decreed without consulting any representative of those who pay the taxes. It makes forcible and sudden entry into people's houses; arrests its critics and throws them into jail; keeps them there without trial; or holds a trial secretly without adequate opportunities for defense. Such actions breed resentment and opposition. People wish to be rid of them. They demand freedom from this abuse, freedom from that one, freedom from all the others. They draft a document in which they spell out their demands. This they may entitle Magna Carta, Petition of Right, Declaration of the Rights of Man and the Citizen, or what you will. They inveigh against specific abuses and invoke specific freedoms. And then they take an intellectual leap of the utmost significance. They generalize their particulars, abstracting a collective noun from the enumeration of singulars. Besides asserting their rights, they plead that Right be done. As redress for injustices, they shout for Justice. They list the freedoms they desire and call this Freedom. Next, as in Euclidean geometry after positing axioms and definitions one reasons about the properties of a triangle, so the philosophers speculate about political concepts delivering therefrom by a "Socratic midwifery" all the content their logic allows. Finally, they proceed deductively to apply the broad symbol to concrete situations that were not included on the original list. Thomas Jefferson, a Virginian and an opponent of human slavery, can proclaim on a nation's birth certificate "that all men are created equal." Ninety-two years afterward, to this nation's Constitution is added the amending clause that no State shall "deny to any person within its jurisdiction the equal protection of the laws." In another eighty-six years, the Supreme Court unanimously interprets this to mean that children of all races shall be educated together in the same schools.

Philosophy, then, is not distinct from the political process, but an integral part thereof. Ideals, however, stand in two opposite relations to the other aspects of politics. Society, as existing at any given time, is both the product of the past and the precursor of the future. Neither tradition alone nor change alone, but both together, are the law of its being. All communities in every epoch, therefore, embody contrary tendencies: one to preserve, the other to progress. Both are represented by the philosophers. Aristotle, Confucius, or Thomas Aquinas expresses in systematic form the ideas that typify his age; and his authority—"the Master of them that know," "the Sage," "the Angelic Doctor"—is then used further to bolster and sanctify the system. Others are the rebels—Plato, Rousseau, Marx— who consider Man corrupt and perverted and propose to straighten him out by revolutionizing his institutions. Thus, the role of philosophers in politics is ambivalent, since partly they supply a coherent rationality to the world of the actual, and partly they point as a signpost to distant, more perfect goals not yet achieved. But in one respect the two groups are alike, for they share a resemblance which is inherent in the nature of all philosophies. Actuality never exactly corresponds with logic. Logic is able to project itself beyond reality by feats of extrapolation. Any existing society is a complex of conflicting principles, checking one another and counterchecked in turn. It is the function of philosophy to develop in the fullness of thought what is potential, but limited, in fact. Philosophy clarifies the location of the halfway houses in which we reside by indicating the direction of the journey's end. Philosophy strives for consistency; actuality is inconsistent. Philosophy perfects; actuality remains imperfect. Philosophy completes; actuality is forever incomplete.

The fusion of these factors—the social context, governmental framework, and philosophical ideals—constitutes the political process. The state can be envisaged as a broker or intermediary which adjusts social issues in terms of philosophical alternatives, and, conversely adapts the desirable to the contingencies of the practicable. To examine each factor in turn and in combination, and thus interpret democracy in the light of this analysis of politics, is the purpose of this book. The chapters are accordingly grouped in a sequence which follows this pattern. The first section traces the historical evolution of the criteria of democracy and the appraisal of its ideals. The next part inquires into the characteristics of the social order which contribute to democracy or impede it. The third section explores the role of the people in democratic politics and the governmental institutions of a democratic state. The fourth part continues the discussion of philosophical values, seeking to assess their modern meaning and significance. The final chapter attempts a synthesis of the relations between society, government, and philosophy which form the core of politics.

The Use of Comparisons

To study so massive a subject, the method I have used is the comparative one. The advantages to be gained from this approach are many. Comparisons, to begin with, extent one's range of information. At the Lyceum, it will be remembered, Aristotle directed the study of one hundred and fifty-eight political systems, whose data provided material for the analysis, and evidence for the argument, of his *Politics*. One's theme waxes strong with what it feeds upon. How much lengthier, then, and how varied, is the menu from which the modern researcher can select! The twenty-two centuries which have elapsed since the *Politics* was written contain a diet whose ingredients are overwhelmingly rich and should be judiciously tasted, but of whose savor one cannot tire. Each people and period that is studied has novel features to add, since all human experience contains something unique. Indeed, it is false to assert that "history repeats itself." It never did; it never can.

Instead of describing various democracies in turn, I have arranged the subject matter analytically by the topics into which it subdivides. Hence, although the book ranges over the principal examples of democracy, both large and small, ancient and contemporary, each chapter picks its examples from the countries whose experience is specially pertinent to the problem under review. The cases which can tell us most, for instance, about the effects of land power or sea power on democracy are not necessarily the same as those which throw light on its connection with religious tolerance or the welfare state. Different countries are therefore selected for closer treatment in different chapters. Also, in order to clarify the character of democracy and the circumstances which sustain it, I have pointed the contrast, wherever appropriate, with non-democratic regimes—e.g., Russia, Prussia, Spain—or with the mixed and indeterminate politics of such a country as Brazil. Because the modern democracies have evolved out of oligarchical antecedents, and because each has matured through different stages and at different rates, I have drawn heavily on the historical record. The present cannot be understood except in relation to the past from which it has grown, and much will be learned about the formative conditions of a democracy by observing the same country at various phases in its development. In particular, the past experiences of communities which now succeed in governing themselves democratically are relevant to those who are venturing along this path today. No people comes to democracy easily, simply, or quickly.

A comparative method throws its light from many angles. Setting side by side a number of political systems reveals their differences and their similarities. Comparison strengthens generalization and explains the exception. It prevents one from taking everywhere for granted what happens momentarily to have been settled in one's own country or culture. It liberates from the dogmatism of single-track thought. It invites appraisal, evaluation, and critical judgment. Not only does this method clarify the answers to the question "how is politics conducted?," but it invites speculation about the causes which have produced the observed results. In addition, after observing a number of countries, one is forced to face the question: Which system is the best? A comparative study of politics finds its natural culmination in a series of ethical judgments. For after assembling and classifying the data, and elucidating the how and the why, we are bound to ask: How good is it? This query involves a reference to the ideal goals which are posited through political philosophy. By their degree of approximation to those ideals we judge the actual states of past and present.

Democracy as a Civilizing Force

The canvas, therefore, on which I am painting this portrait of democracy is broad, and the coloration is ethical. Such a treatment accords properly with a conception of the purposes which politics is intended to serve in democratic states. The object we seek in society is to attain a higher level of civilization. The latter, although depending on knowledge and techniques by which we master our physical environment, consists primarily in the values by which we choose to live. For the distinguishing mark of a civilization is the values which men select, and our success or failure in organizing to attain them. In this process, the role of government is central and indispensable. The fundamental purpose of the democratic state is a moral one. It is to contribute through political activity to human civilization. What we may learn from the study of democratic politics is how governments assist in making humanity more civilized and how misgovernment serves to brutalize and degrade. I have entitled this book *The Democratic Civilization* because I believe that the democratic form of government has brought to the civilizing of humanity a quality which is unique. This is achieved through that union of characteristics—social, political and philosophical—which this book seeks to analyze. Where successfully compounded, their result is the civilization of Democratic Man.

I

The Criteria of Democracy

2

The Classical Tradition

"Call no man happy," ran the Greek maxim, "until he is dead." Similarly, at the outset of a long inquiry, a writer should caution himself: "Define nothing, until you have reached the last page." This is a sensible rule, since definitions, which are almost meaningless at the beginning, become superfluous at the end and can then be eliminated. But in lieu of definition one needs some preliminary sketch, some outline of fundamentals, or delineation of character. It is not wise to reconnoiter in a vast region without a compass and what passes for a map. When we speak of democracy, we should have some idea of what it means. Otherwise, how can it be recognized, when found? Also, the use of the term logically implies both inclusion and exclusion. To certain systems the label of democracy can be applied, but not to others. For the latter, because their nature differs, we employ other categories, such as oligarchy or dictatorship. As a minimum, therefore, we should start with a series of criteria—criteria in the plural, not a criterion in the singular, since something as complex as democracy cannot be reduced to the simplicity of a single principle.

The problem for this chapter is hard to solve, but is easily stated. What are the essential traits of a democracy? What tests, what basic conditions, must a political system satisfy if it is to qualify for the description, democratic? The best way to answer such questions is to examine communities which have considered themselves democratic and have been so regarded by others. By now, sufficient demonstrations exist of democracy in practice to allow the selection of criteria from the record of a rich experience. To understand the categories in which our thought is cast today, and suggest the alterations which future perspectives demand, one must commence with the usages that our past has bequeathed. And to discover these there is no surer guide than history. What, then, does the historical record reveal?

The Athenian Origins

The house of democracy in modern times has many mansions. But its foundations were laid in Greece. The word, democracy, is Greek. The system which it describes developed first among the Greeks and matured between the sixth and fourth centuries B.C., notably in the powerful state of Athens. In the histories of Herodotus and Thucydides; the dramas of Aeschylus, Sophocles, and Euripides; the satirical comedies of Aristophanes; the public orations of Demosthenes and Isocrates; the philosophies of Socrates, Plato, and Aristotle; the buildings, artworks, coins, and inscriptions which have survived both plunder and neglect—there, the living past may still be observed in its pristine vigor. Other states certainly existed before Athens which possessed some democratic features, for nothing political that is wholly new ever emerges at one time and place. But in their case, either too little is known to warrant a full description, or they retained too many non-democratic elements along with the democratic, or they were small and relatively insignificant and stayed obscure. Athens deserves its reputation of being democracy's birthplace. From Solon's time to Demosthenes, it was the Athenians who created democracy. During those two and a half centuries they did more to construct and operate the machinery of a democratic government than is known to have occurred elsewhere before the seventeenth century. They created democracy by theorizing about its principles and inventing its institutions. Any Greek who referred to democracy from the Persian Wars onward had Athens in mind, since there lay the model and archetype for all Hellas.

Moreover, and most important, the Athenians became fully aware of what it was they were doing. Their artists, intellectuals, political leaders, and creative spirits (and also non-Athenians, like Herodotus and Aristotle, who were drawn to the city because of its brilliance) consciously engaged in a lively debate over the principles of a good society and their application. Fertile with ideas, ingenious and restless in spirit, they reasoned and argued. Nor does this mean that their inquiries ended in agreement. Far from it. The Athenian intelligentsia and statesmen were acutely split over the merits of democracy. Praise for it and condemnation, enthusiasm and dread, were voiced with equal eloquence. This process of a continual discussion was the core of their civic life—so much so that on occasion, as in modern France, an avidity for logic produced paralysis in policy and sheer cleverness prohibited the decisions of common sense. Yet this same discussion which they conducted as the designers and practitioners of democracy, and as its eulogists and critics, was their education in the arts of life: Through this their city became, as Pericles pronounced it, "the educator of Hellas."[1] More than that, the inspirational tone of Athenian civic culture has continued to educate the generations down to our own. Nothing has been achieved in democracy's name since the fourth century B.C., which has not incurred some debt to the people of the Owl-Goddess. Indeed, a survey of their democracy will demonstrate that its criteria correspond in many particulars with any twentieth-century formulation. From this one may deduce either that antiquity was truly advanced, or that modernity has invented little, or perhaps that the chief problem of democracy throughout the ages has been, not how to conceptualize, but how to practice it.

The Historians' Judgment: (1) Herodotus and the Persians

Since the Greeks contributed so vigorously to this debate which they started, their authors should speak for themselves and say in their own words what they took democracy to mean. After they have spoken, a summary view of their opinions will be possible. The first in chronological order was Herodotus of Halicarnassus. Thanks to an inquisitive and far-ranging mind, his history of the wars between the Greeks and the Persians becomes a vehicle for much more. Into it he pours his store of information—diffuse, yet extraordinarily fascinating—about the folklore, customs, and politics of the peoples around the eastern shores of the Mediterranean and in the Middle East. Historiography gropes its way toward political science in the celebrated passage where Herodotus evaluates the three forms of government with which his contemporaries were acquainted.[2] It is here that romancing concedes to reasoning, personalities give way to principles, and the annalist evolves into the analyst. Here, too, his imagination fired and his intellect stimulated by the differences he has discovered between Egypt, Scythia, Lydia, Persia, and Greece, Herodotus inaugurates the comparative method.

The occasion is provided by the uprising in 522 B.C. of seven Persian nobles against a Median pretender to the imperial throne. Having assassinated him, and needing to reorganize the government, the conspirators debate what form it should take. The historian admits that some Greeks

1. Thucydides, *Histories*, Bk. II, 41.
2. *Histories*, Bk. III, 80-82.

doubt whether the discussion really occurred, but himself asserts in emphatic language that it did.[3] The arguments are couched in three parallel speeches, which together survey three political systems. Each speaker advocates the merits of one type and stresses the demerits of one other. The three-fold classification did not originate with Herodotus, for there are allusions to it in earlier writers. But it is he who first discusses it systematically and at some length. The classification is based upon a single question: in how many hands is supreme power lodged? The answer expresses the results of elementary arithmetic combined with actual observation. Supreme power may belong to One, to a Few, or to Many. The corresponding systems are accordingly described as Monarchy, Aristocracy, and Democracy. The case for democracy—here argued for the first time, and voiced by a Persian in the writing of a Greek from Asia Minor—is stated thus: "When the multitude rules, firstly it bears the finest name of all: equality of the laws. Second, it does none of those acts which a monarch commits. The multitude distributes offices by lot, makes its officials responsible, and conducts all deliberations where all can take part."[4] Elsewhere, Herodotus specifies another principle of democracy. He comments on the fact that the Athenians won some military successes and expanded their power soon after they had put an end to the dictatorial regime of the sons of Peisistratus. The difference he attributes to their change in motivation. When they were ruled by a despot, they had no wish to exert themselves at his command; but, having made themselves free, each responded to the exertions of his own individual will. "This proves," he remarks, "not in one respect, but in all, that equality of speech is an excellent thing to have."[5]

But Herodotus is not content to leave it at that. Along with the favorable argument he presents the criticism of these same criteria. Not only is this appropriate to his subject, since democracy, which lays such stress on freedom and discussion, invites attention to its own defects; but it is also the necessary *modus operandi* of a Greek intellectual who thinks and writes dialectically and is constrained to balance every "pro" with its re-

3. *Ibid.*, 80.
4. *Ibid.* Here, and elsewhere, the translations from the Greek authors are my own. The word which I have rendered as "equality of the laws" is *isonomia*. J. L. Myres prefers the etymology, "equality of apportionment." See *The Political Ideas of the Greeks* (The Abingdon Press: New York, 1927), p. 355. A. E. Zimmern translates it "fair play." *The Greek Commonwealth* (Clarendon Press: Oxford, 1931), p. 130.
5. *Op. cit.*, Bk. V, 78. What is referred to here in Greek as "equality of speech" (*isegoria*) is generally called "freedom of speech" in modern democracies. To some Greeks equality was more fundamental than freedom and the latter was considered a derivative from the former. For the relation between the two concepts, see Chapter 16.

lated "con." Here, then, are the criteria of the same democracy, as an aristocratic opponent sees them: "Nothing is more stupid or more prone to excess than a useless crowd. It is intolerable that men who seek to escape the excesses of a tyrant should fall into the excesses of an intemperate people. At least the tyrant does whatever he does knowingly. But the people cannot even know what they do. For, how can they be knowledgeable who have neither been taught nor have observed anything that is fine or fitting? The people rush in violently and force matters on without intelligence, like a river in full flood."[6] Thus, ignorance and unbridled violence appear as the stigmata of a democracy to an advocate of government by the best (*aristoi*) who includes in this category himself and the other nobles present.[7]

The context and mood that inspired Herodotus are revealed in the intention expressed in the opening sentence of his work. He plans, he says, to tell of "great and wondrous deeds" performed by Greeks and Persians. Yet his own sympathies lie clearly with the Greeks, and among political systems his own preference is for democracy. Both his theme and his handling of it have the sweep of an epic. He tells of the clash between the two vigorous cultures, expanding in the eastern Mediterranean; he describes the Greek settlements around the coast of Asia Minor, the consolidation of the Middle East in a Persian-controlled empire, the invasion of Greece by Persia, and the victorious Greek resistance. This, and not the Trojan War of Homer's poem, was the true heroic age of Hellas. It was at this time, in the face of their external and formidable foe, that the perennially quarrelsome city-states reached their highest point of co-operation and unity. The valor of the Spartan hoplites and the gallantry of the Athenian seamen, combining together, preserved Greek independence for another century and a half—in fact, until Philip accomplished what Xerxes could not. The generation that still warmed to the afterglow of Marathon, Thermopylae, and Salamis is mindful most of the contrast between Hellene and "barbarian," and to stress it is felt almost as a patriotic duty.[8] Consequently, the differences that did acutely divide the Hellenes, though not ignored, receive less prominence. The Ionian from Halicarnassus is a child of this generation.[9]

---

6. *Op. cit.*, Bk. III, 81.
7. *Ibid.* "For we ourselves will be included among the best."
8. Aeschylus, who fought at Marathon, Salamis, and Plataea, dramatizes this feeling in his play, *The Persians*, a literary act of civic pride comparable in temper to Shakespeare's *Henry* V.
9. Herodotus was born in 484 B.C., six years after Marathon and four years before Salamis.

(2) *Thucydides and Pericles*

The next formulation of criteria is also the work of a historian, who, appropriately, was Athenian: Thucydides. He moves, however, in a different world. The circumstances in which he wrote, the subject itself, and his personality, all lend themselves to an altered outlook. Where Herodotus is a mixture of epic poet and itinerant anthropologist, Thucydides belongs rather to clinical psychology and the tragedians. His topic also is war: but a war of Greek against Greek, a war between two mighty coalitions led, respectively, by the erstwhile allies, Athens and Sparta; of the bitterness and fruitlessness of war between city and city, and the savage ferocity of the war between the factions within. A reader of Herodotus finishes in a soaring mood of exhilaration. Thucydides leaves one brooding over a record of willful self-destruction, speculating why an era of intellectual and aesthetic creativeness squandered its genius in a ruinous act of political nihilism.[10] During the agony of this Peloponnesian War that lasted for twenty-seven years (431–404 B.C.), Athenian democracy degenerated under cumulative strain and desperation of expedient. From the statesmanship of Cleisthenes and Pericles it is a sharp descent to the excesses of Cleon and the moral rot of Alcibiades. Nor should it be overlooked that the man who writes that history has a personal ground for resentment against the extremists who brought Athens to her defeat. When commanding an Athenian force in northern Greece (424 B.C.), he was outsmarted by his Spartan opponent and failed, by one day's margin, to secure control of the strategic city of Amphipolis. Doubtless because he expected retribution if he returned to Athens, he chose voluntary exile—and thereby gained the leisure to collect his data and write his book. A lucky case, as it happened, in which a man's failure in one sphere permitted his triumph in another!

The *locus classicus* in Thucydides for the favorable version of democracy's essentials is, of course, the address which Pericles delivered at the state funeral for those who fell in the first year's campaigning.[11] This was one of those solemn public rites at which on rare occasions an inspired orator rises above the trite. Like Lincoln at Gettysburg, this Athenian

---

10. For the nearest historical parallel one should look at the city-states of northern Italy during the Renaissance. There, too, was the same extraordinary combination of brilliance of the creative spirit and murderous, self-destroying, politics. See Jacob Burckhardt, *The Civilization of the Renaissance in Italy.*

11. Bk. II, 35-46. The whole speech is well translated in Zimmern, *op. cit.*, pp. 200-209.

aristocrat, the first servant of the democracy, is moved to noble utterance by the union of mind and faith. Pericles does more than praise the dead. He gives their sacrificing a meaning and a reason. They died for the city they held dear, and of which they were a part. They loved it for the ideals which had enriched their lives, and these were beautiful.[12] "We use a political system," said Pericles, "which does not emulate our neighbors' laws. Rather than copy others, it is we who set the example. Our system is called a Democracy because it is conducted by the Many, not the Few. In our private disagreements, the laws provide equality of rights for all. But in the civic sphere, our estimate of an individual's worth accords the higher honor, not for his status, but for the skill he displays in some field of distinction. Nor indeed is a poor man, who has anything good to confer on the city, prevented from service by obscurity of reputation. We govern our common affairs as befits free men . . . while we come together in private business without giving offence. In public matters we do not transgress, since we are obedient to both officials and laws—those laws especially which are established to succor the wronged and the unwritten precepts whose breach is acknowledged a disgrace.[13] . . . Our love of beauty does not make us squanderers; our love of wisdom does not soften us. We employ wealth as an opportunity more for deeds than boastful talk. Nor is it a disgrace to admit that one is poor; the greater disgrace is to fail to escape from poverty by work. Our people find it possible to take care, at the same time, of their personal and civic interests, and others who are occupied with labor can have adequate knowledge about their government. For when a person takes no part in his government, only we condemn him as useless—instead of praising him for minding his own business."[14]

Pericles delivered his panegyric in 431 B.C. The next year, when some military defeats had tarnished the luster of his war strategy and the Great Plague brough panic to a metropolis overcrowded with refugees from the countryside, the people stripped him of authority, then indicted and fined him in the courts. The year following, re-elected to office for the last time, as if in belated vindication, the man who had spoken in praise of his city fell victim to the same epidemic, which had already taken two of his sons, and died. Athens was never again so great as in the years when

---

12. To the aesthetically sensitive Greek, Beauty and Goodness are inextricable concepts. Goodness is beautiful and Beauty is good. Even the phrase, *kaloskagathos*, which is their nearest to the ideal of "the gentleman," means literally: "he who is beautiful and good."

13. Bk. II, 37.

14. *Ibid.*, 40.

this statesman, an aristocrat by antecedents and quality, devoted his political genius to the cause of the democracy. Indeed, one may well ask
whether the secret of Athenian success may not have lain in this very
combination—a combination seldom produced, yet irresistible when
found, and one so fortunately repeated in the twentieth century when two
other such aristocrats, Winston Churchill and Franklin D. Roosevelt, presided at the same critical hour over the two most powerful democracies of
the modern world.

Decline of Athenian Democracy

After Pericles, the leadership of Athens descended from the summit to
the mediocre and lower levels of talent and character. Thucydides records
that descent and depicts its seamy side in the sequence of events that he
narrates, in the revealing speeches of men like Cleon and Alcibiades, in
his somber reflections on the ferocities of the civil war within the cities,
and above all in the Melian Dialogue—that climactic passage where this
Athenian historian lays bare an Athens that plumbs the depths of political
immorality. Under the strain of a war that dragged on for a quarter of a
century (because a whale was fighting an elephant and the two could not
come to grips), the Athenians degenerated. Their destruction was at last
encompassed more by their own follies and excesses than by the strength
or virtue of their foes; and by the time they were defeated, they no longer
deserved a victory. The leadership of the seas they had once rightfully
earned by valor when they repulsed the Persian in the service of Hellas.
This they had converted into an empire enforced upon the subject islands
and coastal towns which paid them tribute. Cleon was at least frank when
he told his fellow-citizens: "The empire that you hold is a tyranny."[15]
What he stated was truth, and in it he and his hearers saw no shame.

As they were pressed to extremities in a war of survival, they flung all
caution to the winds and gloried in the arrogance of power. The victims
of their own ambitions, the Athenians themselves removed the moral
foundations of their hegemony. The system which Pericles had idealized
for its devotion to liberty was turned externally into an instrumentality
for enslavement. When the naval force of Athens was pitted against the
fractious islanders of Melos—whose sin it was that they did not wish to
be included among the subjects of a maritime empire—the arguments that
might is right, that naked power acknowledges no limits save those of its
own strength, and that in the governance of mankind he takes who can,

15. Bk. III, 37.

these are established by a consistency of word and conviction of deed that a Hitler could have admired.[16] Hence, where the historian discusses the grim brutalities of the civil strife between the democratic and oligarchical factions, he portrays both groups indifferently as competitors in corruption and equals in evil.[17] When lastly an Alcibiades—the supreme example of talent bereft of character—goes over to the Spartan side, this leader of the *jeunesse dorée*, a scion, like Pericles, of the great Alcmaeonid clan, gives advice to the enemy how most to hurt his native city and with utter contempt spits upon the democracy, which first had honored and then dishonored him, as "an acknowledged madness."[18]

Two other literary documents of this period reinforce, in their different ways, the unfavorable picture which a reading of Thucydides presents. In a series of mordant comedies, the satiric dramatist, Aristophanes, lampoons the leading figures of his day—Socrates, Cleon, Euripides—at public festivals and on the official stage.[19] He ridicules some of the most characteristic institutions of the Athenian democracy—the courts, for instance, with their huge panels of citizen jurors; he expresses the war-weariness of the people and the yearning of many for an ending and an escape.[20] The cumulative effect, if something positive emerges from the catalogue of scathing negations, is a conservative plea for a return to "the good old ways," for counsels of moderation, and for peace. The same theme, more prosaically told, is the burden of the curious, yet illuminating, critique of the *Athenian Constitution* which was written by some champion of oligarchy and has been preserved among the writings of Xenophon.[21] Here, almost everything is said that can be adduced to point out the defects of democracy and at the same time to reject the very features which are ideals to a democrat. Thus, democracy is condemned for its enthronement of ignorance (*amathia*) and indiscipline (*ataxia*). Even the slaves and resident aliens[22] are disobedient and do not keep in their place. The poor use their majority power to plunder the rich, confiscating their property by exorbitant levies. Moreover, they carry equality so far that they expect

16. Bk. V, 85-113.
17. Bk. III, 82.
18. Bk. VI, 89.
19. Socrates in *The Clouds*, Cleon in *The Babylonians* and *The Knights*, Euripides in *The Frogs*.
20. The jurors are *The Wasps*; war-weariness comes in *The Acharnians* and *The Peace*; and the escape in *The Birds*.
21. The author is referred to as Pseudo-Xenophon, or the "Old Oligarch."
22. Athens was noted for the large number of aliens (*metics*) who resided there under its hospitality. They were important to the city's economy because they helped to organize the commercial network of a sea-borne trade.

everybody to participate in office and allow anyone to stand up and speak his opinion.[23]

The Philosophers' Analysis: (1) Plato's Attack

In part, the value of these criticisms lies, not in their content alone, but in the fact that they help us to place in proper perspective the well-known judgments of Plato. Two preliminary points need to be made about the summation of democracy's criteria which that philosopher presents in the eighth book of the *Republic*. His account, in the first place, is wholly a condemnation; and, in the second, is unoriginal in ideas.[24] The condemnation amounts to caricature rather than portraiture. Of itself, it is so unbalanced that one must consider the probable effect of ancestry and personal animus on Plato's judgment. Plato was born of an influential lineage at a time when such families in Athens had shown their alienation from democracy. On the maternal side, he was descended from the great lawgiver, Solon, and was nephew to Critias, one of the "Thirty Tyrants" who took over the government of the *Polis* at the time of the Spartan triumph. Both upbringing and connections had inclined him to the aristocracy, until his bias was irretrievably confirmed by the act which he could never forgive and which decided his future loyalties: the judicial murder of his teacher, Socrates, by the restored, vengeance-wielding *Demos*. As for the content of the Platonic *exposé*, there is nothing in this searing indictment which was not said earlier by his predecessors and was not part of the common stock-in-trade of the anti-democratic schools. Yet, what he wrote has the significance that it bears the authority of Plato's name. For that reason, his statements have influenced the attitudes toward democracy of many subsequent generations which viewed the system only through such books as the *Republic* and not at first hand.

The fundamental assumption of Plato's political philosophy is simple and important. In his own words: " 'Then do we have any greater evil for a city, than that which pulls it apart and makes it many instead of one? Or a greater good than that which ties it together and makes it united?' 'No, we do not.' "[25] In a democracy, the conditions of unity are precluded,

23. These comments occur in the original in (Pseudo-) Xenophon, *The Athenian Constitution*, I, 2, 5, 10, and 13.

24. In style, however, it is strikingly original and brilliant. In this passage and in the account of tyranny that follows, Plato has a richness of phrase, a perfection of artistry, a profusion of imagery, which can only be compared with Shakespeare.

25. *Republic*, Bk. V, 462 a-b, see also 422 e. The stress on unity is an understandable reaction from the horrors of *stasis*.

as he thinks, by the basic principles to which this system adheres. At the center is the principle of liberty (*eleutheria*). " 'Then in what manner,' I said, 'will these people live? And what will be the character of their political system? For it is evident that such men will stand revealed as the democratic type.' 'That is evident,' said he. 'First, therefore, are they not free? Indeed, is their city not chock-full of freedom and of license of speech, and may not everyone in it do what he wishes?' 'That is what is said,' he replied."[26] From this, Plato proceeds to deduce a whole train of undesirable consequences. Because of all this freedom, every kind of personality pattern and mode of living will develop. Then, since the quality of government is rooted in the nature of men, politics will reflect the same contrariety. In fact, the democratic *Polis* will contain not just one brand of politics but countless—"a bazaar of systems," all jostling and colliding with one another. Hence neither in the community as a whole nor in its individual members is there either "discipline or compulsion."[27]

In addition, and no less centrally, democracy is diseased with the canker of equality. " 'Democracy is born' I think, 'when the poor are victorious over the rich, of whom they kill some and expel the others. To the remainder, they share out citizen rights and office on the basis of equality, and offices in general are distributed there by lot.' "[28] What makes this so bad, according to Plato, is that it results in "alloting equality in the same ways to equals and unequals alike,"[29] by which he means that the democracy does not discriminate between those who differ in virtue, knowledge, and ability. In short, Plato attacks the case for democracy by denying that its boasted ideals are ideals at all, by asserting that its roots are grounded in the wrong soil, and by pointing to the resultant growth as one that is sick from faulty nutriment. Therefore, the system is doomed to meet a bad end. Initially, it is bred, by reaction, out of the vice of oligarchy, which is the excessive pursuit of money. Extreme love of acquisition and unequal accumulation provoke the revolt of the underprivileged. Their system, installing equality by loot and plunder, then proceeds to its own self-destruction by permitting an excess of freedom.[30] From this, such anarchy ensues that men flee to the opposite extreme and clutch at the order which a tyrant imposes. The picture is neat; its logic is tidy. The evolution that is described fits well with Plato's theories of psychology and his scale of degeneration from utopia to tyranny. Only in part, however,

26. Bk. VIII, 557 a-b.
27. See the whole passage from 557c to 561e. The concluding phrase is in 561d.
28. *Ibid.*, 557a.
29. *Ibid.*, 558c.
30. *Ibid.*, 564a.

does the analysis accord with historical truth, since, although many of the Greek democracies did emerge through rebellion against wealthy oligarchies, normally a tyranny preceded, rather than followed, the introduction of democracy.

(2) *Aristotle's Summation*

As often happens when a body of argument builds up in the protracted discussion of a complex subject, the last person may have the best of it. Especially is this so if he possesses a system-forming mind with a flair for culling and combining the points which he and others have developed. It is fortunate, therefore, that the analysis which a pair of historians started culminates with a couple of philosophers—and doubly fortunate that the second of these should be an Aristotle. Inferior to Plato as an artist, Aristotle was superior to his teacher in balanced judgment. He utilized well the advantages of living later and of thus being able to garner more historical grist for his mill. The studies of one hundred and fifty-eight constitutions, prepared under his direction, stemmed from the desire, and provided the material, for a broad range of comparisons. A master of the deductive reasoning and examination of *a priori* concepts, in which also Plato excelled, Aristotle is no less pre-eminent for his careful synthesis of evidence gathered *a posteriori*. Indeed, it is his union of the two treatments that distinguishes his philosophical method. He employs historical particulars to test the philosophic universals, while he illuminates the significance of the former by his analysis of the latter. In this, he not only showed the way to a method that connot be bettered, but also proved himself its expert practitioner.

By the time that it reached Aristotle, the three-fold classification of political systems, which the Persians debated, had received an extension. This was a result of the participation in the inquiry by the philosophers and doubtless owes much to the influence of Socrates. The original classification was founded on a single question which permitted three answers. The question itself was one of fact (in whose hands *is* supreme power lodged), and the answers were similarly factual. In the drift of philosophic debate, however, equal attention was paid to the ethical problem: What is the good state? How *ought* a government to be organized and conducted? With the spectacle of civil discord (*stasis*) constantly before them, the Platonic view that unity is the greatest boon could not fail to be attractive. Hence a second criterion was tacked on to the former: In whose interests is the supreme power used by its holders? In their own interest, as a ruling group? Or, in the interest of the whole community—

their subjects included? The moral philosophers, as might be expected, favored the latter. Consequently, when Aristotle presents the classification of political systems that was developed by his predecessors, he has six types to discuss, of which three are the correct forms and three are deviations.[31] Where, then, does democracy fit in this scheme, and why?

First to be noted about the position assigned to democracy is its inclusion among the deviations. The true forms—which exist when either One person, or Few, or Many, rule in the interests of all—are named, respectively, Monarchy, Aristocracy, and Polity. The deviants of the two former Aristotle calls Tyranny and Oligarchy. Democracy is then stated to be the improper version of the system which is a Polity when correctly conducted.[32] It is government by the *Demos*, ruling in the interests of the *Demos*.[33] What makes this labeling significant is that it pins on democracy the stigma of class rule. Granted that the dominant class in question constitutes the majority, its supremacy is still not the ideally best system because the Few are left to the mercy of the Many who exploit them. The best that can be said for democracy is that it is the best of the deviations.

The conception of democracy as the rule of a class (albeit the largest class) becomes abundantly clear in one of the most remarkable passages of the *Politics*. Here Aristotle, after listing and naming the six types of government, proceeds to point out how inadequate is this classification.[34] He does so by putting his finger on its critical weakness—the failure to define correctly the distinction between democracy and oligarchy. Since both are deviations, all that distinguishes them, on the traditional view, is the fact that supreme power belongs in one case to many persons, in the other to a few. But, as he convincingly argues, the mere numbers that compose the ruling group are not the essential criterion of the two systems.[35] What is essential is that the poor rule in a democracy; in an oligarchy, the rich. As an incidental consequence, because the majority of

31. *Politics*, 1279a.
32. *Ibid.*, 1279b. The Greek for Polity is *politeia,* and it is hard to translate. Literally it means "the form of government of the *polis.*" Some translators call it "constitutional government"; others "constitution." In choosing "Polity," I am following Barker. Aristotle himself is aware of the difficulty and tries to explain why he is employing a broad, generic word, as the description of the system where many rule in the interest of the whole. See 1279a.
33. "I mean, for instance, that in democracies the *Demos* is master." 1278b.
34. *Ibid.*, 1279b-1280a.
35. He repeats this later and reaffirms it: "One should not, as some have now become accustomed to do, define democracy thus simply as the system where many have the mastery." 1290a.

the people are poor, democracy is a government by the larger number. Conversely, because wealth is unequally concentrated in few hands, oligarchy is government by a small number. However, in both cases, the fundamental criterion is that political power accords with an economic demarcation.[36] Yet, this factor is entirely omitted from the only two categories in terms of which the traditional classification was conceived: the number of persons who possess supreme power, and the range of interests on whose behalf they exercise it.

Aristotle illustrates his economic interpretation in various ways. In fact, he detects its operation in many of the basic institutions of democracy. Where he discusses the achievements of Solon,[37] who started the Athenian evolution toward democracy, the philosopher carefully traces the connection between the two aspects of his reforms, political and economic. Solon had been entrusted with power at a time of economic crisis which issued in political upheaval. He wiped out the debts of the farmers (*seisachtheia*) and removed the mortgages from their properties, thus forestalling the danger that freemen would be reduced to slavery for non-payment of obligations which they could not meet. Then, under his famous laws, he allotted to all—proportionately to their wealth—a stake in the economy and in politics. In Aristotle's judgment: "The three most democratic features of Solon's constitution seem to be these: first and most important, that no man could offer his own person as security for a loan, next that anybody who wished could come to the aid of the wronged, and third (the feature by which they say the multitude was strengthened most) the appeal to the courts of law. For when the *Demos* is master of the juror's vote, it becomes master of the constitution."[38]

Elsewhere, in the same vein, Aristotle applies the appropriate economic criteria to the composition of the citizen-body and the framework of a democratic government. The ways in which men earn their livelihood and the occupations they pursue both affect the distribution of wealth and influence their outlook toward society. The tone or ethos of a community, and consequently its political complexion, relate directly to the balance among the various vocations or to the preponderance of one group over others. Hence democracies will differ according to the respective numbers and importance of the farmers, craftsmen, businessmen, sailors, fisherfolk, and laborers.[39] Of these, Aristotle's "chosen people" are, like Jefferson's, the farmers, and for them he reserves a special accolade. He considers the

---

36. Aristotle is explicit about this: "The feature in which democracy and oligarchy differ is poverty and wealth. . . . Where the poor rule, it is a democracy." 1280a.
37. Aristotle, *Constitution of Athens*, 4-12.
38. *Ibid.*, 9.
39. *Politics*, 1291b.

best type of democracy, which is also the oldest, to be composed of agri-culturists;[40] the next best, that of the herdsmen in a pastoral economy.[41] However, the reasons for his preference sound like a somewhat back-handed compliment for democracy: "The farmers are kept busy because they do not own much property. Hence, they seldom sit in the assembly. Since they lack the necessities of life, they devote their time to their own work and have no desire for what belongs to others. Indeed, they think it pleasanter to work than to be in public life and to hold office."[42] One can imagine how Pericles would retort to this!

Because democracy is contrasted with oligarchy by the different status accorded to poverty and wealth, Aristotle shows how this basic point af-fects the institutions of democratic government. While an oligarch appor-tions the rights of citizens on the basis of wealth, and permits only the well-to-do to hold office, democracy does the reverse. It requires and en-courages the poor to participate in government, even paying them for at-tendance at the assembly. For filling the great majority of offices, democ-racy relies on the random chance of the lot, and strictly preserves the procedure of election for those posts which require a special skill or com-petence. Oligarchy discriminates against the poor, while democracy does the like against the rich. Under its regime, in fact, the latter run the risk of being penalized and may incur heavy fines for failing to perform the obligations imposed by the poorer majority.[43]

Finally, it is in this same economic and social context that Aristotle places the ideals of democracy. What is the hallmark of this system? The supremacy of the *Demos*. Who are the *Demos?* The poor. What do they value as political virtues? Equality, freedom, and majority rule. Why these? Equality, because materially they are all on one level in possessing either no property or a small amount and they extend their equality in this respect into a general equality of rights. Freedom, because they are all freemen (i.e., not slaves or chattels), from which they derive all man-ner of specific freedoms. Majority rule, because the ruling poor are numer-ous and the solidarity of their numbers is the secret of their power. Thus the values they select follow from the characteristics of those who do the choosing.[44]

40. *Ibid.*, 1318b. "For the best Demos is one that tills the soil."
41. *Ibid.*, 1319a.
42. *Ibid.*, 1318b.
43. These and similar points are argued in an important passage, 1294a-b.
44. This paragraph is a compression of a number of passages in scattered parts of the *Politics*. Some of these are as follows: (1) "But it is a democracy whenever the gov-ernment is controlled by those who are free, poor, and numerous; and an oligarchy when those in control are rich, well-born, and few." 1290b. (2) "For if freedom and equality exist most of all in a democracy, as some suppose, these would mostly occur

The Greek Verdict

Until Aristotle's time, the written accounts of democracy, whether favorable or hostile, had the common advantage of being contemporary observations of a living system. After him, however, the Greek analysis of democracy came to an end—not because Aristotle had said the last word there was to say on the subject, but because democracy itself ceased to exist. The conquests of Philip and Alexander destroyed the independence of the *Polis*, reducing its government to the level of local administration. Government at the center was the military-monarchical rule of a kingdom striving to win and hold an empire. The practice of democracy thenceforth was discontinued. This, therefore, is the right place for a summary view of democracy's criteria, as the Greeks had experienced it.

What is noticeable about this discussion, which ranges from Herodotus to Aristotle, covering more than a century and conducted in turn by historians, dramatists, political leaders, and philosophers, is the considerable volume of agreement about what constitutes a democratic system. The reader must have been struck by the fact that the points made by each author tend to be repeated, with additions and embroideries, by his successors. The descriptions of democracy grow cumulatively until they culminate in Aristotle. Of course, this agreement is made simpler by the reason that democracy in general always meant Athens in particular. No matter what the focus of the argument might be, every picture of democracy had to fit in the Athenian frame or to a Greek it made no sense.[45] Perhaps it is this which explains why the rival schools of thought (those who praised democracy and those who loathed it), while they differ sharply in their interpretation of the facts, agree remarkably in stating what the facts are. With the Athenian example before them, both eulogists and detractors identify democracy's essentials in the same way. They

---

when everybody takes the fullest part in government on the same basis." 1291b. (3) "It is democratic, then, for everyone to deliberate—and about everything—for that is the kind of equality the *Demos* seeks." 1298a. (4) "Democracy was born of people's belief that, if they were equals in anything, they were so in everything. For instance, all who are alike in not being slaves think themselves equal in everything else." 1302a. (5) "There are two points by which democracy seems to be defined: majority rule and freedom." 1310a. (6) "The basic principle of a democratic system is freedom. People are in the habit of saying that this is the only form of government in which they have shares in freedom, and that this is the target at which every democracy aims." 1317a-b. (7) "For democrats say that the just thing is what the majority decides," 1318a.

45. Just as in modern times, although federalism exists by now in many countries, discussion of it must pay special attention to the United States, which was the pioneer and continues to be the prime example of this institutional pattern.

then proceed, however, to judge their data from contrasted viewpoints. Pericles and Plato, for instance, jointly stress the versatility of the citizen of a democracy. But whereas the former approves this and considers it a source of strength to the whole community, the latter as vigorously disapproves because he thinks it produces a chaos of meddlesome and disorderly busybodies. Similarly with the principle of freedom of speech. Herodotus regarded this as an incentive to individual energy and, consequently, to political progress. On the other hand, the "Old Oligarch" dismissed as the supremacy of the ignorant the right of everyone to voice an opinion.

As for the criteria themselves, reviewing them reveals another significant point. Survey the full list of democratic characteristics mentioned above, and what is it that emerges? By their own logic these criteria group themselves, or can be grouped naturally and without forcing, into the analytical pattern that was suggested earlier as a general theory of politics.[46] Admittedly, this is reading into the Greek texts more than their authors actually say. But the rationale suggested here, though none of the Greeks explicitly so formulated it, is nevertheless implicit in their treatment of the subject. It can properly be deduced from their analysis without distortion of either their general meaning or particular details. All the attributes which they detected in a democracy fall under the three headings of social context, governmental system, and philosophical ideals. This can be shown as follows, by simply combining in tabular form the views of the basic democratic traits which are offered by Herodotus, Thucydides, "the Old Oligarch," Plato, and Aristotle.

The Criteria of Greek Democracy

SOCIAL CONTEXT
- Rule by the poor,
- Exploitation of the rich,
- Abolition of debt slavery and of property qualifications for office,
- Opportunity for individual talent, irrespective of family status or wealth.

GOVERNMENTAL SYSTEM
- Public deliberation and decision by all citizens, resulting in majority rule,
- Majority of offices filled by lot,
- All officials held accountable,
- Large citizen juries.

46. See Chapter 1, pp. 8-13.

PHILOSOPHICAL IDEALS
{
Equality,

Equality (= freedom) of speech; viewed negatively as the domination of ignorance,

Freedom and versatility; viewed negatively as license and disorder,

Obedience to the authority of law and of public officials,

Constant participation in civic activities.
}

Some Unsettled Questions

This rearrangement (for that is all it is) of the Greek argument provokes some questions which may be raised here although the proper time to discuss them will come later. In the first place, such a statement of criteria requires some further definitions. Thus, Herodotus says that democracy spells *isonomia*. But so broad a concept contains many nuances, any one of which could possibly receive more prominence than the rest.[47] Democracy is also said to be dedicated to freedom. But how is that to be defined? In the Periclean sense, or the Platonic, or in one of the several ways that Aristotle distinguishes? And if freedom is merely non-slavery, then it should be remembered that Athens throughout its democratic period remained a slave-owning society, that its economy reposed on a foundation of slave labor, that no serious movement was ever started to abolish the institution, and that neither Herodotus nor Thucydides, neither Plato nor Aristotle, speaks out against it. The Age of Greek Enlightenment had its blind spot.

Another difficulty arises because certain criteria on the list are patently ambivalent. A transparent case is the principle of obedience to law. This is included by Pericles among the praiseworthy qualities of Athenian civic life. It is also referred to, with emphasis, by Aristotle who carefully distinguishes the better type of democracy, which is governed by its laws (*nomoi*), from the inferior sort dominated by the demagogues (*demagogoi*). However, the much overworked phrase "rule of law" is full of ambiguities; nor is it necessarily and *ipso facto* democratic. The conventional doctrine which favors "a government of laws and not of men" sounds as if these are opposite alternatives. Actually, far from being self-executing, laws require men for their fashioning, interpretation, and enforcement. Even if it be granted that no system is a democracy where an absolute monarchy or dictatorial clique controls political power and is itself uninhibited by the laws which it imposes on others, there is nothing

47. See note 4 of this chapter.

automatically true about the converse—i.e., that every system where the rulers are under some legal restraints is *per se* democratic. Whether government limited by law is democratic or not depends, not on the procedural point that the laws reign supreme, but on the substance those laws contain. To be subordinated to laws whose provisions are undemocratic in their spirit, intent, and results, does not produce democracy. Law is a tool of government, an instrument of power. It may be used, alternatively, for tyranny, or justice, for equality or inequality, to enlarge freedom or to abridge it. Merely to be law-abiding is never enough; for some laws ought to be broken. There have been laws aplenty, governing all ranks and classes from top to bottom, in the most venal and exclusive of oligarchies; in the most minutely regulated of theocracies; and in the most hierarchical of status-ridden feudalisms, both oriental and occidental. Indeed, the birth of democracy was only possible because some bold men were willing to defy such laws and rebel against the governments which enforced them.

For all this, there is ample evidence in the literature of Greece. A brief, but eloquent, passage was placed by Herodotus in the mouth of a renegade Spartan, who extols the respect for law as it existed, not in democratic Athens, but in Sparta—that dread "garrison state" established by Lycurgus under a militaristic code.[48] So, too, in that moving drama, the *Antigone* of Sophocles, a tragic conflict occurs because a woman is determined to violate the edict of the ruler of Thebes and she justifies her disobedience by appealing to the eternal, higher, laws of her gods.[49]

48. Xerxes asks Demaratus to explain what it is that compels a handful of Spartans to stay at their posts and hold the pass at Thermopylae against hopeless odds. If they are free men, why do they not run from certain death? To this, Demaratus replies: "Free though they are, they are not free in everything. For over them is set a master —the Law—which they fear much more than your subjects fear you." Herodotus, *Book VII*, 103-4.

49. Antigone's brother, Polyneices, led an army to overthrow Creon, the ruler of Thebes, but was defeated and killed. Creon issued an edict that the body should not be buried (in which case, according to Greek belief, the dead man's spirit could not pass into the Nether-World, but must wander forever between the worlds of the living and the dead). Antigone went to the battlefield and buried her brother.

CREON   "Did you then dare to contravene these laws?"
ANTIGONE   "I did. For these were not proclaimed by Zeus,
            Nor did Justice, who dwells with Hades' gods,
            Lay down such laws as these among mankind.
            Nor could I think your edicts have such force
            That you, a mortal man, can override
            Those laws—unwritten, steadfast—of our gods.
            Their date is not today nor yesterday,
            But time eternal. No man knows their span."
         Sophocles, *Antigone*, 449-457. My translation.

Lastly, in the political dialogue that he wrote in his old age, where Plato waters down the extremism of the *Republic* and offers a more practicable, second-best, ideal, he gives the title of *The Laws* to a philosophy of politics whose structure from foundations to apex remains authoritarian, elitist, and regimented. In law, as such, no magic resides. Only laws of democratic content make for democracy.

There are other criteria, besides this one, which are ambiguous and which, on a closer view, reveal their latent inconsistencies. But the appropriate place to examine them will be in a later section[50] where the ideals of democracy are discussed in the light of their modern relevance. Posterity is in debt to Athens not for completing an experiment, but for beginning it.

A Premature Experiment?

From the age of the Greek *Polis,* long centuries elapse before the criteria of democracy are formulated anew. The Athenian achievement was a *tour de force,* none the less spectacular because it was premature. Prevented by its small size from meeting the military and economic conditions of survival, unable to adapt its institutions to a larger population and territory, democracy revealed its potentialities in the *Polis* and then disappeared from view. Nor, in this respect, is its brief but conspicuous record an isolated phenomenon. History provides other examples of attempts initiated too early to endure, yet destined to be revived at a subsequent date when circumstances were more promising for development. Herodotus, for instance, records the fact that the continent of Africa was circumnavigated by Phoenicians in the reign of the Egyptian Pharaoh, Neco. The King equipped their ship and dispatched them south through the Red Sea with orders to follow the coastline and return. In the third year after their departure, the ship arrived on the Mediterranean coast of Egypt. But the crew told a story, which the historian, although he relates it, does not find credible. They reported that at one stage in their voyage, when sailing around Africa to the west, the noon-day sun was on their right. Of course, it is exactly this authentic item of information (one that could not possibly have been invented, since it was so contrary to all the evidence then known) which proves that their report was true and that they must have sailed south of the equator on the surface of an ocean that was curved—although they did not know it. For centuries, Europeans were inhibited from voyaging far afield because they lacked the proper ships and instruments and because they erroneously believed the Earth was flat and feared that at some point they would fall over the edge. Not

50. See Chapters 16 and 17.

until the fifteenth century did Portuguese sailors, inspired by Prince Henry the Navigator, demonstrate anew to a no longer incredulous world that the Cape of Good Hope could be rounded. In their day, moreover, the same voyage could be repeated and regular contacts could be maintained which served an economic use. The same holds true of the crossing of the Atlantic, which was accomplished by Scandinavians via Greenland to Newfoundland at the opening of the eleventh century. But North America had to wait until 1492 for its rediscovery and the establishment of permanent links with Europe. Likewise, in the realm of physics, Democritus advanced his atomic theory as early as the fourth century B.C. But through lack of equipment and experiment, his arguments were supported by scanty empirical evidence and therefore could not be proved. Instead, his physics had to rely mainly on metaphysics—which other metaphysicians, of course, promptly "refuted." Only in the nineteenth and twentieth centuries have scientists been able to show by experiment and more accurate observation that some of the basic assumptions of this theory are correct.

These examples should not suggest the false analogy that the validity of a political system, such as democracy, is tested and shown to be true or false in the same way as explorers can prove or disprove a geographical theory or physicists can verify some of their hypotheses in the laboratory. There is, however, a parallel, and an important one, embracing all these instances—the Athenian invention of democracy, the circumnavigation of Africa, the crossing of the Atlantic, and the atomic theory of matter. An idea or an institution may be conceived and tried long before conditions are ripe enough for its wider application or general acceptance. After its first exposition, it may be discarded or be held in abeyance or even be forgotten. But at some future date, when it is relevant, when it can be retested under more auspicious circumstances, when it can be put to practical use, it may be revived and enjoy a brilliant flowering. Such, indeed, was what happened to democracy.

Hardening of the Literary Tradition

With the obliteration of the democratic system, however, something did survive which could not be suppressed. This was the memory that the system once existed. But that memory was enshrined in the literary record; and later generations which studied it had recourse to writings whose consensus, as has been seen, was in the main unfavorable. Herodotus admires democracy, but he was the earliest to comment and did not witness the Athenian downfall. Thucydides eloquently rewrites the Periclean panegyric, but takes a jaundiced view of the system that lost the war. Aristophanes, the "Old Oligarch," and Plato in varying degrees are hostile to democracy, two of them in a most effective satirical vein; and, though Aristotle is more judiciously balanced, he does after all place democracy among the perversions. To use a modern phrase, Athenian democracy had received a bad press. As with the press of the twentieth century, most of the writing was slanted on the conservative side; and this, composed of the rich and well-born, was inimical to a system which Aristotle correctly defined as rule by the poor.

The consequences of this literary record were as serious as they were far-reaching. For over two thousand years the political judgment of Europe lay captive to a dead tradition. Learned men and heads of states alike judged a democracy, not by what they could see with their own eyes, but by what ancient authors had told them of a single experiment abandoned long ago. Through all the centuries that elapsed from the eclipse of the *Polis* to democracy's relatively modern rebirth, those who wrote political theory judged and generalized about democracy in the terms made classic by the Greeks. Nor was this surprising. What else, after all, did they have to go on? A theory concerning democracy could, of course, be formulated —and was by some—as an ideal conception of what ought to be, as a utopia in short, in which case the argumentation did not have to be circumscribed in time and place. But to the extent that generalization drew for concreteness on actual experience and called history into service to point up the lessons of philosophy, Athens had the field to itself. Naturally so, because until more data would become available, this was the best—nay the only—source there was; and what political experiment in history had ever evoked the reflective judgment of a more brilliantly contrasted group of analysts?

How little the conception of democracy had changed in the course of two millennia can be demonstrated if one refers to the works of the most celebrated political thinkers of the seventeenth and eighteenth centuries. Consider in their chronological order the writings of two Englishmen, Hobbes and Locke; of a Frenchman and a French-Swiss, Montesquieu and Rousseau; and of one American, Madison. What meanings do they attach to democracy?

Democracy Defined by Hobbes, Locke, and Montesquieu

Hobbes has few allusions to democracy in his major treatise, the *Leviathan*. He is, after all, presenting a theory for which democracy, as he understood it, had little relevance. Thinking that self-preservation is a man's primary aim, and that society must be so governed as to impose a coercive order on the dangerous, destructive passions, he pleads for such a concentration of power in one place (which he calls the Sovereign) that all will dread to disobey its commands. Since order requires that the Sovereign be omnipotent, indivisible and unified, the Hobbesian goal is best achieved through the supremacy of a single ruler (who could, of course, be either Charles I or Cromwell, provided he be absolute). Yet, mindful of the possibility that Parliament might emerge supreme in England's Civil War, the cautious Hobbes guarded his logic and his political fences by admitting that sovereignty could be conferred, alternatively, "upon one Man or upon one Assembly of men"—a phrase in which the emphatic word is "one."[51]

When the time comes for Hobbes to distinguish "the severall kinds of Commonwealth," it is evident that in classifying the possible forms of government his thinking has not advanced one iota beyond that of the Greek classics he had studied. In fact, all he does is to repeat the hackneyed threefold division in terms of the location of Sovereignty which may be possessed by one person, or by an assembly of a part of the Commonwealth, or by "an assembly of all that will come together."[52] It is the last that he calls a democracy. His own preference for the rule of one is made clear in two passages. In one of these, he attacks the government of an Assembly: "For the passions of men, which asunder are moderate, as the heat of one brand; in Assembly are like many brands that enflame one another (especially when they blow one another with Orations) to the setting of the Commonwealth on fire, under pretence of Counselling it."[53] In matching vein and in defense of strong government, he argues in favor of a strong monarch and speaks contemptuously of "those Democraticall writers, that continually snarle at that estate."[54]

Interestingly enough, although the political theorists after Hobbes develop philosophies whose contents are so markedly different from his and from one another, in many respects the formal categories in which their thought is couched are similar. Thus, Locke and Rousseau to a very great extent, and Montesquieu and Madison to a lesser extent, drag in the apparatus of the state of nature, law of nature, and social contract—all of

---

51. *Leviathan*, Part II, Chap. XVII.
52. *Ibid.*, Chap. XIX (Everyman ed., p. 97. See also p. 100).
53. *Ibid.*, Chap. XXV (Everyman ed., p. 138). The identical point, that individuals behave worse when assembled than when separate, was made by Plato in the *Republic*, Bk. 6, 492b-c.
54. *Ibid.*, Chap. XXIX (Everyman ed., p. 174).

which they use to support the most contradictory conclusions. Judged in one way, then, the picture of democracy which these men present is disappointing, since it merely reiterates the old, hidebound definitions. Thus, Locke writes a brief chapter entitled "Of the Forms of a Commonwealth." The form, as he says, depends "upon the placing the supreme power" (which is Herodotus all over again) and that power "is the legislative." Three types of commonwealth ensue, according to the number—One, Few, or Many—who make the laws. As for the third of these, "the majority having, as has been showed, upon men's first uniting into society, the whole power of the community naturally in them, may employ all that power in making laws for the community from time to time, and executing those laws by officers of their own appointing, and then the form of the government is a perfect democracy . . . ."[55]

Montesquieu, too, while he is not without an original streak in some matters, merely repeats past platitudes in classifying governments into their principal types. Of these, from the orthodox Greek sextet he picks four to serve his purpose.[56] If there is one man at the head, the government is either monarchical or despotic,[57] depending on whether the law or one man's caprice is paramount. If more than one are collectively supreme, we have a republic. This will be an aristocracy when the power belongs to only a part of the people. But when the main body of the people share it, that is a democracy. Beyond this, all we read in Montesquieu about the criteria of democracy is that these embrace a love of equality. Nor can we avoid noticing that in the passages where he tries to discuss democracy—and to compare it with monarchy, despotism, and aristocracy— every historical illustration that he presents (bar one) is drawn from Greece to Rome.[58] The single exception has some interest in retrospect. He remarks how funny it was in the seventeenth century to observe the futile efforts of the English to institute a democratic government. Torn by faction and weakened by civil war, the islanders were helpless victims of a succession of revolutionary changes, which, the cycle completed, ended in a return to the monarchy they had abandoned.[59] In modern times, when Englishmen have been prone to pride themselves on their own stability and to view with some condescension the spectacle of Gallic turbulence, it is worth recalling that these attitudes were once reversed. However, this English experiment of the period from 1640 to 1660 stands

---

55. (Second) *Treatise of Civil Government*, Chap. X, sec. 132.
56. *The Spirit of the Laws*, Bks. II & III.
57. Despotic government, for Montesquieu, is synonymous with the Greek tyranny.
58. E.g., Bk. II, sec. 2; Bk. III, sec. 3; Bk. V, secs. 3-7; Bk. VIII, secs. 2-4.
59. *Ibid.*, Bk. III, sec. 3.

by itself as Montesquieu's only reference to democracy outside of antiquity. On the other hand, when he speaks about monarchy, despotism, and aristocracy, recent allusions come readily to his pen, since these systems had maintained down to his time the virtually unbroken continuity which democracy had not.

The Direct Democracy of Rousseau and Madison

The Social Contract, published only fourteen years after the Spirit of the Laws, provided political theory with a new and powerful thrust. The tortured personality of Rousseau reacted to the experiences of life with intense emotion, and the principles which attracted his intellect he held passionately. Discerning his ideas by a sensitive intuition, more than by logic, he pressed them into categories which did not always fit. But a fresh, if rebellious, imagination yielded him insights beyond the frontiers of tradition. From such a man a political theory was generated whose connections, though they seemed to close the circuit, were in places loose and frayed. He touched off many fires, some of them accidental. What he had to say specifically about democracy is limited and not particularly novel. This is due in part to the rigidity of his definition, since he takes the term literally, as his predecessors had done, in the restricted sense of a government directly conducted by the people in person.[60] Democracy, so viewed in line with the traditional formula, is one of the three basic types, the others being aristocracy and monarchy. Adhering to that litany, Rousseau is adamant on the point that a representative system is not democratic, because one's will can never be represented by another. It is this insistence which explains his jibe at the English who enjoy political liberty, he asserts, only in the moments of a parliamentary election.[61]

Even if one did not cavil, however, at the narrowness of his category, Rousseau would still be open to criticism on the score of inadequately analyzing direct democracy itself, for which omission he has less excuse than either Montesquieu, Locke, or Hobbes. They, as was seen, derived their ideas about democracy from classical antiquity, being familiar with

60. "In the first place, the sovereign can place the government in the hands of the whole people or its largest number, with the result that more citizens would be magistrates than private persons. To this form of government we give the name of democracy." Social Contract, Bk. III, Chap. 3.

61. "The English people thinks it is free. But it is greatly deceived. It is free only while electing the members of Parliament. Once they are elected, it is enslaved and counts for nothing. The people which so uses its liberty during those brief moments richly deserves to lose it." Ibid., Bk. III, Chapter 15.

no other source. But Rousseau did know another source which he saw at first hand. By birth, he was a citizen of Geneva. Sentimentalist and romantic to the core, he prided himself on the country of his origin and has some sympathetic references to its institutions.[62] Actually, in certain Swiss cantons and communes one little fragment had survived from an earlier Europe where the old Germanic *landsgemeinde*, or mass meeting of adult male citizens, continued to be the supreme governing body. Its spirit and processes could easily have been observed in detail and evaluated in order to correct or corroborate the data drawn from Athens. But Rousseau was not the person for that kind of task. He formed his political judgments, not by conducting research into a system, but rather because a situation evoked an impression to which his feelings responded. It may be possible to read between the lines and to suppose that he had Swiss examples in mind in the passage[63] where he mentions the difficulty of combining the prerequisites for a successful democracy—namely, a state of very small size, of simple manner, of equality in ranks and wealth, and with little or no luxury. Certainly, he is not at all sanguine that these conditions can be widely met. Arguing logically from his definition, he says that in the strict sense no genuine democracy has ever existed or ever will, since "it is contrary to the natural order that a large number should govern and a few be governed."[64] Arguing psychologically, he arrives at the conclusion: "If there were a people of gods, they would govern themselves democratically. A government so perfect is unsuited to men."[65] Never before, or since, was democracy damned with such high praise!

Finally, before leaving this line of discussion, we should notice its influence on the ideology which founded the United States of America. To the majority of those whose support was necessary if the Constitution were to be ratified, democracy was an abusive word. Indeed, in 1786, New England gentlemen with a classical education were sure to associate Shays' Rebellion with the *seisachtheia* of Solon's day.[66] Hence, when the writers

---

62. In fact, though, once he had left home and had started wandering, he spent few years of his adult life in Switzerland; and when he did seek refuge there, after publishing his major works, one canton after another expelled him. Those who contemplate the ironies of history may observe an equivalence in the biographies of Rousseau and Calvin. The latter, persecuted by the French, was imported to Geneva, on which city he succeeded in imposing his horrible system. Biding their time for two centuries, the patient Genevese equalized their balance of trade and scored a revenge. They gave Rousseau to France.

63. Bk. III, Chap. 4, "On Democracy."

64. *Ibid.*

65. *Ibid.*

66. See p. 32. The views of Benjamin Rush are worth quoting. Ruth, a Philadelphia

of *The Federalist* papers were trying to sway the electoral opinion of voters in New York State, they took care to defend the proposed Constitution against the deadly criticism that it would give too much encouragement to democratic tendencies. But since the criteria of democracy had been firmly established along the lines that had become traditional, Madison was able to extricate himself from the difficulty by enlisting the familiar definition in his service. With a doctrinal purity that Rousseau would have applauded, he carefully differentiated a democracy from a republic: "The true distinction between these forms . . . is, that in a democracy the people meet and exercise the government in person; in a republic, they assemble and administer it by their representatives and agents. A democracy, consequently, will be confined to a small spot. A republic may be extended over a large region."[67] It was because of this logic and the fears accompanying it that the word democracy nowhere appears in the Constitution of the United States or in the Bill of Rights. What the Founding Fathers created was, and officially still is, "a republican form of government."[68] The most potent of the modern democracies was born amid a context of thinking which did not permit it, as an infant, to receive the title of democracy.

---

physician and professor, had signed the Declaration of Independence, had served in the Continental Congress, and was a member of the Pennsylvania convention which ratified the draft of the federal Constitution. In 1788, he wrote in a letter thus: "Is not history as full of the vices of the people, as it is of the crimes of kings? What is the present moral character of the citizens of the United States? I need not describe it. It proves too plainly that the people are as much disposed to vice as their rulers; and that nothing but a vigorous and efficient government can prevent their degenerating into savages, or devouring each other like beasts of prey. A simple democracy has been aptly compared . . . to a volcano that contained within its bowels the fiery materials of its own destruction. A citizen . . . of Switzerland . . . refused in my presence to drink 'the commonwealth of America' as a toast, and gave as a reason for it, that a simple democracy was the devil's own government." From *Letters of Benjamin Rush*, Lyman H. Butterfield, ed. (Princeton University Press: Princeton, 1951), p. 454.

67. *The Federalist*, No. XIV, Nov. 30, 1787; see also No. X, Nov. 23, 1787.
68. The same concept of a "republic," not of a "democracy," is reiterated by Jefferson in his First Inaugural Address, 1801.

3

The Modern Rebirth

By the time of the American and French Revolutions, the interpretation of democracy had degenerated into stereotype and sterility. If the concept was to serve any further use, it had to be revitalized. The question then was: Could a new start be made, and, if so, from what quarters would it originate? The answer came from three sources—from new developments in theoretical doctrine, the pioneering of new institutions, and revolutionary changes in society itself. Their interaction resulted in a fresh and vigorous re-examination of democracy's criteria. Let us look at these factors —philosophy, state, and society—and consider the impact of each upon the meaning of democracy.

In the case of the philosophers, perhaps the most interesting point for an assessment of their influence is to compare the results which they did intend with those they did not. Ideas which are born from a person thinking are like the new life created by the union of the sexes. Although forever related to its parentage, the child, as it matures, develops beyond the control of its progenitors, lives a life of its own, and forms its independent connections. So it is with the brainchildren of speculative writers. These, too, by the potentialities inherent in their logic and by their usefulness in practice, can grow in ways which were not foreseen by those who give them birth. Moreover, particular ideas may later be extracted from the whole system of which they were once a part, and may acquire new meanings by being united with a different set. This is what happened to many of the doctrines propounded by the philosophers whose views on democracy were considered above. They advanced the theories which sprang from the felt needs of their time and were consonant with their personal predilections, but which subsequently were adapted to circumstances beyond their anticipation. Neither Hobbes nor Locke, neither Montesquieu nor Madison—nor even Rousseau—intended to pin the democratic label on his philosophy. Looking ahead, they could not foresee the uses to which their arguments might be put. We, however, looking back from the twentieth century with the advantage of hindsight, can trace the links in the chain of development from the seventeenth century to the present. What I shall try to show is how certain doctrines, which were projected along diverging lines toward different ends, were swept up and thrown together as the modern democratic avalanche gathered momentum.

The Authority of the Individual

One example of prime importance is the newly placed emphasis upon the authority of the Individual. Considered as abstract propositions, one might assert with equal sense (a) that society is a unity, which happens to contain individuals as its component parts, and (b) that it is individuals who create society by their aggregation. But if either proposition receives too much priority over the other, the differences in starting point will make a great difference in one's conclusions. A view which holds that the true unit is society, within which individuals are but fragments, will not support the same political relationships as its converse—that the units are the individuals and society is the product of their addition.

Until the sixteenth century, the preponderance of theoretical argument reposed on the former position. For the philosophers of the Greek *Polis*, it was meaningless to speak of an antithesis between society and the individual, since the part cannot logically be antithetical to the whole. As well might one talk of an opposition between a person and his finger! The Greek language—that complex instrument for conveying the subtlest nuances of thought—does not even have a term that precisely corresponds to "individual." A person is either a *polites* (member of a *Polis*) or an *idiotes* (private to oneself). Society's concern is with the *polites*. The *idiotes*, as Pericles said of him, is useless; and, as the English derivative suggests, an "idiot." Plato and Aristotle, who raise between them practically every fundamental issue of social theory, do not debate this one, because to them it is not a meaningful problem. For them, society is the unit; its components are not individuals, but citizens; and that is that! Later in the Hellenistic age, it is true, rather more consideration was paid to the individual in the philosophies of the Cynics, Stoics, and Epicureans. But this trend occurred during that period of turmoil which lasted from the dissolution of the *Polis* and Alexander's short-lived empire until the *pax Romana* was consolidated. With society and its governments in flux, men were cast adrift from their accustomed moorings, and philosophy for a while reflected the mood which felt them to be individuals and not citizens.

Three mighty forces converged, however, to terminate this individualistic deviation. These were: the establishment of the *imperium Romanum*, the victory of the Christian Church, and the spread of feudalism. By their military exploits the Roman legions hammered out the steel structure within which a new political order was designed for the Mediterranean society; and around that framework with ponderous patience the *praetores* and *jurisconsulti* cemented, piece by piece, the legal mosaic of *jus civile* and *jus gentium*. Into this solid edifice, built, like all things Roman, to endure, the faith of the early Christians at first infused the essential quality that had been lacking: an ideal to lift the spirit and unify the whole. But later the Church, which came to institutionalize that faith, deteriorated in ideals once it ceased to be persecuted. By entering into partnership with the Empire, it acquired an investment in the established order and condoned such inequalities as slavery or serfdom. By the suasion of mysticism and superstition men were made to submit to a vast scheme of belief which lay beyond rational inquiry and of which, for centuries, the priest was the sole, self-constituted, interpreter. Lastly, the feudal system completed the social subjection of the individual to a hierarchy of ranks and status that centered around the economic primacy of land. From all these influences the natural product was an emphasis on organic theories which saw the human being as a tiny unimportant cell yielding its minute quota to the plan of the macrocosm.

If the civilization of Europe was to progress, it was necessary to set men free from such dogmas and the duties they imposed. This meant a revolt: revolt against the intellectual categories of traditional thinking, against the ecclesiastical mystique which underpinned them, and against the institutions (the Church and the feudal nobility) whose privileges were their cause and consequence. Those movements—broad-ranging, deep-delving and long-lasting—which we call the Renaissance, Reformation, Age of Enlightenment, and Romanticism, were the different phases of this revolt. Protest took many forms, both because the object of attack was many-sided and because the critics did not agree about the direction of reform. Intellectually, as well as politically, it is always easier to unite against than for; and it was thus that many thinkers who were certainly not for democracy nevertheless helped it along by opposing the Papacy and feudalism. In order to break down the established pattern of author-ity, a new one had to be substituted; in this way, because of the need to reconstitute the social order, the individual came into his own. Appeal could be made to his authority to determine issues that previously were arrogated to prelates and princes. Thus, instead of taking his religion from a priest who intoned in Latin a service that few could understand, the individual might be taught to go directly to Holy Writ, especially when this was translated into German or English and published by means of Gutenberg's invention. The rigidity of status in a land-focused economy had tied the serf to the soil (*adscriptus glebae*). But in a walled city a man might learn a craft and acquire some independence through the solidarity of a guild. He might even, if he could accumulate that fluid commodity, capital, become a merchant-entrepreneur, and write in his ledgers the debts of kings—as, in one extreme case, Jakob Fugger of Augs-burg became banker and paymaster to Charles V and purchased for the Hapsburgs the Holy Roman Crown.

Individualism in the Theories of Hobbes and Locke

How important was the appeal to the individual, and also how ambiguous its implications, can be seen in such theories as those of Hobbes and Locke. The Hobbesian philosophy, as was noted earlier, is not designed for democracy. He hopes for an omnipotent ruler and for unquestioning obe-dience by the subjects, who would destroy themselves if left uncontrolled. Because survival is the greatest need of the individual, the supreme obliga-tion of government is to protect. The government, that can and does protect, must be obeyed. That which does not, forfeits allegiance. Hobbes, therefore, gives no "blank check" to doctrines of Legitimacy. If treason prospers, obey the new masters. In power *de facto*, they rule *de jure*. So far, so clear. But then comes the insoluble problem. Who shall judge whether protection is adequate? The realist, who is unimpressed by claims of Legitimacy, shrinks equally from the Puritans' notion that loyalty must be a decision for the individual conscience. That way, thinks Hobbes, lies anarchy. Yet in final analysis, it is only the individual who can decide whether his government does in fact protect him or not.[1] Hence the il-limitable Sovereign is placed at the mercy of the individual's judgment. The theory, which began by breaking society down into individuals in order the more surely to control them, ends by enthroning them as the final arbiters who must assess the efficacy of Leviathan. The implications

1. *Leviathan*, Part 2, Chap. XXI.

of this logic, whether their author meant them or not, were some help to democracy.

No less revealing are the ambiguities of Locke. His theory had to be artfully constructed because he differed from Hobbes on certain points and disagreed also with Filmer and the Levellers. He does not take the position of Hobbes that the government should have absolute power. He goes out of his way to refute Filmer since he cannot concede that the silly Stuarts had any divine right to England's throne. He rejects the Levellers whose economic and social outlook is too radical and moves further to the extremes of equalitarianism than he is prepared to follow. So, after these negations, what can he affirm? He advances the notion that the individual possesses rights because of his nature as a human being, and that such rights are prior to those which the state guarantees or enforces by means of government. The state exists, therefore, for limited ends, wielding by right only those powers which individuals have delegated by consent. Within the state, however, since law must reign supreme, the paramount institution is that which makes the law—to wit, Parliament.

Now this sounds simple and seems clear. But the simplicity and clarity are deceptive. For Locke is never able to resolve the two great difficulties which beset his theory. In the first place, much depends upon one's picture of the state of nature and on one's conception of its law and of how this is known. He flatly contradicts Hobbes, who had imagined the natural state to be "a warre of every man against every man." But all that Locke offers is a rival conjecture about an admitted fiction. Nor is Locke able to prove his guess correct. We have only his word for it that the state of nature is basically peaceful and that the content of the law of nature is what he says it is. He informs us that this law is "reason,"[2] and, again, that it is "reason and common equity."[3] Finally, he brushes objection aside with the bald assertion: ". . . it is certain there is such a law and that too as intelligible and plain to a rational creature and a studier of that law as the positive laws of commonwealths, nay, possibly plainer"![4]

The sceptical reader, however, is likely to be reinforced in his scepticism when he discovers that, to the rational creature named John Locke, reason is so unintelligible and unplain that he has two different definitions of a term which is crucial for his philosophy. This is the concept of "property." Arguing that the functions of government must be limited, Locke defines "the end of government" as "the preservation of property."[5] Hence

2. (Second) *Treatise of Civil Government*, Chap. II, sec. 6.
3. *Ibid.*, sec. 8.
4. *Ibid.*, sec. 12.
5. Chap. XI, sec. 138.

it is important to know what property means. Unfortunately, the term is used both in a narrow sense and a broad one. The narrow meaning is identical with the modern connotation of the word, i.e., it refers to material commodities which a person may make or acquire and then own.[6] Alternatively, property is extended by Locke to include both the limited meaning and the additional concepts of life and liberty.[7] But, according to whichever of these two senses one selects, the character of one's philosophy will vary enormously. If the true end of government is only to preserve property in the restricted meaning, then we should have to accept a government of, by, and for, the owners of property—in which case the economic context will prescribe a political conservatism and men will count for something not because they are human beings but because of what they own. The implications of this can easily become inegalitarian and thus anti-democratic. But if it is life and liberty, as well as material possessions, which the state should protect, how does one proceed to define liberty, and what is to happen if our physical survival or our interpretation of liberty conflicts with someone else's claim to property? These are vast questions to which certain answers could be democratic. But Locke leaves us guessing. Hence, it is not surprising that a century later both a frightened conservative Burke and an optimistic reforming Bentham can be placed on two forks from a road that leads right back to this plain and intelligible thinker.

The Individual in Rousseau's Community

But, when it comes to ambiguities that can support opposite tendencies, it is Jean Jacques Rousseau who leads the field. His philosophy is a classic example of one whose reasoning appears to hold together, but whose contradictions are actually coated over with rhetoric. What these are must be understood, because some of the principal confusions in modern demo-

6. Chapter V of the (Second) *Treatise* is entitled "Of Property." Throughout this chapter the term means material commodities. In this Locke includes the property in one's own person, for he also has slavery in mind. Elsewhere in the *Treatise* the reader will find innumerable passages, where, as the context clearly shows, property is used in this precise, restricted sense, just as we use the term today (e.g., Chap. XI, secs. 138-140).

7. Locke is also emphatic about his broad definition: e.g. "his property—that is, his life, liberty, and estate" (Chap. VII, sec. 87), and "to unite for the mutual preservation of their lives, liberties and estates, which I call by the general name—property," (Chap. IX, sec. 123). In one passage, too, where he employs the broad definition, he even substitutes the word "property" for "estate" as the third item: ". . . to preserve himself, his liberty and property" (Chap. IX, sec. 131.).

cratic thinking are related to the arguments of Rousseau. The Rousseau-ian theory exerted an influence on Kant, and through him on Hegel, and through him on Marx. In a sense, both Napoleon and Mussolini, both Lenin and Trotsky, are descendants of the gentleman from Geneva. But on the other side, Rousseau can rightly claim to have inspired many of the ideas of 1789, and he could acknowledge among his later offspring such figures as Mazzini or Gambetta. In the political philosophies of Europe, Rousseau supplies the suspension bridge that leads from the eighteenth century to the nineteenth. Toward him, many paths converge; from him, just as many separate. How does this come about? The answers, I believe, can be found in the two fundamental dilemmas which plague the Rous-seauian theory and invite divergent interpretations. Both dilemmas concern the role of the individual: first, in his relation to society, and, second, in relation to his government.

The former problem arises because Rousseau insists on pouring the content of his political doctrine into a form that is not constructed to receive it. He presents a philosophy in which the individual is wholly subordinated to the group of which he is a member. This is what he asserts to be the basic condition of human association: "the *total* alienation to the *whole* community of each associate with *all* his rights . . . *nothing* being held back in the act of alienation."[8] Moreover, the very fact of association is supposed to produce "a moral and collective body" whose characteristics are unity, a common personality, a life, and a will.[9] It is this super-entity, called by Rousseau the sovereign, whose will (*la volonté générale*) is absolutely binding on each person—since his particular will has been absorbed into the general. Hence, it follows that the commands of the sovereign must always be obeyed by the individual, who, if he opposed the sovereign, would only be contradicting the will that incorporates his own. The results of disobedience are plainly stated: "Anyone who refuses to obey the general will, shall be coerced into submission by the whole body: this only means that we shall force him to be free."[10] Or, as he puts it quite bluntly in another place: "When the prince says to him: 'It is expedient for the State that you die,' he must die."[11]

Leaving the content of these remarks aside for the present, one should note the assumptions from which they derive. Like all social theorists, Rousseau has to explain the relation of the individual to the group; and, as many have felt impelled to do, he argues for the priority of the one over

8. *Du Contrat Social*, Bk. I, Chap. VI. My italics and translation.
9. *Ibid.*
10. *Op. cit.*, Bk. I, Chap. VII.
11. *Op. cit.*, Bk. II, Chap. V.

the other. Clearly, for him it is the social grouping which has primacy and constitutes the unit, and the individuals who are merely its parts. Hence, he belongs squarely in the tradition which has interpreted society in terms of an organism, wherein all members are dependent on the whole and are interrelated by virtue of the functions they perform.[12] Consequently, the notion of contract, which he invokes as the principle of social cohesion and even chooses as the title for his treatise, is not merely superfluous, but is in flat contradiction to his teaching. The contract is appropriate to a thinker who considers the individual to have priority over the group and who approves a form of association in which the authority of the group is limited. This is so because a contract is a device for bringing together people who previously were apart. It presupposes the prior independence, freedom, and equality of the contracting parties. It then defines the conditions and purposes which are to bind them and, by inference, the residual areas in which they are to remain free. But the results which Rousseau intends to reach in his philosophy cannot be derived from a contractual premise. One who holds that people are organically interdependent, and that each is totally subordinate to the whole, needs no fiction to unite the parts which, by their nature, are inseparable from the beginning. If they never were apart, nothing is required to bring them together. Nor can a contract, which necessarily implies some limiting conditions and leaves the parties some freedom outside their partnership, endorse the total alienation of each to the whole. Hence, the substance of Rousseau's thought cannot be twisted to fit into this ill-chosen framework.[13]

12. In the *Discourse on Political Economy*, published four years prior to the *Social Contract*, Rousseau explicitly compares the body politic to the human body.

13. On this point, it may be noted that Plato, who was superior to Rousseau as a logician, was fully aware of the doctrine of the social contract. Indeed, in the *Republic*, he puts it into the mouth of a participant in the dialogue, who mentions it, as one suggested explanation for social relationships (Bk. II, 359a). When Plato develops his own explanation, however, he nowhere refers to any contract, but offers a philosophy whose form and content employ the organic analogy throughout. As for Hobbes and Locke, who utilized the contract before Rousseau, Locke does so properly, whereas Hobbes does not. For Hobbes, it is simply the fear of power that holds a state together. No contract is needed for this, since no contract can create it. Indeed, when the power to protect has vanished, so has the "obligation" to obey—an obligation which is strictly physical, and not legal or moral. Hobbes, in fact, brings a contract into his argument only as a *tour de force* with which to taunt his opponents. He is telling them in effect: "Look! I too can use your doctrine and can twist it for my purposes to justify absolute power." But in Locke's case, there is a difference. Unlike Hobbes and Rousseau, Locke is fully entitled to the contractual metaphor. He really believes that the individual takes priority over the group and that the functions of the state must remain limited. For such objectives a contract is admirably suited.

Ambiguity of the General Will

The other major ambiguity in Rousseau comes from his most celebrated concept: the general will. The confusions he reveals here have been many times repeated in the subsequent debate over the meanings of democracy. His belief in a general will flows from the assumption, already stated,[14] that the act of association creates a new entity, "a moral and collective body," one of whose attributes is a will. Just as an individual has a particular will which chooses his private interest, so does the corporate personality will the general interest. As a member of a group, therefore, each person has two wills: the particular one which is private to himself alone, and the general will which is identical for all members and which every person ought to will. Now, even supposing one were to concede the array of intellectual and psychological difficulties which this doctrine raises, and admitting for argument's sake that a general will may exist, there remains the problem of knowing what it is. Amid the competition of policies and proposals, how shall we say which of these ought to be generally willed? By what criterion do we pick the general will?

To this fundamental question Rousseau gives two answers and they differ. This dualism is made clear in the following passage: "This proves . . . that the general will, in order to be truly such, must be general both in its object and in its essence; it must come from all in order to apply to all."[15] What he is saying is that the will, in order to be general, must be so in content by applying to all, and must also be so in its source by issuing from all. Therefore, because the generality of the will itself is two-sided, it is discovered in two ways. One method, corresponding to the point that the general will issues from all, consists in taking a vote; and there are two places in the *Social Contract* where Rousseau explicitly affirms that the general will is what the majority decide.[16] But this view brings him into conflict with another of his doctrines. He is careful to

14. On p. 52.
15. Bk. II, Chap. IV.
16. "The general will is the constant will of all members of the State. By virtue of it, they are both citizens and free. When a law is proposed in the people's assembly, what is being asked of them is not exactly whether they approve the proposal or not, but whether it does or does not conform to the general will which is their own will. In casting his vote, each person states his opinion on that point; and the discovery of the general will derives from counting the votes. Hence, when the opinion contrary to mine prevails, this proves nothing else than that I was in error and that what I thought to be the general will was not so." Bk. IV, Chap. 2. See also Bk. II, Chap. 3.

distinguish between the general will (*volonté générale*) and what he calls
the will of all (*volonté de tous*). In the former case, when people vote,
each is supposed to ask himself: what does the general interest require in
this instance? In the latter, each votes in accordance with his particular
private interest as he judges it, and the resultant addition of votes reveals
the will of all, i.e., the sum of their private interests, and not their general
will. Thus defined, the distinction amounts to the difference between a
collection of wills and a collective will. Hence, when a vote has taken
place there must be a doubt how to interpret it. Can one be sure that the
majority view is the general will, instead of being merely the will of all?

The second method of discovering the general will avoids this difficulty
—but only by creating a new one that is worse. Since one criterion of
generality lies in the content that is willed,[17] the clue to the discovery of
the general will depends on knowledge, i.e., on knowing what the general
interest is and subsequently willing it. But unfortunately, the people are
often mistaken, for they lack the knowledge they need. "How would a
blind multitude, which often knows not what it wants because it seldom
knows what is good for it, perform by itself so great and difficult a task as a
system of legislation? By itself, the people always wants the good, but does
not always discern it. The general will is always right, but the judgment
guiding it is not always enlightened."[18] If the people make errors, then,
through ignorance, and if it takes knowledge to discover the general interest, it is only those with knowledge who are qualified to pronounce
what the general will should be. This line of reasoning leads on to an
elitist view of government, or to something like the Platonic rule of
philosopher-kings. It invites the dangerous Hegelian distinction between
the apparent will, which people think they want, and their real will, which
they ought to be wanting. Whatever it is, this species of general will is
not a government based upon the declared wishes of the mass of the citizens. Thus, the ambiguities of the general will can be alternatively "resolved" by an aristocratic faith in superior wisdom or by the consent of
the multitude expressed in an election. The latter supports a democratic
procedure. It makes Rousseau a proponent of popular sovereignty, as this
is sometimes called. But the other interpretation can justify the most undemocratic control by a minority, or even the dictatorship of one supposedly wise person who claims to know more than the rest. Thus Robes-
pierre could avow that, when executing his opponents, he was executing
the general will. So might Hitler. So might Stalin. No foe of tyranny can

17. "From this one should realize that what makes the will general is not so much the
number of votes as the common interest which unites them." Bk. II, Chap. 4.
18. Bk. II, Chap. VI.

forget that terrible dictum: "When the prince says to him: 'It is expedient for the State that you die,' he must die."

The Democratic Impetus of the Nineteenth Century

This was the point that thinking had reached when the emphasis in politics was shifted from speculation to action. The revolution against legitimacy, absolutism, and traditional institutions that were unrepresentative—this revolution which Englishmen had conducted in the seventeenth century was continued in the eighteenth by Americans and the French. While these events were happening, the British, whose politics then were relatively more stable because they had luckily undergone their civil commotion a hundred years earlier, were plunged into technological change and industrial development so rapid and far-reaching that this, too, has been called a revolution. Hence in the early part of the nineteenth century, when speculative thinkers again confronted the need to justify political changes or resist them, there were new facts with which theory had to come to terms. The institutions of government in some important countries had been profoundly altered and theses cases were proving contagious. The use of steam-driven machines and the organization of the factory system were bringing people together in larger and larger cities, thereby transforming the social context in which the state had to function. Meanwhile, in the New World, a human flood was beginning to pour along the river valleys, over the mountains, into the forests, and across the prairies. Thus, the inheritors of Europe's civilization were remaking their institutions in two unprecedented settings, dissimilar in form, yet not unlike in spirit. For, if they are considered from the psychological standpoint, rather than the geographical, the industrial cities of Britain formed a social frontier in much the same sense as the western rim of settlement in America. In Bradford, Manchester, Birmingham, and Sheffield, no less than in Fort Detroit, Fort Duquesne, and the thousands of lonely log cabins, the static patterns of an old society were giving way before the dynamic processes of new modes of work and life. How this contributed to the building of democratic governments will be discussed elsewhere.[19] Here, I shall try to show how all these movements—the political, economic, and social—produced their impact on the interpretation of democracy and the choice of its criteria.

During the course of the nineteenth century, the meaning and prospects of democracy underwent a dramatic transformation, to which there had

19. See Chapter 8, pp. 204 ff.

been no parallel since Athens of the fifth century, B.C. Even when the nineteenth century opened, the philosophy of democracy was still largely influenced by arguments of ancient Greece. In ordinary political discourse, the term "democracy," in most mouths, was an abusive epithet. Only in Great Britain, the United States, and Switzerland, could significant institutions be found which had a democratic leaning, though even there the actual accomplishment was small compared with the need and potentiality. But by the time the twentieth century dawned, the successes of the democratic creed were everywhere apparent. Democratic ideals were paramount in three of the greatest nations of the world and a growing number of the smaller ones. While the practice of democracy gained fresh adherents with every passing decade, debate had waxed vigorous over its performance and further improvement. Criticism of democracy continued loud and forceful. Difficulties in its application were many. But its fortunes were ascendant, and the future outlook was full of hope. The effect of these changes on the reformulation of democratic criteria is a fascinating fragment of intellectual history.

Representation and the Change of Scale

From what was said before, it is clear that, if the democratic philosophy was to serve any further useful purpose, its concepts had first of all to be stretched. The city-state had been succeeded by the empire-state; the latter, by the nation-state. Was it not high time for the discussion of democracy to be lifted out of its city-state birthplace? This necessary feat was accomplished in the first quarter of the nineteenth century. Democracy now underwent a change of scale. Its dimensions were enlarged; its horizons expanded. Departing from the *Polis*, it embraced the nation. It exchanged Lilliput for Leviathan.

The method employed for accomplishing the transition, as we now see when we look back on it, was simple. The link to connect democracy with the nation was supplied by the principle of representation. Hitherto, the institutional criteria of democracy had always included a requirement that the supreme organ of government must be a mass meeting of the adult male citizens who themselves assembled in person to decide all fundamental matters. Democracy literally meant government by the people. It had to be direct. Indeed, it could not be anything else. But the consequence of this interpretation was to confine democracy to the microcosm, making it inapplicable to the macrocosm. The break with that tradition occurred when statemen and speculators proceeded to graft the new stem of representation on the old roots of the Athenian *Polis*. A distinction was now drawn—which to Rousseau and to the Madison of *The Federalist* was a contradiction in terms—between direct and indirect democracy. The latter, too, could be a genuine democracy, although it solved the problem of governing big populations and vast areas by allowing the people to choose a small number to make major decisions in their name. In this way, the people of the United States could later be persuaded to regard as democratic what Madison (and Jefferson too, for that matter) had earlier approved as republican. Similarly in the United Kingdom, the transition from oligarchy to democracy, under the formal aegis of a figurehead monarchy, could be rationalized in theory and carried out in practice by the progressive extensions of the franchise and the consequent reforms of the House of Commons.

With the inclusion of representation among its criteria, the democratic philosophy now received a new lease on life. Emancipated from both the antiquarianism of the phil-Athenians and from the Utopianism of the Rousseauians, modern democracy could at last enunciate the principles to justify its institutions and build the institutions to embody its principles. In the realm of theory, this result was accomplished by assimilating to the concept of democracy various of the doctrines which, as was noted above, had been formulated in the seventeenth and eighteenth centuries with other purposes in mind. Thus it was that those who cleared their way through the undergrowth of political ideas found themselves cutting a wide swath. They could take from the Levellers the notion of the equal dignity of all men; from the Quakers, the belief in the value of discussion for eliciting agreement; from Locke, an insistence that individuals possess rights which no governments may infringe and that the latter derive their rightful powers from the consent of free men; from Montesquieu, an institutional plan for avoiding an overconcentration of power; and from Rousseau the assertion of a public interest realized through the popular will. Any or all of these, and more besides, could now be combined and blended in a potpourri of many recipes.

In keeping with the political, economic, and social changes which gathered momentum as the nineteenth century ran its course, the symbol of democracy was now put to manifold uses. It is in the United States that the immediate effects on practical politics are first observable. The changing attitude toward democracy—indeed, its positive acceptance by many as their ruling creed—can be traced with fair precision to the thirty-two years which opened with the election to the Presidency of John Adams (1796) and concluded with the defeat of his son by Andrew Jackson (1828). In this period the opposition to the Federalists took for their title the name of Democratic-Republican, whose hyphenation accurately expresses the relation between the two concepts. Thomas Jefferson, in the course of a long and brilliant dedication to statesmanship, science, and philosophy, himself personifies this intellectual evolution from republicanism to democracy. Without ever abandoning the former idea, he comes increasingly to assimilate his thinking with the latter.[20] Jefferson indeed can properly be called the first true democrat to hold the highest elective office of a modern state. Only two years after his death, Jackson was elected President as the leader of a party which now called itself simply "Democratic"—with hyphens removed. Proof enough that the idea of democracy had won a following!

Tocqueville on American Democracy

Performance, while it is preceded by speculation, is followed by analysis and appraisal. Fortunately in this case the analyst was worthy of his subject. Jackson was halfway through his first term when a young Frenchman landed in New York to study the novel phenomenon of the American society and its political system. The result of the visit was a book which has deservedly become a classic: *De la Démocratie en Amérique* by Alexis de Tocqueville. It is doubly rare for a man to enjoy such an opportunity as he had, and then to use it so well. Immediately upon publication of the two initial volumes, the book made an impact everywhere. For Tocqueville was the first since Aristotle—the first in almost twenty-two centuries —to write from direct observation about a democracy in actual operation.

20. Commenting on the Constitution drafted by the Philadelphia Convention, he strongly objected to the powers of the House of Representatives, the only institution of the federal government elected directly by the people. "I like the power given the Legislature to levy taxes; and for that reason solely approve of the greater house being chosen by the people directly. For tho' I think a house chosen by them will be very illy qualified to legislate for the Union, for foreign nations etc. yet this evil does not weigh against the good of preserving inviolate the fundamental principle that the people are not to be taxed but by representatives chosen immediately by themselves." Letter to James Madison, Dec. 20, 1787. *The Papers of Thomas Jefferson*, Julian P. Boyd, ed. (Princeton University Press: Princeton, 1955) Vol. 12, pp. 439-40. Almost two decades later, however, writing in approval of republicanism, what he described and defined is what we would call democracy. "If, then, the control of the people over the organs of their government be the measure of its republicanism, and I confess I know no other measure, it must be agreed that our governments have much less of republicanism than ought to have been expected." See the whole Letter to John Taylor, May 28, 1816 in *The Life and Selected Writings of Thomas Jefferson*, Adrienne Koch and William Peden, eds. (Modern Library; Random House: New York, 1944) pp. 668-73.

In fact, he handled his topic by reviving the Aristotelian method, which no one before him could have done because there was no such democracy to observe. Tocqueville discusses the ideals in terms of their practical consequences, as he illuminates the practice by the ideals it implies. Add acuteness of insight to novelty of subject, and it is small wonder that his work gained such an audience.

Tocqueville had good reason for taking what in those days was a long and arduous journey. As a learned and enlightened man of progressive ideas, he belonged to a country which had just (1830) overthrown the monarchy of the restored Bourbons and had accepted the Orleanist house of Louis Philippe, "the bourgeois king," with institutions that gave more voice to parties and parliamentarianism. He hoped that the politics of his native land would continue evolving along these lines. Convinced that democracy was the wave of the future and was destined to flood Europe, he came to America to inquire, not whether democracy would triumph, but what would predominate when it triumphed—its good tendencies or the bad.[21] His goal, therefore, was first to inform himself and then predict to his fellow countrymen what they must expect. But, although he was quite sure about his prediction of the general trend, a methodological caution saved him from the dogmatism of the determinist. As the title of his work reveals, Tocqueville was intertwining two themes. He had come to look at a democracy, which happened to be functioning in the environment of North America. Constantly, therefore, when analyzing his data, he reminds himself and his reader that it is both democracy and America that he is observing. He invites the query: Are these data generally true of democracy, or do they arise specifically from its American context, or are they in some way the product of both? Hence, he makes it clear that he does not expect a democracy, established in another social environment, to be necessarily identical with its North American form in a frontier society. Thus, the particular structure and traditions of France would place their own individual impress on the general concept—as would the British, the Swiss, and every other historically identified people.

How important it is to disentangle the two themes—democracy and America—is evident when one asks the question: what are the criteria of democracy, as Tocqueville sees them? It then becomes clear that certain points, which are significant in themselves and crucial to his general argument, are related primarily to the American environment of the early 1830's, and not to democracy as such. Thus, he stresses the love of wealth,

---

21. "The organization and establishment of democracy among Christians is the great political problem of our time." *De la Démocratie en Amérique* (Librairie de Medicis: Paris, 1951) Vol. 1, Part ii, Chap. 9, p. 476.

desire for material advancement, restlessness and passion for novelty—factors which have been the psychological accompaniments of some other pioneer communities establishing themselves in a new terrain, and which, though they may well be associated with a democracy, do not necessarily belong to it.[22] Likewise, he asserts that a democracy exhibits weaknesses in the conduct of foreign affairs and in waging war. But at the same time he recognizes the relevant truth that, as he puts it, the Americans have no powerful neighbors.[23] Or, to state this more exactly, after Napoleon had been overthrown, after good relations with Britain had been inaugurated in 1818, and after the Spanish and Portuguese possessions had achieved their independence, the United States had nobody to fear, for the time being, on either side of the Atlantic. It was, therefore, the fortunate circumstance of location, and not the structure or spirit of democracy, which made of defense a minimal function of government. In fact then, what seemed like a defect in democracy was not such at all. The weakness of the military arm was rather the happy result of the advantages of geography.

After allowing for the influence of the environment, what features does Tocqueville consider essential to a democracy? Without any doubt, it is the principle of equality that occupies the central place in his analysis. For a democracy to be established, equality must be enshrined within the state and in the society that surrounds it. So important is this criterion in his thinking that he assigns to equality the supreme position—a most unequal position, one could say—in the hierarchy of democratic values. He regards it as the center of a circle from which other lines extend as radii. All the criteria of democracy which enter his discussion are in some way related to equality as its corollaries or consequences. Whether he is treating the philosophical concepts of the system (whereon, though unoriginal, he has the merit of French lucidity) or its psychological accompaniments (on which topic he has never been surpassed), it is always equality which emerges as the chief determinant. Other factors, to use a metaphor from mathematics, are the dependent variables. Because of equality, as he sees it, quantity outweighs quality and so the majority govern.[24] This also

22. In these respects, the early history of Australia and New Zealand would provide comparisons with Jackson's America, because of the similarities in response to like conditions. On the other hand, the rather static, conservative qualities of Switzerland will indicate that the democracy of an old and long-settled community can generate another psychology.

23. *Op. cit.*, Vol. 1. Part ii. Chap. 5, p. 355.

24. In the legal profession, however, Tocqueville sees an aristocratic element in American politics which combines with democracy so as to mitigate its faults. *Op. cit.*, Part II, Chap. 8, pp. 401-7.

means—such being the distribution of wealth—that the poor rule over the rich. Liberty is subdivided into liberties, which, to be acceptable, must be equalized. Since public office is a trust which the people confer upon one of their number and since almost anybody is considered capable of performing any job, office-holders are to act and be treated as the equals of their fellow citizens. Hence the persons engaged in politics will be a fair sample of the average around them. At any rate, they are unlikely to be manifestly superior.

In a larger sense, however, one notices in Tocqueville the same breadth of interpretation that characterized the Greeks. The meaning he ascribes to democracy is not confined to the structure of government or the categories of politics, but is as broad and deep as society itself. With a penetrating curiosity he inquires into religion, marriage, farming, property, the press, philosophy, science, language, and education, gleaning from each of these its relevance to democracy. He realizes that the threads of society crisscross, as warp and woof, with the processes of politics. He knows that philosophical doctrine is a part of the reality by which men live and that institutions must be explained in terms of principles as well as powers. In short, he sees the essence of democracy in the interpenetration of social context, governmental structure, and concepts of the ideal. If equality, which Jefferson mentioned first in his list of self-evident truths, is successfully pervading the structure and politics of democracy, this is the result of its conformance to the equalitarianism of American conditions, both social and economic.

By the middle decades of the nineteenth century, in the Old World as well as in the New, the democratic idea was gaining a potency which was without precedent in its history. The combined attraction of the democratic values yet to be won and the representative institutions already at work had generated the momentum for a major political revolution. Wherever the notion of fundamental change caught on, it was likely to be clothed in the doctrines, and even the catch-cries, of democracy. Evidence on this point can be found in the contemporary views of two critical observers who recorded, with accuracy, the reality they both noted and deplored. Thus, Thomas Carlyle remarked in 1843: "To what extent Democracy has now reached, how it advances irresistible with ominous, ever-increasing speed, he that will open his eyes on any province of human affairs may discern. Democracy is everywhere the inexorable demand of these ages, swiftly fulfilling itself."[25]

Similarly six years later, a bitter confirmation came from the pen of

25. *Past and Present*, Chap. 13.

Tocqueville's compatriot, the historian Guizot, who had served the monarchy of Louis Philippe as Minister and finally as Premier, only to lose power in the upheaval of 1848. Writing under the immediate sting of defeat, he blamed the revolution for sowing a harvest of chaos which lurked under the name of democracy. This had become the universal term, the sovereign talisman, for all parties to invoke. Monarchists favored a democratic monarchy; republicans a democratic republic. Socialists, communists, and the like, advocated democracy pure and simple. Democracy, he said, derived its empire from sources deep in human nature because its breadth carried an appeal to something in all men. "It is the banner for all the hopes, for all the social ambitions of humanity, be they pure or impure, noble or base, sensible or insane, practicable or utopian. . . . The word 'democracy' is now spoken every day, at every hour, in every place. Everywhere, and constantly, it is heard by everyone."[26]

John Stuart Mill on Representative Government

A cooler appraisal, in a calmer vein, came from Great Britain. John Stuart Mill encountered the same problem as Tocqueville, that of disentangling the generic principles of a democratic system from their specific embodiment in a particular country, and his analysis is contained in the *Considerations on Representative Government* (1861). It is true that the two men differ in the sequence of their ideas. One moves from description of the particular to reflective generalization; the other from broad abstraction to concrete examples. But it is no less clear that Mill's thinking about democracy is colored by the experience of the nation with which he was most familiar. Even when he refers to the United States, Britain remains his standard and model. Now Mill's observations are culled from the three decades that had elapsed since the crisis over the passage of the first Reform Act, 1830-32. In the years of his adult maturity he was a contemporary witness[27] to the initial liberalization of Britain's Parliament and electoral system, to the Indian Mutiny and reforms in Indian government, the expansion of British industries and commerce and the advent of free trade, the beginnings of public welfare services, and the challenge to established tradition in the universities, churches, and physical sciences. Grey, Peel, Russell, and Palmerston were the protagonists in the political drama, while Gladstone and Disraeli were waiting in the wings. Shaftesbury was

26. *De la Démocratie en France* (Victor Masson: Paris, 1849) pp. 9-11.
27. In certain cases, a vigorous participant as well.

humanizing the factories and Chadwick was cleansing the slums, while Marx was writing social theory in the British Museum. The second great installment of parliamentary reform was being actively debated and discussed, and six years after *Representative Government* appeared the legislation actually passed. It was in this setting that Mill's judgments were formed, and the context serves adequately to explain his emphasis.

Two themes constantly recur in Mill's delineation of the character of democracy. Accepting the representative system as the necessary mechanism for converting the popular will into governmental power, he discusses who is to be represented and with what results. Not only are these among the basic constant problems of all democracies, but they were specially pertinent to the stratified society of Victoria's Britain, whose urban working class was then demanding of the middle and upper classes a share in the franchise. Mill views these questions from the twin standpoints of quality and quantity. Of the former, he notes that "the principle of democracy . . . professes equality as its very root and foundation."[28] Hence arises the difficulty of doing justice to unusual talent. Where equality reigns, must quality suffer?[29] The other side of the coin is the matter of numbers. Adherence to equality, coupled with the Benthamite principle that each should count for one and nobody for more than one, must result in the practice of majority rule. Thus, Mill refers to "the rule of the numerical majority" as "the way in which it [democracy] is commonly conceived,"[30] and states elsewhere that "giving the powers of government in all cases to the numerical majority" is democracy's "ostensible object."[31]

But this has frightening implications. Foreseeing as a certainty that the suffrage will be conferred on all adults, he is fearful of entrusting the control of Parliament to a working class as uneducated as it then was. Equality and majorities alarm him if they mean the supremacy of ignorance over knowledge. Hence, while willing to liberate the many from the privileges of the few, he wants to guard the few from the dominance of the many. Let the old hereditary aristocracy pass into history. But substitute forthwith a new elite of the intellectually eminent. The danger lies in the trend to mediocrity. The remedy is to give honor to excellence—to the excellence which the individual has merited, not inherited. Thus, following this

28. *Considerations on Representative Government* (Everyman ed., E. P. Dutton & Co.: New York) Chap. VII, p. 257.
29. "But also democracy, in its very essence, insists so much more forcibly on the things in which all are entitled to be considered equally, than on those in which one person is entitled to more consideration than another, that respect for even personal superiority is likely to be below the mark." *Op. cit.*, Chap. XII, p. 320.
30. *Op. cit.*, Chap. VI, p. 249.
31. *Op. cit.*, Chap. VII, p. 258.

line of thought, Mill draws a distinction between two types of democracy, the "pure" and the "false." "The pure idea of democracy, according to its definition, is the government of the whole people by the whole people, equally represented. Democracy as commonly conceived and hitherto practiced is the government of the whole people by a mere majority of the people, exclusively represented."[32] To save the educated minority from "that falsely called democracy which is really the exclusive rule of the operative classes,"[33] Mill seeks a defense in the electoral scheme of proportional representation. By this method he would balance quality against quantity, knowledge against numbers. In other words, by first taking abstract principles and then applying them in a given social environment, his reasoning concludes with an institutional plan. The equation is clear:

$$\text{Philosophy} \times \text{Society} = \text{Governmental System}$$

The Century of the Common Man

Not long after Mill published these thoughts there took place the decisive events which marked the ending of the old order. In 1865 Lincoln was assassinated and Palmerston died. One had kept the Union united and, in the process, had freed the slaves. The death of the other made it politically practicable to usher in the second reform of Parliament and commence the enfranchisement of the industrial workers. In the two most important democracies of the world the floodgates were down and the tide of equalitarianism flowed strongly. So strongly indeed that, in the last part of the nineteenth century and the first two decades of the twentieth, the impetus to democracy becomes one of the sweeping movements of world history, profoundly affecting the lives of all peoples. Those whose ruling groups accepted the change, no less than those who resisted, were touched by the effects of democracy militant. It is precisely at this stage in its evolution that the formulation of democracy's criteria attains an unprecedented breadth. Whereas earlier it was possible to view the problem through the eyes of a single authoritative thinker, or within the context of some major intellectual system, in the century that has elapsed since the time of Mill one is confronted with a vast array of interpretations and analyses that are comprehensive in scope, complex in content, and contradictory in emphasis.

32. *Op. cit.*, Chap. VII, p. 256. See also p. 266, "In the false democracy which, instead of giving representation to all gives it only to the local majorities, the voice of the instructed minority may have no organs at all in the representative body."
33. *Op. cit.*, Chap. XII, p. 326.

The social evolution of mankind during the hundred years from 1860 to 1960 was distinguished by four major characteristics, for whose simultaneous combination the previous history of the human race affords no parallel. They were as follows:

Everything in society was changing.

The changes reached down to the foundations of the social system.

The rate of change varied from one sector of society to another; but over all was more rapid than ever before.

Welling up from sources in western Europe and North America, the changes rippled out to flood the world.

As a consequence of this unique union of events, it was impossible for innovations to occur in any part of society without at the same time affecting and being affected by the other parts. Hence, the social and intellectual controversies of this period, though each may have originated in one feature of social life, e.g., the economic, religious, or political, become increasingly intertwined. Liberalism confronts conservatism. Capitalism is challenged by socialism. Imperialism is attacked by nationalism, and nationalism by internationalism. Scientific empiricism refutes traditional orthodoxies in philosophy, education, and religion. And withal, the masses of mankind, growing politically self-conscious and articulate, defy the entrenched interests of a privileged few.

Three Views of Democracy: (1) Machinery and Process

The criteria of democracy, at this stage, have a habit of being all things to all men. The argument over its delineation has first to determine whether the terms of reference shall be narrow or broad. In the former case, the meaning of democracy is confined to politics, and intentionally is not extended to embrace the wider social context. Even the political category, however, permits a considerable latitude. Some identify democracy with the machinery of government and then identify a state as democratic if the framework of its institutions is built around an appropriate pattern. Normally, the latter is defined to include, at least as minima, a regularized system of periodic elections with a free choice of candidates, universal adult franchise, the opportunity to organize competing political parties, majority decisions along with safeguards for the protection of minority rights, a judiciary independent of the executive, and constitutional guaran-

tees for basic civil liberties. Such characteristics and their various elabora-
tions are plainly confined to the architecture of the government. In this
way of looking at democracy, what the observer emphasizes is the form of
government. Democracy is a style of procedure. Its primary concern is not
with the results which a government accomplishes, but with the manner
in which they are obtained.

To restrict the interpretation of democracy in this way brings an advantage in greater simplicity of definition. The debate about democracy
becomes more concrete. One can discuss the relative merits of unicameralism or bicameralism, of the presidential or cabinet executive, proportional representation or single-member districts, two or many parties, and
other matters of this sort. The terms of reference are fairly specific. Evidence can be gathered on how such systems function. Then the conclusions, instead of floating in the abstract, will be grounded on empirical
data. Yet when that is done, the ultimate findings are unsatisfying because they are incomplete. Beyond the procedures are the purposes which
they serve. Human beings are concerned with the values to which the
institutions are intended to lead. Analyzing a framework acquires significance when it is construed in the context of ideal goals. Procedure is
good or bad according to the results which it produces or prohibits. If all
the debate over democracy and its alternatives were limited to matters of
structure, why the fuss and excitement? Can people be as aroused as they
are, or become emotionally stirred, over a concept which begins and ends
with a bundle of institutional devices? Patrick Henry could proclaim:
"Give me liberty or give me death." His appeal, even discounting the
rhetoric, would have had less force had he said: "Give me a bicameral
Congress and an independent judiciary, or life won't be worth living."

(2) *The Values of Democratic Politics*

The concept of democracy, therefore, should be extended beyond the
means of government to include the ends of politics. Its criteria are immeasurably broadened when they embrace the purposes to which the state
is directed. What are the values which endow a political system with a
democratic character? The list is a familiar one: individual liberty, equality
of rights for all, supremacy of the people over their officials, the derivation
of authority from the citizens' consent, provision for the public welfare
and social justice. The substance of democracy, thus summarized, comprises the major topics of a political philosophy—the place of the individual in his community, the relations of individuals to one another and to

their government, and the functions which the latter undertakes to promote the general good. The democratic state is distinguished from others
primarily by the solutions it provides for these matters, and secondarily by
its constitutional devices. The life-blood of the system consists in the
values which people enjoy because of the form of government under which
they live.

But further questions at once come to mind. A term like individual
liberty is an abstraction whose breadth elicits wide support. The same
breadth, however, necessitates more detailed analysis if the content is to
become specific, at which point the support will also narrow down. When
closer definitions are attempted of a large concept, one runs into such
problems as those which Mill encountered in developing the argument of
his *Essay*. An inquiry into liberty leads to such related concepts as equality,
and it must then be asked whether the different values are contradictory
or harmonious.[34] In addition, as Mill's treatment illustrates, the political
categories must be considered in relation to whatever aspects of society
are relevant if they are to be realistically understood. Thus, the criteria of
democracy undergo further extension. As a definition restricted to procedures and institutions expands to envelop the substance of political goals,
so must the latter embrace those values of the society which permeate the
political system and condition its character. If one interprets democracy
in the light of philosophical ideals so broadly conceived as liberty, equality,
individualism, or welfare, does not their meaning absorb its color and content from economic, religious, racial, and other considerations which are
not merely political in the narrow sense but also, in the broadest sense,
social? In short, if a democratic theory must embrace a philosophy of
politics, does not the latter involve a philosophy of society?

(3) *Social Democracy*

It is not hard to see why this widening of criteria should have forced
itself upon those who face the question: What do we mean when we say
"democracy"? An example will illustrate the nature of the problem. Let us
grant that a basic criterion of democracy is its promotion of liberty. Suppose, for argument's sake, that liberty means both, negatively, an absence
of restraints, and, positively, a development of each individual's capacities to their full extent. If the positive aspect, the freedom to act, is
thought of in political terms only, then such liberty will include the rights
to vote, to seek public office, to obtain legal redress for wrongs, and to

34. This topic is taken up later in Chapters 16 and 17.

speak and publish without censorship. But there are other rights which liberty nowadays is ordinarily considered to embrace. In the realm of the conscience, there is the right to worship in any faith or not to worship at all. In the sphere of the intellect, there is the right to be educated out of public funds. Then there are the economic rights—the provision of security against such hazards as sickness or unemployment or widowhood and in meeting such inevitabilities as old age and death. The connection between guarantees of this kind and the political freedoms are easily demonstrated. Political liberty is diminished in a community which requires, as a condition of citizenship, that all persons worship in the same way, which denies to some of its citizens the education which enables them to understand issues and exercise an intelligent freedom of choice, or which limits by poverty and fear the opportunity for political participation. Liberty is a formal abstraction unless it can be effectively used. Anything in society, therefore, which impedes its use negates its definition. For, nothing that is socially significant can be politically irrelevant.

Once this is conceded, the way is open for so broad a statement of its criteria that democracy becomes coextensive with society. When it is argued that differences of race or religion should not mar the equal protection of the laws, that every child irrespective of family status or wealth should be educated to the full limit of its intellectual capacity, that employees should be able to bargain collectively with employers through representatives of their own choosing, the concepts of democracy become not only procedural but also substantive, not only political but also social. Such phrases as "social democracy" and "economic democracy" are then used, and they have two connotations. They suggest first that democracy cannot be established in the political sphere unless the rest of society is made to harmonize with its requirements;[35] and second, that such concepts as freedom or equality are transferable from the government of the state to the internal arrangements of the social system (e.g., its schools) and the economy (e.g., the corporation and the trade union). If citizens are entitled to vote together, without regard to sex, color, or creed, should not their children be educated together? If the theories of democracy require that officials be responsible to the people and be controllable by the voters, cannot the same apply to the managers of unions and business firms? Can a democratic state coexist with autocratic private associations?

Such a widening of horizons as these questions imply is not intended

---

35. For example, if all citizens have equal political rights, but an aristocratic notion of three classes prevails in the social order, then there is a disharmony between the equality in one sphere and the inequality in the other. Modern Britain is a case in point.

only in the interest of philosophical symmetry and logical tidiness, though the latter considerations admittedly play their part. The inclusion of social factors within the criteria of democracy—or, alternatively viewed, the extension of democracy to embrace other factors besides the political— does more than pay lip service to consistency of ideals. It also does a service for realism. For the truth is that the politics of democracy are unattainable without the fulfillment of certain economic and social prerequisites. Of what use is it to speak of "equal justice under law" unless the costs of litigation are such that anyone can go to court to defend his rights? What is the meaning of "freedom of contract" if, under conditions of individual bargaining between an employer and an employee, the loss of a job may bring starvation to one party and not to the other? What value lies in the suffrage unless those who vote have been so educated that they can analyze the arguments they hear, inform themselves intelligently of the choices available, and discern their interests over the short and longer runs?

Democracy and Liberalism

As these questions indicate, it became impossible to contemplate the evolution of government from oligarchy to democracy, or to formulate ideals as broad as liberty and equality, without taking cognizance of the entire social framework to which the state belongs. Necessarily, therefore, the other great movements of ideas and action which stirred the nineteenth century could not fail to be relevant to the proponents of democracy or to the opposition they encountered. An example of this is the influence of liberalism. At one stage in their history liberalism and democracy were scarcely separable. They ran on the same track, or at least on tracks that were parallel. The central idea of liberalism was liberty, which is, of course, a basic concept of democracy. But, granted that liberalism overlapped with democracy to the extent of their common concern for liberty, were they identical? The answer, which was not so clear at the beginning of the nineteenth century, became clearer as the century wore on. The movements were not identical. Liberals had to be democrats, but not all democrats had to be liberals.[36]

The reason for this bifurcation between the paths of liberalism and democracy lay in the variety of connotations which freedom could assume

36. As Professor Alf Ross has stated: "Nineteenth-century democracy evolved along with the liberal ideas. . . . But this historical parallelism should not veil the truth that democracy and liberalism are different concepts and are not interconnected." *Why Democracy?* (Harvard University Press: Cambridge, 1952) p. 109.

and the possibility of incompatible emphases which this variety afforded. Among the defenders of liberty there is little occasion for disagreement when the negative side of the concept is uppermost. To an appeal that we should rid ourselves of restraints, the response is usually wide and willing. Over negations there is less disputing. But the same cannot be said of affirmations. "Freedom from" results in "freedom to." After the prohibitions comes the opportunity to act. And there's the rub! The freedom to act positively means competition and clash; and where one side emerges the victor, inequality ensues and with it a loss of freedom for the underdog. Now these contradictions were not apparent in certain of the applications of liberty. The intellectual freedoms, for instance—freedom to speak, think, write, and publish—do not inhibit the freedom of others to do the same. Nor does the active exercise of political liberties, e.g., the right to vote, prevent another from doing likewise. But in the field of economic endeavor this is not normally the case. The economy is not concerned with the distribution of an unlimited, ever-expanding abundance.[37] It deals rather with the allocation of resources which are sometimes scarce in relation to potential need. Consequently, in the sphere of the market not all freedoms can be equally satisfied. The freedom from control by the state which was posited in the classical economics of the Manchester School did have the effect of enlarging productivity. But simultaneously it intensified the maldistribution of the product. Wealth was increased, but it was accumulated more unequally.

At this point the differences between liberalism and democracy became as evident as their overlap had formerly been. The issues were now squarely drawn: in economic terms, over the regulation of business by government; in social terms, over the relations between the middle and laboring classes; in political terms, over the extension of equal voting rights to all adults irrespective of property or income. The socialist movement now entered the field, challenging the liberals as the latter had once challenged the mercantilists and conservative land-owners. The socialist and the liberal looked at the same facts—the relation of the individual to society—but drew different conclusions because their angles of vision started at opposite points. One commenced with the individual and thought of the community's interest as the resultant of individual strivings. The other began with the community and conceived of individual improvement as flowing from the harmonies of general welfare. One was disposed to rely on private initiative as a means of encompassing the common good; the other, on public regulation both to check private rapacity and to

37. Even in an affluent society there are limits to the available resources.

enlarge the public interest. Socialism, therefore, like liberalism before it, had its own relevance to the criteria of democracy. Socialists could argue that democracy spelled both liberty and equality, and they could criticize the liberals for neglecting the latter in the name of the former. With their concern for the equal welfare of all, socialists could readily embrace a concept of democracy which affirmed in the political sphere the equal worth and dignity of all men. But some socialists were impatient to reach their goals. They were ready to take procedural short cuts, if the rate of change could thereby be accelerated. They valued equality so highly that they were willing to sacrifice political liberty. Thus socialism, too, became separable from democracy, and the movement split into social democrats and communists.

Nationalism and Democracy

The same tendency, to gravitate into the orbit of democracy or to swing away, can be detected in the fluctuations of another potent force of modern times, the sentiment for nationalism. Nationalism has many manifestations. It implies the centralization of power in the nation, at the expense both of local interests inside and of the international society outside. It means the converging of individual loyalties into a unity. Also, it can mean freedom. But freedom in what sense? For people who were governed under such a multinational regime as that of the Hapsburgs, or were colonies of Britain or France, freedom had a specific meaning: self-rule instead of alien rule, emancipation from an external, unrepresentative, uncontrollable power. In this sense, there was clearly an area of compatibility between democracy and nationalism. Imperialism negated freedom. It denied a government founded upon the consent of the governed. Consistently, therefore, a Mazzini or a Nehru could be a nationalist and a democrat. But this was not true of all nationalists. Long is the list of dictators who have led their people to throw off the foreign yoke, only to impose their own. Freedom from the distant imperialist can end in the autocracy of the homemade tyrant. There has been too close a correlation between modern nationalism and fanatical intolerance to permit any naïve illusions that "the right of self-determination" will always leave a people freer in fact than they were before. With the switch from colonialism to independence, those who oppose the government may still run the risk of being imprisoned or shot. But there is this difference: in a colony, the jailers and the firing squad do not speak the same language as their victims, whereas, after independence, they do.

The line of discussion pursued in the last several pages would permit extended elaboration and more plentiful examples. But the proper place for those will come in the later chapters. Enough has been written here to show that in the modern evolution of democracy there has been a great variation in criteria from the very narrow to the very broad. The narrower those criteria, the more specific they are and the more comprehensible. With greater amplitude of scope, the concept becomes far richer, though also less clear. At certain points the thinking about democracy, and some of its practices, merge with the aspirations and actions of other contemporary movements; and at their widest and most profound the values of democracy are the goals of civilization. The seamless web of which society is woven does not easily lend itself to the sharp cutting-edge of precise and logical analysis. Categories, to satisfy the intellect, must needs be sharp. But the realities of life are shaded and modulated; their outlines are blurred; their forms can be definite at the center, but are indistinct around the edge.

Theme and Variations

An inquiry into democracy, therefore, is a study of unity and variety. The unity consists in emphasizing freedom and equality as the goals which should permeate a society and animate its politics; in the requirement that the principal leaders of the government should be periodically elected to office through institutions that offer a genuine choice; in the opportunity for individuals to earn that place in the community to which their own service and merits entitle them without regard to their inheritance of family, faith, finance, or face. But important though it is to be agreed on these fundamentals, the variations are also impresssive. Both liberty and equality can receive connotations which are far from coinciding. One principle may be subordinated to the other; and when this happens, it is readily apparent that a libertarian democracy and an equalitarian democracy are markedly different. The institutional structures can vary as much as do those of Switzerland, Great Britain, and the United States. Yet all these are democracies. Moreover, in the application of economic philosophy so much will depend on the resources, both human and natural, which are available that utopian theories of perfect competition, of distributive justice, or of social ownership, must concede to the stubborn necessities of time and place. There is a liberal democracy, as there is a social democracy. Democracy, inherently, is not necessarily either collectivistic or individualistic. It may at times be of the one type, at times of the other, and is normally a blend of both.

To understand the criteria, therefore, let us look at cases. To learn about Democracy, let us compare democracies.

II

The Democratic Society

4

The Spread and Limits of Democracy

One of the strongest influences exerted on a political system is the accumulated force of its own tradition. As the discussion of criteria showed, democratic ideas and institutions have developed over a long period. The analyzing of concepts throws a certain light upon a form of government, since its avowed aspirations thus become clear. But complementary findings emerge from a different set of data—those which are embodied in the logic of experience—for they are the summary of actual achievement. No system can evolve through two and a half millennia without producing conclusions which, besides their philosophical roots, are grounded in the truth of historical happenings. The record of events discloses the conditions under which democracy has grown and then has either flourished or failed. This chapter will briefly summarize a few salient points to serve as an introduction to the social environment of the democratic state.

From Revolution to Evolution

There is one fact which stands out sharply at the beginning. In modern democracies we have eliminated the occasion for revolution, because our constitutional system allows for orderly change and therefore renders a recourse to violence superfluous. One reason, however, which has made this possible nowadays is that, in the countries which were the earliest to move in this direction, democracy had its origins in revolution. In the case of

Athens, this was true both in the time of Solon and later after the Peisistratid dictatorship was overthrown. There, the Many wrested power from the Few, and that is precisely what was meant by *demokratia*—"the people's strength." In Rome, on the other hand, the governing oligarchy of senatorial clans always maintained its grip, even on the institutions of a republic, as was proven in the abortive revolutions of the Gracchi and Marius. Likewise, when democracy was reborn on a larger scale in the seventeenth and eighteenth centuries, its beginnings were everywhere accompanied by violence. The Dutch fight for national liberation, England's Civil War, the Swiss struggles against their cantonal and city oligarchies, the American War of Independence, and the French Revolution, all were the birth-pangs of the modern democratic state.

Only after the foundations of democracy had been laid in uprisings and through deeds of arms was it possible elsewhere to achieve the same result by less violent means. In the British Empire, for instance, the American colonists had to go to war to become independent and self-governing. But the Canadians, after some relatively minor skirmishes in the 1830's, were granted self-government[1] in the next decade, and the Australasian colonies benefited from the same policy without recourse to violence. On the European continent, successful revolutions for democracy had a contagious effect almost everywhere—as in the uprisings of 1830 and 1848. In the twentieth century, after World Wars I and II, democratic constitutions were introduced into the defeated countries, not so much because their own populations had struggled to achieve them, but because there was a reaction against the autocratic governments which had lost the war. As for the colonial areas which have become independent since 1946, the major objective in all cases was to secure autonomy. Internal freedom, in the sense of popular and responsible government, was in most cases the secondary objective. In fact, in many of the recently created states, the result of independence has only been to substitute one kind of authoritarianism for another. In the Gold Coast, a British Governor kept Kwame Nkrumah in prison. In Ghana, the former victim, who now styles himself the Redeemer, does the same to his own opponents.

That democracy originated in revolution is worth remembering by those of us who live in societies where that task was accomplished many generations ago. For us, democracy is part of an inheritance we have received. It is no novelty. We take for granted all of its practices and assumptions. These belong to a *status quo* which we intend to maintain. In our way of thinking and feeling, therefore, democracy expresses not our radicalism, but

1. That is, in domestic matters. Full control over their external relations came after World War I.

our conservatism. We have grown used to it, as one is comfortable in an old pair of shoes. Hence, we find less occasion to re-examine its fundamentals; we pay less attention to the circumstances under which it grew.

Thus we tend to forget—if indeed we ever knew—how slowly democracy evolved and how very recently it has matured. In the case of Athens, while the first steps toward a democratic system were taken by Solon in 594 B.C., the second stage did not occur until the reforms of Cleisthenes at the end of that century, and the third phase came after the Persian Wars with the innovations of Pericles and Ephialtes (461 B.C.) Athens, which was the only important Greek *Polis* to govern itself democratically, attained the height of its power and prosperity between 490 B.C. (Marathon) and 421 B.C. (the Peace of Nicias). Even in that short period, however, the range of democracy was still severely limited. Not only did the Athenians employ their sea power to convert the Confederacy of Delos into a naval empire, but even in their domestic politics the *Demos* was far from including the majority of the adult population. The right to participate in politics did not extend, of course, to women[2] or to resident aliens (the *metics*.) Nor did the principle of freedom embrace the emancipation of slaves. The *Demos* comprised a much more numerous group than the surrounding aristocracies or oligarchies. But it stopped far short of including the whole mass of people. There is some justice in a historian's comment: "To the Greeks democracy meant, not the overthrow of privilege, but merely the extension of its area."[3]

In the modern history of democracy, it is surprising in retrospect to discover how recent has been the achievement of mass participation in politics. Every one of the countries which today are the prime examples of democracy was governed by an oligarchy at the opening of the nineteenth century. By the end of that century the majority of the adult male population had finally won the right to vote. The right of the suffrage, admittedly, is not the only test of democracy. But it is certainly one criterion which is fundamental. To speak of the sovereignty of the popular will, the eliciting of consent, periodic elections, confrontation of parties in the legislature—all this must be realistically interpreted in terms of the numbers of citizens who are legally entitled to vote in elections of the legislature. If that right is restricted to a small minority, the other principles are a façade behind which an oligarchy stays entrenched. One cannot give the name democracy to a system where a dominant elite arranges its internal affairs democratically, but keeps the majority in a subordinate position.

2. Plato's plea in the *Republic* for equality between the sexes was thoroughly unconventional.
3. E. M. Walker, *Cambridge Ancient History*, Vol. V, pp. 102-3.

British Gradualism an Example

Great Britain supplies a specific example which illustrates the point. It is a particularly interesting case because that country evolved from royal absolutism through an aristocratic form into a mass democracy. The process was gradual and there are fortunately sufficient statistics to measure the rate of democratic development. Sir Lewis Namier estimated the size of the electorate which two centuries ago—in 1761, to be exact—could vote for members of the House of Commons. He calculated that there were some 160,000 qualified voters in England's forty counties and approximately 85,000 in the 204 English boroughs. Of the latter, only 22 boroughs contained more than a thousand voters. As to the former: "It would be ludicrous," he wrote, "to talk of any kind of 'democracy' in 39 out of the 40 counties. Taking England as a whole, probably not more than one in every twenty voters at county elections could freely exercise his statutory rights, and the county Members, though a valuable element in the House in that most of them were independent of the Government, constituted the purest type of class representation in Great Britain, to a high degree, of a hereditary character."[4] Such was the state of affairs a hundred years after the death of Cromwell and the restoration of the limited monarchy with an omnipotent Parliament.

The democratization of British politics was, of course, delayed by the French Revolution and the Napoleonic Wars, during which period conservatives could insinuate that reformers were pro-French and, therefore, traitors. But the return of the Liberals to power in 1830 inaugurated a period of rapid institutional change, which accorded with new social and economic conditions. Since the government of the United Kingdom is unitary in form, which has the merit of simplicity, it is possible to trace the evolution of the electorate on a national scale and demonstrate in percentages the steady progress from oligarchy to democracy. The accompanying table tells its own story on this point.

Since the population figures in that table include those under the legal voting age of 21, who make up more than 30 per cent of the total, it is not until the percentage in the right-hand column rises above 60 that one can properly speak of universal suffrage. Specifically in Great Britain, the movement from oligarchical rule to a mass democracy began in 1830 and took a century to complete. Three Acts of Reform (those of 1832, 1867, and 1884) enfranchised the great majority of the adult males. Two more

4. Lewis Namier, *The Structure of Politics at the Accession of George III*, Vol. I, Chap. 2, pp. 92-3.

acts (in 1918 and 1928) made the suffrage universal. As judged by this single basic criterion of the right to vote in parliamentary elections, Britain became a democracy—for men only—after 1884; for the whole adult population, after 1928.[5] The latter date is only one generation back from the time when this is being written.

THE GROWTH OF THE BRITISH ELECTORATE

| Date of Law Extending Suffrage | Registered Voters | | Population at Nearest Census | | Percentage of Voters to Population |
	Date	Number (ooo's omitted)	Date	Number (ooo's omitted)	
1832	1830	440	1831	16,261	2.7
	1833	725			4.4
1867	1866	1,200	1861	23,128	5.6
	1869	2,250	1871	26,072	8.6
1884	1883	2,950	1881	29,710	9.9
	1886	5,000			16.8
1918	1910	7,200	1911	40,831	17.6
	1918	19,500	1921	42,769	45.6
1928	1924	20,650	1921	42,709	48.3
	1929	28,500	1931	44,795	63.6
	1959	35,400	1961	52,673	67.2

Full Democracy a Recent Phenomenon

Similarly on the Continent, to pursue this point further, the trend toward mass participation in politics occupied the century between the close of the Napoleonic Wars and World War I. Because social systems and constitutional arrangements differed, the precise timing varied from country to country. But in most places, the absolute monarchies, aristocracies, and plutocracies lost their exclusive privileges in successive stages—e.g., in 1830 and 1848 and with increasing speed in the period between 1890 and 1914. The Danes, for example, moved rapidly within two generations (1848–1915) from royal absolutism to popular elections for the *Folketing*, univer-

5. "Political democracy in Britain is only a little more than twenty one years old. . . . In 1929, when I was elected to Parliament for the first time, I was a member of the first British Parliament elected by all men and women over twenty one years of age." Aneurin Bevan, *In Place of Fear* (Simon & Schuster: New York, 1952) p. 9.

sal suffrage, and a multiplicity of parties. Likewise, the Swiss people, who were free from monarchy, but were inhibited by their ingrained conservatism, liberalized the cantonal regimes in 1830, adopted a proper federal union with adult male suffrage in 1848, introduced the referendum and initiative on a national scale in 1874, and have been fully democratic (save for the perennial disfranchisement of women[6]) ever since.

In the United States, because this country was a republic and lacked a clutter of traditional institutions with vested interests, democracy sprang up earlier and was able to mature faster. Property or income requirements, as a condition of voting, were generally abolished in the Northeast and Midwest before the Civil War. Thus in 1860, when the total population was 31,400,000, as many as four and three-quarter millions actually voted in the election which brought Lincoln to the Presidency.[7] The enfranchisement of women was largely a Western movement originating in the Rocky Mountain states where women had a scarcity value and greater bargaining power. Nationally, however, it was World War I which brought political equality to women in the United States as in Great Britain. What American democracy has still failed to achieve to date is the complete removal of the color bar from the polling booth. In this respect, the States of the deep South continue to be a retarded region and lag behind the rest of the country. Apart from that important exception, the presidential election of 1920 may be considered the first in the history of the United States at which adult suffrage was the rule.

Nevertheless, when that has been stated, as in truth it must be, other considerations should be included in a total judgment. While it is a fact that democracy evolved slowly, and that its mature expression is a recent phenomenon extending over two generations at the most, in retrospect this may now appear a valuable source of its strength. That which grows gradually sends its roots deep and can therefore rise high and spread wide. The formula for success of the leading, stable democracies of today seems to have been to start with early revolution and continue with gradual evolution. The adoption of new institutions and procedures, admission of new groups and classes to the charmed circle which exercises power, extension of basic rights to all on equal terms—this brings the best results when it is done by degrees. The sudden revolution may bring the swift reaction. Every Brumaire invites its Thermidor. France, after overthrowing the Or-

6. At present (1964) the Swiss ladies vote in cantonal elections in Geneva and Vaud, but not in federal elections. On this point, *la Suisse romande* is tinged with more romantic feelings than the land of the *Schwyzerdütsch*.

7. Contrast the British statistics for the same period. The population in 1861 was 23,128,000. Registered voters in 1866 were under a million and a quarter.

leanist monarchy, adopted adult male suffrage in the Second Republic of 1849. Two years later came the Napoleonic coup and the Second Empire. In the United States after 1865, the victorious North tried to place Negroes, many of them inadequately trained, in responsible positions in the South. But the intention, though good, was too hastily applied and only increased the hostility of the defeated whites.

The Link with Imperialism

Another relevant fact to be remembered is the close connection, until World War II at least, between domestic democracy and external imperialism. By imperialism I mean the imposition of alien rule on a noncontiguous territory and its population. As such, this is antithetical to freedom and self-government. In the two decades between the two World Wars, the largest empires in terms of subjects and area were controlled by democracies: namely, Belgium, France, Great Britain, and the Netherlands. Because of the patent contradiction between the practices of democracy at home and imperialism abroad, the existence of those empires is an item to be entered on the balance sheet when one appraises the whole record of democracy in the modern world.

However, to mention that democracies once possessed colonies is no indictment of the former unless they attempted to perpetuate colonialism. As a matter of fact, the democracies did in the end preside over the liquidation of their empires—with alacrity in the treatment of the Philippines by the United States, with cautious pragmatism in the British conversion of Empire into Commonwealth, with reluctant acceptance of the inevitable by France in Southeast Asia and North Africa, and with poor preparation of their colonies for independence by the Belgians and Dutch.[8] In any case, although nowadays imperialism in most languages is synonymous with sin, a balanced view of the better colonial systems may discern a positive achievement for which there is no need to apologize. Imperial powers exported to the peoples they controlled all aspects of their own society, the good along with the bad. Hence, as democratic ideals and institutions pervaded western Europe, they filtered through or trickled down to subject areas abroad. In the process, the western world has extended its science, technology, and political doctrine to other continents and cultures. The results, in some cases, may bring a lasting good. The United States, half-

8. Spain and Portugal do nothing to prepare their colonies for independence. Why should they? Under Franco and Salazar, there has been no political freedom in Madrid or Lisbon either.

embarrassed after 1898 to find itself with "possessions," applied the principles of the Declaration of Independence to the Philippines within less than half a century and laid the foundations of a democratic system which Spain had never done. India won its independence with an aroused sense of nationalism and by non-violent resistance. Since 1947 the Indian government has tried to keep intact the judicial system and civil service which the British built, and has functioned thus far with a mass franchise, free elections, choice of parties, cabinet and parliamentary opposition. Hence, if present trends continue, India will become the world's largest and most diversified democracy.

Survey of Democracies in 1939

But the possibilities of the future cannot be counted in the performance of the present. It is conceivable that various of the still-developing regions in Asia and Africa will evolve along democratic lines, but the truth is that democracy up to now has always been the exception among political systems. It never was, and is not yet, the rule. Today, as in the past, the majority of the human race are still governed in an authoritarian fashion by oligarchies of one kind or another. This will become apparent if one surveys the world as it was politically when Germany invaded Poland in 1939, and compares that period with the mid-1960's. In 1939, the governments of the following countries could be called clearly democratic:

In North America: Canada and the United States.

In Central and South America: Costa Rica.

In Europe: Belgium, Denmark, Eire, France, Great Britain, the Netherlands, Norway, Sweden, and Switzerland.

In the South Pacific: Australia and New Zealand.

In Asia: None.

In Africa: None.

That list is not very long. There were many countries in which a democratic type of constitution had been introduced before or after World War I, but which reverted to an authoritarian regime in the 1930's. Italy acquiesced to a Fascist leader in 1922 and submitted to dictatorship after 1925. The Weimar government broke down in Germany in 1930 and was ground to dust by Hitler in 1933. One by one, the states of central and eastern Europe reacted to economic disaster by tearing down their democratic façades in favor of Führers, Caesars, or Commissars. The same occurred in the Far East, where Japan, succumbing to militarism and the extreme Right, commenced a decade and a half of aggressive expansion. In Latin America, Mexico was making forward strides with social revolution and political evolution; but republican institutions collapsed in Brazil where Vargas, in imitation of Mussolini, set up a fascist-style corporative state. After the high hopes and idealism of the early 1920's the events of the 1930's were the worst that democracy had experienced in a hundred years. As a consequence, a second war of global dimensions had to be fought to "make the world safe for democracy."

When it was over, and the balance sheet of the 1940's was drawn up, the result was a mixture of gains, losses, and question marks. Most important of all for the democracies was that they survived. The institutions of government and the civic morale endured through initial defeat until eventual victory. Hitler and Mussolini were dead, and Japan's militarists were dethroned. Stalin, however, was very much alive. The Red Army pushed the western frontiers of communism into central Europe, and Mao Tsetung emerged the victor of the Chinese Civil War. The early Japanese successes over occidental forces (1941-42) provided the stimulus everywhere in Asia and Africa for non-white peoples to rebel against European rule. Whether in so doing they would simultaneously reject the political ideals of western Europe was yet to be determined. At this point, where yesterday's happenings merge with today's, the saying of Freeman comes to mind: "History is past politics, and politics is present history." It is always difficult to capture truly the spirit of what is recent and contemporary, particularly when so many situations are fluid or even chaotic. But some appraisal of the extension of democracy in the 1960's must be attempted.

A Contemporary Estimate

Two important differences may be observed between the world's political spectrum now and what it was a quarter of a century ago. One is the sheer increase in the number of states at present controlled by the Communist party in eastern Europe and east Asia. None of these represents a net loss for democracy except Czechoslovakia, which had the double misfortune of being the victim of Hitler in 1938-39 and of Stalin in 1948. On the democratic side, there has been no major addition since 1939 to the catalogue of governments that beyond any doubt can be called stable democracies; and one must unfortunately record the contemporary collapse of parliamentarianism in France, which in 1958 reverted to the autocracy of a single leader. However, there is a fairly long list of countries whose politics have latterly been evolving in a democratic direction or whose institutions convey a democratic appearance. In this category, for example, one might place Brazil, Chile, and Mexico. Their regimes are not completely stable, nor is their democratic character by any means assured. They still exhibit profound oligarchical tendencies and have yet to consummate their basic revolutions—industrial, agrarian, and social. But undeniably they contain a democratic potential.

The same may be said about some of the countries which had only a limited experience with democratic institutions prior to World War II and have renewed the experiment since then. How could anybody at this moment venture a precise judgment about Austria, Italy, Japan, or West Germany? All of them are garbed in the outer accoutrements of democracy. All have functioned with democratic processes since the victors ended their occupation. But too short a period has elapsed to permit any certain opinion about their future. Institutions which do not have the strength of tradition behind them, or have not yet gained wide-spread social acceptance, seldom survive a major catastrophe, economic or military. Also it should be remembered that only one party, or essentially the same coalition, has thus far continuously controlled each of those countries. A genuine alternation in office, between rivals equally loyal to democracy, has yet to be established.

Even more caution must be exercised in appraising the politics of states which have enjoyed less than two decades of independence. India is now practicing democracy on a grandiose scale, Israel on a small scale. But each at the beginning needed the leadership of an extraordinary man and the power of a dominant party. The test for democracy will come when the parties which Nehru and Ben-Gurion respectively led disintegrate or lose power. Elsewhere, throughout Africa for example, it is much too soon to be sure. One may have hopes for a democratic development in Nigeria or in some of the member states of the French Community. But at least two generations must pass before democracy can be said to have matured and to be securely founded. Such instances as Burma, Ceylon, Ghana, Indonesia, Pakistan, and South Korea, supply proof of the precariousness or futility of democratic institutions imported from western Europe and North America. If the leadership of a newly independent state wants first to consolidate its power internally and extend its influence outside, if social and economic changes are pressed with great rapidity in the teeth of traditionalist opposition, authoritarian means are likely to be chosen as short cuts to the desired end. On the other hand, could anyone have offered a sure prediction about the future evolution of British politics, say, in 1640,

1770, or 1790? Was it possible to be confident about the development of the United States either in 1785 or in 1860? In France, at what time since 1789 has there ever been any solid assurance about the durability of the regime? Why then should one expect reliable indications of present or future behavior in communities which have yet to master the peculiarly complex art of self-mastery?

An ounce of history is worth a pound of predictions, because what is done and past can be seen in perspective and judged for what it was worth. What the historical record of democracy undeniably proves is that this system of government was always a rarity and is so still. Saying this does not belittle democracy, for good things are rare. The reason is that to produce a democracy requires not only time, but other favoring conditions. It takes a special combination of circumstances to bring about the genesis of a democratic system and nurture it to maturity. This combination has seldom occurred in the past. Even today it is not widespread. Hence, to inquire into the several factors within society which permit or prohibit the operation of democracy is the next broad theme for this discussion.

The Social Environment of the Political System

A political system cannot be democratic if too many feaures of the surrounding social order are profoundly undemocratic. Both the general ethos of a society and the dominant traits of its particular branches are transmitted to its politics. In a community, for instance, which is strongly imbued with militarism or commercialism, with aristocracy or theocracy, the government will be tinged with the same coloration. You can draft on paper the most democratic constitution in the world and have it officially adopted. But where the social patterns and political traditions are stubbornly antagonistic, that constitution quickly becomes a dead letter. By the same logic, when society exhibits a welter of contradictions—e.g., when equality reigns in some spheres and oligarchy in others—then, since the social order is at odds with itself, politics will constitute an arena for the conflict of divergences. The rival groups will seek to capture the power of the state and use it to make the society and its government either more democratic or less. In the realities of the modern world, societies are seldom all one thing or all the other. Usually, they embody a mixture within which antitheses fight. Moreover, since changes occur continuously, the over-all patterns of a community and of its politics will alter as its various branches evolve, and they do not by any means evolve at the same pace. Hence modernity or progress or liberalism in one sector of society may be retarded by the conservatism or reaction of another. To all these influences politics are susceptible. The flowering of democracy, therefore, is nourished or stunted by its social roots.

It is for such reasons that the present part of this book is devoted to an examination of society. Since democracy affects and is affected by its other social accompaniments, its success or failure may often be traceable to causes that extend throughout the social system. Also, the degree to which democracy is attained may well be due to the opportunities or impediments which society presents. To start, therefore, with a political analysis, and omit the prior social analysis, would be to open this inquiry in the middle instead of at the beginning. The explanation for much that will be discovered later in the politics of democracy lies in the features of the society to be discussed here. But what should these features be? In an ultimate sense all things social, including all things political, are interconnected. In a practical sense, however, no study can encompass everything. Somewhere a line has to be drawn between what is directly and immediately relevant and what has an indirect relation or a remote one. The former must be examined, the latter need not be; and the reader should form his opinion, as must the writer, concerning what belongs to which side of the line.

What are the fundamentals of a community which bear closely upon the problem of democracy? First, there are the people themselves. Their race, religion, and language must be considered, since any of these may have profound political implications. An organized community also stretches over a portion of the Earth's surface. Democracy in space must bow to the compulsions, as it can also utilize the possibilities, of geography. Military survival is conditioned by the physical features and location of the territory which a people inhabits, as is the relation of the central government to its regional and local units. Likewise, there is the economic factor—the availability of natural resources, the scientific technology which converts them for human use, the complex system by which goods and services are produced and exchanged, as well as the ownership of capital and the distribution of income. Each of these several aspects, and all in unison, are involved in a people's politics. As the various features of the human face unite to produce that elusive and indefinable quality, the expression, so do history, culture, geography, and economics, combine with politics in a result to which everything has contributed something. The following five chapters will therefore explore the constituents of society, asking in each case the same questions: What helps democracy? What hinders it? What are the requirements that make a society democratic?

5

Race Relations

The subject of every social inquiry is to study human relationships; its object is to improve our understanding of them. Hence, an examination of the democratic society must begin with the people themselves. Relations between the persons who form a community occur for many reasons and can assume a variety of modes. Certain of these are transitory and superficial. But some are fundamental, permanent, and pervasive. Among the latter are race, language, and religion. Each individual has racial characteristics which are biologically inherited. Similarly, everybody communicates with his fellows through the medium of language. Also, in all periods for which historical information is available, most human beings have adhered to a religion, in the sense that they believed in some power or powers beyond the operation of ordinary natural forces. Religion, so defined, falls in a somewhat different category from either language or race. No one can avoid belonging to a race or mixture of races. Nor, since a minimum level of civilization was attained, has anybody, other than the dumb, been devoid of language. Religion, however, is a matter of faith and doctrine, which many take on tradition and without question, whereas others feel free to accept, reject, or suspend judgment. Practically every organized society in the past acknowledged some religious belief, and, what is more, gave it public official sanction. During the last two or three hundred years, however, the acceptance of religion by individuals has been declining, especially in the western world, until nowadays, though most people still profess a faith, few really practice it.

The Politics of Racial, Religious, and Linguistic Groupings

But what is the relevance of race, language, and religion to democracy or its opposite? What bearing do they have on this subject?

Again one should distinguish between religion and the other two factors. No race, no language, as such, is either democratic or undemocratic. In this respect, however, the world's religions, when they are organized into institutions, exhibit a considerable variation. Some are focused upon the authority of the church; others upon the faith and reason of the individual. In some the priesthood wields great influence over the members; in others the congregation controls the clergy. Some theologies separate humanity into groups, placing their emphasis on differences and inequality. Others see all mankind as equal before the deity. Both attitudes produce immediate social effects and have direct implications for politics.

Granted then that religion, because of the organizations it creates and the ideology it adopts, approaches closer to the core of democracy than either race or language, there is nevertheless an important similarity between the three which justifies their being treated together. The members of a community either belong to the same race, speak the same language, and profess the same religion, or their religions, languages, and races are different. Whether a society is homogeneous or the reverse in any or all of these has a profound consequence for the relations between human beings. The point at issue here is the one that was stated by Aristotle in these words: "A *Polis* wants to consist, as far as possible, of equals and similars."[1] A society that contains deep-seated divergences poses complications for government which are absent from a community of equals and similars. Identity in fundamentals contributes to peace and harmony.[2] Dispute over matters which men hold most dear leads easily to friction and even violence. The quality of tolerance is always included among the democratic ideals. Yet tolerance has no meaning unless it be applied to dissimilars. There is no special virtue in the tolerance of like for like. The virtue consists in tolerating the unlike. But do people ordinarily tolerate disagreement when the substance at stake reaches to the foundations of their social order? Psychologically, can they then be tolerant? Morally, should they

1. *Politics*, 1295b. *Polis* in this passage is normally translated (e.g., by Jowett, Rackham, and Barker) as "state." But it is more than that. It means "city-state-community" combined.
2. Bertrand Russell, who is not noted for his propensity to conform, has observed: "Without some degree of homogeneity, government by discussion is unworkable." *Power* (Allen and Unwin: London, 1938), p. 24.

be? Let us suppose that a community is not fundamentally at one. What happens then? It is admittedly a house divided. Does it always necessarily follow that such a house has to be divided against itself?

The historical record of every civilization abundantly demonstrates that fanaticism and extremism are just as common as compromise and moderation, if not indeed commoner. It is not difficult to persuade an ignorant person, or anyone whose narrow outlook stems from a limited experience, to dislike what is different. Such dislike is compounded with fear; together these yield prejudice. If people are intensely conscious of their racial stock, their religious beliefs, their linguistic heritage and its culture, and if they become convinced that the survival of any or all of these is threatened by a group which differs in such particulars, then the two groups can scarcely coexist within the same society. If you are genuinely persuaded, as were the medieval Catholics, that yours is the one true faith, and that heresy is the work of the Devil, can you truly tolerate the dissenter? If you firmly believe that your race must preserve its biological purity, will you accept members of a different race as your equals and fellow citizens? If you are so proud of your ancestral language and literature, that you wish either to teach it to others or to prevent its elimination by a rival tongue, will speech become an instrument of domination or separatism?

Under these circumtances what role is played by the state? Since politics provides the arena for the public airing of controversy, the state which serves a divided community must either take sides or seek to compose the differences. It is not enough merely to assert that the state, in the time-honored formula, maintains "law and order." Whatever law is imposed must possess a content, and order involves someone giving orders to someone else. For a democracy, therefore, the presence of social diversity postulates a special challenge. A non-democratic regime, which does not value liberty or equality, will not have to change its political character if it uses governmental coercion to subordinate one social group to another. But the democracy that employs the force of the state to sanction a religious orthodoxy or uphold a system of racial or linguistic supremacy denies the law of its own being. Such a policy is a sacrifice of equality and freedom on the altar of uniformity; and uniformity, whether in thought, belief, or conduct, was never a democratic ideal.

Here a clarification is needed, or this argument could soon be misunderstood. Some communities are remarkably homogeneous; others are quite the opposite. Some states are run democratically; others, the reverse. Plainly there is no correlation, inherent or historical, between these pairs of contrasts. Democratic systems of government have existed among societies of similars, and among those with diversity. Dictatorships can likewise be found in both. Empirical evidence does not prove that either type of political system is the product of either a unified society or a pluralistic one. What can be demonstrated, however, is that diversity in fundamentals gives rise to strains and tensions which increase the need for democracy while augmenting the obstacles to its attainment.

Characteristics of a Divided Society

Every society is of course unique in the manner of combining its various characteristics and in the sequence of its historical evolution. But many of the divided houses share some common features which either mitigate or accentuate the effects of division. For instance, where the majority differs from the minority in race, language, or religion, it is important to discover whether the minority is geographically concentrated or dispersed. When it is dispersed, its influence may be diluted by the strength of the contiguous majority. However, a group which is a minority nationally may form the majority within its locality or region. In that case, their physical proximity to one another and their control over a territorial area may increase their separatist feeling and their potency. The pre-Civil War South in the United States and the French-Canadians in Quebec are two examples of this tendency.

A second factor that can influence the relations between groups is a numerical change in the ratio between them. Suppose an established majority finds that its numbers are declining, whether absolutely or as a percentage, and that the minority is increasing in size. Such a shift may provoke alarm among the majority, which fears to lose its ascendancy. It may, as a consequence, become less tolerant while the numbers are altering to its disadvantage. This is most likely to happen when the change is occurring rapidly, either because of different birth rates or because of an influx of immigrants.

Third, the people who form a minority group within an organized community may receive reinforcement from others outside who belong to the same race or religion, or speak the same language. If the external sympathizers form a large and powerful bloc, and if they control the government of an important state, the minority that receives their backing may feel emboldened to resist the majority of their own society. One recalls, in this connection, the support of English and Scottish Protestants for Protestant Ulster; the aid given by Nazi Germany to the Sudeten Germans of Czechoslovakia; the sympathy for the Indian Muslims in what is now Pakistan of Muslims elsewhere; the assistance rendered to Palestinian

Jews by coreligionists in the United Kingdom and the United States. In certain cases, as these examples indicate, the cultural cleavage may run so deep and the gulf become so wide that a community cannot be created or be held together among the discordant members. Ulster chose union with England, Scotland, and Wales, rather than with her southern neighbors. Indian Muslims, although they are geographically concentrated in two regions of the northeast and northwest which are not contiguous, preferred to have their own state independent of the Hindus. Jews and Arabs could not coexist under the same government and the Palestinian Mandate was partitioned. In all of these instances, human beings were divided by religion and economics. But in India and Palestine they were driven further apart by differences of language and culture.

There are more factors, however, than geographical concentration, numerical ratios, and external backing, to explain the effects on politics of social groupings. Whether the relations between a majority and a minority are harmonious or not will also depend on their respective solidarity and cohesiveness. This can be viewed subjectively, in terms of the intensity of feeling on both sides, and objectively, in terms of the effectiveness of their organization. When strong emotion is injected into an attitude or doctrine, its intellectual force is not altered. But its practical consequences are immeasurably increased, since feeling is a goad to action.[3] One has only to re-read the bloody record of religious intolerance in Europe during, say, the Middle Ages or in the period of the Reformation and Counter-Reformation. There one will find abundant testimony to show how fanaticism can rend a community asunder. Conversely in modern times, one cannot fail to observe the lukewarmness or plain indifference with which these selfsame disagreements are ordinarily regarded today. The same contrast occurs in attitudes towards race. If the physical mixing of races is viewed with revulsion, as it is by the majority of whites in South Carolina or South Africa, the prejudices associated with this feeling pervade the entire society. On the other hand, where interracial equality and miscegenation are normally accepted and approved, as in Hawaii or Brazil, the atmosphere makes it possible for different races to create a community. Where passion and prejudice unite one group in opposition to another, the two cannot be mutually tolerant and therefore cannot coexist.

3. "The classic example of power through fanaticism is the rise of Islam. Mohammed added nothing to the knowledge or to the material resources of the Arabs, and yet, within a few years of his death, they had acquired a large empire by defeating their most powerful neighbors. Undoubtedly, the religion founded by the Prophet was an essential element in the success of his nation." Bertrand Russell, *Power* (Allen & Unwin: London, 1938), pp. 149-150.

How Such Divisions Concern Democracy

In such instances, it is the loyalty to the social subgroup which determines the actions of the individual. This happens especially when institutions emerge within the social order, either legally or illegally, to organize "their" group against its opponents. One can call to mind such agencies as the Holy Office of the Inquisition set up by the Roman Catholic Church in Spain, or the Ku Klux Klan in the American South, or the Broederbond in South Africa. Intolerance, when it is widespread but unorganized, will be a factor in public opinion; when institutionalized, it is also a force for action. The effects may take the form, at their mildest, of social disapproval. More seriously, this turns into ostracism or boycott. Most drastic of all are physical intimidation and outright terror. Under such circumstances, the community disintegrates into a civil war between its component groups. The allegiance of the individual is then dominated, not by the claims of the whole, but by the requirements of his peculiar institution. The accompanying politics will be pervaded by militancy and authoritarianism; and when this stage is reached, the relations between the warring factions cannot possibly be democratically governed. For democracy requires that people, to a certain extent, have trust in one another. It is not, and can never be, a condition of war.

These and other relevant points will become clearer when they are discussed in the context of particular countries whose people differ in race, language, and religion. The question at issue is this: Do such differences make it easier or harder to establish a democracy? Conversely, when the government is democratic, how does this affect the relations between dissimilars? For purposes of analysis it would be most convenient if each factor could be studied in isolation from the others. In practice, however, that is seldom, if ever, possible. Normally, a community which is divided in one of these respects is also split in some of the others. Frequently, too, the lines of division do not crisscross, but coincide—that is to say, those who differ on race are separated further by their religion or their language or both. Nor should the economic factor be overlooked. In a society where one racial, or religious, or linguistic group is dominant over another, economic inequality is ordinarily present. Then it is evident that the motives which induce the privileged group to perpetuate its advantages will not be influenced solely by a theology, a racial doctrine, or a language. Calculations of material vested interest will also play their part. Though the variegated fabric of which society is woven may be analyzed into its threads, by themselves the threads do not reveal the pattern of the whole, and it is the latter which has social meaning and political significance. Consequently, in the following pages an attempt will be made to explain the social realities in each of the countries chosen for purposes of illustration, even though this will sometimes involve the simultaneous consideration of groups of factors.

Government in a Racially Mixed Community

Of the three components of society discussed in this chapter and the next, race is the most suitable with which to begin. This is because everybody belongs to a race or else includes a blend of races in his ancestry. Nor is one's race a matter of choice on the part of the individual. It is inherited from his forebears, and will be transmitted to his offspring. When individuals, therefore, receive their social status or are judged superior or inferior in terms of race, the criterion is one in which the individuals concerned have no volition. The classification of races, and the assignment of individuals within the scheme, may be socially, or even officially, determined in a manner devoid of a scientific basis. Moreover, race must be distinguished from language or religion in that its characteristics are externally and immediately visible to the eye. In the multilingual communities, a person's speech is revealed the moment he opens his mouth, though not until then. His religious affiliation, however, may require a long process of discovery. Indeed it is possible for two people to be acquainted for years and not to know one another's religion. But the signs of race are there on the face. Except for complex cases of interbreeding, they can normally be identified at a glance. Those who seek, therefore, to divide a society and construct a barrier of discrimination find in race a patent and easy formula.

Because of these considerations, the relevance of race to democracy can be stated without too much ambiguity. Nobody is free to enter a race; nobody is free to leave it. One is born to a race, and stays in it for life—and that is that. Hence the connection between the problems of race relations and the principles of democracy is not primarily an issue of freedom. It is instead an issue of equality. Granted that a man's race is predetermined for him and unchangeable by his efforts, the choice which society can provide is not the freedom to join or depart, but rather the treatment of different races as equals or unequals. Socially, and a fortiori politically, the controversies over race relations center around this choice: the affirmation of inequality versus the quest for equality. This does not mean that no aspect of liberty is involved at all. On the contrary, a system of inequality diminishes the liberty of the underprivileged. But it should be clear that, when men battle over race relations, equality forms the primary issue and freedom is secondary and derivative. Human beings of different races become free to the extent that they become equal.

Can democracy function in a community inhabited by people of different races? The answer is: yes, it can, if the different races are accorded equality of status, legally and politically; no, it cannot, if racial differences are used as a criterion for unequal treatment and discrimination. When the latter policy is attempted, both the arguments employed to justify discrimination in terms of race and the results produced in practice are incompatible with some of the basic principles of a democracy. A democracy must insist on respecting the worth of each individual and must place a high premium on equality. To classify entire groups as superior or inferior by virtue of their race does violation to the individuality of the members and to the equality of their common humanity. If boundary lines are drawn between groups because of their race, somebody has to draw that line and then police and enforce it. Man-made, socially created differences then arise between the two sides, supervening on the original, biological differences. What you make separate by fiat cannot be made equal, for those who do the separating are the superiors and the separation heightens their superiority. The result is a division in the community between first- and second-class citizens. And whatever this is, it is not democracy.

These generalizations can be illustrated by reference to four cases. They have this in common that differences of race and the questions of race relations are intertwined with the problem of democracy. Two are examples of inequality and discrimination. These are the "Deep South" of the United States (specifically, such states as South Carolina, Georgia, Alabama, and Mississippi), and the misnamed "Union" of South Africa. The former region has been bad, but is slowly improving. The latter is hopeless and is becoming worse. The other pair are dedicated to equality and free intermingling: Brazil and the State of Hawaii. The situation in both, though it is not free from difficulties, contains promise and hope.

Racial Experience of the United States:
(1) Slavery versus Democracy

In the culture of the United States, there are two fundamental difficulties for democracy which this country has thus far been unable to resolve. One is the power and prestige of businessmen and the consequent high standing of commercial values. The other is the racial diversity of the American people. The former will be more appropriately considered in a later part of this discussion.[4] But the latter belongs properly here. To one who sur-

4. In Chapter 9, pp. 267-9.

veys the long record of immigration to the United States nothing is more striking than the contrast between the success in absorbing and assimilating millions who did not speak English and the failure to assimilate the minority whose race is Negro. In the one case, the different elements were fused in the melting pot. The children and grandchildren of Teutons, Latins, and Slavs learned English until it became their mother tongue. The public elementary school and the adult evening class provided the necessary instruments for Anglicizing and thus Americanizing. Linguistic minorities no longer exist,[5] and homogeneity in speech has contributed to nationhood and to democracy.

But with race it is another story. Here the melting pot has failed to discover the right temperature for creating a new alloy. The Negroes are among the oldest of the immigrant groups who came to the New World. By now, they are indistinguishable from the majority in language and religion. But their race has set them apart. They remain an unassimilated element in the American culture. It is true that the nation contains many minorities, constituted by virtue of this or that criterion or organized around this or that interest. The Negroes, however, are distinct from all the others in that their minority is identifiable, permanent, and depressed. They are still, by and large, relegated to second-class status throughout the nation—in the North and West, let alone in the South. Some sociologists have described their position in the American culture as that of a caste, membership in which is acquired by heredity and escape from which (save in very rare cases) is prohibited by the customs and attitudes of the majority.

Since the inception of the Republic, the Negro has presented a challenge in the application of American ideals. Even before it became fashionable and acceptable to refer to this country's political system as a democracy, the creeds of equality and individualism were enshrined among the founding concepts of the new nation. When the young philosopher-statesman from Virginia penned the classic phrases of the Declaration, not only was it equality that received the first mention, but the equality so affirmed was that of "all men." No restrictions, exclusions, or barriers were contemplated. When the Philadelphia Convention was at work, the slavery question inevitably entered the discussions and figured in some of the sectional bargaining between North and South. The resulting text contained three references to slavery;[6] but in none of these are the words

5. Except among recently arrived Puerto Ricans in New York and Mexicans in southern California and along the Rio Grande.
6. Article I, sec. 2 (apportionment of representatives), Article I, sec. 9 (slave trade), Article IV, sec. 2 (fugitive slaves).

"slave" or "slavery" employed—a deliberate omission which may have signified a bad conscience or the hope that the institution would disappear. This latter belief was held by Thomas Jefferson, whose correspondence and other writings are full of abolitionist sentiments, even though he did not minimize the practical difficulties.

These difficulties have admittedly been formidable and continue so today. America's treatment of its Negro minority is a political complex resulting from several factors any one of which would have sufficed by itself to unite strong passion and great principle. For this is a minority whose members are numerous enough to be prominent, yet few enough for oppression to be effective; who have been useful to the economy in menial roles as "hewers of wood and drawers of water"; whose physical distinctiveness has evoked a psychology of struggle, inward and external, over sexual and social commingling. At the time when the first national census was held in 1790, a population of 3,172,000 included 757,000 Negroes (24%), of whom 698,000 were slaves. The national figures, however, are less significant than the regional concentration in the South where 690,000 Negroes[7] formed 35 per cent of a population of 1,961,000. Had it not been for Eli Whitney's invention of the cotton gin, and the consequent extension of the area planted in short-staple cotton, it is possible that the contrast between the economies of North and South and their accompanying social systems might not have penetrated so deep or endured so long. As it was, however, the demands of the Lancashire market and the presence of servile labor united to create a vested interest too potent to resist. On masters and slaves alike, the Cotton Kingdom fastened its imperious sway.

In the year when Lincoln was elected President, the census counted 4,442,000 Negroes (3,954,000 being slaves) in a population of 26,923,000. Nationally, therefore, the minority had dropped to 16 per cent of the total. But in the South, the proportions had remained constant, since 4,097,000 (or 36 per cent) out of 11,133,000 were Negroes and 3,839,000 of these were slaves. The round totals, however, are not the most significant aspect of these figures. More important was the concentration of slaves in the hands of a few owners. On this subject Kenneth M. Stampp has written: "In the South in 1860 there were 385,000 owners of slaves among 1,516,000 free families. Nearly three quarters of all free southerners had no connection with slavery as owners." Eighty-eight per cent of the owners, he points out, had less than twenty slaves. The "typical" planter had a gang numbering between twenty and fifty. Some 10,000 families, living off the labor of gangs of over 50, formed the planter aristocracy, and

7. Of whom 657,000 were slaves.

the slaves they possessed were one-quarter of the total. Within this group, the wealthiest[8] families—owners of more than 100 slaves—were fewer than 3,000.

Apart from its economic power, what is so striking about this oligarchy is the domination it achieved over the minds, mores, and emotions of a whole region. The noble humanity of Jefferson was pushed into the background. To the fore came a swelling chorus of voices—voices of churchmen, scholars, constitutional lawyers, and journalists—enlisted in the cause of justifying the political suppression of the economically exploited. Since that time to the present America has been split, intellectually by an inconsistency of principle and emotionally by a crisis of conscience.

The clearest insight into present difficulties and presage of future dangers was that of Tocqueville, who found in this topic a drama worthy of his talent and did not spare the writing. The chapter containing the discussion of race relations has a title which is at first glance a surprise to one who reads it a century and a quarter afterwards; "Some Considerations on the Actual State and Probable Future of the Three Races which Inhabit the Territory of the United States." Nowadays the Indians have dwindled to so inconsequential a minority that one tends to forget how serious an obstacle they once presented to westward immigration. Tocqueville, publishing in 1835, however, was not only aware of their actual power, but he was able to depict in sharp, if theatrical, contrasts the impact of white European immigrants upon indigenous Redskins and imported Negroes. The liberty of the former in independence, and the servility of the latter in slavery, lead from opposite ends to the same result,[9] the supremacy of the whites. Yet it is the Negroes, as Tocqueville correctly diagnoses, whose problems are the more urgent because of the immediacy of their involvement in the society of their masters.[10] He describes the whole white race in the South as an aristocracy, itself headed by a plutocracy. "They have, if I can so express myself, spiritualized despotism and violence . . . They have violated towards the Black all the rights of humanity."[11] Nor does he feel much optimism for the future. America must choose between equality in freedom or inequality in slavery. But if it is to be the former, then the races must either remain apart or they must intermingle.[12] What he has seen in the North does not lead him to expect that emancipation by itself

8. *The Peculiar Institution* (New York; Knopf, 1956), Chap. 1, pp. 28-33.
9. Bk. 2, Chap. X, p. 486.
10. "The most redoubtable of all the evils which menace the future of the United States springs from the presence of the Blacks on their soil." *Ibid.*, p. 514.
11. *Ibid.*, pp. 543, 545.
12. *Ibid.*, p. 535.

will bring solutions. It will merely substitute the inequalities of custom for inequality under law.[13]

Increasingly the two sections of the United States drifted apart. The North was embracing liberalism and democracy, while the South veered toward aristocracy and authoritarianism. Thereupon, Calhoun supplied the theory to replace the Jeffersonian doctrine—a notion of concurrent majorities which would have enabled the southern whites, controlling their state governments, to defy a national majority in control of the federal government. The doctrine sounds plausible and looks speciouly attractive, until one remembers that Calhoun has cast his philosophy in the mold of white supremacy and will not concede concurrent power, or indeed any right of participation, to the Negroes. Herein precisely lay the dilemma of the South. Slavery was incompatible with democracy; the property of the few could not submit to the votes of the many. To maintain its privileges the oligarchy had to justify a hierarchical social order and negate the principles of the Declaration of Independence.[14]

The very fact that the war came is proof of the incompatibility. Here was the one great issue of the American society which was not settled by the adoption of the Constitution, but instead was postponed with a hope and a prayer. For half a century the best minds in American statesmanship wrestled with the problem and sought a solution. But neither the politics of congressional compromise nor the authority of judicial decision could escape the simple logic of Lincoln. The house divided could not endure unless it became all one thing or the other. The arts of mediation and conciliation could find no middle ground between the positions that affirmed or denied the right of one human group to own other humans as their property. One of the two sides had to be victorious; and if voluntary submission was not forthcoming, force had to determine whose view would prevail. Slavery was therefore ended not by the processes of the Constitution, but outside of them.

13. *Ibid.*, p. 519.
14. "Today is the annaversary [sic] of American independence. I have no doubt in many parts there will be pretensions of great rejoicings, but I cannot really rejoice for a freedom which allows every bankrupt, swindler, thief and scoundrel, traitor and seller of his vote to be placed on an equality with myself. . . . The Northern abolitionists are threatening and planning to take away or destroy the value of our Slave property, and the demon democracy by its leveling principles, universal suffrage, and numerous popular elections, homestead laws, and bribery are sapping the foundations of the rights of property in everything." Diary of David Gavin, a South Carolina planter, entry for July 4, 1856, quoted in Stampp, *op. cit.*, p. 419.

(2) *Democracy versus Discrimination*

Nevertheless, as Tocqueville correctly foresaw, the issue of race relations did not terminate with the Emancipation Proclamation and the Thirteenth Amendment. There are many legal gaps in a federal system, and even the addition of two more amendments, the Fourteenth and Fifteenth, did not close them all. The Negro might be freed from his chains, but he could not walk through any door he chose. Liberty was no guarantee of equality. The intentions of the northern Reconstructionists and the policies of the Freedmen's Bureau contained many features that were excellent. But the programs as a whole were imperfectly applied, or were administered by imperfect agents, or attempted to do too much too fast. As a consequence, the experiences of the occupation by federal troops merely increased the bitterness of the defeated whites, whose sympathy and help were indispensable in any long-range efforts to raise the status of the Negro. At first by extra-legal means (e.g., the terror methods of the Klan), and later by a combination of devices, both official and unofficial, the white oligarchies regained their ascendancy, winning politically what they had lost militarily. White supremacy continued to be the watchword of the states of the Confederacy. The Negro was to "keep in his place"— a euphemism for the acceptance of inferiority.

Judged from the standpoint of its architects, this regime was not without success. It lasted for some sixty years, from the early 1870's to the early 1930's. It resisted one serious challenge, that of the Populists who threatened to unite the poor white farmers with the Negroes and turn them both against the oligarchy of wealth. But the potential union of economic interest was foiled by appeals to racial prejudice. The poor white, who had nothing to save but his skin, compensated for the facts of economic hardship by fictions of racial superiority. For this result the South paid dearly. Fighting against equalitarianism, the leaders of the region were driven to maintain their privileges by subterfuge and perversion. The right to vote was curtailed or corrupted. Judicial and police administration in state and local governments were made to discriminate in terms of color. Social life was cast in molds of segregation. A one-party system dominated elections to public office. With variations in the states around the fringe, the politics of Alabama, Georgia, Louisiana, Mississippi, and South Carolina degenerated into a parody of the democratic ideal. When James Bryce published his penetrating study on *The American Commonwealth*, the conclusions he formed about race relations were these: "Remembering that of the whole population of the Union, one-third is in the southern states and that the majority of that one-third, viz. the lower part of the poor whites and the negroes (nearly one-fifth of the whole sixty millions), has no political knowledge or capacity, nothing that can be called rational opinion, it will be seen how far the inhabitants of the United States are from being a democracy enlightened through and through. If one part of the population is as educated and capable as that of Switzerland, another is as ignorant and politically untrained as that of Russia."[15]

The Struggle of American Negroes for Equality

As late as the third decade of this century, the South could still be correctly described as a section apart from the great nation to which it belonged. Since that time, however, a combination of events, both domestic and international, has speeded the processes of change. The depression of the early 1930's made the southern States depend increasingly on federal aid, at the same time as the excellent programs of the Tennessee Valley Authority (also federally inspired and financed) stimulated the economies of that region and contributed to its industrial development. Correspondingly, in other parts of the South, e.g., Atlanta, urbanism induced a more modern social outlook, while in Florida and the area of Virginia close to Wahington an influx of northerners diluted the strength of southern solidarity. In national politics, the southern bloc, formerly so solid, split in 1928, 1948, 1952, 1956, and 1960. The issues of World War II, in which the United States resisted and overcame the racist doctrines of Nazi Germany, did not fail to affect domestic attitudes. Nor did the politics of the "cold war" and the need for the United States to combat the international appeal of communism to underprivileged peoples in Asia and Africa. Indeed, in the Korean War racial integration was adopted in the American armed forces. Add to all this the unanimous judicial pronouncement of the Supreme Court in 1954, with the simple declaration that, as applied to public education, "equal" means "equal" and does not mean "segregated." Thus the cumulative effect of four decades has been to enlarge the educational opportunities for Negroes, to increase the number of Negroes participating in elections, to strengthen their protection by branches of the federal government, and to improve their economic status.

Nevertheless, great and good though these gains are, and though the prospects for the Negroes are definitely encouraging, the actual results to date are small in comparison with the tasks yet uncompleted. For example,

15. Vol. II, Chap. 82, p. 309 (Chicago: Charles H. Sergel & Co., 1891).

stated as a percentage, the number of Negroes who now vote in the South represents a great increase over the number who used to vote. But it is still a small fraction of those potentially eligible. Negroes are now being admitted, by token integration, into schools whose pupils were formerly all white. The number, however, of such Negroes and of such school districts is, as yet, infinitesimal. Nor can an honest appraisal deny that the conditions of the minority race are far from perfect in the North and West. The laws may not discriminate, but society can. By a mixture of subtle devices, which find their source in the basic problem of housing, whites and non-whites live apart from one another. Theoretically, a school may accept children of all races. But if only one race can acquire housing in the district which it serves, what does integration mean in practice? The real estate interests and mortgage companies, conforming to local mores and then reinforcing established prejudice, become the effective agents of social discrimination. All in all, it remains true that Negroes as a group continue below the national average in income, education, and political participation. The United States has not succeeded thus far in applying the Jeffersonian ideal in the sphere of race. Even in the 1960's the nation is grappling with the solution of issues over which a war was fought in the 1860's.

But a new force is at work in this decade which increases the probability that solutions henceforth with come faster. This is the element of direct action by Negroes themselves. Formerly, their leaders relied largely on appeals to white good will, and their organizations[16] devoted their considerable efforts to litigation in the courts, seeking interpretations of the law which would spell out their constitutional rights. In the 1960's, however, the Negroes have at last become active, mobilized, and militant. Impatient with the slowness of social evolution, they demand that the government—and, above all, the federal authority—should act on their behalf and they demand this action now. New organizations, led by a new kind of leader, have campaigned with different tactics to apply concerted pressure on all fronts. Street processions, boycott of segregated businesses, sitting and staying in restaurants and lunch counters, filling the jails, mass rallies, a march on Washington, all have been used to publicize the felt injustice and heighten the urgency of remedies. A resolute leadership has found willing supporters in a younger generation of educated,[17] self-confident men and women, no longer displaying the submissive and deferential attitude of their parents. They take the words of the Declaration of Independence at their face value and insist that American democracy,

16. For instance, the National Association for the Advancement of Colored People.
17. Educated mostly in segregated schools and colleges.

whose citizens they are, must do the same. Nor can there now be any doubt that they will finally win this struggle to complete their emancipation—political, social, and economic. The guilty white conscience will concede the case of the Negro militant. The power of a liberal idea, enforced through government, will change the practices of society.

South Africa: The Politics of Fear

Anyone who may feel discouraged over the slowness of the United States in achieving equality in race relations may take some grim comfort from a situation where everything is immeasurably worse. There is one country where the relations between races are fundamental to everything that happens in the social order, the economy, and politics, and where these relations have steadily deteriorated to a position of the utmost gravity and peril. This is the hapless, ill-fated, Union of South Africa, the house divided and without hope. It is, at the time of writing, governed—or rather, misgoverned—by a regime impelled to its own destruction by the politics of fear.

Whatever one writes about South Africa consists of variations upon the theme of division. The country is inhabited by peoples of three different races and by their mixed offspring. Relations between them are affected by their contrasts in culture and technology, by the numerical ratios, and by the further complication that the two most important groups—the Africans and the Europeans—are themselves internally divided. The crux of the present problems lies in this simple fact: Non-Europeans outnumber Europeans by more than four to one, but it is the Europeans who are wholly dominant in the government, the economy, and society at large. South Africa is grappling not with a minority problem, but a majority one. The racial composition of the population in round figures is as follows:

ESTIMATED POPULATION OF SOUTH AFRICA,
BY RACIAL AND ETHNIC GROUPS, 1960

Africans (mainly Bantus)		11,000,000
Europeans { Afrikaners		1,700,000
{ English-speaking		1,300,000
Indians (mainly Hindus)		500,000
Colored (of mixed race)		1,500,000
		16,000,000

The political system resulting from contact between these peoples can only be described in a series of negatives. The "beloved country"[18] is not a unity; its peoples do not form a nation; its politics are not those of democracy. South Africa is indeed the classic case to prove that an attempt by a few to impose a permanently inferior status upon a large majority of a different race must end with the loss of democracy for majority and minority alike. Enforcement of inequality upon a huge group is incompatible with liberty for anybody. This is conclusively demonstrated in South Africa, whose governmental regime, as conducted by the Afrikaners of the Nationalist party,[19] has turned into the dictatorship of a police state.

Without assenting to the maxim, *tout comprendre, c'est tout pardonner*, one can explain the circumstances of the past that have led to the tragedy of the present. The story is one of conflicting cultures which have experienced contiguity without community. Organized emigration by Europeans to South Africa started in 1653, when the Dutch officially planted their flag at Capetown. They needed the harbor and its hinterland as a port of call and supply station on the long voyage to and from the East. Settlers could be attracted to move to what was then "the other end of the earth" because of the pressure of population in a small, overcrowded, country and because of the fanatical intolerance mutually displayed by Protestants and Catholics in the religious conflicts of Europe. Some French Huguenots, Flemish, and Germans from the northwest added their trickle to the immigrant stream—most of which ended by the close of the seventeenth century. Thus, a people attuned to the mode of life and mentality of western Europe in the later decades of the seventeenth century were exported to the southernmost tip of the dark continent, were left there, and were lost. Barring the visit of an occasional ship, their links with Europe were severed; and as settlers pushed inland from the coast and upland to the plateau, where they became pastoralists, the attitudes of succeeding generations were deep-frozen in the mold of a bygone era. This mold was reinforced by the severities of the struggle to survive on a semi-arid terrain for whose possession they had to compete with Africans, both indigenous and immigrant. In the south the opposition of the native Bushmen and Hottentots was easily overcome. To the north the martial Zulus and the numerous Bantus, themselves pressing south from central

---

18. *Cry, the Beloved Country* is the title of a poignant novel by the liberal-minded South African, Alan Paton. The title and theme suggest Vergil's line: *Sunt lacrimae rerum et mentem mortalia tangunt*. "Life leads to tears; the lot of mortal men touches the heart."

19. Under the premiership, successively, of Malan, Strijdom, and Verwoerd.

Africa, presented more serious opposition. Uprooted from their old home-land, the bitterness of the Europeans was intensified by the obstacles they encountered in striking new roots and by their isolation in the new habi-tat. The perils of the *veld* and the primitive creed of the Dutch Reformed Church served to tighten the solidarity of these individualistic patriarchs, herding their cattle and their human cattle, imperious, single-minded, in-flexible, insecure, and alone.

For a hundred years, in this environment, habits hardened and customs congealed. Then, early in the nineteenth century, came the succession of shocks which imposed a readjustment on this seventeenth-century people and threatened their hard-won way of life. First, at the end of the Na-poleonic Wars, the British annexed the Cape. This act was followed by a wave of English-speaking immigrants, whose churches and language dif-fered from those of the Afrikaners and whose outlook was more liberal and more modern. The effects of the new order were soon felt in the next challenging event, the Act of Parliament which abolished slavery through-out the British Empire and paid financial compensation to the ex-owners. To this extreme disruption of their society, the Afrikaners' response was equally extreme. They pulled up stakes, piled their families and chattels onto ox-drawn wagons, and migrated (trekked) northwards along the coast and into the interior, founding their own republics remote and apart.

They could not, however, escape the expansion of British imperialism any more than the Mormons, who betook themselves west of the Rockies to a wilderness, could remain immune from the enveloping frontier of the United States. Two magnets drew the Britons upon the heels of the Boers, (as the Afrikaners then called themselves). Because of the military and commercial importance of Durban in the strategy of the Indian Ocean, Natal was annexed. Inland, the two Republics of the Transvaal and the Orange Free State were recognized as independent after the abortive First Boer War. And independent they might have remained had it not been for the fatal discoveries of diamonds at Kimberley and gold on the Wit-watersrand. A flood of aliens poured into the static, slave-holding, pastoral Republics. These newcomers were miners, engineers, businessmen, entre-preneurs, equipped with the techniques and resources of industrialism, urbanism, and capitalism, and reinforced by the might of the British Empire. Since the Republics taxed the undertakings of these *Uitlanders,* but prohibited them from acquiring citizenship and voting rights, a clash was sure to come—as it did in the second South African War of 1899-1902.

The end of the unequal struggle brought peace to the battlefields, but transferred to politics a host of unsettled problems. The government of the United Kingdom, feeling remorse and being led after 1905 by Liberals, made offers of pecuniary restitution and political reconciliation. The latter was accepted on the Afrikaner side by a minority who took their cue from Botha and Smuts. Hence in 1910 the Boer Republics, which had been incorporated into the British Empire, were joined with Natal and the Cape in a new Union of four provinces under a constitution which hovered between the unitary and the federal.

Apartheid plus the Police State

During the half-century which has thus far elapsed, the political process has followed a pattern wherein the bitter memories from the past confront the looming menace of the future. Society and its government have swung around two axes: one, a division between the European minority and the non-European majority, the second, a division among the Europeans between the Afrikaners and the English-speaking. Thus, three guiding themes have underlain the politics of five decades. One has been the persistence of a hard core of unreconciled Afrikaner nationalists, who have forgotten nothing and learned nothing. Second is the presence of the huge African majority, reacting in most recent times to the success of independence movements elsewhere on the continent. Third is the steady industrial growth, conducted largely by the English-speaking and absorbing ever larger numbers of Africans into the labor force and the urban economy. Amid the swirl of these contradictory forces, only two kinds of governments have hitherto proven possible. Initially, the Parliament was controlled by an alliance of the Afrikaner moderates with the English-speaking. Their program envisaged a harmony between the European groups and a progressive, though very slow, widening of opportunities for Africans. Latterly, however, the moderates have been replaced by the extremists. The Nationalist party, under Cabinets composed wholly of Afrikaners, came into office in 1948 and has retained power in successive elections—with increases in its vote. Its social outlook has been expressed in a series of legislative enactments and administrative procedures, all of them comprised in the term "apartheid." The details of this program are far-reaching. They extend to family life, the economic process, social intercourse, and political organization, and their intention is abundantly clear. In a multi-racial community, the Nationalists intend that the races shall remain apart, that the white minority shall remain on top of the heap, and that this group alone shall determine the pattern of discrimination.[20]

These thorough-going conceptions have been matched by a ruthless enforcement which leaves no doubt as to the inflexibility of their authors. Determination bordering on fanaticism, and brutality degenerating into terror, have stigmatized the governmental acts of these willful men, who may justifiably be called the Nazis of the 1950's and 1960's. Not only are their policies morally wrong, because of their inhumanity when put into practice; but even if they were right, they would be unrealistic because they cannot possibly succeed. Condemned by virtually the whole world, alone[21] on a continent where they are hopelessly outnumbered, defying every contemporary trend toward greater interracial equality, espousing a political philosophy which their economic development negates, the Nationalists by their own acts are driving, like a figure from a classical Greek tragedy, inexorably to their own destruction. So blind are men to their self-interest when impelled by the politics of fear.

Nor can it even be claimed that, while seeking to preserve their biological "purity," they are guarding the values of an advanced civilization. The reverse is true. For, in pursuit of policies which are insane because they are foredoomed to fail, the Afrikaners are losing the very ideals they esteem. In denying the dignity of man, they sacrifice more than equality. The rights they refuse to others they must now abandon among themselves. The forcible imposition of privilege, permanently cast in the mold of race, means the abrogation of liberty and of law. The bullwhip and the gun become the sanctions of the state, and Parliament exists but in the shadow of the troops. South Africa, as has been evident in the 1960's, lies under the dictatorship of the police state. Those who prize inequality first must place democracy last.

Brazil's Three Races

To turn from South Africa to Brazil is a dramatic contrast of attitude and spirit. Separated by the width of the South Atlantic Ocean, having little contact and few commercial links, no two countries could be more dissimilar in their social psychology and public policies. The relations which have evolved between the races of Brazil are complex and intricate. It is tempting to oversimplify and overdramatize the broad pattern, and min-

20. For further discussion of the party politics of South Africa, see Chapter 11, pp. 334, 341-2.
21. Except for the support of the white minorities in Angola, Mozambique, and Southern Rhodesia.

imize the contradictory details. Assuredly, Brazil has still far to go in solving its many problems; and the relations between its races could not yet be said to have reached a perfect harmony. But when due allowance is made for present shortcomings, there remains a solid achievement of accomplished fact which has few parallels in this modern world—and no parallel at all on a scale so large and intricate. What is important in Brazilian race relations is the national tendency, the official policy, and the future promise. In all of these there are grounds for hope.

The Brazilians are descended from three races—American Indians, European Caucasians, and African Negroes; and when one considers how these differ, culturally even more than physically, the modern acceptance of racial equality stands forth as a remarkable fact. The Portuguese colonizers of Brazil encountered no significant opposition from the indigenous Indians of the Tupi-Guarani tribes whose social structure and technology did not begin to compare with those of the Incas and Aztecs. Since most of the males who emigrated were unaccompanied by European women, their intercourse with Indians quickly produced a population of half-castes. The ensuing relations between the racial groups were shaped by a combination of varied circumstances. To the credit of the Portuguese it must be said that they had no aversion to color. Not only were they physically attracted, and attractive, to the women of a different race, but in their social tradition they retained the memory of a bygone era when the Iberian peninsula was subject to the sway of a darker-skinned people, the Moors, and when it was advantageous for the whites to intermarry with them.[22] But in another respect, the need of the Portuguese for the Indians was not so easily satisfied. When the colonists turned to the economic development of the country, they discovered a lucrative crop in the production of sugar cane. The Indians, however, were unwilling to work on the plantations, and, if forced into labor, could not be prevented from escaping. The owners had to look elsewhere for a labor supply. Since the Portuguese were sailing regularly around the continent of Africa and had bases on the Guinea Coast, they were able to cross where the Atlantic is narrowest from the bulge of Africa to the bulge of Brazil and transport captive Negroes in a nefarious slave trade.

On the sugar plantations, the *fazendas*, of Pernambuco and Bahia, as Gilberto Freyre has traced their sociology, habits and attitudes developed whose consequences have persisted into the present. Since the *fazendas* were large and scattered, they functioned in virtual autonomy. Their links

22. These points are elaborated by the Brazilian sociologist, Gilberto Freyre. See his *Casa Grande e Senzala*, translated as *The Masters and the Slaves* (Knopf: New York, 1946).

with the colonial government and the distant mother-country were loose. On the plantation itself everything was subordinated to the head of the family, the *dono da fazenda*. The church, too, was an adjunct to the activities of the great mansion, the *casa grande*, and the priest not infrequently was a son of the owner. Socially and economically, a hierarchy of ranks was established, which conformed in many respects to differences in race and color. But the personal relations between the individuals in the *casa grande*, especially between the Portuguese family and their African domestic servants, were often close and intimate. The whites indulged in sexual intercourse with Negresses who were their slaves, and in many cases acknowledged the paternity of their offspring whom they provided with education and an economic start. It was not uncommon, therefore, during the colonial regime, and even less so under the Empire (1822-89), to find mulattoes occupying positions of prominence.

Admittedly, Brazil was late in abolishing slavery; in fact, emancipation was not achieved until 1888. By comparison, the British Empire had ended slavery in 1833; Russia set its serfs free in 1861; while in the United States emancipation was promlaimed in 1863. Yet it must be remembered that, when Brazil finally followed suit under the inspiration of Nabuco, its new birth of freedom was peacefully accomplished by ordinary legislation. The persons who paid the political price for this act of humanity were the Emperor, the wise and progressive Dom Pedro Segundo, and his family. A supporter of emancipation, he lost the backing of the conservative landowners, so that within one year of the act of abolition the Empire had given way to a Republic.

This is now the third generation since those events took place. During the intervening decades, not only have the tendencies of the past persisted, but they have been further strengthened by various forces—by the national dedication of Brazilians to the equalitarian ideal, the impact of economic development, and the influence of a world-wide improvement in the sphere of interracial tolerance. In so large a country, however, the favorable generalizations are qualified both by variations in the over-all pattern and by deviations from it. The regional differences and the stratification of classes which is traditional in the Portuguese society are responsible for serious inequalities, and these have had their effect on race relations.

Equality of Races, Inequality of Classes

Inheriting a complex situation, how are the modern Brazilians proceeding to resolve it? Starting with the fact that their population consists of three races, there are two possible alternatives between which they can choose. They may favor a policy of equality or of inequality, and they have to be explicit about the one or the other. In view of their racial mixture, no compromise or halfway position would ever be satisfactory, because it would not be accepted by enough people and could not last for any appreciable length of time. If the Brazilians were to follow the path of inequality, the consequences would entail the imposition and perpetuation of privilege at the expense of the underprivileged. The elite would then have to devote continuous effort to safeguarding their advantages, and the nation as a whole would suffer from the wastage of potential talent among the depressed group. Alternatively, if equality be encouraged, besides the virtues of tolerance, the Brazilians would clearly be the gainers in internal harmony. Assuming that Brazil is to progress as a country, and that its people are to become more unified as a nation, equality is their first prerequisite for success. In a society composed of three racial stocks, inequality must provoke disunity, whereas equality only can produce unity.

Some such logic, conscious or implicit, underlies the attitudes which prevail in Brazil today. The national tendency is to support equality. Official action encourages it. Governmental action is designed to foster it and to prohibit discrimination. These policies, of course, could not be espoused by the state unless they had social support. Indeed, it is on this point that Brazil is distinctive. Interracial unions in general are not only passively accepted, but positively approved. The ultimate fusion of races into a new compound is considered to be both inevitable and desirable. What will eventually result from sustained miscegenation is summed up in the word *branqueamento*, or "bleaching." Darkening of the light-skinned, and lightening of the dark-skinned, will produce a blended population of intermediate shades, known in a country of coffee-growers as *café com leite*, "coffee with milk.

There is some significance, however, in the use of the term "bleaching" to describe this process, since it stresses the lightening of those who are dark. The same bias occurs in another prevailing attitude where the Brazilian view is the reverse of that found in North America. In the United States, if an individual has a Negro ancestor, social convention calls him "colored"—presumably on the assumption that color stains the white. Brazil prefers to classify a person in the opposite way. When somebody has mixed ancestry, and his skin is on the lighter side, he may be called *branco*, with the implication that whiteness bleaches out the color. On this point, the figures in the national census are revealing. The official classification groups people racially under the heading "according to color" (*segundo a côr*). The enumeration of two recent censuses was as follows:

	1940	1950
Brancos (whites)	26,171,778	32,027,661
Pretos (blacks)	6,035,809	5,692,657
Pardos (browns)	8,744,365	13,786,742
Amarelos (yellows)	242,320	329,082
Não declarada (no declaration)	41,983	108,255
TOTAL	41,236,315	51,944,397

The decrease in the number of *Pretos,* and the corresponding increases of *Pardos* and *Brancos,* are the result both of *branqueamento,* and of self-classification in the lighter groups.[23]

But when due allowance has been made for the wise humanity of these practices, certain stubborn facts remain to be explained. It is a fact that glaring contrasts exist in Brazil between social and economic groups. A minority of the population sit on top of the heap and do very well for themselves. The majority are depressed and underprivileged. It is also a fact that the vast majority of the submerged poor have dark skins, and conversely the vast majority of those with dark skins are poor and submerged. What is the reason for these facts, and how are they connected with race relations?

As has been traditional with the Iberian peoples, and as is common throughout the Latin culture, the social order of Brazil has always been constituted of a smallish elite and a great mass, and the gulf that separates them is formidably deep and wide. Historically, that elite has been white; the Indians and the Negroes have formed the underprivileged. Brazilians are strongly imbued with class differences and are highly sensitive to the significance of social stratification. The elite enjoy their superiority. They are very conscious of their advantages. Their attitude toward their own masses is often quite callous—witness the physical proximity and mutual isolation in Rio de Janeiro of the luxury apartments of the wealthy around the water's edge and the festering *favelas* on the hilltops. Profound inequalities do occur in Brazil. But they are grounded primarily in class differences, and not in a confessed doctrine of racial or

23. In recent censuses, individuals have stated their own color classification, Previously they were classified by the census-taker. Racial data for 1960 were not available in June 1964.

biological superiority.[24] This does not mean that it is easy for an individual to climb upward and thus improve his position. He may accomplish this, however, by one of two means. If he possesses exceptional ability in some professional sphere (e.g., in literature, the arts, or the army), he can rise through his talent. Otherwise, he may prosper in commerce and raise himself socially by amassing wealth. Money counts in Brazil, as it does everywhere. Indeed, it may count enough to alter an individual's race. The Brazilians express this in their saying: "A rich Negro is a white man, and a poor white man is a Negro.[25]

To sum up, one may fairly conclude that Negroes generally live worse in Brazil than in the United States. This is so because even the lowest living standards in North America are appreciably higher than Brazil's worst, and because Negroes in Brazil still have fewer opportunities for education and for economic advancement. It is in Brazil's favor, however, that the discrimination which admittedly exists there is grounded primarily in social and class distinctions and is not reinforced by the further obstacle of racial prejudice. Hence, if the old class distinctions gradually break down in the future, and if the whole country becomes wealthier as a consequence of industrialization, it will at least be possible for the equalitarian ideal to which Brazilians subscribe to be more effectively applied. Plainly, these considerations have a direct and immediate bearing on the political evolution of the country, and its potentialities for democracy. Until now, the Brazilian political system could scarcely be described as democratic. Indeed, it is hard to know which of the conventional classifications would be appropriate. But this at least can be said; the attitude to race relations prevailing in Brazil facilitates a democratic outcome to their political problems. If the Brazilians adhered to the course pursued in South Africa, they would find they could not escape a police state. As it is, their preference for toleration between races will help their development into a democracy, though of course this one factor by itself does not guarantee that they will reach this goal.[26]

24. A distinction exists, however, between the urban centers, which are far more advanced, and the rural areas which tend to be primitive except in the south. One anthropologist has summarized a group of research studies with the comment that "a mild form of racial prejudice exists on all levels of society in rural Brazil." *Race and Class in Rural Brazil*, Charles Wagley, ed. (Unesco, Paris, 1952) p. 149.

25. "Negro rico é branco, e branco pobre é negro." Quoted by Donald Pierson, "Race Relations in Portuguese America" in *Race Relations in World Perspective*, Andrew W. Lind, ed. (University of Hawaii Press: Honolulu, 1955), p. 439.

26. In Chapter 13, pp. 403 ff., there is further discussion of Brazil's constitution and political problems.

The Hawaiian Melting-Pot

The example of Brazil is fortunately not unique. There is another community where the racial components in the population are just as dissimilar and mixed, and where, although everything is on a smaller scale, the same principles are involved. This is Hawaii. Here, too, the possibility of democratic government depends basically on the way in which race relations are treated. Here, too, the economy evolved according to the pattern which is normal for a colonial system, and the social structure was dominated by a privileged elite. Politically, the group of islands, which now make up the fiftieth of the United States, were formerly governed as a Territory. Previously, they had been briefly a Republic, and prior to that a Kingdom. The many ethnic groups which live there today have learned, and thus have earned, democracy. The majority were not born with it, nor did they merely receive it as a grant. The peoples of Hawaii absorbed and accepted the influences of the mainland, which in turn has accepted them.

When Europeans first discovered the Hawaiian group, the principal islands were under separate governments. Kamehameha, the ruler of one of them, was wise enough to discern that all would soon succumb to alien control if they were to stay divided. He therefore unified the group by conquest, thus establishing a single kingdom. As a consequence, the independence of Hawaii was maintained for a century more, since Europeans and Americans, if they sought to trade or acquire land, had to come to terms with the Hawaiian regime which could play off one power against another. Under these circumstances, it was an advantage for a westerner to marry a Hawaiian princess, who endowed him with social position and landed property. Not a few unions occurred of this kind, quite apart from the more casual modes of intercourse. The result was to make the practice of miscegenation respectable and to promote equality in the relations between *haole*, as a Caucasian was called, and Polynesian.

For the labor force which the plantation system demanded, Asia provided the supply. In successive waves, Chinese, Koreans, Filipinos, and Japanese flowed to the islands, and there they remained. As happened with European immigrants to the east coast of the United States, each ethnic group in the order of its arrival entered at the bottom of the ladder, and each in turn has climbed up. But in Hawaii there were far greater complications to be faced than in New York or Boston. The fact that the immigrants from Asia have succeeded both in their personal economic advancement and their absorption into the community represents a triumph for all concerned. Aside from the language barrier, the Chinese,

Filipinos, and Japanese differed from the groups which controlled the islands in race, religion, and civilization, and their political memories had also made them mutually hostile. In every respect that counts most toward a society's unity or division, the peoples of Hawaii were separate and they were unequal. By all odds, and on any reasonable estimate, so might they have been expected to remain.

Life on the plantation was organized into strata or levels, according to a hierarchy which ran from the bottom to the top. The conditions of employment dominated all else. Since the economy was controlled by five big companies and trade unions at first were not permitted, the economic cleavage between owners and laborers was deepened by cultural dissimilarities. Within this general complex, the racial difference was not the only point that mattered, but it was assuredly one of the most important. The plantation manager lived in a big house on some high ground surrounded by a fence. Nearby was a row of smaller houses for the families of the supervisors. Farther away were the huts of the laborers. Everything on the plantation was done under discipline and to the sound of a whistle. I have talked in Hawaii to men now prominent in the social affairs of the community and in its public life who have described the conditions under which their parents and grandparents had to live and work. The authoritarian management opposed every obstacle to the intrusion of any rival which would challenge its power—e.g., the trade union or the Democratic party. Nor was it easy for the Chinese or Japanese, standing amid the alien cane, to secure respect for his rights, or even to learn what those rights were.

The Spread of Interracial Tolerance

Two powerful weights were placed on the scales, however, to equalize the balance. Once they were annexed by the United States and were organized by Congress as a Territory, the inhabitants of Hawaii came under the protection of the federal Constitution and enjoyed its benefits. Whatever the country of origin of their parents, whatever their religion or their race, the children "born . . . in the United States and subject to the jurisdiction thereof"[27] were American citizens. As such, they enjoyed federal rights which were federally enforced and could not be obstructed by a Territorial government. To this juridical equality was added the other essential, the public system of education, without which the younger generation would not have been assimilated to a common culture. In the

27. Constitution of the United States, Fourteenth Amendment.

public schools and on the campus of the University of Hawaii, integration
—racial, social, and intellectual—became an accomplished fact. Four decades saw that task so well done that the Americanization of all groups in
Hawaii was fully demonstrated in World War II. Thereafter, the veterans
who had served in the Hawaiian Battalion and elsewhere were afforded
the opportunities of the "G. I. Bill" and could continue their education
at the best institutions of higher learning on the mainland. From their
ranks came much of the leadership and momentum for the final successful drive to statehood.

Contemporary relations between the races in Hawaii provide evidence
of increasing tolerance and integration. In the public sphere, official policy
outlaws all forms of discrimination based on race or color. Public services
of all kinds—schools, transport, recreation, beaches, housing, etc.—are
open on the same terms to everybody. It is only in the private sector that
some instances of discrimination occur. In certain residential areas houses
may be available only to members of one race. But even where this policy
has been initially introduced, subsequently it can seldom be perpetuated.
There are one or two social clubs—for instance, the exclusive Outrigger
Club at Waikiki Beach—which admit *haole* and Hawaiian members, but
have not hitherto accepted any applicant of Asian ancestry. Some private
schools also are segregated racially. One of these, specifically, is the King
Kamehameha School, maintained by the wealthy Bishop Estate for the
education of Hawaiians and part-Hawaiians. In general, however, social
exclusiveness in private organizations competes with difficulty against the
practice of integration in the public sector. The rise in living standards
of all groups promotes a greater conformity in consumption, just as the
benign climate encourages a common taste for outdoor sports and promotes easy intermingling at parks and beaches. With all these influences
combining, it does not surprise one to learn that intermarriage between
racial and ethnic groups, formerly so exclusive, has become increasingly
common. A leading politician, of Chinese ancestry, described for me the
situation in his own family, where the husbands or wives of his sons,
daughters, nephews, and nieces included *haoles*, Hawaiians, Chinese, Japanese, and more. "Give us another two generations," was his conclusion,
"and we shall all be so mixed that racial prejudice will be impossible!"

Prejudice, however, along racial and ethnic lines has not yet been
wholly eradicated. A glance at the population statistics on the following
page will suggest the form which the problem assumes. These figures indicate that half of Hawaii's inhabitants nowadays are of Asian origin,
and that persons whose ancestors were Japanese form the largest ethnic
group. The Caucasians possess an economic power and maintain a social

influence out of all proportion to their numbers. Although full-blooded Hawaiians (i.e., Polynesians) are becoming fewer and fewer, the census inflates the size of this group by including in it those who are part-Hawaiian. Because the Hawaiians were the indigenous people, some persons take pride in acknowledging Hawaiian ancestry, and there may also be advantages in doing this because the Treaty of Annexation and the Organic Act recognized and confirmed certain legal privileges of the Hawaiians. The census conforms to this in that it permits the classification as Hawaiian of persons whose ancestry is only part-Hawaiian.

ETHNIC ORIGINS OF THE HAWAIIAN POPULATION IN CENSUS YEARS [28]

	1930		1940		1950		1960	
Caucasian	80,373	22%	103,791	24%	114,793	23%	202,230	32%
Chinese	27,179	7%	28,774	7%	32,376	7%	38,197	6%
Filipino	63,052	17%	52,569	12%	61,071	12%	69,070	11%
Japanese	139,631	38%	157,905	37%	184,611	37%	203,455	32%
Hawaiian	50,860	14%	64,310	15%	86,091	17%	119,820	19%
Others	7,241	2%	15,981	5%	20,852	4%		
TOTAL	368,336		423,330		499,794		632,772	

Those who are most vulnerable to prejudice are of course the Japanese. Being the largest group, they form the biggest target for attack. If their solidarity becomes too manifest, others are understandably inspired to coalesce against them. Because of Pearl Harbor, the demonstration of loyalty to the United States was more required of the "Americans of Japanese Ancestry" (the A.J.A.'s) than of any other group. Of this, the Japanese are well aware, and they have intelligently taken pains to remove the causes of criticism, both positively by acting as good citizens and negatively by trying to avoid, in fact as in appearance, the practices of group solidarity. Interestingly enough, I learned after extensive discussions in Hawaii, that the most serious and most vigorous prejudice now active is that of Hawaiians against Japanese. The former once shared with the *haoles* the control of the islands. Nowadays the Hawaiians observe increasing numbers of Japanese entering the professions, business, and government. The former feel themselves pushed out by the late-comers.

28. Military personnel stationed in Hawaii are included in these population totals. The sharp increase in the number of Caucasians between 1950 and 1960 is due, in part, to the trebling of the dependents of members of the armed forces living with them in the islands. The 1960 census did not separate Hawaiians and part-Hawaiians from "Others."

To be sure, there are facts aplenty which reveal the growing participation by those of Japanese descent in all aspects of social life. But this, after all, is greatly to their credit. This is exactly what is expected of any immigrant group as it becomes assimilated. It is characteristic of the Japanese, as it has been of the Chinese, that their traditional culture considered education important and respected scholarly learning. Hence, even poor families encouraged their children to take full advantage of the educational opportunities which were open to them. The University campus has been crowded with students from Japanese homes, in some of which pidgin English is still spoken, who are avid for education, both for intellectual reasons and for purposes of economic and social improvement. The Hawaiians have not been imbued with this tradition. They have been less eager to acquire learning, and less ready to submit to its discipline. As a consequence, there are fewer of them in the professions and in the other higher posts of the community. If their influence is declining, it is not merely because of numbers, but because as a group they were less willing to seize the advantages available to all.

Be this as it may, the current trends of intermarriage and public policy lead one to expect even more integration between the racial groups. The foundations have been well laid in the islands for a social democracy of tolerance and equality. On those foundations, constructed by an enlightened government, a political democracy has been erected. The most striking evidence of this assertion is the result of the first elections which took place under statehood in 1959. At that time, there were five major offices to be filled. The voters were asked simultaneously on one ballot to elect two United States Senators and a Congressman, as well as a Governor and Lieutenant Governor. And the result? The ancestry of one Senator was *haole*; of the other, Chinese. The Congressman was of Japanese descent. The Governor was a *haole*; the Lieutenant Governor, a Hawaiian.[29] Had anyone desired and designed in advance to represent faithfully the racial diversity of the population, it would have been difficult to engineer something better than what actually occurred. This vote was a convincing demonstration of interracial tolerance and political maturity. The moral is plain. In the Hawaiian society, race relations are fundamental, and equality for all races is the prerequisite for political democracy. The people of Hawaii have done, and are doing, the one thing which in such a community is crucial for establishing a genuinely democratic system.

29. As for party affiliation, one Senator was a Democrat, the other a Republican. The Congressman and the Lieutenant Governor were Democrats; the Governor was Republican. The inference is plain that the voters selected individuals across the lines of ethnic and party groups.

Clearly, the four cases which have been considered do not exhaust so vast a subject. To have included every relevant example, however, would assuredly have exhausted both the reader and the writer. But the discussion of the contrasts which exist between the southern United States and South Africa, on the one hand, and Brazil and the State of Hawaii, on the other, suggests a definite conclusion. Where different races coexist in the same society, they must be related either as equals or as unequals. If their relationship is the latter, democracy becomes impossible since much of the system is devoted to the effort of the privileged to maintain their superiority over the inferiors. In a multiracial community, a democratic political system is possible only if the principle of equality between all races is approved by the society and enforced by its government. To impose segregation or *apartheid* can only result in a one-party regime and coercion by a police state. The recognition of every human being in virtue of his merits as an individual, and not because of the racial group to which he belongs, is an essential condition for the politics of democracy.

6

Language and Religion

No less fundamental to society than race, and equally relevant to politics, are language and religion. The successful organization of a state presupposes the existence of a political community. The state and its government are an amalgam of institutions and agencies, of structure and machinery, of powers and functions, of citizens and officialdom. But politics consist in a series of struggles over the beliefs and values which constitute a civilization.[1] In politics men are engaging in controversy about alternative ideals and rival principles. They seek to evoke the emotional allegiance of other men's hearts, the intellectual allegiance of their minds. Anything basic, therefore, that unites human beings makes agreement easier and fosters subjectively that awareness of belonging together which students of politics call a consensus. Conversely, whatever divides men socially groups them in separate camps. Then it is usually but a short step from separation to opposition. It is in this light that language and religion are to be examined here. Sharing the same speech facilitates communication, thus providing the groundwork for co-operation in government. In a Babel of tongues resides confusion; and discords may arise from the sheer incapacity to understand. Sharing the same religion likewise helps to bind people together. The union of a common faith can strengthen the sense of community.

1. I have developed this view of the political process in *The Great Issues of Politics* (New York: Prentice-Hall, 2nd ed., 1960).

Governing People Who Differ in Speech and Faith

The government of men is never a simple task. But it will be rendered that much simpler if people speak one language and worship in one faith. To combine within the same state persons whose speech and faith are not the same injects into politics an added complication. For inescapable questions then arise: Are the different religions and languages to be accorded equality? Shall all be officially tolerated? Or should the state be identified with only one religion, with one language, which will receive official sanction and therefore be superior to the rest? What happens to democracy, especially to its ideals of equality and freedom, if people who are united under government are disunited by religion or speech? Can a divided society sustain a common government? If it can, who will be ruling whom?

Ideally, one might wish that the boundaries of the state would coincide with those of culture. But reality is far from conforming to such a criterion. The geography of politics pays heed to many requirements—to transportation routes, economic interests, defensible frontiers, and the like—which do not correspond either with one another or with the distribution of linguistic and religious groups. The accidents of history, compromises in negotiating treaties, legacies of dynastic marriage, and fruits of conquest, these have all contributed to the size and spread of states, to the consolidation of smaller units into large and the subdivision of big into small. The majority of modern states contain somewhere within their midst the problem of a persistent linguistic minority. Even in those countries which may nowadays appear homogeneous in this regard, one tends to forget that what is now the national language was not always so, and that it was the power of a central government or the unity of an educational system or the prestige of an aristocracy which elevated Parisian French or Castilian Spanish or upper-class English over the provincial dialects. Moreover, in the religious sphere, communities that formerly acknowledged only one church, as did western Europe in the Middle Ages, may later be split into warring ecclesiastical organizations. Statesmen have then confronted the need to restore civic unity when priests and pastors were driving their flocks asunder, and governments have had to choose between policies of uniformity or toleration.

Such perplexities are not confined to Europe. The same intricacies are repeated in the cultural patterns of other areas of the world. Indeed, in Asia, the most populous of all continents, so many languages and religions exist side by side that political unification encounters formidable difficulties. There, as in Europe, the separation of a dominant group from those subordinate to it has often been accentuated by differences of speech and faith. Wherever an independence movement is successful and a new state is built, the linguistic and religious questions loom very large. For, if a state is organized and a government staffed in a society whose members speak and worship differently, will several tongues and faiths be placed on an equal footing? Is there one language which can be designated as national? Will one religion be established as official? Whatever decisions are reached on these matters directly influence the character of the political system. Democracy assuredly requires equality, but in the cultural sphere, does equality mean assimilation to the point of conformity or should it signify a toleration of differences?

When India gained its independence, the Muslims refused to be included in a state which would have had a majority of Hindus. They, therefore, chose partition and formed the separate state of Pakistan. Pakistan itself, however, is split into two geographical regions divided by Indian territory; and their economies and languages are so much at variance that the parliamentary regime at the center collapsed in 1958 and a military man assumed autocratic control. India, too, continues to be beset with the complications of minority faiths and a variety of languages, both local and regional. The structure of the federal system has even recognized the attachment to language by creating the "linguistic state" of Andhra—an experiment of dubious wisdom since it permits national unity to be fragmented into linguistic groups and lessens the need for those within such a group to learn another language. Likewise in Assam, the people who speak Assamese have attempted to assert themselves at the expense of the Bengalis by driving them out and taking over their jobs. Such a policy may promote solidarity locally, but it does not encourage unity nationally.

For reasons similar to those which obtained in India, partition also became the solution in the Palestinian Mandate. The opposition of Jews and Muslims had many facets, among which the economic and technological contrasts between the two cultures was assuredly important. But in addition there were the differences of language and religion, which made impracticable a community of Israeli and Arab. It goes without saying that democratic institutions cannot be applied to the relations between two groups which feel so antagonistic that they prefer a complete separation to any kind of tie. The modern history of Ireland supplies another case in point. The cleavage between Ulster (i.e., the six counties of the northeast) and the remainder of Ireland has its basis in religion.[2]

2. Social and economic distinctions reinforced the religious factionalism of the Irish. George Bernard Shaw recalls from his boyhood experience in Dublin how he ob-

Language scarcely enters into it, since the promotion of Erse has been largely an artificial revival, much of it stimulated since the time of Irish independence. The Ulstermen, having a Protestant majority, chose to be united politically with the Protestants of England, Wales, and Scotland across the water, rather than with the Roman Catholics contiguous to them in the south. If there be sin in such division, it must be laid at the door of the religious zealots on both sides of the line. The political conclusion here was derived from the initial premises of ecclesiastical bigotry.

Where the attempt is made to impose a cultural conformity upon a group that is unwilling to change its ways, the methods employed will become proportionately more coercive to the extent of the determination of the enforcers and the resistance of the opponents. It is not always possible to say for sure whether the motive which underlies such policies originates in society and is thence transferred to politics for a solution by government, or whether it is first politically inspired and thence invades society. Examples could be quoted on either side of the question. Sometimes it appears that warring social groups seek to capture the state in order to win a cultural conflict by governmental means. At other times, what seems uppermost is the political feeling that unity is required and cultural diversity weakens it. But in either case, the methods and the outcome approximate one another. A policy of imposing uniformity upon a divided culture must result in autocracy and dictatorship.

A Comparison of Spain and Russia

Innumerable instances could be cited to illustrate these generalizations. Consider from this standpoint the parallel which exists between Spain and Russia. Of all the countries in Europe which have played a significant

---

served the resulting separation from the Protestant side: "Protestantism in Ireland is not a religion; it is a side in political faction, a class prejudice, a conviction that Roman Catholics are socially inferior persons, who will go to hell when they die, and leave Heaven in the exclusive possession of ladies and gentlemen. In my childhood I was sent every Sunday to a Sunday school where genteel children repeated texts, and were rewarded with little cards inscribed with other texts. . . . What helped to make this 'church' a hot-bed of all the social vices was that no working folk ever came to it. In England the clergy go among the poor, and sometimes do try desperately to get them to come to church. In Ireland the poor are Catholics—'Papists' as my Orange grandfather called them. The Protestant church has nothing to do with them." From "In the Days of My Youth," in *Mainly About People* (London, Sept. 17, 1898). Quoted by Archibald Henderson *George Bernard Shaw: Man of the Century* (Appleton-Century-Crofts: New York, 1956) p. 46.

role in history, these are the two whose political systems have stayed, continuously and decidedly, authoritarian and retain this character today. Both have passed through revolution and civil war, yet neither has conducted a genuinely democratic revolution. Each has experimented, for a short period only, with the formal structure of democratic government—elections, parties, and a legislature—but these institutions were quickly challenged and abandoned. Neither Spain nor Russia has contributed anything of significance to democracy. On the contrary, in their different ways both can be said to typify democracy's antithesis.

There is a striking similarity in the variety of reasons which have pressed the forms of these two governments into a rigidly authoritarian shape. After its conversion to Christianity, each country was influenced by the autocratic traditions of Rome—the one directly from Rome itself, the other indirectly from Constantinople and the Byzantine Empire. The two powerful churches, dominated by priests, maintained a hierarchical conception of society and reinforced the privileges of a social and political oligarchy. Both countries lie at the extremities of Europe and have been exposed, as frontier outposts, to the influences of the civilizations which lay beyond. The Russians and Spaniards succumbed in the medieval period to alien rule by Asian conquerors, the Tartars and Moors,[3] respectively, whom they later succeeded in expelling. Both states, the Russian and the Spanish, expanded by absorption, conquest, and consolidation. Military power,[4] economic enlargement, and cultural penetration extended the area of political union and fostered the centralization of government in Moscow and Madrid. But in this process of incorporating adjacent peoples, variations in language and religion posed an obstacle to unity. What the Ukrainians, Georgians and Poles were to Muscovy, such were the Catalonians, Basques, and Portuguese to Castile.

The Rule of Intolerance

Ruling a society of heterogeneous cultures, the policy of promoting unity through a centralized conformity became habitual for Spanish and Russian governments. Democracy was, therefore, out of the question, since conformity had to be enforced upon the recalcitrant and these were numerous. Roman Catholicism in Spain degenerated into the most extreme

3. The Moors were based upon North Africa, but their culture was derived from the Middle East and their religion was Islam.
4. The effect of land power on the character of Russian government is discussed in Chapter 7, pp. 168 ff.

and least tolerant branch of that Church to be found in a major country. Heresy was stamped out with murderous ferocity by the Holy Office of the Inquisition and their Most Catholic Majesties. The lives of Torquemada and Ignatius Loyola exhibit the inflexibility of the single-minded so convinced of his own rightness that he must cudgel or cajole the dissenter into submission.

But though heterodoxy could be abolished in religion, heterogeneity in language has remained the more stubborn problem. The unity of Spain is an artificial product, painfully constructed in the teeth of a formidable geography and provincial separatism. The peoples on the fringe of the Iberian peninsula do not speak the language of the center. In one case, that of Portugal, a different tongue evolved from the common Latin root, and this has accompanied, as cause and effect, a sense of cultural distinctness and hence of political independence from Madrid. Along the northern frontier, the Basques who inhabit the slopes and valleys of the Pyrenees are a distinctive people with a language unrelated to the other tongues of Europe. Similarly, in the northeast the region of Catalonia, with Barcelona for its capital, has always refused to merge its identity with Castile. Over and above the commercial and industrial interests of this great port—perhaps the most modern in outlook of Spanish cities—the province of Catalonia prides itself on sharing an ancient heritage with parts of south-central France and with the Balearic Isles. The Catalonian demand for autonomy has been persistently pressed. It was voiced with increasing emphasis during the 1920's. It was a potent factor during the civil war of 1936-38, when in fact the final resistance to Franco was concentrated in Barcelona. Even now, in the 1960's, there are Catalonians who continue to defy Madrid and demand the right to use their own language in the schools, the press, and official documents. Here is a clear case where a particularly stupid dictatorship employs the apparatus of the police state in its striving for unity through uniformity. The denial of political freedom is the instrument for a denial of cultural diversity.

The same was true of Czarist Russia.[5] The rulers of that country laboriously built their state from fragments, uniting Moscow with Kiev and Smolensk and pushing outward to the Black Sea and the Baltic. To consolidate such power required agencies of centralization, among which the institution of Czarism itself and the system of military service were crucial. The government, as everywhere, had to grapple with the church and, as its borders were pushed further afield, sought to hold the divergent cultures around the perimeter of its possessions. How to win and keep the

5. On this subject, see B. H. Sumner, *Survey of Russian History* (Duckworth: London, 1944) Chaps. IV-V.

loyalty of the landed gentry and illiterate peasants was a perennial problem for the Czar and his ministers and bureaucrats. Russia was never touched by the movements of the Reformation in western Europe. Its church, influenced by the Byzantine tradition, came to be identified more and more with the organs of temporal power, and the one serious attempt, that of the Patriarch Nikon, to establish two co-ordinate spheres in church-state relations ended in failure. But in "the western lands," as they were called, of Poland and Lithuania, and in the southwestern region of the Ukraine,[6] cultural diversity was an obstacle to political unity. Not only did the Ukrainians, Lithuanians, and Poles speak their own languages, but their ecclesiastical allegiance also was independent of the Eastern Orthodox rite and the Patriarchate of Moscow. Poland was a stronghold for Roman Catholicism, while the Ukraine, situated between the Catholics and the Orthodox, has settled for a compromise in the form of the Uniat Church.

Confronted with the alternatives of assimilation or coexistence, Czarist policy pursued a zigzag course. Severity alternated with moderation, inflexibility with indecisiveness, principle with expediency. In the nineteenth century, the Czars developed the idea of Pan-Slavism, with Russia as leader of the Slavs, and thereby hoped to capture the allegiance of eastern Europe from the Germans, Turks, and Francophiles. Granted the fact that the Slavs were a large and quarrelsome family, Pan-Slavism could be interpreted either as a toleration of differences or as imitation of the head of the family. Eventually, the policy of Moscow veered or drifted in the latter direction and assumed the guise of "Russification." The two areas most critical for its application were the Ukraine and Poland, and the outcome differed in the two cases. Ukraine was amalgamated within the larger unity. But tensions have persisted, and one of their causes has been the separate culture of the part which weakens its identification with the whole. In its extreme phase, therefore, the policy of Russification resulted in efforts to eradicate the Ukrainian language, efforts which provoked intense hostility. Still more repressive, however, were the measures adopted against the Poles—or that section of them whom the Russians had incorporated after the three partitions of the late eighteenth century. The Poles were led or misled into abortive uprisings in 1830 and again in 1863. After crushing the military aspect of the rebellions, Moscow introduced a program of cultural imperialism directed to the replacement of the Polish language by the Russian. As in the Spanish case, the powers of the police state were brought into the service of a program of cultural uniformity

6. A name which means the borderland.

imposed from outside. And again the parallel applies to the results. For, if Catalonia and the Ukraine have stayed within the larger union, they have retained a pride in their distinctiveness. Portugal and Poland, however, were the major exceptions respectively to Slavic and Iberian consolidation. They could be neither assimilated nor co-ordinated nor subdued. But, while keeping independent, they left their mark upon those whose embrace they shunned. The governments at the center, devoting so much of their energy and acumen to repression of cultural autonomy, had less time and still less inclination to evolve democratically.[7]

The Multinational Austrian Empire

The implications of this argument become clearer if one considers the experiences of Austria during the nineteenth century. In a period when national sentiment was rising everywhere throughout central, eastern, and southern Europe, Austria supplied the classic instance of a multinational state. The extraordinary empire of the Hapsburgs had been cemented together through centuries of armed conquest, marital unions, and tortuous intrigue. The result was a medley—it could scarcely be called a union—of a Catholic majority with Orthodox minorities, and of Germans, Magyars, Italians, and Slavs. There had once been a *raison d'être* in this polyglot conglomeration, and it suffices to explain why so many ethnic groups, even if unenthusiastic, had at least acquiesced in government from Vienna. The Austrians had offered a bulwark of defense for central and southeastern Europe against the Turks. A defense, that is, for those who wanted it, since in the religious sphere the Orthodox Christians of the Balkans sometimes received more tolerance from the Muslim Ottomans than from the Catholic Hapsburgs. Furthermore, the Austrians and Magyars were driven together by a fear that the Slavs might unite, and in this they were supported by some Poles who saw behind the screen of Pan-Slavism a prospect of Russian domination.

After the wars of Napoleon the winds of change were swirling over the Danube from all directions. From the west came the revolutionary doctrines of 1789, with their invocation of *liberté, egalité, fraternité,* and the Rights of Man and of the Citizen. From the northeast was felt the Rus-

7. Sumner quotes a statement attributed to Witte during the revolution of 1905. "The world should be surprised that we have any Government in Russia, not that we have an imperfect Government. With many nationalities, many languages and a nation largely illiterate, the marvel is that the country can be held together even by autocracy." *Op. cit.,* p. 122.

sian pressure, increasing with intensity in the wake of the French withdrawal. Contrariwise in the southeast, Turkish power was diminishing as the Ottoman empire declined, and this made it safer and more practicable for the Balkan peoples to display their independence of Constantinople and Vienna alike. Caught among these crosscurrents, the Austrians were forced to choose whether to stay rigid or to bend. But the choice was presented under conditions which foredoomed them to failure no matter which alternative they adopted. For change must entail the dissolution of their empire, whereas not to change spelled its destruction.

The crux of Austria's difficulty was the relation between her many nationalities. All of her governmental problems, in domestic and foreign policy, possessed this common content despite the special guise which a particular issue might assume. In this way and for this reason, any constitutional question, any proposal bearing on the structure of the state, was connected with multinationalism. Needless to say, by temper and tradition the government of the Austrian empire was profoundly autocratic, although the ill effects of its authoritarianism were generally mitigated by its inefficiency. In 1815 after Napoleon's final overthrow, the Austrian regime was re-established on the foundations of legitimacy and absolutism, and Metternich meant to keep it so. But even he could not permanently resist the effects of economic change and the shifts in political sentiment. Responding to the influences of Great Britain and western Europe, the central and eastern Europeans were also awakening to industrialism and liberalism. Simultaneously, however, Austria was the first victim of two great movements of national unification—those of Germany and Italy—to both of which her multinational state presented a major impediment. Under these circumstances, the national question and the question of representative institutions were inextricably linked. Changes in the form of the government could not be considered apart from the social content of the state, and politics consisted in the controversies over these relationships.

In 1830, and even more in 1848, the regime was challenged by a convergence of the different pressures: one for national independence or cultural autonomy, the other for parliamentarianism, a liberal suffrage, and elections. The need for internal reform became still more acute in the 1850's and 1860's when Austria was under attack from Bismarck in Prussia, Louis Napoleon III in France, and Cavour in Piedmont. Up to that time, the ascendant group within the multinational empire had been the German-speaking. Politically dominant, they had also vaunted their cultural superiority. The institution of government which served their purpose was the absolute monarchy—buttressed, of course, by the hierarchies of the church, army, and nobility. Determined to hold their empire, the German Austrians would not make common cause with the moves for German unity, whether of the Frankfurt Liberals or of Bismarck, since, if they joined, they would enter as the junior partner. But if they chose to maintain their multinational union, they could not avoid concessions to their non-German members. This meant a switch from superiority to equality, and from absolutism to liberalism. In that case, how far were Austria's rulers to go in reversing their previous policies? A full-blown democracy, with universal suffrage and majority rule, would mean the equal representation of all cultures and the loss of German hegemony.

The result, inaugurated a year after Austria's defeat by Prussia, was the adoption in 1867 of a new constitutional experiment. The Austrians accepted the second most powerful ethnic group in the empire, the Magyars, as equal partners and converted the state into the dual monarchy of Austro-Hungary. The same king reigned in Vienna and Budapest. Separate legislatures met in the two capitals, and the government of the whole included representation from the two parts. In each half there was a plurality of cultures, but one was predominant over the rest. In Austria, with a population in 1890 of twenty-four millions, the leadership was provided by eight and a half million Germans; in Hungary, which counted seventeen millions, by the seven and a half million Magyars. The potential Slavic majority was weakened by internal subdivisions and mutual feuds. Pride in their respective languages was jealously guarded by the various groups, whose insistence on this form of autonomy sometimes led to absurd results. Thus Lowell relates that, when the Austrian Parliament was convened, the oath had to be administered to the members in eight different languages.[8] In the Kingdom of Hungary the Magyars conceded linguistic autonomy only to the Croats and to no one else. They themselves insisted on a precise equality between Magyar and German in the official transactions of the dual monarchy, and would not permit their own delegates to speak in German. Under such conditions, it is no surprise that parliamentary institutions failed to work. The party system that emerged was inevitably chaotic because divisions into conservative, liberal, and socialist, and rival viewpoints on clericalism, education, and economic policy were crisscrossed by the cultural splits. Ministries were therefore reduced to the futility of unstable coalitions, and much power, both real and residual, remained perforce with the monarchy.

All the ingenuity in the world—and the Austrians had no lack of ingenuity—could not make a system of government function successfully

8. A. Lawrence Lowell, *Governments and Parties in Continental Europe* (Houghton, Mifflin & Co., Boston, 1896) Vol. II, p. 72.

when the character of society precluded it. The state does not have a united body of citizens in a society which consists of divided peoples. To the credit of the Austrians it should be said that they made some liberal concessions. But the concessions came grudgingly, and only after bitter revolts and defeats, and the Austrians were too late in starting. The German-speaking element had occupied first place far too long to share its privileges easily. The other groups, stung by the inferior status accorded to their own cultures in the past, became over-assertive once they had the chance. Not feeling a community of interests, they pushed equality and autonomy to a point where unity was sacrificed. Lowell, with justice, describes Austro-Hungary as "a museum of political curiosities."[9] But it had degenerated into this because, in the first instance, it was a cultural mosaic of ill-assorted pieces.

Russia, Spain, and Austria have been discussed together because their societies were heterogeneous while their governments were autocratic. In each case, a single culture in the mixture sought to dominate the rest, either by imposing an inferior status or by requiring that they assimilate. Authoritarian means were thus employed by the state to promote its social ends; and the character of governments which were already autocratic was made yet more so in the struggle to enforce their policy. Experiments with parliamentary institutions in Austro-Hungary and Spain were unsuccessful, and the failure was due in large measure to the fact that long-suppressed minorities used the opportunity of legislative representation to bargain for more cultural autonomy than the ascendant group was willing to concede. All too often, therefore, politics was composed of factions, and the legislature of fractions, so that the organs of the state were paralyzed by obstruction.[10]

The Democratic State in Mixed Communities

By contrast, let us consider another trio of cases where society is split in language or religion or both, and where democracy has functioned with varying degrees of success. The word "varying" requires some emphasis. The problems which each country has to solve are different, and regimes which follow the democratic type cannot be expected to be uniformly

9. *Op. cit.*, Vol. II, p. 177.
10. Similar calculations inspired the Irish in the period when they were represented directly at Westminster. Parnell's objective in organizing his Nationalists into a solid bloc was to break up the union of Great Britain and Ireland by disrupting the work of Parliament.

successful. Indeed, it can be argued in some instances that the measure of failure or success depends precisely on whether the aspirations of different cultures are frustrated or fulfilled. To examine this question, a convenient comparison is provided by three countries where enough history has elapsed for the results to be observed and judged in perspective. These are Belgium, Canada, and Switzerland. I place them in that order because that is how I would rank them according to the criteria of political stability, mutual harmony between social groups, and the general effectiveness of the democratic system. In every one of these respects, Belgium appears the weakest, Switzerland the strongest, and Canada falls in between. Each country is inhabited by peoples who share the same nationality and live under the same government, but who speak different languages (two languages in Belgium and Canada, four in Switzerland). All three contain a religious cleavage. Canada and Switzerland are divided along familiar lines between Protestant and Catholic. In Belgium, where Protestants are too few to count, the opposition between clerical and anti-clerical, between "good Catholics" and the secular-minded, has almost the same consequences as if there were two religions. It may also be noted that, of the three, the country which exhibits the greatest diversity and complexity is Switzerland. How, then, is this fact connected with the judgment expressed above—that Switzerland ranks the highest in stability, harmony, and democratic effectiveness? Might one not expect the reverse to be the case? To answer this query let us see what relation these countries reveal between social diversity and the politics of democracy.

Belgium's Split Personality

As a political entity, Belgium is very old. The peoples who form the Belgium of today, except for the Liège district, have been governed as a unit since the fifteenth century.[11] But, as an independent state, Belgium is fairly modern. It is a product, in fact, of the uprisings, warfare, and diplomacy of the period from 1830 to 1832. Whether that state is yet adequately unified by a sense of common nationhood is the big question and is still debatable. In the centuries prior to its independence, Belgium was ruled by Spaniards, Austrians, French, and Dutch. It was this succession of alien regimes, therefore, which endowed the Belgians with what they possess in common—the desire to run their own affairs and not to be subject to an external control. When this feeling dovetailed with the

11. On this topic, see R. C. K. Ensor, *Belgium* (Holt and Co.: New York, 1915) Chaps. 1 and 4.

result of rivalries between Prussia, France and Great Britain—none of which was content to see the Low Countries absorbed into the domain of a great power—Belgium was constituted, recognized, and by treaty neutralized.

Could the feeling of difference from their neighbors and resistance to domination from without overcome the diversions that existed within? This has always been the uncertainty of Belgian politics, the question mark attached to the survival of the state. By the same logic, it is also the touchstone of Belgian democracy. For across the unity of Belgium, like some deep and ineradicable scar, runs the line of linguistic separation. Flanders, to the north of the line, speaks Flemish—a dialect of Dutch regarded as "bad Dutch" by the people of the Netherlands. Wallonia, to the south, speaks French, badly according to Parisians. The third region, Brabant, which includes Brussels, lies in the middle and is bilingual. Accompanying this difference in language, and paralleling the same line, are other social contrasts which heighten the separation. Officially, and at least nominally, all Belgium is Catholic. But the Catholicism of Flanders, especially of its rural areas, is devout, traditional, and intransigent. That of the Walloons, because they border upon France and are influenced by French thought and opinion, has been touched by the Enlightenment, the positivists and the anti-clericals. Wallonia is allergic to clerical guidance in secular matters, and its Catholicism is more a form of affiliation than an act of faith. Furthermore, the economies of the two regions diverge in specialization and interest. In Flanders intensive, small-scale farming combines with numerous cities whose fame and prosperity date from the Middle Ages. Shipping, textiles, and craftsmanship have made possible the dense concentration of people on a plain which does not abound with natural resources. The Wallonia of previous centuries was no match for Flanders in economic maturity. The terrain for farming was limited by the forests and hills of the Ardennes, and the cities were not especially flourishing. But that picture changed as a consequence of industrialization. Blessed with ores and coal, Wallonia developed into a natural habitat for industry and mining, and its people soon acquired the secondary characteristics of businessmen and trade unionists.

The division between the cultures is the fundamental fact in Belgian society and therefore permeates that country's politics. Everywhere the dualism crops up. Indeed, it is very hard to strike at anything basic without touching upon the sensitive nerve of cultural pride. What is it that holds Walloons and Flemish together? Presumably, their common reaction to the pressures exerted on them from outside. Instead of a separation and liaisons with the French and Dutch, they have preferred the hazards of life together in lawful wedlock. But this marriage has not endured without friction and discord. Much evidence can be adduced of the incompatibility of the partners and the sterility of their union.[12] The principal agitation has come from the side of the Flemish. In the latter parts of the nineteenth century, these people were concerned for the future of their language. They feared it might be dying out and took measures to revive it. The focus of controversy was, of course, the school. But the controversy also extended—as was natural in a bilingual country —to the machinery of government. The determination of what language is official, the right to use either tongue in the legislature or the civil service, the apportionment of seats and jobs—these and similar questions generated political dissension out of social dualism.

Throughout this conflict it has been the Flemish who have felt on the defensive and who have compensated for this feeling by acting aggressively. The Walloons, after all, have the secure knowledge that their native tongue identifies them with one of the world's great cultures. They have immediate access to the literature of France and easy converse with any French-speaking person. The Flemish lack this sense of identification. Even the resemblance between their speech and Dutch is not sufficient to enlarge the scale of their culture from the provincial to the cosmopolitan. Hence they require constant reassurance of their equality. Before World War I a militant movement of Flamingants, or "Flemishers," was organized, whose aims were particularist and separatist rather than Belgian and national. Similarly, in the 1930's a Belgian species of Fascism was mobilized by two groups of right-wing Catholics. Among the Walloons, these were the followers of Léon Degrelle, whose name, the Rexists, was taken from their invocation of *Christus Rex*. Parallel to these were the Flemish nationalists with their battlecry: "Everything for Flanders, Flanders for Christ." The intolerant fanaticism of such movements was not, to put it mildly, conducive to the democratic process; and a society capable of spawning them had hardly achieved consensus.

Nor did the political events of World War II and its aftermath contribute to Belgium's inner harmony. Severe criticisms were voiced against King Leopold for ordering the surrender to Germany in June of 1940 and for remaining in Belgium when he could have helped the refugee government to continue resistance from outside. After the German defeat, public opinion was deeply divided on the subject of the King, whose abdication was the price for saving the institution of monarchy. In that struggle, Leopold was attacked by the Left, the anti-clericals, and the Walloons. To

12. Their adopted child, the Congo, severed its connection with the foster parents in 1960 under acrimonious circumstances.

his defense there rallied the Right, the Church, and Flemish nationalism. Leopold was forced to abdicate when his person symbolized not the unity of a nation, but the division in its culture.

That cleavage, moreover, is abiding. Its foundations plunge too deeply into the rock-strata of the centuries for its effects not to appear on the surface today. Periodically, over one issue or another, over something important or something seemingly trivial, the forces pent up below produce eruptions in the open. It may be the old, old, matter of tax support for parochial schools, or the inclusion of a linguistic poll in the census, or bringing suburban villages under the jurisdiction of Brussels, or some similar issue. Whatever it is, traditional suspicions and rivalries are at once rekindled, because they never completely die down. If Belgium's two cultures coexist, theirs is a co-operative coexistence against outsiders, a competitive coexistence among themselves. Democracy alone could have provided the institutional framework within which this social dualism can express itself and maintain its uneasy compromise. To this extent, indeed, democracy in Belgium may be considered a success. But it is a conditional success, always perilously poised on the brink of failure. For in those spheres where the division outweighs the union, it is difficult, and at times impossible, to achieve a tolerable relation between majority rule and minority right, government power and opposition dissent, national policy and local enforcement.

The Two Cultures in Canada

Similar perplexities recur in the Dominion of Canada, a country whose situation, both internal and external, affords a striking analogy with that of Belgium. There too, for almost two centuries, two communities have lived side by side without mixing. There too, a nation is potentially in the making, but has not yet been created. The cultures remain distinct and apart, and have not fused. Indeed, both peoples are compelled, or condemned, to perpetuate a partnership which neither sought since they would be too weak, alone, to withstand external pressures. Hence, they abide within the structure of the same state, and share a common government. Nor is the reason for their connection of dualism with democracy hard to find. It is democracy which offers a structure wherein discordant cultures may coexist in relative peace, though even so, as a Canadian scholar has commented, "frictions between them often strain the working of Canadian democracy."[13]

13. Alexander Brady, *Democracy in the Dominions* (University of Toronto Press: Toronto, 2nd ed., 1952) p. 25.

The history of Canada is a sequence of phases: colonization, conquest, competition, commotion, compromise, confederation, coexistence. The French colonized, but the British conquered. The question thereupon arose of determining what law, which language, whose religion, should prevail in Quebec and in the rest of Canada. The outlines of the problem were delineated in an early memorandum of the Baron Maseres, a dignitary who was later the Attorney-General of Quebec. "Two nations," he wrote "are to be kept in peace and harmony, and moulded, as it were, into one, that are at present of opposite religions, ignorant of each other's language, and inclined in their affections to different systems of laws."[14] The French-Canadians in Quebec numbered at that time some ninety thousand. There were but six hundred British. Save for three Protestant families, all the French were Roman Catholics. "But, what is more to be lamented," said Maseres, "is that they are violently bigoted to the Popish religion, and look upon all Protestants with an eye of detestation. This unhappy circumstance has been, and is still likely to be, a ground of enmity and disunion between the old and new inhabitants."[15] A colonial government must be installed. But it should not include an assembly, since, if such a body were truly representative, how could the six hundred British be sure of "domineering over the ninety thousand French"? Only time would produce "that coalition of the two nations, or the melting down the French nation into the English in point of language, affections, religion, and laws, which is so much to be wished for."[16]

The response of the government in London was influenced by the turn of events in the American colonies—a response which can be summarized as a carrot for Quebec, a stick for Massachusetts, and paternalism toward both. The Quebec Act of 1774 pronounced the new policy in Canada. This was a program of social tradition, combined with authoritarian government. The French could retain their language and their civil law. More remarkable still, at a time when Catholics were under legal and political disabilities in Great Britain, their church was accorded equality of status in Quebec. Representative institutions, however, were not sanctioned. There would be no colonial assembly.

The stick failed in Massachusetts, but the carrot succeeded in Quebec. When the thirteen colonies declared their independence and proclaimed the United States, the Canadian French—conquered only thirteen years

14. *Considerations on the Expediency of Procuring an Act of Parliament for the Settlement of the Province of Quebec.* In *Speeches and Documents on Colonial Policy,* A. B. Keith, ed. (Oxford University Press, 1918) Vol. I, p. 12.
15. *Op. cit.,* p. 13.
16. *Op. cit.,* p. 28.

earlier—did not rise in revolt, but stayed under the shelter of the British Crown. During the war, however, and after hostilities ended, those colonists who preferred to remain British migrated northward to Quebec and what is now Ontario, where they were named the United Empire Loyalists. Their immigration began altering the balance of numbers in Canada and spurred the demand for a representative assembly. The latter was therefore conceded in 1791, and for the first time in their history these French of the *Ancien Régime* were exposed to the processes of ballots, bills, and debates. Moreover, by the same Act, Canada was divided into two provinces, called Upper and Lower, respectively. In the former, the majority was English-speaking and Protestant; in the latter, French and Catholic.

The result was a half-century of competition leading to commotion. The competition became acute when British immigration increased after the Napoleonic Wars. Not only did Britishers settle in Ontario, where they had virtually an open field, but also in the French-occupied sphere of Quebec. There, besides acquiring whatever land was available, they congregated in the city of Montreal, applying their skills and capital to its commerce. The French saw their monopoly disappearing, their society challenged, their survival at stake. Nor was this clash of cultures the sole source of Canadian unrest. Both in Quebec and Ontario, as the population increased and the economy developed, colonial opinion grew restive over the division in the governmental structure. The Governor took his orders from London and leaned heavily on the support of the conservative oligarchy in the council of appointed officials. They were naturally opposed by the majority of the representatives elected to the assembly, who were free to criticize but powerless to command. In such a situation the assembly, if it took itself in earnest, was doomed to frustration and futility. Hence it is not surprising that executive-legislative rivalry led in 1834 to attempts at armed defiance in both Quebec and Ontario. For the troops to stamp out the fires of rebellion was an easy undertaking. But to diagnose the political causes and apply a remedy was not so simple. For this task, the Liberal Ministry in Great Britain picked the right man to come to Canada, study the conditions, and report his findings. The result —Lord Durham's Report—is the most famous single document in the evolution of the British Empire into the modern Commonwealth.

The Observations of Lord Durham

Durham's analysis focuses upon the two basic conflicts: the cultural and the institutional. He diagnosed the Canadian malady in terms of the hostility between the French and English, and the further deadlock between an assembly responsive to electoral opinion and a governor who was not. The second problem, as he correctly saw, was different from the former, and was wider in extent. Mackenzie had organized a resistance in the overwhelming British province of Ontario that was similar in motive and aim to Papineau's movement in Quebec. The quarrel over the structure of the government, and the powers of its respective branches, was rooted in a disagreement over political principles which, in itself, had nothing to do with cultural dissimilarity.[17] But, as Durham correctly observed, a connection did develop between the two issues. The English-speaking minority of that province had looked to the English-speaking governor for support against the French-speaking majority in the legislature. Thus, the weaknesses arising from the fault in the structure, i.e., from the collision between two competing sources of authority, were compounded in Quebec by the further, and deeper, conflict—the struggle between the two cultures.

The depth of this latter conflict, and its seriousness, appears to have come as a revelation to Durham when he conducted his inquiries on the scene. "I expected," he wrote about Lower Canada, "to find a contest between a government and a people: I found two nations warring in the bosom of a single state: I found a struggle, not of principles, but of races;[18] and I perceived that it would be idle to attempt any amelioration of laws or institutions until we could first succeed in terminating the deadly animosity that now separates the inhabitants of Lower Canada into the hostile divisions of French and English."[19] The account of Quebec which emerges from his writing is a tale of two peoples, who are neighbors but do not meet. In every respect, as he proceeded to illustrate in detail, the two societies moved along parallel lines and never converged. The roots of the separation lay in language and religion. The two peoples could not converse, since few of the French spoke English, and scarcely any of the latter returned the compliment. They worshipped in different churches, did not intermarry, and did not visit in one another's

17. "It is impossible to observe the great similarity of the constitutions established in all our North American Provinces, and the striking tendency of all to terminate in pretty nearly the same result, without entertaining a belief that some defect in the form of government, and some erroneous principle of administration, have been common to all; the hostility of the races being palpably insufficient to account for all the evils which have affected Lower Canada, inasmuch as nearly the same results have been exhibited among the homogeneous population of the other provinces." Lord Durham's *Report*, C. P. Lucas, ed. (Clarendon Press: Oxford, 1912) Vol. 2, pp. 72-3.
18. Durham refers to the English and French inhabitants of Canada as two "races," which they are not. They are linguistic groups, or cultures.
19. *Op. cit.*, Vol. 2, p. 16.

homes. Even in such matters of common interest as agricultural exhibitions, there had to be separate contests and separate prizes for the two groups.[20] No wonder, then, that in the streets of Montreal and Quebec the quarrels and fights among schoolboys usually arose from the division between the English and the French.[21] Thus it was unavoidable that the social split should be carried over to politics, and that the work of government should be hampered by cultural dissension. "In describing the nature of this conflict," observes Lord Durham, "I have specified the causes in which it originated; and though I have mentioned the conduct and constitution of the Colonial government as modifying the character of the struggle, I have not attributed to political causes a state of things which would, I believe, under any political institutions have resulted from the very composition of society. A jealousy between two races, so long habituated to regard each other with hereditary enmity, and so differing in habits, in language and in laws, would have been inevitable under any form of government. That liberal institutions and a prudent policy might have changed the character of the struggle I have no doubt; but they could not have prevented it; they could only have softened its character, and brought it more speedily a more decisive and peaceful conclusion. Unhappily, however, the system of government pursued in Lower Canada has been based on the policy of perpetuating that very separation of the races, and encouraging these very notions of conflicting nationalities which it ought to have been the first and chief care of Government to check and extinguish."[22]

From this diagnosis there followed the prescription of remedies. For the two types of conflict Durham proposed the appropriate cures. The institutional deadlock could be removed if the principles accepted by Britishers in Britain were exported to their colonies. Canada had been given a representative legislature, but not a responsible executive. In London the practice had been established that the Ministry should be in office because, and as long as, it led a parliamentary majority. Do abroad, Durham urged, what is done at home. Let the governor pick his Ministers, or Executive Council, from those politicians whom a majority of the legislature supported. Thus would executive-legislative harmony be assured. It is on this wise and liberal-minded idea that Lord Durham's fame has rested. The suggestion was radical in its implications, since it was bound to reduce the centralized control of the Empire and would prepare the way for the eventual autonomy of the parts. Hence a whole decade (1839-48) elapsed

20. *Ibid.*, p. 43.
21. *Ibid.*, p. 39.
22. *Ibid.*, p. 63.

before the change was adopted. But once introduced in Canada and later elsewhere, this principle was an unqualified success.

By contrast, Durham's other major recommendation was speedily approved, yet turned out to be erroneous. His remedy for cultural dualism was simple but drastic. Destroy the disease by killing the patient! He had no faith in the efficacy of any institutions to serve two mutually hostile peoples. Nor indeed did he wish to see a dual society perpetuated. Far from it. "I entertain no doubts," he affirmed, "as to the national character which must be given to Lower Canada; it must be that of the British Empire; that of the majority of the population of British America; that of the great race which must in the lapse of no long period of time, be predominant over the whole North American continent."[23] Quebec should be assimilated into an English province.[24] By encouragement and enforcement, the French nationality must be made to disappear, or, in his more expressive word, must be "obliterated."[25] Durham believed that such an objective, moreover, was not merely desirable, it was also practicable. For evidence, Durham mentions the number of French children learning the English language. Then, to reinforce his prediction, he cites Louisiana as a parallel, and points to the triumphal swamping of the French culture by the English.[26] Under the system of an executive responsible to the legislature, what is required to produce the same result in Canada is to make the English a majority and give them the power. At that time, the population of Upper Canada was estimated at 400,000 and that of Lower Canada at 150,000 English and 450,000 French.[27] If the two regions were united, as they had been before 1791, the English would be in the majority. This proposal was acted upon by the British Parliament with great alacrity, and legislation was passed within a year of the report to merge Quebec and Ontario into one.

But the optimistic assumptions which underlay this scheme were falsely conceived. The history of Louisiana was not re-enacted in Quebec. The French did not become absorbed into the English culture. On the contrary, they steadfastly maintained their own ways. In his otherwise discerning study, Durham overlooked three fundamental features of the French: their tenacity, solidarity, and fertility. The effect of all these, with each reinforcing the others, has been decisive. The French have remained French.

23. *Ibid.*, p. 288.
24. *Ibid.*, p. 296.
25. *Ibid.*, p. 299.
26. *Ibid.*, pp. 299-303.
27. *Ibid.*, p. 307.

Diversity Within a Federal Union

It did not take much more than two decades before the merger of Ontario and Quebec became unworkable. A unitary system of government could not be reconciled with social dualism. Though they were a minority of the whole, the French bargained for, and often obtained, an equal status and an equal share in representation, ministerial posts, appropriations, and the like. To the English, who had more voters and who paid the lion's share of the taxes, these arrangements were scarcely welcome. Nor were they fully satisfying even to the French, who preferred the security of constitutional guarantees to the uncertainties of political compromise. Both sides were therefore prepared to consider a new solution (1864-67) and in this they were joined by the Maritime Provinces of Nova Scotia, New Brunswick, and Prince Edward Island. The outcome was both a subdivision and a larger union. Quebec was again separated from Ontario and these two joined the Maritimes in a federal state. Within the new Dominion the majority were Protestants and English-speaking. But the French accepted their minority position, because on the points which to them mattered most their "peculiar institutions" were safeguarded and perpetuated. In distributing their respective spheres of jurisdiction to the center and the provinces, the constitution listed among the "exclusive powers of provincial legislatures" the all-important items of "solemnization of marriage in the province" and "property and civil rights in the province."[28] Thus cultural diversity within the political unity of a federal system became the Canadian formula for managing a divided society.

On this basis, Canada has now been evolving for a century. Some of the political consequences will be discussed in a later section of this book.[29] But certain aspects of this social dualism should be considered here. The cleavage between the two cultures has continued and it remains fundamental for an understanding of Canada. Other circumstances also play their part, however, and these in combination with the cultural division jointly affect the life of the community. Since Confederation, the advantage of numbers has lain with the English, whose ranks have been swelled by immigration from the British Isles. The French have matched this, however, by their rate of reproduction, so that in the future, if present trends are unchanged, they will once again become the majority. But the English ascendancy is more than merely numerical. For one thing, if area and provinces be taken into account, most of Canada conforms to the English

28. *British North America Act*, 1867, Art. 92, secs. 12, 13.
29. Chapter 11, pp. 332 ff.

culture. In the westward expansion, the settlement of the prairies and the Pacific Coast was accomplished mainly by English-speaking people; and when newer immigrants came to these regions from other continental European countries, English, not French, was the language they learned. The French fought to obtain legal recognition of their language in the west on a basis of equality with English (e.g., in the Manitoba school controversy), but were unsuccessful.

Moreover, the English have achieved such a national predominance in commerce and industry that not even Quebec has escaped their influence in the economic sphere. Generally throughout Canada, the owners and managers of industrial enterprises, mines, banks, and other financial institutions, shipping and railroads, are English-speaking—whether they be English-speaking Canadians, or British, or Americans. In the metropolis of Montreal itself, much of the business and capital is owned by the English-speaking, and the commerce of this great port depends largely on English and American firms. The reasons for these facts are not obscure. The British immigrants to North America were the inheritors of the Industrial Revolution, which the French were not. The British were the masters of entrepreneurial technique and of the requisite professional and scientific skills. They had connections with companies in the British Isles whose activities were then "putting a girdle around the world." By contrast, the French were a static, rural, eighteenth-century people, a survival from the *ancien régime*—their links with *la patrie* having been severed by Wolfe's conquest and the Revolution of 1789. Very few of their number received any higher education, and the curriculum was rigidly encased in the classical tradition. Their social outlook, theology, and ideas, remained conservative. The French stayed still, like a rock in the ocean, while the forces of modernity swept over and around them.[30]

It is a miracle then that they have survived. But survive they did— Durham's predictions notwithstanding. They have seen themselves as an embattled minority, resisting innovation because only by not changing could they preserve their identity. Such slogans as "Je maintiendrai" and Je m'en souviens," with their nostalgic yearnings, have been their watchword. This resistance to time and environment, this determination to preserve their inherited ways, has been sedulously fostered by the institution which is most responsible for their survival as a distinctive people. It is the Church which has been the backbone of the French community and the instigator of its nationalism. When French colonial authority was

30. A student of French Canada has written: "The opening of the twentieth century found French Canada almost unchanged from the end of the eighteenth." Wilfrid Bovey, *The French Canadians Today* (Penguin Books: London, 1942) p. 25.

forced to depart, the priesthood stayed. The Church thus represented to the people the chief institutional link with their past, and its priests were the constituted custodians and transmitters of their cultural identity. From this source the people derived their solidarity and determination to cling to their ancestral language, family system, and religion. It is small wonder then that the entire French community was thoroughly permeated with clerical influence.[31] Since the ideas and outlook of the Quebec clergy were old-fashioned and illiberal, the flock simply reflected the viewpoint of the shepherds.

It may be asked then, why two peoples, so dissimilar and antipathetic, should have continued "within the bosom of a single state." Why did not one secede from the other? Also, granted the fact that they have stayed in double harness, how have they managed to pull together more than they have pulled apart? The short answer to the question "why?" is the proximity and power of the United States; to the question "how?," it is the advantage of having a democracy.

If, despite frictions, irritation, and coolness, the English and the French in Canada have maintained the formal links which bind them, it is because both peoples realize that they have more to lose through separation than in union. The principal reason for this feeling is that they face so mighty a nation for their next-door neighbor. If the United States did not exist, or if this country were much weaker than it is, or if the southern Confederacy had succeeded in splitting the Union, it is most probable that the French and English would have parted company. But, viewing the potent omnipresence to the south of the undefended frontier, Canadians have reconciled themselves to the hazards of an ill-assorted condominium. The French, even when they have talked the language of secession or envisaged an independent state of "Laurentia," have been realistic enough to know that their island could not survive in an Anglo-Saxon sea. Culturally, as well as economically, they would be too small a minority by themselves to withstand the rest of North America. They need English Canada for a bulwark against the United States. Different motivations inspire the English-speaking Canadian, but they conduce to the same end. The British who immigrated to Canada retained a sentimental bond with the mother country, for which the crown supplied the ceremonial symbol. Once they were assured of self-government in their new home, they chose a loose connection with a distant Britain rather than total absorption in the United States nearby. By the former arrangement

31. Bryce has remarked: "Nowhere in the world did the Roman priesthood during last century exert so great a power in politics." *Modern Democracies*, Vol. I, Chap. 33, p. 458.

they enjoyed full control on their own terrain while sharing in the larger enterprise beyond. Had they amalgamated with the United States, the Canadian provinces would have been integrated as subordinate units of an enormous union. For geographic and economic reasons French Canada was essential to the well-being of the provinces of English culture. The peoples have been driven together. Thus paradoxically, only their union has preserved their dualism.

As for the question of how that union has been maintained, the explanation resides in the virtues of democracy. The British conferred upon French Canada one inestimable boon: the parliamentary system and the civil and political liberties which accompany it. Furthermore, the two cultures borrowed from the United States the greatest of American contributions to the art of government: the device of a federal union. Combining the two institutions, parliamentarianism and federalism, Canada revealed her true spirit, which is that of compromise. Moreover, the nature of compromise, and the institution of government in a parliamentary federation, both presuppose the political ideals of democracy. Without a democracy, its sense of "give and take," its mutual limits and restraints, the two cultures could not have abided within the same edifice. The coercions of authoritarianism and an imposed uniformity, if attempted from either side, would have shattered Canada into fragments. Only the freedoms and equalities of the democratic system have kept this state in being and may permit, some day, an ultimate fusion into a unified nationhood.[32]

The Swiss Paradox

Strangely enough, as it seems at first glance, a democracy has been firmly established, and a nation truly unified, in a country which is even more diversified in culture than either Canada or Belgium. I am referring, of course, to Switzerland. The government of this country is one of the world's most successful and stable democracies. At the same time, the modern Swiss are divided in religion and separated by language. Three-fifths are Protestant and two-fifths are Catholic. Nearly three-quarters (74%) speak German; for one-fifth (21%) the mother tongue is French; for 4 per cent it is Italian; and 1 per cent cling to Romanche. One thinks of the Swiss as the prime example of a tolerant society where cultural heterogeneity is protected and reflected by the politics of democracy. That this judgment is true cannot be denied. Switzerland is one of those small countries from which great lessons may be learned. Its people have

32. For further discussion of Canadian politics, see Chapter 11, pp. 332 ff.

achieved unity through diversity, and despite their acute divisions they have produced a fairly harmonious democracy. The origins of the Swiss state, the struggles to win independence, and the survival and growth of the confederation, represent a political triumph. When one weighs the odds against the Swiss—the divisions within, the pressures without—it is a miracle that they created Switzerland, that their union endured, and that they evolved as a democracy. Moreover, they have provided the student of politics with an unusual subject to examine, since their country forms the illuminating exception to many a generalization. Switzerland not only proves the rule, but also modifies the truism.

It should be stressed at the outset that the reputation which the modern Swiss have earned is strikingly at variance with much of their history. The Swiss may appear tolerant today. At any rate, they act tolerantly, and from their actions one may infer their attitude. But their harmony comes hardly, not easily. As individuals, they are likely to be strong-willed, slow-moving, conservative, and stubborn. If like coexists with unlike, this is not because they are enthusiastic or eager for differences but because they prudently bow to necessity. Tolerance of diversity, whether welcome or not, is the price they must pay to achieve the greater good of unity and independence.

The tradition of democracy in Switzerland has deep and ancient roots. The basic institution of government in the region which formed the starting nucleus of the Confederation was the mass meeting of the adult male citizens, the *Landsgemeinde*. This primitive folk democracy was inherited from the Germanic tribes of old and resembles the description of them written by Tacitus in Roman times.[33] The people who originally used that system were homogeneous in culture. The Swiss state began when the forest cantons of Uri, Schwyz, and Unterwalden entered into a league for mutual support and collective defense against the Hapsburgs. Victories, alliances, and an expanding influence, produced a confederation which by the fifteenth century had become a formidable military power.[34] But that society was still, in Aristotle's phrase, one of "equals and similars." All the Swiss were Catholic; all spoke German. In the following century, however, the first severe disruption of their unity occurred, and it was due to religious discord. In certain cities and cantons of Switzerland the revulsion against papal politics and clerical corruption generated a sympathy for the Protestant Reformation. Contemporaneously with Luther, and independent of his influence, Zwingli in Zurich pronounced his opposition to Rome; and Calvin not long afterward converted Geneva into his strong-

33. *De Germania*, Chaps. 7, 11, 12.
34. The military aspect of Swiss development is discussed in Chapter 7, pp. 180 ff.

hold. From this time on the Swiss were torn asunder by the furies of ecclesiastical bigotry and popular superstitions.

Why the Swiss Had To Be Tolerant

In writing about these events and the feelings they aroused, a Swiss historian has commented: "We have difficulty today in conceiving the violence of the hatreds which separated Catholics and Reformers in the sixteenth century. . . . For the Evangelicals, the Catholics were not only pagans and idolaters, they were also monsters of corruption, supporters of Austria and traitors to their country. For Catholics, the Protestants were not only heretics and atheists—in a time when crimes of conscience were punished by death—but also the destroyers of the social order."[35] During the wars of religion, the hard-won unity of the Swiss was imperiled almost to the point of dissolution. Protestant Swiss fought Catholic both in their internal feuds and externally as the allies of neighboring states.[36] Each side was intolerant toward its opponents and sought to dominate or exterminate. Society was so broken in two by these hatreds that politics could scarcely maintain a union among the cantons or, in some cases, within them. Under these circumstances, Catholics might practice democracy among themselves, as might Protestants. But it was difficult for democratic procedures (e.g., majority decisions) or principles (e.g., equality) to be applied to a jurisdiction which included both. In the end, through mutual exhaustion, through the inability of either side to eliminate its opponent, and through the clear realization that their confederation would disintegrate if they did not reunite, the Swiss accepted the wisdom of toleration. Rather than kill and be killed, they tacitly agreed to live and let live. Thus, tolerance of diversity became the foundation of their unity, and democracy developed as a *modus vivendi* for the reconciliation of differences.

Nor, although the union survived, have the scars of that combat disappeared. The battle lines—in many areas, even the exact geographical boundaries—inherited from the rivalry between Reformation and Counter-Reformation persist in the Switzerland of today. They reappear in the patterns of a diversified society and the conflicting crosscurrents of parties and politics.[37] To understand the outlook prevailing in modern Fribourg,

35. William Martin, *Histoire de la Suisse* (Librairie Payot: Lausanne, 1943) p. 100.
36. Martin points out that at Malplaquet in 1709, Swiss were fighting against Swiss—the Catholics in the French army, the Protestants alongside the English and Dutch. *Ibid.*, p. 137.
37. On this subject, see Chapter 12, pp. 353 ff.

Lucerne, or Valais, vis-à-vis that which controls in Berne, Geneva or Zurich, one still must recall the centuries-old memory of passion and persecution.

The state which religion had left divided was united through language until late in the eighteenth century. The original members of the confederation were purely German, as were all the adjacent cantons which joined soon afterward. But as the influence of the Swiss expanded, they came in contact with the Italians south of the Alps and with the French along the slopes of the Jura in the west. Some of these areas the Swiss annexed as conquerors. Other Latin communities sought the Swiss alliance, which afforded them a counterpoise to powers which they feared more— e.g., France, Savoy, or Austria. The non-Germans came to be associated with the Germans through a variety of arrangements which followed the logic of convenience rather than consistency. Some of the French or Italians were allies, others were subjects, either of the whole confederation or of particular cantons. Only the Germans were confederates, i.e., full-fledged members. So potent was the German influence in early days that some of the Latins who first joined, or were absorbed into, the confederation proceeded to Germanize themselves. This happened, for instance, with the ruling families in Fribourg and Valais. But the situation changed in the eighteenth century when French diplomacy, French military power, and French culture began to exercise their sway. Then the French language was deemed a desirable asset, and its retention was wisely tolerated by the German-Swiss. Had the men of Berne or Basle or Zurich attempted to impose a Germanization on their French allies and subjects, they would presumably have driven them into the arms of France.

But the political distinction between the confederates and their subjects or allies remained, and the inequality of status coincided with the differences in language. One of the permanent effects upon Switzerland of the French Revolution and the Napoleonic conquests was to sweep these distinctions away. The liberalizing impetus of French ideas flowed into Switzerland through the valleys of *la Suisse romande*. Bonaparte's new order proclaimed the equality of all Swiss citizens and component cantons. Nor, in this respect, was it possible after 1815 to turn back the clock. Henceforth, the Swiss society was to be multilingual, and politics and government had to adjust itself to yet a new division.

Thus upon a society which the schisms in Christianity had already set asunder a diversity of languages was superimposed. It may be said to the credit of the German-speaking majority—and numerically their majority is very big—that they have shown a wise respect for the sensitivity of their compatriots and have made many concessions on the matter of language.

French, Italian, and German have been recognized, in the Constitution of 1848, as national languages and as equal for official purposes.[38] But the Swiss have done even more than that. In the mountainous canton of Grisons in the southeastern corner of the country a minority has survived of some fifty thousand people who speak Romanche, a tongue which is roughly a form of Germanized Italian. This group desired to elevate their speech from the status of a dialect to that of a language. They accordingly sought an amendment to the federal constitution in order to have Romanche recognized as the fourth national language of the country.[39] The referendum on that subject was carried in 1938 by an over-all majority of ten to one, and by majorities in every canton—surely a remarkable demonstration of majority deference to the susceptibilities of an exiguous group.

The Unity of the Unlike

In contemporary Switzerland the problem of unifying a society which is divided in language, and of then governing it democratically, may be considered as solved. This should not be read to imply that multilingualism is free from difficulties and complications. Far from it. What I do mean is that the Swiss have arrived at a balance in which the advantages of diversity offset the disadvantages and may even outweigh them. They have used the techniques of democracy to further its ideals by allowing to each social group the right of self-determination. The principles and practices which contribute to this result deserve a mention and merit reflection. To begin with, the Swiss force themselves to learn at least a second language. In German-speaking areas the schoolchildren have to study one of the Romance languages, usually French. In the regions of French, Italian, and Romanche, they must acquire German, rightly so because it is the language of the national majority. The best-educated Swiss normally are fluent in all three of the principal tongues; or, if they do not speak them all with the same facility, they can certainly read them with understanding.

Their linguistic diversity gives the Swiss a special relationship with bordering countries and, internally, with one another. Through the vehicle of language they have a share in three of the great cultures of Europe, those which are based upon French, German, and Italian. It is only

38. *Constitution of Switzerland*, Article 116.
39. It is also characteristic of the practical sense of the Swiss, and their parsimony, that Romanche was adopted as a "national," but not as an "official," language. In the latter case, government documents would have had to be translated and printed in Romanche—an extra inconvenience and expense.

natural that the Ticinese should feel some affinity with Italy, that *la Suisse romande* should look to Paris, and that German Switzerland should have a kinship with Austria and Germany. Thus, the centrifugal effects of language bind the Swiss to all their neighbors and are a counterpoise to provincialism and isolation. Of all the peoples of Europe the Swiss are, and perforce must be, Europeans. Yet simultaneously, they are Swiss—and most patriotically so. Although one refers in hyphenated terms to German-Swiss, French-Swiss, and Italian-Swiss, it is the second half of that label which takes priority. The Swiss are conscious of belonging to the surrounding cultures, but are even more conscious of differing from them. They take pride in their political separation from their neighbors and are grateful for the peace and prosperity they enjoy. The written and literary languages of the Swiss regions are identical with the written and literary languages in Germany, France, and Italy; but the spoken languages are not. The individual Swiss will cultivate a dialect and a pronunciation which distinguish him from the nationalities next door. For convincing evidence of this, one has only to go to Berne—and listen to the Bernese! Indeed, it may be said with truth that while the differences of language do separate the Swiss domestically, they also serve to divide the Swiss from their surroundings and pull them together. The French- and Italian-speaking Swiss need those who talk German in order to maintain their own identity as distinct from France and Italy. Similarly the German-speaking need *la Suisse romande* to fortify their own sense of rugged individuality.

The internal play and counterplay of these conflicting attractions are manifested in fascinating ways. One cannot travel across Switzerland or live among its people without becoming aware of the cultural enrichment which derives from linguistic diversity. This is a small country, as countries go, in area and population. But it is not a country of uniformity, standardization, and monolithic sameness. Let us extend the words of a Swiss, Jean Jacques Rousseau, and say that in his native land man is forced to be free by being forced to be flexible. Minorities guard their rights jealously, and majorities employ the power of numbers with caution and discretion. The people of *la Suisse romande* feel that they constitute a cultural community, and hence comes this term by which they describe themselves. They will rally together against centralization, if its consequences mean conformity. This is one reason why Switzerland has no national university. If one were established, what would be the language of instruction, and would a national university tend toward a cultural assimilation of the minorities to the majority? Instead, of the seven universities in the country, three are German-Swiss, in addition to the

Polytechnic at Zurich; and four are in the French region.[40] The federal constitution gives recognition to linguistic pluralism in the requirement that the judges on the Federal Tribunal (i.e., the Supreme Court) shall represent the three official languages.[41] As for the twenty-two cantons, three are overwhelmingly French (Geneva, Neuchâtel and Vaud), while in two others (Fribourg and Valais) the French number two-thirds of the whole. The canton of Berne, where it extends in the northwest across the Jura, contains a French-Catholic population some of whom feel that their needs have been neglected by the cantonal government. Ticino is the lone canton where the Italian culture predominates, and in Grisons the population is approximately half-and-half Germanic and Romanche. Political custom and tradition have developed some well-defined practices in the relations between parties and the sharing and distribution of office among the representatives of linguistic groups, to which attention will be paid in a later chapter.[42] All in all, one may summarize the Swiss experience on this topic with a paradoxical comment. Their diversions of language have strengthened their unity, rather than weakened it, and their toleration of differences is both the cause and the effect of their independence and their democracy.

Cleavages in Modern Switzerland

Does the same judgment, it will be asked, apply to the other cleavage in their society—the split over religion? The answer to this question is less sure. Even today, the Swiss are more acutely divided by their two faiths than by their four tongues. The discords of church and doctrine have been assuaged, but not abolished. Latent below the surface are the smoldering embers of fires which were never extinguished and could once more ignite into flame. More passion attaches to this matter than to language, and it is therefore capable of arousing men to more violent action. Furthermore, religions are organized in a way that languages are not. Swiss are separated from Swiss by a clerical curtain. It is possible for an individual to surmount the linguistic barrier. He can learn to be bilingual, or even multilingual. But nobody ever encourages him to be bi-religious; and churches, as institutions, maintain a vested interest in guarding their members from contamination by competitors.

Internecine conflict between Protestant and Catholic Swiss did not end

40. There is no university in the Italian or Romanche areas.
41. Article 107.
42. See Chapter 15, pp. 480-86.

with the Peace of Westphalia or the War of the Spanish Succession. Even in the mid nineteenth century confessional hostilities drove Switzerland into warring factions and led first to an attempt at secession and then to an actual civil war. The struggle began as an issue of church-state relations in the canton of Zurich, where the Protestant church sought to dominate the cantonal government. Soon thereafter the Protestants in Aargau dissolved the monasteries in their territory. Catholic Lucerne then organized for the defense of its church, and with the active aid of the Jesuits formed a special league of Catholic cantons. When this body defied the authority of the Confederation, the latter ordered its destruction. Thus the division between the Protestant majority and the Catholic minority led to a rupture of unity and the suspension of democracy. All seven cantons that formed the *Sonderbund* (Fribourg, Lucerne, Schwyz, Unterwalden, Uri, Valais, and Zug) were strongly Catholic.[43] Against them were all the cantons where Protestantism predominated, and a few where the churches were mixed. The campaign was brief, and the war short-lived, for the two sides were not equally matched in numbers or resources. But the victors were determined that such a breakaway should not be tried again. Consequently in 1848, the year following the defeat of the *Sonderbund*, they drafted and adopted a new constitution in which a federal union replaced the loose confederation. The results of the referendum on the adoption of this document reflected the same political split. Protestants and Liberals voted in favor; Catholics and Conservatives were against. But the former had a decisive majority and therefore their will prevailed.

The law of the constitution reflected the temper of the victors, since it contained provisions which were unpalatable to Catholics.[44] These included, and still include, an absolute ban upon the Jesuits from any organization or activity in Switzerland.[45] Nationally, the religious freedom of the individual is guaranteed. But this does not prohibit a canton from recognizing a particular church as official within its jurisdiction. Consesequently, in modern Switzerland the systems of church-state relations vary so widely from canton to canton that they defy generalization. The churches have not entirely abandoned their old practice of using political power, in the areas where their adherents are the majority, to score an advantage over their ecclesiastical rivals. Of course, the attitudes of ordinary Swiss to religion nowadays run the gamut from devotion to indifference. There are fanatics, as there are moderates, among Catholics and

43. Ticino, however, which was also strongly Catholic, did not join.
44. See Articles 49-54.
45. Article 51.

Protestants alike; and there is also a large number of sceptics. But zealotry of the old-fashioned kind has not disappeared; and the militants, both clerical and lay, can still be expected at times to rekindle ancient prejudices.

The confessional cleavage, it should be added, is further widened by social and economic differences. In general, Catholic Switzerland is poorer and more rural. Since Catholics are forbidden by their priests to limit the size of their families by artificial means, the increase of population presses upon the shortage of land and resources and aggravates their poverty. For this reason, many Catholics migrate from the commune and canton of their home in search of employment elsewhere. They naturally gravitate to the larger cities and manufacturing centers, where they can obtain industrial or white-collar jobs. Today in the city of Zwingli, as in the citadel of Calvin, one-third of the inhabitants are Catholic. Their movement to such cities in growing numbers sometimes arouses the irritation and resentment of the natives, who do not welcome intruders if housing and jobs are hard to find. But in the long run this urbanizing process helps to change the mentality of the ex-rural Catholic. In the city he is more emancipated from his priest than he would be, say, in a mountain village of the Valais. To have a heretic for one's neighbor can be an illuminating experience for both, if the neighbor appears to be a decent human being. Also, a small city apartment lends itself less readily to an expanding family than did the paternal farmhouse. Either economic stringency or a desire for a higher living standard can modify the "theologic" of the birth rate. Thus it is not entirely impossible that in the distant future the two faiths, which once were hotly hostile and since have coldly coexisted, may ultimately be diffused in a general secularism.

Toleration and Neutrality

In the meantime, while the Swiss hold their union intact, two final conditioning factors—one external, the other internal—should be noted. The former is the same point that was observed in the cases of Canada and Belgium. The Swiss accept their differences, and tolerate diversity, because this policy is less painful than the prospect of absorption by their neighbors. The pressures from outside—exerted, as they are, all around the nation's borders—have welded the solidarity within. The Swiss prefer being Swiss, rather than the alternative, which is to lose their identity by becoming fragments of Germany, Austria, Italy, or France. Since independence presupposes unity, and unity in their case posits the acceptance of diversity, the Swiss have learned to be tolerant. Or, let us say, they have learned to be as tolerant as it is necessary to be in order to survive.

Moreover, they are helped in this by one peculiar and fortunate aspect of their demographic design. There is an important feature of the Swiss society which distinguishes it from the Belgian and the Canadian, and contributes to the greater stability of the Swiss democracy. In Belgium and Canada religious divisions reinforce, and tend to follow the same lines as, the divisions of language. This is not the case in Switzerland. Here the religious cleavage, instead of coinciding with the linguistic boundaries, cuts across them. Thus, although the subdivisions are more numerous among the Swiss, their effects are less serious. There are both Catholics and Protestants among those who speak German, as there are Protestants and Catholics among those who speak French. While Berne and Basel and Zurich became Protestant, Lucerne and the Germanic forest cantons nearby remained decidedly Catholic. Vaud and Geneva are Protestant, but Catholicism holds sway in Fribourg, Valais, and Ticino. The Swiss will, therefore, be grouped one way if they are concerned over a question which is primarily confessional, and will cement their political alliances accordingly. But when it is a linguistic matter, they will regroup themselves in different clusters. Since the religious split is the more serious of the two, the Swiss are lucky indeed that Calvin did convert Geneva and that Vaud was reformed by Berne. Had the geography of language coincided with that of faith, the preservation of unity and the politics of democracy would have been rendered so much more difficult and might perhaps have proven unattainable.

Thus, the demographic character of Switzerland not only demands, but also assists, its democratic character. Three of the basic principles of a democratic system—liberty, equality, and tolerance—converge to suit exactly the needs of Swiss society. The individual has the liberty to speak the language of his home, and, as a citizen, the duty of learning one language of his neighbors. He has the freedom of conscience and may worship, or not, in the manner he chooses. Equality is accorded, nationally, to the various sub-groups, linguistic and confessional. Tolerance is required from one and all, since each who wishes to exercise his rights has the duty to respect the rights of others. Thus it is inherent in the logic of Swiss society that, to survive as a people, their government must be democratic. By any other solution, they would not merely have forfeited their equality and surrendered their liberties as individuals. They would also have lost Switzerland.

Equality for Dissimilars

The argument of this, and the preceding, chapter has traversed a broad field, and a summation of some kind is now in order. What, if anything, has been proven? How much of importance has been left unsaid? On the relation between the quality of the political system and cultural homogeneity or heterogeneity there is no country in the world, present or past, which does not have something unique to teach. But since no study could embrace every instance, one must generalize from groups of cases which contain broad resemblances. Such generalization is seldom meaningful, however, unless accompanied by a selection of particulars where special aspects of the main issue can be seen in sharper focus. That is why Brazil, South Africa, and the United States were discussed in the preceding chapter, and why this chapter has taken a look at Spain, Russia, Austro-Hungary, Belgium, Canada, and Switzerland. As these choices indicate, the cases were picked to point a contrast between encouragement of diversity or the imprint of uniformity, between success or failure, between democracy and autocracy. All are examples of social heterogeneity in one respect or another, to which the political order has responded in various ways. All have shared the experience of conflict in attempting to provide a government for a divided society. Indeed in some of these countries the conflicts continue without any solution.

The record of democracy in this sphere is broader, of course, than the contents of these two chapters have revealed. Of the countries which have been discussed, all those which are clearly democratic—namely, Belgium, Canada, Switzerland, and the United States—contain a special problem arising from the divisions in their population. But there are other democracies where such difficulties do not exist or exist in much smaller degree or present fewer cultural complications for political solution. Racial minorities, for instance, are virtually nonexistent in Europe. Or if found, as today in France or Great Britain, they are present in such numbers that they do not disrupt the community as a whole or sow the seeds of discord in its national politics. Similarly in the Antipodes, minority races do not have sufficient force to affect the course of national life. The Australian aborigines have even less effect upon the Commonwealth than have the Indians upon the Dominion of Canada. The Maoris of New Zealand are a more advanced people, and their participation in politics upon a basis of equality is both protected and respected. But they too are not numerous enough to pose a threat or challenge to the majority of British descent. Most of the world's most successful democracies do not face the internal complexities of a racial mixture. Perhaps for this reason, as Winston Churchill has suggested, they are more disposed to maintain a serene and lofty view about the difficulties of those who do.[46]

Differences in religion or language are commoner among the successful democracies, both in Europe and other continents, than the distinctions of race. There is hardly a country which has not had to cope with the problem of church-state relations or which has not at some time embraced a linguistic minority within its fold. In chronological sequence, the usual order has been that the social divisions appeared first and the political system was democratized later. Hence, the challenge for democracy has consisted in its success or failure in promoting harmony between sub-groups and applying to their relationship its principle of tolerance and equality. Success has not been too hard to reach where one side possesses an overwhelming numerical predominance. The majority may then make concessions to the minority without endangering its own position. The pygmy accepts what the giant bestows and is grateful not to be swallowed up. Thus in the United Kingdom, where the English and the Protestants outnumbered everybody else, the existence of diversity did not prohibit the attainment of unity and democracy, save in the case of the one conspicuous failure—the relations of the English with the Catholic Irish. In Denmark, Norway, and Sweden, cultural homogeneity has been the rule rather than the exception. Neither the opposition of the independent Protestant Churches to the official Lutheran church, nor the language question in Norway, nor the Lapps of the Swedish Arctic, can be considered as divisions of comparable intensity to those which were discussed in previous pages. But where the numbers are more evenly balanced, or the feelings are more passionate, it is a different story. Dutch society is nearly bisected between Protestants and Catholics; and since both sides have strong attachments to their respective causes, the politics of the democratic process are hard pressed to maintain a delicate balance. France paid a heavy cost for its intolerance in persecuting the Huguenots, which intensified the absolutism of the old regime and its autocracy. Later on, after the Revolution, the hostility between clerical and anticlerical opinions continued as a bipolar division in French society and was one of the causes of perennial weakness in its democratic experiments.

To conclude then: one may say that, since the tasks of government are

46. "In countries where there is only one race broad and lofty views are taken of the colour question. Similarly, States which have no overseas colonies or possessions are capable of rising to moods of great elevation and detachment about the affairs of those who have." *The Second World War* (Houghton Mifflin: Boston, 1950) Vol. iv, p. 269.

made easier by shared loyalties and understandings, in a society which is culturally homogeneous a democracy is simpler to operate. But so too, by the same logic, is a dictatorship. The real test for both political systems, and a criterion which distinguishes them, is their respective treatment of cultural diversity. A dictatorship could be tolerant of social heterogeneity and still be politically authoritarian. It may recruit some representatives of different sub-groups—racial, linguistic, religious—into the dominant elite, and it may also encourage the manifestations of cultural autonomy. This in fact is how the Russian Communist party has tried to handle the problems which Czarism failed to solve. In that respect the Communists have been wiser than the Czars, whose efforts at Russifying only provoked a bitter opposition. The former, although denying political freedom, have provided some compensation in cultural freedom; also, by tolerating ethnic diversity they have conformed to the maxim *divide et impera*.

In a society composed of dissimilars, alternative policies are possible in respect to both goals and methods. Either the dissimilarities may be accepted as permanent and be permitted to continue, or measures may be used to bring about their disappearance. In the former case, one solution is for the different groups to remain distinct and for all groups and individuals to be accorded equal status. The other policy is for a dominant group to leave the differences as they are, but force the other groups into subordination to itself. The acceptance of diversity can therefore be combined with either equality or inequality. The second pair of alternatives occurs when diversity is rejected in favor of conformity. Such a result may be approached in opposite ways. The heterogeneous groups may be induced to abandon their separate identities and assimilate to a common pattern. Contrariwise, they may be compelled to conform under threat of extermination if they do not.

Two of these policies require an authoritarian system; two make possible a democratic regime. The state will be authoritarian either where dissimilars are treated as inferiors, or where the dominant group imposes conformity. Democracy demands either that dissimilars be helped and encouraged to conform, or that people be allowed to remain dissimilar but be treated as equals. To encourage dissimilars to assimilate is a difficult policy to execute, but may often turn out a wise one. The hardest of all policies to conduct on a harmonious basis for a long time is that of equality for dissimilars. But, enlarging on the Aristotelian dictum, one may offer this judgment, which is not visionary but realistic, that the future *Polis* of humanity will have to be one in which people who are dissimilar can also be equal. In that way, they can also live democratically.

7

Geopolitics

The people who form a political community live on the land. From the earth and the adjacent sea they take their food and make their wealth. What they have thus acquired, they seek to protect for their use and enjoyment. When technology was primitive, many aspects of social organization were derived from the nature of the food supply. Men who hunted or gathered their food were nomads. Even if they lived off domesticated animals, they would still move with their flocks and herds to wherever there was grazing and water. But when agriculture provided the principal source of food, humanity became static. Men had to cultivate the earth, then wait for the crop to ripen. As their food was rooted in the soil, so were the people. For an agriculturist to guard and keep his own was not the same as it was for a nomad. The latter might survive by flight. But since the former had to protect something immovable, his organization for defense was conditioned by its territorial base. In this way, politics came to involve not only the government of people, but the mastery of the area over which their society extended.

Geographical Influences on Politics

Granted these facts, how does the control of living-space affect the character of the political system? More particularly, what is the connection between the territorial foundation of a society and the democratic or undemocratic quality of its politics? It is with this subject—the physical basis of the state and its relation to the politics of democracy—that the present chapter is concerned. The general connection between politics and geography is a large topic which has been variously treated by political thinkers. Some twentieth-century writers, arguing for a certain school of geopolitical doctrine, have contended that this relation is immediate and direct. The requirements of geography, they assert, dictate the political response. The goals and forms of politics are determined by geographical conditions, because whoever would survive must bow to the necessities of securing their living-space. Therefore, they must adopt all means appropriate to that end.

It is not open to dispute that a relation exists between geography and politics and that it is important. But the principal effects of geography on politics are felt indirectly rather than directly. Nor do I think it correct to say that geographical factors determine the political system, if determining means necessitating a particular result or solution in the sense that this alone, and no other, is possible of adoption. The truth is rather that the geographical base presents its human occupants with only a few compulsions in which, strictly speaking, they have no choice. Beyond these, Man's habitat supplies the conditions within which he must solve his problems of production, defense, and transportation; and while there may be limits to his range of choice, the choices nevertheless exist. It is in this sense that geography may properly be said to have an influence upon politics. That influence, however, does not proceed solely in one direction. Our habitat does much to us; but equally we do much to our habitat.

This means no more than that a people will always work with whatever materials lie at hand. In order to survive, they must adapt themselves to those necessities they cannot escape—as the Arabs of the desert must eke out their scarcity of water and the Dutch must hold back the ocean. The inhabitants of an island, if they can command the surrounding sea, will use it for a highway outward. If they do not, it is a highway for others to enter. Likewise, the constant elements of geography inject some continuities into the vicissitudes of political change. It was no series of accidents which, across a span of four centuries, brought Great Britain into conflict with the Spain of Philip II, the France of Louis XIV and Napoleon, and the Germany of Kaiser Wilhelm and Hitler. The islanders, governed by successive regimes of royal autocracy, aristocratic oligarchy, and popular democracy, have always sought to prevent a single major power from unifying the Continent and, especially, from dominating the Low Countries. Likewise the Russians, locked in the Eurasian land-mass, have steadily pressed toward the exits of the Baltic, Black Sea, and Persian Gulf. In this respect, the switch from Czarism to Communism resulted in changes of technique only, but not of aim.[1]

Beyond some obvious compulsions of this sort—and they are not so very numerous—there exists a wide field of choice where alternatives are possible and no result is preordained. Sometimes a river or a mountain range will be enclosed in the interior so that the people on its two sides belong within the same political complex (e.g., the Rockies or the Urals, the Volga or the Mississippi). Or, for convenience and by convention, such a physical line can serve as the political boundary to separate state from state (the Alps or Pyrenees, the Rhine or Danube). Nor is there any sure guide other than the experience of history to indicate whether neighboring peoples who meet at a common frontier will be friendly or hostile. For reasons which were political, not geographical, the United States and Canada could enjoy an undefended frontier when France and Germany could not. Moreover, whereas the data of geography remain constant, except where men dig a canal or turn once-fertile land into a desert, the relations of politics are not. The allies of one century, nay of one decade, are the enemies of another. Witness the Scandinavians, so pacific and mutually amicable today, who were expansive and even predatory powers in years past. The government of Sweden, "the Hammer of the North," once launched its conquering armies upon central Europe. In modern times, it gave Dag Hammarskjold to the United Nations.

That the connection between geography and politics is indirect has already been implied in the preceding argument. The middle of the chain is formed by links which are military and economic. The physical location of a community contains the factors (e.g., terrain, climate, resources, communications, etc.) which are the conditions for its economic development and military security. Of itself, the geographical site which a state occupies implies no necessity that its political values and institutions will subscribe to any particular character. But geography exerts a direct influence on military safety and economic productivity, and, through these, on the survival of a group and its prosperity. Since any piece of territory presents its defenders with strategic features of strength and weakness, these become the concern of the government, which must organize the available forces and allocate resources. Consequently, politics are shaped by the influence of geography as this becomes intertwined in society with other mediating factors—e.g., the economic system, methods of transport, size and growth of population, and the capacity to repel invaders.

1. A Soviet diplomat is reported to have said that, if Russian ships wish to pass from the Black Sea into the Mediterranean, they have to sail through the Bosporus and Dardanelles—a constant in Russo-Turkish relations, irrespective of the systems of government in Ankara and Moscow.

The Physical Foundations of States

As was noted earlier in this book, an analysis of the state is presupposed in the analysis of the democratic state. The form of government which we call democratic must satisfy the general conditions which apply to all governments. If any state is to exist, its primary need is that it should possess the energy to function and the power to survive. Although such ideals as liberty and equality are essential to democracy, there is little point in talking about them unless, as a prior condition, a state is established which can employ the means of government to promote equality and liberty among its inhabitants. Chief among the prerequisites of a state are unity and order. There must be sufficient solidarity for the people to hang together in some kind of structure, and enough order for their society to evolve into a civilization. Viewed chronologically, the qualities of democracy emerge at the culmination of a process, not at the beginning. In the beginning, the art of government consists in the rougher, and sometimes cruder, work of fashioning the raw materials of a community into a cohesive whole. The completed buildings which house a mature civilization may be designed for our comfort and ease and be decorated with good taste. But their foundations lie in plain earth. It is wise not to overlook the foundations.

In other decades, to be reminded of this point, it was sometimes necessary to re-examine the historical accounts of the birth of states in earlier centuries or even in quite primitive times. Alternatively, if one's generation was engaged in major war, the contemporary conflict would yield some valuable insights into the construction or dissolution of a society and its political system. For, when vast organizations of humanity are flung into conflict so that their survival is at stake, one notes more keenly the truth of Aristotle's dictum that the state originates for the sake of life, then evolves towards the good life. But for any observer of politics in the early 1960's, no more telling proof could be sought than what lay open to view in the Congo. After the period of Belgian imperial rule ended in the middle of 1960, the condition of that huge territory plunged sharply and speedily into chaos and anarchy. Too few Congolese had been trained by their Belgian rulers in the methods of operating a modern state, or in the professions and technology of an advanced society. Their loyalties were tribal, not national. When external restraints were removed, they proceeded to fall upon one another and upon foreigners with murderous ferocity. In the fear that the winds of great power rivalries might blow into such a vacuum, the United Nations did what it could, with inadequate supplies of men and money and materials, to hold the fragments together. Throughout the painful efforts to prevent the unilateral interference of foreign powers, it became clear that such terms as "independence" and "sovereignty," or even "state" and "nation" and "government," can have no meaning unless they accord with certain fundamental realities. No society, no state, can be truly founded on fictions. The Congolese did not yet feel, subjectively, as a nation. Juridically, in a formal sense a state could be said to exist by virtue of the recognition accorded by other states and by the United Nations. But internally this "state" was lacking in the institutions, the functions, and the power to command which make a state effective. As for a government, three or four rival groups—all of them based on different regions, tribes, and ideologies—contended for this honor. No leaders had much actual power; nobody possessed genuine authority. Nor could the civil figureheads control their military force, or the officers for that matter control the ranks. In the light of this situation, to speak of a constitution for the Congo, or, more specifically, to urge that a parliament be convened or that new elections be conducted, was meaningless. Until a community of sentiment and interest was created, until the rudiments of a state could be erected and maintained, it was idle to join in debate over higher principles whose preconditions were yet to be established. Before there is some order, it is futile to argue for liberty.

The first essential for any state is to build its internal order and guard against external danger, since if it does not perform these functions it will cease to be a state. In sequence, it is the political achievement of consensus which produces a constitution, a constitution which sanctions the enactment of law, the law which calls for execution, and execution which demands enforcement. Against the domestic lawbreaker and the enemy outside, the community must mobilize the force required for its protection. So far, so obvious—at least as logic goes. But the conclusions of politics conform to no syllogism. It is precisely at this point, when enforcement is operative and protection is secured—in other words, when one set of problems has been solved—that other problems begin. How much force should be organized? What powers shall the enforcers have? Who will control them? Can the community protect itself from its protectors? Will the defense of one kind of liberty (meaning independence from external rule) jeopardize another kind of liberty (the civil rights of the citizen against the powers of officialdom)? The "liberator" who leads a people to freedom from outside control is sometimes the oppressor of his opponents within.

The majority of modern states, particularly the leading ones in power and importance, evolved in earlier centuries from a group of smaller units.[2] Usually, some one unit became larger and stronger than the rest because of advantages in strategic location, economic resources, and political and social solidarity. This one then expanded its sphere of influence among its neighbors; or, as viewed in reverse, it served as a rallying point around which they might cluster for common advantage. To unify and consolidate the whole would call for various means, including alliances, dynastic marriages, and conquest. At some stage, the expansion of the central nucleus generally encountered the resistance of a rival and the two would compete for control of the region that lay between. In many cases, a border area might try to maintain the independence of its own government, especially if its distance from the emerging capital encouraged a feeling of separatism and if it had other outlets for its trade and transport. Such is a generalized summary of a political process extending over centuries, the details of which can be illustrated by comparable episodes in the histories of many countries.

During the growth of a state, as this summary has implied, the line between internal and external politics has often been blurred and hazy. At the most, protection from without has been indistinguishable from consolidation within. At the least, they are aspects of the same process, or the two sides of one coin. When internal divisions exist, a would-be invader discerns an opportunity or invitation. Hence, unity inside augments security outside. If strategic weaknesses along the border endanger one's safety, expansion and the subsequent incorporation of fresh territory may seem the best defense. Like the Roman image of Janus, therefore, the military organization which a community sustains may have two faces and look two ways. The very forces with which a government repels external attack can be employed to bolster its internal domination. After all, you can aim a spear, a musket, or a machine gun in any direction. What counts is the attitude of those who hold the weapons.

Political Types in Relation to Power on Land or Sea

The varieties of geographical location, however, confront each society with different sets of conditions within which the problem of security has to be resolved. All communities extend over land and have the need therefore to control it. But some, in addition, have a seacoast, or are situated on an island. Prior to the twentieth century, the military security of any state was a function of its land power or sea power or both. But there is a difference between land power and sea power which is especially

2. Some have been constituted, however, by fission rather than fusion—by splitting off from some larger aggregate.

relevant to the theme of this chapter. The relation between military organization and the political system must be considered in the light of the contrast between power on land and power at sea. A survey of the historical evidence from the past to very recent times suggests the following propositions. All great land powers hitherto have been autocratically governed. This is to say that the states whose armies have been externally preponderant have been governed internally by one of the various kinds of autocracy—by royal absolutism, an oligarchy of nobles, military condottieri, or some species of dictatorship. The army which was powerful enough to invade others or to repel invasion was sufficiently potent to curb internal liberties. At any rate, there is no clear case on record of the contrary, i.e. of a great land power which was also a democracy.[3] But the same is not true of peoples with a naval tradition. Of the great sea powers, some have been autocratic, others democratic. Although incompatible with land power, democracy has been compatible with sea power. A navy has never been a menace to democratic government. Those who depend on sea power for their military protection do not have to fear their own navy. The military rulers of history have always been the generals, never the admirals.

Such generalizations are founded, of course, on the experience of the past. They apply from the time of classical antiquity to the rise and establishment of the nation-state. Therefore they embrace the birth of democracy in the *Polis* and its rebirth and maturation since the seventeenth century. The advent of air power, however, in this century and the contemporary exploration of outer space, have added new dimensions to geopolitics,[4] both domestic and external. But whatever changes are now required in the solution of age-old problems, the influence of tradition, though doubtless to be modified, will by no means be destroyed. The circumstances of democracy's birth and its subsequent growth have helped to mold and shape the ideas and attitudes and institutions of its full development. Nor, in reflecting on the possible further extensions of democracy, should one ignore the factors which were formative in the cradle period and have persisted since.

Sea Power and Athenian Democracy

A review of some particular cases will support these general arguments. In classical Greece the great example of democracy was also the great

3. The apparent exceptions to this generalization will be discussed later.
4. The present phase could be described as "neo-geopolitics." For a discussion of its implications, see pp. 184 ff.

sea power of its time. Originally a small city serving an agricultural hinterland, Athens grew large, wealthy, and strong. This aggrandizement was accompanied by an economic transformation. For a trading state, Athens possessed two valuable physical assets, the harbor at Peiraeus and the silver mines at Laureium, plus the social assets of her craftsmen and merchants. Using these means, the city became the center for a flourishing commerce which extended from Italy to the Black Sea. The risks of maritime wealth and the long distances to be traversed called for the expansion of the navy. At the time of the Persian invasions, the Athenian fleet was already the strongest in Greece; and after the rout of Xerxes' armada at Salamis, Athenian leadership in the Aegean changed into domination. Attica being a peninsula, the Athenians converted their *Polis* into something as close to an island as it was possible for a portion of the mainland to become. They did this by surrounding the city with a well-fortified wall which was connected with Peiraeus by three long walls. Invading armies, such as those of the Spartans, could plunder the countryside. But the Athenians, secure behind their walls, could import their food and other necessities thanks to sea power. In addition, they guarded their sea lanes by forming alliances with strategically located peoples and by establishing bases. Thus trade followed the trireme, and the trireme protected trade. The whole policy contained its gambles, but was rooted in a rationale intelligently conceived by men of such ability as Themistocles and Pericles. Only a wild and reckless expansionism could turn its understandable risks into sure disaster.

But what is equally noteworthy is the internal concomitant of this external posture. For at the very time when the Athenians were building their sea power, indeed simultaneously with the conversion of their allies into subjects, in domestic politics the constitutional system was steadily evolving toward a more democratic form. Thus it is Athens which supplies the first instance of a union, of which other cases will be noticed later, between democracy at home and sea power abroad. But the relationship goes deeper than a mere coincidence of timing. The actual organization of the navy in Athens made it the political, as well as the military, shield of the democracy. The men who rowed the fighting ships were not slaves in chains but free citizens drawn from the lower income groups. These were the ones to whom full political rights (and specifically the right to participate and vote in the Assembly) had been extended by the reforms of Cleisthenes. Not only were they loyal to the democracy which had enfranchised them, but the character of the majority which would vote at the monthly meetings of the Assembly might differ considerably in its radicalism if the fleet was at home or away. By contrast, the wealthier citizens, who generally were more conservative and less friendly to the democratic system, were particularly influential in the army, where they constituted the principal fighting men, or *hoplitai*. The latter were infantrymen who wore the heavy armor (*hopla*), which cost a considerable amount of money and which the soldier furnished at his own expense. In Athenian politics, both internal and external, a division was frequently observable of democracy, radicalism, and the navy on one side, versus plutocracy, conservatism, and the army on the other. Cimon's policy of sending troops to help the Spartans quell a Helot revolt was an example of one policy. Cleon's adventures in naval imperialism typified the other.

Land Power and the Government of Sparta

The pro-Spartan veerings of the Athenian army were not without reason. If the Athenians exhibited to their contemporaries the union of democracy with sea power, Sparta embodied the merging of land power with autocracy. The contrast between the two states was sharp, and the lines of cleavage ran deep. Politics cast these two communities in the role of erstwhile allies who turned into bitter foes. The character of their institutions diverged in a manner which yielded ample material for historian, philosopher, and dramatist. One was an open society dedicated to freedom, equality, popular participation, and speculative inquiry. The other was a closed society, displaying the results of thought control, secret police, hostility to aliens, inequality, and authoritarianism. The Athenian economy and culture responded to the liberal influences of the sea which makes neighbors of all peoples who have a coastline and encourages the exchange of ideas, as well as commodities, in the ports where travelers mingle. The Spartans were parochial, self-centered, withdrawn, and landlocked.

Founded by tradition on the laws of Lycurgus, the Spartan polity was a byword for Greece. The Spartans were members of the Dorian tribe, who were late migrants into Greece and who pushed south into the central Peloponnesus where they vanquished its Messenian inhabitants. There, as conquerors, they remained. The state of Lacedaemon, originating in conquest, continued as the instrument for perpetuating the mastery of the overlords and quashing rebellion of the underdogs. To this end was the notorious Spartan discipline directed. Outnumbered by their subjects and ever on guard against an insurrection, the Spartans could stay on top only by sacrifice, solidarity, and an inflexible order. For them no distinction existed between civil and military. Their menfolk were hardened from boyhood and trained in martial discipline. Their society, imbued with an ordered hierarchy, was a barracks writ large. Their government was the regimen of an army pervading a community. This is the classic picture of the "garrison state."[5] If any state known to history deserves the title, Sparta does.

The Roman Land Empire and the Loss of the Republic

The argument that large-scale land power has always been associated with autocracy is further exemplified in the history of the state which of all in European antiquity was the most successful and the most powerful. In the course of their evolution from a small farming community with an urban nucleus to the rulers of a vast empire, the Romans ranged the gamut of constitutional systems. At first governed by a monarchy, they overthrew the Etruscan dynasty (509 B.C.) and adopted a republic. This lasted for nearly five centuries, until it was replaced by the Augustan principate. The latter, developing into an autocratic emperorship, continued on for four more centuries in the west and still another thousand years in the east. Two salient facts in that long record are relevant to the present discussion: the outward expansion of Roman power and the internal replacement of the republic by the principate.

Since the politics and constitution of the republic changed so much during five hundred years, to generalize about it can be to oversimplify. But this can fairly be said of it by way of summary. The Roman republic did not begin as a democracy, nor did it end as one. In certain periods of its lifetime, however, the Romans approached as close to democracy as they ever came. The republican system always contained a democratic potential which was never fully realized. Throughout its political history, some principles and institutions which were inherently democratic struggled against others which were aristocratic, oligarchical, and authoritarian. After Caesar and Augustus had done their work, the autocratic element triumphed, and triumphed finally, over the democratic. The *cives Romani* became henceforth the subjects of their Caesars.

The essential reason why the republic failed to make good on its democratic potential lies in the very sphere where it was most successful, namely the use of land power to win an enormous empire. It was, after all, under the aegis of their republic that the Romans became an imperial people. While internally they were at pains to surmount "the struggle of the orders" and to equalize the plebeians with the patricians, externally

5. To employ the phrase of Harold D. Lasswell.

their power was spreading throughout Italy, of which they became the military and political masters. In the next phase they encountered and crushed their principal rivals in the Mediterranean: Carthage and Macedon. The Roman victories over these opponents initiated the acquisition of territories beyond Italy proper, a pleasant taste which formed a habit and terminated in addiction. Moving from each area as they consolidated it to the one next adjacent, the Romans organized their provinces step by step until they found themselves the rulers of an *imperium*. When this process was completed, they had also produced a military paradox. The Romans were landsmen, not seamen. Their natural element was the land, where their infantry distinguished itself. But they were forced onto the water in their duel with the Carthaginians, who, as a Phoenician offshoot, were a seafaring people. The Romans therefore built large fleets during the Punic Wars, though their concept of naval tactics was merely to conduct a land battle on the sea by ramming an enemy ship and sending soldiers to fight aboard its decks. When they had destroyed Carthage, and when the legions had taken possession of every country bordering on the Mediterranean, the consolidation of a continuous empire on land made sea power superfluous. No rival had a port from which he could launch a fleet hostile to Rome. A small naval force was sufficient to overawe the islands and inhibit the pirates. Without the benefits of sea power, the Romans held a land empire around an inland sea.

Meanwhile, the necessities of fighting in protracted and distant campaigns, and the requirements of governing what they had conquered, imposed new strains on their domestic institutions and traditions. The army had once consisted of levies of citizens who served from spring to fall and then returned to their homes, a system which met the needs of combat in Italy. But continuous wars and garrison duty in Spain, North Africa, France, and the Middle East required professional soldiers who had to be specially trained and paid for long service. Also the system of command was altered. In early campaigns, one or both of the consuls of the year could lead the army in person and could alternate between civil duties in the capital and military duties at the front. When later wars were fought at increasing distances from Rome and on so many fronts, the commanders of the legions in the field were no longer the consuls, but ex-praetors and ex-consuls who were sent out to take or govern a province. The separation of the military command from the civil leadership introduced twin problems in the exercise of authority, that of the civil government over its armed forces and that of Rome over the provinces.

To make matters still more complicated, the acquisition of empire transformed the economic base of the Roman society. Conquest brought plunder to the imperial city. The treasure of Egypt, Asia Minor, and

Greece made the Romans rich. The organization of a Mediterranean-wide commerce assured them a lucrative profit, and the abundant supply of slaves from their captives made life easy and luxurious. The flood of wealth, unequally amassed, brought new class divisions into the Roman society. The old nobility confronted a rising plutocracy and an urban proletariat. The tensions between these groups provoked political struggles which the constitution was unfitted to solve.

Under the weight of the burdens which it had assumed, the framework of the republic broke. The Roman constitution, diagnosed by Polybius as of the "mixed" type, had been the work of political compromise and adjustment, not of logic and plan. As their society evolved, the Romans strove to adapt their government by reforming old institutions or sometimes by adding new ones to the old without abolishing the old. By the time the Gracchan revolution erupted (133-121 B.C.), the republic consisted of a network of overlapping assemblies and annually elected offices, in which the principle of the separation of powers, and its corollary of checks and balances, had been pushed beyond the limits of sense. Understandably, therefore, the Roman leaders had to compensate for these excesses in other ways. To provide for continuity of policy, they relied on the Senate, whose functions, which, strictly viewed, had been advisory and consultative, developed into genuine leadership. Also, in cases of dire emergency, they could appoint a *dictator* who superseded the regular officials and for a limited term possessed unlimited powers.

In the century of turmoil which opened with the tribunate of Tiberius Gracchus (133 B.C.) and ended with the battle of Actium (31 B.C.) all these problems came to a head. The fissures in the society resulted in party conflicts between Optimates and Populares. Both sides looked for support in different institutions, the former in the Senate, the latter in the consuls or tribunes. Both turned to military power and brought up the legions against their rivals: Sulla and Pompey for the senatorial oligarchy, Marius and Caesar for the *Populares*. At the climax it was a proconsul with further political ambitions, and a veteran army loyal to him to the death, who marched from their province, crossed the Rubicon, and overthrew the consuls, Senate, and *respublica Romana*. Henceforth the power which prevailed in Rome was authoritarian in character. Propped up by a military underpinning, it was uncontrollable by an ordinary constitutional process. By its army the republic created the empire; afterwards, the army of the empire created an emperorship. The loyalty of the distant legions or the nearby praetorian guard[6] decided the succession to the throne. The

6. On one notorious occasion, some members of the praetorian guard assassinated the emperor (Pertinax). Then, to fill the vacancy they had created, they offered the emperorship at public auction to the highest bidder.

Roman government proceeded upon a syllogism, wherein the rule of law was the conclusion, but the rule of the *imperium* and the army were its premises.

Russia and Prussia

There are some scenes in the drama of history in which the actors change, but the plot remains the same. And this is one of them. The lessons of classical antiquity in the west indicate that sea power can be compatible with democracy, whereas land power cannot. But the experience of the *Polis* could merely suggest, not prove, such a thesis. Confirmation, however, can be found in the experiences of nation-states from the fifteenth century to the nineteenth. Observe the leading states which have contributed much to the modern world, and one will not fail to note the close correlation between land power and autocracy, between seapower and democracy. In this respect, Germany and Russia are the descendants of Sparta and Rome, while Great Britain and the United States have continued the tradition of Athens. It will be fruitful, in order to learn more about the social environment of democracy, to examine these instances and then explore a few special cases and apparent exceptions.

Let us look at autocracy first. Nobody would deny that Germany and Russia are two countries which have exercised a considerable influence, for good and ill, on the modern world. Nor is it open to doubt that modern democracy owes hardly anything to these particular states.[7] In both places the traditions and forms of government have been consistently and profoundly authoritarian. From this standpoint, the substitution of the Communists for the Czars, which in other respects produced many great changes, has altered little. As for Germany, the autocrats and militarists always rode roughshod over the democrats and liberals. The Frankfurt liberals were beaten in 1849, after which they bowed to Bismarck. The Weimar parties ignominiously succumbed in short order to Hitler. Whether the Bonn regime will endure remains to be seen. But at least a generation must come and go before the dominant tradition can be reshaped.

There is much that is similar in the history of Russia and Prussia. Possibly the fact that they were neighbors accounts in part for the influence which each has exercised over the other. For centuries the Teutons and the Slavs have disputed the control of eastern Europe. Across a broad

7. In the realm of ideas, such German philosophers as Kant, Goethe, Schiller, and von Humboldt made an incalculable contribution to notions of freedom, both intellectual and moral.

plain where geography offered no clearly defensible frontiers either to the east or west, security could only come from social solidarity, political organization, and military strength. Human institutions had to supply the shield which the physical conditions did not. Slavs and Teutons alike were subdivided and surrounded. Their safety lay therefore in unity and discipline. Whichever people was superior in these respects could overrun its neighbors—and did so. Both major states, Prussia and Russia, were established by feats of arms. Both developed from a central nucleus (Brandenburg, Muscovy) which expanded and finally enveloped the rest. Both, since their expansion was over land, required strong armies which became closely identified with the creation of the state and the structure of its government. In fact, the growth in the size of the state, the absolutism of the monarch, and centralization at his court were combined with land power into related facets of the same system. When political leadership was interwined with the control of the army, civilian affairs could hardly escape the authoritarian patterns of a military discipline. Nor is it mere coincidence that the titles of Czar and Kaiser both derive from Caesar.

In this triple task of political consolidation, territorial extension, and army organization, a key element was the nobility. When a society was constructed upon feudal principles, those who owned the land commanded the services of those who lived and worked thereon. The merging of feudal fiefs into modern states required a transfer of loyalties from local lord to central overlord. The nobility had to be made submissive to the king. Unless armies were nationalized, nations could not be born. Consequently, at analogous stages in Russian and Prussian history there were similar efforts to accomplish the political and military subordination of the landowners to the crown. The dukes of Muscovy at first extended their sway as payers of tribute to the Tartars, but later formed a focus of resistance to the Golden Horde and attracted the "men of service" to their cause. After Ivan III had repudiated the tribute, thus formally establishing independence, there was bitter conflict between the Czar and the *boyars* under Ivan IV (the Terrible). Ivan IV attempted to reconstitute the nobility into an aristocracy whose ownership of land would depend on their military service to the Czar and would not necessarily be hereditary. The same idea was revived by the early Romanovs when the organs of central power were being rebuilt after the "Time of Troubles." Although the titles of nobility and ownership of land subsequently became hereditary, the obligation of aristocrats to do military service was an implied condition of their privileges and of their allegiance to the Czar. For many centuries, the military exigencies of the Russian *vlast*[8] in its struggles against Tartars,

8. Meaning the totality of governmental power. The term is analogous to the Latin *imperium* and the German *Reich.*

Turks, Poles, Prussians, Swedes, Lithuanians, and Frenchmen provided a major reason for the dominance of autocracy and aristocracy.

But it was Prussia above all which earned its modern reputation as a state where the army was far too potent and the people too impotent. The expansion of Brandenburg, which had barely 600,000 inhabitants in the mid seventeenth century, into the formidable kingdom of Prussia, then the subsequent Prussian expansion into the aggressive German *Reich* of Kaiser Wilhelm and Adolf Hitler, is one of the well-known chapters of modern history. What is abundantly clear in that record is the special combination of techniques employed to secure the result. Both Prussia and Germany were consolidated and governed from the top downward. A remarkable succession of strong-willed and clear-sighted monarchs (Frederick William, Frederick William I, and Frederick the Great) in the course of three long reigns carried out policies which transformed their country. Their principal instrument was the efficient state of which they were both architects and builders. This they supplied with a framework of institutions, the personnel of a new bureaucracy, strong finances, and a strong army. The last of these was a political response to the insecurities of their geographical position. Since the Prussians lived in a region where nature offered no physical defenses, the state and the army had to fill the deficiency. Army and state became indissolubly linked. Together they rose in power and prestige, as with Frederick the Great and Bismarck. Together, as in 1806, 1918, and 1945, they fell.[9]

Army and Autocracy in Germany

From the inception of this policy to its fruition, the army on which the state depended for external expansion left a clear imprint on domestic politics as well. Frederick William I laid the foundations of a national army of citizens, as contrasted with a force of alien mercenaries. He dragooned the Prussian aristocrats into service as officers, and filled the ranks of his regiments by conscripting his own subjects. This was the army

9. "Lacking natural boundaries and with her territories scattered all over Germany, Prussia was uniquely dependent upon strong military force to maintain her independence and integrity. The rulers of Prussia had been aware of this since the middle of the seventeenth century and had poured tremendous resources and manpower into the maintenance of an efficient standing army throughout the eighteenth century. If Prussia, as Mirabeau claimed, was not a nation with an army but an army with a nation, this was because in a very special sense the existence of the army was essential to the existence of the nation." Samuel P. Huntington, *The Soldier and the State* (Belknap Press: Harvard, 1959), p. 33.

which Frederick the Great employed so effectively, but which collapsed at Jena before the *élan* of the French and the generalship of Napoleon. Defeat provided the stimulus for a fresh start—for the political upsurge of a stronger nationalism, administrative improvements in the machinery of government, and a further reform of the army. The new weapon which the army added to its arsenal was an innovation in the system of recruiting, training, and promoting its officers. Henceforth the officers were to be professionalized. They were to be selected for reasons of ability instead of family status. They must receive a general education and then must undergo advanced studies in the art of war. They would be promoted for proven competence rather than mere seniority. For all this, the *Krieqsakademie* provided the school, and von Clausewitz the textbook. Organized around such principles, the Prussian officers were dedicated to military service as a career and they evolved among themselves a strong *esprit de corps*. Their loyalty was to their king; their duty, to serve the state; their special skill, the disciplined use of violence. Ancient Sparta was born anew, this time on the banks of the Spree.

Since the army was the creation of kings, the closest bond developed between the monarchy and the military. Each institution strengthened the other and both together reinforced the authoritarian character of the Prussian government. It is not surprising therefore that democracy made so little headway in Prussia up to 1870 or in Germany after 1871. The government of the Prussian state was essentially a phenomenon of the executive branch, personified by the monarch and embodied in the two professional services, the military and the civil. Democratic ideals assorted ill with such a system, and were less likely to be palatable after 1789, when they had acquired a French flavor. If the Prussian state were to be democratized, the monarchy must be limited or abolished and a representative legislature be made supreme. But to replace so powerfully entrenched an executive branch by a parliamentary body which lacked roots and tradition turned out to be an impossible task. Throughout the nineteenth century the conservative elements in the Prussian society clustered around the king as the best means of preserving their privileges. With them was associated the army, whose leadership viewed with horror the prospect of subordination to elected politicians and the vicissitudes of party alternation and altercation. The army was an *imperium in imperio*, enjoying the right of direct access to the crown, and this position the corps of officers was determined to retain.

Not that the officers did not themselves reflect the growing pains and social diversity of German expansion. Their professionalization had spelled a radical break with aristocratic tradition. The opening of a military career to talent afforded an opportunity to members of the middle class to enter. Indeed, the wording of the decree of 1808 which laid down the requirements for an officer's commission is as socially democratic as one could desire. But it must be interpreted in the light of the fact that the educational institutions through which a candidate could qualify were still restricted and few. In generation after generation the Junker families of East Prussia continued to be the main, and disproportionate, source of recruitment for officers; and those of the middle class who were admitted became indoctrinated with the same loyalties or accepted them for protective coloration. At all events, as party struggles emerged in German politics the army leaders could always be identified with the Right. Liberals and Social Democrats, and any who wished for a constitutional regime, saw in the army one of their main political opponents. In the decisive phase of the revolution of 1848-49, the Liberals of the Frankfurt Assembly lost their chance to unify Germany and to enshrine in its politics the principle of legislative supremacy. Then came Bismarck's turn. He proved that he could expand and re-equip the army even when the legislature was refusing to authorize its budgets. Soon after, by the argument of successive military victories (over Denmark, Austria, and France) he refuted the logic of constitutionalism. German humanism produced its Kants and Beethovens, its Goethes and von Humboldts. But German governments were more susceptible to the influences of their Hegels, Nietzsches, and Treitschkes. As the public, by and large, were persuaded to see it, the army that had built Prussia created Germany. Thus in the twentieth century a reckless Hohenzollern or a Hitler could capitalize on the martial spirit and use the instrument in his hand for anti-democratic aims inside his frontiers and beyond.

The British Navy and Domestic Liberty

If a dependence on land power has molded the politics of Germany and Russia, the security afforded by the sea has been no less decisive in shaping the Anglo-American tradition. The success of democracy in Great Britain and the United States is due in no small measure to the fact that prior to the twentieth century both countries relied more on the sea than on the land for their defense. In both cases, the compatibility of democracy with sea power has been attested by history. Let us review some of the evidence on this point, and the circumstances which led to the result.

Churchill has said, speaking for his own nation: "Whenever we must choose between Europe and the open sea, we shall always choose the open sea." This statement presents the alternatives which are inescapable for a people situated geographically as are the British, or, for that matter, the Japanese. If you occupy some islands close to the edge of a continent, you have the choice of involvement in continental affairs or of seeking your destiny across the water. Up to 1066, beginning with the Romans and ending with the Normans, various peoples were able to enter Britain from the Continent and establish control. This was because the British were not yet sufficiently unified either to command the seas around their isles or to expel an invader once he had landed. After the Norman Conquest and its subsequent consolidation, those conditions changed. William's successors were strong enough to prevent any further invasion. More than that they were able, particularly in the thirteenth and fourteenth centuries, to reverse the procedure and take armies from England to France. For more than two hundred years, English kings were engaged in the futile effort of trying to control a large slice of the mainland from an island base. They failed, and were driven from their last French possession (the port of Calais) in the middle of the sixteenth century.

During the medieval period, when life was localized and power was fragmented, the feudal system with its hierarchical order of ranks corresponded accurately enough to social realities. Since the nobles were interposed between the king and the people, and were powerful in their respective localities, the central authority in general was no stronger than the adhesion of the nobles to the king. The state was pieced together by a process of accumulating blocks of land and thus controlling the people who lived thereon. Land power was the *arcanum imperii*, not merely for winning battles on the fields of France, but for ensuring that the king's writ would run the length and breadth of his realm. The acid test of loyalty consisted in the willingness to fulfill the feudal obligation of military service. Political power, when challenged, was a function of the levy of men-at-arms.

These conditions were fundamentally altered in the two centuries, the sixteenth and seventeenth, which mark the turning point in Britain's evolution, domestic and external. The internal consolidation of England was completed at the very time when the opportunity was presented for expansion overseas. Conflicts between factions of the nobility which had reached their climax in the Wars of the Roses ended with the centralized system of the Tudors. Henceforth, the control of the capital over boroughs and shires no longer depended on the number of men who could be mustered into service. Still undecided, however, was the question as to which institution should prevail at the center. Under the Tudors, power resided definitively in the Crown. But the Stuarts forfeited that position, and brought on themselves a revolution led by the parliamentarians. The civil war of the 1640's was the last[10] serious occasion when fighting took place on English soil. To win the day against the Cavaliers the Puritans had to organize their own army, the New Model, of which Cromwell emerged as the efficient general. So efficient, that when the war was over he ruled the country as its "Protector," without benefit of Parliament—the only case in English history of an army-supported dictatorship. His death, however, and the restoration of two more Stuarts to the throne prepared the way in 1688 for the final triumph of the parliamentary side. This time Parliament made itself master of its own shop, taking effective safeguards (legal, financial, and organizational) against the dangers of a standing army. From that time on, the land forces did not have to be reckoned with as an instrument of domestic power.

Meanwhile, with the dawning of the oceanic age, the British seized the advantage of their insular position and devoted their attention to the sea. Until the sixteenth century, land power was their primary military arm. Command of the sea had been used both for defense and for ferrying the army to France and keeping it supplied. But from the seventeenth century onward, the British turned their backs on Europe and, emboldened by the victory over the Spanish Armada, voyaged to other continents where they colonized or conquered. Sea power thenceforth held pride of place in their calculations. Secure behind a naval shield, the British waxed strong in empire and rich in trade. Armies could be transported on shipboard to scattered and distant theaters, where their activities did not menace the government at Westminster or the civil liberties of the British public. Like Periclean Athens, Victoria's Britain hit upon the lucky formula for success: parliamentarianism at home and imperialism abroad. Paradoxically, the nation was becoming more democratic at the very time it was becoming more imperialist. Conservatives could glory in the one achievement and Liberals in the other, and on the wave of sea power democracy rode the crest. Idealists and "little Englanders" might decry the inconsistency in talking the language of liberty for home consumption and that of empire overseas, but not until after World War I were the British forced to make their choice between the two. Meanwhile in popular feelings the navy acquired a prestige which the army had never enjoyed. Even nowadays, of the three military services, the official titles of two are the Royal Navy and the Royal Air Force, whereas the third is simply the Army; and still the most beloved in deed and myth of Britain's fighting men, ever on the lookout over Trafalgar Square, is an admiral.

10. Except for the abortive Stuart uprising of 1745-46 under the Young Pretender.

Oceanic Safeguards of the United States

Similarly in the United States the flowering of democracy owes much to the benefits of the sea. Even the War of Independence could not have been won without the advantages which an ocean's width afforded the colonists. Nor is it a stretch of fancy to suggest that the Atlantic and Pacific were the two indispensable co-guarantors of the Constitution. The protection of two oceans enabled the immigrants to America to concentrate their energies on harnessing the resources of a continent. Moreover, the improvement in relations with Great Britain after 1818 enabled both countries to abandon their fortifications and withdraw their garrisons from the U.S.-Canadian border, leaving the common frontier undefended except by mutual trust. The Indians were a harassment to those who moved West, but were not a serious obstacle except to small and isolated groups. Had Spain retained the control of Florida or France of Louisiana, or had Mexico developed sufficient power to retain the southwest and California, the history of the United States would have proceeded along quite different lines. For one thing, it would have been necessary to maintain a standing army at the requisite strength. But as it was, the United States could expand during a whole century with the minimum of a permanent land force, improvising its armies as occasion demanded. Indeed, between the winning of independence and the entry into World War I, this nation was engaged in only one conflict which truly imperiled its survival—and that was a civil one.

In the eyes of the Founding Fathers, both the English tradition of the seventeenth century and their own colonial experience were replete with warnings about the dangers of a standing army. When writing the Declaration of Independence, Jefferson included prominently among the specific counts in the indictment against George III that he had used the troops to the detriment of political and personal liberty. So vivid and recent were these memories that special pains were taken when the Constitution was drafted to ensure the supremacy of the civil authorities over the military. Congress was given the means to control the armed forces by its powers of making law and granting money;[11] the President, by his authority of appointment and command. More safeguards were added a few years later

11. Among the powers of Congress enumerated in Article 1, section 8 are the following: "To raise and support armies, but no appropriation of money to that use shall be for a longer term than two years; to provide and maintain a navy." Note that the framers thought it necessary to prescribe a time limit on appropriations for the army, but not on those for the navy.

when the Bill of Rights was adopted. Amendments II and III expressed the ordinary citizen's fear and dislike of the professional soldier. The Navy, however, did not arouse the same political anxieties. The need for a navy to protect American merchant ships was realized very soon after independence had been gained. Lacking the protection of the Royal Navy, American vessels were an easy prey for the piratical powers along the Barbary Coast. Even before the adoption of the Constitution, Thomas Jefferson, as Minister in Paris, was urging on John Adams in London and on other leaders at home the desirability of establishing a naval force. In his correspondence with James Monroe he wrote: "Every national citizen must wish to see an effective instrument of coercion, and should fear to see it on any other element but the water. A naval force can never endanger our liberties, nor occasion bloodshed; a land force will do both."[12]

The political implications of this logic continued to be an axiom, accepted but seldom stated, throughout the nineteenth century. For their unrivaled security and their opportunity to occupy a bountiful continent Americans were the beneficiaries of a peculiar combination of fortunate circumstances. Relative isolation from the principal world theaters of stress and conflict left them undisturbed in the period of early growth. The new *entente* with Britain, which was only temporarily ruptured during the Civil War, had the effect of subordinating the Atlantic Ocean to a joint Anglo-American partnership. Within North America, or indeed in all the Americas—North, Central, and South—no rival power emerged to challenge the hegemony of the United States. Republicanism, democracy, federalism, and civil liberties—all could flourish under such favoring conditions. Understandably, at the end of the century it was an American admiral who drew some correct inferences about the "Influence of Seapower on History." But even Mahan, with all his insight, observed only the external contribution of the sea to national strength and either failed to note, or was unconcerned to stress, its relation internally to political freedom.

Generalization from These Examples

So far, so clear. At any rate, a survey of ancient politics and of four major modern states appears to confirm the thesis that strength at sea has been compatible with democracy at home, whereas strength on land has not.

12. *The Papers of Thomas Jefferson*, Julian P. Boyd, ed. (Princeton University Press, 1954), Vol. X, p. 225. The letter is dated August 11, 1786.

But, like all inductive generalizations, this one too requires more elaboration. There are some ambiguities in the argument, as well as some special cases and an exception to consider.

First, let there be no mistaking what is said and what is not. It is true to assert that some successful democracies have been great sea powers, and that some of the great sea powers have been democracies. But it would be quite incorrect to say that all the great sea powers have been governed democratically. Sea power and democracy have overlapped; they have not been coextensive. For evidence on this point, it is sufficient to remember such cases as Corinth and Carthage in the ancient world, Venice in the Middle Ages, Spain in the sixteenth century, and Japan in the twentieth. Those instances reveal that there have been great sea powers which were ruled domestically by oligarchies of merchants or by feudal aristocracies with a king. The difference in the political consequences of sea power and land power is simply this: the latter has always obstructed democracy, while the former permits either democracy or its opposite.

Second, the democracies which have developed behind the sheltering arm of sea power have not been averse to using that same sea power for the acquisition of a maritime empire, which is of course a denial of democracy to those whom the empire embraces. The Athenians' adventure into imperialism was contemporaneous with their experiment in democracy. Cleon may have shocked his audience, but what he stated in the Assembly was the brutal truth: "It is a tyranny over which you hold sway."[13] In their effort to hold their gains, the Athenians fatally overextended themselves and lost democracy with empire. The European states on the Atlantic seaboard that built their colonial systems between the sixteenth and nineteenth centuries started this process long before their evolution into democracies had begun. Certain of them—Spain and Portugal, in particular——have never yet consummated a democratic revolution, and from the standpoint of political freedom the dictatorships of Franco and Salazar have been as oppressive at home as in their colonies abroad. Britain, France, the Netherlands, and Belgium have all discovered in succession that democracy and empire could not be reconciled, and with varying degrees of grace and disgrace have been jolted into the liquidation or conversion of empire.

Third, there are a few important cases which require discussion because they may seem to qualify the thesis presented here. A closer view will suggest, however, that they confirm, rather than refute, the generalization.

13. Thucydides, *Histories*, Bk. III, 37.

Some Apparent Exceptions:
1. The Rise of American Land Power

To begin with, the United States has been included among the sea powers, and the inference has been drawn from the American case that this fortifies the argument concerning the compatibility between sea power and democracy. But the objection may be raised that the United States has also become a great land power, that in fact it possesses one of the two strongest armies in the world today. Is not this fact a piece of evidence to indicate some compatibility after all between democracy and land power?

In my judgment, that conclusion is not warranted. What is crucial in the American case is the time-sequence in the development of the various military forces. After organizing its land power for the winning of independence, this country was virtually able to ignore its army for a century and a half, except for the Civil War years. The sea power of the Anglo-American *entente* provided the United States with a secure defense. Under these conditions, the practices and principles of democratic government could take firm root without encountering a military impediment. Not until the "cold war" period since 1946 was national policy altered to accept a large standing army and peacetime conscription. Only since World War II has the size, expense, and influence of the armed forces presented a continuous problem in civil-military relations. Had the military branch, and especially the army, expanded at an earlier stage of American history to anything like its present-day proportions, a different tradition might have injected itself into the politics of the federal government. As it is, the principle of civil supremacy was established throughout a long period when matters of security were relegated to the background, when the whole military establishment was small and weak, and when the army in particular was little regarded or respected. The consequences of that tradition have carried forward and continued in the modern period when security has moved into the foreground of national concern, when permanent military forces have greatly expanded, and when all branches, (including the army) have risen in prestige. The modern United States has thus far been able with safety to digest its Pentagon because of the lengthy prevalence of the constitutional system and because sea power guarded the young democracy so well in its formative decades.

2. *The French Army versus the Democratic Republics*

What might otherwise have happened to the United States can be seen in the contrasting circumstances of France. The difficulties which democracy has experienced in France are directly relevant to the topic of this chapter. In military affairs the French have a great seafaring tradition, besides being a strong land power. Moreover, they acquired an extensive empire overseas —the earlier one under the *ancien régime,* the later acquisitions under the Second Empire and the Third Republic. The domestic political record has been variable, since France has traversed the gamut of change through monarchies, empires, and republics. With regard to democracy, Frenchmen have contributed conspicuously to the philosophical formulation of such ideals as liberty and equality. But the application of these doctrines through a workable party system and a stable framework of institutions has not been marked by the same success. May there not be some connection between the recurrent political difficulties since 1789 and the military requirements of security?

Geography has given the French people a long coastline on the Atlantic and another on the Mediterranean, which necessitates their being a sea power. But France is also a part of the Continent. There she must reckon with her Teutonic neighbors and her vulnerability to attack from the northeast. Consequently, it is on the army that the French have primarily relied for their defense, especially since the time when the Prussian Kingdom and the German Reich grew so formidable. Just as the English revolution ended with a Cromwell in control, so did the French Revolution give itself over to a Napoleon. But whereas the English, after the Restoration, were able to place a permanent curb upon their army and keep it weak, the French were compelled to retain a stronger army because of their continental position. Moreover, this requirement necessarily continued the same, irrespective of their regime—were it Bonapartist, Bourbon, Orleanist, or Republican. In the nation's politics the navy has figured little. The army, however, has occupied a prominent, and sometimes the decisive, role. Moreover, the political preference of many of its highest officers has frequently favored the anti-Republican Right. Loyal and devoted to *la patrie,* the marshals and generals in too many instances have not felt the same dedication to *la république,* nor have they willingly acquiesced in the regimes of the politicians who "played musical chairs" in successive governments. In a long series of episodes, therefore, the French army leadership and French democracy have come into conflict. Napoleon and the Bonapartist legacy, Macmahon, Boulanger, the Dreyfus affair, Pétain in the Vichy period, de Gaulle's supporters in 1958, and the officers in Algeria who mutinied against de Gaulle himself in 1960 and 1961— there is a pattern in these names and events too recurrent to be dismissed as purely coincidental. French security has needed a powerful standing army; but the army leadership has been loyal to a concept of the state (*l'état*) rather than to the ideals of democracy. The evolution of a stable democracy in modern France was constantly hampered by the fact that France had to be defended more from the land than from the sea.

The Swiss Case Which Proves the Rule

One important case remains, however, to be considered—the case of a thoroughly democratic community which is completely landlocked, namely Switzerland. Nobody will deny the genuineness of Swiss democracy or the stability of the regime or the perennial dependence of this country upon its army. Is this then an exception to the general rule? Does Swiss history demonstrate that an army can be made safe for democracy?

The answer is that the Swiss owe their security in part to their geography, and in part to a special type of military organization which was effective in past centuries. Their democracy is the product of an old political tradition, reinforced by social tendencies toward equalitarianism. As to the possible antithesis between democratic liberties and army authoritarianism, the Swiss have clearly and consciously protected themselves against domination by their own military and have adopted deliberate safeguards for this purpose. In few places can the influence of geography upon internal politics be detected as plainly—one might say, as visibly—as in Switzerland. Not only did the Alps and the Jura provide an effective defense along more than half of the frontier, but the mountainous terrain has also fostered internally a spirit of localism and engendered opposition to central authority. It is indeed no accident that the two European countries which enjoy the longest continuous tradition of democracy are Switzerland and Britain. This does not mean that the governments of all cantons have always been democratic, any more than England has always been ruled by Parliament or Parliament has always been truly representative. What it does mean is that in both communities certain basic liberties of individuals and localities were fought for and won fairly early and have been retained. Nor is there any reasonable doubt that the geography of each country has had something to do with the results. Indeed, it was an Englishman who expressed this thought in lines of verse which happen to be poor poetry, but good politics:

> Two voices are there, one is of the Sea,
> One of the Mountains, each a mighty voice:
> In both from age to age thou didst rejoice,
> They were thy chosen music, Liberty! [14]

Sympathizing with the Swiss in the period of their conquest by Napoleon, Wordsworth correctly glimpsed the truth that the Alps and the Jura had done for the one people what the sea had done for the other. The mountains and the water each had created an island, within which a certain type of political regime could safely flower.

Machiavelli described the Swiss as "armatissimi e liberissimi,"[15] and he was right in connecting these two traits, for the martial spirit and a rugged feeling of independence have been the keynote to much of their politics. One cannot read the history of Switzerland without constant reminders of two themes—the intertwining of external with internal policies and of civil government with the armed citizen. The Swiss fought for their independence in the thirteenth and fourteenth centuries and won it in a series of epic victories over the Hapsburgs.[16] The secret of their success was the effectiveness of their infantry, composed of their own citizens instead of mercenaries.[17] From their origins among the early Germanic tribes the Swiss had retained the principle that fighting was a regular civic responsibility of the able-bodied male. Military service was considered the citizen's duty and his privilege. Moreover, throughout the centuries when the Swiss were loosely joined in a confederation (i.e., before 1848), the army was strictly cantonalized. When a national force was required, it consisted of levies which the cantons contributed—a fact which made it impossible for anyone to establish a centralized absolutism.[18]

After the confederation was replaced by the present federal union, the Swiss continued some of their traditional practices, but added some new safeguards. The neutrality, which they have so long enunciated and for the most part practiced with success, is an armed one. Every able-

14. William Wordsworth, *England and Switzerland*, written in 1802.
15. *The Prince*, Chap. 12. "Completely armed and completely free."
16. The William Tell myth, celebrating the resistance to the Austrian tyrant, is part of this story.
17. Indeed, it was the Swiss, particularly in the fifteenth, sixteenth, and seventeenth centuries, who because of economic pressure served as mercenaries in the armies of foreign rulers. There they were always in demand, since their prowess had become well-nigh legendary.
18. But this did not preclude the formation of undemocratic regimes in some of the cantons—e.g. the merchant oligarchy in Basel, the aristocracy of Bern, and Calvin's theocracy in Geneva.

bodied Swiss male must undergo a year of military training as soon as he reaches the age of eighteen. Subsequently he is required to spend three weeks in camp every summer for retraining. In order to facilitate a speedy mobilization in time of emergency, the Swiss is allowed to keep his rifle and other small weapons in his own house—something which would be unthinkable in most countries of the world. It would not be easy therefore for anyone to establish a dictatorship over such a people. How can a dictatorship be organized where the majority are trained and armed to resist? Moreover, the Swiss have taken the further precaution of protecting themselves against a military coup which might overthrow the civil power. The permanent professional army is small, and in normal times has no single commander-in-chief. A commander-in-chief is only appointed[19]— and by a vote of the two houses of the legislature meeting in joint session —when an emergency, such as the outbreak of war, exists on the borders of Switzerland.

Thus an examination of Switzerland tends to confirm, not refute, the thesis advanced in this chapter. If Switzerland is an exception to the generalization, it is that kind of exception which fortifies the rule. Land power has been associated among the Swiss with special geographical circumstances. Their military defense has relied upon the nation in arms rather than on the professional army. Their constitution has included effective safeguards against military domination. All very good, one may say in congratulating the Swiss on the rarity of their achievement. But while commending their sagacity, their valor, and their uniqueness, one must also reflect that such arrangements are possible for a small people, situated as a buffer state, and permanently proclaiming their neutrality. These conditions are not pertinent to such countries as France, the United States, or Great Britain, which cannot escape the obligations of active leadership, nor do they apply to small communities like Denmark, Belgium, or the Netherlands, whose geography has rendered them more vulnerable to attack.

Why Navies Did Not Threaten Democracy

If it be granted, then, that the original hypothesis—that great sea powers can be democratic, whereas great land powers cannot be—is reinforced by this survey of cases, let us consider some of the reasons why this is so and certain of its implications.

The potentialities of sea power for democracy are based on the simple,

19. In World War II the man selected as commander-in-chief was, intentionally, French-speaking: General Guisan.

but blessed, fact that navies strike at a distance from home. Within the domestic arena they do not function. Land power, however, can obviously be used either at home or away. To crush a popular uprising, to foil an attempted *coup*, to close the doors of a legislature, the specific remedy throughout history has been to call out the troops. Thus it is that when the civilian government is taken over by the military, it is the generals who wield the power. There have been occasions when a navy rebelled and tried to overturn its own government (e.g., in Brazil in 1895). But such efforts have always been doomed to futility and frustration unless the army took the same side. From the water the ships cannot control the shore against the opposition of the land forces.

Needless to say, the virtue of navies flows from the element in which they operate. Most definitely, whatever compatibility exists between sea power and democracy does not derive from the navy's inner organization. The latter, when one observes the relation of officers to men and the hierarchy of command, is no less authoritarian than the army. In some countries, in fact, the navy is more caste-ridden than the army and more prone to recruit its officers from a restricted social stratum. The army, on the other hand, because of the larger numbers it absorbs, may have some sympathy with the common people. Various of the revolutions of modern times have been engineered by younger army officers, whose social program in certain cases has been markedly radical. Army rule is not necessarily, and *per se*, the worst of all possible systems. Sometimes it is preferable to what it supersedes. At one time or another in the early 1960's, army regimes, or governments led by an active soldier, wielded power in the following countries: Burma, Dominican Republic, Egypt, Formosa, Iraq, Lebanon, Pakistan, Paraguay, Peru, South Korea, South Vietnam, Spain, Sudan, Syria, Thailand, and Turkey.[20] Some of those governments, for example, the Spanish and the Dominican, were backward and brutal. But not all of them constituted a deterioration, even when judged from the standpoint of political liberty. In a few cases, e.g., that of Pakistan, the rule of a general could be called an improvement on the chaos of turbulent parties which had sprouted forth at the time of independence. In many other instances, where no liberty had previously existed, the seizure of power by an army clique did not signify a loss of liberty, but merely the substitution of one species of authoritarianism for another. Depending on

---

20. In addition, there were governments which had attained power through revolution, and whose leader had a military record as a guerrilla fighter, in Yugoslavia and Cuba. Also, the Presidents of the United States (until January 1961) and of France had been professional military men throughout their careers. In de Gaulle's case, the army leadership, especially in Algeria, was instrumental in bringing him to power.

its leadership and goals, an army regime may be socially progressive and administratively efficient, or it may be corrupt, reactionary, and despotic. Yet whatever its quality, and whether its commander be a Cromwell or Bonaparte, a Kemal or Ayub, an army does not govern democratically. Soldiers do not readily brook opposition, accept public criticism, or submit to legal restraints on their physical power.[21] Theirs is a government of swords, not of words.

Questions About Air Power and Space

But a question remains which puts the preceding argument in still another perspective. The hypothesis under discussion has been drawn empirically from the evidence of the past. Taken as such, it is a valid generalization to assert that the birth of democracy and its survival and growth during the cradle period were fostered by favoring physical conditions, among which the geography of sea power was a positive asset. Do the same inferences apply, however, to the contemporary world? Will they be as relevant —or more so, or less—in the later decades of this century? The geographical factor may be a constant, but the requirements of military security nowadays are not what they were in fifth-century Athens or fourteenth century Switzerland or seventeenth-century England or nineteenth-century America. If democracy is to continue as a vital political system, it can no longer rely upon the help of circumstances which have ceased to exist or which now exist in altered combinations. The influences of the cradle period may last into maturity, but maturity in the workaday world grapples with emerging problems. Moreover, new states have appeared all over the map, and few of these are so situated as were the Athenians, English, or Americans. Although some of the principles of warfare are invariable, the modern organization of defense has rapidly evolved into novel forms— principally because our weapons have been revolutionized through science and technology. Not only have we added the third military force of air power, but the army and navy too depend upon a complex of apparatus and equipment which becomes obsolete in each quinquennium. Nor can one safely ignore the implications of space-exploration for power on Earth. Where stand our political ideals, by what values shall we live, in

21. Louis Lévy quotes the following remark from Napoleon (of all people): "It is the nature of a soldier to want to do everything despotically and that of the civilian to submit everything to discussion, to reason and to truth. In social life, therefore, it is the civilian who is entitled to pre-eminence." *France is a Democracy* (Gollancz: London, 1963), p. 153.

this age of nuclear bombs and space rocketry? The cosmonaut and astronaut are beckoning humanity onward, as Columbus did before them. But can we conceive a political response to these limitless dimensions which excite, yet may well confound, the imagination? In view of today's conflicts between political philosophies and institutions, the achievement of our scientists may merely transfer to other planets the rivalries which are not yet composed on this one. As for the governance of men and our domestic tranquility, how will the character of politics be affected by the revolution in weapons, command of the air, and probings into space?

Some of these are queries on which we should begin to speculate, but which at present it is impossible to answer. For men to be traveling from the Earth into space is as much a challenge to our habits of thought and action as were the earlier discoveries that this planet is spherical and that it moves in orbit around the sun. Now that the horizons of a finite world have receded into the vastness of the cosmos, our thinking can no longer be bound by the confinements of traditional categories. True enough—but, how far are we to go, at this present juncture, in rejecting what we accept and grasping at the unknown? A student of politics, dazzled by the technological inventiveness of this era, is dangerously tempted to ride the scientific whirlwind and cry "havoc!" at the experience of the ages. But social progress, although its pace accelerates, does not proceed by leaps. Our man-made systems evolve through a continuous flow. The human race is launched upon a new stage of its journey to a destination we cannot see; but we can only start with the knowledge we now have and from the point which we have thus far reached.

Amid the welter of hypothesis and speculation, a few certainties have already revealed themselves along with a larger number of potentialities. It is evident that air power has rendered all countries equally vulnerable, including those which previously thought themselves secure. But this by itself is not decisive. What saved Great Britain in 1940 was the command of the sea, plus the possession of sufficient fighter planes to make the Luftwaffe pay heavily for its bombing raids. The Nazis' air attack could not reduce the British into submission, and like Napoleon some fourteen decades earlier they could not transport a large army across the Channel. The Japanese at Pearl Harbor could knock out the striking power of the United States in the Pacific, but this blow had only a temporary effect; when the superior industrial resources of the United States were mobilized, the Japanese succumbed. Likewise, the Americans and British commanded the North Atlantic from 1943 to 1945 and their heavy bombers weakened the German military machine; but armies had to be landed on the Continent, opening a second front in the west, before Germany surrendered. Air power, when unopposed in its own element, demonstrated its capacity twice in 1941 when the Nazis took the island of Crete from the air while the British held the sea and when the Japanese destroyed the British fleet which was guarding Singapore. Later on, the dependence of a fleet upon its air force was proven in the Battle of Midway where carrier-based planes fought their duel at longer range than the guns of the capital ships could fire. Japan eventually surrendered without an army having been landed on its shores. But this was only after the American land forces had captured the string of island bases leading up to Japan, after Japanese shipping had been devastated by submarine raids, and after Hitler's Germany had fallen. If all those events point to any conclusion, it is that no single military force—land, sea, or air—can be considered decisive and that the interdependence of all three is needed for defense and victory. Excessive weakness in any one of them results in stalemate or defeat.

In the closing stages of World War II, new weapons were employed which set an augury for the future. The Germans used land-based rockets to carry bombs to England, and American airplanes dropped two atomic bombs on Japan. Within two decades of the end of World War II, each of these weapons had grown up and they were then wedded together. The nightmare of today is the hydrogen bomb placed in the nose of a rocket that can span the continents. Such a rocket can be launched from the land or from a submarine submerged;[22] and if these were ever fired, millions would die upon the instant. This is therefore one of those periods which recur in history when the means of offense have completely outstripped the means of defense. What guards the fragile peace and saves humanity from holocaust is the deterrent prospect of mutual annihilation. In this respect the two strongest governments on earth—one democratic, the other communist—are united by a common dread. A third World War is thus averted as long as both sides are animated by a normal instinct for self-preservation and are led by men who are reasonably sane. But what would happen if a powerful government should ever fall to the control of a madman, of another Hitler?

The Political Cost of Armaments

Apart from this psychological impact, the pervasive influence of contemporary armaments has spread throughout the economy and the political

22. Indeed, one single ship—an atomic-powered submarine carrying Polaris missiles— now contains more destructive power than all the bombs dropped by both sides in World War II.

system. To produce the weapons of today requires an advanced technology, a high level of industrialization, and a government rich enough to support the budgetary burden or strong enough to impose it. Moreover, these weapons are so complex that they must be designed and planned long before they can be delivered for use. As a consequence, a democratic government has to arrange for "defense contracts" with industrial firms whose productive capacity, in whole or part, will be devoted for a number of years to the needs of the armed forces. Nowadays, a significant proportion of American industrial output consists in armaments, atomic power, and space exploration; and in certain specialized branches of the economy, the dependence of private corporations on government contracts is overwhelming. Thus in many cases employment of workers, the profits of owners, even the purchasing power and prosperity of localities, are directly related to military programs. Naturally these facts are fraught with political implications. Firms which receive defense contracts can plan their output and guarantee employment for several years ahead; and when a contract is terminated, they will exert pressure on Congressmen and administrators to have it renewed.[23] There is always the danger, therefore, that when the government buys the products of business, businessmen will try to buy the government.

Besides the risk that corruption may seep into public life from private entrepreneurs, a democracy which supports a heavy load of armaments faces yet another danger. In the historical evolution of the democratic state, it has proven notoriously more difficult to subject diplomacy and military affairs to the democratic process than is the case with domestic policy. Alike in personnel, procedures, and programs, the military and foreign services were the last to feel the breath of reform in the nineteenth century. Even today they sometimes function in a mental atmosphere which bespeaks the etiquette and epaulettes of a byegone era. Surround-

23. The mutual relations of government and heavy industry in the armaments field are clearly revealed in the fact that President Eisenhower picked the head of General Motors for his first Secretary of Defense and President Kennedy took the head of the Ford Company for his. In his Farewell Address to the American People, President Eisenhower issued this warning: "In the councils of Government, we must guard against the acquisition of unwarranted influence, whether sought or unsought, by the military-industrial complex. The potential for the disastrous rise of misplaced power exists and will persist. We must never let the weight of this combination endanger our liberties or democratic processes." Reported in the *New York Times*, Jan. 18, 1961. Four months later, the same newspaper stated that the Defense Department was spending about $42,000,000,000 annually, i.e., over 50 per cent of the total national budget. Adding together the number of that Department's employees and those employed in defense industries, the *Times* estimated that "about 10 per cent of the entire labor force is occupied by defense." May 21, 1961.

ing themselves with an air of mystery and secrecy, they cloak their activities, where possible, from the public eye. Of course, there is a reason for all this, quite apart from the aristocratic antecedents of the military and diplomatic services. Since the security of the nation is linked to the strength of its armed forces, their size and organization and equipment are not as appropriate to public discussion as are other matters on which the survival of a state does not depend. As for diplomacy, not only do its practitioners employ the arts of bluff for which full disclosure would be ruinous, but there is the added difficulty that negotiations between governments involve two or more parties and, whereas one side may be disposed to make its correspondence public, the other side may not.

It is no matter for surprise, then, that modern legislative bodies, such as Congress and Parliament, have been only partially successful in bringing foreign policy and military programs under their full scrutiny and review. The generals and the diplomats have a case for secrecy, up to a point, and it is at this point that the publicity of the democratic process ceases to operate. In a democracy we assert the right to criticize the activities of our government. But since we do not and cannot know in full the technical aspects of modern armaments or the ins and outs of diplomatic maneuver, criticism may be well-intentioned but badly informed. The Chiefs of Staff or Secretary of State, with their superior access to information, may be correct in the position they adopt. But the public may be justified at times in the suspicion that the case for secrecy is abused as a protective screen to conceal mistakes!

Problems of this character present difficulties which are serious, though not, I think, insoluble. From the democratic standpoint, a multilateral system of disarmament—internationally controlled and inspected—is to the highest degree desirable since democracy flourishes best amid the arts of peace. Failing that, however, and on the assumption that wars and alarums of war are likely to plague us for a long time yet, appropriate remedies have to be found for the varied aspects of military preparedness discussed above. The problems which beset a government when much of the economy is geared to defense appropriations belong to the discussion of the general relation between politics and economics, and the ratio of public activity to private.[24] But the conflict between the rival needs of publicity and secrecy is something else. Open discussion of all details of military organization would endanger the security of the state, and full disclosure of all phases of diplomatic negotiations may be undesirable while bargaining is going on, or, in some cases, when it was very recent. Scarcely

24. This topic is treated in the two following chapters. See especially Chapter 9, pp. 252 ff.

any democracy goes as far in informing the public about its military establishment as does the United States. Unfortunately, information intended for the American people is also available to potential enemies. Too much, rather than too little, is ordinarily disclosed in open testimony before congressional committees. The remedy for this would seem to be that more of the hearings at which vital military matters are examined should be held behind closed doors, and the press and the public should be barred from the room. If the elected representatives of the people discover any serious irregularities in administration or have major disagreements over policy, these points should then be debated in the full legislature at a secret session. Such practices are sometimes employed by the legislative bodies of democratic states, and they suggest a workable compromise between excessive publicity and excessive secrecy.

A distinction must be drawn, however, betyeen those countries where the democratic tradition and a stable constitutional regime are in force and others where democratic institutions are young and fragile and still others which live under an authoritarian system. How is the conduct of government affected in these different political categories by the twentieth-century innovations in military organization and weapons? The stable democracies have had new problems to solve, it is true. But these have not been insuperable. Neither the United States nor Britain, neither Switzerland nor Norway, is any less democratic today because an air force has been created, because weapons are more complicated and more costly, or because atomic bombs could annihilate us all. The principle of civilian supremacy over the military arm remains unshaken; and when the American people after World War II elected a professional soldier to the Presidency, he was not of the militaristic type, but rather a man attuned to civilian tastes. Where it is deeply rooted in society and ingrained in the people, the democratic system is not in danger of being overthrown by the military.

Contemporary Military Regimes

The same cannot be said, however, for countries where democracy is a novel experiment or where the choice of a regime does not lie between democracy and authoritarianism but between one species of authoritarianism or another. In the well-established democracies the physical capacity of the armed forces to oust the constituted civilian authority is held in check by restraints which are a blend of the political, social, and institutional. Where such restraints are weak and tenuous, the sheer physical ability of the military to seize power is a fact to be reckoned with. The question which then poses itself is this: Has modern organization augmented or lessened the means by which a military *coup* may be successfully executed? There can be little doubt about the answer to this query. The weapons and tactics in use today have greatly increased the odds in favor of ambitious officers who wish to take over the government. It is an unfortunate fact that a small number of men, well armed and disciplined, can cow a multitude. Nowadays, the weapons which one man can carry and use (e.g., a machine gun), or which a small group can operate (e.g., a tank), possess great destructive power. This has made it much easier for a dictator, in what we called the police-states or garrison-states, to overawe his opponents for a while and to keep millions in subjection to his will. He and his supporters may be only a minority. But a minority can physically dominate a majority.[25] It can do so—if not permanently, at least for a time—by violence and ruthless organization. For recent evidence of this, one need only contemplate the successes of Nazi, Fascist, and Communist parties, and of military juntas, in many of the countries where they gained the control. There is also the air force to be remembered. The air force does not immediately and directly control the ground, which is where the physical basis of power must be maintained. But airplanes can be used in two ways to affect the outcome of a *coup d'état* or civil war or suppress an uprising. They may be employed for terror bombings of a disaffected area, a drastic technique which would be effective only if the opposition were concentrated geographically. Alternatively, air power can quickly transport supplies and men to critical points where extra strength is required. In this sense, the paratroopers are the elite guard or Marines, the shock troops or commandos, of our era.

The experience of the last forty years, both in revolutionary attempts to seize government and in the continuous exercise of power by an authoritarian regime, still indicates that of the three military forces the army is the most important from the political standpoint and can be decisive. Indeed it is noteworthy that the leaders of all the military regimes in power today are soldiers. None of them is a sailor or an airman. Thus, the *arcana imperii* are still at the mercy of the praetorian guard and the legions. Interesting cases arise, however, where a division occurs between the different military arms. So far, the navy alone has been unable to take over a government. There is some evidence to show that navy leaders were influential in the final stages of the movement to oust Peron from Argentina. But most of the army sided with them, or at any rate did not oppose them. In Thailand, an abortive naval revolt was staged in 1951. On that

25. How this affects the attempts to justify majority rule is discussed in Chapter 17, pp. 551 ff.

occasion the army stood firmly with the government and was helped by the air force. In 1962 the navy and air force in Ecuador co-operated in bringing Arosemena to the Presidency, against the army and civilian police who tried to install the Chief Justice of the Supreme Court. That particular military combination contributed to our knowledge of statecraft, if to nothing else.

The insurrection of French generals in Algiers in April, 1961, was the most spectacular political venture by the military of recent times, both because it involved a great nation and because of its international implications and the complexity of the details. The would-be coup was led by four generals of the army, who were encouraged by many professional officers. They were further supported by veteran long-service soldiers, and especially by the Foreign Legion and the paratroopers. Politically, they were backed by the "ultras" among the French colons in Algeria and by organizations of the extreme Right in metropolitan France. During one critical night, Premier Debré in a public radio address charged that paratroopers were planning to fly from north Africa to occupy Paris and other key centers. He appealed, as did President de Gaulle, to the public for help. *Aux armes, Citoyens!* Politically, this appeal, which came more from genuine panic than from any device of tactical maneuver, was triumphantly successful. From the moderate Right to the extreme Left, individual Frenchmen and organized associations rallied around de Gaulle. Rather de Gaulle than *"les paras."* On his side, however, in this ironical situation where a conservative aristocrat summoned the Parisians to the barricades, the President was none too happy about unleashing the tiger of public opinion. Citizens were enrolled for volunteer service, but weapons were not distributed. Nor, as events turned out, did "the nation in arms" have to fight against its own professionals. The insurrection collapsed, not only in the face of this novel solidarity in France proper and foreign declarations of support for de Gaulle,[26] but also because of fortunate divisions within the ranks of the military. There were army men who did remember that President de Gaulle was also General de Gaulle; and, before becoming overt mutineers, many wavered. The regiments that were filled with conscripts—i.e., with young Frenchmen performing their military service as a legal and civic duty—tended to share the political sentiments of their families and friends at home. Above all else, they wanted the war in Algeria to be ended by political negotiation. Some of these units mutinied against mutinous officers, or, in other words, stayed loyal. Moreover, the army was not helped by the navy and the air force. There

26. E.g., from President Kennedy, Prime Minister Macmillan, Chancellor Adenauer.

was some doubt, some fence-sitting, among the admirals. But they tended to oppose the generals.[27] As for the airmen, whose help was needed if the paratroopers were to capture Paris, many of the pilots refused to fly the transport planes and some deliberately took them—empty of soldiers—to airfields in France proper. Thus, the *coup d'état* of frustrated generals failed ignominiously. In that failure, the essential facts which stand out clearly are these. There was no unity among the military forces themselves. The man whom the insurrection sought to depose was himself a general and a national hero. The extreme Right could not overthrow the moderate Right, when the latter was aided by the Center and the Left. Such facts provide an answer to certain questions, although they manifestly do not resolve all of one's anxieties for the future.

The Primacy of Politics over Arms

The events just described contain implications which have a broad relevance and will require watching in comparable situations elsewhere. In the French case, there was overwhelming political strength on one side, and the military forces, being divided, neutralized one another. Had the military been united, they might have succeeded in seizing the government. But, in view of the political opposition to their aims, would they subsequently have been able to govern? It is my judgment that in the long run politics still exercise their primacy over arms. Or, to put the same point in other language, the eliciting and organizing of a common will, which is a function of politics, is eventually more potent than the use of violence, which is the specialized skill of the military. A military junta or dictator can seize the government by physical force. But it can only continue to rule a country if enough support is forthcoming from the public to supplement the use of guns and provide a counterpoise to the opposition. A regime based increasingly on the troops, and decreasingly on popular backing, will eventually lose power. A number of instances have occurred in which a tough military regime has become more and more despotic or corrupt until it was overthrown by the mobilization of a counterforce. Usually, this latter combined a political organization with some military activity by the opposition. In Cuba, the Batista regime was strong for a while, and the dictator's army and police were well equipped and ruthless. But Castro was successful in mobilizing the hatreds of other Cubans. From a remote mountain retreat he conducted a guerrilla war-

27. There is no truth in the report, printed in the newspapers at the time, that one cruiser fired shots against ground forces attempting to occupy a port and supply base.

fare which finally brought Batista down. Similarly, in some Asian countries, notably China, the communists effectively organized popular feelings for the purpose of political action, provided the leadership of a tightly disciplined party, and launched guerrilla activities against the groups in power. Guerrillas, to be successful, must be supported by the society around them. They represent the blending of political aims with military means. In some of the less developed areas of the world they have demonstrated a considerable efficacy against systems whose popular roots were shallow and withered. Indeed, wherever the communists have captured power from within (as contrasted with cases where they imposed a puppet regime through the power of the Red Army), they were successful as conspirators or as guerrillas because they recognized the primacy of politics and turned prevailing discontent to their own advantage.

The lessons for democracy are fairly obvious, although their application to concrete circumstances is far from easy. The replacement of Chiang Kai-shek by Mao Tse-tung, of Batista by Castro, did not represent a gain for democracy. But neither did it constitute a loss, since Batista and Chiang were not conducting democratic systems. When one brand of authoritarianism follows another, it is regrettable both because democracy has missed an opportunity to be the successor, and also because the communists, when they take over from a corrupt regime of army leaders and right-wing politicians, are likely to gain some immediate popularity by sparking a needed social revolution. Mao Tse-tung has remarked that "power grows out of the barrel of a gun." But his own actions, in winning power, were proof that this is an oversimplification. What about the loyalties of the man who holds the gun and aims it? Whose orders will he obey? In which direction will he shoot? Politics, in the last analysis, is a struggle for the minds and hearts of men. Guns contribute to this to the extent that they form a threat to life and limb. Yet men can be captives in body without their allegiance being captured. Democracy competes with authoritarianism, in its many species and varieties. Neither system is likely to succeed unless it has guns on its side. But the guns which ultimately prevail are those with the stronger will behind them. The future of democratic politics depends upon winning the loyalties of men to democratic values.

8

The Economic Origins

Democracy is thought of primarily as a form of government. However, many of its features impinge directly on economic matters and are so closely affected by them as to require an economic explanation. No other institution in society exercises more influence on the economy than government does. Nor is this true only of the regimes called totalitarian, where the state attempts to swallow the economy whole. Alike in countries which blend their socialism and capitalism, and in those whose spokesmen profess to restrict the functions of the state, the role of government in commerce, industry, and agriculture is far-reaching and many-sided. Indeed, in the middle of the twentieth century, there is no democracy, large or small, in which the state does not undertake major responsibilities of an economic character.[1] The forms or structures employed for this purpose are as varied as the functions they sustain—as for instance, the direct ownership and operation by the state, regulation of private corporations and individuals, partnership in mixed enterprises, and indirect inducements and deterrents of various kinds. It follows, when most citizens are keenly aware that their livelihood depends heavily on the state, that much of the controversy which creates the substance of politics consists either in justifying the programs of the government or in finding a reasoned case to oppose them.

1. A partial list of these would include the regulation of credit and investment, the development of basic resources, taxation and tariff policy, issuing money, the maintenance of full employment, the volume of public expenditures, the administration of welfare services, assistance in the location of industry, and the operation of publicly owned enterprises.

The Political Economy

Conversely, the working of economic processes brings results which are immediately relevant to politics. A government will reap the advantage, or bear the criticism, for the volume of production, the level of employment, the supply and distribution of consumer goods, relations between labor and management, and long-term changes in the general standard of living—or its failure to change. Likewise, the capacity of the state to perform any of its services depends on what revenues it can collect and these derive in turn from the efficiency of production and the purchasing power in the pockets of its citizens. Any major economic event or trend will sooner or later be reflected in politics. The parties that compete for power in a democracy are expected to propose solutions for all basic economic questions, and very often their rise or fall in electoral favor fluctuates with the vicissitudes of the economy. Apart from those overriding issues in foreign relations which touch on the security and survival of the state, the results of elections are determined more by the voters' individual assessments of their economic situation than by anything else.

There is no need to argue the general point that an intimate liaison exists between economics and politics. The theme of this chapter is to explore the special relation, if any, between economic factors and democratic politics. In such a relation not all the causes flow from one side, nor are all the effects felt exclusively by the other. There is no economic determinism; there is no political determinism. But there are reciprocal influences galore. Each aspect of society, political and economic, produces causes and receives consequences. The interaction between the two is continuous. It results from simultaneous movements occurring in both directions. A political system which professes to be a democracy postulates a certain ideal for society with which the economy may either correspond or conflict. Similarly, the economic process has its own problems to solve (i.e., those of scarcity or abundance, of production and distribution), and the course of solution gives rise to social relations of which governments must take cognizance and which a democratic government will shape in its own appropriate fashion.

Economic Prerequisites of Democracy

Hence, a number of questions arise.

Does democracy presuppose a particular economic system? Are there some economic arrangements with which democracy can coexist and others with which it cannot? Or is democracy completely neutral in its application to economics?

Are there any economic prerequisites for democracy? That is to say, are there some economic conditions which must be fulfilled before a community can govern itself democratically?

Conversely, do the requirements of the democratic state have a material effect upon the functioning of the economy?

What meaning should we give to the term "economic democracy"? Are there some aspects of democracy and the economy which overlap or are perhaps identical?

The links in the chain connecting democracy with economics can be seen from two viewpoints, historical and theoretical. From the past, both the remote and more recent, there is empirical evidence to demonstrate how the politics of democracy in point of fact have been concerned with economic questions. Likewise, the conclusions drawn from a study of the actual are confirmed by analysis of the ideal. A community expresses its values through a body of principles which can be variously interpreted and applied. These may mean one thing for economics and something else for politics, or they may mutually complement and reinforce one another.

That economic factors were connected historically with the birth and growth of democracy is well attested. In Athens, the reforms of Solon that inaugurated the evolution toward democracy were the political response to a social crisis caused by an economic revolution. Many small farmers had incurred heavy debts for which they had engaged their land or labor as security. When their creditors dispossessed them, there was increasing danger that a free peasantry would be converted into debt-slaves and serfs. Solon, himself a wealthy man, stopped this trend. He wiped the slate clean of debts and removed the encumbrances on the land. Then, along with currency reform, stimuli to external trade, and a revised constitution, he paved the way for a series of later steps in the direction of a fuller democracy. The quality of his statesmanship lies in his grasp of the truth that the political system, the economic order, and relations between social classes are reciprocal and must move together. All his reforms were designed therefore to produce a stable society composed of citizens financially and politically free. Nor did the later developments lose the imprint of these beginnings, although admittedly the culminating forms (of the mid fourth century B.C.) were not what Solon would have approved. The successive modifications, spreading over two and a half centuries, resulted from the relentless pressure of the mass of the poorer and humbler citizens (the *Demos*, the Many) on the old aristocrats and *nouveaux riches.* The struggle between social and economic classes was fought in the political arena, and the outcome of political victories was registered as constitutional change. It is little wonder then that Plato and Aristotle evaluated Athenian democracy in large part as an economic phenomenon, and that its politics were succinctly defined as the domination of the rich few by the many poor.[2]

The same general point—that the rise of democracy as a political system was causally connected with economic change—holds true for the rebirth of democracy in the seventeenth and eighteenth centuries and its subsequent expansion in the nineteenth and twentieth. The modern democratic state is the legitimized issues of the revolutions which occurred in England, Holland, the United States, France, and Switzerland—to mention the prime movers and prime examples. These revolutions were, of course, many-sided, and the various facets were political, economic, religious, military, philosophical, and scientific. In a complex of factors, where the whole of life—both social and individual—is undergoing drastic change, to disentangle an aspect and judge it in isolation may do violence to truth and sense. The economy, then as now, did not function alone, nor was the economic lever the sole instrument at work in loosening society from its feudal foundations. But to underestimate the economic forces which contributed to political revolution would be as great an error as to exaggerate their influences and ascribe to them a basic power controlling all the rest. What one can and must do, so as to understand the phenomenon of democracy, is to separate fact and certainty from inference and speculation. If analysis is to proceed with any sureness, it should voyage into oceans of doubt from an anchorage which is fixed and known.

What is there which can be stated for certain about the connection between economic factors and democracy? Perhaps the only fact which is not disputable and stands out clearly is the chronological relation. Radical changes in the economic system and radical changes in the political system occurred at the same time in the same places. The inference must then arise that movements associated in point of time are somehow causally connected. Nor would it be surprising if this were the case. When politics and the economy are being transformed simultaneously, it is reasonable to suppose that the changes interact and that their influences are reciprocal, immediate, and direct. It is then natural to ask whether one is analyzing two revolutions (one called "political," the other "economic") or two aspects of the same revolution. But, what is not so clear

2. See Chapter 2, pp. 31-4.

is how the causation works, or indeed what is the cause and what is the effect.

A complex situation becomes clearer when its elements can be identified. What then were some of the specific changes whose effects carried over from the economic sphere to the political, and vice versa?

Challenges to Feudalism

Between the sixteenth and eighteenth centuries the feudal system disappeared or was discarded through most of western Europe. Feudalism consisted of a hierarchical structure, in which each person was ranked from birth, with a status corresponding to the rank, and obligations and rights appropriate to the status. Political power, military service, social standing, and economic opportunity—all were graded on descending scales which normally corresponded. Since land was then the principal source of wealth, its ownership, control, and use were not only uppermost among the economic factors but influenced the character of government, law, warfare, and social customs. The major exception to this pattern was, of course, the city. Here, behind a wall which gave protection from the lords of the land outside, was a cluster of other interests—of handicrafts, professions, trade, and commerce. Because it was not self-sufficient, the city depended on its communications both with the rural areas which supplied its food and with other cities which were the markets for the exchange of goods. Urban prosperity needed the organization of wide areas of security, so that its merchandise could be transported without molestation by pirates at sea or brigands and barons on land.

For understandable reasons, it was the city which provided the nucleus for the growth of a new economic order. In the city, the primacy of land yielded to other forms of property. Investment in manufactures, mining, and commerce made new families rich. Capital could be accumulated, whether in coin or shares, and its owners could give financial backing to Emperors and Kings, to Cardinals and Popes. The very mobility of such capital encouraged experiments and offered incentives to enterprising men who were ready to take a risk. Those engaged in these undertakings constituted a group in the middle, between the landed nobility and the lower stratum of peasants, serfs, and artisans. To realize its opportunities, this middle class of burghers, or bourgeois, had to break through the restraints of feudal law and politics and remake society to suit its needs. Cultural renaissance, religious reformation, scientific discovery, political and economic revolution, all contributed in various ways to the same general end.

Along with the economic revolution, which produced the institutions of banks and credit agencies, of insurance companies and joint-stock corporations, came the political revolution and its concomitants. The latter arose both independently of economic changes and in interdependence with them. The government of the feudal system had accurately reflected its social and economic pattern. The realities of power were rooted in the locality where the land-owning nobility was strong. The center was remote and its control was tenuous. In the classic medieval dialogue between the king and the nobles, the advantages at first lay with the latter. The king was *primus inter pares* rather than sovereign. Obedience could not always be exacted from those whom Fortescue described as "over-mighty subjects." The political defects, therefore, of the feudal system stemmed from the vice of localism. The multiplicity of local powers brought rivalries and turbulence, and militated against a general order.

Thus, paradoxical though this may seem, the necessary prelude to democracy was the creation of a centralized order. Liberty (in the sense of self-government by the people as a whole) and equality (in the sense of eliminating traditional differences of ranks, class, and status) had to be wrested from the nobles through the agency of the king. The local bully, potent because he was close, was to be resisted by reinforcing the distant bully, who appeared the less dangerous because he was the more remote. Centralization, sovereignty, state, and nation, were the related expressions of a political transition from the medieval to the modern. The serf evolved into the citizen by the roundabout route of the capital and the court. The architects of royal absolutism held sway for a century or so, but they prepared for their own overthrow. If Henry VIII could dissolve the monasteries, break with Rome, and ally himself with the merchant companies of the City of London, another generation in another century could bring Charles Stuart to the scaffold. The Sun-King might build a pleasure-palace near his capital, where he assembled the *noblesse* of France, separating them from their lands and corrupting them into voluptuaries. But it was not so long an interval, in time or kilometers, from the construction of Versailles to the destruction of the Bastille.

The Pre-Industrial Revolutions

Interpreted as economic phenomena, the political revolutions which created modern democracy occurred in two stages. The earlier of these, it must be emphasized, was pre-industrial. In seventeenth-century England, for example, the Puritan forces which supported Parliament against the King included a coalition of independent small farmers, professional people and merchants. The City of London guaranteed the financial backing; the seaports assured the importation of supplies and the loyalty of the navy; the yeomen and squires of the east and southeast contributed the infantry, the horse, and Oliver Cromwell. This proved to be the winning combination. The political outcome was the end of absolute monarchy and the fatuous notion of the divine right of kings. The temporary regime of the victors was the Cromwellian Protectorate, England's only experience with a one-man dictatorship. Cromwell represented, though he was not controllable by, the groups he had led in war, and his political power, so evident in his contemptuous dismissal of the Long Parliament, was backed by that formidable instrument which he had forged—the New Model Army. Cromwell imposed a curb on the Puritan left wing, crushing the spokesmen for the "have-nots" who advocated equal rights and community ownership. With him, the direction of the revolution swung decisively to the men of property, to the newer forms of urban wealth and the owners of medium-sized farms. His death and the social reaction against Puritan straitlacing made possible a double restoration, that of the strong Parliament and a limited monarchy. If any wondered which of the two had the upper hand, all doubts were removed in 1688. Henceforth, for a century and a half, Britain was to be governed by an oligarchy of wealth and rank, for whose common interests the parliamentary system from William and Mary to William IV provided the convenient vehicle. This was not yet democracy, since only a small fraction of the British people were represented in the legislature or by the parties and groups which found seats therein. But the beginnings of democracy were present, for the principle of parliamentary supremacy had been established. What remained to be done was to make Parliament truly representative of the whole.

The course of events on the continent bears some resemblance to that of Great Britain, but there are important differences in the timing and sequence. In Western Europe, the seeds of modern democracy sprouted earliest in Switzerland. As it was practiced in the small cantons and communes of the Germanic nucleus of the confederation, Swiss democracy was lineally descended from the assemblies of able-bodied males at which the Scandinavian and Teutonic tribes had decided their major questions. The *Landsgemeinde*, like the *Volkmoot* and *Thing*, was deeply rooted in the past. It predated not only the Industrial Revolution, but also the age of mercantilism and the preceding period of feudalism, and had originated with the most primitive economic conditions. In other words, the institutions of direct democracy had functioned in a simpler society where divisions between economic classes were not so sharply marked because there was so little wealth to go around. Could these institutions survive an economic transformation which brought more wealth into the society, and wealth in new forms, first mercantile and later industrial?

The initial answer to this question in Switzerland was negative. After a century of religious controversies, in which Protestants were pitted against Catholics and the survival of the Confederation was imperiled because its unity broke down, the Swiss achieved in the Peace of Westphalia an international recognition of their independent status and determined henceforth on the two conditions which would ensure a future for their state; internally, the coexistence of dissimilars, and externally, a permanent neutrality. On this basis they achieved, if not harmony, at least peace. With tranquillity their country flourished and their commerce widened. But the ensuing wealth was not equally distributed. In many cantons, and in such great cities as Zurich, Geneva, Bern, and Basel, great families emerged which turned riches into influence, influence into power, and power into privilege. Before long the political system registered the effects of socio-economic change. Oligarchies became entrenched in government, and formed themselves into closed corporations. The mass of the citizens were denied equality and excluded from participation in the ultimate authority. The Swiss historian, William Martin, in describing this period, gives it the general name of "le Patriciat." He traces the evolution of "a governing class," observing that "at every epoch of our history, Swiss democracy has been traveling in the direction of oligarchy."[3] Of one canton, Geneva, where an aristocracy of bankers, traders, and lawyers dominated "la cité," a trenchant criticism was written by its most illustrious citizen at a time when the dominant clique had placed a ban on his books. Appealing to his fellow Genevese to recover control of their government, the rebellious Rousseau bade them face reality: "You are neither Romans nor Spartans; you are not even Athenians. Leave alone those great names which avail you nothing. You are merchants, artisans, and bourgeois, each of you occupied all the time with his private interest, his work, his trade, and his profit. You are a people for whom liberty itself is only a means to unhindered acquisition and secure possession."[4]

The revolt against privilege, sparked in Geneva itself by Rousseau's own writing, was fired by the French Revolution and fanned by the Napoleonic occupation. In a blaze of liberté and égalité, the oligarchies were smoked out from their exclusive citadels. They attempted again in some cantons to recapture their privileges after 1815, but lost control once and

3. Histoire de la Suisse, Chap. VII, pp. 150-51.
4. Lettres de la Montagne (1762). Ninth Letter. My translation.

for all in the revolutionary year, 1830. The middle class had wrested political power from the wealthy. Eighteen years later, after defeating the
Catholic Sonderbund,[5] it was able to transform a confederacy into a federal union and establish at Berne a central authority for Switzerland.

The two countries discussed in the preceding pages—Great Britain and
Switzerland—are among those which formed the vanguard of democracy.
Their experiences make it clear that the political revolutions, out of which
the modern democratic state was born, preceded the start of the Industrial Revolution. They were contemporaneous with the economics of the
age of mercantilism. The groups most interested in overthrowing the old
regimes consisted of the small independent farmers, and urban professional men and merchants. Their success was registered in the capture and
exercise of political power on behalf of these interests. Then they refashioned the institutions of government to suit their ascendancy. The parliamentary system was wholly appropriate to this end—but with the proviso
that the boundaries of representation were delimited by the ownership of
property. Within the walls thus erected, a new species of privilege was
established, more diversified and more mobile than what it replaced, but
far from embracing the whole community. Political liberties were still
apportioned upon a scale of economic inequality. Property, rather than
humanity, defined the rights of *homo politicus*.

There is thus a sense of incompleteness which surrounds these earlier
revolutions. Or so they appear to us who, of course, look back at them
with the advantages of hindsight, and can now see that they implied a
later stage. A revolution which abolished absolute monarchy or feudalism
or aristocracy and introduced a legislative system with limited representation had started moving toward democracy. But this was only a start.
What about the rest of the journey? What was to be the place of those
who owned very little property and of the propertyless? Were they to
receive liberty (i.e., freedom from subordination to the wealthier) and
equality (i.e., the same opportunity on the same terms to vote and hold
office)? Would politics become coextensive with community? Would society continue in the mold where the first-stage revolutions had left it,
with a government of the people by and for the middle class? Or would
the state evolve into a democracy which encompassed all?

The Second Stage of Revolution

Although such questions can be expressed and answered in political terms,
no answer is complete unless it includes the economic ingredient. The

5. This subject is further discussed in Chapter 12, pp. 355 ff.

technological advances of the end of the eighteenth century and the beginning of the nineteenth transformed the manufacturing process by means of power-driven machinery. Society now entered the age of industrialization, and much of the content of politics since that time has consisted in meeting and anticipating its problems. When a society became industrialized, more and more people were concentrated in cities where they depended upon the hazards of factory employment and trade. As machinery grew more complicated and more expensive, larger sums of capital had to be accumulated to build it and then maintain and renew it. The livelihood of millions was based on the far-flung operations of a market to whose processes everybody contributed, but which no one person or determinate group directed or controlled. The capacity of machines to produce was almost inexhaustible, being limited only by the supply of raw materials, the stamina of the men who fed the material to the machine, and the availability of energy. But the possibility of a continuous consumption of the product rested on other factors—a complex network of distribution, a sufficiency of purchasing power, and the psychological stimulants of demand. All this is another way of saying that the individual found himself a minute part of a vast system. He enjoyed its benefits when all functioned well, and suffered the disadvantages when things went awry. He did not understand the whys and wherefores. But he could see that some did much better out of the system than others. He was convinced that a person's freedom was a function of how much he earned or owned, that one became freer as one became richer because opportunity depended on money; and that, since money was unevenly distributed, such freedom ended with a return to inequality.

The effect of these changes on democracy varied from country to country. But when their experiences are studied together, a distinction appears between those countries where the first-stage revolution had been achieved before the advent of industrialism and those where it had not. It is always hard for a country to come to grips with industrialism, since the social and economic changes it produces are so drastic and profound as to constitute a revolution in themselves. When all this is compounded with a simultaneous revolution in politics, there is small wonder that the entire society is convulsed in a gigantic upheaval and some extreme solutions are attempted. Where, however, an earlier revolution had already discarded the absolute monarchy and the feudal remnants, had weakened the landowning nobility and the tradition-ridden church, and had invented some of the fundamental organs of a modern government, it was at least easier for the political system to adapt itself to further novelties. Democracy everywhere was created in revolution, but the more successful democracies have been those whose component revolutions—the political, economic, and social—were spaced apart and completed in stages, not telescoped together.

In the course of industrialization—and its accompaniments of technological invention, scientific discovery, and educational experiment—there were urgent situations which required a political response. Two of these must be singled out, because they are central to any discussion of the economic aspects of democracy. In the first place, the factory system and the requirements of capital accumulation created new modes of social organization. Managing this organization and distributing its output generated a formidable power and discovered in the joint-stock corporation a convenient instrument for its exercise. What would be the relation, then, between the two kinds of power—economic and political? Would the state assert its authority over business, or would the captains of industry call the tune for the politicians to play? A second urgent problem was the relation of the industrial workers to the middle class. All of the former were poor or relatively so. Their livelihood was always in danger from hazards against which, as individuals, they had no protection. Only the trade union, in the economic sphere, or the state, in the political, could surround them with a collective shield. Moreover their physical concentration in cities, factories, or mining towns, enhanced their capacity to organize and act in concert. But how would the middle class (a category which included their employers and many of their landlords) react to all this? Would its members lower the barriers of privilege and admit the propertyless? Would there be conflict between classes, resulting in the supremacy of one over the other, or some kind of compromise and harmony? Could democracy overcome the tensions within the economic system?

The answers to these questions were written in the course of the nine decades betwen the middle of the nineteenth century and the outbreak of World War II. Such has been the complexity of this period, and so close is it in time to ourselves, that even its main themes do not readily lend themselves to clear analysis. But at the risk of not seeing the trees for the forest, it is well to try some general summary before exploring in more detail.

Industrial Economies and Maturing Democracy

The economic developments of the last hundred years are definitely linked to the maturing of democracy. This does not mean to imply that democracy has been an effect attributable to economic causes—for in truth there have been many contributors to the modern democratic state besides the economic—but rather that the influence of economic forces has reached into the political process, shaping the conditions under which democracy emerged and creating some of the problems which it had to solve. Conversely, and no less true, where democracy has been achieved, its political effects have altered the social order and affected the environment of which the economy is a part. In the countries which were industrialized first, much of the economic growth was accomplished by individual businessmen or groups of private persons associated under the legal guise of the corporation. The key people, since every enterprise required money and involved risks, were the owners of capital, so that the system which they led is appropriately called "capitalist." In any movement it is the leaders who set the tone, direct its operations, and prescribe its objectives according to how they conceive their interests. Since the men at the top were wealthy, or became so, they could afford to build or buy expensive homes, maintain servants, educate their children in private schools, pay their medical bills, provide for their old age, and endow some church or charity as insurance for the hereafter. It was natural therefore that the doctrine which most appealed to them was individualism. The state was needed only to guard the frontiers, police the poor, issue the coinage, inspect the weights and measures, and enforce those laws which formed the skeletal framework of society. And all this could be subsumed by philosophers under the concept of Liberty.

To the industrial working class, however, and to any who earned little and owned practically nothing, the questions of public policy involved in the relation between politics and economics appeared in quite another light. Individuals who in a money economy are "worth" only a little, as the phrase goes, are less likely to place a stress on the merits of individualism, since as individuals they do not fare very well. Liberty offers few advantages to the weak if its results merely expose them to the power of the strong. Persons who lack education, and therefore are barred from access to the careers for which education is the gateway; persons who lack security, who have other mouths to feed, and who live in fear of dismissal and unemployment; persons who dwell in slums, dress shabbily, and are remote from the amenities and the arts; such persons who in many countries were, and still are, the majority, could be expected to ascribe the causes of their condition to society and to prescribe remedies in the form of collective action by the state. Just as individualism was the philosophy of the middle class, the working class preferred collectivism. Those who counted for nothing individually might count for something collectively. What they needed was organization, and, with this, some institutions, leaders, and doctrines. Many movements flowed from this source (socialism, trade unions, anarchism, early communism, and co-operation) and issued forth into programs, philosophies, and political parties. Since their members were the underprivileged people in society, who had a low position on the totem pole, they wished to remove the ranks and status and discrimination which worked in their disfavor. To help the humble, they must also level the lordly. Hence, as Liberty became the middle-class ideal, the working class espoused Equality.

For democracy, as it evolved from the middle of the nineteenth century, this divergence of interest and ideology contained the potentials of a conflict which had to be resolved. Would the emphasis in its philosophy be libertarian or egalitarian? Could a synthesis of the two be somehow produced? How would the marriage between democracy and the state be consummated? Could the institutions which had been created for monarchy, aristocracy, or plutocracy be refashioned to serve democratic ends, or must they be removed and replaced? On what terms would the state coexist with the economic order? Should the functions of the former be kept to a minimum or be extended to supervising the economy for the public good? Would the working class and the middle class become antagonists or partners? Would class warfare or interclass harmony ensue? Could class distinctions be eradicated?

These queries contained a deeper implication. Until the middle of the nineteenth century, the masses of mankind had almost always stood on the side lines as spectators of a social process and subjects of a political system in which they did not actively intervene. Now they had marched, or had been led, into the center of the arena. The inexorable effect of industrial change was to make everybody relevant and to require participation by all. The remodeling of social relations by economic change had introduced to the world the politics of mass government. What form those politics would take, however, was still an open question. All of the major competitors for our political loyalties in the twentieth century have been different responses to roughly the same situation. Democracy, fascism, and communism alike have had to come to grips with the new facts of mass participation and to provide a basis for the enrollment of all in the governmental process. Thus the modern democracies which have evolved since the mid nineteenth century have been confronted with the basic implications of their own title. If power in a "democracy" belonged to the "*demos*," who were the "*demos*"? Were they all of the adults or not? And if these questions were given a political answer, what did they mean when translated into economics?

The crux of the problem was this. There was an incongruity between the political requirements of the democratic revolution and the economic results of the Industrial Revolution. The former posited the final overthrow of privilege as a principle of government. All adults were to have the suffrage on the same terms. Each person should have one vote. Each vote would have the same value. When the votes were counted, the majority would prevail. But translate this into economics. In the economy, wealth was unequally accumulated, incomes were unequally distributed. A few people owned and received a share which was disproportionately large. A great many owned nothing, and earned but little. Democracy in its fullest sense meant the transfer of power to the latter through the weight of numbers—always assuming that the election campaigns were freely conducted, the voters unintimidated, the balloting honest. If the poor won control of the government, would they not use it to improve their economic position? Would economic privilege survive after political privilege had disappeared? Society could hardly endure as a house divided against itself, with the politics of equality on the lower floor and the economics of inequality on the upper. Presumably, something must give way. If those who benefited from economic inequality were to retain their privileges, either they must resist the introduction of full democracy or, once it had been introduced, they must relegate its institutions to an external façade and reduce its processes to a sham. Alternatively, for genuine democracy to prevail, the citadels of economic power had to be assaulted and subordinated to the state and the state itself be subjected to popular control.

What was implied in these alternatives can be seen in five contrasted cases: the United Kingdom, the United States, France, Germany, and Italy. A survey of these countries will show that the group which was pivotal in determining the outcome was the middle class. Upon its size, power and attitudes depended the issue of the revolution—for democracy or against it.

Class Relations in Nineteenth-Century Britain

Since the United Kingdom was the earliest to be industrialized, it was also the first to face the social and political consequences. When the Industrial Revolution exploded, the British economy was still predominantly agrarian. The social order was oriented mainly to the rural life. Most of the population lived on farms and in villages. Manufacturing was also conducted, but its output was limited by the necessity of using manual power. The prevailing economic philosophy was that of mercantilism, which envisaged a fairly strong state, centrally directed and conceived as a national unity, and state control of economic policy in the national interest. As the name "mercantilism" suggests, a heavy emphasis was placed upon trade, particularly on foreign trade. It was thought that the wealth of a nation could be measured by the excess in value of exports over imports and the storing of bullion to represent the difference. The form of government was an oligarchy, dominated by the richer landowners and the merchant companies of the City of London. The former secured their interests by protection for agricultural products (especially wheat); the latter, by such agencies as the Bank of England, which Parliament had authorized in the late seventeenth century, and the Stock Exchange.

As the technology of industrialism began to affect the social and economic organization, this framework of ideas, assumptions, and policies came under attack. Adam Smith led the assault by exposing the fallacies of mercantilism and excoriating its faults; and his successors, such as Ricardo, turned to the positive work of formulating the rationale for a new philosophy and its derivative program. When this was applied to public policy, the net effect—if one omits the subtleties and refinements—was to advise the government to do as little as possible in the economic realm. Businessmen should be left free to make their own decisions. Their regulation by public agencies, it was assumed, might prevent their doing harm, but could do no positive good. Those who argued in this way were not stupid men or inhumane. They were battling against a tradition and they needed to turn inside out the institutions in which that tradition was encased. The state was viewed as an enemy because it had been constructed and operated for the defense of a different set of interests. It was not to be abolished, since there were irreducible functions which government must perform. But its activities should be kept to a minimum. As for the working class, the factory operatives of the new order, the new gospel was inspired by the Puritans' belief in the virtues of work, and the notions of superiority in a society stratified into classes.[6] The *nouveaux riches* of the industrial cities, being self-made men, were convinced of their right to rule because they had risen to the top in the cut and thrust of competition. The lords of the manor were out; the captains of industry were in. Gradgrind replaced the squire.

6. On this subject Arthur Young expressed the prevailing attitude: "Everyone but an idiot knows that the lower classes must be kept poor, or they will never be industrious." *Eastern Tour*, 1771, Vol. iv, p. 361. Quoted by R. H. Tawney, *Religion and the Rise of Capitalism* (Penguin Books, 1937), p. 241.

Britain's life and death struggle with Napoleonic France provided the urgency for speeding up the rate of industrialization. After the war ended in 1815, the country found itself in a position similar to that of the United States at the end of World War II, the possessor of a well-developed manufacturing plant with a productive capacity for supplying wide markets at home and abroad. The growth in the next decade made challenge and change inevitable. The decisive period when Great Britain entered the modern age was in the 1830's and 1840's. In 1832, the beginnings of political reform were formally registered in the Act of Parliament which extended the suffrage to the urban middle class and began the reapportionment of seats in the Commons. The enlarged electorate, with its bigger proportion of urban members, was able fourteen years later to write the economic results on the statute book by repealing the laws which had protected British-grown wheat against imported grain. The policy of free trade, accomplished in the 1840's, enabled the manufacturers to import their raw materials, and an increasing percentage of the nation's food, without duty. Employers could keep their costs of production down by keeping wages down by keeping the price of food down.

But there was another kind of cost which the individualist policies of laissez faire could not meet. This was the social cost, summed up in the squalid condition of the industrial laborers, who eked out an existence in urban slums, and whose lives, to paraphrase Thomas Hobbes, were overcrowded, poor, nasty, brutish and short.[7] The evils thus generated—poverty, ignorance, disease, and crime—could be removed in various ways. The most drastic remedy was to leave the country and emigrate to some new land. This in fact was what hundreds of thousands of people did. During the same century when Britain was becoming one of the wealthiest and most powerful countries in the world, its population was increasing by leaps and bounds. The figure was 10,500,000 in 1801, 18,500,000 in 1841, and 29,700,000 in 1881. As the business cycle alternated between booms and slumps, the exodus in the bad years swelled from a trickle to a flood, and Britishers tried to start life anew in North America, the South Pacific, or South Africa. A second way to alleviate the lot of the poor was for the rich to dispense charity. This method was encouraged by many moralists and theologians, and the churches approved it since the money was often handed to them for redistribution. But even at its best, charity was a palliative only. Its effects were sporadic and irregular. At its worst, it was a salve for the consciences of the rich, and a further degra-

7. In the *Leviathan* (Part 1, Chap. 13) Hobbes so described the human condition in the hypothetical state of nature, except that he wrote "solitary" where I have written "overcrowded."

dation to the recipient poor. The third method of grappling with the social consequences of industrialism was political. The state must firmly assert its control over the economy to bring some security and decency into the lives of all its citizens. The state was the only institution of society which embraced everybody, had a responsibility for the general welfare, and could apply consistent programs continuously for a number of years. What churches and corporations did not do, Parliament and the civil service might.

Diagnoses by Disraeli, Marx, and Mill

It is significant that three men of unusual ability and divergent outlook were contemplating the phenomenon of British society from the eighteen-forties onward, and we have their diagnoses of its condition and advice about what to do. These were Disraeli, Marx, and Mill. What is surprising is not so much the extent of their disagreement, as the number of points on which they agree. Disraeli had risen to national prominence, or notoriety, in the parliamentary debates of 1845-46, when he had voiced the last-ditch resistance of Tory landowners to the adoption of free trade. Here was the spokesman for conservatism espousing the lost cause of the declining agricultural interest. But in the decades that followed, sitting in opposition and studying the changes in the society around him, Disraeli came to realize that the balance of the economy had forever tilted to the industrial side and that his party, if it was to remain a major one, must do the same. In his political novels he had already probed into the social malaise, saying that the country contained two nations—the rich and the poor—and would cease to be a unity unless they came together. From this he derived the prescription of a "Tory democracy," a system in which the ruling elite would recognize the obligations of society to its underprivileged urban masses, and would adopt programs to improve their position. This was a philosophy which necessarily implied positive action by governments and envisaged the state in a strong role as regulator of the economy and dispenser of social justice.

It may seem odd to include Karl Marx in the same group with a Conservative party leader. But the two did resemble one another in their diagnosis of the trouble, although not in their prescription of the remedy. The root of the passionate Marxian indictment of capitalism is a sense of injustice. As Smith had attacked mercantilism by focusing on its bad effects, so Marx assails the economics of which Smith and Ricardo were the advocates by denouncing the inhumanity of their social by-product. The emotional force of his appeal, irrespective of the merits of its intellectual content, lay in the rejection of inequality. The evil of inequality in the distribution of power, wealth, status, and opportunity—this is the brunt of the Marxian attack. And what of the cure? Marx can find no good in the liberal state, the state of the capitalist bourgeoisie. For him, this is merely the instrument of exploitation by a dominant class. So corrupt is it in essence, it cannot be altered by mere reform. The only thing to do is uproot that state and its supporting institutions and sweep them all away.

On what evidence did Marx develop this analysis and offer his prediction of a proletarian revolution overthrowing the bourgeoisie? Being a Rhinelander by birth, and a Prussian by education and upbringing, he had been able to observe the incipient effects of industrialism on the continent of Europe. But like Engels, who had studied the condition of the English working class in the Lancashire textile towns, Marx derived much of his information from Great Britain, where he resided from 1849 until his death in 1883. What is significant about this is that when Marx was working at the library of the British Museum, collecting the material out of which he produced *Das Kapital,* he gathered a large quantity of data from public documents, notably from the reports of parliamentary committees which were then investigating the social and economic conditions of the British people.[8] In other words, it was a political fact—the power of Parliament as the representative of public opinion and the public interest—which made possible these inquiries into the operation of the economy and the exposure to public view of those results which were evil. But the same power could also be used to remedy the situation. By deliberate intervention the political order could introduce a measure of social justice into the economic order. Capitalism could be humanized by democracy. Even Marx, the arch-revolutionary, condemning the middle-class state and all its works, made a significant exception in the case of Great Britain. In 1886, Engels wrote a preface to the first English translation of *Das Kapital,* in which he said: "Surely, at such a moment, the voice ought to be heard of a man whose whole theory is the result of a life-long study of the economic history and condition of England, and whom that study led to the conclusion that, at least in Europe, England is the only country where the inevitable social revolution might be effected entirely by peaceful and legal means. He certainly never forgot to add that he hardly expected the English ruling classes to submit, without a 'pro-slavery' rebellion, to this peaceful and legal revolution."[9]

8. Marx himself stressed this point in his preface to the first German edition of *Das Kapital* in 1867. He contrasts the inadequacy of social statistics in Germany with the ample information provided by the studies of British parliamentary commissions.
9. Reprinted in *Capital* by Marx (Dent and Sons: London, 1933), p. 887.

As this quotation shows, the predictions of Karl Marx were proven wrong on a number of points. First, Great Britain was not the only country in Europe where social revolution was accomplished peaceably. How about Denmark, Norway, and Sweden, for instance? Second, it was not the case that the "English ruling classes" resisted change with a "pro-slavery rebellion." Far from it. Actually, the Conservative party has incorporated much of that revolution into its program. Marx was right, however, on two major points, in both of which he and Disraeli concurred. He was correct in predicting that the division between rich and poor could not and would not continue. In some way or other, the gulf had to be bridged. As for the means, Marx had enough opportunity to observe British politics at first hand and to reach the opinion that the revolution he anticipated could be legally accomplished in that country through Parliament.

The third in this trio of analysts, John Stuart Mill, also arrived by a different route at a somewhat similar conclusion. The remarkable feature of Disraeli and his party was the spectacle of the privileged espousing the cause of the underprivileged. The equivalent paradox in the case of Marx was the apostle of revolution conceding that salvation was possible by evolution. What was extraordinary in Mill was the conversion of the individualist, who had a bias against the state, into something of a collectivist who admitted the necessity for remedial state action. Because of the rigorous indoctrination to which he was subjected by his father and his father's friends, including Ricardo, John Stuart Mill understandably inherited the philosophy of the Utilitarians in its pristine purism. The results can be read in the first edition of the *Principles of Political Economy*, published in 1848, and in the opening chapter of the *Essay on Liberty* which was given to the world in 1859. There Mill conceives of all good as resulting from the actions of individuals. Society collectively, and the state as one of its organized institutions, can do no positive good to individuals. All it can do is to prevent their suffering any avoidable harm from the acts of others. If something is to be done by the state, the onus of proof is always placed on those who argue for the state to act. Let individuals rise or fall on their merits. Society has no obligation to treat unequals equally. Creativity flowers in freedom. It cannot be organized.

From this early position which regards the political system as something potentially dangerous, but as a necessary counterpoise to other dangers, Mill gradually withdraws. Step by step, he moves to new ground where he condones the need for one state undertaking after another, until eventually—although he never says so explicitly—he accepts the state both as a remover of social ills and as a creator of social benefits. Why this turn-about? The change in outlook occurred for reasons which are greatly to Mill's credit as a human being, although they have earned him the reputation of inconsistency as a thinker. Mill was sufficiently open-minded to recognize facts which did not fit his inherited preconceptions,[10] and broad enough in his sympathies to feel for the lot of humanity. Unlike Herbert Spencer, he modified his philosophy when he could no longer justify the social effects of economic institutions. Hence in the later editions of *Political Economy*, as in the closing chapter of the *Essay on Liberty*,[11] he is arguing in favor of collective action through the state in order to do good to individuals who cannot help themselves. But to accomplish this good, the state itself must be strengthened; and for that to happen, it must be improved. Hence Mill paid increasing attention to the questions of reforming the electoral system, modernizing Parliament, organizing the administrative service, spreading public education, and the like. The logic is clear.[12] The politics of democracy would be invoked to rectify the errors of an unregulated industrial capitalism.

And what of the results? The answer, in the case of Great Britain, is that the laissez faire doctrine was gradually discarded, the functions of the state were progressively enlarged, and the political system did successfully assert its primacy over the economic process. All of this occurred in the half-century from 1865 to 1914. At the same time the institutions of government were further reformed by the steady application of democratic principles. The franchise was extended to the middle class, then to the working class in the factories and on the farms, then to women. The response to the accumulation of economic power and the emergence of social blight was concerted political action. When the traditional oli-

10. Thus, in the first edition of *The Principles of Political Economy*, he stressed the contradiction between the theory justifying private property and its actual distribution. "The principle of private property," he wrote, "has never yet had a fair trial in any country; and less so, perhaps, in this country than in some others. The social arrangements of modern Europe commenced from a distribution of property which was the result, not of just partition or acquisition by industry, but of conquest and violence: and notwithstanding what industry has been doing for many centuries to modify the work of force, the system still retains many traces of its origin. The laws of property have never yet conformed to the principles on which the justification of private property rests. . . . They have not held the balance fairly between human beings, but have heaped impediments upon some to give advantages to others; they have purposely fostered inequalities, and prevented all from starting fair in the race." (1848) Vol. I, p. 253.

11. Chapter V, entitled "Applications."

12. The critiques of Disraeli, Marx, and Mill are reinforced by many others—notably the novels of social protest by Dickens and the aesthetic revolt of Ruskin.

garchy accepted the Reform Act of 1832, they showed that Britain would proceed by evolution, not revolution. In 1832 the middle class achieved its political objectives, and the working class was willing to bide its time. In 1867 and 1884, when the second and third Reform Acts were adopted, the working class was admitted as a participant in the constitutional system. After that, it was a foregone conclusion that the achievement of equality in politics would lead to an assault upon inequality in economics. An uncontrolled capitalism had sown the seeds of its own destruction, because politics had nurtured the seed with the waters of reform. When that seed flowered, the bloom was democracy.

Agrarian Roots of American Democracy

In the United States the economic circumstances have been different and so has been the course of social evolution. But the political results have turned out to be substantially similar in the long run.

The early economic development of the United States was shaped by a group of factors, for most of which there is no parallel in the experience of European countries. In the first place, the American settlements originated as colonies, so that their production and their access to markets were subordinated to British interests. The Declaration of 1776 was an act not only of political, but also of economic, independence. After victory was won on the battlefield, an early task of the young nation was to fight free from the restrictions of a colonial economy. The second characteristic of the United States was the predominance of agriculture. Manufacturing was rudimentary and on a small scale. Commerce, both interstate and external, had stimulated the growth of such ports as Boston, New York, Philadelphia, and Baltimore. But, although merchants, bankers, and lawyers were clustered in these cities, from which their influence radiated outward, the urban interest, numerically considered, was exceedingly small.[13] A third important factor was the vast extent of land to the west, where individuals, families, or small communities could strike new economic roots. Finally, the population (excluding the Indians) consisted of recent immigrants or the descendants of those who had immigrated one or two generations earlier. Because society was younger and newer, its institutions were more fluid than those of Europe. With the challenge of a broad, rich continent, lying at their feet, people might be expected to experiment, create, and innovate.

13. In 1790, the rural population numbered 3,727,000; the urban population, 202,000.

The movement which culminated in independence was led by an odd coalition of southern planters and northern merchants. Washington, Jefferson, and Madison contributed to the final result as did Franklin, Hamilton, and the Adamses. But they had one point in common. Both the War of Independence and the shift from a loose confederation to a tighter federal union were accomplished by men of property. The urban middle class and poor, and the smaller farmers, were scarcely represented in the leadership, nor did their wishes carry much weight at the Philadelphia convention. Indeed, it was the disturbance of Shays' "rebellion," conducted by debt-burdened farmers in western Massachusetts, which produced a climate of opinion in favor of strengthening the government and centralizing it. But, as that statement implies, more than one political choice was expressed in framing the new Constitution and in its subsequent operation, and the various alternatives had different economic and social connotations.

In selecting the political system for the United States, the founding fathers had to decide three basic questions: how much power to allot to the state vis-à-vis the economy and private individuals in general, how much to the union vis-à-vis its component states, how much to the people vis-à-vis their officials. The first of these choices lay between centralism and decentralization; the second, between a strong state controlling the economy or a weak one based on laissez-faire principles; the third, between participation in government by the mass of the citizens or by a limited number only.[14] In the classic conflict that erupted between Hamiltonians and Jeffersonians the dividing lines were sharply drawn. Hamilton preferred centralism, a strong state, and a ruling elite. Jefferson favored the dispersion of powers, limited government, and popular control. Such political choices were, of course, linked to different economic philosophies and rival social values. Hamilton expected the United States to grow along the lines of manufacturing, commerce, and urbanism. He was a mercantilist in economics, as he was a Federalist in politics, because he knew that the prosperity of such an economy required the closer integration of its several states and the services of a government which could provide a national currency, national market, and national transportation. The businessmen of that time, whose cause he espoused, were in favor of government, not against it, since they were a minority interest and they needed its help. But they did not want to place their property in jeopardy or submit it to the vagaries of popular election and legislative policy. Hence they intended to keep the franchise limited, to distribute

14. For the significance of these choices, see my analysis in *The Great Issues of Politics.*

governmental powers at separate levels, and to institute judicial checks upon the legislature and executive.

Jefferson had quite another social philosophy. His well-known, and often quoted,[15] preference was for an agrarian economy and the rural way of life. Cities he viewed with distaste. Indeed, the larger they became the less he liked them. The healthiest occupation for society and the individual was farming, since it brought men closer to nature. The best political system was a community of citizen farmers, each an independent owner possessing enough for the support of his family. Under such circumstances, let government be decentralized and thus remain close to the people. Let it govern little, since the family farm will take care of all primary needs. Let the state be controlled by the people whom it serves. Does not this follow logically from the self-evident truths that the right to liberty is inalienable and that all men are created equal?

The Merger of Jefferson and Hamilton

It is remarkable that the dialectic between these opposites evolved so early in American history. For much of the subsequent politics of the United States can be interpreted in terms of the conflict between these outlooks and the attempts to synthesize them.[16] The result has been noteworthy. In the short run the Jeffersonians had their way on most points; but in the long run the Hamiltonians have prevailed in every respect, with one crucial exception.

During the first seven decades of the nineteenth century the American economy was based chiefly on agriculture, and the character of the country was predominantly rural.[17] All levels of government were severely restricted in their scope, and the localities and the states took care of the bulk of what government there was. Moreover, the ruling aristocracy, the "men of wealth and talent" so dear to the Hamiltonians, were gradually

15. *Notes on Virginia.* Query XIX. "Those who labor in the earth are the chosen people of God. . . . Generally speaking, the proportion which the aggregate of the other classes of citizens bears in any State to that of its husbandmen, is the proportion of its unsound to its healthy parts. . . . While we have land to labor then, let us never wish to see our citizens occupied at a workbench, or twirling a distaff."

16. The synthesizing began early—in fact, with Jefferson's own Administration—for the practical politician was not always consistent with the idealistic philosopher. As President, Jefferson allowed various of the Hamiltonian policies to continue.

17. Actually, the first census at which persons engaged in agriculture were outnumbered by those in other pursuits was that of 1880. But not until 1920 did the total urban population for the first time exceed the rural.

forced to surrender their political privileges and share their control of the government with the less wealthy and less educated. Progressively within the states, and *pari passu* within the nation,[18] the barriers of wealth which kept the poor from the polls were lowered until they were virtually abolished. The driving force behind this movement issued from the frontier region of the West, which was rougher and more rural, more intensely individualistic, and more disposed to accept a man for what he was rather than for his parentage or wealth. In the two political movements which typified the new spirit, those of Jeffersonian democracy and Jacksonian democracy, western radicalism was pitted against eastern conservatism. The egalitarian effect of the former was felt politically in the gradual removal of property qualifications for the franchise.[19] The common man was coming into his own, until individuals who hailed from humble origins—a Jackson or a Lincoln—could be elected to the highest office in the land.

But while the Jeffersonian fruits thus ripened, the Hamiltonian seeds were slowly germinating. True to the mercantilist doctrine that commerce must become national and that exports should surpass imports, the Federalists required a national government strong enough to create the supporting framework of a national market. This explains the concern of Hamilton as Secretary of the Treasury in Washington's Administration to establish confidence in the currency, to stimulate manufactures, and to erect a protective tariff. The same policy is explicit in the principles enunciated by Chief Justice John Marshall in some of his most famous opinions (i.e., *Gibbons v. Ogden* and *McCulloch v. Maryland*), the effect of which was to enlarge the spheres both of interstate commerce and of the federal government. In the rapid expansion that occurred between the end of the Napoleonic Wars and the outbreak of the Civil War, more territory was being occupied and permanently settled and the population was rising both through the birth rate and because of immigration. But the cities were gaining faster than the countryside. In 1820 the urban inhabitants numbered less than 700,000 (compared with a rural population of almost nine millions) and there was only one city of more than 100,000 people. But by 1860, nine cities exceeded that size, and the whole urban population had increased nine times. The rural population in the same

18. Because of the provision in Article 1, sec. 2 of the *Constitution of the United States*, as each State permitted more persons to vote in elections for "the most numerous branch of the State legislature," the electorate which voted for the federal House of Representatives was simultaneously broadened.

19. On the subject of literacy tests, which have the effect of discriminating against the poor, see Chapter 10, pp. 279-80.

period had barely trebled and was but three times as large as the urban. As for political growth, in the presidential election of 1824, which was vigorously contested between John Quincy Adams and Andrew Jackson, a mere 356,000 popular votes were cast. But in 1860, there were 4,680,000 who voted. Democracy was coming to fruition—at least among the adult males and the whites.

Industrial Expansion of the United States

The next phase of economic development witnessed the application of scientific technology to manufacturing and the consequent growth of large-scale industry. As the war against Napoleon speeded the Industrial Revolution in Great Britain, so the war between North and South had a similar result in the United States. The eventual military triumph of the North was due as much to its superior productive power as to any other single cause. Northern industry, sparked by this stimulus, entered upon a period of fantastic growth from 1870 to the turn of the century,[20] with the result that the United States joined Great Britain and Germany in the first rank of industrial nations.

The internal effect was a profound transformation of the social and economic scene. The world of business expanded to gigantic proportions, and within its domain the biggest units acquired control over major sectors of the economy. This was the era of the huge "trusts" that crushed their competitors and then dominated their slice of the market. The laboring force and the consuming public lay at their mercy. Great fortunes were amassed by rapacious men who accumulated wealth and built empires. The concentration of large amounts of capital in the hands of a few intensified the gap between rich and poor, until glaring inequalities prevailed in the country which had preached the gospel of equality. Moreover, as business waxed strong and confident of its strength, its leaders had less need for governmental help than in the time of Hamilton. Seen from the standpoint of power, only a strong government could control the economic system, whereas a weak one would be controlled by the industrialists and financiers. The latter, therefore, embraced the notions of laissez faire and accepted the Jeffersonian doctrine that the best government is that which governs least. Also, since economic processes were nationwide in scope and could be properly regulated only by a national authority, the spokesmen for business now preferred that more power be

20. The annual production of steel, for instance, rose from a mere 19,643 tons in 1867 to 3,339,000 by 1887.

entrusted to the States, which they could more easily divide and dominate, than to the federal government, in which they correctly espied a threat to their hegemony. Thus plutocracy, embodied in the autonomous power of the owners of business, presented a challenge to American democracy.

Big Government for Big Business

The outcome of this challenge exemplifies the observation of Plato that a tendency in any direction which is carried to excess evokes a countermovement in the opposite direction. Against the phenomenon of Big Business, what protection was available for the little man? The possibilities that suggested themselves were these: Big Business could be broken down into smaller units, which was the object of the Anti-Trust laws. Or it could be left big, but be placed under the supervision of government, which was the aim of the regulatory agencies (e.g., the Interstate Commerce Commission). Or the state could itself undertake the functions which private associations were conducting. If such activities were economic in nature, this could be called nationalization or socialism or public enterprise. If the purpose was to promote social justice or enhance the general welfare, then the functions in question could be described as social services.

It now became evident that what was required for challenging Big Business was a Big Government. The truth of this was recognized in the first major legislation to establish a federal Civil Service of career men recruited by merit, the Pendleton Act of 1883, which was adopted in the same decade that witnessed the passage of the Sherman Anti-Trust Law and the establishment of the Interstate Commerce Commission. Furthermore, the political momentum to inaugurate such policies could come only from one source—from those who were exposed to the excessive concentration of economic power and needed the aid of a counter-force. The institution which organized that counter-force had to be the state. The principle which inspired its operation had to be democracy. The political system was required to protect society from the adverse consequences of the economic system. Industry and commerce had to be subordinated to the state; capitalism, to democracy. The power of numbers, possessing the right to vote, could be employed against the power of the economic oligarchy. The results, in the sphere of domestic policy, are contained in a series of programs associated with the names of the more dynamic Presidents of the twentieth century—the Square Deal of Theodore Roosevelt, the New Freedom of Woodrow Wilson, the New Deal of Franklin D.

Roosevelt, the Fair Deal of Harry S. Truman, and the New Frontier of John F. Kennedy. What has happened in the end has been an unforeseen union of a Hamiltonian economy and a Jeffersonian democracy. As for the sequence, it was the political revolution which occurred first and thus laid the foundations for democratizing a republican form of government. When the Industrial Revolution came later, an expanding political democracy was able to correct the social ills of an unregulated capitalism. Thus the particular ingredients—strong national government under popular democratic control, a strong industrial economy subject to the supervision of the state—are those which Hamilton and Jefferson respectively contributed, although the mixture doubtless is one which neither would have wholeheartedly welcomed.

The Experience of Continental Europe

The advent of democracy in modern times to the two largest English-speaking countries should be contrasted with the different development of the largest nations of Western Europe, namely, France, Germany, and Italy. No stable constitutional regime of a democratic kind has yet been established in any one of these countries. France, however, stands in a category of its own by contributing to the democratic tradition in a manner which neither Italy nor Germany can match. When the revolution started in 1789, the French unleashed a liberalizing influence throughout the Continent. In the realm of ideas and principles, no people has written or argued about democracy with more profundity or more variety. But the philosophical achievement has not been paralleled by the establishment of enduring institutions. The only French regime since 1789 which has lasted for more than two decades was a democratic one, the Third Republic (1875-1940), which issued from the defeat by Bismarck and ended in defeat by Hitler. Throughout that period democracy was none too securely based, and was exposed to risks of *coups d'état* from the extremes of Right and Left. As for Italy, after unification had been achieved in 1860-61, an evolution commenced in a democratic direction and some gains were being made in the decade prior to the outbreak of World War I. But the system was too feeble to survive the economic aftermath of war and it succumbed to the assaults of Mussolini's Fascists in 1922. The German experience was even more brief and ended still more disastrously. Under the Bismarckian Reich, a party system emerged which had the privilege of debating without the responsibility for governing. The first serious experiment in democracy was launched in 1919, with the

Weimar Republic. But that was tried under the stigma of military sur-render and the penalties imposed by the Versailles Treaty. For fourteen years the Republic tottered along through occupation, inflation, tempo-rary recovery, and sudden depression. Then it fell prostrate under the wheels of the Nazi Juggernaut.

Assuredly, the modern history of these three nations is not explicable solely or even primarily in economic terms. Others factors were also oper-ating to shape the political development. There were such problems as the role of the army in Germany and France, the power of the Church in France and Italy and the effects of religions division in Germany, the lateness of national unification in Germany and Italy, and the pursuit of expansionist policies abroad by all three. But, over and above these weighty influences, there is still the matter of economic change, and of its social and political consequences. Granted that prior to World War II the French had only partial success with democracy, and the Germans and Italians had total failure, in what way was all this connected with eco-nomic circumstances?

There is no single answer which fits all three cases, but one general explanation may be suggested. The impact of industrialism was felt by all three countries during the nineteenth century. But its political con-comitants varied both because each country had reached a different stage of political development at the time when industrialization started and because the capacity of each to industrialize was different. A major reason why France was able to proceed much further along democratic lines than either of its neighbors was political. The French had already settled two major political problems which neither the Germans nor the Italians had yet solved. France had achieved national unification, and along with it had constructed the machinery of a strong central government, at least two centuries earlier. By contrast, the same results were not obtained in Italy and Germany until the third quarter of the nineteenth century. In addition, the French had rebelled in 1789 against royal absolutism, against the power of the Church, and against the remnants of feudalism which cluttered the social order. Their revolution had demonstrated their un-willingness to acquiesce to the autocratic power of traditional institutions —an attitude which does not alone guarantee the success of democracy, but is certainly one of its pre-conditions. In Italy, something of this kind had been accomplished in the Kingdom of Piedmont, but nowhere else. As for Germany, the liberal-inspired revolution of 1848 both in Prussia and Austria ended in dismal failure. The triple alliance of aristocracy, army, and clerical hierarchy was able to halt the drive of revolution and deflect it into innocuous courses.

The Middle Class in France and Italy

The reasons for this are bound up with economic factors, which also help in part to explain why the French political tradition has been far more democratic than either the German or Italian, but less successfully so than the American or the British. The pivotal group in society was the middle class, which on the Continent as in Britain had expanded in size and influence with the advent of industrialism. Led by merchants, bankers, and manufacturers, the middle class felt itself squeezed between the holdovers of the *ancien régime* and the demands of the working class. Flanked by conservatism on one side and socialism on the other, the liberals were forced to make a choice. In the revolution that erupted in 1848, as later in the uprising of the Paris Commune (1870-71), fear impelled the middle class into alliance with the right against the left.[21] Because of their economic interests, they were reluctant to share political power with those more numerous than themselves. Henceforth, the relations between the owners of capital and the industrial workers were permeated by a fatal distrust. The results of these circumstances provided many obstacles to the attainment of democracy. Political movements, predicated on assumptions of class warfare, were organized along authoritarian lines, and opponents were regarded as enemies. When the antagonism of economic interests leads social groups to compete for political power in order to crush their rivals, it is impossible to agree upon the rules of a democratic constitution or operate its machinery without friction.

The French people, even before they were affected by economic change, were still divided by a revolution which they had started but had never been able to finish. They were pulled asunder by preferences for the principles of the *ancien régime* or for *liberté, égalité, fraternité*; by the choice between monarchy, empire, or republicanism; by the supporters and critics of the clerical hierarchy; by trust or distrust in the army; by a preference for legislative or executive predominance. Superimposed on all these divisions was the Industrial Revolution, bringing complicated subdivisions of its own; urban versus rural, industry versus retail trade versus agriculture, rich versus poor, big landowner versus peasant, big business versus small. Is it any wonder that the French Revolution continued to unfold in a series of phases and episodes, out of which no new harmony has ever yet emerged? Democracy under these conditions was a machinery for expressing disagreement rather than for eliciting consensus. When actions were

21. Guizot's statements in *De la Démocratie en France* testify to the mutual distrust which had developed between the middle and working classes. *Op. cit.*, Chaps. 5 and 6.

required, the result was paralysis. Where decision was wanted, deadlock ensued.[22]

Italy and Germany, as was noted above, were at a still earlier stage of political evolution when they began to experience the effects of industrialism. The consequences of the latter helped at first to speed the movement toward democracy, but later produced a decisive reaction against it. In Italy the political goal which took precedence over the rest in the mid nineteenth century was to achieve national unity. The attainment of democracy was secondary. All the regimes which governed the *disiecta membra* of Italy—there were no less than seven—were autocratic. They had a common interest to preserve themselves by keeping the peninsula divided and by repressing any popular movements which might evoke a national (i.e., an Italian) sentiment. Of the principal powers involved, one was foreign—namely, the Austrians, who dominated the northeast and who were unlikely to be more liberal in the Trentino or Venezia than in Vienna. In the south, with its capital at Naples, was the Kingdom of the Two Sicilies, misruled by a reactionary branch of the less enlightened Bourbons. The Papal States, stretching athwart the peninsula in the center, were subjected to a backward regime in which the Pope functioned as the temporal ruler. The Papacy had always lacked the power to unite Italy, but had been strong enough to prevent anyone else from doing so. In the mid nineteenth century the ruler of the Vatican was especially disinclined to embark on a policy which must entail opposition to Austria. Indeed, the subdivision of Italy actually suited the interest of the Roman rulers who feared their own possible subordination to the government of a united country.

In this depressing picture, a single gleam of hope shone from the northwest. There, the Kingdom of Piedmont evolved along progressive lines after 1815 in both the political and the economic spheres. Piedmont encouraged the modernization of its economy, with the consequent expansion of the business community and the urban middle class. What is more, the House of Savoy, in the person of Victor Emanuel I, was intelligent enough to agree to a liberal constitution in 1830 and to stick by it throughout the revolution of 1848 and the subsequent reaction. With the aid of the clever diplomacy of Cavour, and the requisite backing of France and Britain, Piedmont in 1859-60 took the lead in defying Austria and the Pope and, with Garibaldi's help in the south, created the Kingdom of Italy. The Piedmontese Statuto was then "writ large" to serve as a constitution for all Italy. The influence of the middle class, and especially of

22. For a further discussion of France's perpetual crisis, see Chapter 13, pp. 428 ff.

industrialists and merchants, thus combined with the liberalism and nationalism of men like Mazzini to create an Italian state and launch it into
the modern world.

The same three forces that had secured this initial achievement—
namely, nationalism, liberalism, and democracy—continued to operate,
though not always in harmonious unison, until World War I. Industrialization proceeded as fast as the limitations both of physical resources and
private and public capital permitted. The natural political effect was to
strengthen the vested interests of the entrepreneurs and, by the same
logic, to increase the numbers of the factory workers whose class-con-
sciousness made them hostile to their employers. Slowly at first, but later
more rapidly, the franchise was extended until more of the adult males
were included within the circle of political participation. The Church,
which had forfeited control of the Papal States in 1860 and then of Rome
itself in 1870, remained aloof in sullen opposition—an attitude which it
only abandoned when the organization of the Socialist party filled it with
even greater distaste than did the Liberal state. The South, which lagged
centuries behind the North in social and cultural development, provided
a drag on the progressive regions and a drain on the national budget.
Finally, to compound these difficulties, the nationalists of the Right, led
or misled by Crispi, indulged in risky diplomatic gambits in Europe and
imperialist ventures in Africa. Possessing the resources of a medium
power, Italy tried to live in the style of a great power—a role which lay
beyond its means and overtaxed its capacity. When a divided nation eventually (1915) entered World War I on the western side—in order to fight
against Austria for the *irredenta* in the northeast—the consequences (military, economic, and political) laid too heavy a strain on an as yet imperfect political structure. After 1918, the frustration of demobilized veterans,
an inflation that crippled the lower middle class, and an atmosphere of
political extremism resulting from economic depression provoked a crisis,
into which the Fascist Caesar strutted, presenting himself as the alternative to chaos. With no one else willing or able to oppose, Mussolini and
the *fasci di combattimento* seized the power that other hands had been
too feeble to wield.

Thus in summary, it was a combination of political and economic factors which helped both to unify Italy and to impel it along the path toward democracy. But it was because of the inability to solve the country's
economic problems, plus the political unwisdom manifested in domestic
and external affairs, that an immature democracy abruptly yielded to a
Fascist police state.

Unifying the Germans: The Liberals or Bismarck

The German case suggests some instructive resemblances to the Italian. Certain of the same factors are present in both, though in Germany the degree of success and failure is magnified. In addition, there are special features arising from the historical development of Germany which are not paralleled in Italy.

The principal similarity is that many Germans, particularly after the Napoleonic Wars, desired to unify their nation. The prime question was: Who would be the architects of unity, and by what methods would they build? If the liberals were successful, the German state could be expected to evolve along democratic lines. If the job was done by the conservatives, an authoritarian system was likely to prevail. Nor did the choice lie only between Left and Right (or Left, Right, and Center). Among the many states in which German people lived, only two had developed sufficient power to form a nucleus around which the rest could cohere. These were Prussia and Austria. Austria could not simultaneously govern a multinational state and take the leadership in bringing all Germans together. Determined to keep things the way they were, the Austrian rulers not only forfeited their own opportunity to create a German state, but resisted anybody else who tried. Hence, in Germany as in Italy, national unification had to be accomplished without Austria and against it.

This left the field to the Prussians. Their efficient rulers in the eighteenth century had extended their domains from the northeast westward to the Rhineland, and the internal reforms which were the Prussian response to Jena indicated that the Hohenzollerns and their advisers were serious contenders for further power. At this point, from the 1820's onward, economic considerations became increasingly important. Inspired by, and imitating, the success of the British, the Prussian government assisted and encouraged a rapid industrialization. This had the normal effects of augmenting the urban middle class, adding to the wealth, numbers, and influence of the manufacturers, and creating a proletariat of factory workers. The Prussian Kingdom had been created by the army[23] whose officers were mostly drawn from the same Junker families that gave counsel at Potsdam and filled chancelleries in Berlin. Learning the lesson of their defeat by Napoleon, these people had the sense to see that military strength now depended on an industrialized economy. Hence an

23. See Chapter 7, pp. 170 ff.

alliance of mutual interest was possible between the industrialists and the army, between *Junkerthum* and the Ruhr. But the union also contained its elements of friction. East Prussia was Protestant and largely rural, as Bavaria was Catholic and rural, whereas the Rhineland was Catholic and was fast becoming urbanized. The businessmen, though they welcomed help from the state, did not necessarily share the outlook of a government which functioned as an autocracy and was disposed to regiment all and sundry. Moreover, in Germany at large there were persons of liberal persuasion—in the professions, in literature, in the universities—who demanded more freedoms. While one remembers the Germany of Frederick the Great, of Stein and Scharnhorst, of Hegel and Nietzsche, of Bismarck, Kaiser Wilhelm, and Adolf Hitler, one should never forget the spirit of Beethoven and Goethe, of Schiller and Heine, of Kant and von Humboldt. The tragedy of Faust, as Goethe wrote the drama, is more than a struggle within the soul of an individual. It is also the conflict between opposing tendencies within the German society.

The time of decision was the revolutionary year, 1848; the critical area, the Rhineland; the groups on whose attitude all else hinged, the businessmen and middle class. Both Marx and Engels, be it remembered, were Rhinelanders, the former being born into a family of professional people and the latter the son of a well-to-do manufacturer. Repelled by the rapacity of the capitalists, and sympathizing with the hardships of the employees, these men reacted against one extreme by fleeing to the other. Authoritarianism of the Right bred the authoritarianism of the Left. Marx had absorbed the intellectual heritage of Hegel, then turned him, as he said, the other way up. Living at a time and in a place when all aspects of society were being revolutionized by economic change, he imagined this condition to be universally true and assumed that all societies were always conditioned by material factors. With dogmatism and zealotry, the founders of the organized Communist movement plunged into the revolutionary work of destroying the "bourgeois state," before it had even started, and advocated against the dominance of capital the dictatorship of the proletariat.

Meanwhile the liberals, in Frankfurt assembled, attempted at one and the same time to unify the German states and reform their systems of government (notably that of Prussia) by curbing the monarchy and transferring power to a legislature elected on a broader franchise. The liberals had their chance, but failed. The Prussian king would not accept a German crown from "professors and grocers." In the Rhineland the potentialities of upheaval from below scared the middle class and all owners of property into the embrace of the Right, who responded with the deployment of the troops. Reaction then set in, and in a few years it was possible for Bismarck to flout the Prussian legislature and pay for the expansion of the army without a legally authorized budget. His dangerous gamble was vindicated in the 1860's by the one argument which his critics could not answer—military success. Against Denmark (1864), then against Austria (1866), and finally against the France of Napoleon's nephew (1870-71), the Prussian arms triumphed. The German Reich was immediately proclaimed, and the King of Prussia became the *Deutscher Kaiser*. Unification had indeed been achieved by the Right and in fact by force of arms. The *Machtstaat* had done what the *Rechtstaat* could not.

Weimar or Nazism

The formidable task of democratizing a state founded on "Blood and Iron" could not be undertaken until the Army and the Right had lost their trump card. They were potent in Germany because of military victories. With military defeat, therefore, they forfeited their ascendancy. The first major effort to operate a democratic system was the inauguration in 1919 of the Weimar Republic. Though its institutions were not free from defects, its basic design and governing principles were genuinely democratic. At least, the new constitution would lend itself to a democratic outcome if enough of the German people wished to take advantage of their opportunity. Of the causes which contributed in fourteen years to the collapse of the Weimar regime, the political ones are both well known and obvious. They included the hostility of the Right, the cleavage on the Left between Social Democrats and Communists, and the association of the Republic with the unpopular Versailles Treaty. But there were also the economic factors whose influence was immediate and direct. First, the runaway inflation of 1923-24 brought ruin to many members of the middle class, whose welfare and support were indispensable to the regime. Scarcely did they have time to recover when the economic disaster of the "great" depression struck all Europe and the world. This began in the summer of 1929, and its repercussions were soon felt throughout Germany. It was at this time, and immediately for this reason, that Hitler, whose National Socialist movement had hitherto been but one of the many factions of the extreme Right, leaped into prominence. There is an exact correlation between the worsening of the depression and the strengthening of the Nazis. Simultaneously, at the other end of the political spectrum the Communists were gaining from the Social Democrats. Crushed between the two authoritarian parties, the Center fell apart.

Hitler came to power in January of 1933; an Austrian-born dictator now governed the all-German Reich; and for twelve years a people of vaunted *Kultur* submitted to a party which sloughed off the outer skin of civilization and reverted to barbarism. Mephistopheles had taken payment on his contract. He now possessed the soul of Faust.

Pivotal Role of the Middle Class

This comparison of five countries has included two which, prior to World War II, had combined an industrial with a democratic revolution, two which became industrial but not democratic, and one where industrialization accompanied a partial success in democracy. The subject was treated historically because only thus could the significance of the timing be made clear. The countries which were wise enough or lucky enough to inaugurate their political revolution before the nineteenth century had an advantage when they began to industrialize. At any rate, it was there that the middle class found it easier to accept the working class as its partners in political power. Elsewhere, when the demand for political revolution coincided with the forces of industrial change, the middle class had to choose between different kinds of autocracy. In Italy and Germany this tendency was augmented by the fact that their countries were unified late and that military force was used to bring this about. Certainly the history of European democracy would have been far different if the liberals had succeeded in unifying Germany in 1848. The French have been more successful with democracy than either Italy or Germany because they unified themselves much earlier. But they have been less successful than either the Americans or the British because Napoleon left a military imprint on their revolution and because they never reached agreement about an appropriate framework for a new regime. Where fascist regimes achieved power in the 1920's and 1930's, they drew many of their leaders and followers from the middle class whose allegiance to democratic values had not been wholeheartedly secured. More particularly, the people who felt themselves socially superior to manual laborers, but whose incomes were no longer higher than those of the latter, reacted with violent prejudice against the trade unions and socialist parties. So, rather than submit to parliamentary institutions which a working-class majority might constitutionally control, they preferred to abandon the principles of democracy and surrender to a Leader. What they could not outvote, they decided to smash.

There are, however, other lines of analysis besides the historical from which the connection between the politics of democracy and its economics should be reviewed. Moreover, apart from the matter or origins, and irrespective of what may have caused what, there are significant questions to be raised about results and consequences. Nowadays in the advanced democracies, a mutual interaction occurs continuously between political and economic factors, and the successful removal of some evils that were known has introduced along with new benefits some new difficulties which were not foreseen. An inquiry into these belongs in the next chapter.

9

Modern Economic Policies

If one sure lesson can be drawn from political history, it is this: policies which are adopted as solutions for existing problems eventually become a source of new difficulties requiring further solutions. There is never anything fixed or final in the process of social evolution. From the "remedies" which one generation administers there develops the "disease" which a later generation seeks to cure. Since the consequences that flow from a change in the social system are never fully predictable, governments are ever coping with the unforeseen by-products of actions which cannot be wholly planned or controlled.

Economic Factors Connected with Democracy

These remarks, besides being generally applicable, are pertinent to some of the particulars discussed in the preceding chapter. The philosophy of laissez faire justified numerous improvements in the economy which might not have flourished under the mercantilist system. But much of what resulted from laissez faire was neither expected nor welcome. The same can be said of the measures adopted to correct the new evils. The reassertion of the authority of the state over the economy was a tool, and nothing more. It could be put to various uses. The results depended on who held the tool, how they employed it, and for what purposes. Some of the consequences of a governmental union between industrial power and political power have been disastrous, as in the notorious examples of Hitlerite Germany, Stalin's Russia, and Japan from 1931 to 1945. In other cases, where the state has been infused with democratic principles, the supremacy of political considerations over economic has led to results which are either good or bad, according to the quality of the politics. Democracy has no automatic guarantees that its leadership will always be wise or its masses sufficiently enlightened.

As implied in the previous paragraph, a distinction should be drawn between two modern political developments which happen to have been connected in time and place, but are not necessarily linked in logic. The authority of the state over society has increased everywhere during the last seven or eight decades. This has meant that governments now undertake innumerable functions which previously were exercised by churches, business firms, and other private groups, or were not discharged by anybody. Simultaneously, in those countries which have democratized their political structure, the government has depended on the will of the voting majority for acquiring power and holding office. There is, of course, a direct causal connection between these two tendencies. Because the mass of the people were affected by social and economic conditions they could neither avoid nor control, they sought public correctives for privately generated ills. When political pressure resulted in the extension of the franchise, the right to vote became a power to support those parties and programs which would use the public machinery of the state to regulate the private association and bring help to poorer persons of inferior social status. The positive state of the twentieth century thus succeeded to the negative one of the nineteenth because people who were individually weak found that they could be collectively strong. By political action the general welfare could triumph over private interests.

There has been much confusion about the meaning of democracy and considerable doubt about its adaptation to diverse economic conditions because of the failure to draw an elementary distinction between what is historically accidental and what is necessary in principle. Contemporary views of democracy are understandably colored by the particular circumstances under which it evolved during the nineteenth century and has matured in the twentieth. While it is necessary to take heed of both history and philosophy, we should also take care to separate them. The democratic principle requires that the actions of the government be responsive to the popular will and that the practices of society conform to certain standards. Democracy does not require, *per se*, that the functions of the government be either reduced to the minimum or expanded to the maximum. What it does require is this: whichever alternative is followed, certain other criteria must be satisfied. These latter consist in the ideals of freedom, equality, and social justice. If such goals can be attained for all without an extensive governmental apparatus, the state can be a democratic one. If their attainment calls for a great enlargement of the functions of government, that too can be consonant with democracy. The important point to consider is whether in specific cases a restriction or an expansion of governmental functions is better suited to the attainment of social justice, equality, and liberty for all people.

When the discussion is couched in these terms, certain generalizations about the "causes" of democracy or its supposed connection with this or that aspect of the social system appear valid in a particular instance, but do not necessarily hold true under all conceivable conditions. Thus, the advantage of a comparative review, combined with the proper historical perspective, is that it enables us, in the analysis of democracy, to distinguish between what is necessary and imperative and what is contingent, possible, or accidental. Keeping this caution in mind, we can pose a series of questions about the relevance for democracy of certain economic factors.

Democracy Under Agrarian Conditions

First, is it correct to say that modern democracy is an accomplishment of an industrial society? In other words, was the Industrial Revolution a prerequisite of the democratic state? The answer to these questions is "no"—or rather, "not necessarily so." There are some countries where democracy was achieved within an economic framework which was primarily agrarian, where land was the principal source of wealth, and farming the most important occupation. On the European continent, this category would include Denmark, Norway, Switzerland, and, to a lesser extent, Sweden. In the British Commonwealth, it would embrace Australia, Canada, and New Zealand. The full flowering of democracy in some of those countries was associated with an agrarian revolution in the tenure of land and the type of production. A discussion of two of these cases—Denmark and New Zealand—will illustrate the general point.

1. The Case of Denmark

Denmark, which nowadays is one of the world's most advanced democracies, was governed autocratically by an absolute monarchy from 1660 until as late as 1848. Under such a system, everything depended on the outlook and personality of the king and his choice of advisers. In the

Danish case, certain ministers were able to initiate some enlightened measures. The fundamental problem, if Denmark was to progress, was the condition of the peasants, who toward the end of the eighteenth century numbered 70 per cent of the population. They were uneducated, primitive, and poor, and completely dependent—socially, economically, and juridically—on the big landowners. For democracy to evolve in Denmark, a multitude of ignorant peasants had to be converted into self-reliant citizens.

The beginning steps in this direction were taken, even before the French Revolution erupted, by such royal ministers as Struensee and Reventlow. A series of reforms emancipated the peasants from the feudal bonds of "villeinage"[1] and "adscription."[2] They were then allowed to own land individually, instead of tilling the separate strips which belonged to the villagers in common and were annually reassigned. Good though this was, the peasant still needed more than juridical freedom and a family-sized farm. If he were to function in a true sense as a citizen, he must have education, a sense of dignity in his position, and the right to participate in public affairs. The movement which accomplished this change was due, in a large degree, to the inspiration of an extraordinary man, N. F. S. Grundtvig. Mystic, poet, historian, theologian, and ecclesiastical reformer, Grundtvig brought to Denmark what it sorely needed—a faith in the value of the traditional folk culture. He revived interest in the Old Norse literature and mythology, challenged the Latin-dominated curriculum of the University of Copenhagen, created a new pride in the Danish tongue vis-à-vis German, and above all imparted a Rousseauian belief in the worth of ordinary men and women. Impressed by the dynamism he had witnessed on visits to England, he set about awakening the Danish countryside from its economic and cultural torpor. For this, he invented the Folk High School, which adult peasants would attend in the winter months in order to learn about their country's history and lore and to acquire that precious sense of belonging to its great tradition. The first of these was opened in 1844 as an experiment; it was another two decades before there were enough of such schools to have an effect on farming areas.

Meanwhile, the rural renaissance was caught up with other national movements and with international events, all of which combined to alter the character of the political system. In the Napoleonic Wars, the king chose the wrong side and suffered in consequence the bombardment of

1. Villeins were compelled to lease farms as tenants and to work for the landowner.
2. Adscription required a peasant between the ages of 14 and 36 to remain on the estate where he was born.

Copenhagen, the surrender of the Danish fleet to the British, and the cession of Norway to the Swedish Crown. Such disasters provoked an opposition by liberals to royal absolutism and its policies. Led by city-dwellers, professional people, and intellectuals, the liberal movement campaigned for freedom in state and church alike. Its objectives were gained in the 1840's when the monopoly powers and rigid dogmatism of the official Lutheran Church were broken, and when a new king in 1849 accepted a new constitution with an elected bicameral parliament. But triumphant liberalism was then sidetracked from domestic progress by the nation's involvement in the Slesvig-Holstein question and the claims of Prussia on these provinces of mixed Danish and German inhabitants. When the Danes were defeated by the combined forces of Prussia and Austria in the war of 1864, they were forced to cede two-fifths of their area and population to the Germans, including the predominantly Danish region of North Slesvig. As if that were not enough, a severe economic depression descended on the country already battered and truncated by war. Ever since 1846, when Great Britain adopted free trade, the Danish farmers had exported their wheat to the British Isles. But after the 1860's, they could no longer meet the competition of the abundant, cheaper grain from the prairies of North America. The rural economy plunged into crisis.

Catastrophes of such dimensions would have crushed a truly decadent people. In this case, the Danes responded to shock treatment with a national resurgence. The year 1864 was the turning point in their modern history. With aid from the state and with community initiative, they compensated for the areas they had yielded to Bismarck by remaking the wasteland within their shrunken borders. Across wide tracts of northern Jutland and elsewhere, the sea winds had driven the sand over the earth, converting it into an impoverished heath. There in three decades the Danes reclaimed more acreage than Germany had taken, and everywhere they shifted from grain to livestock, becoming exporters of pork and dairy products. Intelligent legislation aided them in this direction, and they were helped even more by an institution whose principles they imported from England in 1866, the Co-operative Society. For this whole movement, the education and morale and much of the leadership issued from Grundtvig's Folk High Schools. The political élan of the reawakened farmers culminated in the advent to power of the Liberals (the Venstre) in 1901. In the bicameral *Riksdag*, the democratically elected *Folketing* established its domination over the plutocratic upper house, or *Landsting*, and the ministry was made responsible to the popular chamber. Universal adult suffrage in the elections to both Houses was finally achieved in the constitution of 1915. Although there has been further evolution since that date, it is fair to say that full democracy—social, economic, and political —was achieved by the end of World War I.

2. The New Zealand Parallel

A case which is parallel in many respects is that of New Zealand. This country, over which Britain acquired sovereignty in 1840, was granted the powers of self-government between 1852 and 1856. A representative legislature was then instituted; and the ministers were made responsible to it, rather than to the governor. The franchise, by which the lower chamber was elected, became fully democratic in the period from 1879 to 1893, during which years adult male suffrage was introduced, then plural voting was abolished, and finally the vote was given to women. Economic development in the five decades, 1840-90, was devoted primarily to the settlement and exploitation of the land. Apart from a brief boom due to the discovery of gold in the 1860's,[3] and after a wasteful destruction of much of their timber, New Zealanders found that their best resource consisted in their grass, whose growth was replenished by the moisture-laden winds blowing across the Tasman Sea. The temperate climate and the varied elevations of the mountains, hills, and rolling plains formed an environment ideal for sheep. Imported flocks throve so well in the South Pacific that New Zealand before long was deriving most of its wealth from the export of wool. For efficient operation, however, the economics of the pastoral industry favored a large unit of production. It took time for new grass to grow, where the sheep had just grazed; and, because the flocks could be kept in the open all year round, they were taken to the lower altitudes in the winter and higher up in the summer. There was therefore a tendency to acquire huge holdings of land which extended over thousands of acres. These big "runs" were accumulated by "land aggregators," as they were called—that is to say, by wealthy men who owned sufficient capital or whose credit was good at the banks. In various regions, notably the Canterbury Plains of the South Island, these constituted a "squattoc-

3. There is some connection in this period between New Zealand and Denmark, because some Danes emigrated to the South Pacific at this time. Oscar Alpers, who later became a Judge of the New Zealand Supreme Court, landed there as a boy in 1875. The family knew little about the country "except vague stories we had heard of Maori wars, but recently concluded, of 'Hauhaus' and cannibals, and of nuggets of rich red gold to be gathered by the wayside. It was the Land of Hope, where my father proposed to himself to repair his broken fortunes and begin life anew." Oscar Alpers, *Cheerful Yesterdays* (Wellington: Whitcombe & Tombs, 1930), pp. 3-4.

racy"—an oligarchy of rich pastoralists—who dominated the economy and entrenched themselves in positions of political privilege.

The decade and a half between 1879 and 1893 witnessed not only the democratization of the franchise, but also the start of an agrarian and technological revolution. Through the introduction of refrigeration in ships, meat became an export product. The first successful cargo of frozen meat was sent to England in 1882. Henceforth, flocks were produced for their meat, as well as for their wool. But refrigeration presented a second opportunity. The hitherto small dairying industry was expanded, in order that butter and cheese could be shipped to the British market. Dairy cattle yielded good supplies of milk, rich in butter fat, in the regions that received the greater rainfall and grew the thicker grass. Here a farmer could make a living on a fairly limited acreage which he and his family could work by themselves. Suitable land for this purpose was opened for settlement in portions of the North Island where the warlike opposition of some Maori tribes had earlier prevented occupation by Europeans. During the 1880's—the very decade in which these new possibilities became apparent—a depression had spread throughout the country. Wool prices had fallen overseas, unemployment increased in the four principal cities, men wanted land they could not afford to buy, and some families were already emigrating from a country still sparsely settled.

But there was one weapon to be used against economic adversity, and that was political. The men who lacked the land possessed the vote. Democracy was a weapon to be turned against the "squattocracy." Land could be distributed, or redistributed, by the state, which could also offer capital on long-term loans at low interest. And that is precisely what was done. The Liberal party came to power in 1890 and was then re-elected six times in a row with a program which, *inter alia*, legislated an agrarian revolution. A steeply graduated tax was imposed on extensive accumulations of land, so that the owners were induced to sell. The state then bought the land at a fair price, subdivided it, and leased it in smaller holdings to farmers who later acquired the right of ownership.

The cases of Denmark and New Zealand are not identical of course; but they are sufficiently similar to justify some wider conclusions. The economies of both were primarily agrarian, and the interests of the majority of the population were connected with the land. A social and political movement toward democracy had already begun, but was far from being completed at the time when the country was hit by a serious depression. Political means were then adopted to initiate economic and technological remedies, which also resulted in transforming the social order of the rural regions. The government was stimulated to act in this way by the partial progress already achieved in the direction of democracy, and was further encouraged to become more fully democratic because of the success of its reforms. The outcome was a new kind of community, in which the social order, the economy, and the political system tended to conform to the same basic principles and thus had the effect of reinforcing one another.

When the experiences of Denmark and New Zealand are compared with those of such industrialized countries as the United States and Great Britain, there is an evident inference to be drawn. Democracy was not necessitated or even caused by economic developments either in countries that were principally agrarian or in those that were highly industrialized. The possibility of democracy, however, did depend directly on the manner in which the economy—whether industrial or agrarian—was organized. If large holdings of land were concentrated in the hands of a few, if great disparities of wealth consequently ensued, if the landowners formed not only a plutocracy but a social aristocracy, and if political power was proportionate to their property and prestige rather than to numbers, then no genuine democracy could be present in politics because it was absent from the social and economic systems. The same holds true of the industrial countries when disproportionate amounts of capital were accumulated in relatively few hands, when important sectors of manufacturing were dominated by a few giant firms, and when the owners of business held their employees at their mercy by their power to hire and fire. It was inequality of wealth, inequality of social prestige, inequality of political rights, which had to be attacked if democracy was to be achieved. Where such inequality was tied in to the structure of the agrarian economy, an agrarian revolution had to be conducted by political means. Where the organization of industry was similarly oligarchical, again it was the instrument of the state which was used to guide the Industrial Revolution into democratic channels. Democracy could not coexist with plutocracy, whether of the factories or the farms. Alike in Great Britain and New Zealand, in the United States and Denmark, popular government was a form of political power applied to the control of economic power.

Is Democracy the Luxury of the Rich?

A second question related to the economics of democracy concerns the availability of resources. Since the physical assets of different regions vary in quality, character, and quantity, and since so many factors enter into their use by Man, any supposed connection between the existence or non-existence of resources and the adoption of a particular political system must appear tenuous and remote. However, a distinction is frequently drawn between rich countries and poor, between "haves" and "have-nots." Then it is asserted by those who justify authoritarian rule that poor countries cannot afford democracy. Democracy, they argue, is a wasteful method of government, using its resources inefficiently. Among political systems, therefore, it stands out as a luxury model. The rich can afford it, since they possess an abundance beyond their needs and do not miss what they waste. But a people who must organize scarcity and subsist marginally require discipline. What little they have must be strictly allocated and rigidly controlled. Hence, autocracy is the necessity of the poor.[4]

There are many comments to be made on this line of reasoning. To begin with, such terms as poverty or abundance are relative, not absolute. They are, in any case, linked to the size of the population. Resources which can assure plenty for five millions might be inadequate for twenty. Also, the usefulness of resources depends not only on their material character but also on social and political factors. Advances in technology, which are achieved through general education and scientific knowledge, enable us to convert to productive use the assets which were always present but of whose potentialities a former generation or another culture was unaware. Witness the contrast between North America when only the Indians had it and the same continent in 1880, or between North America and Latin America in the 1950's. As a matter of fact, there are some democracies which nowadays enjoy high living standards and which would be included in any list of prosperous and wealthy countries, but which are not endowed with abundant resources and were far from prosperous in earlier times. In Sweden, Norway, Denmark, and Switzerland, the contemporary material well-being is in no sense the "inevitable" result of a rich natural heritage. On the contrary, what the Danes, Norwegians, Swedes, and Swiss enjoy today is the result of human ingenuity and inventiveness combined with social solidarity and political capacity. What explains their high standards of living is not so much the resources lying at their feet, but the resourcefulness of their heads, their hearts, and their hands. Not only have they turned to good account the few natural advantages which they possess, but in some instances they have even converted into a benefit what otherwise would have been an adversity. The Danes, as long as they had the military strength, drew a profit from the tolls which they exacted on ships entering and leaving the Baltic. When they lost this source of revenue, as well as the provinces of Slesvig and

4. Mussolini argued in this way to justify his Fascist regime and corporative state. He contrasted the poverty of Italy with the abundance of the wealthy "capitalist" economies of the United States and Great Britain, which could afford to be democratic.

Holstein, they not only reclaimed waste land and switched from wheat to dairying and pigs, but developed some successful lines of manufacturing for foreign, as well as domestic, consumption. Their modern silverware, porcelain, and furniture are in world demand because of the quality of craftsmanship and the taste that is embodied in the style.

The Swiss have triumphed over a formidable habitat, which would have crushed a less enterprising people. For many centuries, the control of the Alpine passes meant to them what the domination of the Sound meant to Denmark. The traffic which moved between Italy and France and Germany had to pay tribute to the Swiss. But their population always pressed heavily on a limited cultivable area. Some of the surplus of able-bodied males earned an income in the sixteenth and seventeenth century by serving as mercenary soldiers in foreign armies, where the high prowess of the Swiss infantry was richly remunerated. In more modern times, the Swiss have attracted foreign currencies by exploiting their scenery and maintaining good hotels for tourists. Watch-making was traditionally localized in the slopes and valleys of the Jura, especially in Neuchâtel, where a tradition of craftsmanship was handed on to successive generations. Later, by the higher mathematics and applied technology of the Zurich Polytechnich, this process was industrialized and the watches from Swiss factories have held a unique place in the world market. In addition, because of its policy of neutrality, and sustained reputation for political orderliness, Switzerland is both the convenient center for international agencies and conferences and a haven for hoarding private capital in reliable banks.

Sweden and Norway are two other countries whose peoples now have high living standards, but who used to be poor. The mountains, forests, and long northern winters imposed severe restrictions on food production. Many of the families that subsisted on farming, fishing, or lumbering were periodically close to starvation. Indeed it was because of this chronic condition, combined with the completeness of the church registers of births and deaths, that Malthus was able to draw on Swedish statistics as evidence for his larger hypotheses about population growth and limits. Even in the middle decades of the nineteenth century, the inability of the land to feed its people, or of the cities to provide urban employment, was driving thousands of families to emigrate to newer areas of greater opportunity—e.g., to the northerly portion of America's Midwest. Only late in the last century, and in the early decades of the twentieth, did the Swedish and Norwegian economies rapidly improve both in industry and agriculture. The generation of electricity from water power provided energy for factories and railways. The iron-ore deposits were processed into the steel which has formed the basis for engineering, shipbuilding, and diverse manufactures. Scientific studies of agriculture encouraged the efficient use of the limited acreage available. All this—the result of enterprise and skill, both public and private—enabled two of the poorer nations to join the ranks of the rich.

But thus far the analysis is incomplete. Such terms as "rich" and "poor," "have" and "have not," contain an ambiguity. To what do such words refer? Or, more precisely, to which members of the community do they apply? For the sake of clarity, let us imagine a contrast between two hypothetical countries, where the population, area, and resources are approximately equal, but the social systems, forms of government, and ownership and distribution of wealth are vastly different. Assume in one case that a few persons own and control the best resources and enjoy their fruits, and are socially and politically dominant. In the other case, suppose that the most valuable resources are not monopolized by a few, but are managed and used from the standpoint of the public interest and the product is widely spread for the benefit of the whole community. In the former example a gross inequality would exist between the wealth and power of a few and the weakness and poverty of the majority. In the latter, the gap between the extremes would be much smaller; none would be excessively rich or in dire need; a common standard of security and comfort would be assured to all. Which society would you call rich, and which poor? Who are the haves? Who are the have-nots?

Clearly, if such concepts are to make sense, they should apply not only to the total amount of resources which a people possesses, but also to their utilization and the internal distribution of the proceeds. In those countries which today are described as backward, there is generally an oligarchy of wealthy people who live in superfluity amid the surrounding squalor. All the underdeveloped nations contain their quota of overdeveloped individuals. Consider the example of Brazil. In that country, vast regions of the Amazonian jungle, Mato Grosso, and the northeastern *sertão* are still extremely primitive. But in certain districts of Rio de Janeiro, only a stone's throw apart, are the most glaring contrasts between *favelas* and *apartamentos de luxu*, between well-fed people riding in Cadillacs and skinny children with bare feet. In Saudi Arabia, the patriarchal regime of a tribal society with a primitive outlook found itself the owner of an empire in oil which it lacked the techniques to exploit, and much of whose profits it squandered on the support of parasitical princes and millionaire sheiks in air-conditioned palaces. This is a kingdom where the slave traffic still flourishes, and where they punish a thief by cutting off his right hand. Twentieth-century Spain and Portugal are two countries whose backwardness in all spheres—political, social, and economic—suggests some sorry comparisons. Not only do these countries, as they now are, compare unfavorably with such Latin nations as France and Italy; but their present decadence marks a sad decline from their grandeur in the sixteenth and seventeenth centuries. There are cities in the Iberian peninsula which contain gems of civilization and among the inhabitants are individuals of high culture and dignity. But luxury and squalor, sophistication and ignorance, are close neighbors here. And the differences are still more apparent on a journey through the countryside. Travel to the Castilian plateau not fifty miles from Madrid, and you have moved five hundred years back in time.

As far as resources go—if one were to pay attention solely to physical endowment and material assets—there is no reason why Spain, Saudi Arabia, and Brazil should be so "poor," and the United States, Norway, and Switzerland so "rich." The differences that count are explicable, not by nature, but by Man. It is the social system, the economic organization, the technical knowledge, and the political will, which are always decisive. The underdeveloped countries are those in which a minority possesses a disproportionate share of the wealth. The countries with the highest living standards are the ones which have developed their greatest asset—their human resource—and have provided for the well-being of the Common Man. Development springs from knowledge and organization: knowing how to use the assets which are available, plus the proper blend of public morale with individual incentive to apply that knowledge and distribute the fruits.

High Living Standards and Democratic States

Granted, then, that it is not nature which creates the wealth of nations, but nations which put nature to social use, is there a traceable relation between the character of the political system and economic characteristics? What influence does one exercise on the other?

It has often been pointed out that the countries which enjoy the highest living standards happen also to be democratically governed. This relationship was discussed by E. D. Simon shortly before the outbreak of World War II, when he evaluated the success of the smaller democracies. "I have shown how difficult it is," he wrote, "to arrive at an accurate measure of the standard of living of the whole of the people, but few economists would doubt that the following grouping as to the standards of living of the most prosperous countries in the world today is substantially correct. Group I: the United States, Canada, Australia, New Zealand. Group II: Norway, Sweden, Denmark, Switzerland, England, Holland. Group III: includes Finland, Germany, Italy."[5] The significant feature in this classification is that all the countries in the first two groups were democracies. Those which had dictatorial regimes did not rank higher than the third group. The question naturally arises then whether there was a causal connection between democracy and high living standards. Were the countries of the first two groups democracies because their standards of living were high, or was their standard high because their politics were democratic? Simon examined five countries, all of them small and peaceful—namely, Denmark, Finland, Norway, Sweden, and Switzerland. He then concluded that there are "four important reasons" for their success as democracies, one of which he lists as "economic security and well-being."[6]

A more elaborate inquiry into the same topic has recently been undertaken by Seymour M. Lipset.[7] Using the statistical data contained in reports and yearbooks of the United Nations, he has classified political systems on a scale and correlated them with various indices of economic growth and social maturity. The latter include such criteria as the following: per capita income; thousands of persons per doctor; persons per motor vehicle; telephones, radios, and newspaper copies per thousand persons; and measures of industrialization, education, and urbanization. As for political categories, he divides the "European and English-speaking Nations" into the two groups of "stable democracies" and "unstable democracies and dictatorships," and the "Latin American Nations" into two other groupings of "democracies and unstable dictatorships" and "stable dictatorships."[8] According to his findings, the countries that rank highest on the ladder of material possessions, social advance, and industrial development are also the ones which have the stable democratic governments. In those that rank lowest, dictatorships have predominated continuously. What inference should we draw from these facts? That a correlation exists is beyond dispute. But correlation and causation are not the same. We may observe that various factors are connected together, but we still may not know what causes what. Either proposition is arguable;

5. E. D. Simon, *The Smaller Democracies* (London: Gollancz, 1939), p. 172.
6. The others are: "their small size, a long period of peace, and the cool climate of the north." *op. cit.*, p. 184.
7. *Political Man* (New York: Doubleday, 1960), pp. 45-75.
8. The placing of certain countries within these categories is open to question. I doubt that Belgium should be included, alongside of Denmark and Switzerland, under the "stable democracies." Nor does it seem realistic to classify Iceland and France in a group of "unstable democracies and dictatorships" which also embraces Albania and the U.S.S.R. *Op. cit.*, p. 49.

that democratic politics are the result of specific economic and social developments, or that the latter are the consequences of democracy. Or again it is possible that there is no prime or initial cause, that all the factors within the cluster interact and undergo mutual and simultaneous change.

A Warning About Causal Inferences

This problem, because of its intrinsic importance, presents a challenge to the social scientist and, because of its intricacy, will always be difficult to resolve with certainty. The difficulty arises from the complexity of the factors whose interrelations must be traced, and from an ambiguity in the notion of causation itself. When we speak of x causing y, our statement may have one of two meanings. Sometimes we appear to mean that the presence of x has helped to produce the result, or has contributed to the emergence of y. At other times, we can mean that x was necessary for y to occur, in the sense that without y there would have been no x. In the former connotation, a cause is a contributing influence; in the latter, it is a necessary determinant. Nor is this all. Since an argument about social causation is not a statement of fact, but an inference about a relation between facts, we need not only to look forward from the cause to its presumed consequence, but also backward from the consequence to its possible cause. From a given situation called x, there might ensue a variety of actions, namely w, y, or z. If in fact it is y which follows, not w or z, we may be right in suggesting that x was the cause of y. But this should not be taken to imply that y was necessitated by x, in that only y could follow after x and that neither w nor z could have occurred. Even when we feel tolerably sure that y has resulted from x, we are still not positive that y, and y alone, had to be the consequence of x. Indeed, in all these assumptions and inferences which we call causation, only one point can ever be affirmed with any certainty. That is the chronological aspect of the relationship, which is of course a matter of historical verification. If we argue that y was the consequence of x, we are (among other things) implying a time sequence between x and y and affirming that y was the later of the two. It is always much easier negatively to disprove an assumed causal relationship than to prove it positively, and the most convincing line of disproof is to demonstrate that the "consequence" took place before its "cause."

Such caveats and distinctions may help us to avoid some patent errors and reach certain valid conclusions. In the first place, one should not argue that democracy is impossible unless high living standards exist.

There is, as was already noted, a history of democracy prior to the attainment of twentieth-century levels of comfort. Democracy is not merely an outcropping of the private ownership of automobiles, telephones, and television. Some communities had organized themselves democratically when they were far less affluent than they are today. Second, we may note that a community can rank among the leaders on all the indices of economic, social, and technological progress, and yet its government may be thoroughly authoritarian. The most barbaric of all regimes to hold power in an important country in the twentieth century has been that of the Nazis in Germany. But on the figures for industrial production, urbanization, literacy, and higher education, Germany has been very advanced. Clearly then, although material progress may create some of the conditions which support a democratic government, the latter does not necessarily follow from the former. What we can infer from the German case is this: conditions which have combined elsewhere with democracy were outweighed in this case by other circumstances which converted the results of industry and education to anti-democratic ends.[9]

The growth of industry, cities, and literacy, as well as the spread of telephones, automobiles, and other consumption goods, are phenomena which occur gradually and take at least two generations before their full results are felt. The same is true of democracy. This too may start with revolution, but it continues through evolution. At certain stages in the history of modern states, the social and economic changes were occurring simultaneously with the political. In some specific instances, it is possible to point to technological inventions or a rising volume of production which take place before a given political reform. In other cases there are political advances which predate a significant jump or leap in the economy.

For examples, contrast the sequence of events in Great Britain and the United States. Industrialization commenced in Britain at a time when its system of government was still oligarchical in its essentials. Whatever dates one ascribes to such processes, at least one can say that democracy did not reach maturity in that country until after the second and third Reform Acts (1867 and 1884, respectively), which extended voting rights to the majority of adult males. On the other hand, the conquest of illiteracy came after these developments, rather than before them.[10] Not until the Education Act of 1870 was a national policy adopted of establishing public primary schools throughout the country, and even these were designed at first merely to fill in the gaps between the already-existing

9. Joseph Goebbels had a clubfoot, and a Ph.D. from Heidelberg. The prejudices derived from his emotions directed a superior trained intellect into evil work.

10. Except in Scotland, which in the field of education was always ahead of England.

private schools, both ecclesiastical and secular. Only in 1880 was primary education made compulsory for all. Nor were fees abolished in the elementary schools until 1891. With the widening of the franchise, the British middle class acted on the prudent counsel of Robert Lowe: "We must educate our masters."[11] But for millions, the right to acquire "the three R's" came after they had acquired the right to vote. Since it takes time to build schools and educate the children, and then for those children to come of age and begin voting, it was not until the twentieth century—say, in the elections of 1910 or the "khaki election" of 1918—that a majority of adults went to the polls and that majority was literate. In the United States, however, both the sequence and the timing were different. The United States[12] was at least a generation ahead of Great Britain in extending the suffrage and the public elementary schools, but lagged a generation behind in urbanization and industry. In this country, to venture a broad generalization, the advent of political and social democracy predated the period of rapid economic progress. In Great Britain, it was the consequences of economic change which stimulated political progress which in turn produced social reforms.

Thus, the complexity of the historical facts and the differences between various countries should rule out any simple notion of causation. To argue that democracy leads to high living standards, or, in reverse, that the latter lead to democracy, is to assert both too much and too little. Too much, because either assumption would suggest a constant flow in the same direction from cause to consequence; too little, because each statement omits the possible influence of more factors than the one specifically stated. No doctrine of economic determinism can explain the advent of democracy because no clustering of economic conditions necessitates a particular political result. If instead of "determine" and "necessitate" one uses such words as "influence" and "contribute," then it makes some sense to argue that a general rise in living standards and a widespread distribution of an increase in wealth can bring political consequences in two ways. Materially, where more people own at least some property, they have something to conserve and are therefore less disposed to extremist attitudes and violent actions—both of which militate against democracy.

11. When the bill which became the Education Act of 1870 was being debated, the argument was used that Prussia had beaten Austria in 1860 because of the superiority of its education. The schoolmaster, as well as Bismarck, received credit for the victory. Democratic Britain was to learn from autocratic Prussia!

12. This statement applies more to the North and the West than to the South. Slavery was abolished in the British Empire three decades before President Lincoln's Emancipation Proclamation.

Psychologically, where the basic needs of food, clothing, and shelter are satisfied with a reasonable amount of comfort, the resulting sense of security promotes a tendency to compromise and moderation.

But there is a converse to these relationships which requires stating. Too often, democracy is scrutinized and interpreted as if its political character derived from economic or social conditions. This is a one-sided way of looking at the facts. Politics exercise their own original force within the community no less decidedly than the economy, the culture, or what have you. The ideals and institutions of government have their effect on other aspects of society at least as profound as any that operates in reverse. If the notion of economic determinism be an error because it exaggerates some features of the truth, a doctrine of political determinism would be a similar error. But just as many true facts could be selected to justify a contention of the latter type as have been employed to substantiate the former. The higher living standards and more widespread distribution of material amenities which exist in the advanced democracies are attributable in no small measure to political factors. Alike in the smaller democracies and the larger, the positive policies of governments consistently applied during the last sixty years or more have helped to increase the total amount of wealth in the community and to share its proceeds more evenly than in past centuries. From the standpoint of democracy, what counts primarily in a community is not whether, *in toto*, it is poor or wealthy, but whether such wealth as it does possess is fairly distributed and is ultimately controlled for the public interest. The relevant criterion is how the wealth is shared, rather than how much wealth there is. The economic prerequisite of democracy is not abundance but equality, not affluence but justice.

Capitalism, Socialism, and Democratic Government

Much of this same reasoning can be applied to a still more contentious problem. During the last hundred years, in all discussions of the politics and economics of democracy, no question has been more vehemently contested than the merits or demerits of capitalism and socialism. Scholarly research, polemical tracts, party manifestoes, and electoral campaigns have explored all sides to this controversy. Facts and fantasy, dogmas and doubt, principles and propaganda, have been liberally sprinkled across a debate which has enlisted the intellect and passions of opposing groups to a degree seldom equalled in the history of ideological conflict. To search for parallels, one calls to mind the Arian controversy within the early

Christian Church, the bitter medieval disputes of nominalists and realists and the struggles between *imperium* and *sacerdotium*, the deadly antagonism of Protestant and Catholic, and the challenge of scientific experiment to religious creed. In all of those classic feuds, there was the same strange medley of the rational and irrational, the clashing of men in their combat over ideas, the dissent of individuals from organized orthodoxy, and lengthy lists of prophets, martyrs, and inquisitors.

Naturally, what gives an intensity to this modern controversy is the importance of the material interests involved. Both socialism and capitalism have definite views on how the economy should be organized if it is to function at its best. But both are more than economic doctrines. They also express or imply an attitude towards public policy and a preference among social values. Hence the debate over capitalism and socialism is directly relevant to the fortunes of democracy. Not only does each of these economic systems involve a wide range of political presuppositions, but in addition the flowering of modern democracy has been contemporaneous with both movements.

Various queries therefore are pertinent for this analysis: What is the relation between democracy and capitalism or socialism? Is either of these a prerequisite for democracy? Can both be made compatible with it, or not? What can we learn today from accumulated practical experience after a hundred years of thrashing out the pros and cons of this issue?

There is no lack of dogmatic answers to such questions. Authorities of equal weight can be heaped up on each side of the scale. To chronicle the names and the literature would make a grandiose series of footnotes which could not fail to impress a reader. Adam Smith and Robert Owen might start the list; Marx and Mill, Spencer and Proudhon, would follow. Eduard Bernstein and Henry George, Lenin and Coolidge, Sombart and the Webbs, Brandeis and Keynes, belong in the catalogue, as do Laski and Von Mises, Hayek and Galbraith. The roll of fame might be continued indefinitely, and the pairings are not intended to embarrass. The arguments on each side, as befits such names, are not without cogency. Proponents of capitalism frequently say that it is essential to democracy and that democracy is essential to it. They assert that the same social principles—especially, the emphasis on liberty and the primacy of the individual—underlie the economics of the one and the politics of the other. The two, therefore, as they conclude, are mutually reinforcing. Either would fall without its counterpart. Neither can be reconciled with an alternative system.

To this, the socialists argue the contrary. They contend that capitalism is inimical to democracy, because, whatever its aims, its results are undemocratic. Socialism, they maintain, places the public interest or general welfare ahead of the particular interests of private individuals or organizations. Moreover, socialists consider that equality deserves as much stress as liberty and that people will receive more equal treatment under socialism than under capitalism.

Some of the points in debate are concerned with technical economic matters which lie beyond the scope of this discussion. But the political problems are central and important. Foremost among these is the question of power. Since it is the purpose of the economy to produce and distribute wealth, whoever has control over economic institutions will influence decisively the opportunity for others to earn a living and to acquire a share of material possessions. If those in control are private individuals or private corporations, how does a single employee protect himself against arbitrary decisions by his employers? Likewise, how is the consuming public protected? The conventional answers to such questions are well known. The trade union protects the employee; competition safeguards the public. But experience shows that in certain cases these defenses are insufficient. The officials of a trade union may become corrupt. They may exercise autocratic power over their members instead of being responsible to them. Indeed the public may sometimes find itself at the mercy of a wealthy clique in a big corporation, which the mass of the shareholders do not control in fact, or of the bureaucrats or bosses of a large union who dominate the "rank and file." Shall we then say that the public interest, shall we say that democracy, is the result of a power struggle between two oligarchies?

And what about the other answer, that the interests of the consumers (i.e., of the whole public, since we are all consumers) are guarded against possible greed or tyranny or stupidity of producers by the virtue of competition? The reply has merit, insofar as and so long as men actually do compete. But suppose competition is extinguished. Suppose that, instead of the "free market" of individual entrepreneurs, there are corporate giants which construct financial and industrial empires. Suppose that oligopolies, and then monopolies, take over. Trusts and cartels can fix prices by mutual agreement, carve up markets, crush interlopers, and supply or deny a service or commodity—all in the name of an economic holy trinity: "free," "individual," "enterprise." What price democracy then? The ideas of the classical economists, which influenced so much of public policy in the western world during the nineteenth century, were entirely consistent with democracy, provided that two of their basic assumptions were fulfilled. There had to be genuine competition, and it had to be conducted between individuals.[13] But where much of the economy lies in the hands of huge corporate systems staffed by "organization men," the original doctrine no longer has the same meaning.

When the realities of the economy no longer conformed to its philosophy, two remedies or correctives were possible. Either the facts had to be readjusted to fit the philosophy, or new ideals had to be sought which would corespond more closely to the facts. The former method is the one which the United States attempted in the anti-trust legislation. The aim of the Sherman and Clayton Acts and their enforcing agency in the Justice Department was to restore competition in those sectors of the economy where it had ceased to exist. To protect the individual against an excessive accumulation of power, the power would be broken up and competition, it was hoped, would once more prevail. The alternative was to admit that in some fields the individual could not function and even that competition between rival institutions was neither possible nor desirable. There are some services on which an entire community depends (e.g., the supply of water, electricity and gas, or the telephone) and some commodities whose production requires a vast outlay of capital and an intricate organization of men (e.g., railroads and airlines, coal or steel). In such cases, either the ownership could be acquired by the state and the enterprise be conducted by the government; or the ownership and operation could rest in private hands, but the government could supervise and regulate.

In each of the policies thus outlined, the state was called upon to play the major role and perform a positive function. This is true even in the extreme case, that of anti-monopoly legislation, where the public authority is used to restore competition to the private sector. The classic arguments of economic liberalism, which sought to confine the state to a minimal sphere of bare essentials, have become irrelevant in the twentieth century. Indeed the entire balance of the argument has shifted in modern times. Instead of posing the question in terms of "how little can we safely entrust to the state," what we are nowadays debating is how much we can safely afford to keep the state from doing. The powers of the state have been increasingly invoked both to protect weaker individuals from stronger ones and from the big private organizations and to guard the public interest when such organizations are locked in combat.

13. Joseph A. Schumpeter has remarked that "there exists no more democratic institution than a market." *Capitalism, Socialism, and Democracy* (Harper & Bros.; New York, 1950), 3rd ed., p. 184. This is true—for those who possess equal amounts to spend or invest.

The Dilemma of Liberalism

By the same logic, the classic argument of political liberalism faced a contradiction. All liberals are democrats, though not all democrats are liberals. Many of these who fought the early battles both for liberalism and for democracy viewed the state as a major enemy because its traditional organization and spirit was undemocratic. Their revolution was therefore conducted against the state—not only against a state as controlled by certain men who pursued certain policies but against any state as an institution wielding power and using force within society. The way to protect the individual from the tyranny of the state was to diminish its power by limiting its functions. The less there was for it to do, the less the danger of abuse. But power, which develops through people organizing to achieve their goals, resembles the movement of water downhill. You may divert it from one direction to another; you may dam and store it and regulate its flow; but it must find some place to go. Likewise in society, the power that is diverted from one sector or is checked by a countervailing force does not disappear. The problem of its use and flow remains. The evaporation of public power merely left a vacant field for private power to occupy, and a philosophy conceived in the name of equal liberties for all resulted in exposing the weak to the unequal freedoms of the strong. Hence the powers of the state were reasserted, and democracy came to grips with a new reality: the reinstitution of public power in the state, large in scope and formidable in potentiality. Ever since that time, liberalism has suffered a split personality. Should it continue to insist on the minimal state, or should it come to terms with the maximal state? The pressures of democracy were in any case enlarging the functions of government in every decade. There were social demands for the elimination of class distinctions; economic demands for an improvement in the condition of the poor; political demands for the universal right of all adults to participate in politics. The new state had to be strong enough to protect everybody against the power of strong individuals and strong private organizations. But what of the need for protection against the state itself? The liberal dilemma remained, because the phenomenon of power had merely reappeared in a new guise. Who would control the controllers? Could the people adequately protect themselves, if necessary, against the very institution whose powers had been expanded to serve them?

That the dangers are real, and not imaginary, has been proven by the experience of the two most ruthless tyrannies of the twentieth century—Hitler's dictatorship in Germany and Stalin's in the Soviet Union. Although one was fascist and the other communist, the two had much in common. Both extended the powers of the state to an unparalleled degree. Both crushed every kind of domestic opposition. Both murdered human beings by the million. Both exalted, and virtually deified, the qualities of one man. Both used the term "socialism" in their official titles.[14] The history of those two appalling dictatorships shows that the complete concentration of all power, political and economic, in the hands of a clique dominated by a callous egomaniac results in mass enslavement. But there are two fundamental differences between what the Nazis and Communists have called "socialism" and the other brand of socialism that is practiced in Scandinavia, Great Britain, or Australia and New Zealand. First there is a difference in the volume of functions undertaken by the state. In the countries just named, the state does not try to conduct or control everything. The aim of the government is to do whatever is in the public interest, but to leave the rest alone. A second crucial difference is political. The constitutional systems of these countries are democratic. Opposition is legal and open. Rival parties compete for power. Changes occur periodically in the men who control the government and the policies they pursue. There is no tyranny under such conditions because the opportunities for criticism and publicity impose a moderation on the holders of office. Democracy therefore provides a corrective to the excessive powers of the state. Dictatorship, however, from Left or Right, compounds those powers into tyranny. Socialism, when joined to democracy, can be just as safe for the people as capitalism.

Apart from power, another point at issue in the battle of the Isms was the attainment of equality. Equality has many connotations, but in this controversy all of them converged. The founders of democracy attacked the systems that restricted the opportunity for participation in politics to a few. At the same time they opposed all social discrimination based on distinctions of family and class. When capitalism was wedded to industrialism, the inequalities of wealth became, or seemed, more glaring. Either the traditional elite augmented its fortunes or newly rich families emerged. In either case, new or old, plutocracies flourished and, where unrestrained, compounded the earlier kinds of inequality. Laissez-faire capitalism did contain an egalitarian element in its theory. Emphasizing the role of the individual, the doctrine insisted on equal opportunities for all. But as happens in a race, it was expected that those who started from the same line would finish unequally. Moreover, since the individual is born into a family and, as a child, is brought up by parents, people are

14. National Socialism and the Union of Soviet Socialist Republics.

not in fact equal at the beginning of the race. Ofter it is the position and wealth of the family that broaden or restrict the opportunities of the individual.

When luxury and poverty coexisted in the same society, as in the United States or the United Kingdom at the end of the nineteenth century, the proponents of unregulated capitalism gave the answers that the poor were responsible for their poverty, but the system provided a chance to escape that condition. There were indeed some individuals who personified the "rags to riches" myth (Andrew Carnegie, for example). But there were far too many—millions, in fact—for whom the rags remained permanent. Against this, the socialists inveighed with argument and passion. The emotional content of their case should not be ignored because it suffused and colored their doctrine, lending conviction to their logic and sometimes distortion, but always strengthening its intensity. For socialism was not only an economic theory and a political program. Fundamentally it was an ethical protest. It declaimed against social injustice. It asserted that inequalities were not always attributable to the individuals concerned. There were many undeserving poor; there were many unworthy rich. No invisible hand, as Adam Smith had believed, was correcting the system. Private inequities must be removed by public policy; policy meant politics; and politics meant state action. If all men were created equal, could they not be legislated equal?

The Modern Mixed Economies

So much for issues and arguments. Now it is time to view the results. A debate over principles is valuable in projecting tendencies and formulating goals. But in an ultimate sense the logic which counts the most is that of experience. How have the Isms emerged from their century-long encounter? What is their present-day relation to democracy?

The outcome of the opposition between capitalism and socialism has not been a victory for either, but a blending of the two. What actually exists nowadays in all the democracies is a mixture of state and private activity. Public ownership and operation has been considerably extended, but privately owned enterprises still prevail throughout most of the economy. In certain spheres monopolies exist, either state owned or privately owned under state regulation. Elsewhere competition continues, limited in certain categories but open in others. There are also some instances of competition between state and private organizations operating in the same field. The significant discussion nowadays is not between theoretical antitheses. It concerns specific and practical questions. How should this or that aspect of the economy be organized and managed? How should public and private activity be blended? In what proportions should they be mixed? In the mid twentieth century the politics of our economic systems have moved from confrontation of broad principles to practical judgments about detail and degree. The British Prime Minister, Harold Macmillan, stated after his party's electoral victory in 1959, "The class war is dead." In essentials, he was correct. Although the old language is still employed in contemporary speechmaking and editorials, to become excited over capitalism and socialism today is the proverbial flogging of the dead horse. This does not mean, however, that all the systems now functioning in the western democracies have reached a common denominator or that their basic features are identical. As a matter of fact, they exhibit many variations in social and economic policy. There are different characteristics in their respective blends of public and private activity, and differences therefore in general character. The reasons for these, and the results, are worth exploring.

Public Ownership

In the democracies of western Europe and the South Pacific, the modern state generally owns and manages the principal services and utilities on which everybody depends. Besides such older functions of government as the currency and mails, the modern list includes the central bank, telephones and telegraph, radio and television, the supply of water, gas, and electricity, the railroads and canals, and, usually, the airlines. Some shipping lines are run by the state, and various private ones receive a state subsidy. Every state has entered the insurance field in one way or another. It supports those who suffer a temporary loss of income through illness or unemployment, and pays pensions to the aged. Certain governments also sell life and fire insurance on a commercial basis. Likewise in manufacturing, the extractive industries, and the marketing of some basic commodities, the modern democratic state is frequently active as producer and salesman. The coal mines of Great Britain, the Renault automobile works in France, the Norwegian steel industry, some of the forest and lumber mills in New Zealand, grain storage elevators in Canada—these are a few random examples of enterprises which the state conducts.

This summary reveals an underlying pattern which is intentional along with some haphazard features which owe more to history than logic. Twentieth-century democracies have found it necessary for the state to control their currency and credit, communications, transportation, and sources of energy. They have also guaranteed to their citizens a minimum level of financial security against economic or physical misfortune. Beyond these common objectives, the state has done whatever the circumstances demanded. The policies inaugurated in the name of socialism have been due more to the compulsions of a felt need than to those of philosophical doctrine. Thus the British government nationalized the coal mines and the railroads (in 1946 and 1947) because each industry was basic and sick. To bring the plant and equipment up to date required an outlay of capital which only the state could supply. Both industries had suffered in competition with other types of fuel and transport. Both needed to improve the relations between labor and management. When New Zealand inaugurated many state enterprises in the period between 1865 and the end of the century, this was because little private capital was available there for such an investment. If the economy was to be developed and the colonists were to enjoy adequate services, the state had to be the entrepreneur. Private owners initiated the Swiss railroads as a few separate lines connecting some of the major cities. But in order to complete a unified network, to traverse the mountains and build tunnels through the Alps, the federal government had to buy out the private lines and construct the remainder of the system.

It is impossible to say with any precision how much of the economy in such countries is now owned by the state. The figures for capital value offer some guide, though these are often little better than "guesstimates." Another clue is provided by the number of public employees in a country, expressed as a percentage of the total who are gainfully occupied. In Great Britain, for example, two million people, representing 8 per cent of all industrial employees, were employed in 1962-63 by the various nationalized industries. The net output of those industries in the same year was estimated at 10 per cent of the gross domestic product. To complete the picture, one would have to add the enterprises which are municipally owned; also, the figures for non-industrial employment would cover the members of the civil services, both central and local, the armed services, and the state teachers. Hence, some authorities have suggested that in Great Britain, and similarly in France, as much as one-fifth of the economy belongs to the state. For a country so highly socialized as New Zealand, I have calculated that 24 per cent of all gainfully employed persons are working for either the central government or local bodies.[15] Without too much exaggeration, one may conclude that in certain modern democ-

15. In *The Politics of Equality* (University of Chicago Press: Chicago, 1948), pp. 368-9.

racies up to one-fifth of the economy is owned by the public while the rest remains in private hands.

The question naturally arises whether this proportion will continue, or whether the public sector is likely to increase. In general, there is no strong demand in either western Europe or the South Pacific for any significant extensions of public ownership. The majority of the British Labour party are content with what was accomplished between 1945 and 1950, and they recognize that the voters did not respond with enthusiasm in 1955 and 1959 to proposals for more nationalization. Instead of more complete "socialization of the means of production, distribution, and exchange," the Labourites have now settled for the control of "the commanding heights of the economy." A similar development has occurred in the Social Democratic and Socialist parties of the European Continent. The West German Social Democrats have traveled a long way from Marx and Kautsky, and now draw more of their inspiration from Bernstein. They are less concerned today with the title deeds of ownership than with the social distribution of the product. Likewise in Scandinavia, the Danish and Swedish Social Democrats, whose parties have normally been the strongest in the legislature these last two decades, no longer advocate an extension of state ownership. Even in Norway, where the Labor party had a majority in the Storting for over two decades, nationalization is viewed as an accomplished fact rather than as tomorrow's dream.

What does this mean? Has an ideal lost its glamor? Have the doctrinaires grown into pragmatists? Have the visionaries come down to earth? There are some of these elements in the answer, but there is also more. Fundamentally, the socialists of western Europe are evolutionaries, not revolutionaries. Men like Branting and Erlander, Stauning and Hansen, Blum and Attlee, have exercised power with a sensible moderation. They have been disposed to find specific remedies for specific abuses. They have not expected to write a blueprint for a brave new world. Nor on the other hand, have they stood by idly when the authority of the state could be used to produce an economic result.

Experience is always the best test for a theory. Although the meanings of capitalism and socialism embrace more than the form of ownership, nevertheless a preference for either private or public activity is one of the important elements at issue. What has been the actual experience of those societies where the state now owns one-fifth of the economy? From the standpoint of the doctrinal purists on both sides, the results are disappointing because they are somewhat inconclusive. If a system has been operating for a length of time, what one observes is no longer an Ism— i.e., an abstraction—but a specific organization applied to a sector of the economy. In discussing an abstraction, it is easier to generalize because one is unimpeded by the authority of the facts. When concrete cases are examined, the sweeping judgment, though always tempting and often persuasive, does not accurately portray reality. Pure theory demands logical consistency. Empirical research discovers the contradictions within the actual.

The truth appears to be that, for efficiency in operation and service to the general public, there is little to choose between private and public ownership, as such. Assuredly, when particular cases are compared differences reveal themselves. But it is not true that all the "good" cases fall under one category of ownership, and all the "bad" ones under the other. Successful and unsuccessful enterprises may be found in private hands and in the domain of the state, indiscriminately. There are other factors which account for the differences and which seem to count for more than the mere form of ownership. One of these, for example, is the economic health or sickness of the industry itself. Railroads today are in trouble practically everywhere because they require a huge initial expenditure of capital for construction and big continuous outlays for maintenance, and they suffer the competition of airlines and highways. Whether the system belongs to private corporations as in the United States or to the state as in Great Britain, it is unlikely to yield a profit. If a telephone service is provided in a populous metropolitan region, the number of subscribers and the volume of calls should enable any system, irrespective of who owns and operates it, to run efficiently and profitably. But how is anybody to maintain a high level of service and profit for a small population thinly spread over an extensive area? In the latter case, any decision to provide a service of a quality comparable to that of a large city would be based on political grounds or on those of social utility, not on an economic calculation.

When I lived in New Zealand and had the opportunity to observe its government, I well remember how the departments differed in their efficiency and general reputation, even though they were responsible to one and the same cabinet. The Post Office, which conducted a whole range of services for the public, was fairly well run. On the other hand, the railways had been kicked around on the political football field for many decades and were in a sorry condition. In the capital city of Wellington, the municipality operated the streetcars and buses. The service was none too impressive, and relations between the City Council and the trade union were notoriously bad. By contrast, the same city had a virtual monopoly of the supply and sale of milk, and this particular service was a model of excellence.

Exactly the same opposites can be found in the domain of private ownership. The doctrine that such a system always leads, through initiative and competition, to efficiency and quality is an aspiration or a dream. Often it is far removed from the actual. In reality, there are some instances of particular corporations which genuinely serve the public, are progressive, and are efficiently run. In those cases, they are entitled to their profit in return for the services they render. But there are just as many of the opposite character, which are bureaucratic, stagnant, and inconsiderate of the consuming public. To defend the latter firms in the name of "free" "individual" "enterprise" does violence to the facts and to good sense. Experience seems to show that in terms of actual operation there is nothing inherently good or bad about either public or private ownership *per se*. What does matter is whether the industry or service in question is economically healthy or sick, whether its power and importance in relation to the community as a whole subordinates its private character to the public interest, and whether its earlier history of growth and organization have imparted a beneficial tradition. For these reasons, and perhaps others, the question of the form of ownership has ceased to be as controversial as it once was.[16]

The Social Services

The extension of the social services is another topic which nowadays normally consumes less printer's ink and oratorical fervor than it did in the past. In a modern democracy, with its universal franchise and mass electorate, it is politically necessary to use the state to help the poor, the sick, the aged, and others who are in need. No major party can ignore the number of votes which such groups cast. But this is to express the facts of political life in terms which, though realistic, are a trifle crude. There is more justification for the welfare state than the requirement of electoral victory. The voters at large are the people who compose a community, and their ethical outlook determines the prevailing sense of social justice. An opinion which is politic or expedient may coincide with one which is humane and right. As a society rises to higher levels of civilization, one does not leave the victims of economic or physical maladies to the mercy of "market forces," or the charity of strangers, or the generosity of relatives who may be unable or unwilling to support the needy. In addition, the test of a civilization consists in the care it bestows on all its

16. This generalization does not apply to the United States, which is discussed on pp. 263 ff.

citizens, not merely on the grace and culture of a fortunate few. A mature community establishes minimal standards below which no individual should fall, and a measure of its progress is seen in the continuous effort to raise such minima. Hence, the quality and quantity of housing, education, and medical care are among the criteria for judging the "good society."

When present-day democracies are examined from this standpoint, they appear in their most favorable light. Indeed one may hazard the judgment that in no political system known to history have the goals of social justice been more sedulously sought and applied than in the democracies which in the twentieth century have embraced the welfare state. As in the choice between public or private ownership, the debate has now shifted from the principles to the details. For this reason, it is intellectually less stimulating, but socially more constructive. The themes which Mill or Spencer explored have given way to the more mundane and specific aspects of classification, administration, and finance. Shall the school-leaving age be fifteen, sixteen, or seventeen, and for what types of students? Shall old-age benefits be granted universally as a right, or to the neediest through a means test? For public insurance against unemployment or sickness, how much should be contributed by employees, by their employers, by the state? Should tenants in public-housing projects have the opportunity eventually to own the houses they occupy? In a comprehensive state medical scheme, should a doctor be remunerated by receiving a fixed amount annually for each patient on his register or a fee for each particular visit? Such decisions are far from unimportant, but they involve alternatives within an agreed system, and not a choice about the system itself.

In the sphere of the social services, therefore, public opinion and governmental policy are primarily concerned with filling the gaps and removing inequities between groups of different occupation, age, or income. Thus the Swedes in the late 1950's were embroiled in a political controversy over whether the state should introduce a superannuation plan for salaried white-collar personnel in private employment. The Danes have had an acute shortage of housing in the capital city and its suburbs, where a quarter of the country's population are concentrated. To augment the supply of dwellings, all manner of programs have been attempted: e.g., direct construction by the central government or by municipalities and building loans at low interest to trade unions, co-operatives, and other associations. Great Britain has yet to resolve some fundamental questions in the field of education. The school system is still a dual one. The private schools charge expensive fees; and the best of them not only maintain a high standard, but also possess superior social prestige. The great majority of the children go to schools which are supported out of central and local taxation. These schools vary considerably in quality and in curriculum, and some of them are now seeking "parity of esteem" with the better private schools. To date, the division between the two branches of the system has tended to prolong the class distinctions of English society. It continues to be easier for those with more wealth or the right connections to secure a better education for their children.

The relation between democracy and the social services is clear and close. Historically, they evolved, grew up, and have matured together. The achievement of political democracy, expressed in the extension of the suffrage, speeded the advent of the welfare state whose functions have contributed to social democracy.[17] The latter, in turn, has reinforced its political base.

Notwithstanding—or, perhaps, because of—this connection, the welfare state continues to receive its full share of criticism. This comes from different sources, and is inspired by different motives, some of which are quite obvious. But taking what the critics say at its face value, the principal objections run along the following lines. There are some who dislike the welfare state precisely because they reject the notion of equality which it is designed to promote. If you hold an elitist position and divide the human race into the superior few and the inferior many, you will conclude that it is stupid and wrong to provide the latter with services which they are unfitted to receive. Such a view condemns not only the welfare state, but the basic assumptions of democracy. Intelligently formulated, it is the case for aristocracy. Crudely expressed, it is the doctrine of fascism.

Another objection is directed, not against the social services as such, but against having them undertaken by the state. In other words, some feel that it is right and proper to enlarge the sphere of human welfare, both materially and culturally, but consider that this function is better left to the churches or to other forms of private association. Herbert Spencer is dead, but his ghost still speaks through living mouths. The fundamental answer to this contention is that no congeries of private arrangements can add up to a complete program. It will always leave gaps, and large groups will lack adequate housing and education and insurance and medical care. Only the state, because it is the one social institution which has a public responsibility, can care for everybody.

A third criticism is leveled at the mounting cost of the social services.

17. Not all welfare states, however, were produced by democratic regimes. There are many instances of benevolent paternalism conducted by authoritarian governments. On the European continent, Bismarck was a pioneer in certain fields of social security.

Each year they are accused of absorbing more money, and therefore consuming more taxes—both of which points are factually correct. The critics then argue that the financial burden has already become excessive, and that its weight will probably increase. The system, as experience shows, develops a cumulative momentum and generates strong political pressures for extensions and additions. Whether the price we are paying for social services is too high is a matter of opinion, not of fact, and the opinion rests on more factors than an actuarial calculation. Those who are least enthusiastic about the welfare state are usually wealthy individuals who do not personally depend on the state for such services and who pay in taxes to benefit others. What the welfare state costs the community as a whole is usually very small in comparison with the price of military security, which is by far the most expensive of all functions of government. Yet many who consistently oppose the social services on the ground that they cost too much willingly support huge appropriations for tanks, bombers, and missiles. Basically, however, the welfare state is justified not by such comparisons but in terms of its positive contribution to social and individual improvement. No balance sheet can express statistically how individuals are helped to develop their abilities, how they are saved from calamities, and how they are enabled to live with greater comfort and dignity. Throughout all previous centuries, the sheer wastage of human talent has been one of the worst shortcomings of our civilization. The welfare state is eliminating much of that waste.

Planning and Regulation

Apart from public ownership and social services, the state confronts the economy in yet a third relation—that of planning or control. About this there is more uncertainty and room for reasonable disagreement. What can the state sensibly and usefully do in regulating the privately owned sector of the economy? How can it promote economic health in the form of high productivity and full employment, or guard against such economic maladies as prolonged mass unemployment and low productivity? And what bearing does this have on democracy?

To begin with the last question, it is a fact that our economic development gives rise to situations which affect the interests of millions. Business activity may proceed in cyclical fashion with recurrent booms and slumps and an occasional severe depression. Major technological changes may crack the foundations of an older industry (e.g., coal-mining or railroads) and introduce new rivals (e.g., oil, automobiles, airplanes). The accumulation of great power by a big corporation or a big trade union can pose a threat to everybody if such power is abused. Also the interdependence of economies through imports and exports involves their respective governments in negotiations on trade and tariffs, access to raw materials, opportunities for investment, and the like. When economic conditions create a common concern, they generate a political demand to which the government must respond. In a democracy, this is expressed through the media of public opinion, the policies of political parties, and the actions of voters. Individuals who are organized around an interest constitute a political fact. When in addition they are emotionally stirred because of their jobs, their property, or the security of their families, the organization becomes a vehicle for action.

But it is one thing to assert that prosperity, full employment, higher standards of living, are desirable objectives, it is another to decide what techniques to use, when to employ them, and in what degree. These are questions which depend both on knowledge and practical judgment—and, be it added, on no small measure of luck! Nor are the factors which enter into the calculation solely economic in character, although admittedly the economic element looms large. Social and political goals are intertwined with the strictly economic, contributing alike to the complexity and fascination of the art of governing men. Suffice it to say that those in office in a democratic milieu will cope with emergencies or widespread conditions by whatever measures seem likely to succeed—any theory or doctrine notwithstanding. But at the same time, a government is also impelled to act in certain ways because of its attachment to a philosophy. For instance, those who call themselves socialists may believe it right to nationalize an industry, and capitalists may think it good to have the budget balance at the end of each twelve months. Either notion can be a sensible one, depending on the circumstances to which it is applied. But to treat either policy as an economic Eleventh Commandment, and to try to enforce it in all cases, would be doctrinaire and stupid.

It is a normal human feeling to want to run one's own affairs without control by others. Understandably, therefore, a businessman, though he often welcomes and sometimes invites the help of his government, will resist and resent an act of supervision or intervention which he deems unjustified. On the other hand, it is a fact that his activities—and the sum-total of all the acts of others like himself—produce widespread effects which may require a general regulation in the common good. Piecemeal decisions to raise the price of this and that, or to press for higher wages here and there, may appear justifiable to those whose vision is focused on the microcosm of their own concern. But the cumulative result of many such separate actions can lead to an inflationary spiral from which no one emerges with any advantage. Somewhere in society there is a need for a broad perspective on the problems of the macrocosm. People who are adversely affected by economic processes will not patiently submit to the view that they are victims of blind impersonal forces beyond the power of human agency. Rather they regard the so-called "impersonal" as the gross total of millions of personal acts. Is it not reasonable then to suppose that a combination of knowledge with judgment can control events with some purpose and plan?

Right or wrong, this at any rate is the logic or the mood that inspires a growing volume of legislation designed to regulate specific aspects of the economy or to plan its general growth and well-being. A large part of this has a technical character, economic in content, over which economists themselves are seldom agreed.[18] But much of it is also intended to accomplish social ends—e.g., to protect the weaker from the strong, or rehabilitate a backward region—and a great deal has a plainly political source, in that organized groups demand certain measures and a government which needs their support can hardly refuse them. In concrete fashion the democratic form of government contributes to this whole tendency for reasons which are fairly evident. Permitting the freedom of association, and encouraging the free expression of opinions, democracy offers a fertile field for the mobilization of interests and their action as "pressure groups." Also it is widely believed nowadays that governments can take measures to improve economic conditions, and that, if they can, they should. Those in office are therefore held responsible for the prevalent economic atmosphere. They gain political capital if the weather is good and suffer electorally as soon as it turns foul. Action or inaction—both are decisions.

In varying degree, these generalizations apply to all the smaller democracies and most of the larger ones. Older communities whose people are densely congested, as in the United Kingdom; smaller societies which depend on specialized exports, as do Switzerland and Denmark; younger countries with resources still awaiting development, such as Canada; nations whose interest groups are highly articulated and strongly organized, e.g., Sweden; all these exhibit an intricate mingling of the state and the economy under the various forms described above. The state restricts or extends its powers, limits or widens its control, with need and circumstance. One of the relevant circumstances is naturally the partisan complexion of the government. In general, a government that leans on the

18. E.g., What is the incidence of this or that tax? How does the tax system promote or restrict production? When should the interest rate be raised or lowered, and by how much?

Left has fewer inhibitions about using the state to steer and stimulate the economy. One that veers to the Right will be more reluctant to do so, but in practice often employs policies which are indistinguishable in content from those of its opponents. As in the fairy tale of the emperor's clothes, every modern government must appear in public with a plan, whether in fact it has one or not.

The American Economy and State Control

To the foregoing account of relations between the economy and the modern democratic state, a most important exception must be made in the case of the United States. On this subject, I shall start with some statements of fact, inquire into the reasons for them, and then appraise the results. It is a fact that in this country the state[19] performs fewer functions of an economic character than in any other democracy. This is clearly true of public ownership and, to a smaller degree, of governmental regulation. As for the social services, apart from the provision of public education, in which the record of the United States is impressive, the government of this democracy lags behind the rest in the extent and quality of its welfare programs. It is also a fact that the center of gravity in American politics lies further to the Right than elsewhere. American Liberals occupy a position to the Right of the democratic Left in Europe, and American Conservatives are to the Right of European Conservatives. Generally, in the United States the bias against the state is stronger than in other democratic communities, and politics are held in lower esteem. Conversely, there is no democracy where businessmen enjoy such high prestige as they do here.

If these facts are as I have stated them, what is the explanation for the unique position of the United States? The answers are to be found in certain objective conditions, in the late survival of earlier psychological responses, and in the prevalence of certain ideas which have become rooted in tradition. One basic reason is the sheer abundance of the resources with which nature endowed this country. In the soil, climate, and water of North America lay a treasure waiting to be put to use. Adaptive, inventive, and vigorous, the immigrants from Europe who peopled this continent turned their technological skill to its resources and grew rich in consequence. With a wealth of raw materials and a supply of available capital, the Americans had less need than others for the state to take an

19. In this discussion, references to the "state" in the United States include all three levels of government in the federal system.

active role in economic development. The system of private entrepreneurship has proven itself dynamic, creative, and expansive. But it has also been very wasteful. Fortunately (or, perhaps, unfortunately) the United States possessed such a cornucopia until the turn of the century that a surplus could be wasted and not missed. Husbanding of resources, tighter controls, longer-term planning, direction by the state, are more readily justified when there is less to go round for everyone. A TVA would have been unthinkable in the nineteenth century. In the 1930's it was an imperative necessity, and has turned out a superb example of intelligent governmental operation.

Allied to this reason, and reinforcing it, has been the influence of the frontier on American attitudes. Individualism became deeply ingrained in the American character. In its best sense, this reliance on individual energy encouraged that spontaneous outpouring of creativity which has helped to make America great. In its worst light, it militated against community-building and impeded collective efforts even where they were plainly needed. Another contributing cause was the nature of the American Revolution. The Declaration of Independence was itself an act against the public authority. After conducting a successful rebellion, Americans have always regarded the state with ambivalent feelings. Even a regime of their own creation was in a certain sense suspect, because any government must have power and all power was considered potentially tyrannical. Businessmen were willing to invoke the powers of the federal government in the early days to help develop a national economy. But in modern times, they have viewed the federal government as their great potential enemy. Thus, the bias against the state has latterly become a strange amalgam of both the Jeffersonian and Hamiltonian traditions. Finally, there is the importance of material accomplishment in a country which was newly settled and required developing. Such a society most admires the practical men who produce visible and tangible results; and where all are said to be created equal, it is actually the accumulation of possessions which confers status.

These reasons combine to explain why prevailing opinion in the United States has held private activity in higher esteem than public. Their joint effect, as well as the subsequent reaction against the extension of governmental powers during the Civil War, reduced the state to perhaps its lowest level of efficiency just at the very time when the impact of the industrial technology was most sharply felt. Private organizations and individuals were thus able to enter the field, amass wealth, and consolidate power, when the state was in no position either to lead or resist. The timing of America's industrial expansion (roughly, the last four decades of the nineteenth century) also explains the timing of the political response to its results. Large-scale industrialization occurred in the United States about a generation later than in Germany and two or three generations after it had commenced in Great Britain. As a consequence, measures to remedy the social aftermath were taken in the United States at a correspondingly later date. The United Kingdom began to lay the foundations of modern governmental regulation and welfare services in the 1840's, continued in the 1860's and 1870's, and further extended the whole program in the decade prior to the outbreak of World War I. Germany, while guided by the enlightened conservatism and astute opportunism of Bismarck, legislated its pioneering experiments in social insurance during the 1880's. In the United States, a few of the States that contained bad conditions and progressive opinion—e.g., New York or Wisconsin—initiated programs for active intervention by the government, but only to the extent that the Supreme Court under conservative control allowed them to get away with it. Both Theodore Roosevelt and Woodrow Wilson saw the need for national correctives for situations which lay beyond the remedy of the few advanced States. But not until the catastrophic depression of 1929-34 administered a shock treatment to the public was it politically possible for Franklin D. Roosevelt to initiate nationally policies which other countries had earlier established.

But the resistance to an active role for the state in economic affairs remains a potent fact in American public life. Although the accomplishments of the New Deal are now interwoven with the fabric of society, and the acts of government in World War II threaded more embroidery on the fabric, there still are powerful interests in this country which hope to erase the pattern. The TVA has built an impressive record of achievement. But it has not been followed by any similar authorities for the valleys of the Columbia and Missouri, and during the Eisenhower Administration it was subjected to determined attacks by the private power companies. In the sphere of low-cost public housing, much good has been accomplished, as can be seen, for example, in some once blighted areas of New York City. But what has been done is very small in relation to the need. The whole gigantic problem of urban renewal requires active help by the federal government, on which the Congress has hitherto been laggard. The same criticism can be made of the failure thus far to introduce a state medical program to care for individuals who cannot afford the fees of doctors and hospitals in cases of major sickness. The obscurantism of the leaders of the American Medical Association and their success in playing on the fears and prejudices of legislators and newspaper publishers is a sign of backwardness in our society. It is sad to observe the officers of the doctors' trade union aping the politics of witch-doctors.

Contrasts in the Affluent Society

There are some extraordinary paradoxes in today's America which would merit the reflections of a Tocqueville. There is wealth here, there are riches, there is an extraordinary technical capacity and facility in organization. Physical ease and material comfort are enjoyed by more people than in any large country known to history.[20] J. K. Galbraith has called this "the affluent society," whose general abundance has outmoded the assumptions of scarcity in conventional economic thought. But he has also pointed out that, where many individuals are affluent and the majority are comfortable, the community in general may yet show marks of poverty, since the demands of the private sector can crush the needs of the public sector. Governments pay for most of the functions they perform by taxation or borrowing. In a democracy, each of these sources of revenue must be authorized by the people's elected representatives or, in some instances, by the voters themselves. It is possible for a government to be enlightened and for the majority of the citizens to be ill-informed or narrow-minded. In that case, observing its constitutional processes, the government may be powerless to provide the community with services which an objective study of conditions reveals to be necessary. Is this an argument, then, for a benevolent dictatorship? I do not intend it as such. I think it is an argument for better education and higher social awareness in our democracies.

Many individuals are perfectly willing to spend considerable amounts annually on items which are not necessities—e.g., tobacco, alcoholic liquors, gambling—but they object strenuously to being taxed for similar sums to support better schools or hospitals or civic and cultural amenities. Of course, there is an issue here of individual freedom, of the right of each man to do what he wants with his own money, even if he wastes it foolishly. When a public authority takes a portion of one's income, one is predisposed to find fault with some of the purposes to which it is put or the administrative means that the state employs. It is not easy to place

20. Even so, the world's wealthiest country has not yet eradicated poverty. In December, 1963, a National Policy Committee on Pockets of Poverty, created under the auspices of the National Farmers Union, reported that 20,000,000 Americans live in abject poverty and another 26,000,000 subsist at a level of minimum adequacy.

oneself imaginatively in the circumstances of another human being (e.g., of someone reared in a slum, semi-educated, and earning only a little) or to feel a personal obligation to change his situation. However, if gangs composed of such persons disturb our peace, we will then do something about it. But what will we do? Will we rather pay for a bigger police force, or for slum clearance and better education? We are readily shocked when some horrible act of violence is committed by a person who is mentally ill. But would we consent to be taxed to expand our mental hospitals and add to their psychiatric staff or increase the counselling service in the schools and elsewhere? If we own a car and want improved highways so as to drive at faster speeds, we are likely to grumble at the amount of the tax on gasoline which pays for them. And if thousands of car-owners clog the central streets of a big city, causing traffic congestion and noxious fumes, will we then authorize a local government to provide an adequate system of public transportation?

It is possible, of course, to continue this line of argument to the point of exaggeration. No single democracy is perfect in everything, and a larger country with its greater complexities has more problems to solve and contains more than is bad along with all that is good. But it is not exaggerating to say that the case for individualism and for private ownership has been greatly overworked in the United States. Such terms as the "free economy" and "the private enterprise system" have degenerated into slogans and clichés, applied as propaganda and uncritically parroted from mouth to mouth. Often, indeed, they are but a crude mask for blatant commercialism and social indifference. To those who abuse ideas which once made genuine sense, it must be reiterated that the public interest is always paramount over private interests and that the one institution in society with the responsibility for discovering and enforcing the public interest is the state.

The Prestige of the Businessman

There is a corollary to all that has been said above which concerns the character and processes of American democracy. In the social hierarchy of occupations, the politician rates lower than he should and the businessman higher. Great deference is paid to the corporation executive, whose job is the symbol of success and who reputedly has mastered the art of managing men and making money. The attitudes associated with his prestige can permeate a society to its detriment. Other institutions—a university, a church, a government—are supposed to be run on business principles. Salesmanship, advertising, and public relations, then dominate people's mores and (alas!) their thinking. Success belongs to him for whom the ball bounces; and it bounces from the celluloid make-believe of the Hollywood studios to the commercials of Madison Avenue.

Two different, though related, points are involved in this: the mystique of the businessman and the social functions of wealth. How do they affect democracy in this most spectacular instance, the United States? It would be as wrong to suggest that businessmen have no place in government and can contribute nothing to its functions as to assert that they alone are capable of large-scale management. When individual cases of corporation executives holding public office are examined, the results disclose as many failures as successes. What is clear is that the latter have been the men who understood that a government agency is not the same as a business firm, because its powers flow from statutes, it handles public funds, and it has a responsibility to the whole community. Also, to put it mildly, the ability to get along with Congress is not the same as that of running the board of directors or chairing an annual meeting of shareholders. The aura that surrounds the businessman includes many myths which stretch beyond the facts. The same accusations which spokesmen for private enterprise continually level against public administration—charges of patronage, nepotism, swollen bureaucracy, procedural red tape—can be illustrated just as readily from the less efficient private corporations. Enterprise is no less a public than a private function; and freedom, which at times requires resistance to the state by individuals, sometimes depends on protection of individuals by the state.

A different question concerns the effect of great wealth on the processes of democracy, and consequent problems of social ethics. The very rich, being few in number, may be fearful of the power of the majority in a democratic system. If unsuccessful in preventing regulation by the state, they may seek to evade it by corrupting the processes of governmental control. Distortion of political discussion by well-financed one-sided propaganda may be one method. Lavish support for a party or a candidate, with implied conditions of future benefits, may be another. Outright bribery—in cash, favors, or gifts—is a third. Unfortunately, every so often we find a case in which a politician or administrator has abused his public office for personal gain and the donor of the bribe was a private entrepreneur. In the early 1960's the Justice Department brought successful indictments against a group of high executives in some of the greatest corporations in the electrical industry. These men, respected and respectable figures in their communities, were found guilty of illegal conspiracy to arrange prices and thereby to defraud their customers (i.e., other private firms and the U. S. Government) of millions of dollars. A major source of corruption in the public sector is the low ethical standard of numerous persons in the private sector.

The foregoing should not be construed as a blanket condemnation of all businessmen, or even of the majority. Unfortunately it is true that a minority of men who are ruthlessly aggressive, abetted by those who are passively indifferent, can lower the general tone of a community to an alarming degree. As a matter of fact, one should be cautious in judging the role of wealthy men in the democracy of today, since their ranks include benefactors along with malefactors. In the period since the 1930's, there have been impressive instances of multimillionaires who have sponsored liberal causes and dedicated themselves to progressive and humanitarian ideals. Consider the evolution of the Rockefeller family in the last four generations, or of the Harrimans. In the presidential elections of 1952, 1956, and 1960, the chosen candidates of the more liberal party were men of wealth, largely or wholly inherited, whereas the candidates of the party of big business were men of poorer origins and more limited means. Sometimes it appears that those who inherit great wealth may feel the sense of social responsibility more strongly than those who made it themselves. For example, in recent decades some of the most conservative, or even reactionary, individuals have been the *nouveaux riches* of Texas or Southern California. On the other hand, there are some new millionaires, like Henry J. Kaiser, who have been pioneers in social progress as well as in private initiative.

Future Responsibilities of Government

At this point, a reader may well ask whether two chapters of diagnosis lead to any prognosis. Can one offer any reasonably reliable prediction about the future relations between the democratic state and the economy? It is my belief that two of the dominant trends in the present world scene are bound to generate more, not less, activity by the state—in the United States as well as in the medium-sized and smaller democracies. One of these trends consists in the changing technology of military defense, with its requirement of huge governmental expenditures and their impact on major branches of the economy.[21] The other is the decline of the nation-state as an adequate unit of political organization and the need to merge into larger associations both for military protection and for further eco-

21. See the discussion of this point in Chapter 7, pp. 186 ff.

nomic development. The prosperity of the United States is increasingly interdependent with that of other continents where raw materials must be purchased and manufactures must be sold. As bigger political units develop, the government must be the social agency to direct the movement, since no other institution is capable of doing it. Hence, there will be more planning and supervision by the state, not less. Moreover, within the countries which are democratically governed, political pressure for an equitable distribution of the economic product will continue. For our time and for the immediately discernible future, the old controversy between capitalism and socialism is a dead issue. The state will retain and discharge its responsibility to discover the public interest and promote the general welfare, and thereby lead the community to higher levels of civilization.

The combined effect of both trends—the external unification and the internal redistribution—has major implications for the future of democracy. Since the state needs great power to accomplish such tasks, will it continue to conform to democracy's requirements? Will the people be able to control their government, in fact and not merely in principle? And, if that control is exercised effectively, will their government then be strong enough to do what they expect of it? Such questions move the discussion from the sphere of problems which society generates into the arena of politics where they are argued and to the institutions where policies are decided and then translated into practice. Hence, the next six chapters are devoted to the politics of democracy and the framework of its government.

III

The Politics and Government of Democracy

III

10

The Sovereign Voters

Government consists in applying political ideals to social groups and in-interests. Conflicts arise over these ideals because men disagree about what is to be valued and interpret the values differently. It is the nature of politics, therefore, to be continuously involved in controversy. Formulating the ends is an argument about the principles which will govern the relationships of individuals, interests, and groups. Finding and organizing the means is a struggle for power. Shortly described, politics is a duel over principles and the power to achieve them.

But controversy has a character which evokes its own requirements. If it is unchecked, the results can be so ruinous as to be self-defeating. We cannot survive as civilized men unless we limit our capacity to destroy. Hence we find that we must institutionalize our conflicts and subject them to procedural safeguards. Moreover, while debating what ideals we should like to realize in the future, we must conduct our lives in the present within an orderly framework. This order has resulted from the conflicts of all our yesterdays, as today's conflicts will yield tomorrow's order. The continuity of society requires organization by government, incorporating citizens and rules and machinery and powers and officials— in a word, the state. But for this same society to adapt and evolve, the controversies of politics must find a way to respond to change through the institutions of the state and thereby bring reality closer to the ideal. The institutions which function well and endure are those which strike a proper balance between admitting improvements and preserving continuity. Wherever that balance is not achieved, the machinery of government will be at variance with the forces generated in the political process.

Political Dynamics and Democratic Institutions

There is thus a tension between politics and the state. The dynamic features of the former thrust against the latter's more static character. Politics has a fluid, mobile quality. It is an ocean of turbulent forces, seldom easily governable and sometimes uncontrollable. The state, by contrast, is structured. It strives for solidity and solidarity. Law, order, authority, are its hallmarks. It is an aggregate of duties and rights, a complex of institutions and procedures. As in the eternal duet of land and ocean, the waves of politics beat upon the *terra firma* of the state. Their meeting-place is government.

This encounter resembles the metaphysical conundrum of the irresistible force meeting the immovable object. Indeed, on occasions of political upheaval—a revolution, for example—that is the kind of thing which happens. It follows then that a system ought to be designed to resolve that tension. Such a system is democracy. Democracy is unique among forms of government in the spirit and method of its approach to this problem. Part of its purpose is prohibitive—to restrain the conflict of interests, groups, and individuals from being destructive. But the larger task is constructive, to harness their political energy through institutions to generate the public good. The relationship that democracy seeks is one in which politics can be creative and the state responsive. The democratic aim is to make the object movable and the force resistible.

The functions of politics connect it intimately with society and the state. The link with the former is largely one of substance. Much of the content of political controversy derives from the character of the various groups—linguistic, religious, economic, etc.—of which society is composed and from the relations between them. Furthermore, in politics men are competing for power. Besides its appeal to those who wield it, power is important to the groups they lead or represent. Without it, they can neither protect their interests nor translate their ideas into policy. In this way, a connection arises between politics and the state, because power, in order to be effective, must control the state. The energy generated from the raw material of interests is converted into power through leadership and organization. It is then conducted through the machinery of government to the outlets, where it makes contact with the people whom the state is supposed to serve. The currents of politics flow from society, but are harnessed by the structure of the state.

That is to speak, however, in generic terms. Specifically, what is it that gives the state and politics a democratic character? What forms does the political process assume when its content is democratic? What design does the democratic state imprint on its institutions? What are the distinguishing features, substantive and procedural, of a democratic government?

A summarized answer to these questions can be fairly brief, provided that one distinguishes what is fundamental and central from what is secondary or minor. These then are the standards for judging whether a political system is democratic or not:

1. The people should hold ultimate power through universal adult suffrage, each citizen having one vote only.

2. A minimum of two major parties should offer a choice of candidates and programs in honest elections at sensible intervals.

3. The community should guarantee the civil liberties of every member. These include the freedoms to speak and publish and associate with others, as well as protection against arbitrary arrest and imprisonment without a fair trial.

4. Public policy should be directed toward the public interest and should promote the social and economic welfare of all.

5. The state should ensure a balance between effective leadership and responsible criticism. Hence those in office must continually confront their opposition in the legislature, and all citizens may have recourse to an independent judiciary.

6. It must be possible to change any feature of the governmental system by peaceful means through agreed procedures.

Such a list attempts to specify the principal criteria to which the government of a democratic state should conform. In order to be concise, one must employ terms which embrace a general concept, but need more detailed elaboration—for instance, "the public interest." Also, some of the adjectives—e.g., "honest," "effective," "responsible"—involve value judgments about whose meaning people may disagree. But the sense in which such words are used should be sufficiently clear to begin a discussion and will become clearer as it proceeds. The criteria themselves are of two kinds. Some can be factually described and objectively ascertained. Thus it is possible to find out how many persons are registered as voters, how often elections are held, how many parties there are, and so on. Other criteria are abstractions, suggesting ideal aspirations as guides to actual performance. All of them, of course, admit gradations. Since nothing human is ever perfect, and nothing political is ever static, democracy too is a product of flux and change. A particular government, functioning historically in time and place, is not wholly this or wholly that. It will be more democratic or less. The distinctions between one government and another are those of degree. But somewhere on the scale the differences add up to a change in quality and can be evaluated as such.

Participation by the People

The analysis of democratic politics must begin with the people. However, else democracy may be described or defined, it is a system in which the people are considered the ultimate repositories of power and the government is established to serve their needs. It was on this note that Lincoln chose to end his Address at Gettysburg. "Of the people" affirms that the government is theirs and belongs to them. "By the people" signifies that citizens participate in politics and control their representatives and officials, a conception which is similar to the Greek *Demokratia* and the practices of the Athenian *Polis*. "For the people" indicates that it is the government which serves them, and not they who are its subjects. Many of the major problems which arise in the analysis of democracy are expressed or implied in these points. The basic questions are these:

Who are the people?

What political functions do they perform?

Can they in fact control their representatives and officials? If so, how?

The normal form of government has not been democracy, but oligarchy. Traditionally the mass of men have been controlled, in one fashion or another, by aristocrats, by kings and their ministers, by religious leaders, by warlords and military juntas, by landowners, merchants, and owners of wealth. Ordinary persons, the rank and file of the human race, were regarded by such elites as sheep to be kept and fed, and clipped or devoured. Wherever the democratic revolution succeeded, it was aimed at those oligarchies, at the power they wielded and the privileges they enjoyed, at their pretensions of superiority over the Common Man. Democracy affirmed its faith in the inherent worth of every individual and strove for a political order in which all could live with a measure of dignity. The aspiration was noble because its embrace was universal. At this stage in democracy's evolution, it is fair to inquire into what has been accomplished, to judge whether the ideal has become the actual, and to see if the intent has been perverted by reality.

One of the great positive achievements of democracy has been the steady progress in translating the concept of the people into institutional terms with practical effects. Undoubtedly, the most direct evidence of this consists in the extension of the suffrage. Government by the people did not become a reality until the majority of adults had won the right to vote. Generally, it took a century to bring that about. In some western countries this task was not completed until after World War I; in others, after World War II. While it is never possible to state with quantitative precision how democratic a country has become, one relevant yardstick is the size of the electorate. A community falls short of democracy to the extent that any appreciable number of adults are denied the franchise. As a measure of how far the notion of "the people" has been extended, statistics are revealing. When the Constitution of the United States was being ratified the country had a population of under 3,800,000. However, Charles A. Beard has estimated "that not more than 5 per cent of the population in general, or in round numbers, 160,000 voters, expressed an opinion one way or another on the Constitution."[1] In 1960, when the population had reached 180,000,000, as many as 69,000,000 ballots were cast in the presidential election. Likewise in 1830 in the United Kingdom, immediately prior to the passage of the first Reform Act, less than half a million in a population of 16,000,000 were registered on the electoral rolls.[2] But when the general election was held in 1959, the population had grown to 53,000,000 and the registered electorate to 35,400,000. Of course, in terms of sheer size, the most remarkable contemporary experiment with democracy is the Indian. There, in a country whose population in 1950 was 385,000,000, the registered voters in the first parliamentary election under the new constitution numbered 173,000,000. *Mutatis mutandis*, results which proportionately are no less significant have been achieved in the medium-sized and smaller democracies, where nowadays virtually every adult has the franchise.

Removal of Obstacles to Universal Suffrage

There were various obstacles to be broken down before access to the polls was made open to all. Religious intolerance disappeared slowly—it is by no means completely dead yet—as a consequence of the general spread of a secular, scientific, and rationalist outlook during the nineteenth century. Eventually, in all communities which have "gone modern," the idea caught on that civic loyalty is not a function of religious orthodoxy and

1. *An Economic Interpretation of the Constitution of the United States* (New York: Macmillan, 1935), p. 250.
2. See Chapter 4, pp. 80 ff.

that individuals who profess different faiths can be decent neighbors and good citizens. The lowering of economic barriers was a gradual process in most places. Originally, as representative legislatures were tacked on to the formerly absolute monarchies or were introduced into new republics, voting power was correlated with wealth. The suffrage depended on the possession of a sufficient amount of property, and the wealthiest were often permitted more than one vote. By degrees, the franchise was extended to middle-income groups and then to those of lower incomes, until finally it became recognized as a right of citizenship without regard to income or property.[3] In this respect the "frontier democracies" in newly settled lands were generally ahead of their European countries of origin.

The same may be said of political discrimination in terms of sex. The fair sex was politically subordinate to the unfair until World War I. The western region of the United States and the South Pacific democracies of New Zealand and Australia began enfranchising their womenfolk before this startling innovation was acceptable to the diehard masculinity of the Old World and of America's Atlantic seaboard. World War I, however, settled the issue in the ladies' favor, because of the role they had assumed in supporting the armed forces and in civil employment. The Latin countries, however, still clung for another quarter of a century to the notion that politics was man's business. In Canada, Quebec did not allow its women to vote until 1940, and in France and Italy the franchise was first granted to women in the new constitutions after World War II, when the Fascist "supermen" had been discredited. Only one democracy today, namely Switzerland, persists in its curiously old-fashioned ways on this topic.

Racial prejudice has formed another basis for preventing large groups from voting. Most democracies have escaped this issue simply because their populations were racially homogeneous. The United States, however, has always had a struggle of conscience over the politics of a "house divided." The Negroes have never yet been fully incorporated into the American body politic. This continues to be true, notwithstanding the fact that the Thirteenth, Fourteenth, and Fifteenth Amendments to the Federal Constitution were expressly drafted to abolish slavery, to affirm that persons of all races have equal rights as citizens, and to guarantee specifically the right of all citizens to vote. Ever since those principles

3. Until 1963, however, in the United States a poll tax was still in force in Alabama, Arkansas, Mississippi, Virginia and Texas. Its effect was to disfranchise many of the poorest citizens, both Negro and White. An amendment to the federal Constitution, the twenty-fourth, abolishing that or any other tax as a condition of voting in federal elections, was ratified and went into effect in 1964.

were written into the fundamental law, the struggle has been waged between federal enforcement and local reaction and resistance. Once the Reconstruction Era was over, the latter had all the advantages until the economic depression of the early 1930's. In the three decades since then the general improvement in the position of Negroes has been remarkable, and a special case is their political progress. The number of Negroes who are registered as voters, and who actually vote, increases every few years by leaps and bounds. In the 1960's, more Negroes are being elected to public office at all levels of government, and are receiving appointments to executive and judicial posts of high responsibility. Nevertheless, it must be admitted that, though these gains are genuine and impressive, they still go only a small way in removing what has thus far been a serious blot on the record of American democracy. The ideals of democracy are colorblind; the practices, unfortunately, are not.[4]

A further reason for the restriction of voting rights has been the denial of educational opportunities. Many countries insist on a literacy test or some other kind of examination before a person is allowed to vote. In principle, this requirement makes good sense. Since a voter must choose between men and measures, he should be well-informed about the contemporary scene and be able to judge intelligently when he is presented with different proposals. The vote that stems from ignorance or prejudice is no help to democracy. On the other hand, it is sometimes true that a government deliberately neglects to educate a large section of its population in order to perpetuate the privileges of the remainder. Educational tests, as a prerequisite for voting, are morally justifiable only where everybody has equal access to the necessary education.[5] Nor is it true that uneducated persons, or even illiterates, are incapable of understanding politics or forming intelligent opinions about current issues. I have talked in Brazil to men and women who could not read or write, but who had a shrewd grasp of what was going on and held reasoned and reasonable opinions.

Indeed, on this point the contemporary policies of Brazil and India suggest an illuminating contrast. The Indians, after becoming independent in 1949, took a decision which, in view of the size and internal com-

4. See also Chapter 5, pp. 102 ff.
5. A majority of the U.S. Commission of Registration and Voting Participation, which was created by President Kennedy, reported in December, 1963, in favor of abolishing literacy tests. Their opinion was this: "Literacy tests are a remnant of class discrimination. They discriminate against the poor, the aged, and rural inhabitants. It is not the wealthy who can neither read nor write. It is the poor and the depressed. Literacy tests have no more place in a modern democracy than property tests which we have long since abandoned." *New York Times*, Dec. 21, 1963.

plexity of their country, was remarkably bold. In a population which in 1950 totaled 385,000,000 nearly 81 per cent of those over age fifteen are estimated to have been illiterate.[6] Nevertheless, illiteracy did not disqualify a citizen from voting. Such a policy was both an act of faith on the part of its authors and a piece of shrewd realism. The former, because they showed their confidence in the capacity of ordinary men and women to reach valid conclusions about political matters; the latter, because they recognized that, if underprivileged people were granted the vote, they would be more likely to obtain a faster improvement in their condition than if they were excluded from the polls.[7] Brazil in this respect has been more cautious. The constitution that went into effect in 1946 after Vargas was overthrown prescribes that the *analfabetos* may not vote.[8] In 1950 the population had reached 52,000,000, of whom approximately 27,-800,000 were over eighteen, the minimum age for voting. Only 11,600,000 persons, however, were registered on the rolls for the presidential election of that year (i.e., 42 per cent of those above the minimum age). Presumably, the disfranchisement of many of the remaining 58 per cent was due to their being illiterate. We know in fact that, in 1950, some 51 per cent of those over age fifteen were unable to read and write.[9] Nor has the situation improved appreciably since that time, for Brazil's population grows at a rate which outstrips the expansion of educational facilities. Thus by 1960 the population had climbed to 71,000,000 (an increase of 34.5 per cent). Indeed, one cannot escape the conclusion that most members of the dominant oligarchy, who generally despise and fear the submerged illiterate masses, are in no hurry to alter their position and then run the risk of losing their own privileges to so vast a majority.[10]

The gist of the preceding pages leads to a significant conclusion, if one observes the nature of the traditional impediments to voting and considers their source. Those impediments have consisted in racial prejudice, religious intolerance, economic barriers, sex discrimination, educational inequality, and so forth—all of them factors which originate within society. The governmental oligarchies which democracy sought to replace

6. See *World Illiteracy at Mid-Century* (UNESCO, 1957), p. 33.
7. At the first elections of independent India, held in 1951-52, there were 173 million registered voters, of whom nearly 89 million voted. In 1957, at the second national election, the electorate numbered 200 million and 121 million voted.
8. Art. 132(1). Notwithstanding this provision, illiterates do succeed in registering in some areas, particularly where a local boss encourages them to do so. See my article on "Government in Contemporary Brazil," *Canadian Journal of Economics and Political Science*, Vol. 22, No. 2, 1956, pp. 191-2.
9. *World Illiteracy at Mid-Century*, p. 50.
10. In 1963 only 46% of the children were attending school.

were the product and reflection of social privilege. To inaugurate the innovation of democratic politics was to strike at the social roots of the opposing system. Universal adult suffrage has been achieved through politics in the teeth of social backwardness. A political ideal, in other words, has invoked its justice against social injustice. It would be wrong, therefore, to interpret democracy as merely an outcome or offshoot of a certain combination of social conditions. While democracy needs to be associated with the appropriate and favoring society, it is derived just as surely from sources which are political. The democratic institution of the electorate embracing all adult citizens is the application to the state of the concepts of liberty and equality, reinforced by the leveling and inclusive influences of nationalism. Here is a case where politics has been creative, progressive and dynamic; and society, the reverse. Whole communities were segregated for centuries into first- and second-class citizens by such social phenomena as bigotry, ignorance, poverty, class, and caste. Against these divisive elements, democracy emerged as the unifier. Where it has properly lived up to its principles, it has put together those whom society had set asunder.

The fundamental requirement of modern democracy is the right of the mass of the citizens to participate in periodic and honest elections at which they are offered a genuine choice. Establishing that right has constituted a political revolution of the first magnitude. Once this is done, the subsequent exercise of the right produces results which need appraisal.

The Use of the Right To Vote

A few democracies have made voting compulsory. Such has been the system in Belgium since 1896, in certain of the Swiss cantons, and in Australian federal elections since 1924. The enforcement in Australia is thorough, but the penalties are not onerous. The department which administers the electoral law writes to non-voters after each election and asks them to explain why they failed to vote. Certain reasons are accepted as valid—for instance, sickness or absence from the district on polling day. If no satisfactory explanation is offered, a fine of £2 is imposed. Compulsion was introduced at a time when non-voting had reached serious proportions and the political parties, notably Labour, wanted to force their potential supporters to the polls. The immediate effect, of course, was a big increase in actual voting, and over 90 per cent of the Australian electorate does normally participate. There are grave doubts, however, about the wisdom of compelling a person to vote. How does democracy gain if the apathetic or the ignorant are forced to mark a ballot? Must not a vote, to be meaningful, be voluntary?[11]

Voluntary voting is a topic which raises more complicated questions. In view of the struggles which occurred before the suffrage was made universal, it was widely expected that citizens would welcome an opportunity to cast a ballot, would feel a sense of importance in belonging to the sovereign people, and would take part in elections with enthusiasm. The cynics had treated the voting public with scorn. "The notion that a man's liberty," wrote Carlyle, "consists in giving his vote at election hustings, and saying, 'Behold, now I too have my twenty-thousandth part of a Talker in our National Palaver; will not all the gods be good to me?'—is one of the pleasantest!"[12] The results have neither borne out the hopes of optimists nor justified the warnings of pessimists. The record of popular participation in elections is a mixed one and deserves the full examination it has received. For several decades, students of politics have been scanning the electoral statistics to learn about the behavior of King Demos. They have found him a creature of many faces and fluctuating moods.[13]

Because modern democracies possess efficient electoral departments which collect and publish accurate statistics, the facts are well attested

11. The dilemma presented to democracy by the citizen who does not exercise his voting rights is an old one. In Athens, on the day when the Assembly was meeting, the police used to surround the market-place with a red rope freshly colored, leaving open only the road to the Pnyx. Towards this, they drove—or herded—the citizens. Aristophanes alludes in two of his comedies to people rushing to avoid having red on their clothes! *Acharnians*, 22; *Ecclesiazusae*, 378.

12. Thomas Carlyle, *Past and Present*, from Chap. XIII on "Democracy."

13. The first systematic studies of this problem were conducted by two Chicago political scientists, Charles E. Merriam and Harold F. Gosnell. See their *Non-Voting* (University of Chicago Press, 1924) and Gosnell's *Why Europe Votes* (University of Chicago Press, 1930). In 1937 the Swedish political scientist, Herbert Tingsten, published his important work on *Political Behavior* in which he analyzed electoral statistics. Since 1946 scholars in many lands have devoted painstaking research to the factors which induce people to vote or deter them. On this large subject the political scientists and the sociologists have contributed mutual reinforcement in both general and piecemeal analyses. See, in particular, *Voting* by Bernard Berelson, Paul F. Lazarsfeld, and William McPhee (University of Chicago Press, 1954); *Political Life* by Robert E. Lane (Glencoe: the Free Press, 1959); and *Political Man* by Seymour Martin Lipset (New York: Doubleday, 1960). Voting is, of course, the fertile field for those who wish to explain political phenomena in quantitative terms, since the vote is the one significant public act of a citizen which can be identified and measured. Methodological help has come to the quantifiers from refinements in polling techniques and the invention of elaborate computing-machines. Sometimes the connections between the data thus tabulated contain stimulating hypotheses for social speculation. Too often, however, the labor expended consists in the statistical elaboration of the obvious or assertion of the dubious.

and are not in dispute. Certain basic distinctions should be drawn at the outset. When the suffrage was first extended to all adult males, and later to adults of both sexes, the initial effect on each occasion was to increase the absolute number who voted but to diminish the percentage of those registered who took the trouble to vote. Many of the newly enfranchised, being previously unaccustomed to voting, took some time to acquire the habit. Various social groups did not have a ready-made political allegiance, and were therefore slow in responding to the appeal of a party. The number and percentage of voters increased in some countries after World War I, in others after the depression of the early 1930's, and generally after World War II. The conflict between democracy and the fascist dictatorships in the 1930's and early 1940's helped to make many citizens of democratic states more conscious of the value and meaning of a free ballot, and, since 1948, the "cold war" between democracy and the communist dictatorships has had a similar effect. Another difference has revealed itself, not through time, but between places and cultures. In general, the countries which consistently produce the highest percentages of voters are on the European continent. Conversely, the English-speaking democracies show the higher rates of abstentions, with the exception of New Zealand, which will be discussed below, and Australia, where voting is compulsory. What is the explanation of such facts, and what is the significance to democracy of higher or lower voter-participation?

Reasons for Voting and Non-Voting

The factors which explain why the citizens of a democracy either vote or abstain may be broadly classified as social and political. On the former, an accumulating body of research has led to conclusions which are widely documented. These are briefly summarized by Seymour M. Lipset, who writes: "Men vote more than women; the better educated, more than the less educated; urban residents, more than rural; those between 35 and 55, more than younger or older voters; married persons, more than unmarried; higher-status persons, more than lower; members of organizations, more than nonmembers."[14] The causes which underlie such generalizations are fairly clear. Male voters outnumber female because they were enfranchised earlier and developed the habit sooner. Also, as the family "breadwinners," they spend more time outside their home and become aware of conditions in the community at large for which governments may be

14. *Political Man, op. cit.,* p. 182. See the whole discussion in Chap. VI.

praised or blamed. If those with more education vote more, it is because they have a better capacity to understand and they participate from a greater sense of responsibility. Moreover, the better educated often earn the bigger incomes or belong to professions with higher prestige, and they have much at stake in the outcome of an election. City-dwellers go to the polls in larger numbers than farmers for a variety of reasons. People in urban areas breathe an atmosphere which is physically more noxious, but intellectually more bracing, than the country air. In metropolitan centers there is usually a more vigorous discussion of contemporary problems, a more diversified press, and easier access to cultural activities. Moreover, those who live in a city apartment or a suburban street are easier to reach, to canvass, and to organize.

The incidence of higher voting among those aged between thirty-five and fifty-five can also be readily understood. These are normally the most active years in a person's life, the years when individuals establish themselves in their occupations and careers, are married and raise families, acquire property and build up pension funds. Voting, for them, is another expression of their involvement in the community. It is their exercise of a right which signifies their obligations. The same applies to the fact that those with higher status participate in elections to a greater degree. They are conscious of their position and have something to conserve. Realizing as a select group that they are outnumbered, they must nevertheless make their quota count to the fullest extent possible. Finally, the higher voting among those who are members of various organizations arises from the consequences of membership itself and from the conditions which cause it. Organization feeds on and nourishes itself, and its members are more likely to respond to group pressures than is an isolated individual. Also, those who are habitually "joiners" are so because they presumably feel a need to belong to an identifiable group or have interests which they can best protect in concert with others. Hence, the fact that they vote more regularly arises, not from their membership in social groups, but from the same attitudes which caused them to join in the first place.

Besides the social factors just mentioned, one must include the importance of race, religion, and language. When a society composed of dissimilars tries to govern itself democratically, it will simply transfer to the electoral process whatever relations exist between its linguistic, religious, and racial groups. Since democracy in modern times has always succeeded an oligarchy, and since the latter in a heterogeneous society will have consisted of its dominant group, the introduction of universal suffrage will permit a group which was treated as inferior to win equality through voting power. Sometimes the traditionally dominant group deliberately perverts the electoral process in order to perpetuate its ascendancy. Such was the practice of southern whites in the United States until the 1940's. Where this happens, and for so long as it continues, the result is not democracy. Or again, the opportunity which the secret ballot provides for socially subordinate groups to attain equality by political means may encourage the voters to participate for reasons, and along lines, which are strictly correlated to their race, their language, or their religion. It is understandable that if a party espouses a program from which a minority will benefit, and if it nominates a candidate from such a group, the members will feel identified with that party and their hopes will bring them to the polls in greater numbers.

The other principal factors, in terms of which voting and non-voting can be understood, are essentially political. That is to say, they are related to the general attractiveness, or reverse, of party programs and candidates, to the contest for power among politicians, to the "public philosophy"[15] of individual citizens, and to governmental institutions which stimulate or inhibit a willingness to vote.

For example, it stands to reason that more people will vote when something important is at stake. Thus national elections draw more voters than local ones. So does a general election for Parliament in Great Britain as compared with a by-election. The same is true of American presidential elections in contrast with the mid-term elections for Congress and State offices. Likewise in referenda, where a specific issue has to be decided, and no candidates are to be elected, participation naturally varies with the gravity of the subject and the intensity of the discussion. A dramatic occasion or a magnetic personality provides an obvious stimulus to the voter. Great Britain was fortunate to have Disraeli and Gladstone as party leaders during the period when the franchise was being extended, for their personification of opposing principles evoked an interest among those newly qualified to vote. Likewise in the United States, the depression and "F.D.R." brought thousands of once reluctant voters to the polls in 1932 and 1936. At a time of crisis, the individual feels that he is more involved in his community and his vote expresses this commitment. Sentiments of nationalism or calculations of economic interest arouse the lethargic citizen, whether in support or protest, when governments undertake new functions and assume wider powers. Thus in the United Kingdom the debate over socialism and the postwar record of the Labour Ministry elicited a huge turnout of voters in 1950. The more extensive the activities of the state, the more intimately is each individual affected by the character of

15. This phrase is the title of a book by Walter Lippmann.

his government and the folly or wisdom of its policies. This is one of the reasons why more persons habitually vote in countries where there is more socialism, e.g., in Denmark, Great Britain, New Zealand, Norway, and Sweden.

Effects of the Electoral System

The institutions of government have their own effect upon the incidence of voting. One example of this, already cited, is the presidential system in the United States and its equivalent in State elections in the Governorship. Where the entire community forms one enormous electorate to put one man in one supreme office, the choice between organizations and programs is dramatized into a conflict between personalities and thereby a larger vote ensues. In addition, the design of the electoral machinery has a direct influence on voting practices. As a general rule, proportional representation with multi-membered districts increases the turnout of voters. Under this system, all parties and groups, large and small alike, are stimulated to bring their supporters to the polls. The more ballots a party receives, the larger the number of its legislative seats; and when big districts are used to elect several members, the minority interests have some chance to elect a candidate. On this point, the experience of Switzerland is instructive. The Swiss adopted proportional representation as a result of a national referendum in 1918. Prior to that, non-voting had been a chronic feature of their democracy, the number of abstentions fluctuating around 40 per cent.[16] In the first election held under the new system, in 1919, the number who voted increased immediately by 20.5 per cent (from 59.9 per cent in 1917 to 80.4 per cent).[17] Since that date, the percentage has declined,[18] although it has never dropped as low as under the old system.

But the national figures for Switzerland are less significant than the differences within the country. Because of the character of Swiss federalism and the diversity of its component units, the electoral machinery varies from one group of cantons to another. Four of them make voting compul-

16. For greater detail, see the evidence in my article on "Le Système des Partis Politiques en Suisse," *Revue Française de Science Politique*, Vol. 6, No. 4, 1956, pp. 813-32.

17. There were additional reasons for this increase besides the electoral innovation. The country was in acute economic difficulties at the end of the World War, and the conflict between parties was intense.

18. The totals of Swiss participants in federal elections have been: 1919, 80.4%; 1922, 76.4%; 1925, 76.8%; 1928, 78.8%; 1931, 78.8%; 1935, 78.3%; 1943, 70.0%; 1947, 72.4%; 1951, 72.2%; 1955, 70.1%; 1959, 68.5%.

sory.[19] One canton and three half-cantons, which have small populations and are socially homogeneous, form single electoral districts and elect one deputy each.[20] The remainder—fourteen cantons and three halves, containing a majority of the population—use voluntary voting in multi-membered districts. Between these three groups there are significant contrasts in voter participation. The figures in the accompanying table[21] disclose what could be expected. Voting is highest where it is compulsory, and lowest in the small single-deputy districts where proportionalism, of course, does not apply.

	PERCENTAGE OF SWISS VOTERS PARTICIPATING IN CANTONS HAVING:		
DATE OF ELECTION	Compulsory Voting	Voluntary Voting in Multi-Member Districts	Voluntary Voting in One-Member Districts
1919	89.7	79.1	43.2
1922	87.2	74.6	44.9
1925	87.3	75.2	41.7
1928	88.1	77.6	36.7
1931	89.2	77.5	36.8
1935	87.7	76.7	61.6
1943	82.5	67.7	58.0
1947	83.6	70.5	54.9
1951	80.8	67.5	54.0
1955	78.6	68.5	53.3
1959	80.4	66.5	44.1

The effects of the electoral system on voter participation can also be observed in the two largest English-speaking democracies. The United States and the United Kingdom employ the same system in their parliamentary and congressional elections. The country is divided into territorial districts, each of which is represented in the legislature by one member.[22] The victor, if there are more than two candidates, is the person who receives the largest vote (a plurality). There is no second ballot to produce a majority where none was received on the first ballot. In the attempt to subdivide a large country into approximately equal districts it is a natural

19. These are in the north and northeast: Aargau, St. Gallen, Schaffhausen, and Thurgau.
20. These are primarily rural: Appenzell (Inner Rhoden), Nidwalden, Obwalden, and Uri. Three Swiss cantons—Appenzell, Basel, and Unterwalden—are subdivided into half-units for purposes of cantonal government and federal elections.
21. The figures are taken from the election reports of the federal Bureau of Statistics.
22. In some States that have failed to reapportion after the decennial census, a congressman is elected "at large" from the entire State.

consequence that some of the districts will be fairly homogeneous, or at any rate will be strongly weighted one way or the other. Where that happens, a particular political party is likely to exercise a continuous predominance. In Great Britain, the Conservatives possess a number of "safe" constituencies, as does Labour. Similarly in the United States there are localities which are solidly Republican or Democratic. In such areas, the members of the local minority are disinclined to vote since their ballots will not affect the outcome, and it is their abstention which reduces the national total.[23] One reason for the consistently low figures of participation in the United States has been the one-party character of the traditionally "solid South." Ordinarily the elections were decided in the southern States in the primaries or nominating conventions of the Democratic party.

In certain States, many Negroes and poor whites were even prevented from voting by the requirement of a poll tax. The voting in the constitutional election was a mere formality, and few cared to waste their time. The habitual non-voting in the South has always lowered the national percentage.[24] Fortunately, since 1948, the evidence has multiplied that major changes are occurring in the South, both in economic development and in race relations. These changes are already producing their political effects within the Democratic party and have exhibited, in the rising Republican vote, the beginning of what could become a two-party system. Should these trends continue, we may anticipate, among other things, a higher participation at the polls by southern citizens.

Voting in New Zealand, A Special Case

There is one interesting exception to the general statement that fewer persons vote in the English-speaking democracies where the constituencies

23. Even so, the British percentages of voter participation are reasonably high. Since World War II, the number of registered voters actually voting at general elections has been: 1945, 73%; 1950, 84%; 1951, 83%; 1955, 77%; 1959, 79%.

24. There is a further reason why the percentages of participants quoted from the United States are not strictly comparable with those of other democracies. The American figures express those who actually vote as a percentage of all citizens above the legal age, which is eighteen in Georgia and Kentucky, nineteen in Alaska, twenty in Hawaii, and twenty-one everywhere else. State laws, however, disqualify many "eligible" adults through educational or literacy tests, residential requirements, the poll tax, etc. In addition, every citizen who is qualified by law must become a registered voter by a voluntary act several months prior to the election. In fact many who are eligible never register. Registration in other democracies is conducted automatically by the state, and the electoral role is a complete list of all residents known to be eligible.

elect a single member and a plurality wins. This is the case of New Zealand. Universal adult suffrage has been in force in that Dominion since 1893. The accompanying table indicates how New Zealanders have used their opportunity.

THE NEW ZEALAND ELECTORATE, 1890-1960 [25]

Election Year	(1) Population	(2) Registered Voters	(3) Percentage of (2) to (1)	(4) Actual Voters	(5) Percentage of (4) to (2)
1890	625,508	183,171	29	136,337	74
1893	672,265	302,992	45	220,082	74
1908	888,376	537,003	60	428,648	80
1928	1,344,469	844,633	63	743,691	88
1935	1,487,905	919,798	62	834,682	91
1938	1,491,484	995,173	67	924,057	93
1946	1,603,554	1,061,445	66	1,010,778	95
1949	1,780,228	1,113,852	63	1,041,794	93
1951	1,852,216	1,166,375	63	1,036,137	89
1954	1,987,628	1,209,670	61	1,066,810	88
1957	2,117,143	1,202,017	57	1,125,522	94
1960	2,240,892	1,255,488	56	1,139,090	91

To the best of my knowledge, the result in the election of 1946, when 95 per cent of those registered actually voted, is the highest degree of national participation ever recorded anywhere on a voluntary basis. In addition, at five other elections the percentage exceeded ninety, and on no occasion since 1908 has it dropped below 80. What is the explanation?

Two reasons can be suggested why so many New Zealanders habitually vote. The principal one consists in the volume of functions undertaken by the state. "There is no group in the community whose economic interests and social welfare are not positively controlled or else closely affected by what the state does. To a far greater extent than in most democracies the individual New Zealander is a recipient of state-provided services, a subject of state regulation, a competitor against state enterprises, or an administrator of a state activity. Everyone in the Dominion falls into one or more of these categories. The omnipresence and omnipotence of the state explain the keenness to vote. It is partly a sense of public duty, but more

25. This table comprises the Europeans only. The Maori people, who numbered 158,-000 in 1960, are registered on another electoral roll and vote in four constituencies of their own. Among the Maoris, non-voting is about twice as high as among the Europeans.

the awareness of individual self-interest, that draws the New Zealander to the ballot box.

"Yet that is not the whole explanation. The temperance movement, which helped women gain the vote, has also contributed to the large turn-out of voters at general elections. In the year 1894 for the first time licensing polls (or referenda) on the liquor question were held under the principle of local option, and for convenience the same boundaries were used for licensing as for electoral districts. Since 1896 these local licensing polls have regularly been conducted on the very day of the general election—and in the same polling booth. In addition, since 1911 at every general election (except that of 1931), a national referendum on the prohibition issue has also been held simultaneously. At a modern general election the New Zealander votes on three matters. First, he selects a party candidate to represent the constituency in Parliament. Second, in a national referendum he ballots for one of three choices: prohibition, state purchase and control of the liquor trade, or continuance of the existing system of licensing and regulation. Third, there is a local poll to determine whether or not alcoholic drinks shall be sold in his particular district. The keen public interest aroused by the prohibition controversy has often attracted to the polls a class of citizens who were less concerned with party warfare than with social and ethical issues."[26]

Influence on the Vote of Parties and Campaigning

One final point to be mentioned among the influences which bring a voter to the polls is the party organization and campaigning technique. Where a party is efficiently organized and mobilizes its supporters to vote, the participation will, of course, be higher. Historically, the early origins of regular party organization in the constituencies, both in Britain and the United States, were directly due to this desire to bring out the vote. In Britain, the creation of local party organization was an immediate consequence of the Reform Act of 1832, which broadened the qualifications for the franchise. Registration in those days was a voluntary act of the citizen, and the provisions of the law were so complicated that many individuals did not know whether they were qualified to vote or not. Since the potential electorate had been considerably increased, it was in the interest of the parties to find who their possible supporters were and to encourage

26. This passage is reprinted from my work *The Politics of Equality: New Zealand's Adventures in Democracy* (University of Chicago Press, 1948) pp. 172-3.

them first to register and then to vote.[27] For the same reasons, and by the like logic, it was after the second extension of the franchise (1867) that the local party structures were combined nationally into a central organization whose networks covered the country. The Conservatives, under the stimulus of Disraeli, did this first in 1867; the Liberals followed suit ten years later.

In modern times, it is undeniable that electoral success depends on good organization that heartens the stalwarts, encourages the waverers, and attracts the independents. The British Conservative party gained new votes in 1950 and returned to office in 1951 in part because of its internal house-cleaning under Lord Woolton. The Republicans were able to oust the Democrats in 1952 with a popular candidate and a well-financed organization aggressively run. Likewise in 1960 the Kennedy forces scored an upset victory by careful planning and thorough campaigning in the key states. Undoubtedly the spread of the mass media is an aid to modern democracy in this respect, although in some other respects they constitute a danger. No politician underestimates the power of publicity. The newspapers, by simply deciding what they choose to print and where, can promote a candidate or destroy him. They can stimulate or dull the voters' interest. Since the late 1920's, the use of the radio has brought the voices of the party leaders into everybody's living room. The unprecedented succession of four straight wins by Franklin Delano Roosevelt was certainly helped by the eloquent tones of his vibrant personality. More recently still, television has proven supremely important because of its vivid impact on the viewer. The voter appraises the candidate not only by what he says and how he phrases it, but also by the sincerity and nuances of facial expression. In the American presidential election of 1960, a now classic case, the famous television debates between the candidates heightened the general popular interest in the election and gave Kennedy the edge over his opponent.

Even television, radio, and the press are not enough to fulfill the Greek conception of the democratic citizen as an active participant, nor do they recreate the real meaning of Aristotle's dictum that the citizen-body should be only so large as can assemble in one place and see and hear one orator. For when a speaker faces an audience, there is an interplay in mood and thought. Interruptions, questions, the time-honored arts of heckling, are the tests of any man who seeks public office. When people listen to the radio, however, or watch the television, they are scattered

27. "The watchword of the new era was given by Sir Robert Peel in his celebrated advice to the electors of Tamworth in 1841, 'Register, register, register!'" A. L. Lowell, *The Government of England* (Macmillan: New York, 1921), Vol. 1, Chap. 27, p. 481.

physically. As isolated individuals, they cannot communicate among themselves. They are reduced to passive spectators who have no means to answer back. The skilful use of propaganda techniques, exploited with all the wiles of modern advertising, converts what should be a democratic dialogue into a herding of sheep by the practiced shepherds of "public relations." All the dangers of this tendency in its extreme form can be observed in the one-party dictatorships of modern times. They are the ultimate examples of what can happen when an elite of experts, without effective popular checks, keeps control of power by playing on the mass-suggestibility of the semi-educated. The elections, referenda, and plebiscites of the authoritarian regimes do not belong in the same category as those which democracies employ. Such votes are not free, because no genuine alternatives between programs, parties, or candidates are presented and no meaningful conflict of opinion is openly expressed. Voting under a dictatorship serves a special purpose. It is intended as a public ceremony of allegiance to those in power. To vote "No," or not to vote at all, is regarded as treason. Hence the artificial and meaningless percentages (always 99 per cent in favor) which are recorded.

But the techniques of dictators are a warning to those who take their democracy seriously. They indicate what can be accomplished by the use or abuse of modern mass-media when the latter are not properly checked and counterchecked by an objective search for truth and the free expression of contrary views. Whether or not politics should be called, in Henry Adams' phrase, "the systematic organization of hatreds," fears and animosities do play a large part in its processes. At many elections, many persons vote against a man they wish to beat, rather than for someone they hope to win. Especially in times of crisis—when there is war or the threat of it, when the economy collapses, when an ethnic group feels itself encircled or beleaguered—the ordinary citizen votes in accord with his anxieties. The political psychology of dictators consists in prolonging that sense of crisis. For is not this their justification for arbitrary arrests, police terror, concentration camps, and censorship of thought? Does not authoritarianism thrive on perpetuating the fear and suspicion of the enemies without and the traitors within?

Possibly this kind of anxiety, or something akin to it, may explain the fact, on which many writers have commented, that some of the higher percentages of voter participation occur in the very countries where no political regime has much stability and democracy itself, when practiced, is on trial. At any rate, it is true that throughout the fourteen years of the Weimar Republic, which underwent repeated elections during its short life, large numbers of German voters marched solidly to the polls. Frenchmen were regularly voting in the last two decades of the Third Republic and under the Fourth in bigger proportion than were Americans or Britons. Likewise, since their liberation from Mussolini's Fascism, Italians have been active and eager at marking ballots. Hence there is some plausibility in the argument that some of the non-voters in a stable democracy are not necessarily apathetic and should not be written off, in the word of Pericles, as "useless." It could well be that the general feeling of calm pervading a secure and orderly society expresses itself in a certain measure in a disinclination to vote. In a stable community, a change of the party in control is not followed by abrupt reversals of everything that was previously done. On the contrary, the amount of innovation which is usually accomplished by a new government coming to power in a democracy is generally slight,[28] in comparison with the volume of continuity from the past. Some non-voting citizens are realistically aware that what a politician can do in office will be only a fraction of what he promises. Unless, therefore, some special reason at the moment prompts a desire for change or a fear of it, the non-voter can calculate with some confidence, and occasionally some cynicism, that, whatever the outcome of a particular election, life will go on much the same as before.

Political Implications of Mass Voting

An election, however, is the supreme event in which the people speaks for itself. Power is obtained in a democracy by the submission of men and measures to popular approval. It is at this time, and by this process, that citizens who are subject to law affirm themselves the masters of those who make it. When a democracy conducts an election, its citizens are asked to declare, individually and collectively, what it is they want. If they have a will to communicate to those entrusted with authority, this is their moment for its expression. Much, therefore, depends on the conduct of elections, the response they elicit, and the results they yield. For if elections fail us, democracy fails.

The effects of elections can be felt in three directions. They influence the policies of government, the organization of parties, and the votes of citizens. Let us examine some consequences of the system from these diverse angles.

The eminent authority on the British constitution, A. V. Dicey, published in 1905 his well-known *Lectures on the Relation between Law and*

28. But there are exceptions. The innovations of the New Deal were not slight, nor were those of Britain's Labour Government between 1945 and 1950.

Public Opinion in England during the Nineteenth Century. In that work he divided the century into three periods, within each of which he traced a causal connection between the currents of public opinion and the trends in parliamentary legislation.[29] The movements of the former, as he saw, produce the changes in the latter, since lawmakers respond to the ideological vogue. This is an important thesis, and, though it may not sound startling nowadays, was somewhat novel when he introduced it. But a crucial link needs inserting in the causal chain. The lawmakers in a democracy receive their office through election. To retain that position, therefore, they respond specifically to the views of those who have the votes. Hence the currents of public opinion flow into an assembly through the channels of the legislators' constituencies. The size of the electorate determines the attitudes of candidates, and the composition of the representative chamber determines the legislative output. As a matter of fact, the periods into which Dicey divided the nineteenth century correspond exactly to successive stages in the expansion of the suffrage and the redistribution of parliamentary seats. He places the end of the first period in 1830, two years before the passage of the first Reform Act; and the end of the second in 1870, three years after the second Act was passed.[30]

It stands to reason that, when men are seeking elective office and parties are choosing their candidates, they will bear in mind the characteristics of the electorate to whom they must appeal. As oligarchies were supplanted by democracies, more and more citizens were given the chance to express their preferences at the polls. When universal adult suffrage became the rule, the vote of a single individual counted for very little—but still it did count. In political terms, the public became not just an amorphous mass of isolated individuals, but an intricate congeries of groupings, associations, and interests. Some were identifiable and structured—a manufacturers' association, a trade union, a church membership. Others comprised a statistical group, discoverable through the census or other research, but unorganized and unknown to one another as such—the aged, the housewives, the "floating vote." The electoral process under these circumstances involves a response to the organized who make their viewpoints known and the conscious crystallization of the fluid sentiments of the dispersed. The political party is the intermediary. It serves as the broker to unite a

29. Those were, as he defined them in Lecture IV: "1. The Period of old Toryism or legislative quiescence (1800-1830), 2. Period of Benthamism or Individualism (1825-1870), 3. Period of Collectivism (1865-1900)."
30. Dicey refers to the extension of the franchise, though without, in my judgment, giving it the emphasis it deserves. See Lectures VI and VII and the Introduction to his second edition.

diversity of particular interests and groups under the guise of the general good. Electioneering under conditions where every adult may vote requires that programs be broadly conceived and that an appeal be made to every sizable group. Mass participation, by broadening the basis of popular consent to the ultimate limit, has revolutionized the objectives of modern government. The strategy of fighting an election of this kind compels the parties to offer programs which contain something for everybody.[31]

Thus far, the result of achieving universal adult suffrage may be deemed a gain. But there is another direct consequence, implicit in what has just been said, which has elements of danger. The sheer size of a modern electorate makes campaigning arduous, complicated, and, above all, expensive. Everyday language may refer to "the popular will;" politicians canvassing for votes may allude to "the sovereign people." But such phrases involve more rhetoric than reality. "The people" does not act as a singular entity. Rousseau notwithstanding, no corporate personality exists with its *moi commun* and *volonté générale*.[32] Those are the speculations of fiction or metaphysics, with which we become acquainted in the writings of Rousseau or Hegel—but not in real life. In actual fact, the people is a collection, or multiplication, of millions of individuals, each interlocked with others in myriad modes of association. The art of politics consists in taking a huge and often formless multitude and evoking or supplying some coherence and purpose. For this, again, the parties are indispensable. They offer structure, direction, and, I would add, after acknowledging all that is irrational in our politics, whatever modicum it exhibits of rationality.

Nevertheless, we pay a price for organization, even though we are helpless without it. Organization is accompanied by rules, discipline, officials. These are necessary for reaching the millions who form the public. Equally necessary is money, in sums that also reach the millions. To conduct a campaign in a modern election costs a great deal, precisely because the electorate is so vast. Hence all the techniques of publicity must be employed—billboards and leaflets, advertising in the newspapers, meetings and rallies, anything that focuses the attention of voters on the candidate, his party, and their program. Since few candidates possess the requisite funds, and since voters anyway are influenced by the party as much as, or more than, by the man, it is the party organization which spends the money that attracts the votes. Thus whoever controls the organization, and provides and disburses the funds, exercises a disproportionate influence on the people's choice. In this way it becomes possible for an ele-

31. There will be further discussion of this point in Chapters 11 and 12.
32. But there may be a general interest, or a common good, without a general will.

ment of oligarchy to be reintroduced through the machinery a mass democracy requires for its operation.[33] Wealthy individuals who are donors
to campaign chests, business corporations and trade unions, the organized
interests and pressure groups of a complex industrial society, all these
contribute the fuel to the party machine. Inevitably therefore the suspicion arises that a government may be persuaded to give favors to those
by whose help it was elected. By this I do not mean to imply that fate
condemns us to be the victims of an "iron law of oligarchy." There is no
such "law" in the sense of inescapable necessity. But there is in the history of all big organizations a recurrent tendency—more plastic than iron
—for their control to fall into the hands of a few. This does not negate
the practicability or genuineness of democracy. Democracy rests on two
realities: that the majority can always reassert their ultimate power, and
that the possibility of choice between competing oligarchies imposes restraints on the power of each.

The Education of the Public

The element of choice that every genuine election poses contributes not
only to the freedom of the people but also to their education. For when
a campaign is seriously conducted and conscientiously followed, the educative effect upon the voters is incalculable. I am not saying that elections
are always conducted as they ought to be, that all campaigning is high-
minded, and that issues are presented fairly and squarely and debated with
facts and logic. Far from it. Everyone can think of numerous examples to
the contrary. Indeed, as often as not, an election is more of a disillusion-
ment than an inspiration. But even the seamy side—the posturing, half-
truths, false promises, and slick advertising—can teach a lesson to those
disposed to learn. There is a permanent and basic truth in Lincoln's remark: "You can fool some of the people all of the time, and all of the
people some of the time; but you can't fool all of the people all of the
time." The democratic process, because of its freedom to criticize and its
constant publicity, is merciless in exposing demagogues, hypocrites, and
fools. The majority of the voting public are not so stupid. They often succeed in detecting deception and seeing through buncombe. In the long
run, the "hollow men"[34] are generally punctured. Their wiles have a way
of boomeranging. The supreme test of a politician is not what he says in

33. In the American presidential campaign of 1960, Mr. Kennedy spent $912,500 to
secure the Democratic nomination, as much as was spent by all his leading opponents
put together. The post-convention campaign, on the national level, cost both parties
$25,000,000, an increase of 46% over what was spent in 1956.
34. The title of a poem by T.S. Eliot.

an election campaign, but what he does in office. When a man faces re-election, he has a record by which he can be judged. The responsibilities of modern government are inexorable, and opponents are relentless in criticism. The public may sometimes grow cynical as a result; but in a mature democracy most citizens develop a sophisticated sense.

These arrangements whereby we elect those who will govern us and entrust them with office for a determinate period produce a positive benefit when certain conditions are met. There are some things which the people, *en masse,* can do, and can do reasonably well. For other functions they are ill-equipped. What takes place at an election is essentially this. The voting public is presented with a choice between two or more parties whose leaders are known. Each party is officially committed to a program, which will be fairly specific on some matters and vague or evasive on others. When the people come to vote, they are not expected to pass judgment on particular policies or express a preference for the details of one program as against another. This the people should not do, because they cannot do it well. Such decisions would require a range of information and a depth of studied research for which few have either the time or training. What the people are asked is to look at alternative programs whose broad effect involves a continuation or change of governmental policy in this general direction or that. They are also asked to express their confidence in one group of political leaders or another. Then, after a number of years have elapsed, they take a fresh look at the men and their administration and decide again on the general direction and its top directors. To expect more than this is to seek utopia. To require at least this is democracy.

Some of the implications in those comments require more discussion. Every system, however useful, can be misapplied or abused. You can take any good principle, which makes sense in moderation, and ruin it by excess. Elections are no exception. I am not thinking here of so obvious a requirement as honesty. It is essential, of course, that the campaigning, the machinery of registration, the actual balloting, the subsequent count, be honestly conducted. Difficulties arise at each stage of the procedure, but the basic point is beyond dispute. As everyone is against sin, so are we all against corruption. But there are other aspects of elections whose effects are more subtle and which are open to argument from a psychological, not an ethical, standpoint.

The Frequency of Elections

Consider, for instance, the frequency with which elections are held. How long should be the period between them? This is an interesting problem because it involves striking a balance between two requirements which are contradictory. According to good democratic theory, a government exercises authority entrusted to it by the people, and it is the latter's consent which places political power upon an ethical foundation. Since popular consent is the source of the right of a government to act, it follows—on one line of democratic thought—that, the more the people are consulted, the plainer their consent and the purer the ethics of the state. A. D. Lindsay has emphasized the importance of this doctrine to the Puritan founders of English democracy. In later developments, what he calls "the crude theory of democracy" put so much stress on the need for individual assent as to make any government impossible.[35] As the idea of representative democracy replaced the earlier notion of direct decision by the people, in order to preserve consent it was argued that elections should be held as frequently as possible.

In the original form of the Constitution of the United States as inaugurated in 1789, the only democratic institution of the federal government was the House of Representatives, since this body alone was elected directly. The term of office, however, of a Representative was only two years. By contrast, the President was chosen indirectly by an electoral college, and was given four years, while Senators, who also were elected indirectly, were allowed six. In Britain the House of Commons used to be elected for seven years. That period was reduced in 1911 to five, which is the present legal limit, although any Parliament retains the power to extend its own life, as was done during World Wars I and II.[36] In the 1840's, the Chartists, obedient to the "crude theory," were advocating that elections be annual!

If the need to obtain consent requires short terms and frequent elections, the conditions under which modern governments operate require the reverse. To govern effectively in the mid twentieth century, one wants a certain amount of continuity. There are many programs which take a number of years to inaugurate and a still longer time to bear fruit (for example, slum clearance and rehousing). Administrators cannot carry out such programs if their work is suddenly disrupted and the policy reversed. Men elected to public office, however, are under a political pressure to show results. When an election comes around, a politician seeks votes on his record and is anxious to show a positive accomplishment. As a matter

35. See *The Modern Democratic State* (Oxford University Press, 1943) pp. 12, 118-19, 231-5.
36. The Parliament elected in December, 1910, sat until November, 1918. The one chosen in 1935 stayed on until 1945.

of fact, while an election serves the democratic purpose of consulting the people's wishes, it is extraordinarily disruptive of the processes of legislation and administration. When the date for an election is near, those in office are sensitive and nervous. They will do whatever will assure their re-election, and will avoid anything which might be a political liability. A legislative body in an electoral year is highly aware of public opinion, particularly of the moods which prevail in the constituencies. The government at such a time will authorize decisions of policy which make it popular or have a good publicity value. The ticklish or contentious questions it will try to postpone. In effect, the knowledge that elections will recur at fairly regular periods induces a government to conform to a certain political rhythm. The measures which the country may need, but which will be unpopular with various groups (for instance, a tax increase), are best dealt with immediately after an election at the commencement of a new legislative term. The public can then absorb the shock and, as the politicians hope, forget about it or grow used to it by the time of the next election. Popular measures, such as an increase in social security benefits, may be proposed and authorized when an election is just in the offing, so that the voters concerned may react with the appropriate gratitude.

From the standpoint of their effects on the political behavior of governments and representatives, elections should be held regularly, but not too frequently. The regularity is vital in order that politicians will periodically be forced to respond to public pressure on major issues. The frequency, however, should not be excessive, so that between upheavals they may raise their sights to the far-off horizons of national progress.

Can all of these contradictory requirements be adjusted, and, if so, what would seem to be the most sensible interval between elections? Nobody nowadays, if the Constitution of the United States were to be rewritten anew, would dream of limiting the term of a Representative to a mere two years. A man in that office has only one year of respite, and already he has to think of the next foray. Conversely, although on this one cannot be so positive, many would consider a six-year term to be excessive. A United States Senator, for instance, is even more secure than he should be, and often acts too independently of the President—even when the latter is of his own party. The reasonable compromise appears to be the quadrennial elections required in the United States for the Presidency and for an increasing number of the governorships. There are many other democracies, large and small, which operate nowadays on the basis of quadrennial elections. The Swiss used to elect their National Council for three years, but in 1931 extended the term to four. New Zealand has adhered to triennial elections ever since 1881.[37] But the results are not so good, because the party in power is virtually forced to concoct some vote-catching proposal in every third year. In Great Britain, where the Prime Minister determines the date at which the election will be held, Parliaments seldom last for their full five years. As a matter of interest, it is worth remarking that since the end of World War I, their average duration has been three years and nine months, which is almost the same as the four-year term of an American President.[38]

Of all the democracies, the one in which the electorate is most over-worked is Switzerland. In that country the federal system itself requires the holding of elections for three separate levels of government, and these take place at different times. In addition, the Swiss fondness for the referendum and the initiative adds to the voters' responsibilities until the burden becomes well-nigh unbearable. In the majority of cantons, people are expected to go to the polls too often. As a result, they tend to become bored with the system.

The Popular Initiative and Referendum

The experience of Switzerland invites discussion of a related topic: the use of the initiative and referendum. These are not peculiar to the Swiss. They can be found in various forms and to various degrees in several countries. On the Pacific coast of the United States, for instance, they are extensively employed. But it is the Swiss who have carried such procedures furthest and have systematically incorporated them into their methods of government at all levels. What is the significance of the referendum and the initiative? How valuable are they to democracy? How do they work? What have been their results? The questions do not permit a simple answer, for here is one of those problems in which one may give assent to a principle, but have doubts about its practice. The principle is at its strongest as applied to the adoption or amendment of the constitution. In countries which distinguish between their constitution and ordinary legislation, giving legal priority to the former, it makes sense to argue that anything which is truly fundamental should be decided by the people. Hence if a

37. In World War I elections were postponed until hostilities were over. During World War II the elections were deferred from 1941 to 1943. On both occasions, this was done by agreement between the parties. In the depression of the early 1930's, however, a Conservative government, over Labour protests, postponed an election for one year and was punished by the voters in 1935.

38. Between 1918 and 1963, twelve elections were held.

new constitution is to be approved, it should be submitted to popular vote. Once that has been done, the text of the basic law should only be altered in the same manner. Likewise, since all power flows from the people, the constitutional machinery, which they have themselves adopted, should include an opportunity for them to initiate change as well as, subsequently, to accept or reject it. In a democracy, the people are not expected to remain passive. Their role can also be active.

There is merit in this argument, and its logic is consistent. But the same merit and consistency do not apply to the use of the initiative and referendum in the ordinary sphere of legislation. The argument in this case was voiced, at the time when democracy was embracing the representative principle, in order to reserve important functions for the people. The regular kind of election in which the public votes for party nominees to sit in a legislature was considered insufficient. At such an election, the people have no way of expressing their opinions about specific measures. They can do this, however, through the initiative and referendum. By the former, they can themselves propose something. By the latter, they can have a law submitted to popular ratification. Implied in this, of course, is no small distrust of the legislature. If the people had full confidence in their representatives, they would have no need to take matters into their own hands. Indeed, when the referendum and initiative were adopted in the western region of the United States, it was for this very reason. State legislatures too commonly had fallen under the domination of special interests—e.g., the railroads, banks, and privately owned utilities. The people wanted to be able to countercheck what was done at the State capital. In a sense, therefore, while indirect democracy was established through representative government, direct democracy was reintroduced through the initiative and referendum. The people were taking back with one hand what they were giving with the other.

The results of the system in operation have been a strange mixture. Some good has come out of it, along with many disappointments, and some surprises. The greatest good unquestionably is the educative effect on the general public. If people take their duty seriously—that "if" is a big one—they learn a lot about their society and the problems of governing it. The public debate, articles and reports in the press, the distribution of propaganda materials pro and con, all this can heighten the civic sense of awareness and responsibility. But by the same reasoning, many voters can be duped. The appeals which succeed may be those directed to their prejudices. How interested the voters are depends on the inherent importance of the topic and the intensity of the campaigning. In Switzerland, between 1918 and 1947, the people voted on twenty-five initiatives to amend the federal constitution, of which only three received the requisite double majority of the total popular vote and more than half the cantons. On seven of these occasions, the federal legislature offered counterproposals of its own, five of which were approved.[39] The percentage of voters ranged from a low of 41.8 to a high of 86.3.[40] In fact, the two issues which elicited most participation were controversial measures proposed by the Socialist party in 1922 and 1935, both of which were rejected. William E. Rappard sums up the results by observing that the majority of initiated amendments which were accepted brought fewer voters to the polls and were successful because of the amount of abstentions rather than of participation.[41] In the case of constitutional referenda, where the measures originated in the legislature itself, more are adopted, but fewer people vote. Only two out of nineteen were rejected between 1918 and 1947. On three occasions, less than 40 per cent of the voters took part, and on no occasion did the participants exceed 80 per cent.[42]

One of the surprising results of the system has been the discovery that the majority of the public are cautious, even conservative. When the initiative and referendum were being proposed both in the Swiss federal government and in American States of the West, it was the radicals—or those at any rate to the left of Center—who supported these devices. Right-wing groups generally were opposed because they feared that wealth would be penalized by poverty. As things have turned out, such anxieties were groundless. While the referendum and initiative have sometimes been used to help the underprivileged or curb the strength of economic oligarchies, the people have not pushed their voting power to the extreme of social revolution. In Switzerland, many measures which would be considered progressive have been defeated by popular referendum. Sometimes it has taken thirty years and three votes before a program won approval.

In Sweden, only three referenda have occurred since the system was made possible by constitutional amendment in 1922. That same year, a little over half the electorate voted on a proposal to prohibit the sale and consumption of alcoholic liquor, which was rejected by a slight majority. On the second occasion, which came three decades later in 1955, the gov-

39. Without the initiatives, however, the legislature would probably not have been stimulated to act.
40. On these thirty-two initiatives and counterproposals, the percentage of registered voters participating was between 40% and 50% on six measures; between 50 and 60% on nine; between 60 and 70% on fifteen; and over 80% on two. See William E. Rappard, La Constitution Fédérale de la Suisse (A la Baconnière: Neuchâtel, 1948), pp. 329-30.
41. Ibid., p. 331.
42. Ibid., pp. 347-8.

ernment submitted to the public the question whether to switch from left-hand traffic to driving on the right. Such a change was plainly desirable in view of the fact that Sweden in this respect was "odd man out" on the Continent. Nevertheless, with only one out of two registered voters participating, a decisive majority preferred to retain its accustomed ways. Soon afterward, in 1957, the voters were again consulted with a choice of no less than three different schemes for a system of national pensions. To this bait, as many as 72.4 per cent of the voters responded—a turn-out which was large for a referendum, though much less than occurs at general elections. The result, as could be expected when the ballots were divided three ways, could scarcely be called conclusive.[43]

Distrust of the Legislature

One aspect of the use of the referendum which may appear surprising is that the people have not hesitated to reject measures which have been adopted by the legislature. When this happens, what are the implications for our theories of representation? Ideally, the legislature is supposed to represent the public—to be, in effect, a microcosm of the people at large—and to know what the people want and respond to their wishes. When the majority of the legislators vote one way, and the majority of the people another, something is evidently out of kilter. The reasons for this are varied. Sometimes the electoral system can produce a result in the legislature which distorts the proportions of viewpoints among the public.[44] This can easily occur, of course, under the American system. But in Switzerland, which has proportional representation, it is supposed not to happen. Or a new question may have arisen which was not uppermost in the minds of the parties or the voters when the last election occurred. Or it may simply be that the legislators, who take part in committee hearings and have access to reports from the civil service and elsewhere, are better informed. Their vote may be based on superior knowledge; that of the public, on ignorance and inertia. Certainly, there are cases on record where the legislative sentiment has been ahead of public opinion; and there are reverse instances where the majority of voters are ahead of a legislature which is controlled by special interests. But, whatever the cause may be, the fact remains that the "representative" body does not always and accurately represent. That is proven by the experience with the referendum and initiative.

43. For information on this subject, I am indebted to Professor Eric C. Bellquist.
44. For a discussion of this problem, see Chapter 14, pp. 442 ff.

The question of the knowledge that underlies a vote is relevant and important. Indeed it raises an issue which is fundamental not only to democracy, but to all politics. If all the available information points strongly to one conclusion, but the majority of the people want the opposite, which view should prevail?[45] Through the initiative and referendum measures may be submitted to the people whose content is inherently technical. In that case, is it wise to have such matters decided by a majority vote of the general public? A few years ago, in the area of California where I live, the people were asked to vote on a proposal to add fluoride to the drinking water as a protection against dental caries. A campaign of considerable intensity was conducted for and against the measure, which eventually was defeated. My point is merely that on such a question the people should not be voting. The problems relevant to the decision are those for which scientific knowledge is required. In this field the opinions of hydraulic engineers, public health officers, chemists and dental scientists, are germane; those of John Q. Public, myself included, are not. Only a legislative body, advised and buttressed by the necessary data and reports, can weigh the technical evidence and reach a reasonable conclusion in the public interest.

This line of criticism can also be directed against the distinction mentioned earlier between using popular votes for adopting or amending a constitution and employing the same device for approving ordinary legislation. In principle it would seem that one can agree to the former, while being dubious about the latter. But even the wisdom of submitting constitutional amendments to the people can be questioned, because of the way in which in some cases the principle has degenerated in practice. Ever since the referendum and initiative were incorporated into the Swiss federal constitution in 1874, their use has resulted in cluttering up the document with amendments, some of which are essentially legislative in content. Since the federal constitution, unlike the constitutions of some cantons, does not permit a popular initiative in legislation, the public have reacted by proposing laws in the form of constitutional amendments. To a greater degree, and with worse results, the same has happened in the western United States. In this particular respect, the State of California has a constitution which is notoriously at fault.[46] It was originally adopted in 1879, at a time when Kearneyism had made some stir in San Francisco,

45. This problem is discussed in Chapter 17, pp. 551 ff.
46. I have no hesitation here in comparing California, a State within a federal system, with the Swiss Confederation. California's population is four times that of Switzerland; its area ten times as big. In its economic development, both agricultural and industrial, and its regional and social diversity, this State forms an empire in itself.

and the railroads and various governmental agencies were under attack. Even when Bryce published the first edition of his *American Commonwealth*, he reprinted this extraordinary document in an appendix and directed the reader's attention to its abnormal contents. The motive which dominated the drafting was distrust—distrust of the big corporations and of all officials, whether appointive or elected. The outcome was a structure in which powers were carefully circumscribed, often in great detail, and care was taken to prevent the future repetition of past abuses. Not long afterward, when the wave of direct democracy washed the Pacific Coast, the already weak foundations of the State government were flooded with the popular initiative and referendum. Now, after seven decades of their operation, the whole edifice is strewn with their flotsam and jetsam. Here is a classic case of a principle ruined by its practice.

The moral is plain, although politics even in a democracy does not always conform to its morals. Ultimate political power in a democracy resides in the people, meaning all the adult citizens. Their consent gives to government the moral authority from which its legal powers are derived. The principal procedure through which the people make their wishes known is a general election. On this occasion, the voters fill the legislature for a determinate number of years and express approval for a broad direction in the sphere of governmental policy. So far, the people are doing what they can do, and what no one else can do for them. Beyond that, the people may intervene in decisions on which their judgment is not enlightened. The freedom of the people lies in their power to elect and, if they are so convinced, to refuse a further term of office to the same men next time. Democracy is not helped if burdens are placed upon its institutions which they are not fitted to support. An election is conducted both to educate the public and to entrust certain men with official powers. That is the great purpose of the electoral system, and that is enough.

But a further problem still remains. The referendum and initiative were adopted at the very time when the functions of all governments were beginning to increase. There is a rough logic, or a rough justice, in what these devices attempted to accomplish. If governments were receiving additional powers in order to give new services to their citizens, the latter should redouble their means of controlling their government in order that those powers should not be abused. The reintroduction of direct democracy was not a happy solution. But it was directed to a real problem. Nor is that problem solved yet. The nature of a solution must depend on the party system and its relation to the formal institutions of the state. To these matters, therefore, the next two chapters are devoted.

11

The Two-Party System

In the government of a modern democracy, political parties occupy the
central position. The functions they perform are indispensable since without them the representative institutions which we know today could not
work. Viewed in terms of its organization, a democratic government consists in the rule of the majority party or coalition, aided by a corps of politically neutral administrators, and criticized continuously by the opposition party or parties. The civil service supplies efficiency and expertise;
the parties contribute responsibility to the public and criticism on behalf
of the public.

In some of their functions, and certainly in their internal structures,
parties are a modern invention. They are modern, that is, in the sense that
their present character was formed in the last hundred years. But like the
civil service, which has its antecedents in authoritarian Prussia and the
Chinese mandarinate, parties too are the product of a long evolution in
which the continuity is no less significant than the change. Wherever
sufficient diversity occurs among the interests which compose a society,
and the political system affords them an opportunity to combine, men will
cluster into groupings, more or less formal, more or less cohesive. They
do this in order that by union of the like-minded they may protect whatever they have at stake and extend their influence to wider spheres. It is
the constant interaction of such organized groups—through the representation of interests, formulation of policy, competition for power, control of
government, or criticism of the government—it is this which constitutes a
party system.

The Ancestors of Parties

The origins of parties can be traced back a long way. At least they were present in the first known democracy. The Athenian *Polis* in the fifth century B.C. was divided not only on occupational and economic lines (between rich and poor, farmers and city folk, fishermen, retail tradesmen, merchants, and the like), but also along lines of broad social classes and divergent philosophies. The aristocrats, or Eupatrids, were pitted against the Demos. The former were conservatives, since, after all, they did have something to conserve; the latter were radicals who had little and wanted more. Leaders of the radicals were Themistocles, then Ephialtes, next Pericles, and later Cleon and Agyrrhius.[1] Their successive opponents on the Right were Miltiades, Aristides, Cimon, who was Miltiades' son, and Thucydides (not the historian, but his namesake, the son of Melesias). It was this Thucydides, in opposition to the policy of converting the Delian League into an Athenian Empire, who urged his supporters to sit together in the Assembly, to applaud or jeer in unison, and vote as a bloc. These were the elementary, yet fundamental, tactics of a political leader mobilizing his followers into a party for a show of strength.

Similarly, in the last agonizing century of the Roman Republic, from the Gracchi to the Battle of Actium, Rome wrestled with its problems of adjusting to imperial expansion and revamping its constitutional arrangements to accord with social and economic change. The opposition between classes and movements broke out into violence when the struggle between Gaius Gracchus and the senatorial oligarchy ended with the assassination of the people's tribune, and was then resumed in open warfare between armies under Marius and Sulla. Cicero, a clever lawyer and gifted orator, who climbed from modest origins as the spokesman for the ruling clans, defines and distinguishes between the parties which he labels *optimates* and *populares*. Their contest was conducted in the consular elections of the *Comitia Centuriata*, in the institutional conflicts between the senate and the tribunes, and finally in a test of authority between the central government and proconsuls holding provincial commands. In the climax, it was Caesar, an aristocrat of the Julian clan, who espoused the cause of the *populares* against the senatorial clique and its military champion, Pompey. The civil war between these men, later continued and completed between Octavian and Anthony, marked the climax of a party

1. Pericles belonged to the great aristocratic clan, the Alcmaeonids. Cleon and Agyrrhius, in the days of the advanced democracy, were called by the opprobrious epithet "leaders of the people"—demagogues.

struggle whose politics reflected the military and economic changes which existing institutions could neither absorb nor regulate.

In the Middle Ages the relations between Empire and Papacy perennially erupted into discord, and each institution, temporal and ecclesiastical, found its supporters among different clans of the nobility. The long-lasting rivalry of Guelphs and Ghibellines originated in Germany and spread through Italy. From the twenfth century onward, regions and cities were pitted against one another and were split internally by the partisans of these famous names.The Guelphs took the papal side; the Ghibellines, the imperial. Beyond that, locally prominent families, which for one reason or another[2] were competitors or foes, identified their mutual enmities with these broader warring factions. But there was little in their struggles, apart from their preference for Pope or Emperor, which expressed a political principle; nor did they represent a cleavage of interests between social and economic classes. The same can be said of the Wars of the Roses in fifteenth-century England. In that protracted duel, the two houses of Lancaster and York competed for possession of the crown and the nobility were forced to take sides. The result, not unnaturally, was to produce a reaction against feudalism and to usher in the centralizing monarchy of the Tudors.[3]

In England, France, and Spain the stronger kings of the sixteenth and seventeenth centuries conducted a personal type of government, in which they served as active and authoritative heads. Under these conditions, parties as such were not permissible, and their inception was discouraged. To be against the king was not ordinary political opposition. It was treason. Nevertheless, within the royal entourage there were men who tendered different advice and jockeyed at the court for positions of influence. In a broader sense, the courtiers and ministers would be representative of certain of the interests existing in the country at large—particularly the ecclesiastical and economic—and might, to enhance their own strength, be spokesmen for those viewpoints. Organization was lacking, of course, with the one exception of the church, which could at will produce a clerical party. Nor were there formal procedures for consultation or evoking opinion, save for the English Parliament. Anything that resembled a persistent combination or developed the rudiments of structure was frowned upon and stigmatized as faction—an epithet which connoted division of the country and disruption of its unity. As party systems emerged in the

2. Shakespeare has depicted their feuding, and its pettiness, in *Romeo and Juliet*.
3. At the end of the Middle Ages, Jack Cade's Rebellion in England (1450) and the Peasants' War in southwest Germany (1524-26) were symptoms of deeper social conflicts, and expressed the grievances of those whom politics did not yet seek to represent.

eighteenth century they had to emancipate themselves from the sinister reputation which factions had earned. And positively, they had to demonstrate that they could remain opposed to one another within a system which claimed their joint allegiance.

Why Parties Are Essential to Democratic Government

The revolutions that marked the beginnings of modern democracy threw up new problems for political solution—new in their scale and dimension, new in their internal complexity. Governing is never a simple task, and it was not even easy to operate a stable or harmonious government when the principal viewpoints to be reconciled were limited to those of rival families among the nobility or rival factions at a royal court. How much more difficult, then, to govern a people when all members of the community claim some voice in the determination of the policies which affect their lives and livelihood, and when the principle that underlies the system asserts, not merely that the people are the recipients of what others decide, but are themselves in some way the agents in a process of self-government. The circumstances and character of democracy created two needs. First, as the circle of political participants broadened, some means was required of organizing their relationships and imparting to their actions a pattern of purpose and coherence. The recording of millions of votes, without some common focus of policy and program, would only yield chaos. It could not serve as the durable basis for a government founded on the consent of the governed. Second, the institutions of the democratic state had to provide in some crucial place for the representation of the voting public and the reflection of its cross-pressures. This was clearly the task of an assembly (a Moot, Thing, or Congress), which served as a forum for debate and discussion (a Parliament, or speaking-place) and then as a body for authorizing high policy and enacting laws (a Legislature).

The party system evolved to meet both needs and provided the link, otherwise missing, between their solutions. It has been the vehicle for organizing millions of citizens and it has lent substance and direction to the work of the representative assembly. Elections are the mechanism for ascertaining the wishes of the former about the membership and product of the latter. The parties make up the core and center of politics. Everything which is politically relevant—be it social, institutional, or ideological—converges here. A party system serves democracy as a bridge, uniting society and the state. Consequently, it is susceptible to influences from both ends. From society, the parties derive much of their substance; from the state, much of their form. The mobilization of interests in groups, their opposition or overlap, provides the raw material out of which parties can grow, and these, as their perspectives widen, formulate ideals in the terms of a political philosophy. But parties, while they draw their content from society, are molded to the structure of the state. Not only the methods of election, but the design of the institutions through which policies are devised and executed, have some effect on party strategy and tactics and on the power to fulfill promises with programs.

Interestingly enough, this fact that parties have a dual aspect and play a double role is accurately expressed in an ambiguity of our language. The word "party" in ordinary English usage may refer to one or both of two things. It can describe an organization of the members of a legislative body, who acknowledge a common label, co-operate through the same leadership, and in general believe in similar policies. But a "party" can also mean their supporters outside the legislature. An association of citizens who agree substantially about the broad lines of governmental policy and habitually vote together constitutes a party. Indeed, in the literature on the subject there is sometimes confusion because the term is intended to apply in certain contexts to legislators and in others to voters. The French, being more precise, distinguish between the meanings by using *groupe* or *groupement* for the former and *parti* for the latter.

Two further distinctions are needed to clarify the subsequent analysis. For one thing, a party is not the same as a pressure group. The latter is an association of individuals united around a common interest, which can be economic or occupational, ethical or religious, or may correspond to any of the numerous facets of a pluralistic society. An organization of manufacturers or trade unionists, the growers of wheat or grapes, a church, a temperance movement, any of these may legitimately represent the viewpoint of an identifiable group on matters that fall within its sphere of concern. They may seek to influence governmental policy, endorse candidates for public office, and request the passage of laws. Obviously, these are activities in which parties are also engaged. How then are they distinguishable from pressure groups? The answer is primarily a difference between the general and the specific. The membership of a pressure group is limited, as are its aims. It protects an interest or promotes a cause. Its *raison d'être* is not political, and it intervenes in politics only for the reason, and to the extent, that the government can help or harm it. A party, however, has functions and purposes which are directly political. It seeks to govern. To that end, it must concern itself with the public interest, or at least appear to do so. Simply in order to attract enough support, the party must enlarge its viewpoint above and beyond the specific and the particular. It must review the narrower, and often competing, claims of pressure groups and private associations, and then moderate, compromise, unify them within the broader framework of the general welfare. Society, in its infinite diversity, creates the pressure group; politics, through its responsibility for the government of the whole, creates the party.

Something else which needs clarifying is the innocent-sounding word "system." What does this term imply? Without doubt, it refers to the number of parties and the relations between them. According to some scholars, party systems are of three kinds. There are those which contain only one, those which consist of two, and those which embrace three or more. Such a classification, in my judgment, not only involves bad semantics, but also imparts confusion to the understanding of the subject. A party is, by definition, a part of the whole. As such, it signifies the existence of other parts, i.e., a coexistence of parties. To speak of a one-party system, therefore, is to employ a contradiction in terms. A party system, properly so-called, must include more than one. Dictatorships do, it is true, mobilize their more ardent followers into a party where they are subject to an authoritarian discipline. But that kind of party serves a special purpose and has a peculiar character, because it functions primarily as the service arm of a dominant elite and enjoys a monopoly of political power. The parties in a democratic regime survive or fall under the conditions of competition, and their political being is fundamentally altered when they live by challenging others and being challenged in turn. The significant distinction is that which exists between dictatorial regimes, employing a single party, and the party systems of the democracies, which must always contain more than one. The difference between two-party and multi-party systems is, of course, important. But it is not nearly as profound as the difference between the party systems of genuine democracies and the one-party regime of the modern dictatorship.

Democratic philosophy places a high premium on the virtues of freedom and diversity. It is readily assumed that these are connected, since, where men are free, they will exhibit their individuality and variety will ensue. What is true of individuals applies also to their associations. When men are free to combine with one another, when they may voluntarily choose to join or not to join, the results in organizational terms will be almost bewildering in their number and complexity. Nowhere is this more evident than in the sphere of party politics. To know a democracy is to understand its politics, and to know its politics is to understand its parties. They contain the clues to everything else. Look at a party system and you see the community reflected in a mirror; and though the glass may distort and the frame be too small, this is the best reflection available.

The first point which impresses itself on the student of the subject is that individual parties, and *a fortiori* party systems, are so extraordinarily different. No two parties anywhere are alike. Within the same country, they differ—even though presumably they share some national characteristics in common. Between countries they are also unlike. Pick any two democracies you wish, and you observe that conservatives and conservatism are not identical, nor are socialists and socialism, nor liberals and liberalism. Every party has features which are unique in its support, its structure, its history; if each is dissimilar from the other, much more so are the systems which they form. The contrasts in the character of parties and party systems are a consequence of the democratic emphasis on the importance of freedom.

The Causes of the Party System

That being so, however, we are confronted with a problem. To the extent that something is unique, can it be compared with something else which also contains its elements of the unique? In a subject where so much is idiosyncratic, what generalizations can be valid? Is classification possible unless the type overshadows the particulars? If every case is an exception in some respect, what is the rule? These are difficulties which inevitably arise in applying the comparative method of political analysis to the diverse data of historical experience; and an inquiry into party systems poses such questions in perhaps their most acute form because of the complexities inherent in the topic. I do not believe it illuminates the subject to start, as is too frequently done,[4] with elaborate categories couched in a jargon which covers too much and explains too little. A conceptual scheme is useful when it helps to make reality more meaningful. It serves no good purpose when, instead of deciphering reality, it diverts discussion to what the concepts are meant to mean.

The most promising place to begin is with party systems in individual countries. Thence, one can proceed inductively to broader generalizations, reexamining them in the light of new situations and exceptions. In this way, whatever hypotheses emerge will have grown out of the facts, instead of the facts being interpreted to fit the hypothesis. The only classification that is needed at the beginning is the one which is the safest because it is the simplest. This is the distinction between two-party systems and those containing more than two. I propose to look at certain countries which

4. Principally by those who regard the study of politics as a science to which the consideration of values is irrelevant.

fall under one heading or the other, dealing in this chapter with the two-party system and in the next with multipartism, and shall raise this question in each instance: What was it in this country which caused this kind of party system to develop there? After that has been discussed in various cases, the answers can be compared. Such is one of the ways in which a comparative method can yield fruitful results. Inferences about causation which are based on a single instance are never so securely based as those derived from several. By comparing a number of cases, one discovers in what respects they are alike and in what respects they are unlike. It should then be possible to explain why this is so; that is to say, to pick out one set of causes which makes them similar and another which makes them different. The detection of similarities and dissimilarities, and the explanations for each, can only develop through comparisons properly made.

Political scientists in many lands have devoted close study to party systems in recent years, and considerable speculation has arisen over their causes.[5] It is precisely because the parties are located in between the state and its society, and belong in some measure to both, that scholars may reasonably disagree about which factors are the prime determinants of party politics. The arguments ordinarily advanced to explain why a particular system evolves where it does are of two kinds. Either the primary causes which mold the party system are located in the institutions of government, or they are attributed to the issues arising in society over which people take sides politically. It is the word "primary" in that sentence which requires some comment. None would deny that something as complicated as a party system may be influenced by several factors in varying degrees of immediacy and strength, or that an effect may later react upon its cause and help to reinforce it. Thus scholars who, like Professor Duverger, rely heavily on institutional interpretations make some allowance for social factors;[6] and others who, with M. Lavau, put their stress upon

5. Much discussion was stimulated by Maurice Duverger's Les Partis Politiques (Armand Colin: Paris, 1951). A contrary thesis was presented by G. E. Lavau in Partis Politiques et Réalités Sociales (Armand Colin: Paris, 1953). The literature on the subject is now voluminous, one important contribution being Modern Political Parties, S. Neumann, ed. (University of Chicago Press, 1956). My own published research on this topic can be found in the following articles: "The Two-Party System in British Politics," American Political Science Review, Vol. 47, No. 2, June, 1953, pp. 337-58; "Common Ground and Emerging Conflicts between the British Parties," Political Quarterly, Vol. 27, No. 1, April-June, 1956, pp. 182-93; "Le Système des Partis Politiques en Suisse," Revue Française de Science Politique, Vol. 6, No. 4, Oct.-Dec., 1956, pp. 813-32; and "Party Systems in the United Kingdom and the Older Commonwealth," Political Studies, Vol. 7, No. 1, Feb. 1959, pp. 12-31.
6. E.g., in Les Partis Politiques, pp. 263-4.

the latter do not regard the governmental framework as wholly irrelevant to its party politics.[7] What is really in dispute is which kind of cause, if any, is original and fundamental and whether it continues subsequently to be the most influential.

The countries I intend to discuss are Australia, Canada, Denmark, France, Great Britain, New Zealand, Norway, South Africa, Sweden, Switzerland, and the United States. Except for South Africa, all of these are democracies. South Africa is included, however, because its party system exemplifies the problems of a minority governing a racially divided state. France is a special case of another kind. Its party system could not produce a stable government during the Third and Fourth Republics and yielded to the strong presidential regime of the Gaullist constitution. The nine remaining countries contain a mixture of similarities and differences. All are unquestionably democratic; all have stable regimes. Their political institutions, however, are markedly different. In size, they are ranged along a scale from small to huge. In economic character and cultural composition they vary from simple to very complex. The same can be said about their party systems. These too are widely diverse, and yet their diversities reveal some repetitive patterns. Taking the elementary distinction between two-party and multi-party systems, one notes a fact which suggests a paradox. The two countries with the largest populations, the United States and Great Britain, have two-party systems, whereas some of the smallest require from four to six. Why is this? For the answers one should examine each system in turn. This I shall try to do with an extensive analysis in a few cases, and a briefer one for the rest.

The Classic Two-Party Model: Great Britain

The classic home of two-party government is Great Britain; nor is any feature of the system which has developed in that country more distinctive than its long duration. Although there is room for disagreement among historians about the time and circumstances of its birth, it would be difficult to deny that two-party government was established earlier, has lasted longer, and is still more firmly rooted there than in any contemporary state. Indeed, the practice of reducing the contest for office to a pair of major claimants has endured in Britain through a catalogue of changes which would assuredly have wrecked a less effective system. It has survived the evolution from an oligarchy of aristocrats to a democracy of all the people; the transfer of power from monarchy to parliament and

7. E.g., in *Partis Politiques et Réalitiés Sociales*, p. 45.

thence to the cabinet; the rise of large-scale industry with its social after-math; the switch in economic policy from mercantilism to laissez faire and from that to state planning; and withal, the expansion and later shrinkage of Britain's international might. Especially in recent decades, moreover, both major parties have developed a strength of organization and discipline to which New Zealand offers the nearest parallel inside the British Commonwealth and no similar approximation exists elsewhere.

The preceding argument could be challenged, however, on one of two grounds. It could be said, for instance, that more than two parties nor-mally exist in Britain contemporaneously, so that to speak of a two-party system is a misnomer. A word of definition is therefore in order, since otherwise discussion can be sidetracked and mired down in a semantic bog. Any state has a two-party system if it satisfies the following condi-tions:

1. Not more than two parties at any given time have a genuine chance to gain power.

2. One of these is able to win the requisite majority and stay in office without help from a third party.

3. Over a number of decades two parties alternate in power.

Such a statement has the merit of being politically realistic. It recog-nizes that, even where two giant organizations are dominant, some Lilli-putian groups may exist alongside of them. Only if one of the latter should succeed in holding the balance between the principal contenders does the two-party system cease, as for instance in contemporary Aus-tralia. The list of conditions further permits the possibility that a major party may dwindle and decline and eventually be replaced by a new-comer, as the British Labourites supplanted the Liberals. While this is hap-pening, of course, a three-party system may emerge temporarily (witness Britain in the period from 1918 to 1931). It is also compatible with a two-party system for a major party to suffer a prolonged eclipse and be overshadowed by its rival in a series of elections, as the Whigs over-whelmed the Tories from 1715 to 1760 and the Liberals led the Con-servatives between 1845 and 1874 and the Conservatives in their turn pre-vailed from 1885 to 1905. The presence within the system of minor parties which are unable to affect the control of power; the lengthy ascendancy of one party; even the extinction of a major party and the rise of a new one; these phenomena do not signify the abandonment of the two-party system provided that the previously stated conditions are fulfilled. What really matters is that over the long run government through two parties be clearly revealed as the norm, from which any departure is only temporary and to which the system always returns.[8] Judged by these criteria, Britain may be said to have operated the two-party system for two and a half centuries. Thus the long Whig ascendancy that began in 1715 did not prevent a Tory resurgence in 1760. Domestic conservatism during the Napoleonic period and immediately afterward did not prevent the Liberal-sponsored reforms of the 1830's. The Conservatives split in 1846 over the protection of home-grown wheat, but were reassembled by Disraeli to triumph in 1874. The Liberals were splintered in 1885-86, but came firmly into power in 1905. Labour was divided and routed in 1931, yet returned to sweep the country in 1945. A three-party system existed in the later decades of the nineteenth century because of the Irish question and the talents of Parnell, and again in the 1920's when Labourites were rising and the Liberals were declining. But the two-party system reasserted itself after each of these seeming deviations.

Another possible objection can be raised against the assertion of the longevity of the two-party system in Britain. This is assuming that certain basic features have persisted unbroken for centuries and that these comprise a continuous system. But was there in fact anything in the politics of the eighteenth century which can properly be called a party? Should the same term be applied to the varied political associations that mark the eras of the Pelhams and the Pitts, of Grey and Peel, of Gladstone and Disraeli, of Asquith and Balfour, of Attlee and Churchill? The truth is too plain to require argument that the lapse of more than two centuries has wrought profound and substantial change. British politics a couple of hundred years ago were decidedly oligarchical, and the government of those days was cast in a wholly aristocratic mold.[9] A century later,

8. In suggesting that British politics are characterized by a two and a half party system, Carl J. Friedrich overemphasizes the deviations. *Constitutional Government and Democracy* (Ginn and Company: Boston, rev. ed. 1950), p. 414.

9. Namier's work, *The Structure of Politics at the Accession of George III*, has provided evidence for the view that clusterings of nobles, cemented by patronage and position, do not amount to a party system. But any general conclusions to be drawn from this study are limited by its method of analysis. Namier operated on history as a surgeon, cutting through the evolutionary process and placing a cross section under the microscope. The truth he revealed was the truth of that moment. But this does not disclose the historical reality which consists in the flow of events through time and the sequence which unites the past, present, and future. Namier's observations were of a period when the long Whig hegemony had ended and their interests were less cohesive, while the Tories were clustering although their grouping had scarcely crystallized. Comparing the years 1760-61 with what preceded and what followed, one can discern, among the fluidity of groups and interests, some nascent bipolarity of outlook and direction. Many aristocrats were individualists or functioned as members of splinters. But there were two larger groupings, or sides, identified and labelled as Whig

the urban middle class had broken the earlier monopoly of aristocrats, but the majority of the public were still denied an influential voice in decisions that affected them. Nowadays, when every adult can vote, the coalescing of millions and the harmonizing of their interests have become the job of the political party. Naturally, the principal differences between the older and more modern parties are due to the range of interests which they represent and the philosophies to which they subscribe. The parties of today cohere in a disciplined fashion which assuredly has no earlier parallel.

But when all this is said, is the existence of parties to be denied before the modern era? No such conclusion is necessitated by the facts. The point that modern parties are greatly changed from their predecessors applies not only to them but to every institution of British government. The twentieth-century Parliament, the cabinet, the monarchy, the judiciary, civil service, and local authorities have all evolved into forms unlike what existed earlier. But though the cabinet under Macmillan differed from its archetype under Walpole; though the figurehead monarchy of Elizabeth II is a far cry from the personal supremacy of Elizabeth I; though the Commons of Gaitskell and Bevan was many stages removed in functions, work-load, and membership from that of Pym and Hampden; nevertheless the identical terms are rightly used because of the unifying theme that has persisted throughout the variations. This may be done without abuse to language or to sense, provided that there be a substantial continuity of the institution concerned and reasonable comparability of the functions it performed then and performs now. Do the parties meet this test? In my judgment they do. Essentially a party is a group of people who are sufficiently like-minded to work together in order to secure control of the government and apply the policies that promote their interests. Within the breadth of that definition may be included a clique of aristocrats, an association of middle-class entrepreneurs, or a mass movement drawing millions to its banners. In that sense the label "party" can be applied alike to the gatherings that followed a Walpole, Peel, or Baldwin, for though these differed in the nature and number of their adherents, there is an unmistakable continuity that underlies the objectives they sought and the role they played.

---

and Tory, which spoke for different elements in the country, adhered to contrasted philosophies, and preferred opposite constitutional arrangements.

Institutional Explanations of British Parties

Many reasons have been offered for the persistence in British politics of two-party government. The various explanations are broadly of two kinds. Sometimes the system is interpreted as the outcome of specific institutions which supposedly lend themselves to the formation of two major parties and no more than two. Alternatively the roots of the two parties are traced to the foundations of British society and economics. Let us examine each of these suggested "causes" in turn.

(1) *The Cabinet and the Power To Dissolve*

The theories which seek to derive the two-party system from the structure of British political institutions have not failed to pay honorable mention to the cabinet. Indeed it was only to be expected that attempts to solve the riddle of the party system would connect it in some way with the cabinet, the latter being the key institution in British government. To assert, however, that a relation exists between factor A and factor B is one thing; to prove that in that relationship A is the cause and B the effect is quite another. This difficulty is well borne out by the course of the discussion over this very assumption that cabinet government was the cause of two-party government. When A. Lawrence Lowell wrote his *Governments and Parties in Continental Europe*, he argued: "The result (so long as the ministers cling together) is that the members either group themselves about the ministers, and vote with them through thick and thin, or else they attach themselves to an opposition party, whose object is to turn out the cabinet, and then take office itself and carry on a different policy. The normal condition of the parliamentary system, therefore, among a people sufficiently free from prejudices to group themselves naturally, and possessing enough experience to know that the practical and attainable, and not the ideal, is the true aim in politics, is a division into two parties, each of which is ready to take office whenever the other loses its majority. . . . A division into two parties is not only *the normal result* of the parliamentary system, but also an essential condition of its success."[10]

By the time that he published *The Government of England*, Lowell's position had shifted. He was still convinced that a causal connection existed between the cabinet and the party system. But he had now veered

10. Vol. I, pp. 71-2 (1896 ed.). My italics.

round to the view that, instead of the cabinet system causing the formation of two parties, it was the parties which preceded and caused the cabinet system, though he did think that the consequence had later reacted on its cause. "Neither the parliamentary system nor the party system" wrote Lowell, "neither the responsibility of ministers to the House of Commons nor the permanent division into two parties, grew up in a day. Throughout the eighteenth century the principle of cabinet responsibility was but dimly recognized; while parties at times disintegrated, and the wheels of government were kept going by means of corruption, which has served in all ages as a lubricant for ill-adjusted political machinery. But little by little, with halting steps, the rivalry of parties built up the responsibility of ministers, and this in turn helped to perpetuate the party divisions; for the parliamentary system, like every rational form of government, reacts upon and strengthens the conditions of its own existence. It is based upon party, and by the law of its nature tends to accentuate party. . . . The parliamentary system, as it has grown up spontaneously in England, is *in its origin* and nature government by party, sanctioned and refined by custom."[11]

Lowell's afterthoughts were more accurate than his first impressions, for the notion that the two-party system is a by-product of the cabinet system encounters some fatal objections. There is, for example, the elementary chronological fact that the clustering of political factions into two major groups occurred at an earlier date than the emergence of the cabinet and thus could not have been caused by that institution. Like complex tapestries, the Whig and Tory combinations were woven of many strands, some of which connect directly with the Civil War between Parliamentarians and Royalists, while others may be more deviously and tenuously traced to the religious controversies of the sixteenth century. It is certain, however, that after the last and most stupid Stuart was compelled to abdicate, the reigns of William and Mary and of Anne did witness the more orderly beginnings of bipolar politics with its essential corollary of alternation in office. Thus it was the Whigs who saw that Britain had an interest in the War of the Spanish Succession, who pitted the nation's strength against the Sun-King and who discovered the first genius with the surname Churchill; whereas the Tories divined when the time for peace had come and negotiated the Treaty of Utrecht.

The cabinet system, however, postdated these events. Its central principles—that the Crown should select as ministers only those who are supported by a parliamentary majority and that these should be collectively

11. *The Government of England*, Vol. I, pp. 457-8, and Vol. II, p. 86 (1921 ed.). My italics.

responsible for the acts of one and all—could be applied in practice only because the parties were already there to make them work. Indeed, as G. M. Trevelyan has observed, the party was the vital difference through which Cabal was converted into Cabinet.[12] Add to this the fortunate accident that a Walpole's talents were available to exercise among Englishmen the arts of leadership which a German-tongued Hanoverian prince could not, and thus the same party system which produced the Ministry endowed it with its Prime Minister.

Comparative evidence presents another difficulty to adherents of the view that the cabinet produces two-party politics. Such evidence, it is true, must be cautiously employed since it is impossible to prove that something must have, or could not have, happened in a particular country by means of imported data. Nevertheless, the fact remains that virtually all the countries of continental Europe which have adopted cabinet government also have multi-party systems. This suggests that the cabinet, *per se*, was not the prime cause of the party system in Britain, for, were that the case, it might reasonably be expected that, when cabinets were installed elsewhere, they would give rise to the same consequences. Since the cabinet system, however, can be found associated in more cases with multi-party systems than with a two-party system, and since the latter instances occur only within the Commonwealth which Britain founded, the existence of two parties would appear to be the product of other elements that are peculiar to the British tradition.

One such element, which some political scientists have proffered in argument, is the Cabinet's use of the power to dissolve a Parliament. How this is supposed to discourage the formation of more than two parties is thus explained by Harold F. Gosnell: "In Great Britain the two-party system is also perpetuated by the type of parliamentary government which the British have evolved. The Prime Minister can dissolve Parliament and declare new elections. This gives the party in power a firm grip over its members in the House of Commons, and discourages their trying any insurrections or new ventures, since re-election is a troublesome and uncertain matter. In doubtful British constituencies, winning an election is difficult, and the support of a major party is almost a necessity. The party in power keeps its members in the House from straying, and the opposition

---

12. "The party bond introduced a principle of unity among Cabinet Ministers other than that of mere individual obedience to the orders of the King. For that reason, party is the real secret of the step upwards from Cabal to Cabinet. The mutual loyalty of members inside the Cabinet was a reflection of the habit of party loyalty among the same persons in the world outside." *The Two-Party System in English Political History*, Romanes Lecture. (Clarendon Press: Oxford, 1926).

party is well disciplined because this is the only way that it can hope to come to power."[13]

This line of reasoning scarcely supports the pretended conclusion, since it omits a number of considerations that point in another direction. The argument assumes that a Ministry is better equipped to enforce party regularity among its followers in the Commons because it alone can take the initiative of deciding when to hold a general election and, if defeated in Parliament, it may prefer to go to the country rather than tamely resign. But precisely how this flexibility in the timing of elections strengthens the disciplinary control of the Cabinet is not proven. Such a control does, of course, exist. But it rests primarily on other foundations: i.e., on the cost of winning a general election; the centralization of party finances; the dependence of many Members on their salaries; the power of the party leadership to endorse local candidates; and the absence of any requirement that a candidate must reside in his district, which makes him depend for his seat more on the leaders and less on his constituents. In the light of such potent considerations, it makes relatively little difference to most back-benchers whether a general election will be called this year, next year, or two years hence. At some time, as he well knows, the day of reckoning must come. Whenever it does, he depends for renomination on the favor of the leadership, and that dependence would still hold good in Britain even if elections were held there with the clock-work regularity of the American system.

Furthermore, if the power to dissolve were actually such a deterrent to party rebels as is believed, how does one explain the cases of defiant party members and actual splits which have occurred? The ministerial power of dissolution did not deter Disraeli from rising against Peel in 1846, or Chamberlain and the Liberal Unionists from crossing over to the Conservatives in 1886, or Henderson and his cohorts from breaking with Macdonald in 1931, or the Bevanites defying Attlee in 1950. Indeed, there may even be occasions when a group of dissidents, so far from coming to heel, withdraw their support from Ministers and deliberately provoke a dissolution in the hope that an election may work to their own advantage, as was clearly Parnell's stratagem when he switched from Gladstone to Salisbury in 1885.

(2) The Electoral System

Of all the attempts, however, to interpret the parties as the product of other political institutions, the most popular view attributes the existence

13. *Democracy: the Threshold of Freedom* (Ronald Press: New York, 1948), p. 242.

of two parties to the operation of the electoral system. Perhaps no commonplace is so widely held, and so seldom questioned, among students of politics, as the notion that single-member districts combined with plurality victories foster a two-party system, with its corollary that proportional representation promotes a multiplicity of parties. Thus M. Duverger has this general comment on the importance of the electoral system. "Its effect," he says, "can be expressed in the following formula: *the simple-majority single-ballot system favors the two-party system.* Of all the hypotheses that have been defined in this book, this approaches the most nearly perhaps to a true sociological law."[14] V. O. Key has written: "Among the influences leading the electorate to divide itself into only two major groups, great weight must be attributed to the system of choosing representatives from single-member districts by a plurality vote in contrast with systems of proportional representation which, of necessity, are based on multi-member districts. In a single-member district only two parties can contend for electoral victory with any hope of success; a third party is doomed to perpetual defeat unless it can manage to absorb the following of one of the major parties and thereby become one of the two parties itself. Parties do not thrive on the certainty of defeat. Faced by this prospect the only alternative is to support one or the other of two parties. The single-member district thus molds parties into the bipartisan pattern."[15]

How does this argument apply to the case of Britain? Does it fit the facts of that country's politics? There are some important respects in which it fails to do so.

In the first place, the effect of the plurality requirement has to be considered. If victory in the election required a majority of the votes cast, it is true that a two-party system would be more likely to arise since groups would be encouraged to coalesce in order to build up the necessary strength.[16] But that is not the British system. On the contrary, the mathematics of victory by a bare plurality, if not counteracted by other influences, would foster the politics of a multi-party system, because the larger groups could expect to win seats without entering into wider unions. As for the single-member districts, the proponents of the theory ignore the awkward truth that in Britain these postdated the rise of the two-party system. Prior to the Reform Act of 1832, the House of Commons contained a total of 558 members, of whom only 74 (13%) were returned from single-

14. *Op. cit.,* p. 217.
15. *Politics, Parties, and Pressure Groups* (Crowell: New York, 2nd ed., 1947), pp. 218-9.
16. As happens in the election of the President of the United States through the electoral college.

member districts.[17] As a result of the redistributions of 1832, 1867, and 1885, districts with a single member were gradually substituted for those with two members. But it was not until 1885 that the former became the rule.[18] From that date through 1963, twenty elections have been conducted in this new style. What has been the effect of the change?

It is customary to point to the decline of the Liberals in the 1920's as definitive proof of the hypothesis that single-member districts, plus election by plurality, operate adversely upon the weaker or weakest group and thereby cause a two-party system. The argument owes much—too much indeed—to Ramsay Muir's Book of Lamentations, which has been uncritically accepted at its face value.[19] Thus E. E. Schattschneider in his brilliant and provocative study of American party politics allows himself to write: "Many other instances of the operation of the single-member distric system could be found. Outside the United States the most conclusive demonstration is to be seen in the fate of the Liberal party in England under an analogous election system. Here was a party that had every advantage—money, prestige, able leadership, a glorious history, and a large body of devoted followers—yet it was strangled by the election system. The Liberal party had the great misfortune to become a third party and, once caught in this position, was destroyed by the statistical tendency of the single-member district system."[20] To say that it was the electoral process which "strangled" or "destroyed" the Liberals is a gross exaggeration. Their demise was due primarily to other, and far weightier, factors operating quite independently of the method of apportionment and voting. One has only to study the history of the four decades from 1884 to 1924 to see what these factors were. The Liberals declined as a party because cumulative changes overcame the British economy and social order for which neither their philosophy nor the combination of interests they had erstwhile represented permitted a solution. The swing of manufacturers from free trade to protection, because they suffered increasingly from German and other competition; the pressure of the newly enfranchised masses for social services and further regulation of business; the consequent need to substitute a positive program of governmental action for the negativism of *laissez faire*; the task of governing an Empire (and

17. See L. B. Namier, *The Structure of Politics at the Accession of George III*, Vol. I, Chap. 2, pp. 79-80.
18. Note the comment of Morley in his *Life of Gladstone*: "The election [of 1885] ran a chequered course (Nov. 23–Dec. 19). It was the first trial of the whole body of male householders, and it was the first trial of the system of single-member districts." Vol. II, Bk. IX, Chap. II, p. 486 (2nd ed. Macmillan's; New York, 1906).
19. See his *How Britain Is Governed* (4th ed., London, 1940), Chaps. 4-5.
20. *Party Government* (Rinehart: New York, 1942), p. 79.

especially Ireland) which gave no qualms to Conservatives, but did give to Liberals a sense of guilt; the impact of World War I and the experience of a coalition in which some Conservatives were liberalized, but rather more liberals were conservatized; and finally the sorry spectacle of discordant leaders squabbling among themselves and hence splitting their followers; these were the long and short term causes of the Liberal debacle. As compared with them, the electoral machinery *per se* had no more weight than the proverbial last straw. The Liberals, like the camel's back, could not have been broken without the accumulation of the innumerable and much weightier straws preceding the last!

But in any case, to use the decline of the Liberals as "proof" that Britain's electoral system perpetuates its two parties by driving the minor groups to the wall fails to explain how Labour ever succeeded in getting its start and becoming a major party. Schattschneider, who contends that "the American two-party system is the direct consequence of the American election system," also emphasizes that "no minor party in American history has ever become a major party, and no major party has ever become a minor party." This is not true at all, however, of Britain. The "statistical tendency" of the electoral system, which is alleged to have strangled the Liberals in their old age, ought to have suffocated the Labourites in their cradle. Why did this not happen? From 1900 through 1910 Labour won a smaller percentage of seats than the percentage of their votes—the fate that befell the Liberals in the 1920's. Yet the one party surmounted this handicap, while the other did not. Does it not appear then that the causal significance of the electoral system has been greatly overrated?

The Social Roots of British Politics

If this line of reasoning has been correct, the character of the party system must derive primarily from other than institutional factors. To understand what these are one must turn to the society within which the parties have their roots and grow. The party structure takes its substance from the interests which men engender in society and the relations that are organized between them. This poses the question: what sort of divisions can be found in British society which provide the basis for partisan opposition? If sectional, cultural, religious, or economic cleavages occur, how have these been represented by the parties?

It is an arguable hypothesis that the two-party system emerged in

Britain because the social order of that country was relatively homogeneous and offered little possibility for a multiple splintering of parties. This is to say that in a number of matters which are fundamental to society such a preponderant majority existed on one side of the question that the arena of practicable controversy was much restricted, and, conversely, the remaining issue on which two sides were opposed in nearly equal strength were few and the divisions between them fairly simple. Thus, if the small territorial expanse of the British Isles precluded the formation of sectional groups, the numerical superiority of Anglo-Saxons and Protestants prevented the rise of a Celtic or Catholic party. Likewise the dominance of agriculture until the end of the eighteenth century, and of urbanism since the middle of the nineteenth, clarified the battle-lines of economic conflict since it was impossible in the earlier period to dedicate a party wholly to the interests of city-folk or, more recently, to those of farmers.

These generalizations are true in the main, but they need to be explained and in certain particulars qualified or corrected. Take, for example, the question of sectional influences on British party organization. It is, of course, doubtful whether parties are ever founded anywhere on a purely sectional base. Even in states that cover a huge area a section acquires much of its political relevance from other factors which happen to be reinforced by geographical concentration. Certainly in a country whose total area slightly exceeds that of Oregon, and where even the hillier terrain does not approach the contours of Switzerland, there is less occasion for that sense of a separate political identity which physical remoteness can at least abet or aggravate. To the extent that sectional forces have obtruded into British politics, they have done so because they largely coincided with the boundaries of cultural and religious diversity and represented a genuine economic antagonism. The one clear instance of a party confined to a single section where it predominated is that of the Irish Nationalists. In nine successive elections from 1885 to 1918 their parliamentary seats showed a small variation between a high of 86 and a low of 80. The decision to form a separate bloc, instead of working inside one of the major parties, was based on Parnell's calculation that he could hold the balance between the Liberals and the Conservatives and disrupt the United Kingdom by obstructing its Parliament. Theirs, however, was a solitary and special case and serves as the exception to point the rule. Stemming from cultural, religious, and economic differences, the ardent nationalism of the Irish was fostered by the existence of a water barrier and by embittered memories of past warfare. But the significance of the religious cleavage in this whole complex can be gauged by the fact that Ireland ceased to be politically solid in the counties of the northeast where Protestantism was strong and the opponents of Home Rule voted Conservative.[21]

The contrast between Ireland, on the one hand, and Scotland and Wales, on the other, is instructive. The two latter communities, though both belonging to the "Celtic fringe"[22] and maintaining their own brands of nationalism, did not develop a separate Welsh or Scottish party. Why was this? One may suggest that a hilly border has produced among Scots and Welshmen less of an isolationist psychology than a sea channel would, that their economic grievances were less acutely felt than those of the Irish, and that the divisions between Protestant churches were more easily bridged than the gulf between Protestant and Catholic. Instead of creating sectional parties, the Scots and Welsh have preferred to pursue their objectives within the fold of one or other of the two major organizations. The commonly accepted generalization assigns the Celtic areas to the Liberals at least during the nineteenth century, which was true in the main, though Disraeli was able to make inroads on the Liberal strength at the time of the Conservative victory of 1874. But the generalization does not apply to Scotland in the eighteenth century, and of course, has little force today. In the first half of the eighteenth century Scotland had a politically split personality. Its Jacobite sympathies endowed it with Tory leanings; while those who were antagonized by the Stuart preference for Catholicism sided with the Whigs. Later in the same century the talents of Dundas and his skillful use of jobbery consolidated the Scottish votes into a solid Tory bloc, which was placed—for a price—at the disposal of Tory Ministries. The Liberal decline in the twentieth century proceeded more slowly in Scotland than in England, and still more slowly in Wales than in Scotland. What little is left of the Liberal organization nowadays might be called the last protest of the Celt against the Anglo-Saxon. Those Celtic constituencies where it formerly dominated have been partitioned between Labour and the Conservatives. To the former have gone the Welsh coal mining areas and most of the "industrial waist" of Scotland; to the latter, the Scottish counties.

Sectional and cultural differences have had less effect on the general development of the British party system than religious dissension. Not

---

21. Outside of Ulster the Nationalists almost always carried every Irish constituency, except for two in Dublin. Outside of Ireland the only seat they could win was the Scotland division of Liverpool where many Irish resided. See Lowell, *Government of England*, Vol. II, p. 128.

22. As K. B. Smellie calls it in *One Hundred Years of British Government* (Duckworth: London, 2nd ed. 1950), p. 126.

only the origins of the Whig and Tory parties in the years from 1660 to 1700,[23] but their continued rivalry in the following century and the subsequent opposition of Conservative to Liberal, would be inexplicable unless viewed in the light of those religious controversies that plagued the country since the reign of Henry VIII. But how did this issue contribute to the growth of a two-party system? On this point Carl J. Friedrich has commented: "England escaped the religious division (and the consequent development of a Catholic party) on account of the overwhelmingly Protestant nature of the country, buttressing this religious uniformity by depriving Catholics and other religious dissenters (nonconformists) of political privileges until well into the nineteenth century." However, if being "overwhelmingly Protestant" means having "religious uniformity," why did some Protestants think it necessary to deprive others of "political privileges"? What "political privileges" were these, and, if uniformity was so securely "buttressed," did the relations between churches cease to be relevant to the strife between parties?

Dualism, Religious and Economic

The fact is that in the seventeenth century the kingdom was split by religion into three segments. In the middle stood the adherents of the Church of England, who were flanked on one side by the large group of Puritans and on the other by the smaller Catholic group. When the monarchy was restored in 1660, the Anglicans turned the tables on the Puritans, who had predominated in the Cromwellian decade, and wrote their triumph into the Clarendon Code. Though subsequently challenged, the central principles of that Code continued in force and formed the line of demarcation between those Protestants whose church was established and those whose churches were not. The threat of a Catholic revival under James II temporarily solidified the Protestant ranks. But when their victory was assured in 1688, the old cleavage re-emerged. In essentials the politics of the revolutionary settlement amounted to a deal between the two major factions. Parliamentary supremacy was accomplished by the Whigs, Anglican supremacy by the Tories. Neither party was wholly satisfied with this *modus vivendi*. Both, therefore, strove to undo that portion of it which favored their rivals. But the balance of forces was so nearly equal that two generations had to elapse before the agreement could be fundamentally amended. With George III on the throne the Tories as-

23. On which see W. C. Abbott, "The Origin of English Political Parties," *American Historical Review*, Vol. XXIV (1918-19).

sisted in the recrudescence of monarchical power. Owing to the debacle of his American policy, however, and his later fits of insanity, the principle of parliamentary authority was rammed down their throats.

To secure a Tory acceptance of religious toleration took longer. Throughout the entire eighteenth century and the first two decades of the nineteenth, the Tories were identified with the Church of England and championed its establishment. The Whigs were thus cast in the role of representing the Protestant nonconformists, whose numbers were notably swelled by the impact of the one great spiritual force that appeared in eighteenth-century Britain—to wit, John Wesley. The political disabilities of the nonconformists were not total, however, and their influence was far from negligible. The intent of the Test and Corporation Acts was to debar dissenters from holding public office. But by no statute were they disfranchised. Still less were they prevented from giving financial assistance to the Whigs. Even the ban on their taking office was not rigorously enforced, and regularly after 1727 an annual Indemnity Act was passed by Parliament to exempt from legal penalties those office holders who did not swear the necessary oaths! The truth is, therefore, that eighteenth-century Britain contained not religious uniformity, but religious dualism; and this was carried over directly into a two-party system. Nobody has expressed this with greater clarity than G. M. Trevelyan: "From the Restoration to the latter years of the nineteenth century, the continuity of the two parties in English politics was very largely due to the two-party system in religious observance, popularly known as Church and Chapel. . . . The dualism of the English religious world, and the disabilities imposed on Dissenters, form a large part of the explanation of the peculiarly English phenomenon of two continuous political parties in every shire and town of the land, surviving even when obvious political issues seem asleep or settled, or when the party programmes seem in certain important respects to have changed hands. . . . The dualism in the religious life of the nation reflected itself into a political dualism."[24] Because this political inequality survived on the statute-book for over a century and a quarter, the time-hardened pattern of a Tory affinity for the Anglicans and a Whig alliance with nonconformists continued to exist long after the decade of the 1820's when the disabilities of the nonconformists and of the Catholics were at last removed. Even in modern times, therefore, it has made some sense to generalize about the church-frequenting Conservative and the chapel-going Liberal or Labourite.

How was this split over a religious issue connected with conflicts of eco-

24. *Op. cit.*, pp. 26-7.

nomic interest? Or, to put the question another way, what "durable sources of faction" were present in the sphere of economics which could give rise to partisan opposition, and especially to a division into two parties and not more?

Until the end of the eighteenth century British society was primarily rural and the farming interest predominated in the economy. The commercial interest, though far from negligible, was secondary. Under such circumstances party opposition admitted only one possibility. The landowning aristocracy divided into a majority who formed the Tories and a minority who united with the commercial interest to constitute the Whigs. Since the country squires were mostly Anglican, while the leaders of commerce were largely nonconformist, the religious split complemented the economic—a fact that contributed materially to a two-party system. Thus founded and fortified, the system had more than a century in which to settle down before encountering its severest test—the impact of rapid technological changes on the economic and social order. The cumulative effect of such changes has been to substitute an overwhelmingly urban society for one that was rural and to make farming yield pride of place to industry.[25] How did the parties adapt themselves to so major a transformation? Were the old bottles able to hold the new contents?

Response of the Parties to Industrialism

The answer is that the system, though subjected to an agony that was acute and prolonged, did in the end survive the strain. But during the course of readjustment, both great parties were respectively the victims of a major shock, whose results crippled one party for thirty years and killed the other. The first of these crises occurred when the manufacturing interest had grown to such proportions that it could challenge the farming interest and assert its predominance by altering to its advantage institutions which formerly favored the owners of land. That was done in the political reform of 1832, which amended the franchise and the apportionment of seats in the Commons, and the ensuing economic reform of 1846, which abolished the protective tariff on food. The immediate sufferer was the Conservative party, which cracked under the blow. The Peelites, including Gladstone, split away and within a few years coalesced with the Liberals. The Conservative residue followed Disraeli. He, having correctly prophesied the permanent decline of British agriculture and

25. In recent British censuses less than 20% of the population are classified as rural; about 6% of the gainfully employed are engaged in farming.

knowing that a party devoted to a minority interest could not win majorities, looked around for a new source from which to replenish its strength—a task that occupied three decades.

At the very time that the Conservatives were emerging with renewed vitality, the crisis of the Liberals was beginning; for the same causes that helped the former now harmed the latter. The contest between manufacturers and farmers amounted to a vertical division in the British economy wherein industrial wealth was arrayed against landed wealth. But with industrial predominance secured, a horizontal fissure soon opened in urban politics and poverty now challenged riches along class lines. The factory workers, in order to obtain improvements in their living and working conditions, besought the same voting rights that their Liberal employers had gained in 1832. On this issue there occurred in 1866 the first of the splits that were to prove fatal to Liberalism, since many a manufacturer was unwilling to see his employees enfranchised. When the suffrage was extended in 1867, the statute was enacted by a coalition of the minority Conservatives and the progressive wing of the Liberals. To whom would the huge new Labour vote be given? For several decades it was actually divided between the two parties, since some working men voted for the Liberals as champions of nonconformists and social progress, while others were attracted to the benevolent paternalism of Disraeli's "Tory democracy" and to the hope of an imperial market for their products. Gradually, however, as the Liberal party weakened after a further split on the Irish question, and as tariff-conscious manufacturers drifted over into the Conservative camp, many working men became disillusioned with both parties. The birth of a separate Labour organization ushered in temporarily a three-party system which lasted until, and ended with, the depression of the early 1930's. Even as they broke asunder, however, the Liberals continued to serve their country well, for, by entering the other parties, they made reform more palatable to the Conservatives and the constitution more palatable to Labour.

Throughout this entire process, the timing and the order of events has evidently been crucial to the retention of a two-party system. Its early development, as Friedrich has stressed,[26] gave the system an initial advantage, and it was particularly fortunate that the main outlines of the constitutional system were already settled before the social order was convulsed by industrialism. But there is another important aspect of the timing which has received insufficient emphasis. What distinguishes Britain's political history in the nineteenth century is the gradualism whereby the franchise

26. *Op. cit.*, p. 413.

was extended to successive waves of new voters. The great reform acts were spaced at such intervals—1832, 1867, 1884—that the two-party system, already in existence prior to the first reform, was able to guide, absorb, and assimilate each fresh increase of the electorate. Every extension stimulated more intensive organization by the parties in order that the newly enfranchised might be registered and captured, and better organization reacted upon and fortified the system.

This survey of the causes of the British system warrants the conclusion that the parties were primarily the product of their society, and only secondarily the offshoot of governmental institutions. The latter influenced the party structure, mainly in that they braced and buttressed a system whose foundations were deeply embedded in the cultural, religious, and economic components of a nation. Instead of the electoral system causing the party system, it would rather appear that the latter was the cause of the former. Then, once the effect was produced, it reacted upon its own cause, helping to perpetuate the two-party form. But there are also factors in the analysis of this case which are uniquely the product of British history, and it is very difficult to subsume the unique under a general law. What was special about the British development was the nature of the issues which its society generated and the correspondence between the groups which these issues yielded. No less special was the chronology of events, for it is the time sequence in confronting and settling problems which always distinguishes the history of one people from that of another. The British case is important, and deserves this somewhat lengthy treatment, because it is the prime example of a long-enduring two-party system and has supplied a model to others. The British did not plan, or consciously aim, at the result, and a retrospective analysis may therefore detect as causes events, or trends, or accidents which were not so regarded at the time they occurred. But what is accidental in one nation's experience can be observed by others and be deliberately imitated. Let us then examine some of the effects to which the British model has given rise when transported elsewhere.

The Model Exported to Canada, New Zealand, Australia, and South Africa

As the Romans brought their culture and their law to the provinces they organized, so the British exported their political ideas and institutions to the territories they colonized or conquered. The four countries which were the earliest to attain full self-government within the Commonwealth—

Canada, Australia, New Zealand, and South Africa—provide an instructive group for comparative study. In Australia and New Zealand the indigenous populations were either too few in number or too retarded in culture to affect the imported system. But elsewhere, the British tradition had to coexist with what it could not eliminate: in Canada with the descendants of France's *ancien régime*, and in South Africa with an offshoot of seventeenth-century Holland and a large majority of tribally divided Africans. Here then was a situation where a common political pattern was introduced into areas remote from the place of origin and scattered from one another. As it struck new roots and grew, the exported system retained some of its inherited features, but mingled them with the characteristics acquired in the new environment. Also, as the process of nation-building required amalgamation into larger units, the federal principle was borrowed from the United States and adapted to the circumstances of Canada and Australia. Thus, after the lapse of four or five generations, it was possible to observe both similarities and differences in this group of countries. An examination of these will take the analysis some steps beyond where it was left after the discussion of Great Britain.

First, it is necessary to look at the politics of Canada, Australia, New Zealand, and South Africa, and describe the party system which has evolved in each place. The one which provides the closest parallel to Great Britain is New Zealand, the smallest country and the most distant. Party politics emerged there during two formative decades (1856-76), in which the principal problems to be solved were those of immigration and public works, the Maori Wars, and central-provincial relations. The contest between groups then became polarized into a Conservative-Liberal fight. As the working class came of age politically and universal suffrage was achieved, the Liberal party broadened into Liberal-Labour. Later, this hyphen lengthened into a split, and contemporaneously with Britain (from 1905 to 1931) New Zealand wrestled with an unstable equilibrium of three parties. The depression of the early 1930's restored the two-party system by impelling a coalition between the Conservatives (then called Reform) and what was left of the Liberals. Since that time to the present, a normal alternation in office has continued between Labour and their opponents, who currently are named National. Minor parties have occasionally formed themselves during the last sixty or seventy years—usually in order to express and organize a special interest or some extreme viewpoint. But they have always evaporated quickly.

Canada, being a more complicated country than New Zealand, has experienced more complications in maintaining a two-party system. Within a few decades after federation, political contests had already fallen into the classic pattern. Two principal parties emerged; but Canada's size, along with the diversity of its groupings and their regional concentration, has always facilitated the breakaway of special interests or areas. As a consequence, third and fourth parties have been organized fairly frequently. Often, these have been able to capture control of a province and there to maintain themselves in office throughout several elections, contemporary examples being Social Credit in Alberta and British Columbia and the Cooperative Commonwealth Federation in Saskatchewan. At the Dominion level, however, Conservatives and Liberals have been alternating in and out of office for three-quarters of a century, and it has been a rare exception for a third party to hold the parliamentary balance.[27] Of recent decades, the most remarkable feature of Canadian national politics was the long supremacy of the Liberals, which was accompanied by a decline of the Conservatives and some fragmentary representation for the Social Credit and the C.C.F. After the two federal elections of 1957 and 1958, however, the Liberal reign terminated abruptly, and the political pendulum since that time has swung back and forth along a shorter arc.

Australia became a Commonwealth thirty-three years after Canada was created a Dominion. Hence, national party politics in Australia count less than seven decades. But a definite pattern has already emerged in this period. The facts are easy enough to state, although their meaning is in dispute. The first decade of this century was occupied with putting the federal system into motion and with a coalescing of groups. The fight between protectionists and free traders tended for a time to overshadow the other divisions and to twist the political interests into its particular mold. But once that issue had been resolved in favor of protection, the Australians developed the kind of party system with which they have now lived for five decades. On one side stands the Labour party. Its history has been a series of battles between a central discipline and the revolts against it. Arrayed against Labour are two parties. The chief of these, after frequent changes of name, has now resumed the Liberal label. The other is the Country party, which has maintained a separate existence ever since the early 1920's. How should the Australian system be classified? Plain though the answer seems, it is nevertheless in controversy. Some say that Australia has a three-party system, for the simple reason that the system does contain three! But others argue that this arithmetic has to be interpreted politically. The third member of the trio, the Country party, does not

27. This did happen, however, after the election of 1921 when a revolt of the western prairies produced an agrarian movement called the Progressives, and again in 1962 when the Conservatives needed votes from either Social Credit or the New Democrats to keep a majority in the House of Commons.

function in complete independence, nor does it fill the role of a balancer. It operates instead in a permanent coalition with the Liberals. Never does it combine, either electorally or in office, with Labour. Hence, with a substance of truth one can assert that Australian politics are divided along the axis of Labour versus non-Labour. The latter side maintains two organizations, of which the weaker partner represents and increases the bargaining power of the rural elements. The Australian system, therefore, is a trio in form, a duet in function.

In South Africa, where government is the exclusive preserve of a minority which is itself acutely split, the party system functions amid a nightmarish network of restrictions and distortions. Since the minority has a monopoly of political participation, the parties "represent" only the dominant fifth of the population. Yet, all their calculations are powerfully influenced by the presence of the other four-fifths—who are disfranchised, discriminated against, and demoralized. Thus, in describing South Africa's party system one must allow for, but never forget, these basic limitations. Within their framework, a complex of tangled groupings has tended to sort itself out into a rough alternation between two parties. One party is formed by the majority of the Afrikaners, and they are opposed by the minority of Afrikaners combining with the majority of those whose tongue is English. This division between groups, which runs primarily along linguistic and cultural boundaries, is widened by a difference of attitude toward the submerged majority. On the problem of race relations the fanatical extremists oppose the more moderate gradualists. Then, too, within the minority of dominant Europeans there are minorities which form splinter movements of their own—a Labour party to oppose the owners of capital, a Dominion or Federal party to resist the supremacy of Afrikanerdom over the English, a Liberal party to plead (valiantly, but forlornly) the noble doctrine of human equality. Such groups have hitherto been unable to make much of a dent in the strength of the two big organizations—National and United.[28] At present, since every election from 1948 onward has recorded rising percentages of the votes in their favor, the Nationalist fanatics unfortunately have had everything their own way.

Such, then, is a short description of the four systems. It justifies a generalization that they conform principally to the two-party model. But the variations and deviations are quite as significant as the norm. What there-

28. In the mid-1920's, however, Labour had sufficient votes to enter into coalition with Hertzog against Smuts, on a policy of monopolizing the best jobs for the white workers. Also, when Malan's Nationalists first came to office in 1948, they needed the parliamentary backing of the small Afrikaner party under Havenga which they later absorbed.

fore remain to be explained are the reasons both for the norm and for the departures from it. Let us proceed in the same order as in the discussion of Great Britain, taking the institutional interpretations first. The initial question to be asked about the four countries is this: How uniform, how different, are the institutions which could have a bearing on the character of the party system? And is there a discernible connection between these institutions and the parties?

Institutional Patterns of the Four Countries

At the outset, one is struck by the amount of over-all similarity in the institutions by which the four countries are governed. But at the same time certain differences are apparent and it is the explanation of the reasons for them which calls for further analysis. To begin with, there is complete uniformity in the use of the cabinet system. The fusion of parliamentary and executive leadership in the hands of the same persons is a distinctively British contribution to the art of constitution-making and is invariably followed throughout the Commonwealth. Rule by cabinet is the rule. To this there are no exceptions. Differences do exist, however, in the effects of the cabinet's power and in the techniques by which it is exercised. In certain of these countries, for example, the threat of dissolution has virtually atrophied and can no longer be considered essential—if indeed it ever was —either for maintaining discipline in the majority ranks or for perpetuating a two-party alignment. Seventy years elapsed in New Zealand (1881 to 1951) before a general election was called prior to the expiration of Parliament's full term. The reason for this is simply that New Zealand's elections have been triennial, and it was therefore unnecessary to shorten the life of a Parliament. Notwithstanding this fact, both the two-party system and the discipline within the parties have continued in force.

In Australia, too, early dissolutions have become superfluous because the regular federal elections are held triennially, as in New Zealand. But in one important respect the Australian Parliament differs from those of Great Britain, Canada, New Zealand, and South Africa. It retains its original bicameral character, in fact as well as in form. Following the pattern of the United States, the six States are represented in the Senate as equal units, and the terms of Senators are staggered. Consequently, a conflict between the two Houses can occur if Labour controls one House while the non-Labour coalition controls the other. Because of this situation, Prime Minister Menzies, the Liberal leader, took advantage in 1951 of the constitutional provision that authorizes a double dissolution. But this did not take place because of any defect in the working of the party system as such. It was the result, rather, of an institutional contradiction. Cabinet government, to be effective, requires not checks and balances, but a concentration of political authority in one place. Hence, wherever it functions in full force, the cabinet has either crippled or crushed bicameralism; and the ability of one chamber to eliminate its rival has been reinforced by the logic of the two-party system which necessitates a majority for one party over its opposition. Thus the power of dissolution, to the extent that it survives nowadays in Australia, is a consequence of the party system and not a cause of it.

The Australian case, however, contains other implications whose broad effects should be comparatively viewed. Australian bicameralism is the product of Australian federalism. One must therefore consider whether the institutional difference between a federal and a unitary constitution has any effect on the number of parties within the political system. Let us suppose that one were to rank the United Kingdom and these four countries on a scale according to their proximity to the poles of unitary or federal government. The order would be as follows:

UNITARY

New Zealand
United Kingdom
South Africa
Canada
Australia

FEDERAL

How does such a ranking correlate with the party system of the same countries? In my judgment, fairly closely. The countries in which the two-party system is most firmly established are the very two whose institutions are most definitely centralized and unitary.[29] On the other hand, the states which are federal or quasi-federal are precisely those in which the problem of the third, and even the fourth, party has continued to present itself. A person who favors the institutional argument will, therefore, be disposed to contend that federalism is an impediment to two-party monopoly. Just because an intermediate level of government exists, a party whose prospects for national power are slender may prevail in a state or province. Hence, it would seem to follow that federalism tends to encourage a multiplicity of parties. If so, this indicates how the governmental structure helps to shape the party system.

29. The case of the American party system is discussed in pp. 343 ff.

Certainly it would appear that the party system is correlated with the degree of centralization or the reverse in the machinery of state. But to assert that one factor causes the other is an unproven inference. Rather, it may be held that both factors—the type of party system and the pattern of institutions—are themselves the joint product of another, more fundamental determinant: namely, the character of the society. Should this be true, the correlation between the parties and either a unitary or a federal government would resemble the relation between siblings and not that between parent and child.

One further institutional arrangement to be considered is the electoral system. What has been its relation to the party system in the four countries under discussion? Three of them—Canada, New Zealand, and South Africa—elect their parliaments in the same manner as Great Britain. That is, they use single-member districts, in which the winner is the candidate with the plurality of votes. As in Britain, this system was acceptable to the two largest parties because its very lack of proportionalism helped them win majorities in turn and impeded the growth of new parties. However, as happened with the Labourites both in Britain and New Zealand, a new party can become powerful, notwithstanding the electoral machinery, if it has adequate social support. When the New Zealand Liberals saw the writing on the wall, and while they retained their parliamentary majority, they changed the law and experimented with the second ballot,[30] hoping thereby to forestall the rise of Labour. But electoral jugglery could not arrest a political movement which had its own strong economic and social basis. After two elections under this system (1908 and 1911), the voters of Reform (i.e., Conservative) and Labour increased, while those of the Liberals declined. A Reform Ministry came into office and reverted to the single ballot with victory by a plurality.

In New Zealand, the third party (Labour) grew potent enough to replace one of the existing major parties and thereby restore the two-party system. That being so, the old electoral system was retained because there was no need to abandon it. But if a third party is added permanently to the other two, the party system itself changes. In that case, it is convenient and sensible to modify the electoral system subsequently. Indeed, this is what occurred in Australia, the one country of this group which forms the exception that proves the rule. There, the Country party was organized after World War I to increase the political power of the farmers on the anti-Labour side. The electoral system was then changed to conform with

30. Under this system, a candidate had to receive a majority of votes to be elected. In districts where there were more than two candidates and none had a majority, the two leaders contested a second election soon after the first.

the altered character of the party system. Since it was expected that farmers would give their support first to the Country party, and next to the other non-Labour party, the electoral method which was adopted was that of the single transferable vote—a device precisely suited to the politics of a tri-party system wherein two of the members were normally expected to coalesce against the third. Clearly in this case the party system formed itself first and then modified the electoral machinery to conform to its political requirements.

Their Social Structures, from Simple to Complex

To summarize the comparisons thus far, one notices an over-all similarity in the governmental institutions of these countries. The significant exceptions are the electoral system in Australia and the federal structure there and in Canada. A relation certainly exists between these institutional differences and the variations in the party systems. Let us now see whether the respective differences and resemblances both in party systems and institutions are related to other factors more pervasive and more penetrating. For this, I turn to the composition of the societies in question, since it is these which give politics their content and the parties their being. It is reasonable to suppose that the more homogeneous a society, the simpler its party system; the more heterogeneous the former, the more complex the latter. Is this supposition borne out by the facts? In terms of homogeneity and its opposite, New Zealand and Australia are evidently more homogeneous than Britain, whereas Canada and South Africa are more heterogeneous. Are these social variations reflected in the party systems?

The simplest in structure of all these societies is the one in New Zealand, the country whose party system is the closest akin to the British. The people of New Zealand are homogeneous to a rare degree. They have the population of Philadelphia spread over an area as big as Oregon. The Europeans, who outnumber the Maoris by ten to one, are drawn, to the extent of 98 per cent, from the British Isles. Of these, the great majority were English or Scots and Protestant, and are descended from emigrants of the working class and lower-middle class. Although farming provides nine-tenths of the country's export wealth, farmers ceased long ago to be in a majority and have also lost the advantage of special apportionment under the electoral law. The demand for higher living standards, equally spread, has led to a moderate urban development. But, instead of one dominant metropolis, New Zealand has four main centers, spaced apart from north to south. For political purposes, the people divide along two axes: the city folk versus the farmers, and those who have less against those who have more. The farmers form a bloc which seldom[31] splits. But, being insufficient to win an election, they need to coalesce with some urban interests in order to produce a majority. The result is their alliance with importers, businessmen, and higher-income professional people. Thereby, the National party is cemented together. On the other side, the Labour party enjoys the full allegiance of the industrial workers. With these, it unites in the cities many of the lower paid white-collar employees of government and of private firms. For the National party the problem is to hold together its rural and urban wings; for Labour, its industrial and white-collar supporters. A loosening of either tie is usually enough to produce an electoral swing and thus to change the party in power.

What New Zealand politics would be like if its social structure were projected onto a larger screen can readily be seen in the case of its neighbor, the Commonwealth of Australia. In many of their basic characteristics the two countries are identical. But the sub-groups which exist in Australia are proportionately larger than their New Zealand counterparts. This fact has intensified their sense of separateness and aggravated their frictions, with consequences which are immediately observable in the party system. In terms of race, language and national origins, the Australians are remarkably homogeneous. In religion, however, because rather more Irish emigrated to Australia than to New Zealand, the number of Catholics amounts to 21 per cent as against 14 per cent in the smaller Dominion. This is politically relevant because the bulk of the Catholics (for the same reasons that formed them into Democrats in the U.S.A.) early joined the Labour party, where their concentration makes them a powerful force. Also, owing to their geographical distances from one another, regional sentiments are more pronounced in Australia than New Zealand and explain why one country adopted, and the other abandoned, a federal constitution. The antagonisms between classes, and between city and country, are also more sharply felt in Australia. In practically every state over two-fifths of the population are to be found in the capital city; and in the rural areas the pastoral industry had to adapt to conditions of climate which required huge "runs" for the sheep to graze and led to cleavages between the owners and their laborers. Hence the Australian party system accurately reflects the same two lines of social division as in New Zealand—but with two important differences. The city-country conflict has fostered two parties on the anti-Labour side. The Country party represents many of the farmers, while a minority of them join with the urban business interests in

31. Occasionally, however, and in times of falling prices overseas, the dairy farmers may break from the sheep farmers, and, as in 1935, some will vote Labour.

the Liberal party. Labour has the backing of the industrial workers and many of those in the lower paid clerical jobs. Maintaining unity on the Labour side, however, has proven difficult. The party was split acutely in World War I on the issue of conscription, in the depression of the early 1930's over the choice between radical or orthodox finance, and after 1947 between its Catholic right wing and a left wing that veered close to the Communists. When the Labour factions are divided, the other side is sure to hold power. When they are unified, they can take advantage of the city-country feud and oust their opponents from office. Thus, the system described above as a duet in function and a trio in form corresponds appropriately to the patterns of the Australian society.

The country which comes next in order of social complexity is Canada, consisting of two cultures which have coexisted for nearly two centuries but have not fused. They are divided by language, religion, and political memories, and the capacity of the minority to survive is reinforced by its geographical concentration and the Church. The art of governing Canada is exceedingly difficult. So far, only three men—Macdonald, Laurier, and King—have fully mastered its secret. For the politics of the Dominion require the maintenance of a delicate equilibrium among forces which are for the most part centrifugal. Externally, Canadians are drawn to influential poles both east and south. The English-speaking are pulled by trade and sentiment to Britain; the French-speaking to France—but of the *ancien régime*. Southward, the natural alignment of the North American continent has attracted Canadians to the United States for the mutual benefits of trade, defense, and propinquity. Internally, Canada is a country whose north is sparsely settled and whose people are stretched east-west in a narrow band from Newfoundland to Vancouver Island. This band is divided into the five well-marked regions of the Maritimes, the St. Lawrence and Great Lakes, the Laurentian Shield, the Prairies, and the Pacific slope of the Rockies. The function of the federal government at the center is to hold the balance between the two cultures, among the domestic regions, and between the United States and western Europe. Under these conditions, the party which keeps in power is the one which can discover a lowest common multiple of the contending interests. Thus, statesmanship in Canada becomes synonymous with compromise.

The two main parties of Canada are best described as federal unions within a federal union. The strategy of their opposition is dictated by two recurring factors: the unity of Quebec, and the tendency for people to vote one way provincially and another way nationally. For many decades Quebec was the "solid South" of Canada. Each of the major parties owed its long period of ascendancy to support from that province. But the retention of power at Ottawa has been consistent with continued opposition from the provincial capitals. What was so significant during the long Liberal hegemony was that effective party conflict virtually ceased at the federal level and also within most of the provinces, but was still conducted between the two levels. Only a decade ago, many provinces for all practical purposes had produced one-party regimes, since for many elections in a row there had been no political change. Equally significant was the fact that the Liberals, though lording it at Ottawa, did not control the majority of provincial governments. Thus, Duplessis' Union Nationale was ascendant in Quebec; the Conservatives ruled Ontario; the C.C.F. was dominant in Saskatchewan, as was Social Credit in Alberta. Yet some of the very districts which chose these parties provincially were voting for the Liberals nationally. What this must mean is that in Canada the effective line of political division is drawn between the nation and its component regions. Indeed, even when the party that controls the province is nominally the same as the one prevailing at Ottawa, conflict can still occur between province and Dominion—a striking example being the fight in the 1930's between Prime Minister Mackenzie King and Premier Hepburn of Ontario.

It is these fundamental tendencies that are reflected in the history of Canadian politics. Because of the regional diversities in the Canadian economy and the geographical distribution of languages and religions, Canadians express their preferences on one set of issues locally, on another set nationally. Hence, as many as four or five parties may dominate the several provinces. At the center, however, that party prevails which cements a winning coalition by compromises and conciliation. Thus, following the same line of argument, one can see why the federal system, as such, is not the cause of the Canadian party-complex. Both the party system and federalism are the consequences of the same social factors. The federal structure is well-suited to the diversities of Canada's regions and cultures; the parties, major and minor, which flow from these very diversities support and use that structure for their political ends.

Last to be considered is one of the most heterogeneous societies in the world. Viewed cumulatively, South Africa exhibits all of the diversities of Canada—plus the tremendous complication of the size of the non-European majority. In two other respects the position of the English-speaking South Africans differs from that of English-speaking Canadians. In the former country they are the minority group within the European minority, whereas in Canada they still outnumber the fertile French. Also, in South Africa the memories of armed conflict between English-speaking and Afrikaners reach back to as recent a date as the beginning of this century, and the bitterness of military defeat has increased the determination of extreme Afrikanerdom for political revenge. Because non-Europeans are not permitted to participate in elections (save to the limited extent that the Coloured may vote in the Cape), the pivot for South African parties lies at the point where the Afrikaner group splits into fanatics and moderates. When there were enough of the moderates, their alliance with the English-speaking minority could produce victories for the United party—the party of which Botha and Smuts were leaders. But the Afrikaner moderates are always threatened by their own extremists. In this way, Hertzog rebelled against Botha, as Malan did later against Hertzog. Since 1948 the program of *apartheid* has served as the rallying cry for the fanatics, who have thus far outmaneuvered their opponents by appeals to prejudice, fear, and white supremacy.

South African society is subdivided both vertically and horizontally. The horizontal layers are racial, with the whites occupying the narrow apex at the top of the pyramid. Vertically, they are themselves split by language, religion, economic status, and the bitterness of the past. Since all lines of cleavage tend to coincide, each reinforces the other. In this way, there has arisen among the dominant whites a system of two major parties flanked by a number of splinters. But the nub of this party system is that it does not include and represent the majority. Instead, it serves merely to organize the fear of the majority which the minority entertain. Since South Africa comprises not one society, but several which have been superimposed in a hierarchy, the party system reflects the restrictions by which the country is crippled. Clearly, if the Liberal viewpoint were ever to prevail, one would expect to see many more parties in the arena.

Summary of Experience in the Older Commonwealth

To what conclusions do these comparisons point? In the process of transplanting the British way of governing, what has been retained is perhaps more striking than the modifications. The latter, however, were bound to occur, since structures and processes do not emerge the same when their social accompaniments are altered. The British who emigrated were not an exact statistical cross section of the society they left, for the upper-class element was far smaller and less influential. Moreover, in Canada and South Africa the English-speaking people had to coexist with other cultures which they had forced under their jurisdiction. In the homogeneous communities, party politics are founded, almost exclusively, on economic divisions. Hence it is in the United Kingdom, Australia, and New Zealand that a Labour party became strong, but not in South Africa or Canada.

Where language, religion, and race create their own affiliations, party politics are as strongly influenced by these groupings as by the economic.

It is these crosscurrents within society which inject the motive force into the party system and, through it, determine how the institutions of the state will function. This comes out very clearly in the point around which so much controversy has raged, the operation of the electoral system. Chronologically, as well as logically, the party system is prior to the electoral system. The dominant parties pick the electoral arrangements which suit their interest and foster their own perpetuation. In the sense of primary origination, the party system is produced by the relations between social groupings and it in turn produces the machinery which will help it survive. Governmental institutions, as such, do not provide the party system with a content, save on the one point that the professional politicians wish to control whatever institutions there are and to prevent their opponents from doing so.[32] But institutions do give shape and structure to what otherwise would be amorphous. Because of the requirements that it must govern, the state gives firmness of outline to the formless. It is in this manner, as an important yet secondary cause, that institutions contribute to the character of the party system. Such, at any rate, is the inference I draw from Great Britain and from four countries whose politics were wholly or largely derived from the British model.

The Two Party-Systems of the United States

An instructive case to consider next is the United States. Self-evidently, no interpretation of party politics is worth much if it does not embrace the most important of contemporary democracies. What is the nature, then, of the American party system? And what have been its causes?

Conventionally, the United States is described as having a two-party system, and ordinarily it is classified along with Great Britain. Since both countries employ the same type of electoral system (i.e., victory by plurality in single-member districts), the line of reasoning for those who explain the parties by institutional factors is straightforward. The same cause is responsible for the same result. Is this view correct? Or is it possible that there are two errors in this reasoning—that both "cause" and "re-

32. A French writer, who studied Australia and New Zealand at the turn of the century, reported that on a visit to an Australian State legislature he asked an opposition leader what his program was. The latter pointed to where the Ministers were sitting, and replied: "To turn them out!" Albert Métin, Le Socialisme sans Doctrines. (Paris; F. Alcan, 1901), p. 73.

sult" may have been wrongly assessed? To begin with, let us review the facts. Before any hypothesis about causation can be reliably advanced, one should first be clear about the nature of the effect which it has supposedly produced. Hence the initial problem is to diagnose and classify the American party system.

In politics appearances can be deceiving, and labels are especially deceptive. To apply the names "Democrats" and "Republicans" to two huge conglomerations may suggest more than exists in actuality. It may express a hope for unity or an intention which some facts confirm, but others belie. Here is one of those interesting problems which arise in the course of political analysis where what is in dispute is the degree of emphasis to be attached to different facts, and the degree depends on one's angle of vision. If the standard of comparison for judging American politics is France or Switzerland, the United States can be said to have a two-party system. If Britain or New Zealand is the standard, the actual workings of the American parties have some measure of kinship with the multi-party systems of the European continent.

It may be possible to clarify such contradictory judgments in this way. The United States contains, not a two-party system, but two party-systems. One of these reflects its origins within society and corresponds with reasonable accuracy to the diversity and complexity of this huge country. It consists therefore of a multiplicity of groups which combine differently over different issues. These groups are observable in their greatest variety at the time of the congressional and state elections—especially those which occur in the middle of the presidential term—and when votes are taken in Congress on matters of public policy. In these instances, the American party system does not function with the disciplined predictability of the British. Republicans and Democrats lack the cohesion of Conservatives and Labour, and the unity of each party is regularly broken. When the House of Commons is due to divide, the result is always[33] a foregone conclusion. In the Senate and House of Representatives, there are many divisions of which no one can predict the outcome.

The other party system in the United States is based on the same social components and consists of the self-same numerous groupings. But in this case the latter are pressed into a special mold by the nationalizing tendencies of certain aspects of the federal Constitution. The one which is uniquely important is, of course, the Presidency. To capture this office is the supreme prize of American politics—not only for the ambitious hand-

33. It is rare for an individual member or dissident group to cross the floor and vote with the other side. Strong disagreement with the majority prevailing in the party is ordinarily expressed by abstention.

ful who dare to climb the pinnacle of public life and wield power at the summit, but also for the thousands who are concerned to improve a specific situation and want the authority to execute their programs. The character of the office and the method by which the President is elected have an effect upon the multi-group system. The majority which actually elects the President is that of the Electoral College, not of the people voting; and in the college each State comprises a single district in which the candidate who receives the largest number of popular votes wins all of the votes assigned to the State in the Electoral College. Only if the Electoral College fails to produce a majority is the election transferred to the House of Representatives, where each State delegation casts one vote. This latter procedure, or "run-off" election, has been used only twice (1800 and 1824) and both occasions were in the early period when the Republic was growing and before its party system and institutional practices were fully formed. Since then, in fact, great care has been taken to see that the Electoral College will produce the requisite majority and that the President will not be elected by the House.

The result is both curious and fascinating, since it illustrates an effect of a constitutional office on political processes. A multi-party system—based on regional, racial, religious, ethnic, and economic diversities—is generated by American society, and that party system tends to dominate for nearly three years out of every four. But in the fourth year, when the presidential election is due, the multi-party system separates into two huge coalitions. These display their internal differences to the full before the presidential candidates are nominated. Once the nominees are chosen, however, all emphasis is placed on party unity and concord without which the electoral college majority cannot be won. Unity prevails during the campaign and for varying lengths of time after the election. On the losing side, disintegration starts earlier. A defeated candidate is a titular leader without authority, and the odds are against his renomination. The victors hold together somewhat better, since they can feast upon the fruits of victory. Normally, however, by the summer of the first year of a presidential term the disintegrative tendency is already at work in the party which has the nominal majority, and when votes are being taken on key items in the legislative program the multi-group system reasserts itself. The Republican and Democratic parties are neither centralized, nor disciplined, nor unitary. Essentially, like the Canadian parties, they are two federal unions operating within a federal union, and producing their maximum cohesion at the time when it is necessary to elect a President and primarily for that purpose.

If the American party system is understood in this way, the salient facts can be adequately interpreted and the apparent contradictions explained. Analysis and classification are always beset with difficulty whenever reality is particularly complex. But even though our categories are sometimes too neat for the untidiness of real life, the classifier must take the world as he finds it and make sense of its inconsistencies as best he can. Actually, with all their lack of logical symmetry and precision of principle, the party systems of the United States faithfully reflect the community that created them. The tension between the particularism of the parts and the unity evolving through the growth of common interests and the lapse of time is one of the major themes of American history.

Alignments in Modern American Politics

The parties in the United States have been the agents for the political incorporation of the groups within society and have represented their divisions. Thus the criss-crossing splits of urban and rural, exporters and importers, rich and poor, earlier and later immigrants, Protestant and Catholic, white and non-white, have yielded their quota to the general pattern. The modern system was formed in the 1850's when the sectional conflict overshadowed all other questions and the Democrats were divided between north and south. The Republicans then forged an alliance of the urban, manufacturing, and commercial interests of the Northeast with the farmers of the Midwest. This coalition found Lincoln for a leader, saved the Union, and won the Civil War. Afterwards, the Republican strategists sought to perpetuate their control by enlisting support in three directions. One was in the defeated South, whose States were to be reconstructed by pro-Republican factions. This attempt failed completely. The second hope lay in the region from the Rockies to the Pacific Coast where territories were due for admission as States. Here the Republicans were moderately successful, in that they did attract widespread and continuous support in many States of the West. But their greatest success lay in their appeal to the manufacturers and owners of the big corporations who spearheaded the industrial expansion in and after the Civil War. Beyond that, the Republicans in general were a party of Protestants, tolerant of the Negroes whom they had emancipated, favoring high tariffs to protect their manufactures, and welcoming a flood of immigrants for a plentiful supply of cheap labor.

The Democrats, as was natural, rebuilt their fortunes from the 1870's on by forming a rival coalition of all who were or considered themselves to be the underprivileged. This category included the white southerners who regained supremacy in their section when northern troops were withdrawn, the industrial workers and the poor of the big northern cities, new immigrants as they gained citizenship, and Catholics. An alliance of such disparate elements could only cohere through a common antipathy to those who ruled the roost. Republicans could use economic power to bolster their political position. So Democrats had to wait for a depression or a cleavage between the manufacturers and the farm bloc, and thus attract the extra votes to augment their collection of minorities into a majority. After the turn of the century, the two basic domestic issues were the absorption of the recent immigrants and their children into the main stream of the national culture, and the reduction of the gap between the very rich and the very poor. The events of World War I focused on the first question through the rise of nationalist feelings and some resentment against "hyphenated Americans." The subsequent decision to restrict immigration by the quota system converted the land of opportunity into a relatively closed society. But it carried the implication that those who had already arrived now belonged together and shared equal rights.

It was the depression of the early 1930's which demanded solutions for the economic malaise. Because the Republicans had held power for the ten preceding years, the political blame fell squarely on them. In any case the Democrats were the party whose supporters and ideas disposed them to take novel and energetic measures and expand the powers of the federal government accordingly. Roosevelt's New Deal forms the watershed dividing modern American politics from the earlier formative phase. In a sense, the domestic issues raised in all presidential elections and sessions of Congress since 1933 have been variations on the one theme, what to do with the legacy from the New Deal: how much of it to retain, which of its programs to contract, which of its principles to extend. For this reason, the Democratic coalition, because it was responsible for initiating the New Deal and has most vigorously applied its ideas, has taken the political offensive. Reviewing the six and a half decades of this century, one cannot fail to note that the Democrats have developed into the majority party. Between 1900 and 1932, the Republicans held the Presidency for twenty-four years as against eight for the Democrats. But from 1933 through 1964, the figures were exactly reversed. Moreover, the only candidate elected President under the Republican banner during the last three decades was a popular soldier with no prior party connection, and not a professional politician or party regular. As for the Congress, between 1901 and 1932, Republicans controlled the Senate during twenty-six years and the House for twenty-two; the Democrats, for only six and ten, respectively. But from 1933 to 1964, the Democrats had a majority in both chambers for twenty-eight years, and the Republicans for a mere four. Continuously in recent decades the Republicans have been driven, or have driven themselves, on the defensive, until they have become limited to a posture of niggling negations.

Because both organizations are so loosely articulated, however, when one speaks of a party as "controlling" the legislature, the term must be interpreted and qualified. There is political meaning in the party label which is genuine enough. For instance, the designation affects a candidate's prospects of election, his committee assignments and seniority, and so forth. But it regularly appears that another factor, running across party lines, exerts an equal influence on the behavior of the voters and of those who represent them. This is the distinction, not between Republican and Democrat, but between conservative and liberal. These two divisions are far from being synonymous. Each party contains its liberal wing and its conservative wing—albeit with the significant difference that liberalism is proportionately stronger among the Democrats, as is conservatism among the Republicans. On major issues the liberals of both parties frequently join forces in the Congress while their conservative opponents do the same.

That the two great American parties should be broken down and then regrouped in terms of a liberal-conservative line-up has been suggested many times as desirable and has sometimes been predicted as inevitable. Although sceptical of inevitability, I can nevertheless subscribe, as a personal judgment, to the desirability of such a change. The old labels accord oddly with some of the newer characteristics of the changing American scene. The gap between rich and poor, the split between urban and rural, the antipathy between Protestants and Catholics, the separatism of sections and regions, the discrimination against minority races—these older cleavages, though undeniably they still exist, have been growing less acute and in varying degrees are being reduced. In this classic land of individualism and diversity, we are gradually, yet discernibly, becoming more homogenized. And these long-term trends in the evolution of our society have permeated and modified our politics. One-third of us, perhaps, are liberals; perhaps another third are conservatives. The remainder straddle in between and are non-aligned. The party organizations compete for the favor of this uncommitted group, and whoever captures the Center holds the power. Since 1932 the Democrats have continuously represented the Left, and, with the single exception of the Eisenhower interlude, have attracted the Center. But while they are in office, their effectiveness is handicapped—in the Congress, at least—by the conservative, and even reactionary, interests of the southern oligarchies.

One final point is relevant to the analysis before this part of the discussion, and this chapter, are closed. If one searches for the party system which most nearly resembles that of the United States, the closest is the Canadian. Scholars in Canada have themselves drawn the analogy between these two systems.[34] In the early decades after confederation, the Conservatives with their "national policy" were similar to Federalists of the Hamiltonian variety. Their opposition, bringing together the small farmers of Ontario and the anti-centralist, anti-clerical, *rouges* of Quebec, resembled the Jeffersonian alliance of western small farmers and states' righters. When later Conservative policies provoked ardent hostility in Quebec, that province became as solidly Liberal as the South after reconstruction was solidly Democratic. The influence of the Catholic Church in Quebec has provided Canada with its "peculiar institution," as have slavery and the emancipated Negroes for the United States. Thus in the twentieth century the circumstances of political history drove into the Liberal party the most conservative force in Canadian life, just as the white supremacists, defending an outmoded *status quo*, have found themselves oddly aligned in the Democratic party with the liberal elements of northern urbanism and western radicalism. Both countries have also experienced the phenomenon of third- and fourth-party movements, based largely on regional interests which could capture a state or provincial government. Thus Populists, Progressives, and Farmer-Laborites in the past could break away from the two big coalitions in the United States, as have the United Farmers of Ontario, the Western Progressives, Social Credit, and the Cooperative Commonwealth Federation in Canada.

The major Canadian parties call themselves by British names, but their ingredients are essentially of this hemisphere. In the realities of their political behavior, both the United States and Canada conform to the influences of the North American continent. The geography of continental dimensions and its accompanying regionalism, the broad range of economic interests, and the social composition of an immigrant population—these are the factors mainly responsible for the similarity between the party systems north and south of the undefended frontier. If this category admits an accurate description, one might suggest the title: duopoly under difficulties.

This chapter has been concerned with the two-party system and those closely approximating to it. The most notable examples happen to occur in the countries which belong in the main to the English-speaking tradition both in politics and culture—a fact which in itself suggests that sharing a common historical origin has something to do with similarities in subsequent growth. But a different cultural pattern, and other historical influences, have shaped the democracies of the European continent. It is there that the classic cases of multi-party systems can be found. To the causes and character of these systems, therefore, the discussion will turn next.

34. For instance, Alexander Brady in *Democracy in the Dominions* (University of Toronto Press), Chap. 5, p. 101.

12

Politics with Many Parties

A Danish Prime Minister once made the comment that people often exaggerate the difference between a two-party and a multi-party system.[1] Politics, he argued, consists in reaching agreements through compromise. You make your compromises in a two-party system inside the party; where there are many parties, you compromise between them. The results amount to much the same.

Characteristics of Multipartism

This opinion is important because of the man who held it and for what it states. The experience of a seasoned politician (and a highly successful one), who was presiding over a three-party coalition, is worth a great deal. He knew, as only a veteran really can, that the art of governing in a democracy involves the mobilization of support and that the interests of separate groups must be continuously harmonized through give-and-take. True enough, and yet that does not complete the matter. This viewpoint focuses on politics as a process which conducts a certain activity—constructing agreement through compromise. But politics involves more than process. It includes the element of organization, whose character influences the process and its outcome. Let us grant that all democratic politics require the building of consent among individuals and groups. The fact

1. This Premier was the late Mr. H. C. Hansen. I had heard this remark attributed to him, and once asked him if this was indeed his opinion. He confirmed it, and spoke along the lines indicated above.

still remains that the character of the building blocks affects the patterns in which they can be arranged and has a bearing on the life and strength of the structure. It makes a difference to a political leader, to parliamentarians, to party members, to the general public, whether the groupings which must be taken into account are loose, informal wings of a larger body, or whether they are separate, structured, formal entities. The differences between insiders are normally easier to reconcile than those between outsiders. Publicity alone supplies one compelling reason why this is so. The factions that form within a party will ordinarily press for what they want in private session behind closed doors. Those who argue against one another in caucus or cabinet can still preserve some appearance of unity when they are in the public view and face their opposition. But parties which exist as distinct organizations, which present rival candidates for election, which announce their own programs, and denounce all others —for some of those to combine in coalition is made more difficult because their disagreements are public and are on record. The art of compromise is more easy or less depending on when, where, and how the differences are stated.

The multi-party system has hitherto been characteristic of the democracies of Europe, for nowhere on the continent has a two-party alternation been definitively established. But the term "multi-party" can be misleading. The systems which comprise more parties than two are not all alike. They vary in their individual components and over-all character. Some (e.g., Italy) contain a powerful movement which is anti-democratic in spirit and allegiance. In some (e.g., Norway) a single party has maintained a long continuous ascendancy over a splintered opposition. In one borderline case, that of postwar Austria, two old rivals joined in a coalition which has virtually eliminated effective opposition, as has also happened in the Latin American democracy of Uruguay. It is possible, of course, when referring to multi-party systems to exaggerate the element of multiplicity. These systems naturally include a fringe of very small parties—as does the British two-party system for that matter—which normally have little or no effect on the outcome of an election. Hence, although one may sometimes count as many as six or more, the figure has to be reduced to terms which are politically realistic. In general, a multi-party system is made up of four, and politics revolves around their various relationships—be they relations of competition or of coalition. Nor are the coalitions haphazard or accidental. In Switzerland a powerful party which was once dominant joined with others in a permanent coalition, which for many decades controlled the seven-membered Federal Council. In Denmark the alliance of Social Democrats and Radicals on one side is as traditional as that of

Venstre and Conservatives on the other. There are some long-lasting marriages in these multi-party systems, as well as some bigamous connections and temporary liaisons. Divorces occur also, as in the case of the Swedish Agrarians, who severed their ties with the Social Democrats. Nowhere is the human capacity to contrive and survive more fascinatingly displayed than in politics, and nowhere in politics more ingeniously than under conditions of multipartism. The respectable and the petty, the serious and the frivolous, meet here in imperfect balance; and the public observes a performance whose scenes may switch rapidly from grand opera to opera bouffe.

To an observer who is accustomed to the apparent simplicity of a two-party system the initial impression of multi-party politics is one of bewildering complexity. It is not easy to understand at first glance what each party stands for and whom it represents. Nor are there always convincing answer to the inevitable, yet seemingly naïve, question: Are so many parties really needed? A citizen of a Continental democracy, who grows up with the system, understands its nuances and accepts it as reasonable and normal. He is likely to turn the argument around and suggest that his form of politics is the truly representative one since it honestly reflects the pluralism of a democratic society. The two-party system, though its simplicity may be enviable, marks in his view an artificial bifurcation which does not accord accurately with the facts of political life. No democratic baby, as W. S. Gilbert pointed out, is necessarily born to be either a little liberal or else a little conservative. The "either . . . or" dichotomies, beloved of some logicians, seldom fit reality.

Nor should the supposed superiority of two parties over many be taken for granted, as is usually done by writers in the Anglo-American tradition. There is only one irrefutable argument in favor of the two-party system. It has the great merit of focusing responsibility. The dividing line between government and opposition is clear and sharp.[2] The people know whom to praise and whom to blame. By contrast, when a multi-party coalition holds office, responsibility is divided and evasion is likelier. This contention appears to me correct. But the other principal criticism of multi-party politics is an example of erroneous generalization from one much-publicized case. This is the argument that multipartism breeds instability and is the parent of governmental weakness. Such a conclusion is derived primarily from the history of France under the Third and Fourth Republics, when the recurrence of ministerial crises became a byword.[3] Contrary in-

2. It is not at all clear or sharp, however, in the United States because of the existence of the two party-systems described in the preceding chapter.
3. Even in France, however, as I shall argue later (pp. 377 ff.), multipartism was itself the consequence of causes which lay deeper in French society.

stances, however, can be found in Switzerland and Scandinavia, where multipartism and political stability go hand in hand. Indeed, I would venture the judgment that no democracy anywhere is more stable than the Swiss and none has a party system whose multiplicity is more intricate. Certainly there are several states in which the multi-party system is used with considerable skill and has given general satisfaction. Most Danes, Swedes, and Swiss consider that it suits their needs no less than the two-party system has suited others elsewhere. On this topic their views are entitled to a respectful hearing, because, when it comes to democracy, these countries have much to teach the world.

But this argument is moving to conclusions when it has not yet delved into causes. Before exploring the results, one should try to explain why they have occurred. Can the multi-party systems be interpreted in the light of the analysis of the preceding chapter? To what extent are they influenced by social phenomena or by institutional factors? I shall begin with a discussion of Switzerland because the very complexity both of society and government in that country poses some basic questions. The multi-party politics of the multi-social Swiss will then be compared with the multipartism of Scandinavia where society is more homogeneous and the structure of government is also simpler. Finally I shall turn to an examination of France—the crucial case on which many hypotheses must stand or fall.

Reasons for the Swiss Party System

Switzerland is a complicated country to govern. It is small in scale, in population and area. Yet internally everything is unbelievably intricate. The Swiss are a tenacious people. The product of a long tradition, they are slow-moving and firm; and, especially if they are Bernese, they can be very stubborn. In the center of Europe, influenced by the crosscurrents of their powerful neighbors, they have survived defiant and distinct. A long laborious effort, prudently and patiently conducted, has brought results which are envied in many lands. They enjoy wealth, stability, freedom, and peace. At the same time they suffer the obverse of such virtues. Their wealth can be accompanied with parsimony; their stability with dullness; freedom with exclusiveness; and peace with inertia. The governance of such a people well repays study, for if Europe can be said to contain a political miracle, it is the *Confederatio Helvetica*.

The party system of Switzerland is highly pertinent to the topic of this chapter. In 1964 nine parties had some representation in the National Council. Only three of these—the Socialists, Radicals, and Catholic-Conservatives—could be called major parties, in the sense that each collected over one-fifth of the vote. Together, at the election of 1959, they received the support of 73 per cent of the voting electorate. Fourth in importance come the Peasants, Artisans, and Bourgeois, who used to win 16 per cent of the votes, but have slipped to under 12 per cent and are therefore only half as strong as the Conservatives. Moreover, they are less of a national party than the "big three," since in 1959 they presented candidates in less than half of the cantons and gathered half of their electoral support from the one Canton of Berne. Accordingly, they should be classified as a medium, not a major, party. Last, there are five small parties—the Independents, formerly led by Gottlieb Duttweiler, the Liberals, the Democrats, the Communists, and the Evangelicals who manage to elect a single deputy from Canton Zurich. These five polled, altogether, 14 per cent of the votes in 1959. They occupied 12 per cent of the seats in the National Council.[4]

The problem, then, is to explain why this kind of party system has grown out of Swiss conditions. The peculiar significance of Switzerland is that it permits a plausible argument to be made for either a sociological or an institutional view. Those who explain the Swiss party system by the nature of the society reason thus. If the groupings around which parties cohere originate in the interests and issues that divide society, a multi-party system, it is reasonable to suppose, must be the product of considerable social fragmentation. How does this apply to the case of Switzerland? The answer admits of little doubt. Cultural diversity is the distinguishing hallmark of the Swiss people. No other nation in Europe is compounded of elements so heterogeneous. The Swiss are split into two camps by religion, share in three of the surrounding cultures, acknowledge four national languages, and are further crisscrossed by the conventional distinctions of economics. How can they do otherwise than sustain many parties? Only if a two-party system existed in such a society would it be baffling to the inquirer.

But the institutionalist is not satisfied with all this. He is convinced that the structure of the state supplies the channels into which the forces of party politics are poured, like molten metal into forms; and that of all institutions the one that is nearest to the parties and influences them most directly is the electoral system. Now, is it not a fact that for several decades prior to World War I the Radicals had a majority in the National Council over all other groups combined? Is it not also a fact that since 1919 no one party has ever again predominated? Instead, an equilibrium has been maintained among four bigger parties and another four or five

4. Candidates were also presented in a few cantons by some even smaller splinter groups.

smaller ones. What happened to produce this transformation? Surely it could have been nothing else than the change in the electoral system which was altered in 1919 from the requirement of a majority, after two ballots if necessary, to proportional representation. Here then is a clear case of a change in the electoral system which induced a corresponding modification of the party system.

In order to assess the correctness of these conflicting interpretations, one must trace the fortunes of the parties, both before 1919 and since, and estimate how the manner of their evolution is related to the composition of society or the organization of the vote.

Formation of the Parties Before World War I

The party system of modern Switzerland was formed in the six critical decades between the end of the Napoleonic regime and the revision of the federal constitution in 1874. Four major problems were faced and surmounted during that period. These were the creation and strengthening of the central government, the extension of democratic principles and procedures in the cantons and at the center; the relation of the state to the churches; and the role of government in the economy. Each of these matters produced conflict since in each case opposite positions could be, and were, adopted. It was from this mélange of issues that the fluid lines of controversy took shape in persistent groupings and, as they solidified, acquired the semblance of parties. The future of the democratic system, challenged by the aristocracies and oligarchies which sought after 1815 to regain their former privileges, was assured in the upheavals of 1830. But the government of Switzerland was still essentially that of its cantons, and the switch from a loose confederation to an articulated federal union had yet to be accomplished. The precipitating cause of the change-over was the confessional struggle between Protestants and Catholics, which broadened out into the bigger issues of the relations of the state to the clergy[5] and of the union to its parts. Defeating the Catholic Sonderbund in the short-lived Civil War of October 1847, and spurred on in the next year by the revolutionary turmoil among their neighbors, the victorious majority drafted and ratified in 1848 the federal constitution that is still in force.

5. The problem of clerical power, though the climax of the struggle focused on the Catholic priests and monasteries and especially on the Jesuits, was by no means confined to Catholicism. Indeed in 1839 fanatical Protestants in Zurich had overthrown the lay government by force. See George Grote, *Seven Letters Concerning the Politics of Switzerland* (John Murray: London, 1876), pp. 34-5.

In the new federal assembly and through the periodic elections which its two branches required, the way was now open to organize the combinations of cantonal groups into parties that could become national in character and coverage. The Catholic-Conservatives held their power in the seven cantons which had attempted secession and there maintained, like the Democrats in the southern states of the United States, the tenacious solidarity of a defeated minority. The alliance of Protestant centralists which carried the day in 1847-48 continued to govern Switzerland for some decades. But the union that had been cemented in the religious struggle began to weaken as the importance of economic programs increased in national politics. The new question revolved around using the power of the central government to promote economic growth and to regulate the acts of private entrepreneurs. On this point the wealthier, more conservative Protestants (called Liberals) parted company with the numerous, less wealthy Radicals who were more disposed to favor active state intervention in the economic process. In this way, a difference of economic interest crisscrossed with the religious split to generate a three-party system—the Radicals being on the Left, the Liberals in the Center, and the Catholic-Conservatives on the Right.

It was the continuation of economic change which stimulated the next development among the parties. During the last quarter of the nineteenth century and the opening decade of the twentieth, industrialization came fast to Switzerland; and of course, as manufacturing establishments increased, the number of factory workers rose correspondingly. The political representation of their interest not only produced a new party, but stimulated a realignment of the old ones. The new party were the Social Democrats, who added to the indigenous Swiss associations of workingmen (the Grütli) the philosophy and militancy of Marxism imported by German immigrants. The spread of socialist ideas and the creation of a disciplined socialist movement called for a new strategy on the part of their nearest competitors, the Radicals, and their most distant opponents, the Catholic-Conservatives. Hitherto, the Radicals had enjoyed a quasi-monopoly[6] of the Left and Left Center. Now they found themselves compelled to resist the socialist effort at capturing the Left, and to compensate for any losses in this quarter by equivalent gains at the Center. The result was a progressive weakening of the Liberals to the benefit of the Radicals and a gradual rapprochement between the latter and the Catholics. For whatever antipathy Catholicism might feel for the Radicals was exceeded by the fear and revulsion which Marxian socialism provoked.

6. A splinter group, called the Democrats, had however broken away from the Radicals in Canton Zurich.

Thus, on the eve of World War I, Switzerland possessed four principal parties, in addition to some splinters. Of the four, the Radicals were still much the strongest, with the Catholic-Conservatives in second place, the Social Democrats ranking third, and the Liberals a declining fourth.

How the Electoral System Originally Operated

Under what kind of electoral system did these parties operate? The method in use before 1919 had two essential features. First, to win a seat in the National Council, a candidate had to obtain an absolute majority of the votes cast in the election. In the absence of a majority, a second ballot was held. If that too failed to produce a majority, a third poll occurred at which a plurality elected. This excessive solicitude for a majority was, however, modified after 1883 by a reduction in the number of ballots from three to two and acceptance of a plurality on the second turn. The other characteristic of the system was that in nearly all the districts several members were elected, and single-member districts were in fact extremely rare. Thus, in 1917 the 189 National Councillors were chosen in 49 districts. These were distributed as follows:

ELECTORAL APPORTIONMENT FOR THE SWISS NATIONAL COUNCIL
BY DISTRICTS, 1917

Number of Members Elected in the District	Number of Such Districts
1	6
2	7
3	10
4	10
5	6
6	3
7	5
8	2

Hence, three-quarters of the districts were assigned as many as three or more deputies to elect.

In the discussions of this system, most attention has been directed to the requirement that a majority should elect and to the provision of a later ballot where no majority was forthcoming the first time. Surely though, whatever relation may exist between the electoral system and the parties, the size and shaping of the districts will influence representation as much as the number of votes required for victory. The actual results of the system are instructive. For many decades the Radicals maintained a continuous majority in the National Council over all other parties. This success appears to have been due to two circumstances. First, the Radicals enjoyed the tactical advantages of position in the political spectrum extending from Left to Right. Originally their power was derived from their supremacy on the Left. But subsequently, after the emergence of the Social Democrats, the Radicals occupied a position similar to that which the Canadian Liberals so skillfully exploited from 1935 to 1957. Astride the Center, though inclined to the Left, they mastered an opposition that was scattered into groups on either side of them. Secondly, they reinforced this advantage by the skillful use of "electoral geometry."[7] The districts were determined after each census by federal legislation. The Radicals entrenched themselves in power for as long as possible by gerrymandering in their own favor—a charge commonly voiced in Switzerland around the turn of the century.

Representation thus suffered a distortion. What was essentially a multiparty system among the public was artificially converted into a continuous one-party dominance of the National Council. Little wonder, then, that the opponents of the Radicals felt themselves the victims of an injustice. Little wonder that, with the system manipulated against them, a large section of the public boycotted the elections[8] and turned to other devices as a counterpoise. Of these the most important were the referendum and the initiative. Since the constitutional revision of 1874 the optional referendum had made it possible for the people themselves to overrule the legislation enacted by their representatives, and this happened with some frequency. Further, the use of the initiative to propose amendments to the constitution gave the voters a means of breaking the vicious circle whereby the Radicals perpetuated their majority in the National Council by drawing the boundaries of the constituencies. Here was a weapon of which the opposition parties could make use. An amendment requiring that elections to the National Council be conducted under proportional representation was first initiated and proposed to the voters in 1900, but was decisively defeated. Ten years later, however, when the same proposal was resubmitted, it came near to being accepted. Both Socialists and Catholics favored proportionalism, which, they hoped, would bring them more seats in the National Council.

Events now moved toward the climax. In 1909 the Gothard convention

7. *Le Journal de Genève* wrote on Oct. 28, 1917: "In Zurich, one of the districts has been carved for the bourgeois parties, the other for the socialists. There you have one of the beauties of the majoritarian system and of electoral geometry." p. 1.
8. See Chapter 10, pp. 286-7.

was signed with Germany. Under it, as many Swiss believed, that country gained a favored position in the Swiss economy. The debates over ratification were long and bitter; and, when the convention was ratified in 1913, there were loud protests, especially in *la Suisse romande*. Immediately a third attempt was launched to change the electoral system, so that within a few weeks over 120,000 signatures were obtained for the initiative.[9] The Radicals resisted by delaying tactics, in which they were helped temporarily by the outbreak of the war. In the long run, however, it was the war's effect on Switzerland which broke their political supremacy. The dislocation of the country's economy led to a sharp increase in the cost of living and a conflict of interest between the city dwellers and the farm population. In order to offset the advances of the Social Democrats, the Radicals adopted policies to allay the discontent of urban workers. Their measures, however, were only sufficient to alienate the peasants, and were insufficient to satisfy the factory employees. At the election of October 1917—the last that was held under the old system—the Radicals still clung to their majority, but with increasing difficulty. In many electoral districts they arranged with other parties to present joint lists of candidates in order to keep the Social Democratic representation down to a minimum. Thus, in the fourth *arrondissement* of Canton Zurich, embracing Winterthur, a common list was offered by three parties, containing one Radical, two Agrarians, and two Democrats.[10] In Fribourg, the Radicals were allied with Catholic-Conservatives in the twenty-third *arrondissement*.[11] In Geneva, the Radicals and the Democrats jointly sponsored a list of six candidates, three being from each party—an act which is described as "an event which is wholly new in the annals of Genevese political life."[12] In Bern Mittelland, comprising the capital city and the communes nearby, a bitter struggle was fought between the Socialists with seven candidates and a list composed of three Radicals, two Young Radicals, and two Liberal Conservatives.[13] Similar details could be cited about other districts.

The Switch to Proportional Representation

Electoral alliances of this character supply evidence for these points—a multi-party system was already firmly established; the Radicals, who had

9. *Journal de Genève*, Oct. 11, 1917, p. 1, and Oct. 11, 1918, p. 1.
10. *Journal de Genève*, Oct. 23, 1917, p. 6, and Oct. 25, 1917, p. 4.
11. *Ibid.*, Oct. 23, 1917, p. 6.
12. *Ibid.*, Oct. 25, 1917, p. 1.
13. *Ibid.*, Oct. 28, 1917, p. 1.

inflated their own group in the National Council, were now forced to depend on other parties; the Social Democrats were challenging the older parties with considerable effect. Indeed, the results of the 1917 election left little doubt that an era was drawing to an end. Despite alliances between parties, the Radicals were noticeably weakened in districts where they had once dominated. For many of their seats they required a second ballot to win. As the *Journal de Genève* grimly commented after polling day: "The elections of 1917 have given the finishing blow to the majoritarian system."[14] Consequently, in 1918 the Radicals could no longer postpone the submission to the voters of the constitutional initiative in favor of proportional representation which had been launched for the third time in 1913. Its adoption now appeared likely. Throughout 1918 the economic condition of the country imposed still more hardships on poorer people. Frequent reference was made in the press to "economic difficulties," "increasingly distressing social problems," and "the high cost of living."[15] The minority and opposition groups—the Catholic-Conservatives, Socialists, and *la Suisse romande* generally—favored the change. So did the Agrarians, who at this time were splitting away from the Radicals, particularly "the Peasants' parties recently founded in Cantons Zurich and Berne."[16] But on the conservative wing there were misgivings among those who had earlier sponsored the proposals, for they began to fear the gains that would accrue to the Socialists. The *Journal de Genève*, a paper of Liberal persuasion, tried editorially to allay these fears, pointing out that everybody—and not merely the extreme Left—would benefit at the Radicals' expense.[17] Anyway, said the paper: "Will the socialists thereby gain some seats in the National Council? No matter: it is not in Parliament that they are dangerous! . . . Now, under the present majoritarian system, thanks to which they can portray themselves as martyrs, the activities which they conduct in their menacing Soviets is infinitely more pernicious. The injustice committed at their expense increases their strength and pushes them in a revolutionary direction."[18] Nevertheless, though hopefuls, they expected six and a half cantons (Schaffhausen, Glarus, Appenzell R.E., Grisons, Thurgau, Aargau, and Vaud) to oppose the change, and Fribourg and Basel-Land were rated doubtful.[19] Conse-

14. *Journal de Genève*, Nov. 1, p. 1, in an article entitled: "Towards Electoral Reform."

15. E.g., *Journal de Genève*, Jan. 1, 1919, article on "The Year 1918 in Switzerland."

16. *Ibid.*, October 8, 1918, p. 1.

17. *Ibid.*, Oct. 2, 1918, p. 1.

18. *Journal de Genève*, Oct. 13, 1918, p. 1.

19. *Ibid.*, Oct. 8, 1918, p. 1.

quently they, like everybody else, were astonished at the size of the majority in favor of proportionalism when the vote took place.[20] At the moment when Imperial Germany was sinking to its knees, peaceful Switzerland sought to strengthen its democracy with "electoral justice."

From this analysis so far the conclusion that emerges is plain. It was not proportional representation which created the multi-party system, but the latter which antedated and produced the former. Multipartism has its roots in the pluralist character of Swiss society and in the fact that the line of its various subdivisions did not correspond. A series of issues—religious, economic, and political—generated a number of parties. Although for several decades a single party, capitalizing on the memories of 1847-48 and its own genuine services to the nation, was able to outmaneuver all its rivals, their combined opposition in the end proved irresistible. They then adopted the type of electoral system which more appropriately conformed to the social mixture of the country.

Nearly four decades have elapsed since proportionalism came into force, and twelve federal elections have thus far been conducted under its auspices. During this same period Swiss society has adjusted to the aftermath of World War I, the depression of the early 1930's, World War II, and the postwar tensions. It has confronted the challenges of Nazi aggressiveness and revolutionary Communism, and has continued a slow, yet steady, industrial development and population growth. In what way have the parties reflected or registered these facts?

There is certainly one change, attributable to the adoption of proportional representation, for which students of politics can be most grateful. The federal Bureau of Statistics has published since 1919 a series of thorough reports on each election, including a full statistical analysis and an excellent commentary. It is relatively easy, therefore, both to observe the evolution of the party system as a whole and to trace the fortunes of an individual party. Unfortunately, data of similar quality are not available prior to 1919, a fact which precludes exact comparison between the two periods. Nevertheless, this much can be said with certainty. If one compares the results of the 1917 election with those of 1919, one is impressed with two striking differences and one equally striking similarity. The first difference is in the number of voters who participated in the election.

20. Yes, 265,194; No, 149,037. Only in Vaud, Thurgau, and Appenzell R.E. were the majorities for the *status quo*. Said the *Journal de Genève:* "Sunday's vote is an historic date. In effect, it sounds the death-knell of the regime which has governed Switzerland since 1848. In a general fashion, it marks the end in our country of the whole regime of single-party domination." Oct. 15, 1918, p. 1.

Prior to 1919 the chronic abstention of over 40 per cent of the electorate had marked a serious blot on Swiss democracy. In 1919, however, the number of participants amounted to 80.4 per cent of those eligible, a rise of 23 per cent over 1917. The other great difference is the existence in 1919 of a separate party of Peasants, Artisans, and Bourgeois, which won 15.3 per cent[21] of the votes and thus became the fourth largest group in the National Council.

To what extent were these differences associated with the adoption of proportional representation, or did they spring from other causes? It would be unreasonable to deny that the change in the system was a factor that contributed to the rise of the votes and the success of the Peasants. Many citizens who had been aggrieved at the inequities in representation were prepared to give the new system a trial. But, in my judgment, both the increase in voter participation and the formation of the Peasant party were more profoundly influenced by the same social, economic, and political trends which had made proportionalism itself acceptable. The tensions generated by the war even in a neutral nation, the ever-rising cost of living, mounting sentiment against the Radicals, and the militancy of the Bolshevik-inspired wing of the Socialists[22]—all these circumstances led to a heightened interest in the party struggle. Moreover, the split of the Peasants from the Radicals in Bern and Zurich happened earlier than the adoption of proportionalism and was not the consequence of the latter. Even without the change in the electoral system, the agrarian ferment, being geographically concentrated, could have maintained its separate identity.[23]

Relative Strength of Swiss Parties Since 1919

That the differences between the results of 1917 and 1919 are attributable even more to economic and other social factors than to electoral reform is further borne out by the profound resemblance between the two elections. Switzerland had multipartism in 1917, and the same was true in 1919. The system of parties did not change. What did change was the relative posi-

21. Of their total, 57% came from Canton Berne and 22% from Canton Zurich.
22. In November 1918, their committee at Olten had attempted a general strike, which the government resisted with strong measures (including troops), and defeated.
23. At the close of World War I or in the early 'twenties, due to similar economic pressures, the farmers in Australia, Canada, and elsewhere, developed their own political parties. The electoral systems of the countries concerned were of various types. It was a common economic situation, not a common electoral system, that gave rise to these agrarian parties.

tion of the parties within the system. Between 1917 and 1919 the Radicals declined in strength (a decline in part explained by the splitting away of the Peasants) and the Socialists and Catholics gained. Switzerland now had four principal parties, finely balanced from Left to Right, and another four or five small ones. It is equally instructive to compare the relative positions of the parties in 1919 with their standing in later years, and especially in the elections of the 1950's. The accompanying table depicts the evolution of the parties over four decades. Again one is impressed with the stability of the multi-party system which continues unaltered. All that does change is the relative strength of the parties. The Socialists have become stronger than the Radicals, and have occupied the first place for the last thirty years. The Conservatives have made a modest advance, while the Peasants have slipped back. The smaller parties, all told, win only 13 per cent of the votes; and the largest of them, the Independents, show signs of weakening. Swiss government today is still necessarily conducted by coalition, as it was at the close of World War I.

PERCENTAGE OF VOTES CAST FOR SWISS PARTIES
IN ELECTIONS FOR THE NATIONAL COUNCIL

	1919	1928	1939	1951	1955	1959
Radicals	28.8	27.4	20.8	24.0	23.3	23.7
Socialists	23.5	27.4	25.9	26.0	27.0	26.3
Catholic-Conservatives	21.0	21.4	17.0	22.5	23.2	23.3
Peasants	15.3	15.8	14.7	12.6	12.1	11.6
Liberals	3.8	2.9	1.6	2.6	2.2	2.3
Democrats	2.0	1.9	2.7	2.2	2.1	2.2
Evangelicals	0.8	0.7	0.9	1.0	1.1	1.4
Communists	—	1.8	2.6	2.7	2.6	2.7
Independents	—	—	7.1	5.1	5.5	5.5
Others	4.8	0.7	6.7	1.3	0.9	1.0

Such differences as can be noticed between 1919 and 1959 are explained accurately enough in terms of the development of Swiss society and public opinion. Industrialization has continued perforce, since, apart from emigration, it has provided the only means of livelihood for an increased population. From this fact, assuredly, the Socialists have benefited. Correspondingly, the peasants and agricultural laborers have formed an ever-smaller percentage of those gainfully employed. Thus the party of Peasants, Artisans, and Bourgeois, being the political expression of a numerically dwindling group, has contracted rather than expanded. However, in a country like Switzerland, the law of whose being is its internal diversity, national totals tell only one side of the story. Though the whole is more

than the sum of its parts, to understand Swiss domestic politics a knowledge of the parts is crucial. It is the interlocking of territorial units, the
cantons, with cultural and economic groupings which produces the issues
and organization of party politics. Luckily, in tracing these connections
one is again helped by the statistical work of the federal government. The
census reports contain for each canton and its subdivisions exact data on
religion, language, and occupation. These I have correlated with the voting
patterns in the same areas. The following analysis of the modern party
system is based on the combined results of this study and of interpretations supplied in interviews by scholars, news editors, and men in public
life.

There are, to begin with, some conditions of Swiss political life which
govern all parties. After a century of federal union the center of gravity of
politics is still closer to the base of the pyramid than the apex. Parties are
more strongly knit in the canton than they are nationally. Indeed it is approximately true to say that Switzerland does not have a single party system, but as many party systems as there are cantons. Then too, the opposition of nearby or contiguous cities creates complications to which the
parties must needs adjust: e.g., the rivalries of Basel and Zurich, Geneva
and Lausanne, Lugano and Locarno. The national parties, as in the United
States and Canada, are essentially federal unions within a federal union.
Their names vary from one canton to another, as does their relationship
with other parties. The Radicals, for example, are the farthest to the Right
in Canton Zurich; whereas in Basel-Stadt it is the Liberals who occupy the
Right, thereby pushing the Radicals nearer to the Center. The Radicals
of Canton Lucerne, where they are also in the Center, joined with the Socialists in 1955 to oust a Catholic-Conservative from his seat in the Council of States. Such mutual aid between Radicals and Socialists would be
unthinkable in Zurich, where, however, the Radicals and Democrats who
are rivals in cantonal elections support a joint list in federal contests. Of
these differently twisted threads is the national fabric woven!

The Radicals and the Socialists

Recognizing the risks of generalization, then, let us survey the parties in
turn. The one that stands alone by virtue of historical prestige and experience is the Radical party. They are the party of 1848, that created the
federal constitution. They are the governmental party par excellence, who
for over a hundred years have played a larger role than anybody else in
shaping the policies of the Federal Assembly and the Federal Council. Be-

cause of this long and intimate association with authority, the Radicals are a protean organization, varying in character with the circumstances of the canton. Geographically, they continue to be truly national, in that they are well represented in virtually every canton and in each of the linguistic areas. Though primarily an organization of Protestants,[24] they have their adherents also in Catholic strongholds. Thus, in 1959, they won over one-fifth of the votes in Fribourg and Valais and almost two-fifths in Lucerne, which in this respect, as in certain others, is the Virginia of Switzerland. In the representation of economic interests, however, the Radicals have become narrower with the passage of years. They lost the Left, first to the Democrats, then to the Socialists, thereby proving themselves unable to hold the allegiance of the industrial working class. Similarly, they lost the Peasants in the important cantons of Zurich and Bern. What they retain is the backing of most businessmen, especially in Zurich, where their influence has pushed the party over to the Right; of professional and salaried people; and generally of the *petit bourgeois*. Many of the industrious, thrifty Swiss, whose savings accounts are modest and hard-earned, bring to the Radicals their sense of individual independence and cautious conservatism.

While the lapse of forty years has left the Radicals somewhat weaker, the Socialists have grown stronger and on several occasions have received the highest percentage of the votes. But growth and time have changed the Socialists in other ways besides. As the Radicals have been pushed from Left to Center or Right Center, the Socialists have moved to the Left Center from the extreme Left. In the domestic sphere, they have exchanged militancy for moderation, helped in the early 1920's by the breakaway of the Russophile Communists. In external affairs, long hostile to the national military program, their attitude altered in the 1930's because of the Nazi threat. Today the temper of the Swiss Socialists is comparable to that of the British Labour party. Structurally, however, the two are markedly different, since in Switzerland there exists no organic link between the Socialists and the trade unions. A large number of trade unionists favor the Socialists; and some of these and many of the union officials are members of the Socialist party. But collectively the unions, which in general are weak vis-à-vis the employers, and which in 1937 abandoned the strike weapon in favor of "social peace," prefer to have no direct participation in party politics.

24. For instance, in Canton St. Gallen, whose population has a mixture of Protestants and Catholics, the coefficient of correlation between Radical votes in 1951 and Protestantism is 0.916. It is −0.931 between Radical votes and Catholicism. (These figures are calculated from the 1950 census and the 1951 election.)

Not all the industrial workers vote Socialist; but more of them vote for this party than for any other. In addition, there are a number of intellectuals, teachers, and secretaries of organizations who are Socialists. Understandably, therefore, this party is the strongest in the urban areas.[25] But since a large section of Switzerland is rural, a national party cannot confine itself to the urban areas; and, as a matter of fact, the Socialists in 1951 gathered 55.3% of their votes in the rural communities.[26] There are two reasons for this. One is that the policy of the Radicals in the government has helped commerce and manufacturing. There has been a tendency to allow agricultural prices to fall in order to keep urban wages down. Hence, in some cases, the discontent of the rural areas has been expressed through a Socialist vote—particularly in *la Suisse romande*, where the Peasant party scarcely exists. Equally important is the gradual blurring of the occupational distinction between urban and rural residents. In many peasant families the husband now supplements his earnings by commuting for work in a factory. Thereby, he acquires the interests and viewpoint of the "worker." As a consequence, there are at present some villages, especially in Aargau, where the Socialists possess a majority.

In other respects, too, the Socialists are as broadly national in their appeal as the Radicals, since they collect a sizable percentage of the vote in practically all cantons. While they are strong in German-speaking Switzerland (notably Bern, Zurich, and Aargau), they have made great gains in Vaud[27] and they obtain a higher percentage of votes in Neuchâtel than in any other canton. As for religion, the Socialists have extended their influence more easily among the Protestants (who also have the bulk of the industry) and their strength still varies in inverse ratio with that of the Catholic priesthood. Nevertheless in the overwhelmingly Catholic cantons, to the extent that there is industry and anticlericalism, the Socialists do not lack support. Thus they received in 1959 a tenth of the votes or more in Fribourg, Lucerne,[28] and Valais, and a quarter of the total in Schwyz and Zug.

25. In 1951, the Socialists received 30.8% of the votes cast in the large cities, 35.7% in the medium, and 33.2% in the small. Report on *Elections au Conseil National*, 1951, by the Bureau fédéral de Statistique (Berne, 1954), p. 25.
26. *Ibid.*, p. 24.
27. The Socialists in Vaud received 21.5% of the votes in 1951, 29.6% in 1955, 30% in 1959.
28. An eminent news editor in Zurich told me this about the intense party struggles of Lucerne: Socialists seldom go to Church, Radicals go more frequently, Conservatives go regularly.

The Catholic-Conservatives and the Smaller Parties

The Catholic-Conservatives have displayed remarkable tenacity in the last forty years. In 1919 they had 21 per cent of the votes; they sank to 17 per cent in 1939; and recovered to 23.3 per cent in 1959. There are seven cantons and three half-cantons in which over 80 per cent of the population are Catholics; it is these that provide the original and continuing base of the Catholic-Conservative party. Hence, in 1959 they obtained over half of the votes in Lucerne and Fribourg, and more than three-fifths in Valais —percentages which, for Switzerland, are extremely high. Yet, as such figures prove, the Catholic-Conservative party has no more succeeded in mobilizing all Catholics than have the Socialists organized all the industrial workers. Generally, the strength of the Conservative party is correlated in the Catholic cantons with clericalism and ruralism. For instance, there are some villages in the Valais where, if the census returns are compared with the election results, the number of males aged 20 and over, of registered voters, of actual voters, and of Conservative votes, is identical in each case. But such perfect mobilization is rare. The party meets new problems when it confronts urbanism and industry. Indeed, the truth is that, in the long run, while the Catholic birth rate is the party's major asset, industrialization is its greatest challenge. The higher birth rate of the Catholic cantons produces a surplus population, which their limited resources and relative poverty cannot absorb. Hence there is a drift to the more prosperous Protestant areas, where commerce and industry offer employment. So much so that in traditionally Protestant cities like Zurich[29] and Geneva, 30 and 40 per cent, respectively, of the inhabitants are now Catholics.

Under these altered conditions a fascinating political rivalry emerges. The Church has to compete with the trade union; the Conservative party has to outbid the Socialists and the Independents. Over the outcome of this struggle, conflicting opinions are expressed in Switzerland. A prominent Socialist, when I asked him which of the other parties was his most serious competitor, answered immediately: "The Catholics." He went on to say, optimistically from his standpoint, that the priests gradually lose influence over many of their faith who move to the cities, and that another party can capture them. But I have heard other well-informed observers express a contrary view. Indeed, the importance of this problem is indicated by the division or split that is occurring within the ranks of the Catholic party. Originally called Conservative, and still so named in

29. In fact, Zurich today is Switzerland's largest Catholic city.

many cantons, its traditional outlook is deemed too static by many Catholics who face the issues of industrialization. Consequently, a wing of the movement, which prefers the title "Social Christian," has been organized in several cantons. It is this that competes in the cities with the Socialists and Independents in sponsoring social services and protesting against the urban cost of living. And, after all, since most of the industries, business, and finance in Switzerland are Protestant-owned, what does the Catholic party stand to lose? However, their gains in this quarter may be offset by losses due to another emerging controversy. Of recent decades the bitterness of the confessional struggle has greatly subsided. But new attempts are periodically made by Catholics, particularly in cantons where they are in a minority, to amend the constitutional provision that bans the Jesuit order from Switzerland. If this initiative proceeds further, it is likely to arouse vehement opposition among the Protestants, renewing their solidarity and reviving the unhappy discords of the nineteenth century.

The fourth of Switzerland's principal parties—the Peasants, Artisans, and Bourgeois—is half the size of the Conservatives and lacks a national coverage. Of 113,600 votes which it received in 1959, 81,000 were cast in Bern and Zurich. To all intents and purposes, if the Conservatives have represented rural Catholicism, the Peasant party, which split away from the Radicals in the two biggest cantons, represents rural Protestantism.[30] In numbers, however, theirs is an ebbing tide. Thus, in Bern, the census shows a total of 185,503 persons occupied on the land in 1920 and only 154,804 in 1950; and these figures are reflected in a decline in the absolute votes of the Peasant party in the same canton from 65,657 in 1919 to 54,517 in 1959. Like the Country party in Australia, the Peasants continue their separate organization in the two principal cantons in order to bargain better with the urban interests and protect their insecure economy.

Of the small parties, two are survivors, for special reasons, from the pre-1919 period. The Liberals offer lists of candidates in only three and a half Protestant cantons, of which three (Vaud, Neuchâtel, and Geneva) belong to la Suisse romande. Here they represent the older families, the professional élite, and some of the urban wealth. Quantitatively insignificant, the Liberals are important qualitatively. They have given Switzerland

30. This can be demonstrated from Thurgau, where the population is two-thirds Protestant and one-third Catholic. There, the area with the highest percentage of Catholics (54.2% in 1950) is Münchwilen, and there in 1951 the Conservatives won their highest percentage of votes in the canton. Conversely, in Weinfelden, the most Protestant area, the Peasants party fared best of all. Münchwilen and Weinfelden are alike in the proportion of agriculture and industry. The significant difference here is religion.

some of its great men, (Dufour, Ador); they publish at least two of the country's best newspapers; and they are well represented among holders of university chairs. But their individualism, political as well as economic, prevents them from leading a mass party. The total number of votes that go to the Liberals (23,000) is about the same as the Democrats receive. These latter exist only in Zurich, Grisons, and Basel-Land. In Zurich, whence half their votes come, they have a double *raison d'être*. They are a left-wing splinter of white-collar workers that broke off the Radicals, as these moved across to Center and Right. In addition, they represent the rivalry and resentment of Winterthur against the powerful metropolis of Zurich. So strong is this inter-urban feeling that in Winterthur even many businessmen, who in Zurich would certainly be Radicals, support the Democrats against the party of their competitors in the bigger city. In Grisons the Democrats organized themselves for another, and equally simple, reason. There the Radicals had been continuously in control of the cantonal government and some corruption developed. An opposition arose which took the name of Democrat, and has persisted as a group in cantonal politics.

Since the adoption of proportional representation two new small parties have come into existence. The Communists contested their first election independently of the Socialists in 1922. Outlawed during the war, as was the pro-Nazi organization, the Communists were again permitted to present candidates after hostilities ceased. In 1959 there were Communist lists[31] in Zurich and Basel-Stadt, and in Vaud, Neuchâtel, and Geneva. Their supporters are found mostly in the big cities and more in *la Suisse romande* than in the German-speaking parts. A reason for this that was suggested to me, is that *la Suisse romande* is strongly influenced by France, which has a powerful Communist party—some of whose influence percolates across the frontier. The Swiss Communists have followed the Moscow line in all its twists and wriggles. They are a nuisance, but not a danger.

More interesting, because more original, are the Independents. This is a remarkable phenomenon, because, in a country where an eminent personality is a rarity in politics, here is an organization that was created by a unique individual who saw and responded to a social need. Gottlieb Duttweiler developed a thriving business with a chain of grocery stores (Migros) dedicated to the aim of bringing prices down. From this he branched out into other ventures, all of which attack the non-competitive practices of Switzerland's highly cartelized economy. On this account he

31. Under the name of a Labor party.

was much admired by urban consumers, and much disliked by other businessmen. Having a broad social outlook, and being concerned over the Nazi menace, he founded a political movement in 1935 which injected a vigorous and polemical note into the placid politics of the nation. At their best, in 1939, the Independents received 7.1 per cent of the votes. In 1959, they were given 5.5 per cent in five German-speaking cantons, half of the total from Zurich. This was a vote of city dwellers who protested against the high cost of living by following Duttweiler instead of the Socialists or Christian Socialists. There were less than a dozen Independents in the National Council during the 1950's. But the strength of this movement is seen not so much in the size of the legislative group as in the measures they have carried by means of the initiative or blocked in the referendum.[32] As Switzerland's conscience, political gadfly, and leading individualist, Duttweiler accomplished much good; but it is doubtful whether his movement, as an organized political group, can survive his death (1962).

Such is a panorama of the contemporary parties. And does it not point to a self-evident conclusion? Swiss multipartism is the product of social pluralism.[33] The one is the direct consequence of the other. Multipartism, growing out of such a soil, was able to break through an electoral system which did not suit it and to substitute one that did. Nor is this true of the electoral system alone. Several of the major institutions of Swiss government—federalism, the initiative, and referendum, as well as proportional representation—flow from this identical source. Given the facts of political freedom, whereby the Swiss could choose their form of government, on what other basis was any consensus possible?

Finally, it should be observed that while we may affirm this causal sequence—social pluralism produced multipartism, multipartism produced proportionalism—it is true that the effect reacts upon, and has reinforced, its cause. The party system growing out of society adopts the electoral system that corresponds best to its own character and is then strengthened by it. Certainly, proportional representation has permitted the multiplicity of parties to continue. It has prolonged the life of the party system of 1919; it has slowed the rate of decomposition of pre-existing small groups, and has allowed representation to two new ones. Under this system, and because of it, the sense of injustice over the membership of the National Council, which was acutely felt prior to 1919, has disappeared. The Democrats and the Peasants have clung to their own organizations in defiance

32. This point was emphasized to me by Gottlieb Duttweiler in a conversation held in 1956.
33. As is well argued by G. E. Lavau, *op. cit.*, pp. 107-14.

of the Radicals. Government by coalition has become a permanent habit, and opposition has to be expressed by the people themselves, when they are sufficiently aroused, through the referendum.

Stable Multipartism in Scandinavia

The Swiss case has merited this detailed discussion because, despite its intrinsic interest, it has been infrequently studied. What distinguishes Switzerland, however, is its cultural diversity. Even without the economic factors, this by itself would explain why a multi-party system arose and lasted. For purposes of comparison, the Scandinavian trio—Denmark, Norway, and Sweden—will be considered next. These countries are similar to Switzerland in successfully combining multipartism with stability. But they differ from it markedly in their social character and governmental structure. All three, in fact, impress the observer with their cultural homogeneity and the relative simplicity of their governments. Although a linguistic controversy persists in Norway;[34] and although independent Protestants throughout the region have opposed the official Lutheran Church, divisions of speech and faith have not occasioned political dissension as serious as that among the Swiss. In Scandinavia, therefore, the pluralism which a multi-party system presumably reflects cannot be attributed to cultural diversity. The explanation must be sought elsewhere.

Since the end of World War I, the party politics of Denmark, Norway, and Sweden, have settled into a regular, definable pattern. Each country has produced, in essentials, a four-party system, with some splinter groups around the fringe. At every election, four parties collect over 85 per cent of the popular vote and over 90 per cent of the legislative seats. The strongest of the four are the Social Democrats, who ordinarily receive around 40 per cent of the votes in Denmark, and between 46 and 50 per cent in Norway and Sweden. Consequently it is they who have the best chance of holding office, either alone or in coalition with some smaller group. In Denmark, as might be expected of a country where agriculture is so important, the second strongest group is the Venstre, a mixture of farmers and liberals. The Conservatives are in third place, and the Radicals are a dwindling fourth. In Sweden, the Conservatives (Högern) were ahead

34. Because Norway was under the Danish Crown for centuries, the official and literary language was close to Danish and differed from the spoken folk-tongue. Attempts to reconcile the two have created an artificial "new Norwegian." Denmark, of course, used to have a large German-speaking minority in Slesvig-Holstein, a few of whom still remain in northern Slesvig.

of the Liberals until World War II, since when their positions have been reversed. The Farmers, who made an alliance with the Social Democrats in the depression of the 1930's, stayed in coalition with them for a quarter of a century. Then they tried to arrest the decrease in their votes by ending the partnership and changing their name to Center. In Norway, the opposition to the powerful Labor party consists of four unimpressive fragments. The Conservatives, Høyre, are the biggest of these. After them come the Venstre (liberals) and the Farmers. A party which calls itself Christian has also further divided the opposition during the last two decades. Likewise in Denmark there was a splinter movement named the Justice party, composed of single-taxers, which at one time had enough seats to bargain for a place in the governing coalition. The Communists reached their peak in all three countries in 1945, winning approximately one-tenth of the votes. But Stalin's policies quickly brought them into disrepute, and nowadays, because of the triumphant success of social democracy in Scandinavia, the Communists appear more ludicrous than dangerous.

What are the causes which generated and have sustained this kind of party system? To an external view the Scandinavian communities look peaceful, progressive and stable. They are an oasis of sense and civilization in a turbulent and dangerous world.[35] The multiplicity of parties might seem to contradict this character. What are the differences which the various parties seek to represent? The answer is that the modern parties correspond to economic divisions in terms of occupation and wealth, which before World War I were accentuated by distinctions between social classes. In addition people have disagreed about philosophical principles and their application to society and politics. These factors have been sufficient to produce four parties, remake the institutions of government, and turn class antagonisms into harmony through political moderation.

There are two primary divisions in Scandinavian society—the vertical cleavage between urban and rural, and the horizontal one of richer and poorer. Here is the fundamental socio-economic source for a four-party system, and it does in fact correspond to some basic features of the political groups. One must remember in the case of Scandinavia that the modern evolution toward democracy commenced quite late, but then

---

35. In a remark which he presumably did not intend as a compliment, Lenin observed: "If a proletarian revolution had just broken out in Sweden, the first act of the new government would be to invite to dinner the members of the bourgeois government whom they had overthrown." Quoted by Raymond Fusilier, Le Parti Socialiste Suédois (Les Éditions Ouvrières, Paris, 1954), pp. 1-2.

proceeded very rapidly. The dominant oligarchy which shared the privileges of an authoritarian regime consisted of the nobles, who usually were also big landowners, the military leaders and rulers of the church, and the hierarchy of officialdom. These were naturally the Conservatives, or, as they are still called in Norway and Sweden, the Right (*Høyre, Högern*). Their opponents, from the 1840's onward, demanded that the government be liberalized. They wanted a representative legislature, elected from territorial districts, with a franchise which would broaden out until it became universal. Their support was derived from an urban middle class of commercial and professional people, which was naturally large in the capital city; from those who objected to the state-supported monopoly of the Lutheran Church with its rigid orthodoxy; and from rural interests and those who urged the need for social revolution in the countryside. These were the ingredients of the Left—Venstre as they are still called in Denmark and Norway, or Liberals as in Sweden.

As generally happens in such movements which prepare the transition from oligarchy to democracy, all kinds of diverse groups and interests coalesce in common protest against the entrenched elite. Their initial objectives are to capture the citadels of power and change the structure of government. When that is done, the power thus acquired has to be used and policies have to be adopted and applied. Divergences then appear and secessions, splits, and splinters form. Political controversy now centers on economic matters and on the social relations between occupational groups and new forms of wealth. Those who are the earliest to be satisfied have acquired something to conserve, while their former partners may press for yet more reform. Hence the Left or the Liberals split, either along urban-rural lines or in terms of the distribution of wealth. The Danish Venstre, for example, broke into two in 1905: one part consisting of the more prosperous farmers, the other (taking the name Radical) representing peasants with smaller holdings and urban intellectuals. Last to emerge were the Socialists, who organized the swelling body of industrial workers with a militant philosophy and a deeply-felt crusade for social justice.

The emergence of this multi-party system became, as it were, the point of focus for a revolution at three levels—social, political, and institutional. Previously underprivileged groups, such as peasants and factory workers, were seeking improvements in their economic and social status. The democratic development permitted and encouraged their mobilization into parties. The constitutional framework then had to be redesigned to accommodate them. Confident that it counted for the majority, the Left wanted universal suffrage, a unicameral legislature, and an executive responsible to the legislative body. The Right, fighting a rear guard action and surrendering its privileges piecemeal, sought to extract concessions and safeguard its minority position. A principle of checks and balances might restrain an otherwise omnipotent majority. This could be done by keeping the executive in some ways independent of the legislature, presumably through the retention of an element of royal power. Alternatively, bicameralism might be continued in order that one chamber could offset the other. Both of these methods were used in the three countries at one stage in their transition to a complete democracy. Thus the Swedish king was still actively intervening in the formation of governments until the end of World War I, and the Danes were engaged in controversy about the supremacy of the lower chamber over the upper on the eve of World War II. Nowadays, however, the subordination of the cabinet to the Parliament is fully accomplished in Denmark and Norway, both of which have adopted a unicameral legislature. Only in Sweden, which in these matters is usually more conservative than its neighbors, does bicameralism survive and the executive function with some independence of the Riksdag.

But there was yet another way in which a minority might protect itself against an all-powerful majority. It could employ the electoral machinery to subdivide the potential majority and make it extremely difficult for a majority ever to be mobilized. The natural device to achieve this objective was proportional representation. Since a multi-party system was already in being prior to its adoption, the various parties—except perhaps the strongest—were likely to agree on a system which gave "justice" to each and every one. Hence the introduction of proportionalism was often an item in a general political bargain, as in Denmark in 1915. There, when universal suffrage was accepted by the Right, the Left agreed to take proportionalism and, at least for the time being, to retain the upper house.

The consequence has borne out the expectation. In Denmark the four-party system has managed to survive, and undoubtedly the electoral methods in use for nearly half a century have saved the weaker parties (e.g., the Radicals) from complete absorption by the stronger. But the political dialectic, corresponding to the balance of economic interests, has generated two customary coalitions. Normally, the Social Democrats, representing the urban workers, combine with the Radicals, who speak for the less wealthy farmers and some of the intellectuals. Against them, the Venstre and the Conservatives unite the majority of more prosperous farmers with urban capital and commerce. The control of the Folketing and the cabinet shifts from one pair of parties to the other. Something of the same pattern is repeated in Sweden, though with certain variations. Sweden has more industry than Denmark and is more urbanized. Consequently, the Social Democrats win a larger percentage of votes there than they do among the Danes, and were able to stay in office even after the Farmers' party decided to dissolve the coalition. The opposition to the Social Democrats in Sweden is divided into two groups, of whom the Liberals have latterly shown more strength than the Conservatives. It would seem sensible, and politically advantageous, for them to merge. But a tradition of separation dies hard.

The Case of the Norwegian Labor Party

From the standpoint of party politics, the most surprising of the three countries is Norway. Here is one very powerful organization, the Labor party, facing a splintered opposition of five discordant groups. A Norwegian scholar described his country's party system to me as "Anglo-French": on one side a single, disciplined, party as in Great Britain; on the other, an assortment of incompatible fragments as in France's Third and Fourth Republics. What is unusual about Norway's politics is the strength which the Labor Party has been able to organize and maintain. Ship-building and the merchant marine, lumbering, mining, and fishing, have been the principal sources of the country's wealth. Although newer industries of a diversified nature have been expanded since World War II, Norway would not ordinarily be classed as a highly industrialized country, and in any case the power of the Labor party predates the most recent development of industry, which in fact it helped to stimulate. How then has this particular party been so successful under such conditions?

The answer is that the Labor party alone has succeeded in welding together a national coalition of three different economic groups, which are so distributed geographically as to collect around half of the popular votes and legislative seats. Like a tripod, the party is supported on three legs. One of these, naturally, consists of the industrial workers, who were strongly imbued with class consciousness in the first three decades of this century and embraced the Marxian philosophy with alacrity. But this group, being a minority, required the adhesion of others. A second leg, therefore, is based on a segment of the rural population. Good agricultural land is limited in Norway; and, until modern communications were introduced, the families which lived along isolated fjords and inland valleys between rugged mountains subsisted on a precarious margin. To them the Labor party offered what they wanted most: economic and social security through state programs. Third, the triangle is completed by the inclusion of the fishermen who operate in the Arctic north.

The latter's enrollment under the socialist banner is a curious and fascinating episode in political history. In the 1890's and at the turn of the century, the government of Norway (then under the Swedish crown) was conservative. The income of the northern fisherman had declined in that period because the supply of herring was diminishing. The reason for this is uncertain, but it may have been connected with changes in the temperature of the sea. The fishermen, however, put the blame on their government which had entered into an international convention to limit the annual catch of whales. The consequence of this attempt at conservation, as the fisherfolk reasoned, was that the whales ate more herring. In addition, the government antagonized the northerners by its policy toward Russia. Communications with the south of Norway were poor, and the food supply in the Arctic was inadequate. The Czarist regime had exported grain to that area at low prices and was consequently popular. But in the Norwegian capital the Russians were suspected of designs to detach that slice of territory and bring it under the control of St. Petersburg. Hence the conservative government placed restrictions on the imports of Russian grain. Simultaneously, the same ministry was preparing for eventual independence from Sweden. To this end, it was devoting more expenditure to armaments in case Norway should find it necessary to fight. The people of the north were pacific, or at any rate disliked the increase in the military budget, and developed still more hostility to their government. Hence, for all these reasons combined, their political sentiments turned toward the movement which at that time signified the most extreme opposition to the established order—namely Marxian socialism. The Labor party thus built up great strength in the region, which it has never lost. Indeed, in more recent times, with the Soviet regime controlling Russia, the Communist party competes powerfully with Labor in the Arctic area.[36] Thus does politics, irrespective of ideology, rethread the same patterns at an interval of half a century.

The lapse of time, however, brings changes to a party system. Labels, organization, and doctrine may persist, while the social and economic realities to which they once corresponded become modified. Scandinavian multipartism had more meaning when applied to the class divisions and economic differentiations of the period preceding World War I than when it continues in the kind of community which has been evolving since 1950. If one attempts such a chronological comparison, the con-

36. It may be noted both in Norway and Sweden that the conditions of the far north produce extremes of all types. People are heavy drinkers or strongly prohibitionist. They adhere to fundamentalist religions, or violate religious and ethical conventions. Similarly, their politics tend to the extremes.

temporary scene differs from the earlier in three major respects. First, there is nowadays a greater degree of social egalitarianism. Occupational differences remain, of course, but they are less associated with a horizontal stratification of classes than heretofore. Second, the extremes in the distribution of wealth and income are not so glaring. Fewer persons are very rich or very poor; many more, absolutely and relatively, belong in the middle. Nor is the urban-rural division as sharp as it once was. The influences of the city radiate out to the rural areas, both from the metropolis and from secondary centers. Regional economies are diversified by the decentralization of industries. Different members of the same family may be working as agriculturists, as lumbermen, in an office, or in a factory. The same individual may be employed in one job in the winter and in another during the summer. A person's outlook varies with his interests; and as his interests become more mixed, his ideas or ideology grow less rigid and less clear cut. Third, political changes have naturally accompanied these developments both as cause and effect. Groups which once were acutely hostile learn the need to tolerate and coexist. Policies and points of view become less distinguishable, and party programs offer all things to more men—and women. A Scandinavian socialist of the 1910 vintage would not find himself at home among the tranquil Social Democrats of the 1960's. Still less would a pre-World War I Conservative embrace what contemporary Conservatives accept. A Liberal today is asking himself what middle ground remains for him to occupy when the former extremes of Left and Right have expanded so much toward the Center. Likewise an Agrarian, alert to the changing technology of food production, is troubled about the future of separate political organization for a diminishing minority.

All in all, the multiplicity of parties in contemporary Scandinavia represents, as it does in Switzerland, a triumph for democracy and not its failure. Multipartism in some other countries signifies the inability to combine and compromise. But in Denmark, Norway, and Sweden, these parties have grown up together and are accustomed to compete within a framework of co-operation. The justice of a humane society, and a flair for moderation in government, are the popular attributes which explain the peculiar success of democracy in this corner of the world.

French Politics in the Third and Fourth Republics

Thus far the examples under discussion have been those where multipartism works reasonably well or at least does not create serious disadvantages. But there is a case to consider in which the results of multi-partism have been notoriously poor. This is, of course, in France, the country which people have generally had in mind when they think of multipartism and on which they base their unfavorable conclusions about that kind of politics. Two different, yet related, questions must be asked about the French parties. What have been the causes of the multi-party system in France? What was there about the system, as it developed there, which led to such unsatisfactory results?

Although this may sound like beginning at the end, the results should be mentioned first. Throughout the Third and Fourth Republics (1876-1940, 1946-58), a multiplicity of parties competed for votes at every general election and a multiplicity of groups received representation in the national legislature. On no occasion did a single party receive as much as 51 per cent of the votes or seats, or indeed approximate even closely to that figure. Since the formation and support of a government required a majority of votes in the lower house,[37] every ministry was of necessity a coalition. Ministerial politics consequently was based on the outcome of the relative strength of the participant groups, the equilibrium which could be maintained among them, and their willingness to continue as a team versus their tendency to pull apart and recombine in altered patterns. Under these conditions the short duration of French cabinets became a by-word. "You go to London," as the travel agent advised his customer, "to see the changing of the Guard; to Paris, to see the changing of the Government." Nearly a hundred ministries held office under the Third Republic, their average tenure lasting for eight months. Only eight, all told, survived more than two years. The same history was retraced by the Fourth Republic. From January, 1946, to May, 1958, the French people watched twenty-one ministries come and go. Two only were tenacious enough to survive a year; the average life-span was but seven months.[38]

Of course, there were mitigating factors which offset this impression of utter impermanence. In the first place, when one ministry succeeded another, there was by no means a total change of personnel. Many of the outgoing ministers were frequently reappointed, a few of them in some instances (especially Foreign Affairs) to the same portfolios. Normally, a new ministry was composed of a mixture of holdovers and newcomers. Nor did the policies, adopted under these circumstances, exhibit on all occasions a break with the past. On the contrary, the changing of the

37. Called *Chambre de Députés* in the Third Republic, and *Assemblée Nationale* in the Fourth.
38. The statistics are subject to some interpretation. One should exclude from the list of governments those attempts to form a ministry which lasted for only a few days.

ministers often meant that the programs did not change. In any case, since somebody had to be responsible for governing France, it followed that ministers, whose appointments were short-lived and who were therefore impotent, surrendered control *de facto* to the *fonctionnaires*, who were steadfast and permanent. Although parties were numerous, and their relations fluid, they could be grouped by their programs into three positions on the political spectrum—Left, Center, and Right. Some scholars would further reduce that trifurcation to two. Professor Goguel argues that the Third Republic exhibited the opposition of two tendencies, the parties of Order and those of Movement.[39] Likewise, Professor Duverger contends that the Center is an unreal abstraction, and that there are only "superimposed dualisms."[40]

But when all that is said, it remains true that the manner in which the system functioned in the public eye earned it an ill-repute which overrode its more stable features. The French people, and foreign opinion, paid less attention to the persisting continuities than to the overt *crises ministerielles*. If the same ministers survived through successive cabinets, this fact was lampooned as "the waltz of portfolios." When governments fell in Paris, some enemy (Hitler, for example) would take advantage of France's difficulties while the country was headless. Moreover, when a general election was held under these conditions, the voters did not know whom they could properly hold responsible for what had been done or omitted, nor whom to entrust with power for the future. A collection of office-holders, temporarily holding portfolios which they must soon relinquish, was a feeble substitute for a genuine cabinet. The boldness and integrity—in a word, the leadership—which must inspire a government that is worthy of its name were not to be found under the rules of *le jeu politique*. Rarely, and then on the occasions when an exceptional man stood forth (Gambetta, Clemenceau, Poincaré, Blum) did the republican regime rise to the needs of France. In the general public an attitude developed toward politics and politicians which was compounded of cynicism, indifference, ridicule and contempt. The crux of the difficulty for French democracy was how to operate a set of institutions which did not repose on a solid foundation of popular esteem and respect.

For this state of affairs much of the blame rests with the political parties. Not only were they too numerous, but their points of disagreement were so many and varied, that a broad and enduring consensus was hard to elicit. If multipartism means merely that compromises are made between the parties, instead of inside them, under the higgling of the politi-

39. François Goguel, *La Politique des Partis sous la Troisième République, passim*.
40. *Op. cit.*, p. 215.

cal market in France the practice of low-level huckstering predominated over high quality statesmanship. Yet to assign responsibility to the parties, to *le système* as President de Gaulle has called it, only explains in part the malaise of French democracy. It may be argued with considerable truth that the parties reflect the people and that the failure of the parties to sustain a government is the people's fault. At any rate, a diagnosis (or autopsy?) must raise the question: What caused the parties to be such as they were?

"Proving" an Untruth

To begin with, I shall propound an absurdity. Suppose, for the sake of argument, that the French party system in the Third and Fourth Republics had been of quite the opposite kind. Imagine that France had two well-disciplined parties like the British and that these had alternated in office with reasonable stability and strength. If such had been the truth, how would we political scientists explain that fact? To what would we point as "causing" the result?

There is no lack of "causes" which could be adduced to prove this "consequence." Indeed, both sociological and institutional factors come readily to mind. Let us remember that the French are one of the oldest nations in Europe, and that their unification was accomplished long ago. Theirs is a mature country, devoid of racial, ethnic, or linguistic divisions, and containing a politically sophisticated population. In domestic affairs, as in their external diplomacy, the French are wise with the experience of centuries. Culturally, they stand in the forefront of Western Civilization, of which at certain periods they have clearly been the leaders. Much of the world has looked to France for ideas and inspiration in the creative realm of the spirit, and has not looked in vain. Democracy itself cannot be appraised without giving full due to the French contribution since the time of Montesquieu, Voltaire, Rousseau, and Diderot. Geographically, the country is compact and well-knit—not elongated and rugged as Italy or Norway, not physically separated into provinces by mountains like Spain. Fine navigable rivers gave access from the coast to the center long before the age of smooth roads and steel rails. Internally, France is strongly unified by the luster of its magnificent capital, the city which has no near-equal and no rival. As Islam turns in prayer to Mecca, the emotions of all Frenchmen focus on Paris. Endowed with a fertile soil, France is both a beautiful garden and a bountiful farm. Nor, when it entered the age of modern industry, was its agriculture sacrificed. With an economy better balanced than that of Britain, it has been less vulnerable to external vicissitudes and is therefore more stable. The ownership of land, of business firms, of factories, is more widely distributed among a larger number of persons than in Germany, Britain, or the United States, so that more French families possess a material stake in their country. Nor can one ignore the effect of foreign relations on the domestic regime. The long tradition of Franco-German hostility has unified the people. Particularly after 1870 they sank their internal differences and rallied together against the menace of German power.

Then, for full measure, the institutional arguments can be added. Under the Third and Fourth Republics, the relations of the legislature to the executive were based on the fusion of powers through the cabinet which, as in Britain, promotes a two-party system. Since the constitution[41] gave that cabinet the power to dissolve the lower house, the *Députés* were as disciplined as the Commons, for they feared to bring down the government and place their own seats in jeopardy. Lastly, one must never omit the influence on the parties of the electoral system. The latter, as a matter of fact, was changed on several occasions. But in the first decade of the Third Republic (1876-1885) the Anglo-American method of single-member districts with victory by plurality was used. Later (1889-1919 and 1927-40), when the legislature again substituted single-member districts for that of the list system in larger constituencies, a majority was required to elect; and, in the districts where this was lacking at the first election, a second ballot was held after a short interval. Naturally, the electoral system had the effect of encouraging the parties to coalesce and the citizens to concentrate their votes in order to win the election.

Such are the lines along which we would be reasoning if France had actually produced a two-party system. The trouble with the argument, however, is patent: I have been connecting the real with the imaginary. I selected a number of facts which are true, grouped them, and linked them as the "causes" of a "consequence" that never existed. All the features cited above to explain the false conclusion have been genuine characteristics of France. They are those which, when found in other countries, are always identified as contributing to a stable two-party system. In this case, however, they did not combine to produce the same result as elsewhere. How can this be explained? What interpretation are we to follow if similar causes appear to lead to dissimilar effects?

This paradox, if such it be, suggests that, in the search for explanation, the analysis must probe deeper yet. Since all the factors mentioned are truly present in the French case, but do not there produce the conse-

41. In the Third Republic, according to the Law of February 25, 1875, Article 5. In the Fourth Republic, under Article 51 of the Constitution.

quence attributed to them elsewhere, three hypotheses should be considered. Perhaps it is not enough to catalogue a list of factors as promoting unity and stability and then add them together as if they were of equal significance. Possibly, in different countries, they need to be differently weighted. It is conceivable that their priorities vary from place to place. In country A, factor X may count for more than factor Y; in country B, the reverse could be true; and that may alter the character of the complex. Second, there may be some further points to consider which were not mentioned in the analysis earlier, but which might properly be relevant in the case of France. Third, it is arguable that a fundamental assumption is in error. Inferences about causation are at best speculative, even in a single country. A *fortiori*, therefore, a comparative treatment of the subject is highly problematical. Is not each case individual and unique? Can the multiplication of such cases support a valid generalization? With these cautions in mind, let us look at French multipartism, for this is either the exception which proves the rule or the rule wherein everything is an exception.

Institutions Molded by the Party System

First, there are the institutional factors to examine. It will be easy to dispose of these, since in a discussion of France they explain nothing. Take the cabinet, for example. Even if it were true that this system influences a legislature to divide into two sides—an argument which I rejected in the discussion of Britain[42]—the functioning of French cabinets from 1876 to 1940 and from 1946 to 1958 certainly could not be used as evidence to prove that contention. Actually, the cabinet type of legislative-executive relations that existed in London and Paris was not one and the same, but two different systems. On one side of the Channel the cabinet controlled the legislature; on the other side, it was the reverse. And the reason is plain. The character of the cabinet was determined in each case by that of the parties, and not the other way round. A French ministry was necessarily weak because it was formed by a temporary alliance of groups which knew, as in a Hollywood marriage, that they would not stay together for long. The multiplicity of parties among the *Députés*, and their unwillingness to coalesce in lasting unions, maintained the ascendancy of the legislature over the cabinet. In other words, the facts of political life determined the relationship of the institutions.

Exactly the same can be inferred from another institutional feature, the

42. Chapter 11, pp. 318-20.

power to dissolve the lower chamber and order a general election. The notion that this intensifies the discipline which party leaders can exercise over their followers and thus contributes to a two-party system was earlier discarded when Britain was analyzed.[43] Again, however, if we concede the possibility that this power might operate differently elsewhere, what discernible effect did it have on the party system in France? Absolutely none. Instead of the power of dissolution having an influence on the parties, it was the latter which caused the former to atrophy with disuse. Historically that power was used only once in the Third Republic, and once in the Fourth. The reasons why it was used on these occasions, and never again, provide an instructive lesson in political history.

In the Third Republic, the Law of February 25, 1875 provided that the President, with the consent of the Senate, could dissolve the Chamber of Deputies before its legal term had expired. This was actually done as early as 1877 during the famous Seize Mai affair. At that time, the monarchists who still controlled the Senate and had a President sympathetic to their side thought they could reverse the republican majority of the Chamber. They therefore used the opportunity of a parliamentary maneuver to install a rightist Premier, whom the majority of the Deputies did not support, and grant him a dissolution. But the weapon which was wielded as a bludgeon to crush the republicans turned out to be a boomerang which curved back and struck the monarchists. The people elected a chamber more strongly republican and more to the Left than before; and the President, bowing to necessity, resigned. The effect of this event was to leave in the minds of the Left and Left Center the memory of an unscrupulous trick. For them, henceforth, Article 5 of that law was a dead letter. They would neither invoke it themselves nor allow their opponents to do so.

When the Constitution of the Fourth Republic was debated in 1946, there were many who drew the inference from Britain that cabinet government required an occasional early dissolution and urged the revival of this procedure. Consequently, the power was written into Article 51, although it was hedged around with conditions to prevent its being abused or used too frequently. No dissolution was permitted in the first eighteen months after an election. Subsequent to that, if two ministries were forced to resign in any eighteen-month period as a result of a vote of censure by the Assembly or the failure to win a vote of confidence, the Council of Ministers could decide to dissolve the Assembly with the concurrence (*avis*) of its presiding officer. The only time when this was done was in December, 1955. The ministry led by Edgar Faure was running into diffi-

43. Chapter 11, pp. 320-21.

culty in domestic economic policy and in North Africa. Finding it increasingly hard to maintain a majority among the Deputies, the government chose to dissolve, which constitutionally it was able to do. Actually, the election, held on January 2, 1956, was advanced only six months—the previous one having taken place in June, 1951! Nevertheless, even this minor acceleration provoked a clamor in the Assembly, many of whose members attributed high-handedness to the Premier and the groups in his coalition; and the results of the election were adverse to those who launched it.

The lesson of the Third and Fourth Republics is clear. The legislature was dominant over the ministry because of the multiplicity of parties and their unwillingness to stay in the same combination for long. This being so, the power of dissolution, though constitutionally permissible, became politically impossible. The members of a transitory coalition could not agree about employing a device which might recoil on their own heads and from which they were unlikely to gain any positive advantage. When many parties occupy the arena, and every government is an alliance, it is evidently harder to dissolve than when the leadership of a single party makes the decision. Thus, it was the party system which led to the disuse of the power; the latter was unable to influence the former.

What the Electoral Permutations Reveal

But, there is now the electoral machinery to look at. Cannot this be considered a cause of the party system? The answer, in my judgment, is quite the contrary. In France, the parties determined the character of the electoral system, and not the other way round. What is more, they also determined how any type of electoral arrangements which they adopted would function in practice. The evidence for this contention can be found in a reference to history. If the politics of Republican France, from 1875 to 1940 and from 1946 to 1958, be viewed in a single sweep, two facts stand out clearly and irrefutably. The French were continually changing their electoral system. They did so after every two or three elections. The party system, however, did not change. Individual parties might grow or decline within the system; the power pendulum might swing between left, Center, and Right; but the same kind of party politics persisted throughout. Altering the electoral machinery had the momentary effect of helping or harming this or that party or combination. It had no effect on the fundamentals of multipartism. On this point, the details speak for themselves. In the first decade of the Third Republic (1876-85) single-member districts were used with victory by plurality. This method was favored by the monarchists and adopted over Gambetta's opposition. By reaction, therefore, in 1875 the republicans, comprising the Left and Left Center, introduced a list system (*scrutin de liste*) with proportionalism. When General Boulanger, however, illustrated the danger of twisting such elections into a Bonapartist plebiscite and thereby emerging as dictator, the Chamber again reverted to the single-member district (*scrutin d'arrondissement*), though this was now combined with *ballottage* (a run-off election in districts where no candidate had a majority on the original ballot). Immediately after World War I, the Right thought it would work to their advantage to change back to a list system, allowing for preferential voting for individuals on the list. Accordingly, in 1927 the Left swung over to the single-member district with *ballottage*. Thus in the final decade of the Third Republic, Left and Right respectively preferred the opposite to what they had advocated in the 1870's. *Plus ça changeait, plus c'était la même chose!*

In the Fourth Republic, the new National Assembly (successor to the Chamber of Deputies) was soon up to the old tricks. In 1946 they adopted proportional representation, with fairly large multi-membered constituencies, assigning legislative seats to each party in the district according to its percentage of the votes. This arrangement, tending to favor the strongest parties, was appropriate to the politics of a period when Socialists, Communists, and M.R.P. were temporarily overflowing with mutual goodwill and cooperation. Four years later, however, everything had changed. The Communists had broken with their coalition partners; all moderates were chilled by Stalin's Cold War; and de Gaulle, leading the R.P.F., had re-entered the fray and resuscitated the Right. To preserve itself in the middle, the governing coalition formed its "Third Force" extending from Left Center to Right Center. But, in order to entrench themselves in office, the groups which comprised the alliance thought it advisable to alter the rules of the game prior to the next election. This they did by permitting alliances (*apparentement*) between different parties in a district. All the seats of that district were assigned to any alliance which gained 51 per cent of the votes, and the allies then distributed them according to the proportion of the votes which each partner received. Since none of the Third Force was willing to join an alliance with either the Communists or the Gaullists, the system was devised to increase their own representation and decrease that of the extremes. And the results worked out exactly as the planners had hoped.

However, in 1955 when Edgar Faure was preparing for the third (and, as it turned out, the last) election under the Fourth Republic, the political relationships had again altered. Though there was still a menace from the extremes, the Third Force was disintegrating. By this time, the Socialists, M.R.P., Independents, and Radicals were more animated by discord than harmony. The Radicals themselves were split into hostile factions owing allegiance respectively to Faure and Mendès-France. Faure took the initiative of proposing changes in the electoral law, as did others. Throughout November and early December of 1955, the National Assembly drafted, debated, and in turn rejected by different combinations every known kind of electoral system. It was always possible to produce a negative majority against everything, never a positive majority for something. Consequently, when the election took place, after the dissolution had been invoked, the district alliances no longer operated as they had done in 1951. The result was an increase in the representation of the extremes (including this time a quasi-fascist group of Poujadists) and a drop in the strength of the Center. Two and a half years later, the Fourth Republic was dead.

To sum up this stage of the argument, the institutional interpretations of the party system, as applied to France, prove nothing. Whatever causal connection may exist between the type of party system and the type of electoral system, in France quite definitely the party politics were the prime cause and the electoral arrangements were their consequence. Similarly with the cabinet and its constitutional power to dissolve the chamber. The groupings in the chamber controlled the cabinet and made a rarity of dissolutions. Such institutions were impotent to modify what its critics called *le système*.

One is forced then to turn to other explanations of the French party system. If the institutions of government were themselves effects rather than causes, the causes must presumably have resided in political factors and in the composition and character of French society. What is there to be said on this score? Obviously there is a great deal to be said; so much, that it is easy to become submerged in the sea of argument. In order to keep afloat, therefore, and see where one is going, it is wise to concentrate on the basic points. If that is done, the minor ones can then be readily fitted into the general pattern.

Disagreements About First Principles

From a broad survey of the whole sweep of French politics since 1848, two facts of fundamental importance emerge. First is the notorious propensity for changing, not merely the government, but even the constitution. Traditionally, the French people, since the time when their revolution was inaugurated in 1789, have been unable to agree on their form of institutions. A *fortiori*, therefore, one may deduce that a people who were divided over what type of constitution they wanted were unlikely to evolve a stable and coherent party system. If they could have done the former, they could have done the latter; if the latter, the former. The instability of the constitutions presumably flowed from the same source as the multiplicity and mutual incompatibility of the parties.

There is a second fact which serves as a corollary to the first. If the French have changed their constitutions with a frequency which is rare for an advanced modern community, it follows that, at any period when a given constitution was in force, there were individuals and groups whose allegiance it did not command. They did not accept it as binding on them. They disputed its legitimacy. Hence, there were movements in society, frequently producing parties in politics, which did not merely compete with other parties within a settled framework, but rather embodied a challenge to that framework itself. During the Third Republic movements were organized on both extremes which rejected the constitutional laws of 1875 and saw them as a provisional expedient to be discarded whenever the moment was opportune. On the Right were the monarchists and Bonapartists, whose influence continued throughout the Dreyfus affair and was reinforced after 1918 by the organization of *Anciens Combattants* and after 1930 by the spread of fascism both outside France and within. On the Left were the survivors of the Paris Commune, to whom not only the monarchists, but also conservative republicans like Thiers, appeared a gang of butchers. Violence, justified by such a writer as Sorel, continued to be a phenomenon of French public life—witness the tragic and wanton murder of Jaurès by rightists. When the Communists split from the democratic Socialists in 1921, they matched the extreme Right in their hostility to the regime, their proneness to conspiracy, and their readiness to use violent methods. The Vichy period, while it represented an interlude from the standpoint of normal politics, did express the enduring hatred of the far Right for the symbols of 1789 and the principles of *la république française*.

Again, from 1946 onward, antagonism to the republican regime was voiced from the extremes. The Communist party operated within the system only in order to cripple the machinery whenever an opportunity occurred to damage, delay, or disrupt. Likewise the Right, mobilized by de Gaulle, did not cease to harry the parliamentarians of the Assembly. At times they joined with the Communists in joint opposition to the Third Force. The Gaullists, too, rejected the constitution under which they lived. Finally, when their chance came, with the help of the army, they happily overthrew it. How could a multi-party system function on the same lines as it does in Scandinavia or Switzerland when so many Frenchmen were not yet committed to the principles of a parliamentary democracy? At the election of 1951, the Communists received 26 per cent of the votes, while the Gaullist R.P.F. won 22 per cent—altogether, 48 per cent of the votes going to the regime's relentless opponents. Manifestly, the party system cannot function in the normal democratic way when two of the largest groups are working for its overthrow.

Such facts are symptoms of a malaise which has been endemic in the French body politic since the revolutionary agony commenced in 1789. The fever-chart has sharply fluctuated up and down, never settling for long enough at normal. Rather than embodying a co-operative and healthy pluralism, as in Scandinavia, the French parties have signified the pathology of a society simultaneously at war with itself on many fronts. There was a division between those who embraced the ideals of 1789 and those who still hankered for a return to the *ancien régime*. There were those who espoused republicanism and those who preferred either monarchy *à la Bourbon* or empire *à la Bonaparte*. There were the advocates of parliamentary supremacy, cabinet leadership on the British model, or a presidential system of the American type. Inevitably in a country where Catholicism was traditionally so strong, people were for or against the Church as an organization and clerical influence in secular affairs. This topic cut a deep fissure in French society and politics, since it necessarily extended to disputes about the family, the position of women, education, property, and divorce. Likewise, as was noted in an earlier chapter,[44] the army on which France relied for its defense became identified politically with a rightist orientation. If you were republican, socialist, or belonged generally to *la Gauche*, the military was suspect. In the Dreyfus affair, whose episodes tore France apart for a decade, all these points of dissension cumulatively overlapped in the dramatic conflict between the claims of order and justice.

In addition, as France embraced the modern technology and developed its industries, the complexities of divergent economic interests were superimposed on the other social cleavages. Not only were there the regional distinctions between the northern plain and the Midi, between the Rhineland and the West, but the urban and rural sectors were themselves subdivided. Paris, buttressed perhaps by Lyons and Marseilles, had metropolitan interests to which the inhabitants of small provincial towns and

44. See Chapter 7, pp. 179-80.

villages were strangers. Agriculture was split, not merely according to the crop (e.g., wheat or wine), but by the rivalry of big landowners and the farms of peasant families. On the urban side, the small shopkeepers, conservative with but little to conserve, were jealous of financiers, *négociants*, and manufacturers whose range of operations spelled wealth and power. Lastly there were the factory workers, inevitable outcrop of an industrial revolution, who viewed their employers as class enemies and whose *syndicats* the latter treated as criminal conspiracy. Such ingredients in any case were the mixture for a piquant political sauce, not a bland one. But why did it turn out that so many were incapable of blending, while others positively curdled on contact? One needs to explain not only why there were so many parties, but also why they were mutually so antagonistic.

Three points are essential to the answer. The first is concisely stated by Professor Duverger. He refers to the various antagonisms—political, social, economic, and religious—existing in France and emphasizes that these crisscrossed and overlapped in all directions. "Multipartism arises," as he says, "from the mutual independence of sets of antitheses."[45] The individual citizen found himself associated with one group on one issue, with another group on a second, with yet a different group on a third, and so on. The net effect of the sheer multiplicity of divisions whose boundary lines did not coincide was to promote a political fragmentation. Parties tended to be small, homogeneous, and doctrinally pure.

This leads to a second, and related, explanation. The tendency has been greater in French public life than in that of the English-speaking or Scandinavian democracies to give priority to matters of ideology and focus the membership of a party around the acceptance of a principle. Some writers refer to this as a trait of national character. But I for one hesitate to use this term because I question its validity and doubt that it explains anything.[46] However, it is a commonplace in the analyses of French politics, alike by French scholars and non-Frenchmen, to stress the importance of theory and abstraction. Possibly this preoccupation with doctrinal questions may be due to the Latin educational tradition which so predominated in the *lycées* and in the universities. Whatever its source, it encouraged among politicians a propensity to combine around principles which must be kept logically consistent. This may be sound in philosophy, but may not be sensible in politics. At any rate, it discouraged the pragmatic approach of Anglo-Saxons, who are less given to speculation and

45. *Op. cit.*, p. 232.
46. In the national character argument, when you seek to explain the reason for a mysterious phenomenon, you assert that it is an attribute of national character. Then you deduce the result from this assumed location of the cause.

perhaps for that reason are successful in achieving some solidarity by co-operation.

Timing and Sequence of French Political Events

The third point is historical. It concerns the timing and sequence of events, which of course is unique to each people. The French Revolution started somewhat late, one hundred and fifty years after the English. When it occurred, it developed into a more deep-seated upheaval, as was the still later Bolshevik Revolution in Russia. All society was convulsed in the course of this tremendous cataclysm. Property, the church, the middle class and the laborers, political principle, and institutional structure—everything was swept up in the same whirlwind; and, once uprooted, France found difficulty in settling down. In a true sense—and this differentiates the French Revolution from those of England and America—what began in 1789 has never ended. For almost two centuries the nation has been enacting new scenes in a drama for which it has not yet found the *dénouement*. The successive phases of the Directory, Terror, First Consulate and First Empire, are one act in this story. Others are the restoration of 1815, the revolutions of 1830 and 1848, the *coup d'état* of 1851, and the traumas of 1870 and 1940. French multipartism corresponds with some accuracy to the habits of a strongly individualistic people whose political groupings, like geological strata, are the deposits of specific problems, periods, and principles. Old parties, in France, never die; their labels and programs merely fade.

There is an additional factor to be mentioned which illustrates both the idealistic and the unwise in French political history. Under the Orleanist monarchy of Louis Philippe, inaugurated in the revolution of 1830, elections were held on a franchise strictly limited to the owners of property—which in fact was no different from the contemporary British franchise established by the Reform Act of 1832. The groupings in the French legislature, however, had not yet evolved as far as their British counterparts, and the French king still retained a more genuine power over the government and over the selection and direction of ministers than was then tolerated in London.[47] As a consequence, the parliamentary parties in Paris were restricted to criticizing what they could not control. As with the German parties in the Bismarckian Empire, a system which does not face the responsibility of actually governing tends to degenerate into squabbling.

47. In the famous events of 1834, William IV discovered that he could no longer pick a ministry at his will and force it on a reluctant House of Commons.

This is further borne out by the crises of 1848-51 and 1870-75. When the Orleanist monarchy fell in 1848, France embraced its Second Republic. Brimming once more with *liberté, égalité,* et *fraternité,* the constitution-makers threw open the gates of the franchise and admitted all adult males. Under this principle, prematurely adopted before the party system was ready to receive it, Louis Napoleon was elected to the Consulate and in three years' time converted the Second Republic into the Second Bonapartist Empire. Similarly, after his regime collapsed at Sedan, and the Third Republic was accepted by default in 1875, adult male suffrage was once more introduced. The result in the Third Republic was the same as in the abortive Second Republic. A forest of parties sprang up in the richly fertile soil of universal suffrage. They represented faithfully the pluralism and particularism of the French people. But they could not govern France. The British, by contrast, did things more gradually. The beginning of their two-party system, as was noted earlier, preceded the extension of the franchise. The latter movement was spread out slowly— 1832, 1867, 1884, 1918, 1928. It took half a century (1832 to 1884) before the majority of males were enfranchised, and another generation (1884 to 1918) before the male suffrage became universal. The women, too, received the vote in two installments, 1918 and 1928. Throughout this process, the party system evolved and expanded with the successive extensions of the vote and was capable of absorbing the newly enfranchised. French democracy, however, tried to run before it could walk. So it stumbled and fell. British democracy crawled for a long, long time. Eventually, it walked firmly and erect.

And, as if the lessons of the Third Republic were not sufficient evidence, the Fourth Republic proceeded again to repeat the pattern. Such institutional innovations as its constitution contained did not in fact overcome the fundamental divisiveness of the parties, reflecting once more the crisscrossing of issues and the fragmentation of parties. On the question of carrying through its policy of "decolonization," especially in Algeria, the Fourth Republic foundered. Hence, when the party system could offer no built-in stability, the people abdicated and entrusted their fate to the abilities of a single individual. General de Gaulle had never failed to voice his contempt for *le système* and its practitioners. In French history, he stands in the tradition of the two Napoleons, of Boulanger and Pétain. Thus the excessive individualism of a gifted people, which produces such wonders in the realm of the arts, the intellect, and the spirit, contributes in politics to a turbulence from which people retreat to authority and order. For more than a century, the government of France has fluctuated between two alternatives: multipartism or Bonapartism.

The contemporary Bonaparte, who lords it while this is being written, is now doing his best to destroy the party system he has so despised. France therefore still faces an uncertain future, since Bonapartism, embodying the prestige of One, must produce a succession of Bonapartes.

An examination of France would seem, therefore, to support the contention advanced here and in the previous chapter. The party system is the consequence of the social divisions, political propensities and historical traditions of the people. The institutions of the state—legislature, executive, and electoral machinery—are molded to conform to the requirements of the parties (rather than the other way round) because the dynamics of politics are always more potent than the statics of structure.

Toward an Unscientific Generalization

But having said that, let me immediately add a caution and a disclaimer. I would not want this generalization to be interpreted as some "law" of politics or to be endowed with some pseudo-scientific validity. The findings of history may be assorted and classified to lead by induction to conclusions which seem generally true. But to suggest that this is the discovery of laws founded on the assumed regularities of political behavior is to assert far more than the known data can possibly support. The fascination of politics is akin to that of the history of which it is a part. Its consistencies encounter the inconsistent. Its regularities concede to the irregular. Its symmetries are defied by the asymmetrical. There are in history two factors at least which no amount of scientific law can subsume: the fortuitous and the traditional. One cannot deny in politics or ignore the element of mere chance—the *fortuna* of Machiavelli. For instance, without subscribing to any Carlylean apotheosis of heroes, one must admit that the accidents of individual personality can make a crucial difference to party politics. What leaders emerge, and when, has a vital bearing on the system as a whole. The time at which they happen to die is also important. The Republican party was permanently affected by the fact that Lincoln was assassinated before Reconstruction had really started, as were the Democrats when Franklin D. Roosevelt did not survive to guide the nation into the post-war period. The ascendancy of Bismarck profoundly affected the Social Democrats, Catholic Center, and Liberals. Hitler's demonic mania, coming when it did, left an imprint on German politics and on Europe which will be visible for generations. In Victoria's Britain, at a critical stage in the transition from oligarchy to democracy, party conflict was dramatized by the confrontation of two contrasted, yet towering, personalities—Gladstone and Disraeli. Those to whom the labels of Liberal and Conservative meant little, and the programs of liberalism and conservatism meant even less, could nevertheless be drawn to an awareness and an understanding of politics by the dramatic debates between "Dizzy" and "Mr. Gladstone." It was lucky for the country that the incorporation of new voters into the party system happened to coincide with the simultaneous presence of two such remarkable men. These accidents do occur. They are a portion of the real stuff of politics. But they exemplify and conform to no law.

Nor can our contemporary "model" builders and "science" seekers find comfort in that other omnipresent political fact—the force of tradition surviving into and influencing the present. In the United States, the continuous party allegiance of the dominant minority of white Southerners affected both Democrats and Republicans nationally for three-quarters of a century. The sheer antipathy to the Republican party, arising from their authorship of the northern victory and the policies of reconstruction, drove the southern voter irrationally to the Democratic side. A parallel to this exists in Canada, where the voters of Quebec acquired a similar prejudice against the Conservatives for what they did to Riel and for enforcing conscription in World War I. Hence for a whole generation in national elections they voted solidly Liberal. Equally remarkable is the allegiance of Norway's northern fisherman to Labor for the reasons which were discussed earlier, or the refusal of the French Left and Center under the Third Republic ever to agree to a dissolution. Facts like these abound in politics. They differ from country to country. But everywhere some examples of this kind can be found. Party systems are influenced by them, as they are by the careers of exceptional men. Such data can be described, analyzed, explained, and understood. But they yield no law and fit no science.

It has been said that the function of Art is to hold a mirror up to nature. Adapting this, one might remark that in a democracy it is the function of party politics to hold up a mirror to society. The analysis which has been attempted in the preceding chapter and the present one interprets the parties as the product of their social environment, shaped by the stresses and pressures arising from the circumstances of political combat. Whatever the disagreements over inferences about causation or the merits of one type of party system versus another, the undoubted conclusion emerges that only in writing about democracy would this analysis be possible and relevant. Autocratic regimes, of no matter which Ism, strap the community in a governmental strait jacket and thereby restrain the spontaneous movements of the members of the body politic. The internal complexity and diversity which the party systems of democratic states exhibit are authentic as a picture of life. If you want, therefore, to learn in a democracy about a people and its government, observe their party system. For here lies the heart of the matter.

13

The Constitutional Order

If parties are the actors, playing out their several roles in the democratic drama, the state through its institutions provides the stage and scenery. The stage has its limitations. It is finite in size and shape, and plot and action must conform to its requirements. The scenery appeals to the imagination and creates an illusion. Partly it is make-believe; partly, aspiration. Stage and scenery together impose a form for action. To dramatist and players they mean ordered opportunities.

The Rationale of Constitutions

Thus it is with the structure of government. We fashion our institutions so that the goals of politics may be achieved within a set of rules that are known and accepted. The framework embodies a logic of its own. Intricate though its sections may be, they incorporate an over-all design and combine in a pattern. This, in essentials, is what one calls the constitution. A constitution includes those features of the form of government which are fundamental in importance, widely accepted, and reasonably enduring.[1] In that sense—and it is a realistic criterion—every settled state has a constitution, irrespective of its type of politics or the character of its particular government. This chapter is concerned with the requirements which give a constitution a democratic quality. But the discussion of this topic cannot

1. Elsewhere I have defined a constitution as "the basic design of the structure and powers of the state and the rights and duties of its citizens." *The Great Issues of Politics*, 2nd ed., p. 262.

be separated from the more general question of the functions which every constitution must fulfill. Its sources and context are as relevant as its purposes.

The analysis of constitutions is one of the oldest themes in the history of political thought. The systematic treatment of the subject begins inevitably with Aristotle, and, although the empirical data he compares are restricted to the experiences of the *Polis*, he raises problems which are still among the central ones to be considered. Polybius carries the argument further by applying the Greek classification to the strange medley of institutions in the Roman Republic. In fact, his hypothesis of the "mixed constitution" was later resuscitated by British writers, under similar conditions, to explain the newly acquired power of their nation and the liberties of its citizens. Because the period from the mid seventeenth century to the end of the eighteenth was one of political ferment, the pros and cons of constitutional principles and institutional structures were vigorously debated by Locke, Montesquieu, Rousseau, Burke, Jefferson, and Madison. In the nineteenth century and the first half of the twentieth, the emphasis shifted from speculation about the principles to the construction and operation of workable machinery. Because the advent of democracy always spelled a revolutionary challenge to the pre-existing regimes, its literature has been much occupied with constitutional questions. When traditional modes of government are rejected, and men apply their reason to the deliberate formation of something new, they necessarily confront the issues that are fundamental. The organization of the state and the powers of its agents, the rights of its citizens and their duties, all have to be examined. It then becomes necessary to obtain some measure of agreement about how the government will be constructed and will function in the future. Democracy does not supersede the classic questions that have been asked about the constitution since Aristotle. But it does have its own views on content and method, and it poses some new questions. In this chapter, I shall examine the subject of constitutions from the standpoints of society, politics, and law; and then look at various types of democratic constitutions. Certain particular cases will provide important insights, notably those of France, South Africa, the United Kingdom, and the United States.

There are three major functions which a constitution must fulfill and three influences to which it must correspond. In the first instance, a constitution is a way of organizing and giving formal recognition to the interests and groups of which society is composed. Second, it serves the state as the skeleton serves the human body, offering a hard structure round which the dynamic processes of politics can operate.[2] Structurally viewed, the constitution is several things in one. It is a complex of official powers and functions plus private rights and responsibilities. It erects a framework of institutions, branches, and agencies. It further embodies the philosophical principles which underlie a community's conception of its form of government. Third, a constitution is endowed with the paramountcy of law. It marks the apex in a hierarchy of legal gradations. Here is the focus of the supreme law of the state and the fount of its subordinate laws.

Aristotle's Analysis

To consider the relevance to democracy of these various aspects, let us begin by looking at what Aristotle had to say. His observations, as one restudies them after twenty-two centuries, are indeed remarkable. Not only does he go to the heart of the subject, but he balances his formulation of the ideal with insight into the real.

The Greek word in the *Politics* which we translate as "constitution" is *politeia*. To a Greek, however, as Ernest Barker points out,[3] this did not signify the same as our English term which carries the connotations of its Latin origin. *Politeia*[4] is an abstract noun derived from *Polis* and refers to the general pattern of organization of the city-state-community.[5] Endowed with this generality, and helped by Aristotle's deftness in definition, the term becomes a many-sided concept embracing topics which today would be called social, political, institutional, and legal. The effect of the social foundations on both the political system and the constitution is made explicit in the portion of Book Four where he analyzes various types of oligarchy and democracy according to the classes that compose the society.[6] Political power, as Aristotle sees it, is connected with wealth and social status. Hence the relation that exists between classes arising from these factors has a bearing on the control of the government. But this is

2. "The constitution itself is like a skeleton which politics endows with flesh, blood, and the breath of life. . . . More specifically, politics involves the translation of social pressures into public policies." Peter H. Odegard and E. Allen Helms, *American Politics* (Harper Bros; New York, 2nd ed. 1947), p. 1.

3. *The Politics of Aristotle, op. cit.*, p. lxvi.

4. When Aristotle introduces the six-fold classification of governments, *politeia* is also the name for one of the forms. It is the good type, of which *demokratia* is the perversion. See Chapter II, p. 31 and footnote 32.

5. "The *politeia* is the form of organization of the inhabitants of the *Polis*." Bk. III, Chap. 1, 1275b.

6. *Politics*, Bk. IV, Chaps, 2-3, 1289b-1291a.

not all. Besides interpreting the constitution in the light of social classes, Aristotle stresses the significance of inequalities in the distribution of property. It is difficult, he notes, to be law-abiding if you are very rich or very poor.[7] The former can break the law with impunity because their wealth protects them. The latter are tempted, or driven, to steal because they are desperate. Thus he concludes that the most stable segment of society is the middle class.[8] Wherever this group is proportionately large, the prevailing temper is moderate and the laws are normally obeyed. In addition, the general character of the constitution is affected by any particular occupation which is important to the whole community and in which many persons earn their livelihood.[9] Classifying the various types of democracy according to their economic components, Aristotle draws the conclusion that the best kind of democracy is based on agriculture.[10]

These economic and social features are reflected in the structure of the government. Here the *politeia* is expressed as an organization of offices and authorities capped by whatever element is politically supreme.[11] This notion involves an accurate insight into the form which institutions assume and the spirit in which they are used. On one side, Aristotle observes the realities of political power; on the other, the machinery of the state. The constitution is the junction of the two. Through its agency, the latter is charged with the former's energizing force. But a word of caution is added. Experience shows that the structure may be designed according to one pattern, but can work according to another. Aristotle sagely comments that it is possible for a democratic constitution to be administered oligarchically, and the reverse.[12] The inference is plain. If you seek the truth, look behind the façade. There you will find the working reality. There lie the *arcana imperii*.

To complete his summary of essentials, Aristotle makes two further points, derived from empirical research, which have been considerably amplified in subsequent history. When the machinery of the state is broken down into its components, three parts[13] can be distinguished. One of these deliberates, one administers, one adjudicates. The first-named is su-

7. *Ibid.*, Bk. IV, Chap. 9, 1295b.
8. *Ibid.*, 1295b-1296a.
9. *Ibid.*, Bk. IV, Chap. 4, 1291b.
10. *Ibid.*, Bk. VI, Chap. 4, 1318b.
11. This description of *politeia* occurs more than once. See Bk. III, Chap. 4, 1278b, Bk. IV, Chap. 1, 1289a.
12. *Ibid.*, Bk. IV, Chap. 5, 1292b.
13. Since the reader will detect in this statement the embryo from which the doctrine of the "separation of powers" later evolved, it should be noted that the Greek word is the neutral and descriptive *morion*, meaning a part or portion.

preme, when its jurisdiction includes external affairs; the enactment of domestic laws; inflicting sentences of death, banishment, and confiscation; and the audit of official accounts. Hence, whichever citizens participate in these functions are in fact the rulers of the state. Finally there is the legal hierarchy. The authority of law proceeds in descending order from the supreme to the subordinate. The *politeia* incorporates the fundamental design to which *nomoi* (laws) must conform. Hence the justice or injustice of the latter is relative to the constitution which promulgates them.[14] The laws in turn, being of general application, are superior to the decrees or rulings (*psephismata*) which govern the details of a particular case. The full citizens of a community are those who share in the responsibility for establishing the *politeia* and enacting its *nomoi*. By the same principle, they are subject to the laws which they themselves helped to formulate. So, *a fortiori*, are the officials who occupy public positions in government. They are "guardians of the law and its servants."[15]

What is noteworthy about this Aristotelian analysis is its clear grasp of essentials. It can well stand as a model for those who study politics by a comparative method. Aristotle based his account of constitutions on empirical data taken from historical research and contemporary observation. Some of his conclusions are evidently inductive generalizations from instances in various city-states. Others again are grounded on one special case, that of Athens. But the lessons of history are united in his thought with the ideals of philosophy. Aristotle not only makes explicit the concepts which are implicit in actual systems of government, but evaluates these by his criteria of political virtue. Viewing the development of humanity from animalism to civilization, he depicts his ideals of the good society, the good state, and the good citizen. All these enter into the notion of *politeia*, taking its content from the potentialities inherent in the historical process and clothing the latter with a significance which the bare political event would otherwise lack. Few thinkers, having the advantage of stepping early into uncharted territory, have blazed so useful a trail for others to follow.

The Social Content of Constitutional Forms

Let us pursue the Aristotelian line of reasoning further and look at constitutions in a democratic context. The following propositions are central to my argument:

14. *Ibid.*, Bk. III, Chap. 6, 1282b.
15. *Ibid.*, Bk. III, Chap. 11, 1287a.

> A constitution embodies the political design of the institutions of government and the citizens' relations to them.
>
> Part of its substance comes from the quality of the society in which it functions; part, from the principles by which people think their government should be conducted.
>
> Politics produces the constitution and endows it with legal sanction from which lesser laws flow.

The element of democracy, or its opposite, in these propositions depends in each case on the character of the content. The social fabric may bear a pattern which helps to make democracy possible or may prevent it. The principles which animate the institutional design can be those of liberty and equality or of privilege and authoritarianism. The legal order will reflect one set of aspirations or the other. Furthermore, the relationship between these factors, particularly the processes employed for adaptation and change, are not only relevant to democracy, but are frequently a major ingredient in its success or failure.

A constitution may be considered initially the political expression of an equilibrium or hierarchy of social forces. It recognizes the co-ordinate or subordinate position of social groups in terms of governmental structure and legal powers. When subordinate groups seek to improve their status, or when new groups emerge for which the old order had no place, a disequilibrium arises and one of two consequences follows. Either a constitutional change is brought about by revolution or reform; or reaction ensues and the *status quo* is reconfirmed. In a society dominated by a traditional or hereditary elite whose members control a disproportionate share of the property and military force, the structure of the state will be arranged to correspond to the facts of their political supremacy. Numerous instances come readily to mind. One recalls in classical antiquity the privileges (and harsh discipline) of the minority of Spartiates and the system which Lycurgus devised to fasten their ascendancy upon the submerged population of Lacedaemon. The early Athenian constitution reserved a monopoly of political power for the land-owning aristocracy and Draco's code dealt severely with the underprivileged. The laws of Solon, being only the first stage in the course of liberalization, apportioned the functions of citizenship according to the distribution of property, the richest class being classified as *pentacosiomedimnoi*.[16] The domestic history of Rome during the first two centuries of the Republic revolves around "the struggle of the

16. A *medimnos* was a unit of measurement of about 1½ bushels. The richest citizens, rated in terms of land alone, were those whose estates produced annually over 500 *medimnoi*.

orders." Every family in the Roman *populus* had the hereditary status of patrician or plebeian. The former had superior legal rights and social standing and they alone originally could fill the highest elective offices. The plebeians battled politically for equal access to all positions, dramatizing their demands on more than one occasion by seceding *en masse*. The patricians were forced to give in, primarily because of their shortage of manpower. Rome's constitution evolved under the Republic by registering these changes. Domestic harmony, or *concordia ordinum*, was not finally achieved until full equality was gained. The plebians secured recognition for their own assembly, the *concilium plebis*, and the ten tribunes were elected annually to protect their rights.

The feudal order in medieval Europe was entirely constructed on the principle of gradations in rank. Relations between men were hierarchical; and whether in the tenure of land, in the obligations of military service, in legal rights and responsibilities, or in access to government, the same hierarchies coincided. When the kings of France chose to consult with representatives of their subjects, the latter were grouped into the three estates —nobility, clergy, and commoners. The third of these included, not the "common people" in its modern sense, but the richer townsfolk, the *bourgeois*. The views of the urban and rural poor were excluded from consideration.[17] Sometimes these systems restricted the privileges of full participation in government to a small elite perched at the apex of the social pyramid. An example is the merchant-oligarchy which ruled Venice, amassing its wealth from the maritime commerce of the eastern Mediterranean. As with the Corinthians in classical Greece, property ownership served as the initial qualification for a share in politics. The oligarchy thus formed then converted itself into a hereditary nobility of a limited group of families. These intermarried with others whose names were inscribed, appropriately enough, in the Golden Book. At a certain date that book was closed and no new names could thenceforth be added. Under such circumstances, what else was the constitution of the Republic of St. Mark but a written code and framework of institutions to reflect and ratify the privileges of the socio-economic plutocracy whose palaces lined the banks of the Grand Canal?

A similar situation—varying only in degree and in the ease or difficulty with which a *parvenu* might break into the charmed circle—lasted in all countries of western Europe until the dawning of the democratic era.

17. See Chapter XIV, pp. 439-41. England's famous Magna Carta was drawn up by the nobility, primarily to reassert their privileges against the King. Only by later extension, and because of the generality of some of the phrasing, did it become a charter for the liberties of all.

Great Britain was governed oligarchically by an aristocracy whose primary wealth was vested in the land although some profit also accrued from commercial ventures. The same institutions of the Crown, Lords, and Commons, existed in the sixteenth, seventeenth, and eighteenth centuries, as are to be found in the nineteenth and twentieth. But political revolutions, responding to social and economic change and movements in ideas, have transformed their character. The power of royal absolutism was broken in the period from 1640 to 1690, and the so-called constitutional monarchy which survived that fiery ordeal has been whittled down in the last hundred years to the forms of a ceremonial etiquette. The grip of the landowning aristocracy on the Houses of Parliament was broken in the years of crisis, 1830-32, and legal relations between the two chambers were made to correspond to the new realities in the later crisis of 1909-11.[18] The somewhat facile generalizations which say that power was transferred to the middle class in 1832 and to the working class in 1884 contain their substratum of truth, although they are vitiated by the inevitable vagueness of such broad sociological expressions.

Many more instances of this kind could be cited. History is replete with them. But my purpose here is to confirm the main point by reference to sufficient examples, and not to detail an exhaustive list of all the cases that ever were. "The constitution," as a British scholar has aptly written, "is society in its political aspect. We cannot understand its nature without reference to the chief characteristics of society."[19] This is perfectly true— or rather it correctly refers to those constitutions which have lasted for at least a couple of generations and have therefore, as the phrase goes, "stood the test of time." In such cases, the constitution and the society have grown together and are intertwined with one another. If a constitution is to be thought of as embodying the fundamentals of the political system on which a majority of the people are agreed and to which they give their allegiance, then in a certain Burkean sense no constitution can be deemed effective until it has been consecrated by time and tradition. The Constitution of the United States, thus viewed, had acquired a deeper meaning for the American people in 1889, and will possess a still deeper one by 1989, than it had in 1789, when all that it portended was a noble promise.

Of itself, a constitution has no force or binding character. In the twentieth century we are unfortunately only too familiar with paper documents which have been drafted, promulgated, and quickly disregarded, for any

18. See below, pp. 410 ff.
19. H. R. G. Greaves, *The British Constitution* (Allen and Unwin: London, 1938), p. 11.

doubts to remain on that score. If a constitution is actually to be in force, it must be rooted in society and be nurtured by political custom. Moreover, the people must feel that it is theirs, that it belongs to them, that it is not alien.

The Brazilian Experience

In this context, a relevant case to consider is that of Brazil. The dilemma of Brazilian politics can be summarized as a conflict between an inherited tradition and a choice of imported products. During the colonial period, the Portuguese regime was an oligarchy. The country was run by an aristocracy of big planters (*donos da fazenda*), military officers, and civilian officials, whose relations with the governed were authoritarian, but not inevitably despotic. Their system might be described as authoritarianism tempered by inefficiency—the least objectionable species of that genus. Ever since independence, Brazilians have tried repeatedly to improve the design of their government; but in every case they have had to go abroad for their models. There was nothing they could learn on this subject from Portugal, and they did not produce new ideas or institutions from within. As a consequence, although the systems they introduced might be good in principle or might work successfully in their land of origin, they did not always harmonize with an unfamiliar and exotic environment. Also, the imports were open to criticism on the score that they were alien.

During the reign of its second Emperor, the sage and humane Dom Pedro Segundo, the government evolved in imitation of Great Britain at a time when British naval power, diplomatic influence, and economic strength, were paramount. Thus, the Emperor was envisaged as a male Portuguese-speaking Queen Victoria; a Parliament was started with a carefully restricted franchise; and the two principal political clusters were named Conservative and Liberal. Naturally, when the Empire was replaced by a Republic in 1889, Brazil looked northward for its model and, through the virtuosity of Rui Barbosa, imported a Portuguese version of the Constitution of the United States. Thus federalism, the presidential system, and judicial review, were essayed in Rio de Janeiro and the regions to which its writ extended. But the plant that had grown from seed in Massachusetts and Virginia was not yet acclimatized to its tropical soil when it was struck by the economic hurricane of the 1930's and uprooted. Getúlio Vargas then conducted a *golpe*, installed himself as dictator, and established a regime with fascist trappings. For this, he too looked abroad —to Latin Europe understandably—and found in Mussolini's corporative state a system worth importing. His *Estado Novo*, however, could not survive the end of World War II, which encompassed the downfall of fascist regimes, and Vargas himself was eased into retirement by the discreet intervention of the army. Once more, the Brazilian politicos and intelligentsia set to work to write a constitution, and restored the North American model with federal union, separation of powers, and popular elections.[20]

That constitution stumbled along for almost two decades, but broke down in March 1964. Its forms, intent, and proclaimed ideals were democratic; and the democratic potential was consistent with various features of Brazilian society—the mature and tolerant policy in race relations; the vivid intelligence of the best-educated Brazilians; the capacity for self-criticism that is revealed in conversation and the press; and the balance and proportion which come from possessing a sense of humor. But, as Aristotle reminded us, an institution may have a democratic façade while the realities which lie behind are oligarchically run. Modern Brazil is still controlled by an elite whose members possess and direct a disproportionate share of the country's material and social goods. It consists of an economic plutocracy of rich *fazendeiros*,[21] industrialists, and businessmen; a professional corps of individuals who are highly educated and cultivated; a social aristocracy of great families or clans whose names reappear in bewildering combinations. To this minority of the population, who are qualitatively important, but quantitatively few, the egalitarianism required by political, economic, and social democracy, with its consequences both of leveling up and leveling down, is not cordially welcome.

Under these conditions, a constitution can either spell out the dominance of the few, or offer a channel for the hopes of the many, or provide an arena for the conflicts between an actual oligarchy and a potential democracy. In 1964 the constitution collapsed as Leftists launched a social revolution and the Right defended its privileges. Supported by leading governors, the army seized control and, violating its best traditions, installed a marshal as President with autocratic powers. The resolution of tensions is not made any easier when the whole community is simultaneously undergoing change, but the rates of change are different in its various sectors.

20. In a few years' time, when the presidency of Dutra was drawing to an end, Vargas emerged from retirement and became a candidate for that office under the new constitution. He was duly elected. Only George Bernard Shaw could have written the script for the dictator-emeritus serving as president under a regime akin to that which he had earlier overthrown.

21. In 1950, less than one-tenth of the landowners possessed as much as three-quarters of the explored area—and this in a country where 63% of the people live, or subsist, on the land. Data cited by Fernando Henrique Cardoso in "Tensões sociais no campo e reforma agrária," *Revista Brasileira de Estudos Políticos*, No. 12, Oct. 1961, p. 11.

Fastest of all in Brazil is the economic development, particularly in the sphere of heavy industry and diversified secondary manufacturing. The economy plunges ahead at a dizzy speed, dragging everything after it, and the never-ending inflation destroys the security of those on fixed salaries and wages. Meanwhile, the traditional institutions of society are changing much more slowly. The Church, though it contains some progressive elements, for the most part is rural-oriented and rooted in traditional values. The family system, with its emphasis on kinship connections, competes with the political conception of the public interest. Educational opportunities, although considerably expanded, barely keep up with the population increase. In between lies the political system. This has been changing faster than the family, Church, and education, but more slowly than the economy. Pulled forward by the needs of economic growth, the political system is held back by social conservatism. To arrive at an appropriate constitutional order under such circumstances is truly a formidable task. It is rendered more difficult when corruption pervades the government, and when the ideals and institutions to which innovators aspire are not indigenously Brazilian but foreign imports.[22] Hence a Brazilian friend, whom I asked to define his country's politics, replied: "What we have in Brazil is confusionship." Indeed, he was right. Though not included among the accepted categories of classification, confusionship is a dreadfully common form of government.

Requirements for a Democratic Constitution

There are some important implications for democracy in all this. If a country like Brazil is now at an intermediate stage of development and could evolve in the future along either democratic or authoritarian lines, the same was once presumably true of states which today are mature democracies, but had to change in this direction from their oligarchical past. For the constitutional order, therefore, to be democratic in actuality as well as in form, certain requirements must be satisfied in combination. It is evident that a constitution cannot function democratically if the surrounding social context is imbued with oligarchy and authoritarianism. But it is not society alone which makes the constitution democratic. The form of government influences society, as in turn it is influenced by society. The government is a composite of popular demands organized into interests and parties, of structured public institutions, and of philosophical

22. The same would hold true if the Communist party should ever gain control in Brazil.

ideals to which a community subscribes or aspires. The raw materials of social groupings are fed into the constitutional system where the creative processes of politics endow them with shape, coherence, and purpose. Judged from a democratic standpoint, the crucial problem for a constitution is to register the relations between social groups, machinery of state, and valued goals which make democracy an operative reality.

The first political requirement for a democratic constitution is that all persons who are subject to the jurisdiction of the state must be equal as citizens and in that sense must have the same share in the choice and control of their officials. This is to say that a democracy cannot allow a constitutional distinction between citizens and subjects, or between first- and second-class citizens.[23] In terms of fundamental rights and obligations, it must not discriminate between human beings because they happen to differ in race, faith, tongue, sex, birth, or wealth. A democracy embraces all —as its citizens—equally. From this it follows that any who are deliberately excluded, or are permanently relegated to an inferior political status, cannot acknowledge the constitution to be representing them. To the extent that any such group exists, the constitution fails to be democratic. If such groups oppose the constitution and refuse it their allegiance, they are morally and politically justified because it has rejected them. Democracy, therefore, cannot be applied by constitutional or any other means between groups which deny one another's common humanity or repudiate a common identification. The constitution of a democracy must first embody the unity which is accepted by all.

On this point, having earlier paid tribute to Aristotle's analysis, let me here emphasize that the constitutional scheme which he envisaged was far from being democratic. Or, to be more exact, what he favored was a system where an elite would govern itself democratically, but rule the mass of the community aristocratically. Aristotle accepted and explicitly justified the institution of slavery. Unlike Plato, he did not concur in the principle of equality for women. Poorer persons, and those who earned their living in manual and menial occupations, he excluded from his concept of *polites*, or citizen.[24] The principles of democracy, though better understood at the Lyceum, were scarcely more respected there than at the Academy.

The argument that a democratic constitution must recognize the unity

23. However, this does not mean that the concept of citizenship includes non-citizens, i.e., aliens whose allegiance belongs to another state. Nor does a person acquire equal political rights until he or she reaches whatever age is considered by law to confer maturity—conventionally twenty-one in many places.
24. "For the truth is that we should not include as citizens all those who are needed for a state to function." *Politics*, Bk. III, Chap. 5, 1278a.

of the whole membership of the state is the theme of a much-quoted statement by Lord Balfour, the British Prime Minister and Conservative party leader at the beginning of this century. In an essay written as a foreword to an edition of Walter Bagehot's *The English Constitution,* he commented: "Our alternating Cabinets, though belonging to different Parties, have never differed about the foundations of society. And it is evident that our whole political machinery presupposes a people so fundamentally at one that they can safely afford to bicker; and so sure of their own moderation that they are not dangerously disturbed by the never-ending din of political conflict. May it always be so."[25] One may re-echo Balfour's hope. Happy the country which has attained to that level of tolerance and maturity. But what about those whose people is not fundamentally at one? Can democracy then be made to work? Is a stable constitution possible? After all, let us not forget that British politics in former centuries did not exhibit the qualities which are so remarkable today. In the medieval period, there was frequent turbulence and disorder, culminating in a protracted civil war. The Tudors produced a strong monarchy, at the very time when the community was split by religious dissension. This division continued under the Stuarts, until for this and other reasons civil war again ensued. It took the country half a century to settle down, and only after 1690 was a new constitutional pattern achieved which thenceforth could evolve in an orderly manner. Twentieth-century Britons can safely afford to bicker because Englishmen and Scotsmen, Welsh and Irish, Protestants and Catholics, aristocrats and commoners, landowners and industrialists, finished their persecuting, exploiting, and slaughtering in bygone eras. Today's consensus is the fruit of yesterday's crises.

But, let us revert here to a point which Aristotle makes. In the six-fold classification of forms of government, democracy is listed on the side of the perversions. The latter, it will be remembered, are characterized by a class dominating in its own interest. In a democracy, the poor plunder the rich, whereas in an oligarchy the situation is reversed. Of the two, the former is less reprehensible simply because the poor outnumber the rich. Ideally, however, those who rule should do so in the interests of all. How does this standard apply to societies which are stratified or otherwise divided into classes?[26] Democratic principles cannot allow a permanent domination by a group which treats others as inferiors and excludes them from a share in politics. Hence the founders of democracy in every land were necessarily engaged, from a constitutional standpoint, in an act of

25. In the World's Classics edition (Oxford University Press, 1928), p. xxiv.
26. The term "class" is ambiguous. Sometimes it signifies a horizontal section, or stratum, spreading across the community; sometimes, an occupational group which may run vertically from high to low.

revolution. Granted the plural character of a society composed of various groups, a democratic regime had to establish equality of status between the groups and freedom of opportunity for their individual members. An oligarchical constitution had to be imposed from above by an elite intending to prolong its own supremacy. A democratic constitution had to be accepted by all groups, which they would only do if it accorded them fair treatment and a fair chance. This criterion is the key to consensus in a system which aims at embracing everybody.

Of course, the enunciation of a philosophical ideal is one thing. Its application through history is another. The constitutions of the democracies which are now mature and successful did not spring, like Athene in the Greek myth, fully armed from the popular godhead. Characteristically, they evolved after an initial revolution which broke the barriers of ancient privilege. The subsequent evolution was often slow, but it had the merit of being orderly. The ultimate end was implicit in the beginning and was foreseeable. The former ruling class had time to adapt to the new circumstances; and its members—or the wiser of them—could learn to accept the inevitable with the best grace they could muster. Reciprocally, the spokesmen for newly emergent groups, though to noble ears their voices might sound strident and their accents uncouth, were more careful students of the *ancien régime* than their opponents realized, and they did not totally reject its every feature. All they insisted on was that benefits once reserved to a few be spread abroad and made available to each and every one.

It has been noted earlier that gradualism was a major ingredient in the democratic formula for success. Its advantage, from the standpoint of reaching agreement on fundamentals, was that different sections of society could accustom themselves to the rules of the game and grow familiar with the implied understandings which permit the rules to work. In this respect, Gladstone's famous comparison of Great Britain and the United States combines a pair of half-truths. "The two constitutions of the two countries," he wrote in 1878, "express indeed rather the differences than the resemblances of the nations. The one is a thing grown, the other a thing made: the one a *praxis*, the other a *poiesis*: the one the offspring of tendency and indeterminate time, the other of choice and of an epoch. But, as the British Constitution is the most subtile [*sic*] organism which has proceeded from the womb and the long gestation of progressive history, so the American Constitution is, so far as I can see, the most wonderful work ever struck off at a given time by the brain and purpose of man."[27] There is both overstatement and understatement in this remark. In the case of Britain, Gladstone does not mention the revolutionary fer-

27. W. E. Gladstone, "Kin beyond the Sea," *North American Review* (1878), No. cclxiv, p. 185.

ment of the seventeenth century which prepared and preceded the later evolution. As regards the United States, he overlooks the amount of inherited tradition which was incorporated into the Constitution and the "organic" growth which had already occurred in the nine decades from 1789 to 1878 and which is doubly evident in the 1960's. The British constitution has evolved successfully during the last three centuries because it absorbed enough change to satisfy progressives, while containing the potential for more; also, it retained enough of the old, mainly in its institutional forms and outer ceremonies, to satisfy traditionalists. The American system likewise did not accomplish everything at one go, nor was this even attempted. The prevailing mood at the Philadelphia Convention was a concern for basic principles tempered by a practical sense of the possible. It was an aristocracy of wealth and intellect which wrote the document of 1787, but in language broad enough to allow latitude of future interpretation and including as its most important single article, Number Six, the procedure for proposing and ratifying amendments.

Another relevant comparison is that between Great Britain and France. De Fleuriau relates a conversation between himself, when he was Ambassador in London, and the then head of the Liberal Government, Campbell-Bannerman. "When we conduct a revolution," said the Prime Minister, "we do not destroy our house completely. We take care to preserve its façade, and behind this we rebuild a new house. In France, you do things differently. You tear down the old structure and then reconstruct the same house, but with a new exterior and under another name." On this the French diplomat comments: "There is some truth in this sally."[28] Democratic Britain did not abolish such patently undemocratic institutions as the Crown and House of Lords. It merely left them powerless. It preserved the shell, but removed the kernel. There are certain advantages in conducting affairs this way. A reasonable respect for continuities may make transitions easier—provided always that the general public do not mistake the illusion for the truth. Walter Bagehot was writing news for his generation when he informed the readers of *The English Constitution* that their government was not in fact administered by the Queen; that the real locus of power was in the cabinet; that the "dignified" parts, which served for outward display, should be distinguished from the "efficient" parts which did the work.[29] And if one is to base conclusions not only on ideal principles, but also on practical results, one must confirm the judg-

---

28. From the preface which de Fleuriau wrote for J. Magnan de Bonnier, *L'Empire Britainnique, son évolution politique et constitutionelle*, p. 6. Quoted by K. C. Wheare in *The Statute of Westminster and Dominion Status* (Oxford: Clarendon Press, 5th ed. 1953), pp. 9-10. My translation.
29. *Op. cit.*, Chap. 1, pp. 3 ff.

ment that such countries as Great Britain, Denmark, Holland, Norway, and Sweden, which have chosen this combination, are hardly less democratic on that account than the republics of the United States or Switzerland.[30]

Besides maintaining an appropriate and continuous correspondence between social groups, governmental structure, and legal authority, the constitution of a democratic state must solve a second major problem. This concerns the method of procuring changes and of exercising political power. Constitutions are political devices for regularizing the use of power and harnessing it, by means of institutions and rules, to legality.[31] Any form of government must come to terms with the phenomenon of power. A democratic form attempts to provide machinery and establish procedures, on which agreement is reached in advance, whereby men and movements peacefully compete for power, peacefully wield it when won, and peacefully concede its transfer when lost. The link between this problem and the former is created by their common relevance to a principle of justice. The only possible constitution which is acceptable to all and therefore is basically stable, is that in which all individuals and interests feel that they stand a fair chance. Without such a feeling, and the realities which give it substance, no democracy is possible.

Both problems can be explained by examining two cases of profound controversy: the struggle in Great Britain which led to the curtailment of the powers of the House of Lords, and the fight in South Africa over the removal of colored voters from the common electoral roll in Cape Province. Let us review those events and issues, and explore their implications.

The British Constitutional Crisis of 1909-11

In the history of every ancient constitution, there are moments of severe crisis when all branches of the state collide head-on, and their previous equilibrium is brusquely broken. Such crises occur when new demands

30. The argument about a harmless monarchy does not, however, apply to the continuation of a social aristocracy focused around a "Court." This can be seriously harmful because of its false pretensions and appeals to snobbery. A hereditary aristocracy is an offense to democratic egalitarianism. Of the monarchies which survive today the least undesirable are those of Scandinavia because they are socially democratic and not too expensive to maintain.

31. Carl J. Friedrich has defined a constitution, in its functional sense, as "a technique of establishing and maintaining effective restraints on political and governmental action." *Constitutional Government and Democracy* (Ginn and Co.: Boston, rev. ed. 1950), Chap. 7, pp. 121 ff.

confront an old tradition and the state must thenceforth accommodate itself to innovation or reaction. At these times, as when a flash of lightning illuminates the night, outlines and positions which could only be guessed at are vividly seen and relations which were formerly uncertain become suddenly clear. This is what happened in the United Kingdom between 1909 and 1911. The events of those years form the last major constitutional crisis which Britain has undergone and the only one in this century thus far. In terms of structure, the conflict was conducted between the two Houses of Parliament. The result was a legislative enactment altering the powers of the Lords by statute. What it all really signified was the maturing of British democracy, both political and social, and its triumph over the entrenched privileges of the oligarchical past.

The British constitution consists of a collection of institutions and of rules for governing the relations between them. Both rules and institutions repose on a political foundation in the sense that they are either tacitly accepted or actively supported by enough individuals and groups to ensure an effective capacity to govern. The authority of these rules and institutions is derived from one of two sources, custom and law. The monarchy, for instance, is lineally descended from the tribal chieftainships of ancient times. It survives today because, through the symbolism of a royal family, the institution now serves to personify the continuity of a people's past and present and its unity at any particular time through a common identification. The strength of the Crown was broken in the revolution of the seventeenth century; and, although its forms were restored after the Cromwellian interlude, the throne was never again the seat of power. Nowadays the monarchy survives only if the monarch is politically innocuous. Above all, whoever lives at Buckingham Palace must remain studiously non-partisan—which means, under the conditions of modern democracy, taking no part in what is important.

Those who resisted the Crown in the seventeenth century made use of Parliament as the vehicle for their opposition.[32] Although Cromwell, who was as authoritarian as Charles I, brought his soldiers to close the doors of

---

32. Milton may be alluding to this in *Lycidas:*
> "The hungry sheep look up, and are not fed,
> But swoln with wind, and the rank mist they draw,
> Rot inwardly, and foul contagion spread:
> Besides what the grim Woolf with privy paw
> Daily devours apace, and nothing sed,
> But that two-handed engine at the door,
> Stands ready to smite once, and smite no more."

The "two-handed engine" may mean the two Houses of Parliament.

Parliament, this body became the legatee of power when his dictatorship ended. Thereafter, for reasons which were essentially political, parliamentary supremacy was the central fact of British public life; and from this fact, because politics produces law, a flow of legal consequences ensued. Since Parliament was politically dominant, it established the principle of its legal omnipotence. It acknowledged no higher legal authority inside Great Britain or without. No other institution, no official, could override its will declared in statute form. At any time, under its ordinary procedures, Parliament could make, remake, or unmake, any portion of the constitution.

These statements, however, though technically correct, require a more exact definition. When one refers to the legal omnipotence of Parliament, a constitutional lawyer will add that Parliament, thus defined, means "the Crown in Parliament," because a bill which has passed through Parliament must be signed by the monarch before becoming a law. Indeed, it is still true today that the royal signature is necessary, as a legal form, to ratify an act of legislation. The political realist, however, will note with emphasis that no monarch has refused to sign a bill since the first decade of the eighteenth century, when Queen Anne withheld her assent. It is therefore politically certain that what has not been done for two and a half centuries will not be tried again. If it were tried, either the monarch or both monarch and monarchy would go. Political reality, therefore, dictates the way in which a traditional legal form is actually used.

But, excluding the Crown, how about Parliament itself? Since the legislature is bicameral, what is the relation between its two Houses? In particular, what happens if they disagree? These questions have a special relevance in a country where the membership of the two chambers represents two entirely different aspects of society. The House of Lords was designed as a citadel for the hereditary nobility and the highest prelates of the Anglican Church. The House of Commons has been so transformed by successive extensions of the franchise (1832-1928) that it now represents everyone else. Once the Commons had been democratized—and this it was, at least for the male half of the population, after 1884-85—a clash with the Lords became highly probable. Indeed, that probability became a political certainty in the light of the party affiliation of the two chambers. By virtue of the interests it represented, especially landed wealth, the Lords contained a permanent majority of Conservatives. The control of the Commons, however, would alternate between that party and the Liberals. Naturally, when the Commons had a Conservative majority, its relations with the Lords would be harmonious. The contrary would be true when the Commons supported a Liberal Ministry. The Liberals could not be expected to view with equanimity an important branch of government—one half of the supreme legislature, to be precise—in which their opponents perennially held power. By the turn of the century, the two chambers were fundamentally opposed because they embodied the antithesis not only between liberalism and conservatism, but also between an aristocratic conception of government and a democratic one.

The Liberals had won a landslide victory in the election of 1906. Together with the Irish Nationalists and the emerging Labour party, they held an overwhelming majority in the Commons. The Lords soon demonstrated their hostility by amending or rejecting various measures which were sent to them from the lower House. But in 1909 they fell into a trap which Lloyd George, then Chancellor of the Exchequer, had prepared. In his budget proposals for that year, he included an income tax more steeply graduated than before and a new tax on land. After these had passed the Commons, they were rejected by the Lords. This particular action constituted the most extreme defiance of the Commons which the Lords could possibly have displayed. It had long ago been firmly established as a rule of custom that the House of Commons, being the elective chamber, took priority in financial matters; and the Lords, though they might disagree with the Commons' viewpoint on financial questions, must submit. To challenge a major revenue-raising feature of the budget was to throw down the gauntlet to the Commons in the most arrogant and contemptuous fashion.

The Liberals took up the gauntlet. But how were they to make their will prevail? The Lords had done nothing illegal. They had simply committed a breach of a custom that was long-established and clearly recognized. By what mechanism could the rule of the superiority of the Commons in the sphere of finance be reaffirmed and the Lords be made to bow? The problem was a political one; the techniques for solving it had to be political. Accordingly, the Liberal Prime Minister, Asquith, decided to appeal against the peers to the people. He asked King Edward VII to dissolve Parliament, which was done, and to order an election for a new House of Commons. This election was held in January, 1910. The Liberals lost a hundred seats to the Conservatives, partly because their majority in 1906 had been disproportionately large and the pendulum was now swinging back to a more normal position. But the votes of the Irish and Labourites, added to those of the Liberals, created a clear majority both in the electorate and the Commons. The Liberals then reintroduced their tax proposals. The Commons accepted them and the Lords most reluctantly allowed them to pass.

That was only the end of the first stage, however. In the election campaign, Liberals, Labourites and Irish, had attacked the Lords with might and main. They had proclaimed their view that the power of the Lords to obstruct the will of the Commons must be destroyed. The upper House, it was said, must be "ended or mended." The noble lords, observed Augustine Birrell, represented no one but themselves and they possessed the entire confidence of their constituents. The Liberals had lost patience with a chamber in which conservatism always ruled the roost. The Irish had not forgiven the Lords for defeating Gladstone's Home Rule Bill of 1894. In the Labour view, the Lords were a feudal relic, a bastion of ancient privilege and hereditary wealth, which must be swept away. With this backing, Asquith counterattacked. He introduced the Parliament Bill under which the legislative powers of the upper House would be reduced by statute. By its provisions, any bill which the Commons had passed on a financial matter would be sent to the Lords, but would become law at the end of a month with their consent or without. On all other types of legislation, the Lords were granted what amounted to a power to delay for two years. If they rejected or amended a bill which the Commons had approved, and if the latter passed it twice more at consecutive sessions within a space of two years, the bill would then be law despite the Lords' objections.

This Parliament Bill was passed by the Commons. The next problem was to push it through the Lords. In this situation there was a reserve weapon which could be employed in the last resort to force a surrender of the recalcitrant peers. All constitutions have their loopholes. One of these, in the case of Great Britain, is the absence of any fixed limit to the membership of the upper House. Actually, its size is always fluctuating. Whenever a new peer is created, the size is increased by one; and if one dies without an heir to whom the title may descend, the size is similarly reduced. On certain occasions, the Crown has created a number of new peerages simultaneously. Thus arises the possibility that the political impasse of a deadlock between the two chambers can be removed by flooding the upper House with enough new peers to alter its majority. Naturally no monarch wants to do this, because it is similar to printing a large supply of new notes and thus depreciating the coinage. But the political pressure can be sufficient to induce a reluctant sovereign to swallow the distasteful. Or at any rate, he may announce his readiness to do it if necessary—in which case the Lords can bow to the Commons on the issue in dispute and thus accept a lesser evil. There were precedents for this in earlier controversies. Queen Anne had actually created a dozen new peers in 1713 to ensure the ratification of the Treaty of Utrecht. In 1832 during the struggle to enact the Reform Bill, King William IV promised the Liberals that he would authorize enough new peerages if necessary, and before this threat the Conservative opposition in the Lords grimly retreated.

On this weapon the Liberal Prime Minister relied for victory. Indirect discussions had taken place with representatives of the King, even before the election of January, 1910. The King, however, would give no promises in advance—least of all on the merits of a bill which had not yet been introduced. But hints had already been dropped that the King was unlikely to agree to swamp the Lords unless a second election were held on the specific issue of reform of the second chamber. After the Commons had passed the Parliament Bill and before it was introduced in the Lords, Asquith resumed negotiations with the Crown with a view to breaking the inevitable deadlock. It was just at this time (May, 1910) that Edward VII died. He was succeeded by his son, George V; and after the customary period of national mourning and political truce the controversy continued. Asquith discovered that the new King, like his father, would not agree there and then to create new peers. Hence a second election was necessary, which the Prime Minister requested and obtained. Simultaneously, he received from the King a secret[33] commitment that, if the Liberals won and the Lords maintained their opposition, new peerages would then be granted. The election—the second in a single year!—was held in December, 1910. The parliamentary results were virtually unchanged from January. Together, the Liberals, Labour, and Irish had a clear majority over the Conservatives and against the Lords. Events then moved to a now foregone conclusion. While the Lords were debating the Bill, with a majority of their House clearly opposed, it was made known to the Conservative leaders that the King would authorize new peerages if necessary. In the face of this unwelcome possibility, the opposition did what it had done eight decades earlier, at the bidding of the Iron Duke. Enough peers abstained from voting to permit the bill to pass. Thus did the Parliament Act of 1911 become law.

The Lessons of Those Events

Various conclusions can be drawn from that famous controversy. It is evident that when British politics, and to a lesser extent the social system, had acquired a democratic character, traditional institutions which embodied a contrary principle were compelled to conform. The two heredi-

---

33. This understanding was kept secret before the election in order that the King's name might be kept out of the party struggle and the campaigning.

tary branches of government, the Lords and the Crown,[34] had to bow to the popular will as represented in the Commons. The method by which the change was accomplished was certainly democratic. The innovation was expressed in statute form, and went into law because a majority of the electorate had twice recorded their support for the Liberals and their allies. One might even say that for the Crown to require two elections in one year was an excess of democracy. But on a clear issue of "the Lords versus the People," the odds were in the Liberals' favor. For their part, the Liberals could not be expected to tolerate an institution which claimed a half-share in the legislative power, but where their opponents, the Conservatives, were permanently entrenched. If the machinery of state is to conform to democratic principles, and if democracy is organized through a party system whose different sides alternate in power, any branch of the government which decides on major matters of policy must be susceptible to such alternations. This was not true of the House of Lords. Its hereditary character made it unrepresentative, and self-interest made it irresponsible. The second chamber was not ended—simply because the British have an aversion to destroying anything old. But it was mended, mainly by being reduced to the position of a dignified debating society for elder statesmen.

Custom is a major element in any operative constitution, and naturally it bulks largest in the older ones. The accumulation of precedents creates a rule. People then expect that what was previously done in a certain way will be done the same way whenever a similar situation recurs. Or at any rate, the burden of justification rests on those who wish to act differently. These are the understandings which imbue a system with a certain orderliness and regularity. But circumstances arise, as in the process of change they are bound to do, which alter the context that gave rise to the understandings. "Gentlemen's agreements" posit a spirit of mutual trust. At least they require the harmony of equals. But what is to happen when the underprivileged seek an equality never accorded them before? What should be done when an exclusive set of interests is based upon an institution from which it wields a power disproportionate to its numbers or social utility? Actually, in the struggle over the budget of 1909, it was the Lords who violated tradition and the Liberals who sought its enforcement. As the controversy developed, the Liberals went further. They wrote into a rule of law what had previously been left to a rule of custom, and then realistically incorporated into that law the modern relation between the

34. I include the Crown in this statement because both Edward VII and George V were clearly most reluctant to do what the Liberals wanted. Their political sympathies were with the Conservatives and the Lords.

two chambers. Whereas Parliament had earlier won political supremacy over the Crown, now the Commons achieved the same over the Lords. The Parliament Act of 1911 wrote down in a precise and specific text the details about which there should be no uncertainty for the future. A political will affirmed a legal change. The law of the democratic constitution issued from the politics of democracy.

Why then was there all the fuss? Is the Conservative opposition to be attributed solely to shortsightedness, to a failure to face facts, to a selfish attempt to perpetuate a bastion of oligarchy and guard within it the interests of property? There were such elements in the policy of the Conservatives. But there was something else which merits more serious attention. They had one major argument, essentially political in character, which touches the core of the problem of making a constitution consonant with democratic principles. Looking to the future, the Conservatives could see very clearly that subordinating the Lords to the Commons would convert the Parliament, for all practical purposes, into a unicameral legislature. Since the Crown was already bereft of political power, the Commons would be undisputed master of the machinery of state. Since Parliament was legally omnipotent, if no checks and balances existed, the majority in control of the Commons could—conceivably—do anything. Beyond the Liberals, whom they opposed but did not fear, the Conservatives could see the emerging Labour party whose socialist program inspired them with dread. Suppose these wild men should one day win a parliamentary majority? Ought the institutions of government to be such that a temporary majority could fundamentally alter the economic and social system without the possibility of effective constitutional restraint?

In other words, although the Conservatives were cast in the impossible role of defending a hereditary chamber, the principle which they argued was an important one. In the Liberal and the Conservative positions were two contrasted conceptions of how a democracy should organize its government. The logical projection of the Liberal view affirmed the need for universal suffrage, a representative assembly, and the untrammeled power of the majority. The other side argued that majority power at any time was limited by minority rights, and that institutional devices must be built into the structure of state to prevent a majority of either party taking the bit between its teeth and running amok. Although Balfour had expressed the opinion, cited earlier, that the British constitution presupposed a people fundamentally at one, he and other Conservative leaders distrusted that very assumption. Fearful of the Labour party, they were unsure of what would happen when the working class asserted the power of its numbers. Precisely because British society was not yet fundamentally at one, because in fact it was still permeated with inequality, they had no confidence in that version of democracy which left the majority free to work its will. This was the same fear which had so alarmed Aristotle that he had classed democracy among the perversions. By the same logic, Polybius, when looking for the secret of the Romans' success in the character of their government, ascribed its excellence to the fact that its form was mixed. Instead of being of one type or another, the Roman constitution supposedly blended the best features of all three classical types—government by One, by a Few, by the Many. Each offset and complemented the others. Together, they produced an effective blend. The same notion was resuscitated in eighteenth-century Britain to explain the country's domestic stability and imperial triumphs in terms of the balance between Crown, Lords, and Commons. But in the twentieth century, these restraints were being thrown to the winds. The power of the Many would henceforth be uncontrollable. Was modern democracy to repeat the pattern of fourth-century Athens? Were the underprivileged poor, by weight of numbers, to despoil and dominate the wealthier, better-educated, socially superior, few?

In politics, the fears of one generation are frequently the source of indifference or amusement to the next. From the retrospective light of the 1960's, one can look back upon the fears and angers of 1911 and dismiss them as groundless. The Liberals have ceased to be a major party. By the end of the 1920's they had shrunk to a splinter. Labour took their place and, when in power, behaved with due respect for the constitution. Actually in 1949 they amended the Parliament Act of 1911 so as to reduce the delaying powers of the Lords on other than financial bills from two years to one. The Conservatives, after returning to power in the 1920's and again in 1951, did not restore the Lords to their earlier position. In fact, the Conservatives did very little to reverse what their opponents had enacted. Since World War II, the "lower classes" have been less lowly, the "upper classes" less uppish. The British people today, though differences persist among them, are more at one fundamentally than they have ever been in their history. Hence the enormous legal powers of the House of Commons, which lie politically at the disposal of the party with the majority, have not in fact been abused. Contemporary Britain exhibits a paradox in the relation of its law to its politics. The legal categories of its constitution theoretically would permit the most completely totalitarian system amounting to utter despotism. Political practice, however, is characterized by careful restraint and cautious moderation. This is therefore a case where the politics of a genuine democracy triumphs over the potential dangers of abuses sanctioned by law.

The British formula for success, or rather the reasons for this outcome, will be examined in the next chapter. But it is relevant here to contrast the experience of the United Kingdom with that of another country where some of the forms of the British constitution have been adopted without any of the accompanying spirit, and where, not unnaturally, an authoritarian police state is now in the making. I refer to South Africa, whose political history during the 1950's supplies an invaluable comparison with that of Britain. From Asquith it is a far cry and a long descent to Malan and Strijdom. Let us see then what happened in a controversy where some of the same constitutional principles were invoked as in Britain four decades before, but where the surrounding context was wholly different.

The South African Controversy of 1951-56

The crux of the difference, briefly stated, is this: the population of South Africa is not fundamentally at one. On the contrary, as has been discussed above,[35] the inhabitants of that tormented country are deeply split by race, religion, language, living standards, and social opportunity. How does one govern such a country? How can a constitution be constructed which embodies the reverse of harmony or agreement, which in fact is intended as a weapon for domination of many by a few? Under such circumstances, what is the relation between law and politics, between branches of government, between minority rule and majority rights? Whose will shall prevail when there is no general will?

All of these questions were acutely raised in South Africa after the Nationalist party acquired control of the government in 1948. In the course of carrying out their declared policy of *apartheid*—segregating the different races physically and socially, and ensuring the supremacy of the White minority—the Nationalists included one specific change which involved a break with constitutional tradition. The ensuing controversy lasted for half a decade, from early in 1951 until the end of 1956. The point at issue concerned the voting rights of the Coloured population (i.e., persons of mixed race) in Cape Province, one of the four provinces which compose the "Union." When the Cape was governed as a British Colony prior to 1910, the franchise was limited by criteria of income and literacy, but it did not discriminate on the basis of race or color. Hence a number of half-castes who satisfied the educational and economic requirements had gained the right to vote. When the British Parliament combined the two colonies of the Cape and Natal with the two recently conquered

35. See Chapter 5, pp. 104 ff., Chapter 11, pp. 334-5, 341-2.

Dutch Republics of Transvaal and Orange Free State to form the Union of South Africa, the Act of 1910 which was the constitution of the new Dominion contained special safeguards on two points: the established voting rights of the Cape Coloured and the equality of the two European languages. Henceforth, the Union Parliament could not alter either of these principles except by a two-thirds majority in a joint session of its two chambers, the House of Assembly and the Senate. The section of the constitution providing for this procedure was known as "the entrenched clauses."

In 1931, however, the British Parliament, conforming to the recommendations of the Imperial Conference of 1926, had enacted the Statute of Westminster, whose provisions the South African Parliament immediately adopted. Under that Statute, the Parliament of the Union was placed on a legal level co-ordinate with the British Parliament. South African legislators henceforth could pass laws on any domestic or external topic, and no statute could be declared void in the courts on the ground that it conflicted with a British statute. Nevertheless, at the time when the South African Parliament was discussing the application to the Union of the Statute of Westminster, it was clearly stated by the then Prime Minister, General Hertzog, and affirmed by a resolution, that the procedures of the Constitution of 1910 were still in force, so that the Union Parliament could not amend the entrenched clauses except by a vote of two-thirds in a joint session. Some doubt was later cast on the legal obligation (as distinct from the moral one) to observe this restraint, when the South African Appeal Court wrote a judgment in 1937 stating that the Union Parliament had become fully sovereign since the adoption of the Statute of Westminster and implying that any law it enacted by any procedure would be accepted as valid.[36]

In the racial divisions of South Africa's population, the Coloured people occupied an anomalous position. Traditionally, the more liberal-minded whites had regarded them as an extension of their own race and were willing to share with them some of their own political privileges. In the constituencies of the Cape Province those of the Coloured who were entitled to vote were registered on the same electoral roll as the whites and voted in the same constituencies for the same candidates. Generally it was believed that they supported the United party against the Nationalists and there were a few constituencies in which their votes, if cast as a group, might decide the contest. The Nationalists were determined for two reasons to remove the Coloured voters from the common roll and place them on a separate register where they would vote for different candidates. At

36. The case was *Ndlwana v. Hofmeyr.*

the election of 1948 the Nationalists had received fewer votes than their opponents, but the over-representation of the rural areas in which they were strong had given them more parliamentary seats than the United party. By alliance with the small Afrikaner party, led by Havenga, the Nationalists were able to take office. But their hold on Parliament would be lost at the next election unless they could manipulate the constituencies and assure themselves a majority in the legislature. At the same time the registration of Coloured voters on the same roll as Europeans violated the principle of racial segregation and its corollary of white supremacy. The Nationalists were thus doubly motivated to alter the established voting rights of the Coloured and were convinced that they were not legally bound by the entrenched clauses.

Accordingly in March 1951, the Government introduced in the House of Assembly a Separate Representation of Voters Bill. Under its provisions the Coloured voters in the Cape were to be taken off the roll where they were listed with the Europeans and would be registered separately. They were then to vote at regular periods of five years, but not at the general elections, for four Europeans to represent them in the House and for one in the Senate. As soon as the Bill was introduced, the Opposition leader, J. G. N. Strauss, protested that the Government was violating the procedure required in the Constitution and asked the Speaker to give a ruling. When the latter did so, he took the position that since the adoption of the Statute of Westminster the Parliament was freed from the restrictions of the entrenched clauses and could henceforth enact any law on any subject by any procedure. The debate then proceeded with intense heat and bitterness, in the House, in the press, and in the country at large. The Government justified its action by the principles of *apartheid* and the legal omnipotence of Parliament. It viewed the entrenched clauses as a relic from the period when the Parliament at Westminster had the authority to legislate for South Africa, and it denied their validity in the 1950's. The United party opposed on grounds which were both legal and moral. It pointed to the understandings and promises which had been made by leaders of both major parties when the Statute of Westminster was adopted. On the strict point of law, the opposition agreed that the Union Parliament was now sovereign, but argued that it could not alter the voting rights of the Coloured or the equal status of the two European languages except by a two-thirds majority in a joint session. Morality, however, was stressed even more strongly than law. The Coloured voters in the Cape had enjoyed this electoral status for more than half a century. Special means were taken to protect their rights when the Cape became a Province of the Union. The law of the constitution must be founded on good faith. Majority power should be restrained by respect for minority rights. If these established rights were altered, was anything sacred or safe?

As was to be expected, the Bill, though hotly contested on party lines, received a majority of votes in the House, and then in the Senate. Immediately a test case was brought to challenge its legality in the courts. In March, 1952, the five judges of the Supreme Court decided unanimously that the "law" was unconstitutional. The entrenched clauses, in their view, were still binding. The reaction of the Nationalists to this rebuff was simple and direct. If the Supreme Court would not decide in their favor, they would remove this matter from the Court's jurisdiction. Consequently, the Government's next tactic was to introduce a High Court of Parliament Bill. Its provisions were little short of farcical, if the principles of judicial review mean anything. The bill would have established a committee of Members of Parliament, described as a High Court, to whom an appeal could be taken from the Supreme Court against any decision that an Act of Parliament was null and void! The same bitter controversy continued over this Bill, which of course was adopted by the same partisan majority in both Houses. At once, it was challenged in the courts; and, when the case reached the Supreme Court, all five judges declared unanimously against it (November, 1952).

The next move brought the contestants directly into the political arena. Since the last general election had taken place in 1948, the country was ready for another election in 1953. The question of the voting rights of the Coloured was one of the issues in the campaign, as was the whole policy of *apartheid* and the attitude toward the Constitution. After the balloting, the Nationalists increased their popular votes, receiving a higher percentage than before (though less than 50 percent), and gained a clear majority of the House of Assembly. However, they did not have enough seats to win a majority of two-thirds in a joint session with the Senate.

Thus reinforced politically, the Nationalists returned to the attack. They now conformed to the logic of the Supreme Court and convened a joint session of the Assembly and the Senate. It was their hope that they could detach enough votes from the Opposition to secure a majority of two-thirds. This stratagem failed. On the final vote, the Bill to take the Coloured voters off the common roll was defeated by 122 to 78. Nothing daunted, the Nationalists tried again, and by the same procedure. They reintroduced a new measure which met some of the objections of the United party. But once more, it fell short of a two-thirds majority. At this point (late in 1954) the Nationalist party changed its leader. Malan retired, and was succeeded as Prime Minister by J. G. Strijdom—a man who was still more extreme and had even fewer scruples about constitutional restraints. Strijdom then launched the final assault, employing a tactic which had been threatened in previous stages of the controversy. Thwarted by the existing Court, unable to take appeals out of its hands, and lacking the necessary votes in a joint session, only one way was left. This was to increase the bench of judges and pack the Court with new appointees, and at the same time raise the number of Senators. Both steps were accordingly taken. The Appellate Division of the Supreme Court was expanded from five to eleven, and a new Act laid it down that all eleven must sit on any case that dealt with the constitutionality of a Union statute. Soon afterward, a Senate Bill passed into law by which the membership of that body was raised from forty-eight to eighty-nine, including eighteen who were to be nominated by the government. By these devices, the problem of satisfying the constitutional requirements of the entrenched clauses was now reduced to a mere formality. A joint session was duly held, and over two-thirds of the enlarged Parliament voted in favor of a separate register for the Coloured voters. This Act was contested in the Courts. But in November, 1956, the bench of eleven judges upheld it by a majority of ten to one. Strictly on the basis of law, they could not at this point do anything else. The Nationalists had worked a "numbers' racket," but they had duly observed the procedural forms! Politics had triumphed; the law of the constitution was changed.

The Two Cases Compared

There is much food for thought in a comparison of these two controversies. They exhibit both similarities and contrasts which are equally significant. The major resemblances lie in the outward forms and procedures and the methods adopted in overcoming an institutional deadlock. Except for the differences that the British Liberals had to get around the Crown, whereas the South African Nationalists had to circumvent a Court, the mechanics of the two cases approximate one another closely. The party which held a majority of the seats in the lower House of Parliament was trying to enact into law a principle to which its rivals were strongly opposed. In both cases, there was an appeal to the electorate in the midst of the struggle—two such appeals, in fact, in Great Britain—and the verdict of the voters upheld the Government.

But after that is said, the resemblance ends. In Britain the Liberals were supporting custom against the Conservatives who were breaking it. To reinforce the traditional rule and then make future violations difficult, they changed the law so as to spell out the rules with precision. In South

Africa, the Nationalists were determined to reverse a situation which had the backing both of custom and law. By new legislation they sought to alter vested rights. The most important of all differences, however, is not the question of law or custom or overcoming deadlock between the branches of government. The fundamental distinction between Asquith and Malan resides in the conception of democratic principles and morality. Asquith was seeking an objective whose substance was wholly consonant with the requirements of democracy. He wanted an elective chamber to be paramount over an hereditary one. He wanted the Parliament, as a whole, to reflect the declared will of the popular majority. He would not tolerate a branch of the legislature permanently representing the interests of a privileged class. Hence, his opposition to the Lords and his determination to wring concessions from two reluctant monarchs were fully justified. Without his victory, the evolution of British institutions from oligarchy to democracy would not have been consummated. Nothing of this kind can be said about the objectives or policies or spirit of the Nationalists. This party has been led by a bitter group of frightened men, who hate the English and fear the Africans. They are fanatically determined to use the powers of government, including all its weapons of coercion, to prolong the supremacy of their own race and deny equality to Africans, Indians, and Coloureds. What the Nationalists were trying to accomplish was inherently anti-democratic. Even the appeal to the electorate during the South African controversy does not have the same moral equality as the two British elections of 1910, because the voters in the "Union" are so small a minority of the whole population. Hence there is an unreal, nightmarish, aspect to the debate in South Africa. Arguments were used which sound democratic enough if read by themselves, but acquire a totally different character when they are studied in context. What are we to say about the "sovereignty of Parliament" or the "majority will" in a situation where a small minority of the voters is denying basic human rights to the remainder? The same procedures, the same institutions, can be made to function in opposite ways to yield opposite results.

Actually, recent political history supplies convincing proof that a constitution of the British model is ill-adapted to the circumstances of South Africa. Democracy cannot coexist in that country with the domination of a minority race. As was argued above, the constitution of the United Kingdom exhibits a paradox. Because of its central legal principle of the omnipotence of Parliament, plus the political fact of party discipline, and the absence of institutional checks and balances, the way is potentially open for a majority to establish a totalitarian regime in due legal form. What prevents this happening is neither a legal protection nor a separation of

powers, but a virile political safeguard. The dangerous potentialities of
the British constitution are kept in check by the presence of an active Opposition, buttressed by an alert and vigorous public. The guarantee of
British democracy is the certain knowledge that there are some things the
people will not stand. What these are is never explicitly stated, and quite
obviously they elude precise definition. But the basic point is that Britain
traditionally admires fair play, is allergic to bullies, and always reacts
against abuses of power which affront the ordinary citizen's sense of justice. It is this that makes the powers of the British Parliament safe for
British democracy. But what is true of Britain is not true of another people
whose ethos and traditions are different. In South Africa the constitution
which Britain exported has degenerated into a thin veil for a police state.
For a divided country this was the wrong kind of system. What was
needed there was a set of checks and balances, with such a distribution of
powers that no party temporarily holding a majority of the seats in Parliament could have done what the Nationalists succeeded in doing after
1948. There is no "general will" in South Africa at present; there is no
popular consensus; in fact, there is no union. Hence there is no democracy.
The "best" kind of constitution for such conditions is that which leaves
the government too weak to do much evil.

Political Evolution of the American Constitution

The reference to checks and balances will, of course, bring to mind the
Constitution of the United States. How should the constitution of the
largest western democracy be interpreted? What version of democracy
does it incorporate? Along what lines has it evolved? The obvious and immediate answer to these questions is that the American Republic, after an
unsuccessful experiment with a league that was too loosely structured,
adopted "a more perfect union" whose principles form a democracy of a
special kind with institutions designed in opposite fashion to those of
Britain. The essential difference is this. The English revolution ended
with the supremacy of Parliament; the American revolution, with the
supremacy of the Constitution. The victors of England's civil war established a regime which would be strong enough to govern effectively, while
respecting the rights of individuals. In the United States, the work of the
founding fathers was designed to protect individual rights, while providing the national services through which the states could coexist and multiply. The circumstances, as well as the doctrines, of the American Revolution tended to make all government suspect. Hence the less of it, the

better; and what there was should be distributed in safe amounts. This was accomplished by separating level from level (federal, state, and local) and branch from branch (legislative, executive, and judicial). Purposely arranged as an obstacle to tyranny, this system of dispersion made positive action of any kind difficult—except in the sphere of foreign relations where the President could exercise rather more discretion.

Such a Constitution, conceived under the notion of an antithesis between individual freedom and governmental power and with a bias toward the former, was naturally adapted to the physical conditions of North America in the first half of the nineteenth century. Its distance from Europe and Asia, and the start of friendly relations with Great Britain, made the United States secure. From the Atlantic to the Pacific there lay a continent to be peopled, resources to be put to work, an empire to be won. With such abundance at human disposal, individual energies were adequate to the task with a minimum of direction and assistance by government. When people crossed an ocean, plunged inland into a wilderness, then founded settlements in a territory where they had no roots, what held them together and recreated the bonds of society was the memory of the culture they had left which they carried within themselves, plus the need to survive on a frontier which was hostile and, as yet, untamed. The somewhat loose articulation of the American constitutional system served its purpose by providing the minimal framework which was necessary and leaving it to individuals to make and take the rest by their own initiative.

Seven decades after it was inaugurated, the Constitution broke down, while the two sections of the country fought a long and bitter Civil War. Had there been a sufficient political will to resolve the slavery issue, the mechanisms of the Constitution would have been adequate for the task. Either by Act of Congress or by judicial decision or by constitutional amendment, a way could have been found to abolish slavery. The South, however, was not disposed to surrender its economic interest in its "peculiar institution" and refused consent to major innovations which would work to its disadvantage. As long as the newly admitted States could be divided, more or less equally, between slave-holding and "free soil,"[37] North and South could coexist within the framework of an unstable equilibrium. But when all the area in the southwest available for the extension of the Cotton Kingdom had been occupied and the remainder of the West lay open for settlement primarily by northerners, southern attitudes became rigid and intransigent. No cause in politics arouses such

37. This meant equal voting power for the southerners in the Senate.

fanaticism as a losing one. The cleavage in society over what was essentially a moral question produced a political impasse and with it a retreat from constitutionalism to arms. When the shooting ended, and the victors spelled out the results, the Missouri Compromise and *Dred Scott* were replaced by a trio of Amendments and *Texas v. White.*

In the aftermath of fratricidal bloodshed came a new birth of nationalism, a psychological change with political consequences. The potent forces of mechanization and Americanization transformed the social context which the framework of government was called upon to serve. Understandably, therefore, the dynamics of the constitutional system during the last six decades have consisted in a push and pull between functions and structure. The needs of the space age are not easily satisfied by a machinery whose basic pattern was designed before the age of steam. The principle which requires three separate, and theoretically co-ordinate, branches is less suited to the alarums and excursions of the twentieth-century politics than it was to the slower tempo of seventeen decades ago. Indeed, by virtue of its plan and processes the American Constitution sometimes make inaction easier than action. It places a premium on opposition by multiplying the opportunities for delay. It allows the rival parties simultaneously to control the different branches of government whose co-operation is the condition of political success. Despite these obstacles, marvels have been accomplished in adapting American democracy to the imperatives of modernity. But much time and ingenuity must be expended continually on circumventing the blocks which the institutional structure creates.[38]

There is a genuine sense in which the conception of the Constitution held by Jefferson and Madison is still relevant for containing a conglomerate of persons, interests, and groups. The frame is large and loose-limbed, as befits a giant. There are many minorities in so big a nation, which need protection of different kinds from different threats. Majorities are variously reconstituted as issues change. For all this the Constitution in its traditional format makes due provision. But the Hamiltonian concept has acquired increasing relevance with the lapse of time and the circumstances of growth. Since 1932, the themes of national direction and executive vigor, of big government and broadening responsibilities, have been heard and heard again, and the Constitution of the contemporary United States must therefore function with a different political climate. With the single exception of race relations (an important exception, I grant) the American people are now more fundamentally at one than in any other decade

38. I shall have more to say on this topic in Chapters 14 and 15, where the legislature and executive are discussed.

of the last twelve. Hence the national, centralizing aspects of the Constitution can be developed at the expense of those which are local and individualist. Indeed, this growth of a greater sense of common identity has been largely stimulated by the political use of the powers of the federal government. These were the powers which saved the Union when threatened by secession, and abolished slavery. These same powers converted a Babel of alien immigrants into a people of English-speaking American citizens. The same powers narrowed the widening gulf between wealth and poverty and laid the national foundations of social and economic justice. The same powers are once more being used to eliminate discrimination against any individual on grounds of race, and eventually they will win that struggle. All these are instances of society being unified by the political process, of the state creating a community. The Jeffersonian goal of the dignity and freedom of the individual will in large measure have been furthered by Hamiltonian means.

France's Perpetual Revolution

There is an unhappy contrast between the constitutional experience of the United States since 1789 and that of France. Only one crisis has struck the United States during this period with a vehemence sufficient to wreck the Constitution, but that danger was fortunately averted. In fact, the failure of the attempt to secede resulted in the subsequent removal of some imperfections in a far from perfect union. The vicissitudes of France are the more distressing because even now finality has not been achieved, nor is it yet in sight. Let us first be clear that the statistics in a chronological table of French regimes can be misleading, or at any rate their interpretation can be exaggerated. Three of the constitutions of France were discarded because the country was defeated in war (1815, 1870-71, 1940). Two of these were the Napoleonic Empires, involving a species of personal power which in the nature of the case cannot be transferred or transmitted. The other was an unglamorous parliamentary regime, being Number Three in the republican series. It had survived the early monarchist maneuvers and Boulanger, the Dreyfus affair and the Panama scandal, World War I and the depression of the early 1930's. But it could not defend itself against Hitler. For the rest, the substituting of one constitution for another has resulted from dissensions which were primarily domestic in source and character (1830, 1848, 1851, 1958).

The trouble is that the French have never succeeded in finishing the revolution they began in 1789. What is the reason for this? It would be easy to repeat the trite statement that the French lack a consensus. But what does this mean? It is only another way of summarizing the whole historical development since 1789, and generalizing from the facts that many constitutions have been tried of which none has outlasted two generations. To say that France has not arrived at a consensus adds nothing. Obviously there is no consensus. To affirm that none exists does not provide the known data with a cause. The statement is merely a tautologous use of the same facts to explain themselves. Nor does it help to attribute the continual French searchings for a constitution to the loss of legitimacy. This concept, too, has a breadth and generality which conveys the appearance of explanation. But is it a relevant description of the historical circumstances? On this point, suppose we compare France with Britain. The English revolution was followed by a republican commonwealth over which the autocratic Cromwell presided. Since that system could only last his lifetime, the Crown was brought back to Westminster—as was Parliament—and the two learned to coexist. If the British case is taken as proof that legitimacy was restored, how does one account for the failure of the French to do the same? The fact is that France definitely tried between 1815 and 1830 to do something analogous to what England had done from 1660 to 1688. A Bourbon king reoccupied the throne, as the Stuarts, a century and a half earlier, returned to London. True, the Bourbons were ousted in 1830—but so were the Stuarts in 1688. France nevertheless clung to the legitimist tradition and still preserved its crown. As the English transferred the royal functions to William and Mary, so the French accepted the House of Orleans in the person of Louis Philippe—who proceeded to struggle with ministers and legislatures as did King William and Queen Anne with theirs.[39] The *mystique* of monarchy was given a new trial in France for a whole generation, 1815-1848, as it was in England after 1660. The concept of legitimacy, by itself, is too mechanical a formula to serve as an explanation. Why did it work its presumed magic in London and not in Paris? And, equally important, why was it not needed in the United States? Why did the American Revolution dispense with a

39. Besides the similarities, mentioned above, there are differences between the course of events in England and France. The French Revolution was a deeper social upheaval than the English, and Napoleon's Empire left the nostalgic memory of a period of military glory to which latter-day Bonapartists could revert. Nevertheless, the analogies between France and England (1815-48, 1661-88) are close. In particular, there were French political groups in 1830 which were strongly conscious of the resemblance between their act in substituting the Orleanists for the Bourbons and the English ouster of James II in favor of William and Mary. Students of causation will note that this appears to be an instance of similar "causes" not producing the same "consequences."

monarchy and proceed satisfactorily under a republican form of govern-
ment? Was not legitimacy also desirable in the United States? And if the
Americans and the Swiss could make a republic work, why could the
French not?

The case of France, I readily admit, is a puzzle. The facts are clear,
but their explanation is obscure. Presumably, however, the inability of the
modern French to produce an enduring regime must be ascribed to a
cause or causes which are absent in the successful democracies or, if present there, exist in a much smaller degree. The truth is that ever since 1789
authoritarian tendencies and democratic tendencies have been in conflict
in French politics and society. This has happened, of course, in other political systems[40] where the latter have triumphed over the former. But in
France the authoritarian profile was strengthened by two prominent features. This is a Latin and a Catholic country, and, being geographically
part of the Continent, it has depended on its army. Neither of these factors was an aid to democracy, as was proven in the nineteenth century and
by some episodes in the twentieth.

It is a fact that the traditional combination of the Latin culture with
the Roman Church did not provide a context favorable to democratic
growth.[41] None of the major Latin countries of Europe has yet produced a
successful democratic regime. Even now, when this is being written, Spain
and Portugal are still being misgoverned by a pair of senile Fascist dictators, France is ruled by an intelligent autocrat, and Italy after two decades
of Fascism is making a fresh attempt at democracy on which a judgment
would be premature. From the democratic standpoint, the record, over
all, is not impressive. Certainly, it does not bear comparison with that of
the English-speaking countries and northern Europe. There is something
in the union of the Roman Church and the Latin culture which has militated against democracy. Both have served as custodians of the tradition
derived from ancient Rome in which liberty (*libertas*), law (*lex*) and republic (*respublica*), became subordinate to authority (*auctoritas*), order
(*ordo*), and empire (*imperium*). The educational system implanted these
ideas in each successive generation; and the structure of the Church,
emphasizing the power of the priesthood and using Latin in its services,
prevented control by the congregation. The result of this blend was to
perpetuate the dominance of an elite, composed of aristocrats in society,
oligarchy in politics, and hierarchy in religion.

40. Think of the survival, for instance, of what the British call "the Establishment."
41. It would not be correct, however, to generalize that Catholicism and democracy,
as such, are inimical. In Switzerland, for example, the origins of democracy are associated with the central, German-speaking, Catholic cantons.

Naturally such a system generated its rebels, as the emphasis on authority will always do. It would be quite wrong to conceive of the Latin countries as being peopled only by rulers and subjects. On the contrary, one cannot fail to be impressed with the evidences of vigorous individualism. Outstanding individuals who think for themselves and do not conform to authority have been prominent in the history of the Latin world. Many scholars who analyze these countries (e.g. Siegfried on France, Salvemini on Italy, Madariaga on Spain) have stressed, and themselves exemplify, the admirable individualistic traits of their citizens. Here then would seem to be a paradox. How does this individualism coexist with authoritarianism? The answer is that the one feeds the other and each, in reaction against its opposite, runs to excess. But it is noteworthy that the individualism of Latin Europe has yielded most fruitful results in the arts, in literature and philosophy—in the spheres which call for imagination and intuition as well as intellect, and where the individual works best alone and must create on his own. The same genius has not been applied with similar success to the constructive tasks of social co-operation. Latin individuality, in fact, has produced in politics more discord than community. When the outstanding individual applies his talents to the work of government, he frequently operates as an authoritarian. France has its Bonapartes and de Gaulles. It has lacked the Churchills and Roosevelts. The genuine abilities of a Mussolini in another context might have developed into those of a democratic leader. In the turmoil of post-1918 Italy, they ran to seed in Caesarism.

The second factor contributing to the same conclusion, and fortifying it, is the historic dependence of the French state on its army for protection. The implications of this fact were discussed earlier.[42] Here it suffices to note that the importance of the army created an additional obstacle to supporters of republicanism, and was a stumbling block in the way of co-operation between Right and Left. Ideologically, the army has reinforced the authoritarian tendencies in French culture. Socially, its officers have been more identified with the upper class. Politically, its weight was normally thrown to the conservative side. Taken together, army and Church are corroborative examples of the point that, when French talents are applied to large-scale organization, they find an authoritarian system more congenial. In politics, therefore, the pendulum swings between the two opposites. The individualism which is creative in the arts becomes destructive in government. It degenerates into the disorder of the Third and Fourth Republics. Disgusted, and with a sense of relief, people then turn

42. See Chapter 7, pp. 179-80.

to the Bonapartes and de Gaulles, supporting or accepting the hero for so long as his energies bring success. They abandon their quest for the General Will, and accommodate themselves to the Will of the General.

When the French problem is judged in these terms, the discussion of institutions, though not irrelevant, is relegated to secondary importance. Much ingenuity has been devoted to debating the rival merits of a parliamentary or presidential system and its efficacy under French conditions. But the argument over structure misses the point. Either system could be made to work if the party politics were less chaotic than heretofore, and that situation will not be remedied until the French acquire the habit of co-operating in big organizations without surrendering to the alternatives of authoritarianism or instability. The Fifth Republic, which is the one currently in vogue, is not a solution, but a breathing-spell. Its constitution was tailored, like a suit of clothes, to fit one tall man. No other person, now known in public life, could wear that suit or would be allowed to, although some hopefuls might wish to try it on for size. When de Gaulle departs or dies, his personal power will have to be transferred to a party system if democracy is to survive in France. But since his ascendancy has broken the old parties, and has not yet replaced them by new ones,[43] the political foundations of future stability have not been laid.

The Control and Transfer of Power

In contrast with the successful democracies, the French have not been able thus far to subject the transfer of power within society to an orderly and acceptable system. That is why, whenever deep-seated changes are due in policy and personnel, they are likely to throw out the constitution with the government; and, when they are defeated in a major war, their institutions are too discredited to survive. A society at peace with itself has attained the political maturity of tolerating the periodic shifts of power from side to side. When men were ruled by kings, or wherever nowadays an autocrat or dictatorial junta holds sway, it may appear that power is momentarily consolidated and internal opposition silenced. But there is a nightmare which haunts all such regimes, the anticipation of the day when monarch or dictator is incapacitated or dies or when a split develops within the ruling clique. On such occasions, can power be transferred to new hands without convulsions in the state and society?

To solve that problem, the monarchies employed the hereditary prin-

43. The Gaullists of the Fifth Republic (the U.N.R.) are camp followers of the General, not a party, and have no meaning without him.

ciple. This had no other possible justification, since it is an indefensible absurdity for a single family to reign continuously over a community. But if it was known that the eldest son or daughter would succeed to the throne, struggles between rival claimants could normally be eliminated. Likewise, a self-perpetuating oligarchy, such as the merchants of Venice, was able annually to elect the Doge from their own circle and could safely permit rotation of their leading office. In contemporary states, where a ruler or ruling group has taken power through revolution, the risk of internal bloodshed—and even the threat to external security—is always severe whenever the leaders or basic policies are changed. One may recall in this connection how long it took for Stalin to capture control after Lenin died and for Khrushchev to establish his ascendancy after Stalin's despotism.

The democratic states, however, have solved this problem by concealing a revolution in the interstices of procedure. In Washington or London, in Berne or Copenhagen, one never needs to speculate on the possibility of sudden *coup d'état*, because changes of government and of the constitution itself have been made to conform to a body of rules on which there is widespread agreement. While this conveys the appearance of being a triumph of law and is frequently so described, fundamentally it is a triumph for politics. By now, we have grown accustomed to the system of nominations, campaigns, and elections; we take it for granted that competing parties will share in ruling and being ruled; and we expect the losers to accept defeat with the best grace they can muster, knowing their turn will come later. Actually, as the record proves, no principle of democratic politics was more original in conception or more daring in operation than that of the loyal opposition.

These are achievements whose profundity is perhaps belied by the seeming simplicity with which we now practice them. Thus, in the United States, the replacement of Democrats by Republicans in 1953 and the return of the former to office in 1961, was conducted with a smoothness which is all the more remarkable in the light of the size and complexity of the American government. Likewise, in the tragic circumstances of November, 1963, a world that was shocked at the horror of a presidential assassination also observed how speedily and skillfully the Vice-President grasped the reins of government. What would have happened, one may ask, had the head of the Russian government been slain, or of the Chinese? Are there comparable shock-absorbers built in to the machinery of authoritarian regimes?

To conclude, this discussion of constitutions has not attempted to cover every aspect of the topic because this book is primarily concerned with understanding and clarifying the nature of democracy, and to this broad subject much of the mechanics of how a particular constitution operates is not directly revelant. A democracy must provide a constitution that guarantees a fair chance to all its citizens, and, having done this, it can safely guarantee the orderly exercise and transfer of power. These are two fundamental conditions which must be met. Beyond them, there is no single pattern to which the constitution must conform. One discovers, in the smaller countries, that such dissimilar institutions as those of Denmark and Switzerland contribute equally to democracy; and the same can be said for larger units as the United States and the United Kingdom. However, while different structural designs can be equally democratic, this does not mean that they are equally appropriate for dissimilar conditions. It is self-evident that the Swiss would not want to adopt the Danish constitution, or vice versa. The former have evolved a system which respects their historic particularism and toleration of diversities. It is replete with institutional checks and popular safeguards, as befits a slow-moving nation which is perennially suspicious of its officials. The Danes, being fundamentally at one, like the British, have streamlined and simplified their institutions; for their protection against the abuse of power they rely upon their sense of decency and justice and the freedoms of responsible criticism and publicity. Where such qualities exist, the powers which look formidable on paper will be applied with proper restraint in practice. The United States at the beginnings of its independent history needed arrangements which would allow for sectional diversity and give free play to local initiative. Nowadays, the effects of nationalism, of centralization, of majority power and external pressures, are more strongly felt than they could have been in any decade before this century.

The old argument on behalf of the "mixed" constitution, like the Madisonian conception of a government whose agencies are balanced in delicate equilibrium, has less and less validity for a developed democracy in the second half of the twentieth century. But such principles are by no means outmoded or inappropriate elsewhere. In a politically underdeveloped country, or wherever the transition from oligarchy to democracy has not been completed, one shudders at the possibilities of introducing powers which it has taken others several centuries to learn to use with safety. In South Africa or the Congo, in Haiti or South Vietnam, as presently composed, one only stages a farce by writing a script for actors who read the letter and do not understand the meaning. No constitution can rise above the level of achievement of its citizens. No institutions can save a nation from itself. The spirit of the laws, as Montesquieu discerned, consists in the character of the people they serve.

14

Representative Chambers

The study of legislatures abounds with paradox. Of all branches of government, this is the one which in a democracy occupies the pride of place.
When the expansion in area and population had made it impossible for
the people to assemble in person and themselves determine policy, the
legislature, in terms of democratic principle, became the pivotal agency of
state since its task was to represent the people. Hence there is a long and
respectable tradition in democratic thought which gives the priority
among political institutions to the legislature. Locke considered it the supreme organ of state.[1] The Constitution of the United States lists the
Congress first when establishing the three branches. Mill likewise asserted
the primacy of the representative chamber.[2] The function of a legislature
is to stand for the whole people and speak in their name.

High in Importance, Low in Reputation

Admittedly, that is the statement of an ideal. But it is all the more important for that reason because our avowed ideals are intended as goals to
which our practice should be directed. Moreover, the ideal is not an unattainable utopia. On the contrary, it is grounded in hard political fact. Let
us contrast the components of the legislature with those of the other
branches. The judiciary in a democratic state is deliberately placed apart
from the political process and judges are granted security of tenure to help

1. *Second Treatise of Civil Government*, Chap. X-XI.
2. *Representative Government*, Chap. V.

435

immunize them from the temptations of partisanship and power. The executive, including in this the conception of political leadership,[3] is necessarily controlled by those who for the time being enjoy the support of a majority. The minority party is not represented in the White House, nor does Her Majesty's Opposition have offices in 10 Downing Street. But the legislature is differently conceived from other branches and therefore is differently organized. Its political purpose is basic and unique. This is the one institution which exists as a forum where government and opposition, power and criticism, confront one another continuously and in public. The legislature has seats for the minority, or minorities, as well as the majority, for the Outs as well as the Ins, and from these seats all parties can stand up and give voice. The Congress, Assembly, Ting, or Moot—the place where people come together—is also the Parliament or Agora—the place where people speak both for and against.

Hence the legislature is the crucial institution which distinguishes a democracy from a dictatorship. That form of government which does not tolerate opposition and which prohibits public criticism cannot allow a legislature to function with true independence. If any such body exists at all, it performs the role of a subordinate, deliberating council or of a periodic rally for the adherents of the dominant clique. Witness the Supreme Soviet in the U.S.S.R., the Reichstag under Hitler, the Cortes under Franco.

Nevertheless when all is said that needs saying about the primacy of the legislature, such assertions confront a serious and unpleasant truth. Although its functions, if properly carried out, are of an importance second to none, in most democracies the legislature is not highly regarded. In some it is the object of continuous ridicule. A belief prevails in public opinion that the legislature has adapted itself to the circumstances of the twentieth century less successfully than the judicial or executive branches. The most acute example is that of France, whose *Chambre de Députés* had little prestige under the Third Republic and whose *Assemblée Nationale* fell into similar disrepute under the Fourth. In no small measure, the French people attributed the weakness of their country in 1940 to the inadequacies of *la République des Députés*. General de Gaulle achieved his position of one-man rule in 1958 because the public was again tired and disgusted at the inability of the parliamentarians to sustain a government. The French case is, admittedly, the extreme one. But unhappily, it is highly relevant because this is a country which figures so prominently in the democratic tradition and has contributed brilliantly to the formulation

3. This topic forms the subject of the next chapter.

of democratic ideals, but whose experiments with democratic institutions have never worked effectively. In varying degrees, one must acknowledge the fact that legislatures elsewhere have failed to retain the public confidence to which the hierarchy of democratic values entitles them. The United States Congress, as an institution, has a much lower place in public esteem than either the Presidency or the Supreme Court. The two latter have responded to the needs of modernity with more evidence of statesmanship than is normally displayed in the Capitol. I state this as a personal judgment and wish the facts were otherwise, but I believe this view to be widely shared. The same can be said of Westminster as of Washington, though with the difference that Parliament's prestige in Britain has not declined relatively by as much as that of Congress in the United States. But though Parliament today may have more to commend it than Congress, its present standing does not compare favorably with the position it occupied in the two generations from Peel to Asquith. Has the "Mother of Parliaments" grown and over-ripened to the stage of grandmotherly superannuation?

These doubts must be squarely faced, for they raise questions which demand some answer. The generality of the phenomenon—for it holds true in most of the smaller democracies as well as the larger—is one of its most disturbing aspects, and perhaps provides some clues for diagnosis. At any rate, the discussion of the representative chamber commences with this paradox: the institution whose functions are central and crucial to democracy is not adapting itself with notable success and commands less public respect than it should enjoy. Here therefore is a contradiction between need and performance, which requires a scrutiny. How is this result manifested? What are the circumstances which have brought it about? Can a remedy be found?

In order to understand the nature of the problem, I shall try in this chapter to explore the following topics: First, the principle of representation and its effects on the composition of legislature; next, the internal structure of the legislative body, in particular the number of chambers; third, the influence of the party system on legislative groupings; and lastly, the functions of the legislature.

The Medieval Parliaments

Institutions and ideas which survive historically have a way of growing beyond their origins. In the course of development, although a retrospective view can see the continuity from step to step, a later stage may acquire a character which differs from the beginning. Frequently, the form which an institution attains, and the functions it comes to conduct, are not produced by design or intent, but in the casual manner of accident or expedient. Hence the rationale which may serve in one age to justify an institution can be a far cry from earlier notions of its use or purposes. I am saying this because, in reflecting on representative chambers in the modern democracy, one is cognizant both of their long evolution and of their having been founded in a period whose spirit and ideas were anything but democratic. As a matter of fact, the institution of a Parliament is one of the two great legacies which we owe to the Middle Ages[4]—the other being the university. The need from which a Parliament arose was political. In order to carry out major policies, somebody needed to mobilize support. Hence a meeting was summoned. This was done by Simon de Montfort in 1265 when he was rallying the barons. This was what Edward I did because of his financial necessities. In ensuing centuries, Parliaments met at the summons of the King to give him backing. But those who convened might have other ideas than his and could reinforce one another in assembly. Thus Parliament could grow apart from the King and assert a will of its own. Therein lay its potentiality. Therefrom flows its history.

The summoning of a Parliament required some basic decisions. The most important involved the principle of selection. Who were to be invited—or commanded—to come? How were they to be chosen? Whom, or what, were they supposed to represent? Some large issues are raised in these queries, and they have been the subject of long debates which are not ended yet. In modern democratic theory, representation is considered a privilege or a right. But it was not so regarded in the pre-democratic beginnings. Then it was a duty, and one which frequently was onerous and dangerous.[5] A locality might not wish to pay the expense of sending one of its residents to the distant capital, and the person chosen might prefer to avoid so dubious an honor. There were physical hazards in traveling to

4. There has been some controversy among English historians as to whether the medieval Parliament was a direct lineal descendant of the Anglo-Saxon councils, or whether it was something new. The weight of evidence inclines to the latter view, although some of the same purposes were served by both bodies.

5. "Representation was not the offspring of democratic theory, but an incident of the feudal system. . . . The boon of representation is not in election to serve, but in the licence to stay away; it consists in the immunity obtained through the vicarious service of others, and centuries elapse before the service becomes a privilege and the burden an object of envy and a source of pride. In the twelfth and thirteenth centuries the difficulty is to enforce the attendance of representatives. . ." A. F. Pollard, The Evolution of Parliament (Longmans, Green & Co.: London, 1920), p. 109.

and fro, and political risks for any who incurred the King's displeasure or that of a powerful neighbor. It is, in short, to this odd combination of contradictions that the modern democratic state owes the genesis of its central political practice—the election of representatives and their meeting in a national legislature. Neither the institution of Parliament nor the principle of representation, as originally conceived, was designed to work out the way it did. Democracy's central institution is the paradoxical latter-day outcome of non-democratic circumstances.

According to our ideal conception of democracy the legislature is a representative body. But what is it to represent? One may say that it represents "the country," "the nation," "the people," that it is a small-scale sample of the whole, and so on. Such generalities, however, are devoid of specific content. The macrocosm consists of parts. Should they be reproduced in the microcosm? If so, how exactly and in what proportions? And which parts are significant and deserve the representation?

Early Schemes of Representation

A survey of the systems which have actually been used will show at least six ways of answering such questions. Three of these belong to the medieval beginnings. A King who needed to organize his support and raise money had to turn to those who were influential and wealthy. Naturally, therefore, he would invite the nobility and the clergy. Beyond these, how widely should representation extend and how far down the pyramid of feudal society should it descend? The practical solution to this problem was to bring to the capital those who were prominent in their localities— on the assumption that they spoke for the remainder of the population and in the hope that they could commit "the folks back home" to decisions taken at the center. Such, at any rate, seem to have been the ideas in the mind of King Edward I when he convoked what has been called the "Model" Parliament of 1295, and instructed the sheriffs to arrange for the election of two knights from every shire, two citizens from every city, and two burgesses from every borough.

In the medieval genesis of Parliament, and in the early growth of this body and similar ones on the continent of Europe, one may observe a clear illustration of the analysis applied to the subject of democracy in this book. Here is an institution which is organized to meet a political need. It draws its content, inevitably, from the character of its society. Yet the form and rationale embody principles which become a basis for discussion and develop a logic to govern future action. In the England and

France of the fourteenth century, certain distinct and different ideas can be detected whose influence can still be felt today. There is first the notion that major occupational groups, performing important functions, should be represented in the government. Thus Maitland described the Edwardian Parliament as comprising those who pray, those who fight, and those who work.[6] A second notion starts with the fact that society is organized as a hierarchy with layers or levels superimposed from the top to bottom. The legislature then, to accord with reality, should represent each major stratum. With rough simplicity, and for convenience, these can be reduced at least to three: upper, middle, and lower. Or again, it is realistic and sensible to recognize that a kingdom or a large country is subdivided into localities, each possessing an identity and organized in some appropriate fashion. Hence corporate communities can be represented, these being composed of persons who live fairly close together and belong to the same social and economic aggregate. A county, a city, a medium-sized town, fits this description.

These three notions—the representation of functional groups, or social strata, or corporate communities—can be treated analytically as separate. But when applied historically to an actual people, they are bound to merge or overlap; and the institutions which embody such concepts will rather display the compounds of practical need than the precision of philosophic categories. A group may be differentiated by the occupation of its members, which is an observable fact; but occupations can be classified as higher or lower according to the opinions prevailing in the society. Also within each group there may be a hierarchy of position and power. One can distinguish the higher nobility from the lesser; the cardinals, archbishops, and bishops, from the ordinary priests; the rich landowners from those with modest holdings. Edward I, for instance, ordered his archbishops and bishops to bring to his assembly "the heads of their cathedral chapters, their archdeacons, one proctor for the clergy of each cathedral, and two proctors for the clergy of each diocese."[7] Only the highest of these, however, (i.e., the archbishops and bishops) were subsequently included in the permanent membership of the Parliament, and the Church developed its own representative Convocation for deliberating on internal matters. The title of the House of Commons has two connotations, of which the later one was not the original intention. In a social order dominated by an aristocracy, the "Commons" suggested a popular chamber belonging to the commoners, i.e., to those who by definition were excluded from the peerage. But the medieval idea was to represent the

6. Cited by C. P. Ilbert, *Parliament* (Holt & Co.: New York, rev. ed. 1913), p. 13.
7. C. P. Ilbert, *Parliament, loc. cit.*

communes (*communitates*) through which the King's government was conducted locally. These were considered, perhaps arbitrarily, as equal units. Hence the Edwardian summons to two knights, citizens and burgesses, from each borough, city, and shire.

On the Continent, notably in France, the conception which took shape and acquired a structural form was that of the estate. The kingdom was thought to be composed of estates which the King should consult. This term is primarily associated, of course, with the related idea of status and connoted a stratum of a hierarchy. But at the same time, because a status implied responsibilities and rights, the members of an estate were performing a function for society, of which their rank was the consequence. Out of all this the French developed their three estates: *noblesse, clergé,* and *bourgeoisie.* The last of these, famous later as the "Third," consisted originally of the richer merchants only who, as *bourgeois,* enjoyed full civic rights in the urban oligarchy.[8]

Apart from their historical significance, are these notions of representation in any way relevant to a modern democracy? Are they still of some use, or have they been superseded along with their feudal associations?

In the case of one concept there can be no possible doubt. To make representation correspond to social strata—i.e., to inequalities of rank and status—is inherently anti-democratic. It was against the privileged position of the nobility and clergy that the democratic revolutions were, in part, directed. The less stratified a society, the more democratic it is. In a democratic state the power of politics should be used, not to reproduce and strengthen the forces of social inequality, but to counteract and minimize them.

The second notion which conceives of representation in functional terms has something, *prima facie,* to commend it. The occupations through which we earn our livelihood constitute a valid interest for each of us individually, and the services thus performed create, we hope, some social benefit. In principle, there is no reason why democracy, as such, should not accord representation along the lines of occupational groupings. Actually, this doctrine enjoyed a certain vogue in the early decades of the present century. It was revived in England by G. D. H. Cole, whose theory of guild socialism bore evident traces of its debt to the medieval world. The Webbs also were attracted to its possibilities, and thought of a Parliament or Congress reconstituted from districts into industries. In practice, however, no democratic legislature ever was constructed on this

8. Charles Seignobos, *Histoire Sincère de la Nation Française* (Presses Universitaires de France: Paris, 1946), p. 147. André Maurois, *Histoire de la France* (Éditions de la Maison Française: New York, 1947), Vol. 1, p. 144.

basis, because of a strong argument against it. Everyone would agree that economic interests tend to bring out the utmost of egoism and selfishness in each of us. Organized groups of this character—consider the record and viewpoint of associations of businessmen, trade unionists, and farmers— are not in the habit of subordinating their narrow aims to the public good. There is no reason to believe (in fact, there is good reason not to believe) that a functional Parliament would care for the general welfare any better than is done under present arrangements.

Next, there is the idea that local communities should be represented in a central legislature in their organized, corporate capacity. Theoretically, this sounds sensible and actually it did make sense in earlier centuries when much of men's lives was concentrated on the locality. When populations were small and communications poor, the town or rural region created a feeling of community which was genuine enough. Today this is no longer true. Indeed, psychological propinquity nowadays may be in reverse order from physical proximity. Though living in California, I personally feel closest to Washington (because of the interest and importance of what happens there), next to Sacramento, and furthest from the doings of the local city hall. Moreover, since our contemporary society is so highly urbanized, and many cities are so large in themselves or belong to enormous metropolitan clusters, the local "community" has changed into an intricate and overlapping complex of subcommunities. Countless individuals live in one city and work in another. The simple idea of having "communes" represented at the center belongs to a bygone age. It does not fit the present-day facts.

Representing a Modern Society

There are still other aspects of society, however, which can be selected as the basis of representation. When a country is inhabited by peoples of different race, religion, and language, they can be classified according to these various characteristics and be grouped accordingly for purposes of voting and legislative representation. Such an arrangement gives frank recognition to the significance of these factors and admits that they are the primary ones to be considered in the exercise of citizenship. This explicit separation by virtue of language, religion, or race has been employed in certain polyethnic societies as a transitional device for introducing democratic institutions. For instance, the Lebanese, who are divided into Muslims and Christians, have used this system. It was also one of the methods employed in India by the British government because of the religious susceptibilities of Hindus and Muslims. The Colonial Office, too, repeatedly experimented with this system in its African territories. All one need say of it is that it has never been favored in any of the successful democracies. Its results tend to keep peoples divided instead of unifying them as a people. It accentuates, instead of softening, the divisive influences which race, religion, and language can exert on men's minds and loyalties.

Yet another basis for representation is area. Granted the fact that the state wields its jurisdiction over a finite portion of the Earth's surface, it may be deduced that the government is that of the territory and of all the human beings—citizens and non-citizens alike—who happen to reside there. Thus land can claim its representation and the legislature will be a map of regions and districts. The implications of this argument are clear to see. It always has strong adherents in countries where a great deal of land is owned by a few, for the power of the big landowners will be prolonged if the legislature represents their latifundia. In such cases there is a direct antithesis between democracy and the political and economic self-interest of an oligarchy. Elsewhere, however, the recognition of area as a basis for representation can mean something different. Indeed, under certain conditions it can even be justified in the name of democracy. These conditions are worth considering, since they do raise an important issue.

That issue can best be stated by referring to the ultimate of all methods of representation. It is the system of having a legislature which represents a people strictly on the numerical basis of population. In nineteenth-century Britain, when the Liberals argued for this principle, they called it representation by population, which was abbreviated in discussion to "rep. by pop." Parliamentary seats, they said, should not be assigned on the basis of land, wealth, communities, or tradition. The whole population should be included in the count, and every person should count for one. Electoral districts should contain, as nearly as possible, an equal number of people. Each district should then be assigned one member in the Commons. The result would be a House that reflected the nation in miniature. Democracy would thus rest on its proper foundation—the equal worth of all its individual members. From the standpoint of democracy, there is no denying the general validity of this principle. The individual citizen is certainly the unit with whom democratic politics begin and end. If citizens are to be treated equally in the determination of their fundamental rights, there is no other way to distribute representation than on the basis of numbers. This criterion, then, may be accepted as the standard, any exception to which should be justified by special arguments pertinent in the particular case. What are the deviations from the norm which occur in practice? And is there any which can be reconciled with democratic requirements?

Certain of the objections to the principle just stated, and some of the actual departures from it, can be dismissed or discounted on the ground that they are irrelevant or antithetical to democracy. Thus, a Conservative who argued in Britain in 1830 that Old Sarum should continue to be represented, while he was unconcerned if no members sat for Leeds or Birmingham, was either placing a nostalgic regard for tradition above the needs of the present or he was crudely asserting the political self-interest of a declining rural minority. For democracy to triumph, his viewpoint had to succumb. Similarly in the 1960's, wherever the boundaries of legislative districts are deliberately misdrawn in such a way as to make the votes of citizens count unequally toward the result, this "gerrymandering" must be condemned as the offense against democracy which it is. Unfortunately this is an all too common practice, especially in State legislatures in the United States, some of which habitually cheat their own citizens for partisan advantage.

Apart from indefensible practices of this sort, there are certain arguments against basing representation solely on numbers which merit a serious hearing. Ideally, representation must be fair. But how is fairness, a quality, translated into figures, a quantity? It is a fact that population, seen geographically, is not evenly distributed. In particular, people are densely concentrated in cities and spread thinly in rural areas. The urban concentration confers certain political advantages, because proximity makes organization easier. Campaigning is simpler in a city; candidates can reach their constituents; the latter can make their collective wishes known. Farmers are usually fearful and suspicious of the power of urban masses and their influence on the policy of governments. They believe— sometimes with justice—that as between rural and urban districts the unqualified recognition of numbers does not make for equal conditions. This attitude is especially strong in countries where agriculture or the pastoral industry is important to the national economy (e.g., because its products bulk large in exports), but the percentage of persons engaged in such occupations is a minority. Then the farmers are likely to demand a disproportionate share in representation on the ground that national living standards depend so heavily on what they produce. But, over and above this special case of politics conceding to economics, there are the well-nigh universal sentiments of difference and distinctness which exist between city and country, the capital and the provinces, the center of power and outlying regions. All this can be illustrated by examples everywhere. The feeling that results is based on physical separation, fortified by economic and sociological divergences. That it exists genuinely is a fact, and, as such, it has had political relevance.

Sometimes, therefore, as a matter of political wisdom it may be sensible to modify the application of the principle which accords representation to numbers and to these alone. It is part of the statesmanship of a mature democracy to mitigate those situations which would otherwise rankle as a grievance or give rise to feelings of injustice. However, this same counsel applies also to minorities, which should not be allowed to exploit an entrenched position to thwart the reasonable claims of the majority. In any case, the circumstances which underlie this argument have been rapidly changing in the advanced democracies since World War II. The earlier separation, which was due to remoteness or a city-country cleavage, is less of a reality nowadays. Internal communications have been revolutionized by better highways, mass transportation, and the private automobile. The radio and television, the cheap press and popular magazines, contribute to a common market in taste and ideas. There are dangers in this development, as well as benefits, most dangerous of all being the encouragement of conformity. But from the standpoint of representing a people in a central legislature, the more they grow alike the less the difficulty!

The general problem of what constitutes fair representation must also be viewed from two other angles. There is the precise character of the electoral system to be considered, and there is the further question of bicameralism. Let us discuss these in turn.

Apportionment and Proportionalism

Electoral systems are of many kinds. Indeed their detailed variations display to its fullest the remarkable ingenuity of *homo politicus*. Apply the mathematics of vote-counting to the politics of apportionment, and many odd equations ensue. But all the innumerable ways of voting are designed with the same end in view and can be judged by their effectiveness in contributing to the desired goal. The prime purpose of an election is to find out what the people want and then see if there is a clear majority of citizens who wish their government to act in a certain fashion. Electoral systems are therefore intended to discover such a majority, if indeed it exists, and at the same time to accord enough representation to minorities so that they can adequately protect themselves. When it comes to the mechanics of doing this, all systems of voting face the same problem, which they solve in one of two ways. Either the territory of the state and, *ipso facto*, the electorate are cut up into a large number of small segments, each of which elects one person to represent it in the legislature; or that same area and people can be subdivided into a smaller number of larger slices, each electing several candidates. There may also be a difference in the number of candidates for whom the citizen is allowed to vote. He may have only one vote to cast, or he may vote for several in the order of his preference.

Each of these two systems has some advantages to commend it and suffers from some defects. The single-member district system possesses the great virtue of simplicity. It brings the candidates as close as possible to their constituents. It clarifies the voter's task by narrowing his choice. Since democracy stipulates the control of government by the people, and since the people cannot possibly control what they do not understand, the most easily comprehensive system is by this logic the most democratic. The voters under modern conditions choose between the competing parties, but at the same time they can pay some attention to the qualifications of the rival candidates since these are near enough for scrutiny. However, there is an inescapable element of arbitrariness in this way of voting. When the size of the constituency is thus reduced to the minimum and there is only one representative to be elected, what do you do if you find no candidate to your liking? Moreover, after the results have been tallied and somebody is declared the winner, in what genuine sense does he "represent" those who voted for his opponents? This objection was of course more serious at the time when people assumed that a close link existed between the representative and his local constituency, and that voters cast their ballots according to their appraisal of the qualifications of individual candidates. Nowadays, however, because of the development of party organization, the party program and philosophy generally influence the voter more than the characteristics of individuals. Thus the minority in a particular constituency can feel that it is represented in the legislature by members of the same party who were successfully elected in other districts.

The alternative system purposely enlarges the field of choice. Its constituencies embrace more voters and cover a wider area in the expectation that scattered minorities can thereby pool their strength and win the representation which they would otherwise lack. Normally it follows from this system that many parties divide up the bulk of the seats in the legislature and that no single party wins a majority. Adherents of this electoral method claim that it faithfully represents the nuances and diversities of public opinion without distorting the results. In this way, they feel the system conforms to the requirements of justice. The people can be satisfied that various points of view are adequately recognized and that no segment of opinion is grossly over-represented. At the same time, admittedly, these advantages are offset by one corresponding defect. The meticulous care in providing for representation of significant minorities takes less account of the need to elicit a majority. In fact, the techniques of voting under proportional representation make it exceedingly difficult for any one party ever to control a majority of the seats. Hence, the governments which hold office under this system are normally coalitions in which several parties combine.

A choice between the two systems will necessarily be influenced by one's conception of what democracy requires and by the appropriate balancing of contradictory goals. What is at issue is a judgment about the functions the legislature should perform and whether certain of these take priority over others. It goes without saying that in a democracy the legislature must represent the people. But one can apply some common sense in distinguishing between the representation of those interests, groups, and concepts which are of major importance and the representation of every identifiable grouping and outlook according to its exact mathematical strength. If the latter is attempted, the legislature will be reduced to an absurdity since, if it contains an excessive proliferation of factions and splinters, it cannot be organized. For a legislature serves another need besides that of representing the public. It has the responsibility to sustain and support a government. It is not only a deliberative body, but also one whose deliberations are supposed to end in authoritative decisions. Hence its internal organization, while containing a diversity of significant viewpoints, should foster—and not unduly impede—the mobilizing of a majority. The failure to perform this function adequately is the great vice of the innumerable systems of proportional representation. Too frequently, in the name of electoral justice, they sacrifice utility to futility.

The Parliament of the United Kingdom is the classic case with which to argue this point. Those who put electoral justice first and insist on mathematically fair representation of the principal opposition party and of all minor parties are bound to criticize the Parliament at Westminster for its evident failure to accomplish either of these purposes. But the British electoral system is designed for other purposes, which it fulfills extremely well. Its first objective is to produce a majority with enough power to govern for a period of four to five years; the second is to accord to the government's leading rival enough voices in the House of Commons to ensure continuous and effective criticism. The British draw a careful distinction between criticism and obstruction. The former they demand; the latter they forbid. They had plenty of experience with the techniques of parliamentary obstruction when those were employed by the Irish Nationalist, Parnell. As a result, the Standing Orders of the House of Commons were revised so as to prevent endless filibusters. The majority must tolerate the right of the minority to criticize its actions and must provide ample opportunity for the free discussion of any topic which the opposition wishes to debate. But the government, precisely because it is supported by a majority of the votes, always remains in control. Thus the British parliamentary system is excellently designed to balance the power of strong government and the power of strong criticism—leaving it to the public ultimately to judge between the two sides. When it is kept in mind that these two needs are equally important, one is justified in concluding that the mathematics of proportionalism fulfill only one purpose and neglect the other. In order that the opposition may make their criticism tell, there is no substantial difference whether they hold two hundred seats or two hundred and eighty. In fact, in any debate all major points are likely to be stated and answered by the first ten speakers on each side, and prolongation of oratory after that usually amounts to repetition of the same arguments in other language. Just because the single-member district system produces disproportional results in the legislative representation, it satisfies the need for strong government admirably by increasing the size of the strongest party. But at the same time it leaves an opposition which is sufficient to criticize the ministry, without being able to encompass its overthrow. The latter task is properly left to the people, if they so wish, at the next election.

How Many Chambers?

Another feature in the organization of the legislature which bears on the same general problem is the number of its chambers. In modern times it has been normal to have a central legislature composed of two Houses. But there is nothing particularly sacrosanct about the number two. Nor is there any compelling reason to regard this figure as immutable. Historically there have been experiments with one, two, three, and even four chambers. In England, the Model Parliament of Edward I was unicameral. A formal separation into two houses only occurred after gradual and fortuitous developments spread over two centuries or more. The medieval description of the parliamentary system, the *Modus Tenendi Parliamentum*,[9]

9. In the edition of this work which I have used (edited by W. Hakewel and published in London by Abel Roper in 1671) the six degrees are described on p. 31 and the reference to the two Houses is on pp. 33-5.

refers to six ranks or degrees among the members of the Parliament, and states, when specifying their judicial functions as a High Court, that "this honourable Assembly consists of two houses, Upper and Lower." The latter is identified as the "House of Commons," whose principal officer is its spokesman or Speaker. Not until the time of Henry VIII is the other chamber first called the "House of Lords." The crucial fact which influenced the grouping of the six degrees into two houses was a political one. It was a sense of common interest uniting the knights of the shire with the representatives of the cities and boroughs which led the former to sit and deliberate in the same body with the latter.[10] This left the higher nobility and the top clergy, the "upper crust," to support one another in a House of their own. Thus, by a lucky occurrence, the chamber which originated as a body of communes could develop into a representative House of Commons and eventually become truly national.

Contrariwise, the French adhered to the conception that society was subdivided into estates. Hence, their medieval kings created the States-General, containing three houses for the nobility, clergy, and bourgeois, respectively. This trifurcation not only kept the various representatives apart and reinforced their sense of being separate classes, but it enabled the monarchs more easily to play off each estate against the others. The growth of royal power under the English Tudors was actually accompanied by an increase of the power of Parliament, so that this body could later challenge and subdue the Crown. But in France the cumbrous States-General grew weaker until the absolute monarchs of the seventeeth and eighteenth centuries were able to dispense with it completely. It is significant, however, that when Louis XVI was trying to introduce reforms which would stave off a revolution he summoned the defunct States-General—its first meeting in 175 years. When the members assembled, they faced at once the question of organization and voting. Should they vote as three separate orders, or as persons belonging to one body? The Third Estate, being the most numerous, favored the latter, in which they were supported by the lower clergy and a small minority of nobles. The higher prelates, who were removed from the people, and the great majority of nobles, wanted to meet and vote separately, so that their two orders could prevail over the third. The decisive point in the Revolution occurred when the Third Estate proclaimed itself a National Assembly and proceeded to adopt the initial measures of France's Revolution.[11]

10. See A. F. Pollard, *The Evolution of Parliament, op. cit.,* pp. 66-7, 75, etc.

11. Jefferson, serving at that time as American Minister in Paris, describes the political relations of the Three Estates in his letters. See *The Papers of Thomas Jefferson,* Vol. 15; letter to James Madison, May 11, 1789, pp. 121-2; to Thomas Paine, May 19,

Even more extreme, and more absurd, than the French States-General, was the Swedish Riksdag as it functioned until the seventh decade of the nineteenth century. There, the legislature had traditionally been subordinate to the monarchy which ruled with absolute power. It was subdivided into as many as four estates—these being composed respectively of the nobles, clergy, burghers, and peasants. To manipulate four such bodies, and play upon their divisions, was simple enough for Sweden's kings. Not until 1866 were the four chambers abolished and a bicameral legislature was substituted. Two generations later Sweden had arrived at the institutions of a democratic state.

The Bicameral Habit

During the nineteenth century, as old legislatures were being reorganized and new ones founded, bicameralism became the general practice. Two main reasons may be suggested for this. In traditional societies, permeated by class divisions and dominated by an aristocracy, the use of two chambers made it possible for the mass of the people to be represented in one and the nobility in the other. Thus the elite, which formerly had wielded exclusive control over the government, could accept the introduction of popular elections while still retaining a grip on one branch of the legislature. In new states, or in older ones which underwent a revolution, bicameralism either served to embody some political principle (as the Congress

---

1789, pp. 136-7; to Madison, June 18, 1789, pp. 195-7, etc. The following extract is from the last of these: "Committees of conciliation having failed in their endeavors to bring together the three chambers of the States general, the king proposed a specific mode of verifying their powers; for that having been the first question which presented itself to them, was the one on which the question of voting by persons or orders was first brought on. The Clergy accepted unconditionally. The Noblesse accepted on conditions which reduced the acceptance to nothing at all. The Commons [i.e., the Third Estate] considered this as a refusal on the part of the nobles, and thereupon took their definitive resolution, to invite the other two orders to come and verify their powers in common, and to notify them they should proceed with or without them to verify, and to do the business of the nation. This was on the 10th [of June]. On the 15th they moved to declare themselves the national assembly. . . . Among the commons there is an entire unanimity on the great question of voting by persons. Among the noblesse there are about 60 for the commons, about three times that number against them. Among the clergy about 20 have already come over and joined the commons, and in the course of a few days they will be joined by many more, not indeed making the majority of that house, but very near it. The bishops and archbishops have been very successful by bribes and intrigues in detaching the Curés from the Commons to whom they were at first attached to a man. The Commons are about 554 in number, of whom 344 are of the law."

of the United States was meant to reflect the essentials of federalism) or was justified by elementary arguments of a cautious conservatism. Leaving aside the force of tradition and the sentimental attachment to inherited forms, let us examine the reasoned case for two chambers and the arguments against it.

Clearly, if the legislature is to consist of two Houses, there is no point in having them unless the people are represented under different guises. Where one such House is composed of persons who owe their seats to hereditary status, it is inherently undemocratic. Naturally in countries which have tried to combine a popularly elected House with a hereditary body, a conflict eventually ensued; and the results were the same wherever the democratic principle triumphed. The hereditary body was either abolished, as in Denmark; or allowed to linger on as a subordinate appendage of the elected chamber, as in great Britain. In fact, the Danes, being a more genuine social democracy than the British, carried the development to its logical conclusion and have accepted a unicameral legislature. In Britain the Lords are permitted to survive as a pale shadow of their former selves, and the institution is supposedly made somewhat less offensive to democracy by the inclusion of life peers and women.[12] For similar reasons, what has happened to hereditary second chambers has also occurred to those which were filled by appointment. New Zealand had a Legislative Council whose members were originally appointed for life, and after 1894 for terms of seven years. That body was abolished in 1950, since when the Parliament has been unicameral. Canada continues with its appointive Senate, but this chamber has no real power or independence. Only in name does it resemble the Senate in the United States or Australia.

Apart from such relics of the earlier aristocratic or colonial regimes, which nobody is going to defend in the name of democracy, can a bicameral legislature, both of whose chambers are elected, be made compatible with democratic principles? I am going to argue that, with the exception of the federal systems which form a special case, democracy is best served by a unicameral legislature. The bicameral bodies cannot fail, in some respect or another, to deviate from the requirements of democracy.

There is a basic truth in the much-quoted remark of the Abbé de Sieyès on this subject. "Of what use," he asked, "will a Second Chamber be? If it agrees with the Representative House, it will be superfluous; if it disagrees, mischievous." Bryce, who cites this statement, points out that, like all dilemmas it omits the possibility of third or other choices.[13] This

12. And, more recently, by allowing a peer to renounce his title and seek a seat in the Commons.

13. *Modern Democracies* (Macmillan: New York, 1921), Vol. II, Chap. LXIV, p. 399.

objection is valid when one is considering the functions which a legislature performs (e.g., reaching decisions on matters of public policy). It has less force when it is applied to the mode or principle of representation. In the latter respect a representative chamber is either fully democratic or it falls short of this by varying degrees. To be fully democratic means that all adult citizens have the same voting rights and also that each single vote counts the same in contributing to the result. In all mature democracies, the popular chamber or lower house has evolved in this direction during the last hundred years. In the sphere of voting rights, apart from the one major exception of Negroes in the southeast of the United States, the needs of democracy have been satisfied. But the same cannot be said of the connected requirement that all votes should count equally, because of continuing inequities in apportionment. However, the logic of Sieyès remains. When one chamber does become fully and completely democratic on both points, what is to be done with a second chamber? An elective second chamber must either be filled in the same manner as the first, in which case it is superfluous; or in a less democratic manner, which is mischievous.

Pros and Cons of Unicameralism

This dilemma explains why in every democracy which has a unitary constitution the second chamber has either declined in power or disappeared during the twentieth century. When the first chamber becomes fully representative of all the people, it will not and cannot tolerate a rival. The attempts which are made to continue an elective second chamber with genuine powers of opposing the first derive from some fear or distrust of popular majorities. Usually such efforts emanate from the conservative Right or from rural areas and the small towns—in other words, from those sectors of society which do not embody dynamism and change. A second chamber can easily be given a different political character from the first by a method of indirect election, by electing its members for longer and staggered terms, or by deliberate distortion in the apportionment so as to increase the representation of minority interests. The French *Sénat* of the Third Republic is a good illustration of this, and its built-in conservatism led to frequent obstruction of the Chambre de Députés. That is why the question of unicameralism became so crucial in the debates over the Constitution of the Fourth Republic in 1946. A draft Constitution with a provision for a unicameral assembly was actually submitted to the voters, but was defeated because of the objections of the M.R.P., of General de

Gaulle, and the whole of the Right. The Constitution which was later adopted did include a second chamber, although it was intentionally meant to be subordinate to the first. The Gaullist Constitution of the Fifth Republic purposely made the Presidency, not the Assembly, the focal institution of government; and in keeping with the traditions of French conservatism it was only natural that the General originally had himself elected indirectly through a college in which rural districts and smaller towns had a disproportionate weight. Without any doubt a contemporary democracy which wants its institutions to register the majority will and reflect a modern outlook must accord full power to the fully representative house. Any departure from this does violence, in some respect, to democracy.

There is, however, one valid type of exception to this generalization. What I have been saying applies to unitary states. Other factors should be considered in the case of federal systems, where a reasonable argument can be made for the continuation of genuine[14] bicameralism. A federal constitution is constructed around the principle of balance. It is appropriate to a society where such an equilibrium exists among a diversity of groups, interests and regions that the search for a majority must proceed through moderation and compromise. Under such conditions, some of the component groups aim at the center to make their will prevail, while others rely on maintaining control of local or regional strongholds. Hence a federal system properly ascribes a special constitutional status to the intermediate layer in a three-level hierarchy of governments. Be they cantons, provinces, or states, they represent and by their structure reinforce the centrifugal factors within the nation. Consequently the composition of the central legislature reflects these facts. As everybody knows, when the members of the Philadelphia Convention were drafting the Constitution of the United States in 1787, one of the latent conflicts was that between the smaller States and the large ones. No agreement could have been reached unless that issue was in some way resolved. Only late in the Convention was a formula adopted which produced an acceptable draft and obtained the subsequent ratifications. The Congress was made bicameral; the Senate was to represent the States as equal units; the House would represent the people in proportion to population. This principle, which appears to be one of the essentials for the successful operation of a federal system, has been followed elsewhere[15] in countries which have imported their federalism from the American model.

14. By "genuine" I mean that not only does the central legislature contain two houses, but that both possess real power and either may effectively oppose the other.
15. E.g., Switzerland and Australia.

Bicameralism, therefore, has a special justification under a federal system. The internal homogeneity of a Denmark or a New Zealand does not require either federalism or bicameralism. But both these are needed in the United States and in Switzerland. They buttress one another and they correspond to the same social and political realities. Even so, when that justification is conceded, it remains true that bicameralism presents a problem to democratic government which a unicameral legislature escapes. Inevitably the geographic pattern of federalism assigns a disproportionate share in the government to the less populous, or economically dependent, regions. Zurich and Zug are represented as equals in the Council of States at Bern, as are Tasmania and New South Wales in the Senate at Canberra and Alaska and California in the Senate at Washington —and in these arbitrary arrangements there is an element of the ridiculous. What happens, therefore, in the practice of federalism is that one chamber gives more weight to urban and industrial interests and crowded population centers, while the sparsely inhabited regions predominate in the other house. The national interest and public good must then be sought by compromise between the two bodies.

Actually, however, from the standpoint of city dwellers the situation appears still worse than that statement would suggest. It is common for the rural districts, which did once contain a majority of the population, to keep a grip, if not a stranglehold, over the machinery of government long after their voting strength has dwindled to a minority. This is notoriously so in the United States and explains, in part, the conservative bias of public policy in this country. In the House of Representatives, the total membership is redistributed among the States after each decennial census on the basis of population. But it is left to the State governments to draw the boundaries of the districts for congressional elections. As a consequence, the metropolitan centers seldom receive their fair share of representation. At the State capitals, the distortion is still more serious—and there are several classic cases of big cities being unfairly treated by State legislatures in which farmers and small-town lawyers control too many votes.[16]

Deliberate gerrymandering of this kind is a symptom of the pathology of democracy, not of its health. But even if we could assume for the sake of argument that a legislature had two elected houses, each of which was as fairly representative as the other, would this be the best possible system for a democracy to employ? The argument in favor of bicameralism contends that it necessitates a second look at legislation, that this prevents rash and overhasty decisions, and that it permits one chamber to discover

16. Examples are New York City in New York State, Chicago in Illinois, and Los Angeles in California. The Supreme Court has now declared these practices unconstitutional.

inadvertent errors in the work of the other. There is some merit in these points in the sense that all of us would want our legislatures to be both deliberate and careful. But it is not proven that a bicameral system actually fulfills these objectives or that it fulfills them better than a unicameral body. There is no evidence to show that the Danish Folketing or the New Zealand Parliament, since becoming unicameral, has been driven headlong into foolish actions by sudden gusts in the winds of public opinion. The errors or inconsistencies in statutes, which occur through careless drafting of the original or the adoption of later amendments, can be discovered and corrected by reference to a committee of legal experts before a bill is finally passed into law. A unicameral legislature can safeguard itself against hasty and ill-considered action by the adoption of procedures which allow for sufficient time and reflection. In other words, there is not one of these supposed advantages of bicameralism which cannot also be secured with a single chamber.

Moreover, there are definite disadvantages in bicameralism from which the alternative is exempt. A bicameral legislature, instead of taking extra care, sometimes acts more carelessly than it should because one chamber may vote thoughtlessly and leave its errors to be rectified in the other house. When there are two chambers, each is tempted to dodge its responsibility by "passing the buck" to the other.[17] In addition, a bicameral structure lends itself too readily to obstruction and delays. By contrast, in a unicameral body responsibility is fixed, the organization is simpler, and legislators have fewer alibis for inaction or evasion. Remembering that it helps democracy to simplify its government and to focus responsibility clearly on its public officials, one may conclude that a single chamber generally is better than two.

Once a representative body has been elected and assembled, it must be organized. A chamber which may vary in size from 80 (the New Zealand Parliament) or 100 (the United States Senate) to 435 (the U. S. House of Representatives) or 630 (the British House of Commons) needs to have structure, rules, and leadership, or it can accomplish nothing. Much of the character of the results which come from a legislative session will depend on the internal effectiveness of the system and the use to which it is put. The factors which shape the organization of the legislature can be considered from two aspects. Certain features follow from constitutional requirements which determine the legislative structure and which may govern its relations with the executive branch. The other features are

17. These arguments used to be stressed by Senator George W. Norris when he persuaded Nebraskans to adopt unicameralism.

political in nature and derive from the party system. Each set of factors has an influence on the other. Party politics must function officially within whatever channels the constitution prescribes; and, conversely, the legal powers of the legislative branch will be exercised according to the will of the prevailing party or coalition.

Organization in the United States Congress

A few examples will make this plain. The working of Congress in the United States is unmistakably influenced by the differences in the mode of electing the two chambers. A House which must face re-election in entirety every second year cannot be as secure or function as independently as a continuous body, one-third of whose members are elected at a time and all of whom enjoy a longer term than the President. For this reason, and also because the Constitution requires that the Senate[18] consent to treaties and to presidential nominations for high office, this branch has evolved as the more powerful half of the Congress. In fact, Congress is unique in this respect among the bicameral legislatures of democratic states. This is the only instance in the world where the smaller, second, chamber has grown stronger than the one which was intended to represent the country on the basis of population. To some extent, this state of affairs could be altered by lengthening the term of office of Representatives from two years to four—a change which is certainly needed, but which would call for a Constitutional Amendment. Without amending the Constitution, however, the House could augment its own political strength when the boundaries of congressional districts are redrawn within the States so as to give their due representation to the most populous areas. The weight of numbers at the polls would then have its effect on the composition of the House and would enable this body to mobilize majority opinion more effectively in its relations with the Senate.

The other major constitutional provision which affects the congressional system is the exclusion of the President and other executive officers from membership in the legislature. This does not mean that the President has no influence on legislation or on legislators.[19] Far from it! But it does mean that, because of the absence of the Administration from the Capi-

18. The main special prerogative which the Constitution confers on the House of Representatives is that "all bills for raising revenue" must originate here. Art. 1, sec. 7. The Senate, however, can initiate its own financial ideas through amendments to the bills it receives. The House, in addition, has "the sole Power of Impeachment." Art. 1, sec. 2.

19. For a discussion of the President's legislative role, see Chapter 15, pp. 493 ff.

tol building, Congress has to create its own substitute organization and produce its own leaders from within. The result is a complex machinery in which the power of initiative and decision is not concentrated in any single person or office but is subtly dispersed in various places. Because every bill is sent to a committee which conducts hearings and considers amendments before reporting it to the floor, the respective committees do much to shape the ensuing legislation. So great are their powers that they can substantially rewrite a measure, or doom it by an adverse vote, or simply allow it to die by failing to report it.

In this system, the key person is the committee chairman, since it is he who calls for the hearings and arranges the agenda. A chairman with strong opinions of his own on policy matters is a force to reckon with. Cabinet Secretaries, and the President himself, will try to persuade him, but they cannot compel him if his political base is secure in his home State. At regular intervals in American political history there emerges some potent figure—usually a Senator—whose voice is dominant in a certain field because of his control of the relevant committee.[20] What compounds the difficulty is the political custom which seats a man in the chair according to his seniority of service on that particular committee. Sometimes, as a consequence of this practice, the chairman may become a genuine expert in his particular field and, through accumulated knowledge and experience, can make a valuable contribution to public policy. But there are glaring instances of the opposite, where a politician of narrow, parochial outlook holds the key to decisions of national or international importance. Unfortunately in both major parties seniority usually accrues to diehard members of the more backward-looking wings—the southerners among the Democrats and the rural or small-town Republicans. Such groups do not represent a majority of the American people. Nevertheless, they hold a disproportionate share of committee chairmanships and their coalition wields a crucial influence in the Congress in the direction of a negative conservatism.

Besides the committees and their chairmen, the other important officers in Congress are the leaders of the majority and minority parties in both chambers and the Speaker of the House of Representatives. Because the latter body is over four times larger than the Senate, it requires more leadership and a tighter discipline in order to function effectively. Hence the Speaker wields greater power than either the Vice-President or the President *Pro. Tem.* of the Senate. At times, in the past, this power has been carried to excess, as occurred notably during the reign of "Czar"

20. E.g., Senators Smoot, Borah, Connally, Vandenberg, McCarran, Taft, Russell; Representatives Smith, Cannon, Passman, Vinson.

Cannon, whose arbitrariness provoked rebellion and led to changes in the House rules. But when a Speaker combines wisdom with strength, and is a dedicated custodian of the prerogatives of the House, he can acquire unparalleled influence in the legislative field and in the counsels of his party. This was true of Speaker Rayburn, whose long ascendancy in the House coincided with the continuous majorities for the Democratic party. A master of the fine points of organization and procedure, he was also skilled in the subtle art of leading without driving. His power, however, derived as much from his personality as from his office, and the former is not transferable with the latter.

The Senate is much harder to lead than the House. Its smaller size, longer terms, and staggered elections, give this extraordinary chamber the corporate character of a club in which each member jealously guards his individual privileges and must likewise respect those of his colleagues. Very rarely does the Senate apply the rule of closure to end debate. Seldom indeed does it censure a member who goes beyond the bounds, although it did deliver this ultimate rebuke to Senator McCarthy. If the majority party can find a floor leader of trusted judgment and parliamentary skill, he and he alone can give this chamber such cohesion as it will tolerate. The roles of Senators Robert A. Taft among the Republicans and Lyndon Johnson among the Democrats are conspicuous examples, and somewhat exceptional. In the Senate it is always difficult to apply party discipline to recalcitrant members, although the withholding of patronage in a Senator's State may have some effect. Presidents who have tried at election time to "purge" their ranks of senatorial opponents to their programs have not met with much success—witness the failure even of Franklin D. Roosevelt in 1938. If a man succeeds in being re-elected to the Senate for two or more terms, he builds a strong following of individuals and groups who owe him a personal loyalty. This may clarify the curious fact that some big and important States where the two parties are evenly balanced may be simultaneously represented in the Senate by a Republican and a Democrat both of whom at intervals of two years have received clear majorities—as in the case of Senators Dirksen and Douglas of Illinois, or Keating and Lehman of New York.

The battle lines in congressional politics are seldom clear. Normally they are confused; on occasion, they are even chaotic. Influences of four different kinds, which shape and reshape their groupings, are brought to bear on Members of Congress. First, of course, is their party affiliation. Second is the distinction between liberal and conservative. Third is the influence of the State or region—the most potent of all regional blocs being that of the Southern Democrats when civil rights are in issue.

Fourth, there is the medley of economic interests, some of which coincide with a region while others bring together a combination of congressmen from widely scattered areas. With so complex an interplay of forces, it is not at all surprising that a multi-group system prevails in both Houses, giving rise to coalitions and alliances which solidify, then melt and form again, according to the topic or pressure which is uppermost at the time. It is a system which faithfully reproduces in the political arena the pluralism of American society with all its many facets. The spectacle of the Congress at work is a frustrating experience to those who wish for a clearer direction, greater unity, and decisive policies. But the numerous pieces which make up this legislative mosaic are authentic fragments collected from the length and breadth of the United States, from the lower depths and the loftier heights.

Discipline in the British House of Commons

To switch one's attention from Washington to Westminster affords a sharp reversal of mode and mood. For Parliament is strong where Congress is weak, and weak where the latter is strong. The commonest complaints about the Congress are that the parties are insufficiently disciplined, that individual members are too independent, and that minorities can obstruct action on matters of national importance. The commonest criticisms of Parliament assert that party discipline is excessive, that backbenchers have lost both independence and initiative, and that the Commons has surrendered too much of its power to the Cabinet. When the House divides on a major question, e.g., a vote of no confidence, there is no uncertainty over the outcome, since the result—given the facts of party discipline—is always a foregone conclusion.[21] The only matter of interest to political experts will be to watch any variations in the size of the Government's majority or of the Opposition's muster. For if serious disagreement erupts within the ranks of either party, this will normally be expressed, not by crossing the House to vote with the other side, but by abstaining from the division altogether.

The reasons for the strength of party discipline in Great Britain are worth examining. As was noted earlier,[22] a two-party system developed from the history of the issues over which the British people were most

21. This refers, of course, to the normal situation where there are two major parties, one of which has a clear majority. The situation from 1918 to 1931 was different, since temporarily there were three parties, one of which held the balance of power.
22. See Chapter 11, pp. 324 ff.

acutely split. This would only explain, however, why British politics have
been dominated by two major groupings, but not why each of these
should maintain so high a degree of internal discipline. The factors which
influence a member of the public to vote consistently for the same party
are not completely identical with those which lead a Member of Parliament consistently into the same lobby with the same group. There are
some additional motives which animate the parliamentarian, who, as a
professional politician in public life, has his own career to think about as
well as the good of the country. A member who hopes to stay in Parliament will do whatever helps him to be re-elected; and one who has ministerial ambitions will try to attract the favorable notice of his party's
leaders. To be nominated and renominated by a constituency, a candidate
needs to be *persona grata* to the central headquarters as well as to the
local organization. Fighting an election nowadays is so expensive—because
of the cost of campaigning and advertising—that few can meet the expense out of their own pocket. Since the national treasury of the party has
to produce most of the necessary funds, the central committee will naturally have some say in the selection of a candidate. It may provide a list of
suitable nominees from which the constituency can pick, and it can on
rare occasions prevent the selection or renomination of somebody ob-
noxious.

The American and British systems differ significantly in certain of the
limitations they impose on the choice of a candidate. In the United
States, either by law or custom, a Congressman must reside in the district
he represents. No such requirement exists in Great Britain. Since British
voters are picking the party label rather than the individual candidate,
they do not expect the latter to reside in his constituency. This element of
flexibility means that somebody who is useful to his party can be given a
safe seat in order to keep him in Parliament. A Congressman, in order to
be re-elected, must ever be mindful of local interests and susceptibilities.
If he offends too many in his home area he may lose his seat and then is
not eligible for another. But a Member of Parliament who hopes for re-
election will normally follow the central leadership rather than the local
pressures, since, if defeated in one district, he can stand again elsewhere.
In fact, an examination of the parliamentary careers of some of the greatest figures in British politics reveals that it is quite common for a man who
has served for many years in the House to have sat for two or three constituencies. Moreover, since promotion to ministerial rank depends on
the goodwill of the Prime Minister, and since the latter, before bringing
a back-bencher down to the front, will count his voting record among his
qualifications for office, a Member will hesitate many times before dis-

obeying the party whip. Failure to march into the same lobby with his colleagues when the bells sound for a division is the deadliest sin which a Member can commit. He may even be pardoned for occasionally disagreeing with his party in public—just so long as he always casts a loyal vote when the time comes.

Hence the discipline which is so characteristic of the parliamentary parties is the product of the conditions which shape a man's political career and of the circumstances under which the House of Commons does its work. If in the United States Congress the House with its 435 members requires a more centralized organization than a Senate of one hundred, it follows that the Commons consisting at present of 630 has even more need for direction. So large an assembly could not conduct the nation's affairs without some mechanism to supply cohesion and control. That instrument, of course, is the Cabinet. The secret of its strength lies in this combination of facts: all its members are chosen from within the walls of Parliament, comprising the leading lights of the predominant party, and they continue to serve in Parliament while supervising the administrative departments. These are political reasons of the first order of importance. When you multiply together the power of the leaders of the majority with the legal authority of Parliament and the resources and skill of the civil service, you know why the Cabinet has evolved into the central organ of British government. Under such a system it is also evident that the parliamentary committees are in no sense comparable to those of Congress. The one all-powerful committee is the Cabinet; it functions inside Parliament; and it brooks no rival. The Cabinet controls the legislature in this sense that it has the votes to obtain what it wants and to prevent the enactment of what it does not want. The politics of Cabinet government depend on maintaining the constancy of this equation. A Cabinet is in office and remains there for as long as it is backed by a majority of the House of Commons. If for any reason that majority disappears, one of two consequences must ensue. Either the Ministry resigns, and a new one takes office supported by the majority which threw out the old one, or the Ministry which has lost the confidence of the House will take its appeal to the people by asking for a general election. Then the result of the popular vote decides which party will form the Ministry in the new Parliament.

Nevertheless, although these points are correct as statements of constitutional principle, the political practice of a disciplined two-party system has all but eliminated the possibility of a Ministry being defeated in the House on a vote of no-confidence. A group of members who are dissatisfied with their own leaders may abstain from a division, as was noted above. But they will not let their dissatisfaction extend to the point of bringing their own Government down. The Cabinet's power is founded on the premise that, however disgruntled some back-benchers may become, they will still choose to keep their own party in office rather than invite in the Opposition. Here, as so often in *Realpolitik*, the practical alternatives are not between two goods or between good and evil, but between two evils of which the sensible will opt for the lesser.

The logic of this argument has indicated that in the normal operation of a two-party system the Cabinet's power over Parliament is unassailable. Does that support the criticism leveled by Ramsay Muir and others that a "dictatorship of the Cabinet" has grown up in Britain? I think not, and regard the use of that term and its implications as exaggerated. Great as is the power of the Cabinet, it is not absolute nor does it corrupt. For it must operate within boundaries of restraint which are well understood on both sides. In essentials, the British form of government functions in this way. The men who run the country for the time being are the leaders of the party which won the larger number of seats in the Commons at the last general election. It is recognized that while they constitute the Government, it is for them to lead, decide, and act. But their actions, decisions, and leadership are conducted under continuous surveillance and publicity. They must argue their case in the Commons and answer the worst that their rivals can say in attack. Although each side addresses the other in Parliament, in reality they are both speaking to the nation outside. Their court of judgment is public opinion; the jury is the electorate; their verdict comes at the next election—which is never far off and never forgotten. Hence, a Ministry which would trample rough-shod over the Opposition, abusing its mastery of the procedures of the House, would violate the public's sense of decency and justice. In practice, therefore, a Government is careful to exercise its wide parliamentary powers with due circumspection. It displays its wisdom, or statesmanship if you will, by knowing at what time to be forceful and firm, and when it is better to show restraint and deference. This is the merit of a democratic state where power in the long run must be founded on persuasion.

Yet, while rejecting the notion that the Cabinet is a dictator, I would stress one aspect of the contemporary system which has been carried to excess with some unfortunate results. The discipline of the two parties is necessary for the Cabinet system to work, and up to a point it is good. But certain of its side effects are regrettable. A minority group within a party must follow the party line, sometimes in violation of deeply held convictions. The price paid for party loyalty is the sacrifice of the individual conscience.

At the same time, the Cabinet's monopoly of legislation has been accompanied inevitably by the atrophy of the initiative of the private member. Whereas in Congress too much scope continues to be given to the independent initiative of the individual Congressman or Senator, the British Parliament demonstrates the opposite extreme. The time allotted nowadays for debating private Members' bills is ridiculously inadequate, and the odds against any of these ever becoming law are very high. Naturally I am not arguing for private Members' bills to encroach on the spheres of public policy which are properly the responsibility of the Government. But there are innumerable matters, apart from economic issues and foreign affairs, which are important to individuals in a modern society, but yield no political dividend to those in power. Questions of morals, the family, sexual behavior, the sale and consumption of alcoholic drinks, religious instruction in the schools—these are examples of topics on which a great many people have deep feelings and where the results of individual actions can lead to social consequences. Politicians, however, instinctively shrink from subjects of this kind because they do not necessarily involve a party viewpoint. On the contrary, they frequently relate to aspects of private conduct or belief which cut across party lines and play havoc with discipline. If you try to modernize the divorce laws, you bring the churches after you in full hue and cry—which any prudent Ministry tries to avoid. Conversely, if the Church of England, which suffers the pains as well as the privileges of being "established," wishes to alter its prayer-book, it must seek the approval of Parliament, where it will inevitably encounter some critical representatives of the non-conformist conscience. In such fields it would be better if private Members still retained some of their former initiative. They could grasp the nettle with impunity, while Ministers enjoy the fruits of office.

The Illogicality of French Legislatures

In their internal organization, as this discussion has suggested, Parliament and Congress are polar opposites. Each legislature might be improved by borrowing some features from the other. Congress could benefit from more party discipline; Parliament, from more initiative by the backbenchers. But these are matters of degree. The two legislatures are organized differently because of the fundamental fact that one includes, and the other excludes, the political heads of the executive branch. What cannot be done, however, is to blend the two systems together in equal doses and expect the result to work satisfactorily. Yet that is exactly what was tried by the French, who have curiously gained a reputation for being a logical people. Under the Constitutions of the Third and Fourth Republics, the legislature was purposely made the central institution with the greatest power. The idea of the omnipotence of the popular assembly has survived as a tradition from the last decade of the eighteenth century, when the French initiated their long series of governmental experiments. In the two Republics which spanned the period between Louis Napoleon and Charles de Gaulle, the Deputies gloried in their authority and made the most of it. Rousseau's acid criticism[23] of the representative system as it functioned in eighteenth-century England could be better applied to the *Palais Bourbon* from 1875 to 1940 and from 1946 to 1958. In the Chamber of Deputies and its successor, the National Assembly,[24] the legislators maintained a continuous supremacy. They did so through their control of organization and procedure. The former consisted of an elaborate network of specialized committees, each concentrating on a field of public policy in which its members became experts. Besides the committee chairman, the person who had great influence on the content of a proposed bill was the member assigned to be its *rapporteur*. He was placed in charge of investigating the subject; he could initiate amendments before the committee; and it was he who spoke first when the measure was debated in the Chamber. In addition to their control of the organization of the legislature, the Deputies could dominate or disrupt its procedure by the device of interpellation. Based on a motion which called for questioning a Minister, this method could develop into a debate on general policy and might lead to the Ministry demanding the confidence of the Assembly or the latter voting to censure its Government. Like Damocles in the myth, the French Ministers dined at the banquet table, but the Deputies' sword dangled overhead and willing hands were ready to cut the string.

With these realities of legislative predominance France attempted to combine a Cabinet system imported from across the Channel. But French Cabinets could never acquire the mastery of the Deputies which British Cabinets are wont to wield over their rank and file. The different results were due, of course, to the contrast between the two party systems. British parties behave in Parliament like regular troops under the command of seasoned officers. French parties (except for the Communists) resembled

23. *Contrat Social*, Bk. III, Chap. 15, quoted above in Chapter 2, p. 43, n. 61.
24. There may be some confusion of the nomenclature on this point. In the Third Republic, the *Assemblée Nationale* was the bicameral legislature composed of a *Sénat* and *Chambre de Députés*. In the Fourth Republic, the bicameral *Parlement* was composed of the *Conseil de la République* and *Assemblée Nationale*.

insurgent guerrilla bands whose leaders were as likely to be shot down from the rear as from the front. Given these political facts, it was hopeless to expect the Ministers to control the Deputies. The institutions could not function in a manner which the character of the party system prevented. Hence, in the futile attempt to wed the committee system of the United States Congress with the Cabinet leadership of Britain's Parliament, the former inevitably triumphed because that was appropriate to multipartism. Had a two-party system ever emerged in French politics, the Cabinet would have succeeded in dominating the committees and drowning the *rapporteurs*. This, therefore, is clear. One pattern of organization or the other had to prevail. They could not be harmonized or compromised. What was to prevail was determined, coldly and simply, by the logic, not of principle, but of the party system.

How Parliament's Functions Evolved

The aspect of the legislature which remains for discussion is its functions. What is the representative chamber intended to do? What does it actually do? How well is its job done? On this subject, as was suggested at the opening of this chapter, dissatisfaction is widespread. The representative chamber in many democracies is the butt of satire rather than a focus for respect. The complaints and criticisms, though merited in some particulars, go further than is fair, in my judgment, and are based in part on a public misconception of the role to be performed by the legislative body in modern times. In order to obtain perspective on this problem, let us look at the functions of the legislature in their historical evolution and then survey current performance in the light of current needs.

To begin with, our judgment of the legislature is colored and may to some extent be misled by its title. An organ of government which is said to exist for making laws will necessarily be evaluated by its output of legislation—and by its omissions in this same field. As a matter of fact, however, the enactment of laws was not an original function of the bodies which are called legislatures today, but a later accretion to an institution which assembled for other purposes. This may sound paradoxical, but it may be demonstrated from the seven centuries of development of Britain's Parliament. The primary reason which led to the summoning of Parliament was the King's need for money, and the assembled representatives used their opportunity to present their grievances and ask for remedies. These then were the original functions of a Parliament—to authorize the raising of revenue and provide a national forum for expressing complaints.

The former gave rise to inquiries into the objects of expenditure; and thereby "ways and means" and "supply," as they are called in Britain, broadened generally into the power of the purse. Likewise, the airing of grievances evolved into what has been termed "the grant inquest of the nation"—a continuous scrutiny of what is done, or not done, by those who hold the reins of office.

After this pair of functions came the third—that of making laws. In the Middle Ages very little legislation was enacted by Parliament. But the activities of Tudor monarchs, particularly Henry VIII and Elizabeth I, required parliamentary endorsement for political reasons. Henceforth, the Crown could no longer govern the realm by Orders-in-Council, using the royal prerogative as the source of law. This was proven, politically again, by the opposition and rebellion against the Stuarts, from which Parliament emerged supreme as the maker of laws. Finally, between the early part of the eighteenth century and the third or fourth decade of the nineteenth, a further power was added. It was in this period that the Cabinet emerged in keeping with the crystallization of parties. Party solidarity in Parliament deprived the monarch of the freedom of choice which he had earlier exercised in selecting Ministers. Thenceforth, a Ministry held office, not because it had the favor of the King, but because of the support of a Parliamentary majority. By these steps the institution, which was first called together at the royal bidding, matured enough to defy the royal will and eventually appropriated the royal function of administering the government.

Modern Parliaments, therefore, have inherited four major responsibilities as their political legacy from past centuries—the power of the purse, ventilation of grievances, law-making, and Cabinet-making. Now the question is: What do they do with these responsibilities in the present?

There is no denying that in three of those categories the Parliaments of the twentieth century have had much less say than their predecessors. This is clearly the case, for instance, in the sphere of finance. In essentials, the decisions concerning revenue and expenditure are made by the Cabinet with the assistance of the Treasury. The budget is ratified by Parliament in the form in which it is submitted, because the Ministry regards the acceptance of its financial program as a matter of confidence by which it stands or falls.[25] Naturally, the Opposition presents whatever criticisms it

25. Very rarely indeed the Government may withdraw a particular item or accept an amendment, while the House is debating the budget. This occurs only if opposition develops from groups whose support is needed. In 1938 Chamberlain withdrew a proposal for a new tax to finance the cost of rearmament against Hitler, because of an outcry from the businessmen of the City on whom the tax would have largely fallen.

can, building its record for the next election. But it will, of course, be out-voted in the House. Indeed, the only place where the House still operates effectively in the financial field is in the post-audit. There is a Public Accounts Committee, chaired by a member of the Opposition, which receives the annual report of the Comptroller and Auditor General. This official is appointed to serve at the pleasure of Parliament and is independent of the Ministry. He inquires solely, however, into the legality of the expenditures which have been incurred. The wisdom of the policies themselves does not come within his competence or that of the Committee.

A second sphere in which Parliament has virtually lost its earlier power is the formation of a Government. During the period from 1832 to 1884, when the franchise was extended in stages to adult males, and when party organization was developing, the parliamentary parties were not yet as cohesive or tightly disciplined as they are today. Back-benchers in the House of Commons could not always be counted on to follow their leaders; and there were several groups, and various independent members, whose support might temporarily switch from one major party to the other. Under these circumstances, Ministries could be made and unmade in the House of Commons by changing coalitions. But those circumstances have long vanished. Not since the 1920's, when the Liberals held the balance in two Parliaments, has a Ministry taken office whose party did not have a majority of the seats. Nowadays, the House of Commons plays much the same role in selecting the Government as the Electoral College does in choosing the President of the United States. The British people, when they vote at the polls, choose between the two major parties. Then the leader of the party with more seats in the Commons is appointed Premier and he picks his Cabinet, which remains in office until he resigns or asks for the next election. Similarly in the United States the constitutional majority which formally elects the President is that of the Electoral College; but this body—according to law in some States and usage in others—serves nowadays only to ratify the result of the popular voting in each of the fifty States. A majority in the Commons is required for the formation of a Government. But this does not mean that the choice of Government is really made in the Commons or by its members—any more than the Electoral College really decides who is to be President. Needless to say, the fact that the power of the House of Commons to make or break a Ministry has atrophied, in the same way as that of the Electoral College to select the President, does not signify a loss from the standpoint of democracy. On the contrary, this is one vital matter on which it was essential to modern democracy that the choice should be transferred from the Commons and the College to the People. The citizen voters must keep in their own hands the choice of the elected officials whose powers are the greatest. In an earlier day, the method of election was indirect, with the College and the Commons acting as filters to strain and "purify" the voters' preferences. The modern method has become the more democratic one of direct popular voting at a nationwide election.

The third of Parliament's functions is to make laws. How effectively does it discharge this duty? Or has this too suffered the same erosion as the others? My answer would be that Parliament has retained its role in shaping legislation to a greater degree than the other powers which have been discussed. But its authority in this field has declined by comparison with what nineteenth-century Parliaments did. All bills of importance are introduced nowadays by the Ministry; and the majority become law in substantially the same form that they had at first reading. The real law-making body today consists of the Cabinet and the heads of the civil service, in the sense that their collective judgment is decisive in formulating legislative policy and drafting the actual contents of future statutes. Parliament serves as the debating chamber where the proposals which come from the Cabinet and civil service are given publicity and full discussion. During the argument, it will sometimes happen that the Government is persuaded to agree to amendments. These are likely to be adopted at the committee stage, if the press and pressure groups display hostility and the opposition advances some telling criticisms. Then it becomes a sign of wisdom on the Government's part—or call this prudence or bowing to the public will, if you prefer—to make concessions that dull the edge of the attacks. In 1962, for instance, this happened during the protracted debates on the controversial measure to restrict immigration to the United Kingdom from other countries of the Commonwealth. Parliament then acts in the manner intended for it as the body which represents and re-echoes the sentiments of groups of citizens on public questions. Since it controls the House anyway, the Government is free to decide if it can safely ignore its critics both inside and outside. But if it becomes convinced that its opponents are sufficiently numerous and feel rather deeply on the point at issue, it may demonstrate its dedication to democracy by retreating with the best grace it can muster.

Because Parliament's total work-load has increased so much, it must try to save its time for the matters that are important. The criterion of importance, however, is flexible. A topic will be important if it clearly affects the national interest, or is politically sensitive, or arouses public controversy. Much of the subject matter of legislation does not fit in any of these categories. There are many clauses which deal with the machinery of administration, about which there is sometimes no dispute. Since Parliament exists for debate, it should only occupy itself with what is debatable. The rest it can pass over. Hence, at the committee stage of a bill, by prior agreement between the two sides, the discussion may skip over several clauses and concentrate only on those where the Opposition wishes to make a point. In addition, Parliament has increasingly delegated to the Ministry the power to issue subordinate regulations or orders to supplement in detail the broader features of a statute. This practice evoked much criticism in the 1920's and culminated in a book by the then Lord Chief Justice attacking what he chose to call *The New Despotism*.[26] As a result, a Royal Commission was set up to inquire into the subject of Ministers' Powers.[27] They reported that some abuses had occurred for which safeguards were needed, but that the charges in general were grossly exaggerated. Further, they recognized that the proliferation of governmental activity in a modern society called for greater administrative discretion which Parliament could not possibly hope to supervise in detail. Much of the content of modern law has a technical character which only experts are qualified to understand. Members of Parliament should, therefore, concern themselves with general policy and broad principles, leaving the technical matters and specific details to be spelled out elsewhere. The consequence is not so much a surrender of its authority by Parliament, as a division of labor which makes sense.

The Ultimate Power

Finally there is the fourth of Parliament's functions—to provide a national forum where grievances can be aired in public. What should be said on this score? Has there been a decline in the discharge of this duty or do Members still prosecute it with full vigor? I would answer the latter, emphatically. There is no substantial evidence to show that genuine grievances, of individuals or groups, are no longer accorded a public hearing through the machinery of the House. In fact, one might plausibly argue the opposite: that, while Parliament has seen its share in other functions dwindle, it has deliberately insisted on continuing its full prerogatives as the watchdog of the public interest and the inquisitor into signs or symptoms of administrative tyranny. A major responsibility of backbenchers is to serve as intermediaries between their constituents and the departments in Whitehall. Because of the tremendous extension in the activities of the modern state, the individual citizen is the subject of laws

26. Cosmopolitan Book Corporation: New York, 1929.
27. London, Cmd., 4060, 1932.

and regulations and decisions which in countless ways, direct and indirect, remote and intimate, affect his welfare and define his opportunities. A person may feel that a rule was applied harshly in his case, that he has rights which were overlooked, that he is entitled to a favor, that he is being pushed around by bureaucrats. Such notions may be grounded in fact or they may be illusory. But it is a fact that they are felt, and they arise naturally from the position of an individual confronting a hugh machinery whose intricacies and size seem incomprehensible.

It is here that the much-despised politician—*homo parliamentarianus vulgaris*—fulfills an essential function. He is the channel of communication between John Doe and H. M. Government, seeking out information, requesting that an application be sympathetically considered, humanizing the impersonality of the law. Members who do their duty conscientiously spend much time in writing and telephoning departments at their constituents' request—and when an inquiry is received from a Member of the House of Commons, a careful reply is always forthcoming. For the ordinary Members hold the trigger of that ultimate weapon which they have never abandoned. They have the power of public criticism under procedures of the House which can be fully reported in the press. The system is in fact formalized in the Question-Time, a one-hour period with which Parliament opens its afternoon session. On this occasion, by procedures which are now carefully regularized, Members receive answers from Ministers to questions which have previously been submitted in writing and may, at the Speaker's discretion, follow up the reply with a few "spontaneous" (i.e., carefully prepared) supplementaries whose purpose is to hit the Minister where he is weakest.[28] It is significant that the power of Members to put questions directly to Ministers developed historically during the very period when the Cabinet was acquiring progressively more control over Parliament's other functions and when party discipline was tightening. The back-benchers to some extent compensated by this gain for their losses in other spheres.

By and large, however, a conclusion of fundamental importance remains valid. Parliament's power has not declined at all in the field which is basic to its dignity as an institution and to the spirit of the democracy which it represents. Originally convoked by the Crown, and using the occasion to its advantage to seek redress of wrongs, the contemporary Commons turns the weapon of publicity on the work of the Crown's Ministers. Hence the great combination of legal authority and political power which the Cabinet holds is exercised with the caution that flows from the fear of public

28. On this whole subject, see the useful study by D. N. Chester and N. Bowring on *Questions in Parliament*, (Clarendon Press: Oxford, 1962).

exposure and disapproval. In this sense, the Parliament continues its ancient, historic function. It is still the place where the people's representatives speak out with impunity, and where the strength of government is tempered by the strength of criticism. This role which the legislature plays is possible because it gives constitutional expression to the political dialectic of the party system, just as the latter is able to function because of the freedoms to associate and express opinions on which the people insist in a democracy.

Mutatis mutandis, much of what has just been said about the Parliament at Westminster applies to other legislative bodies of the democratic world. The variations which they exhibit conform to a general pattern. The legislature, as such, retains proportionately greater strength *vis-à-vis* the ministry wherever multipartism prevails. Where the chief executive is constitutionally separate from the legislature, there will either be an equilibrium between the two as in the United States, or the legislature will be reduced to the impotence which has befallen the French Assembly under President de Gaulle's authoritarian regime of plebiscites and personality. A plurality of parties has the natural consequence of weakening the ministry because its survival depends on a coalition between groups which may only be temporary. Hence the real focus of power is situated in the legislature, where the committees or commissions do much to shape the bills which ministers or members introduce. The Swedish Riksdag is a notable example of a legislature operating in the political context of multipartism whose commissions are famous for the thoroughness of their investigation and research.[29] In a genuine sense, therefore, although the Ministry proposes its drafts of bills, these may be substantially redrafted in the Riksdag before passage into law. Elsewhere, in the smaller democracies of western Europe—in Belgium, Denmark, the Netherlands, and Switzerland—much the same holds true. In none of them is the Ministry (or, in the Swiss case, the Federal Council) as potent as in the United Kingdom. The nearest continental approximation to Great Britain in this respect is Norway, for the simple political reason that its Labor party has been as strong as all the others combined and its solidarity has usually enabled it to control the Storting.

29. I was once discussing with a member of the Norwegian Storting a problem which they had been considering for some time. "The Swedes," he said, "are studying the same matter, and we're waiting for them to finish. When they've done research on something, there's no need for anybody else to repeat it."

The Need for Congressional Reform

The American Congress is perhaps at the opposite extreme to Britain from the standpoint of legislative independence. This is due to the reasons which were mentioned earlier—the multi-group character of the congressional parties and the constitutional exclusion of the President and Cabinet officers from the Capitol. Because it is created as a co-ordinate branch of the federal government, distinct in its personnel and drawing its legal authority from the Constitution, the Congress is wont to act politically in a manner which follows psychologically from the sense of separation. Senators and Representatives are acutely sensitive to the charge of being a "rubber-stamp." They resent any impression that they are dominated or driven by the occupant of the House at the other end of Pennsylvania Avenue. No President can use the big stick on a stubborn Congress. He has to proffer whatever carrots he can find. But even so, there are always some mulish members who will not budge for all the vegetables in the garden. A former Secretary of State, John Hay, once remarked in a moment of deep frustration that sending a treaty to the Senate for its consent was like watching a bull charge out into the arena. One thing you knew for certain: it would never come out alive. A similar comment could be made about the President's budget and many of his legislative proposals when they arrive on Capitol Hill. Some of these meet their death in committee or on the floor, and many emerge so mangled by congressional surgery or butchery that their original features are hard to recognize.

Nor is this true only of the role which Congress plays in law-making and finance. A wide range of functions is assigned to the legislative branch and it has many vantage points from which it can overlook and undercut its rival in pre-eminence—the Administration. The Congress is influential in foreign policy, not only because of the special senatorial powers to consent to treaties and to approve ambassadorial nominees, but also because of the annual need to appropriate large sums of money for military, technical, and economic assistance to other governments. In addition, like the British Parliament, Congress is the national forum for debating the questions of the hour, for expressing the grievances which citizens may suffer or imagine, for inquiring, probing, and investigating. Since the Congress is empowered to conduct hearings on any matter which falls within the scope of its constitutional authority, it may start an investigation into almost anything. Thereby it can detonate the ultimate weapon of a democratic state—the power of publicity. Somebody or other can always be found to undertake this task. The members of the opposition party will be looking constantly for campaign issues in the year or so preceding an election. But inquiries may also be started by a member of the majority who has an independent streak or is at odds with the White House, and occasionally his investigation may yield disclosures which embarrass his own party.[30] As with all examples of the use of a constitutional power, everything depends on the wisdom of its exercise. The investigating power is a necessary one and can be wholesome when it focuses attention on a matter which requires governmental action or when it exposes corruption which might otherwise remain secret. But it is often carried to excess and abused for purposes which are solely partisan (in the worst sense of the term) or even personal. On such occasions, individual citizens may suffer severe injustice through public attacks by legislators who enjoy congressional immunity.

It is always difficult, when summing up an evaluation of a great historic institution, to arrive at a judgment which is not unduly influenced by purely contemporary events and the passing mood which they evoke. I say this because, at the time when this is written, the reputation of the Congress has fallen especially low—so much that public confidence in the capacity of the legislative branch to meet the needs of the American people has been seriously impaired. In the general view, the Congress has been dilatory and even negligent in acting on proposals of national importance (e.g., in such fields as taxation and civil rights) submitted to it from the White House. Even when one recognizes that major interests in society and powerful organized groups are arrayed on opposite sides, it is still true that the legislature is hampered in reaching decisions by its own defective structure and customs. Congress itself could remedy such internal abuses as the powers of the House Rules Committee, minority filibusters in the Senate, and the appointment of committee chairmen by seniority. Most observers are agreed that the Presidency and Supreme Court genuinely try to formulate a national outlook on issues which really are national, whereas the Congress can seldom raise its vision from the parts to encompass the whole.

This is a judgment which I share, since recent Congresses have been all too plainly derelict in some of their duties to the American nation (notably, in failing to authorize better assistance for the needy aged, a government-supported medical program, and public transport in cities).[31] Still, it should be remembered that institutions with a long life span pass

30. E.g., Senator Kefauver's inquiry into organized crime during the Truman Administration, and Senator McCarthy's search for Communists in government positions as continued during the Eisenhower Administration.

31. In 1964, however, a bipartisan majority did enact the Civil Rights Law.

through these cycles of vigor and stupor. There have been periods in our history when the Presidency lamentably failed to produce a succession of men of high quality. Likewise, during the 1920's and early 1930's the Supreme Court was far from being regarded with the same respect as today. Both of these institutions, however, have risen nobly to their responsibilities in recent times, and we can only hope that the Congress will similarly react to the prods which its current inadequacy has brought upon itself. If it does not, the ultimate consequences for our democratic system could indeed be grave.

Taking a longer view, one may perhaps conclude that, if the modern legislature is mixed in quality and performance, this only indicates the fact that it is truly performing its proper function of representing the people. There is some rough justice in the argument that every nation gets the government it deserves. The twentieth-century chamber is a bundle of virtues and vices because it is a more or less accurate sample of the human beings who elect it. Few legislators will discourse with a Ciceronian eloquence. Few will counsel with the wisdom of a Solon or Solomon. Still fewer will be saintly men. The most one can expect is that the restless currents of democratic politics will take this rough-hewn material of ordinary human nature and then the educative responsibilities of public office will apply the polish, rather as the ocean wears off the sharper edges of its rocks and tumbles them into smoother pebbles. Any legislature contains its quota of professionals and specialists, of men who arrive there with some expertise or acquire it through their service. But in a broader sense, the function of the representative chamber should be to utilize our technical knowledge for the general welfare and harmonize particular interests through some notion of the common good. The legislature of a politically free society does more than merely check on abuses of executive power. As a miniature of the people, it reflects their aspirations and imperfections, fashions the justice they produce as a community, and formulates into public policy their level of civilization.

15

Political Leadership

In 1943, the six individuals who wielded the greatest influence in world politics were Churchill, Hitler, Pius XII, Roosevelt, Stalin, and Tojo. Twenty years later, the heads of the American, British and Russian governments, and the Pope, would be on the list, along with Mao and Nehru. The power which each of those men possessed was a complex in which several elements combined, and the combinations varied according to which factor assumed more prominence. In some cases, irrespective of the type of person who occupies its leading office, it is the size and importance of his country which primarily explains his stature. Whoever serves as President of the United States or is the principal figure in the Soviet Union's Politburo is bound to carry weight. If in addition he is somebody with the magnetic attraction of a Franklin D. Roosevelt, he will be heard and followed at home and abroad through the appeal of his own personality. The characteristics of the individual affect the office by determining the way in which its potentialities are developed. The American Presidency with Kennedy in the White House was not the same as under Roosevelt, and it differed again with Hoover, Truman, and Eisenhower. Likewise, the peacetime Premiership of Macmillan employed other arts than the Churchillian wartime dynamism. The Soviet leadership as exercised by Khrushchev has changed markedly from the cold-blooded tyranny of Stalin. Hitler was the product of an aggressive nationalism into which he injected the demonic force of his personality and a murderous madness. He, Mao, and Stalin are akin in that each arose with a revolutionary movement which overthrew an established system and, after seizing power, imposed its own institutions. Each therefore enjoyed a wide field for maneuver among the ruins of the past. In marked contrast is the Papacy.[1] This is the oldest continuous political organization in the world, endowed with traditions and precedents which have accumulated for more than sixteen centuries. Thus when the Cardinals elect one of their members as Pope, he acquires at once the powers invested in an authoritarian office, and is the custodian of its system. But there, too, as an astonished world observed in John XXIII, the individual can create a difference.

Leadership of the Democratic Style

Of the men who were mentioned in these lists, only five—two in 1943 and three in 1963—were functioning in a democratic milieu. The President of the United States, and the Prime Ministers of the United Kingdom and India, achieve office as a result of a national election in which the mass of the citizens take part and alternatives are presented. They hold or lose their positions by the same method at periodic intervals. In the authoritarian regimes, the political leader is either chosen by a small oligarchy and depends on their support, or exercises power with a personal domination reinforced by terror and the secret police. Hitler and Stalin in this century pushed the rule of One to a limit seldom, if ever, equalled in history, and millions died because of them. At the end of World War II in Europe, a general election removed Churchill from office at the moment of his greatest triumph—at a time, in fact, when the British public at large felt unbounded gratitude and admiration for his indomitable courage from 1940 to 1944. Yet, looking to the future, a majority of the voters preferred, not the man, but the party and the program more likely to foster economic and social justice. Democracy could go no further in demonstrating the ultimate power of the people over the individual—however great he might be. When the Potsdam Conference recessed in the summer of 1945, in order that Churchill might go to London to await the electoral verdict,[2] it was Attlee who rejoined Stalin and Truman as Britain's Prime Minister. Stalin must then have reflected on the transitory character of power in a democracy. In his case, as he knew from his own

1. The Papacy is unique and forms a special case. Its primary raison d'être is religious, but its influence on politics and the scale of its political operations are undeniable. Staffed by a clerical hierarchy, its type of government is theocratic. The Pope has traditionally reigned and ruled in the style of a monarch.

2. The election had been held earlier, but the results were not tallied until the ballots of military personnel stationed overseas were brought back to Britain.

experience and Hitler's, nothing could remove him from his position but defeat in war, an assassin's bullet, or a natural death.

These considerations suggest the nature of the problem with which this chapter is concerned. A discussion of the legislature concerns an institution which is unique to democracy. Only in a democratic context can it be what it is and do what is characteristic of it. But that is not the case with political leadership. Here is a generic phenomenon comprising many species, ranging from the democratic to the despotic. It makes a certain sense to talk of the political functions performed by Churchill and Roosevelt, by Hitler and Stalin, as belonging to the same broad category, whereas it makes no sense to group together the American Congress, the British Parliament, the Nazi Reichstag, and the Supreme Soviet. When Machiavelli wrote his classic essay on political power, he illustrated his general maxims with historical examples of successful cases to imitate and failures to avoid. They covered a wide range of types and forms—tyrannical and benevolent, autocratic and responsible. No system of government can dispense with the requirement of political leadership. This has always been true. But the need for it is even greater in this century than it was in the past because of the increase in population, the incorporation of the masses of mankind in the political process, and the continual extension of the activities of government. All these trends, which are unlikely to be reversed, have the result of multiplying the situations which evoke discussion and decision, and the cumulative pressure of more and more decisions accentuates the need for coherent and therefore unified direction.

Leadership is not the same in a democracy as in a dictatorship. It cannot be—or there would be no democracy. Even under the stresses of a World War, Roosevelt and Churchill functioned in a political milieu which contrasted sharply with those of Hitler and Stalin. The crucial differences between the leadership that is exercised in the democracies and in the non-democratic states consist in the manner in which it is acquired, employed, and lost, and in the purposes to which it is put. Nevertheless, the fact that all types of leadership exhibit generic similarities does confront democracy with a difficulty. Leadership always involves some concentration of power in one institution or in one person or group. How then can we be sure that this power will not grow beyond the limit of safety? What guarantee is there that a democracy can mobilize enough power to serve the people in the way they want, but not so much as to impose a tyranny which they cannot escape?

The Ambivalence of Leadership

Here is a genuine dilemma whose solution is complicated by the nature of the problem. It is not a simple choice of either-or. The alternatives of having some leadership or none are an exercise for purely theoretical discussion; they are not valid in real political life. Leadership there must be, and the only practical question is: How much? When we are talking about a matter of degree, the criteria of logic and clear-cut principle are less relevant than those of judgment, prudence, and common sense. All democracies have to cope with a contradiction which is inherent in power itself: if used, it may be abused. How does one provide for the former and prevent the latter? The gradations by which a power which is organized to serve can become a weapon wherewith to dominate are observable, but undefinable. Plato put his finger on the problem in the passage of *The Republic* where he commented on the origins of tyranny and located its source in the person who poses as the spokesman or champion of the *Demos.*[3] Generalizing, as the dialogue shows, from the political career of Peisistratus, he describes the stages and stratagems in a dictator's climb to power. In his relationship with the people, the crucial question is always: Who controls whom? Is he their servant or do they serve his will? The turning point occurs when they can no longer remove him except by force—and when even that requires such abnormal circumstances as domestic revolution, assassination, or foreign war.

The ambivalence in the phenomenon of leadership is aptly illustrated in a story of the French Revolution. A political group was meeting in a house when a mob rushed past in the street. Seeing them, one of the politicians rose to leave, explaining as he went: "I am their leader; therefore I must follow them."[4] Leadership implies supporters, and the dynamics of their relationship operate in both directions. The institutions of the democratic process are designed to find out what people want and it is then the duty of those in public office to fulfill their wishes to the extent that they can. It would seem simple to distinguish between democratic and authoritarian leaders by saying that the former obey the popular will, whereas the latter bend the people to their own will. But the facts are not

---

3. " 'Is it not always the people's custom then to put forward some champion in a pre-eminent position and nurture him so that he grows to great stature?' 'It is.' 'This indeed is clear,' I said, 'that whenever a tyrant is born, he sprouts from no other root than that of the people's champion.' 'Abundantly clear.' " *Republic*, Bk. VIII, 565b.
4. In *The Gondoliers*, it will be recalled, the Duke of Plaza Toro always led his troops into battle from the rear.

as simple as that antithesis would suggest. The people are not a single, homogeneous whole. They consist of many groupings, of various minorities; and a majority may not always be discernible. Even in a dictatorship of the most despotic kind, the tyrant has his supporters. There were men who worked willingly with Hitler or with Stalin, who enjoyed the privileges which his power bestowed, who threw in their lot with his and shared in his crimes. The point about a democracy which makes its leadership different is the freedom inherent in the system. Producing a majority is a creative task, because the majority will is seldom ready-made or self-evident. Moreover, the groups of which society is composed can recombine and form a new majority which will throw out old leaders and select new ones, and elections are held regularly to give an opportunity for this to happen.

The dangers which result from the abuse of leadership make it suspect in democratic eyes. Acton's famous generalization, to the effect that all power tends to corrupt and absolute power corrupts absolutely, incorporates an emotional bias against power, and his judgment goes beyond the historical evidence (even with the saving qualification that this is a tendency only).[5] One could not say that Jefferson or Lincoln or Franklin Roosevelt, that Gladstone or Churchill or Nehru, were corrupted by exercising power. Opponents may disagree with their policies, or query the wisdom of this action or that; but corrupted those men were not. And when there are such exceptions to cite, one doubts the soundness of Acton's rule. Yet the suspicions remain, and they are justified by the fact that power is sometimes abused with consequences which are horribly cruel. Power, like fire, is a good servant, but a bad master. A democracy is a political system which keeps the power of its leaders always under control.

The argument for leadership of some kind or another is a blend of necessity and convenience. There is work to be done; a government must be run; organization is required. In a legislature, somebody must preside and somebody must take an initiative. In a committee or a cabinet, someone must occupy the chair and policies must be proposed. During an election, programs must be presented and discussed and votes must be actively sought. These are the activities which add up to the sum of leadership.

---

5. Acton is usually quoted as saying that "all power corrupts," the word "tends" being omitted. However, another eminent historian, Burckhardt, did write as follows: "Now power is of its nature evil, whoever wields it. It is not stability but a lust, and *ipso facto* insatiable, therefore unhappy in itself and doomed to make others unhappy." *Force and Freedom* (Pantheon Books: New York, 1943), p. 184. There are Platonic echoes in this.

They are not always well conducted. On occasion, there is a lack of wise judgment and effective personalities. At such times, democracy suffers. The plight of American politics between Wilson and Roosevelt offers an example, as does British politics between Lloyd George and Churchill. Without subscribing to Carlyle's exaggeration that history is the record of the deeds of heroes, one should not go to the opposite extreme and deny the need for political individuality and greatness. Democracy gains something when it is temporarily led by a man who evokes respect and trust.

How then is this produced? What is it that makes possible the kind of leadership which stays within the bounds of democracy? How do we escape the sharp horn of Plato's dilemma? How does the people's spokesman remain their champion and not evolve into their master? The answer to these questions, as in all matters political, depends on a group of factors. These consist of the people's social composition and prevailing ideals, of historical tradition and institutional structures. I propose to compare three types of political leadership, which are different yet equally democratic. They can best be studied in the context of the countries which have produced and exemplify them. These types are the Swiss, the American, and the British. To characterize them briefly: The Swiss have a system which leaves the least scope to individual leadership, the United States places the greatest reliance on the qualities of the individual, and the British method lies in between. From this standpoint, let us examine the Federal Council, the Presidency, and the Cabinet.

The Swiss Type of Collegial Executive

In Switzerland, nothing is normal.[6] The Swiss are the only nation in the modern world, of those with stable and democratic institutions, which expects their leadership to come from a committee. They object strongly to any arrangements which accord pre-eminence to a single person. In their political behavior they aim at minimizing, or even effacing, the force of individuality. In this respect they are at the opposite pole from the Iberian peninsula and Latin America, where *caudillismo* and *personalismo* are the stigmata of politically backward peoples who have not developed the arts

6. Some evidence for this assertion: the degree to which the initiative and referendum are used, a federal state without judicial review of federal laws, the disfranchisement of women, the collegial type of executive, and a multi-party system combined with frightening stability.

of collective self-government.[7] The Swiss are fervent believers in democracy, of whose principles and procedures they possess an experience that is second to none. From a history which has involved them in repeated struggles with Emperors, Kings, Dukes, and Popes, they have derived a rooted aversion to personal aggrandizement, whether of the inherited or the self-made variety. Hence it is their invariable practice to employ a collegial executive. Distrustful of leaders, they consider power as necessary but dangerous, and have put it into commission. Thus, their contemporary system merely continues and conforms to one of their oldest traditions.

When the Swiss were converting their loose Confederation into a tighter union in 1848 and were debating how to organize their executive, they had little difficulty in reaching agreement on its essentials. As Rappard has observed, they borrowed some features of federalism from the United States (e.g., bicameralism). But when it came to the executive branch, they followed their old customs.[8] In the communes and cantons they had long been accustomed to the collegial executive. This they transferred to their central government. The commission which prepared the draft of the federal Constitution in 1848 considered, but rejected, a presidential office of the American type. The argument of the report deserves quotation: "We are cognisant of the advantages which a presidency would offer in promoting unity and continuity in public affairs whether from the standpoint of expressing the national will or in keeping officials responsible. Nevertheless, the committee could not dream of proposing to establish an office so antithetical to the notions and customs of the Swiss, who could see in it a step in the direction of a king or a dictator. We Swiss adhere to councils, and the democratic sentiment amongst us rejects any form of pre-eminence which is too exclusive."[9]

The institution which these traditions and suspicions produced has now

---

7. Two small exceptions to this statement are Costa Rica and Uruguay. The latter, like Switzerland, is a pacific buffer state between much larger neighbors, which is internally stable and enjoys high living standards. The two-party system of *Colorados* and *Blancos* has been institutionalized in a collegial executive modelled after the Swiss.

8. "Although the organization of the executive power in Switzerland habitually arouses and holds the attention of foreigners more than that of the legislative power, it exhibits much less originality when one views it solely in the light of national tradition. . . . Collegial government was as old as the cantons themselves." William E. Rappard, *La Constitution Fédérale de la Suisse*, 1848-1948 (A la Baconnière: Neuchâtel, 1948), p. 153.

9. From the Report of the Preparatory Commission (Lausanne, 1848), p. 65. Quoted by Rappard, *op. cit.*, p. 154, and in *The Government of Switzerland* (Van Nostrand: New York, 1936), p. 76.

settled into a well-defined pattern. Certain of its features are specified in the Constitution. But where this document is silent, political custom has filled in the gaps with rules which are no less binding. The Constitution provides for a Federal Council (*Bundesrat, Conseil fédéral*) consisting of seven men. They are elected simultaneously for terms of four[10] years by the two Houses of the federal legislature meeting in a joint session. On the question of a Councillor's elegibility for re-election, the Constitution says nothing. Custom, however, has spoken eloquently. The legislature traditionally re-elects a Councillor for continuous terms until he dies or volunteers to retire. No elected official in a democratic state has more security of tenure than a Swiss Federal Councillor. As a consequence, vacancies occur rarely and the composition and character of the Council change very slowly.

Since every committee, even in Switzerland, must have a chairman, the legislature at a joint session designates one of the seven to be presiding officer of the Council with the title of President of the Confederation. It also elects a second Councillor to serve as Vice-President. Each man holds this office for one year at a time; he may not succeed himself, although later he may serve again in one of these offices. To these constitutional requirements, custom has added its inevitable extra. The Presidency and Vice-Presidency are filled in rotation according to seniority—the Vice President of one year being the President in the next. The Constitution confers no special powers on the President. True, he is Head of the State, both for domestic ceremonial and for external relations. But this is an honorific position, not one of greater power. A man who is king for twelve months, and then must ordinarily wait six more years before his turn comes round again, cannot be too overbearing while dressed in such little brief authority. If he is too domineering to his colleagues, they have six opportunities to his one to make his life unpleasant. Hence the rules of the system, both formal and informal, encourage collegiality and minimize individuality.

Not only do the Swiss take elaborate care to see that no man becomes *primus inter pares*, but they have erected ingenious safeguards to stop one group or interest from predominating over the rest. This is accomplished by a careful plan of rationing the seats on the Council and distributing the segments of power which each incorporates. One such principle of distribution is cantonal. The Constitution prohibits the election of two Councillors from any one canton, which prevents the biggest units from dividing up the spoils—if they were so minded. But again political custom

10. Originally, three. But in 1931 the term of the National Assembly, and that of the Council, was extended to four.

has supplied other details which add up to a predictable regularity. Because Berne and Zurich are the two largest cantons, there is always one Councillor from each of these. In addition, the German-speaking majority recognizes the legitimate claims of the French- and Italian-speaking areas for representation on the Council. Hence at least two Councillors are elected from *la Suisse romande*. Either both of them are picked from French cantons, or one could be French and the second could come from Ticino.[11] Since Vaud is the most important of the French cantons, one of these Councillors will ordinarily be a Vaudois.

Party Composition of the Federal Council

The other factor which governs the distribution is derived, of course, from the relations between the parties. Here, if anywhere, the Swiss version of democracy is seen in its most characteristic form, and the political genius of this people has generated a system which few others could imitate with success. For not only is the executive power of their federation lodged in the hands of a seven-membered committee, but this body has evolved into a permanent multi-party coalition. Originally, this was not the case. When the federal Constitution went into effect in 1848, its political architects, the Radicals, the same who had stopped the secession and won the civil war of 1847,[12] at first monopolized all seven seats on the Council. Like the Federalists in the United States, they were the men responsible for planning the new machinery and they meant to operate it in the early years until it was running smoothly. Thus Radicals and Liberals[13] between them furnished all the Councillors for four decades (1848-92). Then came the reconciliation with the Catholic Conservatives—inspired by fear of the Socialists—and first one Catholic was welcomed to the Council (1892-1919), and in the next decade (1919-29) two were elected—the remaining seats being still occupied by Radicals. In 1929 the Radicals surrendered one of their five seats to the Peasant party, which was strong in Canton Bern, and solved the problems of representing that particular party and that Canton. Thus, for a decade and a half (1929 to 1943) the Federal Council functioned as a three-party coalition.

Meanwhile the Socialists were pressing their claims for a seat. Since 1931, they have normally polled a higher percentage of votes than any

11. The latter happened during the long period when Giuseppe Motta served as Councillor.
12. See Chapter 12, pp. 355-6.
13. For this distinction, see Chapter 12, p. 356.

other party, and have frequently held a larger block of seats in the assembly than their nearest rivals, the Radicals. Yet they were long excluded from the Federal Council, even when so small a group as the Peasant party was included. Hence the Federal Council had all the appearance of a coalition composed of parties whose common aim was to gang up against the Socialists—thus forcing the latter into the role of a permanent opposition. Not until 1943 did the situation change. Then the first Socialist was elected to the Federal Council, and later, when his seat became vacant, another Socialist was elected to fill it. The latter, however, did something un-Swiss. He resigned (1953) after the legislature rejected a bill he had sponsored. Consequently, for the next six years, the Council again functioned without a Socialist member.

In discussions about the Supreme Court of the United States, people often echo Mr. Dooley's opinion that this judicial tribunal "follows th' ilection returns." This is true in the long-term sense that the thinking of the Court's majority responds eventually to the same basic movements of opinion as are recorded in the popular votes. The Court is not, however, bound either in law or political necessity to reverse itself whenever a new Administration takes office or the Outs become the Ins on Capitol Hill. Generally, the same can be said of the Swiss Federal Council. Although its members are elected by the legislature, the practice of continuous re-election has meant that this body registers the fluctuations of party strength with majestic slowness. The clean sweep of the higher political leadership that occurs in London under the alternations of the two-party system only horrifies the Swiss. In Berne, the composition of the Council changeth at the speed of the Rhone glacier, not as an Alpine avalanche. Hence, when the Socialists won extra seats in the National Assembly at the election of 1955, and again replaced the Radicals as the strongest group, they looked at the Federal Council, completely controlled by their rivals, and claimed two seats as their fair proportion. The answer of the coalition and their newspapers was highly characteristic. In effect they said: "We are very sorry, but that is not our system. At present there is no vacancy. You will have to wait. When a vacancy occurs, then we shall see." [14] In 1959, the unusual happened. Two vacancies occurred simultaneously, and two Socialists were placed on the Council. Since then, the Council has functioned as a four-party coalition—consisting of two Radicals, two Catholic Conservatives, two Socialists, and one from the Peasants. To all outward

14. Professor Rappard told me that he had given an answer on these lines to M. André Siegfried, who had inquired about the representation of Socialists on the Council. Siegfried had implied that the Council should be changed in conformity with the electoral results. Rappard affirmed that this was not expected or required in Switzerland.

appearance, the members of this strange consortium have managed to co-operate without undue friction. On the part of the Socialist newcomers, that result seems to be due to their policy of not pressing for measures which really embody their philosophy. Nowadays they talk little, and do even less, about designing a brave new world, and are content to repaint the old one—in a soft pink.

Such being the formative conditions which shape the Federal Council, how does it function in practice? Theoretically the Council is subordinate to the legislature and is duty bound to execute its decisions. In practice, however, the policies approved by the legislators are normally those which the Councillors have initiated and proposed. Federal Councillors do not have seats in the legislature; but they appear in either House and speak there. It is customary, when a vacancy occurs on the Council, to fill it by the election of a member of the national legislative body. In fact, a man becomes a Councillor because he has the confidence and respect of his party group. The practice of re-election for an indefinite number of terms gives him experience; and since he ordinarily continues in charge of the same department, he becomes a professional in the knowledge of its subject-matter. Thus, when the Council as a whole confronts the legislature, it does so as a body of experts in relation to an assemblage of amateurs. Seldom, therefore, will the latter overrule the former. It is the consensus of observers that this collegial executive which in principle is the servant of the legislature has developed into its leader. Bryce thought that the Federal Council provided almost as much leadership as British Cabinets do.[15] Rappard considered the influence of the former to be even more decisive than that exercised by the Cabinet over Parliament.[16] But the collective responsibility of the Federal Council is not as hard and fast as in Britain. Nor could it be, in view of the fact that the Council is a multiparty coalition. When unanimity is lacking, decisions are reached by a majority and the minority is bound by their view. Dissenters, however, may make known the fact that they disagreed and state their opinions in the legislature. But this is a rare occurrence. As skilled politicians, the Federal Councillors are aware that their strength is their solidarity. If they part company too often and voice their divisions in public, their leadership

15. "Legally the servant of the Legislature [the Federal Council] exerts in practice almost as much authority as do English, and more than do some French Cabinets, so that it may be said to lead as well as to follow." *Op. cit.*, Vol. I, Chap. 28, p. 354.
16. "We would be inclined to go even farther and to suggest that the influence of the Federal Council on the Federal Assembly is, if less spectacular, actually more rather than less decisive than that which the British Cabinet exercises on the House of Commons." *The Government of Switzerland*, p. 82.

of the legislature will go by default through splitting among themselves.

This system embodies some undeniable advantages. Admirably it expresses in a concrete institution the need of a pluralistic society for a form of government which will create harmony out of diversity. The collegial character of the Federal Council, and its multi-party composition, encourage the search for compromise and the practice of moderation. Experience, continuity, and pragmatism are its virtues, and they are not to be minimized.

But the pleasant picture also has its negative side. The continuity is excessive in degree. More frequent infusions of fresh blood would do some good at the head of the Swiss body politic. The lack of a single chief executive prevents the aggrandizement of One. But it tends toward slowness of decision and confusion of direction. In a sense, the Swiss have carried to the ultimate the art of political anonymity. For the most part, these Councillors are faceless men. Most Swiss do not know the name of their President-for-the-year. Few could name more than a couple of the Seven. In modern Swiss politics one searches in vain for great names and big men. The other smaller democracies have thrown up some outstanding statesmen, whose reputation and influence extended beyond their borders. The creativity of individual Swiss is felt, if at all, in other fields than the exercise of public office—as Pestalozzi, Dunant, Hodler, and Honegger, bear witness. Under the special circumstances of a buffer state, whose unchanging foreign policy is permanent neutrality, this type of organization has worked successfully. It is undramatic, prosaic, sensible, and reasonably efficient. It would be ill-adapted, however, to the needs of a community actively immersed in world affairs and requiring dynamic direction amid turbulent currents.

The American Presidency

If they had to be invented in fiction, once could scarcely conceive a greater contrast in form and function than the two types of democratic executive operating in fact in Berne and Washington. Where Swiss leadership is collegial, multi-party, and nameless, the American system is designed for the leadership of One. The Presidential office makes the greatest possible demands on a single individual. Indeed it is the political apotheosis of individuality among a people who have set much store by this principle. The personal qualities of the man who happens to occupy the White House make a crucial difference in how the government functions in the United States.

These aspects of the office will be discussed here: the bases of presidential power, the quality of the men who have served as President, and the various roles a President performs.

I begin with the sources of a President's power, since everything else stems from these. Three distinguishable factors enter into the compound: his personal attributes, the strength of his party and his position in it, and the legal authority he derives from the Constitution and acts of Congress. These elements differ in their significance at various stages in a man's climb to power and his eventual exercise thereof. When politicians are being mentioned as possible candidates for their party's nomination, and when the active campaigning starts, the personality of the individual counts heavily in the scales. The several media through which opinion is formed—newspapers, magazines, radio, and television—produce a composite impression of a man's general character and special characteristics.[17] He is dissected and analyzed *ad nauseam* in terms of family connections, education, religious affiliation, the state or region to which he belongs, his wealth, training, and occupation, and prior public service. All the news that is fit to print is retold by scribes with wearisome reiteration. The rest is circulated by the gossips, calumniators, and opponents. Then, when a human being has been minutely classified as one would a botanical species, and is delineated by a scatter of oblong holes on a punch-card, such details become blurred and merge together as the campaigning proceeds and the voter focuses in the primaries on a few traits that stand out. This candidate is folksy and has courage; that one is cold, intellectual, and conservative. Here is an idealistic liberal and a veritable "egghead"; there, an old soldier with a wide grin. He is a young Irish-Catholic multimillionaire's son from Harvard; or he is self-made and opportunistic. So millions of spectators, who cannot have personal contact with these actors on the stage, decide somehow that they admire Truman, like Ike, distrust Nixon, and cannot comprehend Stevenson.

But once the candidate is picked, the party of which he is titular leader becomes an essential item in the aggregate. The individual is now more than F.D.R. or Ike or J.F.K. He is the Democratic or Republican standard-bearer. Thus, he must act as the representative man who pulls together the internal wings and factions and interests and pleads for unity in the face of the enemy. In the campaign which follows the nominating conventions and precedes the November election, the people will be swayed by the political appeal of the party as well as by the personal attraction (or reverse) of the candidate. Millions will vote for X or Y be-

17. In the jargon of the Madison Avenue advertisers, this is known as the "public image."

cause they habitually vote Democratic or Republican and this is their party's nominee. But other millions will assess the individual and his party separately. Independent voters may judge that X is the better man for the job and vote accordingly. Others again will think in the larger terms of the kind of Administration which a Democrat or a Republican would lead, the appointments he would make, the programs he would espouse. A general indefinable atmosphere condenses into a mood so that people are influenced by the argument that it is time for a change, or we should get America moving, or A is soft on communism, or B will save us from war, or C will spend more on welfare services. In that case, the voters are expressing their preference for a certain direction, and for the party and candidate who are more likely to follow it.

The most important political fact about the Presidency is that a man wins the office in a popular nationwide election. He must go directly to the people and seek their votes. His power comes from them. An electorate of more than a hundred millions chooses between two of its citizens for the highest office in the land. It is a formidable matter, and awesome in its implications. Moreover, this development has occurred as a consequence of the democratization of the American system. It was not the original intention of those who created it. The majority of the Founding Fathers were afraid of having the President directly elected by the people since they despised the ignorant and distrusted the poor. Consequently they devised the method of indirect election by a College specially created for this sole purpose. But its elitist connotations were ill-suited to the advancing democratic spirit. Nor could the system be harmonized with the growth of parties. In 1800, and again in 1824, the parties made havoc of the Electoral College. Either the voters, with the parties serving as intermediaries, had to pick the President, or the College had to be free to make an independent choice. One system or the other had to prevail. The result has been one in which the legal forms have been smothered by the political realities. The parties nominate; the candidates compete; the people vote; the College ratifies. A modern President has power because he has won support among the public. That is the source of his strength.

But as soon as the victorious candidate has taken the oath of office, a new element is added to the compound. He now acquires an authority conferred on him directly by the Constitution, as well as certain specific responsibilities under Acts of Congress which he is duty bound to execute and enforce. This is the legal aspect of his office. He is lawfully empowered, or obligated, to do certain things because of the position he fills. This kind of authority comes to him from the Constitution which is the supreme law of the land. But the reason why he, and no one else, has it is political. The contest between parties and personalities decided which individual would wield the powers entrusted by the Constitution to the President.

The Quality of Presidents

The possession of legal authority, however, is one thing; its use, another. The actual use—except in those functions which are mandatory—involves a considerable degree of judgment and discretion. Again this comes back to the qualities of the individual. He has advsiors galore, and he will receive far more reports and memoranda than he has time to study thoroughly. But he, and he alone, must decide. This is a matter of judgment. It involves the intellectual ability to discriminate between the wise and unwise; a political flair for tactics, timing, and the handling of men; and, one hopes, the statesmanship which discerns the larger interests of the country. How far a President succeeds or fails in these matters depends, first on his own character, next on the public assessment of his capabilities, and third on his effectiveness in leading his party and exploiting divisions among the opposition.

The presidential system, therefore, is a resultant of several factors, and it is their variations in force and content which give each Adimiistration its unique character. The legal authority fluctuates, on the whole, less than the others. Although there is a steady tendency to increase the scope of constitutional powers, which are broad, but undefined (e.g., that of Commander-in-Chief), these form as it were a solid continuum which a President takes over with the office much as he acquires a staff, a house, a plane, a yacht, and a fleet of cars. In its political aspect, the Presidency is more changeable. Its strength ebbs and flows with the vicissitudes of party combat and the demands of the times. Most volatile of all is the influence which a President exerts through his individuality. This is no constant. It cannot be measured or predicted. It can swing sharply up or down. Compare the ways in which Truman was regarded by the public in 1946 and 1950, or Eisenhower in 1953 and 1958. Some men grow in the office; others do not measure up to its demands. Some are successful in winning elections, but incapable of governing. Some are over-shadowed by members of their Cabinet or by powerful Congressmen. A few, such as Abraham Lincoln and Franklin Roosevelt, respond to an emergency by demonstrating a greatness far beyond the earlier expectation.

When James Bryce wrote *The American Commonwealth*, he included a chapter with the title: "Why Great Men are not Chosen Presidents." [18]

18. Vol. I, Chap. 8.

That was published in 1888, just when Cleveland was ending his first term. The judgment which Bryce expressed was undoubtedly influenced by the general mediocrity of the Presidents who followed Lincoln.[19] He was also impressed by the arguments of Woodrow Wilson, who had published his *Congressional Government* three years earlier. Wilson's theme was that Congress had become the predominant branch of government; that the character of Presidents had declined, and therewith the prestige of their office. Moreover, he considered this "inevitable." [20]

It is, of course, difficult to evaluate the men who have served as President on a scale, since objective criteria are lacking and nobody can eliminate his subjective preference. Recognizing such limitations, I shall nevertheless try to list the Presidents whom I would call great and those of the second rank, who were still above the average and can be called big. Suppose we take the year 1860 as the dividing line and group together those who served in the first seven decades (1789-1860) and those who followed in the century from 1861 to 1960.[21] In the earlier period, two Presidents—Washington and Jefferson—could certainly be described as great. A third, Jackson, might be classified as big. Some would be tempted to include John Adams and James Madison in the latter category. But my opinion would be that they were big men in other respects, but not in their tenure of the Presidency. In the hundred years since the Civil War erupted, the clearly great Presidents have been Lincoln, Wilson, and Franklin Roosevelt. Theodore Roosevelt could fairly be described as a big man in the office. Some might say the same of Cleveland, though this is arguable; and I suspect that, as time goes by, Truman's stature will steadily increase because of his genuine courage and epochal policies.[22]

The over-all record, then, is not so bad. In a hundred and seventy years, exclusive of the doubtful cases, there have been five great Presidents and at least two big ones. Together, they held the office for a total of almost fifty-six years—i.e., for a third of the period since the Constitution went

19. I.e., Andrew Johnson, Grant, Hayes, Garfield, and Arthur. Whether he intended his criticism to cover Cleveland is doubtful.
20. *Congressional Government* (Houghton, Mifflin & Co.: Boston, 4th ed., 1887, Chap. 1, pp. 42-3.
21. I am excluding President Kennedy because the emotions aroused by the brutal tragedy in Dallas make it impossible, as yet, to judge him in perspective.
22. *The New York Times* published, in Section 6 of the Sunday edition, July 29, 1962, the results of a rating of Presidents conducted by seventy-five American historians. Their conclusions were that five Presidents belonged in the highest class of "great." These were, in descending order: Lincoln, Washington, Franklin Roosevelt, Wilson, and Jefferson. Six others they ranked in the next class of "near-great," in the following sequence: Jackson, Theodore Roosevelt, Polk, Truman, John Adams, and Cleveland.

into effect. Anybody writing in the late 1880's would have had to express the same opinions as Bryce and Wilson. But there is definite ground for encouragement in the fact that the first six decades of the twentieth century have yielded three men in the higher classifications (including the author of *Congressional Government* himself).

There is a sense in which the office educates and develops the man. Some were already proven great in other spheres before their election, e.g., Washington and Jefferson. That they were remarkable Presidents is therefore no surprise. Two of the very greatest, however, namely Lincoln and F. D. Roosevelt, were surprises. They grew in the office, measuring up to its exacting demands. Among recent Presidents, Truman is a case of a man who did not seek the office and was ill-prepared for its responsibilities when he was catapulted into it by Roosevelt's death. In his first two years he badly mishandled a number of situations and his public reputation fell to a very low point. From 1947 onward, however, he grasped the nettle of statesmanship and acted with a new vision and boldness. Eisenhowever, by contrast, though always popular with the public and winning his elections easily, never rose to the dimensions of the office. Inexperienced in politics and poorly informed on civilian affairs, he delegated too much to strong personalities and powerful minds among his official subordinates.[23] Thus the Presidency he handed on to his successor was a weaker institution than what he had himself received.[24]

The Functions of a President

So numerous and exacting are the duties of the Presidency that it is indeed hard to see how any human being could fulfill them adequately. It is not only the size of the country and its ramifications through the world which make the presidential burden well-nigh intolerable, but also its unusual concentration of functions. If "one man in his time plays many parts," so in his four or eight years does a President. He is head of the state, Chief Executive, chief legislator, Commander-in-Chief, party leader, and the prime mover in foreign relations. These different parts call for varied talents; and nobody can be expected to excel equally in them all, especially when they must be played simultaneously and their requirements are contradictory. To begin with, no one is going to have the chance

23. He was also handicapped by two major illnesses.
24. The judgment of Tacitus on the Emperor Galba, who also was a soldier, could be applied to Eisenhower: "Omnium consensu bonus Imperator, nisi imperasset." (Everyone would have judged him a good Emperor, if only he had never reigned.)

of showing what he can do in the other roles unless he can first fight a political campaign and win elections. Hence a successful President must initially be an acceptable party leader and an attractive vote-getter. The magnetism of Roosevelt, the geniality of Eisenhower, the youthful charm of Kennedy—these were political assets in the rough and tumble of the electoral arena. These were qualities which drew votes. They can also be used by a clever and determined President to mobilize support for his program after he has entered on his office and must persuade reluctant Congress that he has the people behind him. Franklin D. Roosevelt was a past master at this technique. His "fireside chats" on the radio, and his press conferences, brought the presidential face and voice and ideas directly and continuously before the electorate. No wonder that he won the office four times in succession.

But other qualities are needed, say, for administration. As Chief Executive, the President bears the direct responsibility for supervising and managing the great majority of the federal agencies. He administers an annual budget of around one hundred billion dollars. Over two and a half million civil servants are controlled by his directives. In this sphere, for elaborating programs and enforcing laws, the arts of the politician, which are needed for example to win approval of the budget in Congress, have to be supplemented by another set of techniques. All the sacred dogmas of the efficiency experts (span of control, clear lines of responsibility, delegation to subordinates) are treated with scepticism or outright irreverence at the political level where supporters must be kept happy, interests placated, compromises negotiated, and bargains transacted. Roosevelt again is the classic case in point. Brilliantly though he functioned as politician and statesman, he was a sorry administrator. During his Presidency, Washington was notorious for the multiplication of agencies with overlapping functions, the reshuffles of personnel, and reorganization of bureaus.

There are two supreme tests nowadays of a President: the measure of his skill in handling Congress and his success or failure in international diplomacy. The institutional arrangements of the American form of government strengthen the President in that his tenure is independent of the will of Congress; but they weaken him in that he depends on a co-ordinate branch for revenue and statutory authority. The relations of Presidents with the Congress have seemed at times to follow a cyclical pattern with phases of presidential leadership, congressional ascendancy, and balance of power. In the nineteenth century, there were a few, such as Jefferson, who exercised a strong influence over Congress, welding together the executive and legislative branches through the instrument of the party which they led. Others again—including as great a figure as Lincoln—were engaged in continual struggles with Congress and faced criticism and obstruction from within their own party as well as from the opposite side. Indeed, when smoothness or harmony characterizes the relations between the two branches, this cannot be cited as certain proof of the President's ability or skill. It may actually signify the reverse. The President may be weak or inexperienced in politics and therefore ineffectual, and may abdicate from his opportunity to lead in deference to dominant Representatives and Senators.

The Presidency of the twentieth century differs from that of the nineteenth in this important particular. From Washington to McKinley if a President exerted leadership in Congress, it was because he was an extraordinary man or the times were extraordinary and required his initiative. Since Theodore Roosevelt, all Presidents as a matter of course have been called upon to take a more active part in proposing legislation and influencing legislators. And the public nowadays expects this. Theodore Roosevelt was the first to argue strenuously in season and out for what he referred to as "my policies." His example has been increasingly followed, both by those who were temperamentally disposed to inject a dynamism into the office and also, though to a lesser extent, by those who elevated passivity into a constitutional principle. A modern President must appear to be a leader even if in fact he is not. He campaigns for the office in terms of a program which, if elected, he promises to introduce. When installed, he appeals to the Congress to support the measures which the citizens are supposed to have approved at the time they voted for him and rejected his opponent. When seeking re-election, or when his would-be successor is nominated, he runs on his record, asking the people to endorse what was accomplished during his stewardship and therefore, supposedly, because of it.

The Chief Legislator

Traditionally, the President has been known as the Chief Executive. That is a phrase which nowhere appears in the Constitution, although its meaning may be inferred from the clause conferring "the executive power." The title of Chief Executive accords accurately with that aspect of the office which places the President—and him alone—in a position of supremacy over the executive branch and entrusts him with constitutional functions which he can share with no one else. But in their more literal and restricted sense, the words would be utterly misleading if taken to imply that a President merely executes what others have decreed as law or chosen as policy. For a President in fact is a prime mover—and particularly so in the sphere of legislation. Not only that, but he wields by himself as much influence as an entire House of the Congress. Quite appropriately, to complement the title of Chief Executive and offset any wrong impression it might create, the President has been described as Chief Legislator.[25] Indeed it is not stretching the truth to say that in the domestic arena the people judge him most by his performance in this field. His executive decisions, to a large extent, are hidden from the public eye, or are prosaically buried in the detailed documentation of thousands of particular cases. But relations with Congress (though these too are conducted behind a screen of secrecy at White House breakfasts and in Capitol corridors) compel proponents and opponents to commit themselves in the glare of publicity. There is an element of high drama in the practices whereby a President must declare himself on the issues of the day, making known just where he stands and what course he favors. Nor is it possible for him to evade this responsibility, whatever his preference or the political risk to his personal standing. Whether he advocates, equivocates, or stays silent, he will be noted and judged both for acts and omissions. The prestige of his office, the fortunes of his party, his own place in history, are committed at each political move he makes. Using separate means for the several portions of his program, he must seek those combinations of votes which will add up to a majority in each House.

The use that he makes of the means at his disposal is an indication of his tactical skill as a politician. His judgment must tell him when to drive and when to bargain, where to hold out the carrot and where to brandish the stick. The techniques which contribute to the sum of his legislative leadership are as varied as they are numerous. Certain of them flow immediately from the Constitution; others, from the realities of political power. The Constitution does not say very much about the President's role in legislation, but it says enough to indicate that all legislative powers, despite the opening clause of Article 1, were not given to the Congress. For the President is required annually to report to the Congress on the state of the union; he may recommend to that body such measures as he thinks fit; he may convene both Houses in a special session; and he must either sign or veto all bills which majorities of the two Houses have approved. Taken together, this mixture of duties and opportunities gives the President a direct *entrée* into the legislative field. Historically, the power to initiate and propose was sparingly used throughout the nineteenth century and was then normally confined to general statements of policy.

25. By H. L. McBain in *The Living Constitution* (Macmillan: New York, 1934), Chap. 4.

Only during the last several decades have Presidents made it their regular practice to recommend specific drafts of bills to serve as a basis for congressional action. Actually, the constitutional power which Presidents traditionally used most to influence legislation was the one which ostensibly brings them into the process at the very end. Because of the difficulty of obtaining a vote of two-thirds in each house to override a veto, a President could have his wishes heeded by the threat that he might not sign a bill he did not like. Hence, this negative force—the veto—was converted into a positive weapon of great potency; and its actual influence cannot be fully measured since its effectiveness has been the greatest in the cases where it was never used.

The techniques of legislative leadership which accrue to a President from the political process are different again. When the spoils system of allotting government jobs to loyal partisans came into vogue, it produced simultaneously two contradictory effects. It lowered the level of administration, thereby impairing the capacity of the President to execute the laws efficiently and impartially. But it provided a lubricant to grease the gears of the institutional machinery and help them mesh. Presidents entered into bartering arrangements, trading departmental jobs in exchange for votes on legislative roll calls. The civil service reformers and political moralists decried the practice and they were, of course, correct in castigating its cruder manifestations. Yet it served its purpose in overcoming, to a partial extent, the frictions built into a system of separated branches and divided powers. Even the greatest of Presidents, and the noblest, employed the practice—Lincoln, for example—since they had to survive politically in the real world of continuous combat, and they stocked their arsenal with whatever weapons would serve.

The more significant, however, of the political techniques was the formation of the party. A man becomes the leader of his party in the United States as soon as he is chosen as its presidential nominee and because of that fact. He continues in that capacity until his successor is selected, but his power dwindles rapidly as that event draws nigh. The degree and character of the leadership, which a President exercises because of his party and over it, vary so much and depend on so many factors that generalization here becomes impossible. A President is more likely to control his party if the following conditions are satisfied: internally, the principal groups and interests are fairly cohesive or, at any rate, are not mutually disruptive; the opposition is reasonably strong and therefore presents a genuine threat; the President himself is a man of stature who has won a public following in his own right; and he personifies or incorporates those elements on which his party is most agreed.

In the present century, the use of patronage as a lever to shift reluctant Congressmen has progressively diminished as more posts in public employment have been filled on the basis of merit and occupied with security of tenure. The party has provided, in general, a more significant means of linking the executive and legislative branches than in the nineteenth century, although it must be remembered that Democrats and Republicans bow less to a unitary discipline than the centralized parties of some other democracies.[26] The capacity of a President to influence congressional votes through his party leadership will depend on various motives and inducements. Certain Congressmen will vote for a President's program because they share his views and agree in principle. Others will be thinking about the next election and will try to estimate whether supporting the President will redound to their advantage. They may need his national popularity and prestige (if he has them) to help them win in their respective localities. Or on the contrary, their constituencies may be of the marginal kind where a show of independence can sometimes pay higher dividends than an undeviating record of party regularity. Since the party organization is built around favors given and received, men who hold elected office expect reciprocal aid for the assistance they render. If they vote along with the President, and do so fairly consistently, they can claim his backing when they have need of it. The President has more to offer than any other single individual in the country—and every politician knows it.

Moreover, the last three decades have added yet another weapon to the presidential stockpile. This is the power of publicity, which is a formidable force in a democracy as susceptible to the stimuli of mass media as the United States. Any journalist will tell you that the Presidency is top news. Whether its occupant seeks it or not, publicity will attend him as surely as Mary was followed by her little lamb. All that goes on in the White House, the private aspects of the family as well as the public activities of the head of government, all is grist for the press, radio, and television. A President never experiences any difficulty in attracting attention to his statements. Indeed, he could not prevent it even if he tried. The more skillful among the recent holders of the office have utilized the press conference, the radio talk, and the television appearance to establish a direct contact with individual citizens. The power to mobilize and mold the amorphous material which contributes to public opinion is lodged in the Presidency beyond the challenge of peer or rival.

It is more realistic to describe the law-making body in the federal gov-

26. See Chapter 11, pp. 320 ff. on this point.

ernment of the United States as consisting of four houses rather than two. The four in question are, of course, the House of Representatives, the Senate, the President, and the Supreme Court. The first two of these can overrule the third if two-thirds of the members concur in each House; otherwise, he alone can overrule them. Then, even if the Congress and the President are agreed, five out of the nine Justices of the Supreme Court can reverse the other three agencies if someone challenges the constitutionality of a federal statute. The White House, consisting of One, is obviously more powerful politically than the two Houses of Congress or the Court. As the democracy of the American Republic grew in size and the electorate increased to nine figures, all trends and tendencies combined to enlarge the importance of the office in which a single figure presided.

The Responsibility for Foreign Relations

What has been said thus far applies primarily to the operation of the Presidency on the domestic scene. But in a most interesting way, the external pressures have moved in precisely the same direction and have fortified the general trend. Whenever foreign affairs present problems that are urgent and critical, the President necessarily takes the center of the stage. He is Head of State, Commander-in-Chief, and Diplomat Plenipotentiary. Only he can speak with official authority for the government of the United States and the American people. Of course, this was always true. In that sense there is no difference between the Presidency of the 1950's and 1960's and that of the 1790's. But what has altered fundamentally is the scope and relevance of affairs which once were truly foreign, but now are interwoven with the threads of national life. In the switch from a policy of isolation to one of active participation in a network of alliances, in the acceptance of the responsibility for international leadership, in the shrunken dimensions of a more congested planet, the American system of government has placed an ever-increasing load on its Chief Executive. He alone can authorize and guide the discussions between heads of governments. He alone can negotiate at the supreme level with the Chairman of the Soviet government, the French President, or the British Prime Minister. He alone can properly represent his country when it is necessary to travel abroad and cultivate good will by parades and speeches and handshakes in London, Paris, Bonn, Vienna, Caracas, or wherever else the vicissitudes of international diplomacy attract a busy man.

But in that last phrase lies the crux of the difficulty. Thus far, this discussion has emphasized the strength of the office, and the opportunities which befall a man who can develop its potentialities. But may not this same argument suggest the conclusion that the duties of the Presidency have in fact become excessive, that its functions are too many and too complex, and that the whole array of responsibilities has expanded into an unsupportable burden? Can any human being—not excluding the greatest—do justice to such an office?

This indeed is my one major doubt and reservation about the Presidency, that its demands are too exacting, and that any President, measured by the length of his duties, must somewhere fall short. Sheer size has placed the government of the United States quite beyond the effective span of any one man's control, and virtually beyond the limits of anyone's intellectual capacity to keep abreast of current information. A President is responsible to the public for millions of actions about whose substance he can know nothing, and concerning which he will never hear a thing unless some political quirk drags the details from obscurity into the limelight. Ambitious men in public life will always seek this office because they are fascinated by its prestige and tremendous concentration of power and influence. But when serving in it, those who remain self-critical will surely ask themselves how close they can come in fact to satisfying the impossible sum of demands which the Presidency imposes, and the honest ones will be disappointed at the answer. Of the half-dozen personages mentioned at the beginning of this chapter as wielding the greatest political influence today, the man who serves as President of the United States—just because he is operating in the environment of a democracy, and a very large one—has the hardest job to fill. Mr. Khrushchev does not encounter such a problem as working with the Congress. The Prime Minister does not have the President's responsibility of deciding whether to store and whether to use the bombs from which millions could die. In an ultimate sense, there can be no completely successful President nowadays. There are only varying degrees of approximation to a standard which is unattainable.

The British Cabinet System

The institutional arrangements by which the British handle these problems differ from those of Switzerland and the United States. There is, of course, the constitutional distinction that the two latter countries are republics, whereas Britain has retained the monarchy. Its continuance, even in figurehead form, produces consequences for government of a legal, social, and ceremonial nature. But the political influence of the Crown nowadays is nil—except that politicians pay public respect to it as they do to God, motherhood, the Boy Scouts, and the fight against cancer. When it comes to what Bagehot called the efficient part of the constitution, leadership is produced by methods which amount to a cross between the Swiss and American types, since some features of both are combined in a blend which is original and unique. The British system resembles the Swiss in placing a heavy emphasis on collegiality. Bagehot was the first writer of note to identify the Cabinet as the central organ of political power.[27] Since then, an extensive literature has grown around this institution. Books have been written with such titles as *Cabinet Government*; and the type of democracy where the legislature and executive are related as they are in Britain is referred to as the Cabinet system.

But the corporate character of the Cabinet is only one side of the story. For this is not the Swiss Federal Council, one degree removed and operating under another name. The Premiership is an office for which no parallel exists in Berne. In fact, it brings the practice of British democracy close to that of Washington. A Prime Minister is by no means identical with a President in the range of his power. In some respects his is the stronger office; in others, it is weaker. But there is a strong similarity between the pair to the extent that one man occupies a position of pre-eminence, outranking all others in public life. In Britain, this primacy of the Prime Minister has been variously described with metaphors and classical quotations. He is said to be *primus inter pares*, or *inter stellas luna minores*.[28] He is "the keystone of the cabinet arch,"[29] and so on. Perhaps the reason why people have recourse to these indirect allusions is that the facts defy a simple explanation and will not yield to clear-cut analysis. The office of the Prime Minister is flexible and changeable—certainly to the same degree as the Presidency. Located in the midst of complex relationships, it exercises an influence in many directions and responds to many pressures.

Two points are central to a discussion of political leadership in Britain: the position of the Cabinet vis-à-vis the Departments and Parliament, and, second, the place of the Prime Minister within the Ministry.

The leadership which a Cabinet provides is due to the pivotal role it fulfills in the British Constitution. Its members are selected from within the walls of Parliament and, retaining their seats there, they do double duty. They lead the Parliament and also control the administrative departments. If the American Constitution has sought to enshrine the principle of the separation of powers—to the extent that the President and his

27. The Cabinet forms the subject of the opening chapter of *The English Constitution*.
28. "A moon among tiny stars."
29. This was Morley's phrase.

Cabinet cannot sit in Congress—the British system embodies the opposite notion of a fusion of powers. The political heads of the Ministries along Whitehall must be members of Parliament. It was with this in mind that Bagehot called the Cabinet "a combining committee—a hyphen which joins, a buckle which fastens, the legislative part of the state to the executive part of the state," and, in another succinct definition, "a committee of the legislative body selected to be the executive body."[30] The latter phrase was amended by McBain, who argued that the main duty of the Cabinet is its legislative leadership. "The Cabinet," he wrote, "is a committee of the legislative body selected primarily to lead the legislative body."[31] Nowadays, one might suggest, each author is only half correct. The function of the contemporary Cabinet is to lead both branches, legislative and executive. Hence, the test of efficiency in British government depends on whether the same persons can perform the two jobs.

Party Influence on the Cabinet

Since the question of how the Cabinet conducts its functions is connected with why it succeeded in acquiring them, a glance at its political history will help explain the sources and conditions of the Cabinet's power. It is somewhat ironical that when Montesquieu developed his notion of the separation of powers, he based it on the English model. What he did not discern was the political trend which would soon substitute fusion for separation, so that the country on which he drew to illustrate the concept abandoned it in later practice. The fact of political life which determined the particular form and functions of the Cabinet in Great Britain was, of course, the growth of the two-party system. The crystallization of parliamentary cliques into the Whig and Tory clusters had the effect of limiting the royal choice whenever a Ministry was to be appointed. The King could invite the Tory heads or the Whigs. If all else failed, he would try for a coalition. Essentially, it was a growing sense of solidarity among the leaders of the two main parliamentary factions which turned the Cabinet from an arm or extension of the monarchy into an institution ruling by its own political force. All that a Cabinet had to do was to close ranks and stay united. With impunity it could then defy the King. Ministers could dare him to accept their collective resignation and call in the Opposition. Collective responsibility became the operative principle of Cabinet action, the secret of its power, and the method of its survival in office. Later, by

30. *The English Constitution, op. cit.,* pp. 9, 12.
31. *The Living Constitution, op. cit.,* p. 121.

the same logic, the weapon with which the Cabinet had emancipated itself from royal control was directed against Parliament, and with the same effect on that body. If Parliament voted down the measures which a Cabinet proposed, the composition of either the Cabinet or the Parliament would have to be changed. What controlled everything was, of course, the party and its increase of discipline which accompanied the extension of the franchise during the nineteenth century. The Cabinet dominates Parliament as well as the Departments because it dominates the dominant party. Wherever this fundamental political condition is lacking, the institutions of Cabinet government will not operate in the same way because they cannot. The French imported the institution, but never linked it to the same kind of party system. Hence in Paris the institution did not work successfully.

Consequently, when discussing the role of the Cabinet in Great Britain and its fusion of legislative and executive leadership in the same hands, you are speaking of two different, but related, topics. Or rather, you describe one set of facts, while referring to another. The structural and constitutional aspects of Cabinet leadership in Parliament and the Departments have to be realistically explained in terms of the political relations between the majority party and the Opposition. The Cabinet possesses powers in law because of the power it draws from politics.

The same considerations of party union which affect the Cabinet in its external relations with political opponents have their influence internally on the members of a Ministry. The responsibility which all assume collectively for the acts of each is only another way of recognizing the political truth that they are in the same boat and must sail or sink together. A success by any one helps them all, as all are harmed by the failure of one. The Cabinet, be it remembered, is the small body or nucleus within the larger membership of the Ministry. It consists of men who are senior in terms of service to party and Parliament, and normally includes all who are politically important and have acquired some public standing. For the most part, these are politicians who have worked as colleagues for a long time. They have grown up together, politically, in Parliament and have become accustomed to co-operation. This does not mean that their relations are wholly inspired by friendship or that sweetness, light, and harmony forever prevail in their councils. Some personalities will jar and grate on one another; and, since these are all ambitious men who hope to climb higher up the greasy pole, each will outsmart his rivals in competitive situations. Periodically, the system will throw up its strong characters whose individuality will attract special loyalties or breed peculiar animosities. One recalls the careers of Joseph Chamberlain, David Lloyd George, Winston Churchill, and Aneurin Bevan. Such men do not make easy or comfortable colleagues. Their actions can divide a Cabinet and split a party. But these can also, when the time comes, be the great leaders. The general run of Ministers, however, are ingrained with the virtues of the team spirit. Whether they were drawn from the social class which played cricket on the fields of Eton, or that which organized the factories and built the banks and shipping fleets, or that which organized trade unions and conducted strikes, solidarity within the group is a feature of British public life which reposes on deep foundations of character and tradition. The Englishman's home may be his castle; but once he walks outside his front door his defenses and his status are dependent on the group. The Cabinet's unity is a translation to the Treasury bench in the House of Commons of all the group pressures which pervade an old and stable society. The Club, the Church or Chapel, the Cricket-Team, the Old School Tie, the Trade Union and Co-op, the Party, and finally the Cabinet—they are all of a piece and they fortify each other. Like the Fellows in the senior common room, Cabinet Ministers are condemned to live together and to make the best of it.

The Prime Minister

So much for the arch. But now what about the keystone? How much weight does the Prime Minister exert? If he is really *primus*, in what sense are other Ministers *pares*? And what is the meaning of parity in this context? Like the President of the United States, a Prime Minister holds in his hands a bundle of powers. Some of these come to him from the procedures of the Constitution; others derive from his post as party leader; and others again are attributable to his personality.

In law, the Prime Minister owes his office to an appointment by the Crown. Because the monarch is Head of the State, and because a British Ministry is officially Her Majesty's Government, certain functions of supreme importance require the royal signature to make them legal. The Prime Minister's pre-eminence in law over his colleagues stems from the fact that he is their channel of communication with the Crown. Only he can initiate the processes which are central to the Cabinet system. Thus it is the Premier, and he alone, who nominates other Ministers for appointment to their posts. He is the one who must request that Parliament be dissolved and a new House of Commons be elected. At any time he chooses, he can submit his resignation and, with it, that of the whole Ministry.

The legal powers, however, are his because of his political standing. To move the analysis one stage further back, the reason why the monarch invites him to assume the post of First Minister is that he leads the party with the majority of parliamentary seats. Hence the indispensable political conditions of leadership are his ascendancy in a major party and its victory in a general election. But the term "party" contains an ambiguity in this context which needs clarifying. As was observed in an earlier chapter,[32] it may refer to an organized group within the legislature or organizations of like-minded citizens scattered throughout the constituencies of the country. In Britain it is the parliamentary party which controls the party organization outside, and the parliamentary party in turn is controlled by the parliamentary leaders. Here then we reach the bedrock of the British political system. Parliament is the institution where politicians receive their advanced training in the arts of government. A person is promoted to ministerial rank, thence into the Cabinet, and finally to the Premiership, only after serving a long apprenticeship in Parliament. All the Premiers of this century had sat in the House of Commons[33] for several terms and had served as Minister in someone else's Cabinet before becoming Prime Minister.[34] They were therefore experienced men who knew the problems of campaigning, who were thoroughly familiar with the ways and moods of Parliament, and who had previously administered some major Department. Nobody who is politically untrained climbs to the top in Westminster.

But climbing is a sport at which lightweights, as well as heavyweights, may be successful. The British system throws up men who are technically well trained. Only a few of the Premiers, however, are statesmen of genius. Certain of them have been distinguished above the average. Some, like Eden, were successful Ministers, but failed to handle the bigger job. Others have been downright mediocrities. Actually, on a scale of quality of leadership, the resemblance between the results of the American and British systems is remarkably close. During the last hundred years, Great

---

32. See Chapter 11, p. 310.

33. Until 1963, the last peer to serve as Premier was the Marquis of Salisbury, who left office in 1902. When Macmillan resigned, the Conservative party was plunged into a contest for the leadership, in which the two protagonists were Butler and Hailsham. However, the man eventually selected was Lord Home, the Foreign Secretary. In choosing a peer to lead their party and serve as Premier, the Conservatives broke a sixty-year-old custom. The new Premier, who had briefly served in the Commons before inheriting his earldom, renounced his title and was then elected to the Commons in a safe Scottish seat.

34. Except Ramsay Macdonald, who formed the first Labour Ministry and, as leader of a new party, had no previous experience as a Minister.

Britain has produced four truly great Prime Ministers: Disraeli, Gladstone, Lloyd George, and Churchill. A fifth, Asquith, was outstanding, at least before war broke out. At the other end of the scale, Baldwin, Chamberlain, and Macdonald are a worthy match for Harding, Coolidge, and Hoover. Thus the parallelism is striking. The two contrasted party systems and constitutional structures have yielded about the same quantity of great, big, and mediocre figures and at approximately the same times.

To carry the comparison further, however, one can discern some equally significant contrasts and similarities between these offices. A Premier is far stronger than a President in that he is sure to win parliamentary support for his legislative proposals, whereas no President can ever count on the Congress. But a President is much more potent than a Premier in that the method of his election amalgamates the entire nation for his constituency, and the Constitution accords him an incontestable supremacy in the executive branch, as Head of the State, and in foreign affairs.

The Premier's Position in the Ministry

The point that a Premier is strong because he leads the parliamentary party can also be viewed from another angle. What is a source of strength can also supply a limitation on his power. This is where the institutions of British government differ from the presidential system of American democracy. For though the Premier comes first in political importance, he presides over a Cabinet, and, despite his primacy, there is a genuine collegial aspect to the British arrangements which is absent from those of the United States. In British politics the men who count are those who in the course of their careers move down to the front benches of the parliamentary party. Hence, when a Ministry has to be formed, although the Premier is the Cabinet-maker, he does not have a completely free hand in the choice of his materials. Anybody who is prominent in the parliamentary party has a claim to be included. Or, to state this negatively, if such a one is excluded, there must be special reasons why. Baldwin and Chamberlain kept Churchill out from 1935 to 1939 because he was too big a man for them to manage, and they knew it. When Attlee formed the Labour Ministry in 1945, there was no question that Bevan, Bevin, Cripps, Dalton, and Morrison had to be allotted the major posts. Likewise in 1951, Churchill was bound to find room for Butler and Eden. This is due to the fact mentioned earlier that the leaders of the parliamentary party have been accustomed to work as a team—in opposition as well as in office. Hence it is as a team that they constitute a Ministry. In this sense, to speak of the Cabinet system as a corporate body accords with an element of political reality. Yet the team still has to have a captain, and it is his function to decide where the individual members shall play. Attlee in 1945 could not have excluded any of his important colleagues. But it was he who decided which posts they should occupy. Two or three of them had eager eyes on the post of Foreign Secretary, but it was the Premier who picked Bevin.

Because of the reality of the collegial factor in the British system, a delicate equilibrium is always maintained between the Premier and his Cabinet. The time is long since passed when the Premier could closely supervise each of his fellow Ministers and be conversant with the operations of their respective Ministries—as is reported to have been the case with Sir Robert Peel. A twentieth-century Premier is responsible for holding the team together, for leading it, for supplying the general political direction, and for building public confidence in the government at home and abroad. But the niceties of constitutional principles and the maxims of political wisdom will be adjusted to the accidents of individuality. It is the chances of personal biography and political vicissitude which bring a group of half-a-dozen men together into prominence within their party at the same point in history. And together they must hang, or be hanged. Sometimes through sheer force of personality, because of his public following, by responding to the emergency of the times, one of these will tower above the rest. He is then unassailably the First, without rival or competitor.

But on other occasions, when there is less of the dramatic and the dynamic, and when three or four individuals are equally strong and influential, the Prime Minister is likely to be a less colorful figure. He may do his job by serving as committee chairman with dignity and decency. Without being personally impressive or even outstanding, he may have qualities of tact and fairness which enable him to apply a gentle rein to otherwise unruly steeds. Everybody remembers the names of the two whose energies galvanized the British nation in the grimmest years of World Wars I and II. But nobody, except the curious scholar, recalls that Liverpool was the Premier in the final years of the Napoleonic Wars and for twelve years thereafter. When the Liberals returned to power in 1905, their Ministry combined perhaps the most brilliant cluster of talents and intellect which ever held office in the United Kingdom.[35] But the man who sat in the chair for the first three years, Campbell-Bannerman, was the one with the seniority as party leader in the House of Commons and who

35. Among its members, in senior and junior posts, were Asquith, Birrell, Bryce, Churchill, Fisher, Haldane, Lloyd George, and Morley.

was trusted because he was no threat. For similar reasons, an Attlee could preside over a Cabinet which contained such doughty stalwarts and personal rivals as Bevin and Bevan, Cripps, Morrison, and Dalton because none of those could have tolerated one of their ilk in the chair.

The Choice of a New Leader

This is another way of saying that the British system provides the opportunity for leadership if the times require it and if the right man is available. Actually, the system is sufficiently flexible so that, without resorting to an election, the Premier can be changed by an internal reorganization of the Cabinet. Thus Lloyd George succeeded Asquith and Chamberlain gave way to Churchill, and in both those instances a new all-party coalition was formed. In 1956 Eden resigned because of his failure at Suez, and Macmillan was selected on the advice of Conservative elder statesmen and a poll of the Cabinet. In those cases, be it noticed, the political situation, both domestic and international, was one of emergency, and the majority party was sorely split over policy and tactics. A change of leader was needed if unity was to be restored inside the party and confidence revived among the public. On other occasions, however, the succession to the leadership is arranged by procedures which vary between the parties and depend to some extent on whether a party is in office or opposition. Labour follows the democratic method of conducting a ballot within the parliamentary party. Candidates are nominated; they and their backers solicit votes; and a majority elects. In that way, Hugh Gaitskell was chosen over Bevan and Morrison; and, after Gaitskell's death, Harold Wilson defeated Brown and Callaghan.

The Conservatives prefer to do things differently. In keeping with their aristocratic and oligarchical affinities, they abhor the notion of an outright election. By contrast, they contrive, if possible, to elevate a successor to the position of heir-apparent where he is clearly designated as the next in line and so cannot be overlooked. In this way, Chamberlain followed Baldwin, and Eden came after Churchill. The Premier can do much to influence the choice of his successor by virtually making him his deputy and by leaving him temporarily in charge when he is out of the country. At other times the *éminences grises* of Conservatism—such men as Churchill and Salisbury in 1956—will take it upon themselves to sound out opinion in the small elitist circles of the Establishment and will then discreetly tender advice to the Sovereign. The possibility of an intra-party revolt cannot be discounted, however, even in an organization as well disciplined as the Conservatives like to be. Thus in 1922, on the issue of continuing in the coalition under Lloyd George or fighting the next election as an alternative government, enough of the Conservative M.P.'s rebelled against Austen Chamberlain so as to force his resignation and replace him with Bonar Law.[36] Also in May, 1940, what finally brought about the downfall of Austen Chamberlain's inglorious younger brother was the abstention of many Conservative M.P.'s on a vote of confidence in the House plus the Labour refusal to enter a coalition Ministry unless a new Premier was found. But the significance of such episodes, apart from the fact that they can happen, is that they are extremely rare.

Since the appointment of Home to succeed Macmillan in 1963, the Conservative method of picking a leader has been strongly criticized by those who in this case considered the result a political blunder of first magnitude. Indeed, two of the brighter members of Macmillan's Ministry, namely Macleod and Powell, were so disgusted that they refused to take office under Home. Not only had they been loyal supporters of Butler, but they were leading spirits in the more progressive wing of the party which had liberalized Conservative policies in the preceding decade. Such men saw in the selection of Home an insult to the House of Commons and an internal *coup d'état* by the party's right wing. Controversies have already erupted over the procedures which led to the outcome, and certain points are still in dispute. But it appears definite that the retiring Premier authorized a canvas of opinion by four different persons among four separate groups—in the Cabinet, among Conservative members in each House of Parliament, and in the constituency organizations. At the start, Home was not seriously considered and was not a contender; and, quite late in the proceedings, he was the first preference of only a minority of the Cabinet. Both the methods used, and the conclusion, presented to the public eye the appearance of manipulation and maneuver by the inner circles of the Tory Establishment, where the decision was steered in favor of a man of their own stripe as against the party's intellectuals, progressives, and middle-class representatives.

The American Administration

By contrast with a Prime Minister, an American President has greater freedom and security in one respect, and less influence in another. Within the executive branch he is raised on so high a pedestal that he juts out in

36. For a recital of these events, see R. T. McKenzie, *British Political Parties* (St. Martin's Press: New York, 1955), pp. 83 ff.

splendid isolation.[37] His official family, as the members of his cabinet and heads of important agencies are called, does not consist of colleagues, but of subordinates. Ordinarily, when he makes his initial appointments and fits together the jigsaw puzzle of his Administration, the leading politicians of his party are not included—particularly those who were his rivals for the presidential nomination. Roosevelt could not have brought Al Smith into the New Deal. Wilson did appoint Bryan as Secretary of State, but theirs was not a happy relationship and it did not last long.[38] When a newly elected President selects his cabinet, the men he picks are generally either technicians and specialists in a particular field or ex-Governors or former Congressmen who represent some major interest or region. Hence a President cannot always obtain the best political advice from within the executive branch,[39] and this may explain why certain Presidents of this century have relied on individuals whom they specially trusted to serve as their "eyes and ears." House was to Wilson, for a while at any rate, what Howe and Hopkins were to Roosevelt. More recently, a brother has been co-opted to fill the role. Witness the cases of Milton Eisenhower and Robert Kennedy.

Beyond the executive branch, the President must deal with innumerable

37. The first wartime meeting of Roosevelt and Churchill provided evidence on this point. "The Atlantic Conference gave Hopkins an opportunity to observe more clearly than ever the differences between the American and British systems of democracy. This was the first time he had seen both the President and Prime Minister in operation away from their own home bases. He remarked on the fact that whereas Roosevelt was completely on his own, subject only to the advice of his immediate and self-selected entourage, which advice he could accept or reject, Churchill was constantly reporting to and consulting the War Cabinet in London, addressing his communications to the Lord Privy Seal, who was then Clement Attlee." Robert E. Sherwood, *Roosevelt and Hopkins*, Vol. I, Chap. XVI. (Harper's: Bantam ed., New York, 1950), Vol. I, p. 438.
38. The relations of Adlai Stevenson to the Kennedy Administration also seemed to be the reverse of intimate.
39. The comments of Harold L. Ickes, Secretary of the Interior under Franklin Roosevelt, are pertinent: "The first hour of the Cabinet session was taken up with the relief bill. . . . Aside from this, only the barest routine matters were discussed. All of which leads me to set down what has been running in my mind for a long time and that is just what use the Cabinet is under this Administration. The cold fact is that on important matters we are seldom called upon for advice. We never discuss exhaustively any policy of Government or question of political strategy. The President makes all of his own decisions and, so far at least as the Cabinet is concerned, without taking counsel with a group of advisers. On particular questions he will call into his office persons directly interested, but it is fair to say that the Cabinet is not a general council upon whose advice the President relies or the opinions of which, on important matters, he calls for." *The Secret Diary of Harold L. Ickes*, Vol. I. (Simon & Schuster: New York, 1953), p. 308. Entry under the date March 3, 1935.

difficulties. Unlike a Premier, he has to anticipate friction and obstruction from Congress at some time or other. Here in the Senate and House of Representatives, the floor majority leaders and committee chairmen are frequently powerful enough to assert themselves in their own right. To a President with a legislative program, these form the equivalent of what his colleagues on the Treasury bench are to a Premier—but with the important difference that the Premier and his fellow ministers have at least been teammates for many years, and he not only distributes their portfolios but can switch a man from one Ministry to another. By contrast, when Eisenhower became President, he depended in Congress on the rival whom he had just beaten for his party's nomination, Senator Taft. Similarly, President Kennedy had to enlist the support of Speaker Rayburn, a veteran in all respects his senior. Presidents have little influence on the selection of the Speaker and the floor leaders, and none at all on the appointment of committee chairmen because of the seniority rule. Hence the Chief Legislator must work with material much of which is intractable. However he has this consolation. No matter what feelings are entertained towards him on Capitol Hill, Congress can do nothing to remove him.[40] For four years he is in and stays in, whether Senators and Representatives like him or not. A British Premier or Opposition Leader is very strong as long as his party is united behind him. But any serious split or debacle can force him out—as Austen and Neville Chamberlain, Asquith and Eden, could testify.

The Growing Resemblance of the Presidency and Premiership

In one final respect, the political forces in this second half of the twentieth century are tending toward a closer approximation of the Presidency and Premiership. I refer to the decline of the nation-state and the steady removal of crucial decisions on economic and military matters to a level of inter-state agreements. Since the dividing line between domestic and foreign affairs has grown so thin, the heads of governments are in ever closer contact. Nowadays, they maintain a stream of correspondence which they reinforce by visits and conferences. Just as an active[41] President is deeply immersed in foreign relations, so is a Prime Minister. Of course,

40. Impeachment is not a politically realistic device. The only time when it was used (against Andrew Johnson), the attack failed—as in that case it deserved to do.
41. To distinguish him from the inactive kind. President Eisenhower left the conduct of foreign affairs to Secretary Dulles and that of domestic economic policy to Secretary Humphrey.

this phenomenon has its parallels in the past. Whenever an issue of external policy was uppermost, the Premier was bound to be concerned; and certain Premiers, like some Presidents, flung themselves into the international arena because it was to their taste. Thus Palmerston threw his weight around in all directions as Theodore Roosevelt was wont to do, while Disraeli, Gladstone, and Salisbury continually asserted themselves in foreign affairs because the promotion of British interests was their duty.

In the twentieth century the Premier's participation in foreign policy has become increasingly a habit and a necessity. During the two World Wars the activities of Lloyd George and Churchill were in vital respects indistinguishable from those of Wilson and Roosevelt. Similarly, after hostilities ceased, Truman and Attlee were pressed into regular consultation by the need for joint action in matters of common concern. The small-gauged Premiers (Baldwin and Chamberlain), like the small-gauged Presidents (Harding and Coolidge), have been the modern exceptions which prove the rule. They exemplify an out-dated throwback to the self-centered preoccupations of the different world of the mid nineteenth century. With Eden and Macmillan, there was no doubt, any more than there was with Churchill, of the deep involvement of the Prime Minister's office in international affairs. The case of Eden may sound an unfortunate one to cite in this context because of the mess he made at Suez.[42] But my concern here is to emphasize the truth that a contemporary Premier is forced to be an active participant in the world scene. Whether his policies happen to succeed or fail is not the point. Macmillan, who followed after Eden, not only supplied evidence on this score by his acts, but realistically stated the responsibilities of his post in so many words. He did, in fact, serve largely as his own Foreign Secretary, for the men who nominally filled that office during his Ministry were far from being the more talented of its members. Indeed, on one occasion when the Premier reshuffled his Cabinet, substituting the Earl of Home for Selwyn Lloyd at the Foreign Office, he was criticized by the Labourites for selecting a peer who was not answerable to the House of Commons. Macmillan's answer was forthright and honest. Contacts between governments, he argued, required continuous attention at the highest level. The Premier therefore had to take personal responsibility. Under these conditions, a Foreign Secretary was reduced to the secondary role of executing policies or conducting negotiations along the lines decided by his superior. Thus the inference followed that this portfolio no longer required a man of outstanding ability.

42. The tragedy of Eden's Premiership is due to the fact that a man whose whole public life was spent in diplomacy, and who was profoundly experienced in international problems, failed as Premier in this very sphere.

In this way and for these reasons, the dynamics which inhere in the functions of government exert a pressure on constitutional structures and affect the practical application of their supporting theories. Although the President was allotted powers which made him a participant in legislation, he was not intended to serve as Chief Legislator. But lapse of time, emergence of parties, the mass franchise, and expansion of state activities have converted the White House into the legislature's Third House. The President must therefore try to exercise from the outside a leadership which the congressional structure is ill-equipped to admit and which various Congressmen in both parties are psychologically habituated to resist. The Premiership originated as the office of the first servant of a monarch who actually governed as well as reigned. It evolved into the chairman of a Ministry which could emancipate itself from royal control by relying on the continuous pledged support of a parliamentary majority. Later, with the extension of the franchise, the formation of more disciplined parties, and the increase in the functions of government, the Cabinet developed its mastery over Parliament and the brighter Premiers outshone their colleagues. Finally the need for democracy to survive in battle against autocracy, and the subsequent revolutionary challenges of the 1950's and 1960's, have placed demands on British governments whose response has lifted the Prime Minister still further to the fore. If Bagehot one hundred years ago could stress the dissimilarities between the Presidency and Premiership, today one is more impressed by their new-found similarity and tendency to approximate to a common pattern.

Comparison of the Three Systems

This comparison of three types of institutions for democratic leadership suggests some concluding comments. The Swiss system, although highly interesting in itself, functions under such special conditions that it can hardly be considered a model for extensive imitation. The presidential and cabinet types are the alternatives which merit the serious attention since each has been used effectively by the two largest and most powerful democracies of the modern world. In comparing them, one is struck by certain prominent characteristics which throw some light on the general subject of leadership. Historically, both systems have evolved since the last quarter of the eighteenth century into forms which are greatly changed from the originals. There has therefore been sufficient elasticity in the institutions for them to be stretched according to need and purpose. Washington, Adams, and Jefferson would presumably be as astonished to observe what the Presidency has become since 1933 as Walpole and the Pitts would feel in scrutinizing the agenda of Cabinet meetings since 1940. What is truly impressive in this development is that offices which were shaped by members of the upper class to fit the limited ends of oligarchical rule have proven themselves adaptable to the expanding goals of the democratic civilization.

All acts of government presuppose the creation and use of authority. The democratic principle accepts an authority which is founded on consent and is revocable, but resists an authoritarianism which is imposed by fiat. To apply the principle to a structural form and there make it work depends more on practical judgment and a mature civil outlook than on philosophical acuity—which is where the English-speaking and Scandinavian peoples have been superior to the Germans and Latins. But two purely quantitative factors will influence the circumstances in which leadership is exercised and the conditions for its success. One is the size, both of area and population, that is organized under the state's jurisdiction; the other, the volume of activities which the political process demands of its government. As the size increases, both structure and functions grow more elaborate, as do the techniques for managing the whole. In the original democracies of the city-state or mountain-valley variety, it was just possible for enough of the people to assemble in person and decide the major questions, after which they could entrust the administration for short periods to officials and committees. Sheer numerical expansion appears to necessitate as a consequence more efforts at unifying an organization which becomes ever more complex and, at the summit, more remote from those whom it is designed to serve. This may explain why the largest democracies have witnesssed the steady concentration of effective leadership. The British Parliament could not, as a whole, do the job which the Ministry does; and, although formally in control, it is in fact controlled by the smaller body. Likewise the Cabinet is paramount within the Ministry, and in times of war a still smaller War Cabinet has exercised the supreme direction under the dynamic impulses of one man's energy and flair. Characteristically, too, the United States has seen the Presidency grow in conformity with the expansion of the United States and the functions of the national government.

The advantages which accrue from this are evident. A unified system, a clear direction, a common purpose, should be easier to attain. A citizen-body of two hundred millions, or even of fifty-five millions, would be a chaos if it lacked adequate organization and the leadership which attends it. But the disadvantages are also manifest and manifold. The leadership may then be tempted to dominate, and the public must be prepared to re-assert its ultimate primacy. Even without that risk of authoritarianism, there is the ordinary, everyday certainty that the burden of decision at the center becomes intolerable. The work-load of the Presidency and Premier-ship imposes a strain, both nervous and physical, from which all grow fa-tigued and some collapse. Wilson, Roosevelt, and Eisenhower are ex-amples of this danger; as are Macdonald, Eden, and Macmillan. Moreover, the political qualifications which enable a man to reach the pinnacle of power may not be those best suited to its intelligent exercise. This is par-ticularly true of the American system because the President must win an election which is nationwide. Popular government places a premium on popularity. The intellect of a Stevenson was not a vote-getting asset—at least, not in competition with the Eisenhower grin. Eisenhower always re-mained popular and could win elections with big majorities. But he was not a success in his exercise of office. One wonders whether in the 1960's a Jefferson or Madison could be elected to the White House. Probably not.

Finally, in assessing these systems one should remember to assess the effects of the constitutional structure and the party politics, respectively. The design of the American Constitution has the obvious result of giving the Congress a separate identity. The interests of State and locality are as naturally expressed there as the national and international interests are focused on the White House. Political figures who belong by virtue of their office to a distinct branch of the government are bound at times to feel the need to assert their distinctness. The British framework avoids that tendency for executive-legislative disagreement which is inherent in the American pattern. But it can never be forgotten that structure alone does not determine how an institution will operate. The Cabinet would be something quite different if it were not for the associated party system, as the French experience proves. The smaller democracies of Scandinavia have succeeded in operating a Cabinet system, with some variations, in conjunction with a multi-party system. In their case, one may suggest that the beneficial results are due to such circumstances as the size of their fairly homogeneous communities and their more limited external commit-ments. The question which should be raised, but which cannot yet be answered in the absence of historical evidence, is how the presidential system would function if combined with two parties as disciplined as those of Great Britain. Perhaps in the future we shall observe the answer if the Democrats and Republicans subdivide and then recombine in two group-ings more consistent than the present: one liberal and internationalist, the other nationalist and conservative.

IV

The Democratic Values

16

Liberty and Equality

Democracy is conspicuous among political systems for the importance it attaches to questions of philosophy. In this respect, the closest modern parallel is provided by communism, which has developed its own elaborate body of doctrine and dogma. There is a reason for this similarity. At their inception, both democracy and communism were revolutionary innovators. Any political movement imbued with this character is bound to do much explaining. Seeking to overthrow established regimes, it must justify its decision to condemn them and to substitute something different and supposedly superior. Throughout the history of democracy, the time-sequence in the relation of philosophy to practice has varied. Sometimes the philosophy was written before the acts of revolution began. In that case the new institutions which were established afterward were intended to conform to earlier statements of principles. At other times, action preceded advocacy; and in that case the philosopher found himself generalizing about the accomplished fact.

The Purpose of a Philosophy of Democracy

Democratic ideals, as was noted in Chapters 2 and 3, have been variously formulated and discussed during two and a half millennia. But the most intensive period of philosophical creativity spanned the two hundred years from the mid seventeenth century to the mid nineteenth century. The last published work which has gained a definitive place among the classics of

517

democratic thought is Mill's *Essay on Liberty*,[1] and that is already more than a hundred years old. Evidently there is a significance for our understanding of politics in the fact that so much theorizing about fundamentals was carried on from the age of the Levellers and Locke to that of Mill, whereas so little of a similarly fundamental character has been produced since. Whenever men are challenging the *status quo*, it is important, if not imperative, politically to re-examine what is ordinarily taken for granted. Those who deny the validity of vested interests and refuse to be bound by tradition must base their criticism of the existing system on reason and ethics. Intellectually, they must demonstrate that the established order is not rationally defensible. Morally, they must show that it conflicts with justice. Thus they win and hold the allegiance of their supporters by enlisting their reason on the side of revolution and freeing their consciences from any feelings of guilt. At the same time, since something new must be put in the place of the old, the innovations should be ethically and rationally satisfying. When that task is substantially completed, however, in the sense that new ideas and institutions have prevailed, the work of government grows more prosaic. With the major values settled, the community is preoccupied with the details of their application. Philosophy then gives way to policy. Ideals acquire concrete form through institutions, and principles are buried in programs. A successful system has less occasion to inquire into its own credentials, and in the second generation after its revolution is accomplished democracy becomes the *status quo*. The treatises of Locke, Montesquieu, Rousseau, and Mill were as necessary in the circumstances of their time as the Acts for Public Education, Social Security, or Public Housing have been in ours.

But if principles are normally enunciated before they are spelled out in programs, it is also true that the elaboration of the latter eventually requires a fresh look at the former. Ideals may, and should, be used for a stimulus to action. But as experience accumulates, the record may suggest that the initial ideals be reformulated in the light of what is possible. Hence a continuous interchange should be occurring between political practice and political philosophy. Programs which are applied continuously produce effects on society and its politics because people change under their influence. The crusading appeals of the grandfathers are trite incantations to the grandchildren. Abstract ideals must be adaptable in content to altered particulars.

1. I have taken the *Essay on Liberty*, not the *Considerations on Representative Government*, because the former is an inquiry into basic principles, while the latter is more concerned with the institutions in which they are embodied.

The discussion earlier in this book on the criteria of democracy[2] was focused on the evolution of the concept and the conflicting views which grew up around this form of government before the present century. To a large extent, the ideals to which we subscribe today are the product of this long history, and much of the controversy which still surrounds the evaluation of the democratic record resounds with the echoes of ancient arguments. Contemporary democracies, therefore, are based on a supporting theory which has come down by inheritance. Certain particular doctrines have entered into the democratic tradition and now belong to the common stock-in-trade of democratic thinkers. I have in mind such principles as the foundation of government on popular consent, majority rule, equality of opportunity for all. In addition, a few men—of whom Locke, Rousseau, and Mill are the most notable—have developed philosophies of the systematic kind. In these, they seek to provide a coherent rationale for justifying the whole scheme of values of a democratic state.

Here I am not primarily concerned with the origins of democratic ideas, with the ascription of authorship, or with ferreting out who first said what on which point. In studying the history of political thought or the biography of individual thinkers, such topics are important. But they do not help us judge the validity of the ideas in question or appraise their present meaning and utility. The subject of this chapter and the next is to examine some of the fundamental notions of modern democracy and estimate their influence on politics.

Contradictions Among the Traditional Concepts

When the topic is approached in this way, two points are apparent. First of all, we do not have a democratic philosophy, if the singular is taken to mean a set of ideas worked out as a consistent whole and generally accepted. What we do have is a variety of philosophies, in the plural, and a potpourri of doctrines. There is no one ideal of democracy. There are many democratic ideals. Each has its own supporters, its classic exposition, its institutional embodiment. The numerous concepts, and their still more numerous interpretations, are similar to the rock strata which in the geological lapse of time have been superimposed to form the Earth's crust. But a series of layers is not a fusion of substance, and the need to synthesize the materials of democratic theory remains. The task of synthesis, however, is complicated by a second consideration. It is the simple truth

2. Chapters 2 and 3.

that the respective philosophies and the various principles are in certain respects contradictory. Some doctrines, if pressed to their logical conclusion, would negate others. Likewise, the systematic philosophies, while containing points of agreement, are poles apart in some matters which are basic. The individualism of Locke and Mill, for example, can hardly be reconciled with the organic and collectivist assumptions of Rousseau. Yet all these are branches of the democratic family tree.

The ideals of modern democracy flow then from a rich cornucopia. This is a source of advantage in that the wide selection can cover a variety of situations. But these riches can also bring embarrassment. The same doctrinal multiformity which contributes to flexibility may encourage opportunism. Is democracy to be all things to all men? Is it truly the political "bazaar" which Plato derided? These are not rhetorical questions, nor should they be dismissed as the plaint of the intellectual whose occupational habits set a high premium on consistency of principle. Whether the concepts of democratic thought form a coherent whole, or whether they are a mixture which has a historical, but not a philosophical, unity, is as pertinent at the grass roots of *Realpolitik* as in the outer spaces of metaphysical speculation. How are we to test our actions by their conformity to principle, when we are in doubt or disagreement over principle itself? If communities which have newly won their independence are looking around for a model to imitate, and we who say our government is democratic invite them to follow our splendid example, how are they to know what democracy means when we, its creators and practitioners, embrace a group of incompatible ideas? I am aware that thought can be pushed to a degree where one preserves the logic, but loses touch with life. No sensible person would want to go so far. On the other hand, in a governmental system which explicitly appeals to Man's reason and morality it makes good sense to strive for clarity as an aid to understanding. What the citizens can clearly comprehend, they have a better chance to control.

There are certain fundamental topics to which every political philosophy, be it democratic or other, must address itself. The character of a particular philosophy derives from the values it selects in each case. The fundamentals are these: the position of the individual in the community, relations between individuals, their relationship, severally and collectively, to the government. On all these matters the student of democratic thought will find no lack of solutions. The difficulties arise from their mutual contradictions. There are sharp conflicts between the different concepts and conflicting implications of the same concept. Thus it is sometimes possible for two people to argue on opposite sides of a question and for both to claim that what they advocate conforms to democracy. And as far as the theories go, they may both be partially right. This point can be illustrated by referring to several of the central doctrines of democracy. Whichever one affirms, the antithesis can also be maintained. The emphasis on consent must yield somewhere to the right of dissent. The majority rules, but minorities must be protected. The dignity of the individual is paramount; nevertheless, we should promote the public interest. Does democracy attempt to have it both ways? Are our theories at cross purposes? An answer of some kind is needed to these questions, but should give us pause. It would be folly to suppose that one will readily discover solutions to problems which were treated by Rousseau, Locke, and Mill, and have been repeatedly debated by able minds. Possibly the problems are insoluble. But to inquire into the character of the contradictions may help towards eventual clarity.

Each of the basic issues of democratic theory is connected with one of the fundamental subjects of political philosophy mentioned above. The individual's position in his community is essentially the question of his liberty. Equality, on the other hand, is a matter of the relations between individuals. Both equality and liberty are political concepts in that they are profoundly influenced by the type of government and its activities. But in a broader sense they are coextensive with society since their substance also comes from other groupings besides the state. The remaining topics— i.e., the majority's power, eliciting consent, provision for the general welfare—are directly political. They affect us in our public capacity as citizens, authorizing and receiving the services of government. What I propose now is to inquire into these concepts in turn and examine the contradictions they present.

The natural place to begin is with liberty and equality. Without this pair of ideals it is impossible to conceive of democracy, for, if they cannot be satisfactorily explained, the rest is unlikely to be clear. Usually, liberty and equality are considered separately,[3] and this is perhaps the source of some of the confusion. While they are logically distinguishable, they cannot meaningfully be treated apart. When either one is examined, the analysis shades off into the other, as the following pages will attempt to show. Hence it is possible that they may ultimately appear as different, yet related, aspects of one and the same concept.

3. Much more, however, has been written about liberty than about equality. There is no classic treatment of the latter to match the *Essay on Liberty*.

Critique of Mill's Analysis of Liberty

The complications of liberty originate in two points which were noticed in the preliminary discussion of this subject.[4] Freedom has its negative and positive sides. The former, in the sense of removing restraints, occasions fewer disputes than the latter. When I am free from restraint, I am free to act, and my actions are bound to clash somewhere with those of someone else. To argue for the liberty which involves the absence of restraint is excellent. But subscribing to that formula will not take us very far, because it leads only to the point where the difficulties begin. Nor does it help the argument to continue, as Mill does in the *Essay*, with the assertion that the object of removing restraints is to facilitate the "free development of individuality." That is a fine-sounding phrase, but it is a formal category devoid of substance. People can develop their individualities in a manner that is detrimental, or even disastrous, to others. Hitler, for instance, exercised his capacities most freely, with the result that millions were enslaved and murdered. Mill's doctrine, of course, would not justify a Hitler, because he insists that society is entitled to restrain those actions which are harmful to others. But he limits the force of this principle by an assumption and a condition which are hard to accept. He assumes that all acts are divisible into those which concern only the doer and those which concern others. In the former, society has no right whatsoever to intervene. It may do so in the latter, but only on condition of protecting others from being harmed.

The objections to these provisos are fairly obvious. There is scarcely an act, except of quite a trivial nature, which does not produce consequences for other people. Hence, if there are persons affected by the results, they have an interest in whatever caused it. With his characteristic candor, Mill himself raises this objection in Chapter IV[5] of his Essay. But he does not meet it squarely or resolve it satisfactorily, because the objection is unanswerable. Hence one is forced to conclude that society, which means simply others besides oneself, has some interest in every act of everybody. If that is so, it follows that actions which have social consequences are proper objects of social regulation. Mill would agree—but only to the extent that an action may be controlled if its consequences are harmful. What he refuses to admit is that society may limit an individual's liberty for the purpose of doing something to him which is good. In other words,

4. Chapter 3, pp. 70-71.
5. Entitled, "Of the Limits to the Authority of Society over the Individual."

social restraint is acceptable for the negative object of preventing injury, but not for the positive one of promoting welfare.

It is strange that a humane man of lofty ethical ideals could tie up his thoughts in such a straitjacket. For his logic is so one-sided as to land him in some extraordinary positions. Admittedly, in arguing this way he presents a reasoned case. He distrusts the principle of allowing society to regulate its individual members on the pretext of doing them good, because this can leave the door open for all kinds of tyrannical controls. The most cruel of regimes, and the most regimented, always justify themselves with the argument that they know what is good for the community and are doing it. Against this, Mill's defense rests on the point that each individual knows best what is good for himself and his will should be paramount.

Undeniably there is a wealth of historical evidence which should make us sceptical of the would-be do-gooders, particularly when they are dogmatic and assume their own infallibility. But Mill has trapped himself in an inconsistency which leads to plain distortions of sense. He does not wish society to decree what is good for its members and then do what it so decrees. Nevertheless, he does permit society to stigmatize what is harmful and take positive measures to prevent it. I do not see how one can postulate a category of the injurious without implying, by the same logic, the opposite category of the beneficial. The society which acts according to a notion of what constitutes harm is not merely subscribing to a negation. It is making a positive affirmation that the antithesis is good. As a matter of fact, this is precisely what Mill does throughout the *Essay*. His entire argument is based on some definite conceptions of what is socially desirable. "The worth of a State," he says, "in the long run, is the worth of the individuals composing it."[6] To develop their individuality to the fullest is the criterion of the good society. To that end, liberties must be maximized and restraints minimized. These are positive assertions, and together they add up to a notable philosophy.

Furthermore, in the course of his discussion Mill is open-minded enough to advocate policies which contradict his own first principles. When he writes about the applications[7] of the latter, he considers various issues which were controversial in the Britain of the 1850's. One of these was the notion of compulsory schooling for all children at public expense. To his great credit, Mill argues in its favor with emphasis and eloquence. Not to educate a child, he proclaims, "is a moral crime, both against the

6. This is the beginning clause of the closing sentence of the *Essay*.
7. In Chapter 5.

unfortunate offspring and against society." No one could phrase it more strongly. But how is this to be reconciled with the basic principles of the *Essay?* When children are required to attend school, certain liberties are being restrained. One of these is the liberty of the child, who might prefer to play all day in the streets or work underground in a coal mine. But since all would agree that children do not yet have the maturity to decide what is good for them, somebody else must make the decision. It is, therefore, the parent whose liberty is curtailed when the law obliges him to send his child to a school. And Mill may seem to save his logic by virtue of the fact that such a law does prevent harm to others—i.e., the parent forfeits the opportunity to injure his child by denying him an education.

By such reasoning the *Essay on Liberty* may retain the self-consistency of its logic. But it does so at the price of sense and, I would add, of truth. Such an argument twists around the meanings of words and does violence to our natural way of thinking. When the law sends a child to school, it is not the liberty of the parent which is curtailed, but his authority. In this case his authority within the family is over-ridden by a larger authority, that of the state. The purpose of sending the child to a school is not the negative one of preventing his being harmed. It is rather the positive aim of doing him some good. The principle of compulsory education at public expense rests on the notion that it is good for every individual to be educated to the full limits of his or her intellectual capacity. Thereby the individual is enriched and improved; and so thereby is society. Actually, Mill agrees with these objectives. They are wholly consonant with his philosophy. But his insistence that society may restrain the liberty of an individual only in order to forestall harm to others gives his thought an artificial twist and falsifies its obvious meaning. It is sensible, clear, and direct to argue that education is valuable in itself, that you educate a child to do good to the child, and the state—as the public expression of organized society—is responsible for seeing that everybody gets an education.

Why does Mill land in these contradictions? The answer is that he invites them because of the basic assumptions from which he can never extricate himself. He conceives of the individual as the true unit and of society as an artificial aggregate. Consequently, because of his bias toward individualism, he must always seek special reasons for condoning actions by the group. Taking the individual for his starting-point, Mill reaches out from there to a philosophy of politics. Liberty is good because it is the assertion of individuality. By the same logic, restraints *per se* are bad. They must be explained as the lesser evils which drive out the larger. So conceived, liberty is the product of a collection of negations; and the role of the state is eventually defined, in a monstrous phrase, as "the hinderer of hindrances to the good life." At that point, a theory of liberty couched in individualistic terms had reached the ultimate in sterility. Use two negatives rather than let yourself affirm a single positive!

Certain inferences can plainly be drawn from this critique of Mill's *Essay*. The concept of liberty should be couched primarily in positive terms, since the test of liberty is how one uses it. When the positive is stressed, it becomes clear that the liberty which originates with the individual terminates in relations which are social. Hence it is necessary to regulate such relations in conformity with the values which the society deems good. If these several criteria can be summed up in a definition, it might be this: liberty consists in opportunities to act for socially beneficial ends.

The reference to opportunities, in the plural, requires further explaining. Freedom, as we have seen, is a compound of many particular freedoms. But generically, these can be classified into a few groups. The primary concern of democracy is with the intellectual, political, and economic, which I shall discuss in turn. The character of liberty, and its conditions, differ in each case.

The Case for Absolute Intellectual Freedom

What is meant by intellectual freedom? Some have called it freedom of thought.[8] But that is a misnomer because it is too narrow. Thinking is an internal activity, as much as digesting a meal, which no amount of external coercion can prevent. But the freedom to think requires the attendant freedoms for communicating one's thoughts to others, and such communication is a social action. Freedom to speak, to discuss, to publish, are examples. These are the freedoms which historically have been limited by authority. The institutions mostly responsible for the restraints have been the state and the organized religions, which have imposed their controls either to preserve the power of a ruling group against its opponents or to safeguard a theological dogma from queries and rational criticism. Political and ecclesiastical bodies, however, are not the only offenders. Other organizations—e.g., those with vested economic interests to protect—have also sought to influence the channels of communications, frequently by methods more subtle and indirect than those of outright censorship.

The case for intellectual freedom is simple and irrefutable: it is the necessary condition of human progress. The evolution of *homo sapiens* as a species has been the work of the mind. Without free inquiry followed by

8. E.g., J. B. Bury in his masterly book A *History of Freedom of Thought*.

free discussion, we can neither master our physical environment nor improve the institutions of civilized society. This was what Milton meant when he affirmed: "Give me the liberty to know, to utter, and to argue freely according to conscience, above all liberties."[9] Voltaire and Jefferson have argued the pre-eminence of this freedom, as have Mill and Russell. Broadly viewed, it is the prerequisite for the political freedom embodied in the democratic state. The classic statement on freedom of discussion is still the one contained in the second chapter of Mill's *Essay*. Perhaps this is because of its uncompromising character. What Mill advocates is an absolute. He entertains no reservations. Let us therefore reconsider his arguments.

Mill divides all opinions into three classes. Some are true; some, false; and some, a mixture of truth and falsehood. All kinds should be expressed with complete freedom. Why? The correct opinions, for the obvious reason that they are the truth; the incorrect, because the error can best be discovered by collision with truth; and the mixed, because by open discussion the true portions can be disentangled from the untrue. The contrary policy, which employs authority to ban opinions of a certain kind, Mill rejects because it assumes the infallibility of the censors. He points out that some ideas which at one time were thought absurd have later been proven correct, and that many people will hold their views merely because these happen to prevail in the area where they live.[10] Hence, to emancipate ourselves from the accidents of time and place, we should submit only to the authority of our own reason. And for this to function properly, it must have complete freedom. "The peculiar evil of silencing the expression of an opinion is, that it is robbing the human race; posterity as well as the existing generation; those who dissent from the opinion, still more than those who hold it."[11] Consequently it follows: "If all mankind minus one were of one opinion, and only one person were of the contrary opinion, mankind would be no more justified in silencing that one person than he, if he had the power, would be justified in silencing mankind."[11] These are noble ideals. The outlook they express is tolerant, mature, and intelligent. Trust in reason is faith in Man.

Principles of this absolute character, however, depend on exactness of

9. In *Areopagitica*.
10. ". . . The world, to each individual, means the part of it with which he comes in contact; his party, his sect, his church, his class of society; . . . and it never troubles him that mere accident has decided which of these numerous worlds is the object of his reliance, and that the same causes which make him a Churchman in London, would have made him a Buddhist or a Confucian in Pekin." *Essay on Liberty*, Chap. II.
11. *Ibid*.

definition. The argument contains implications which are ambiguous. In addition, the century since the *Essay* was published has furnished experience with problems which Mill barely considered. Let us pose the question in this way: What is it that we advocate under the name of freedom of discussion? Does it really mean that anybody is entitled, under all circumstances and at all times, to communicate any sort of statement to anyone on any conceivable subject? I doubt that Mill himself would say "yes" to that. The relevant distinctions should be drawn if the principle of free discussion is to be socially applicable.

The Consequences of Expressing Opinions

Communicating a thought produces a relation between the source and the recipient. Thus it is an action with social consequences. Men are responsible for the results of what they do, and the abuse of liberty may be dangerous or even pernicious. A few examples will make this clear. Justice Holmes pointed out in a celebrated opinion that one could not tolerate a person who falsely shouted "fire!" in a crowded theatre. This is because the falsehood is compounded by the circumstances under which it is spoken and causes injury to others. Similarly, a false attack in speech or writing on the character of another individual is punishable as slander or libel, not only because of the intellectual error but also for reason of moral irresponsibility. Parents and teachers are responsible for the tutelage of the young; and, on the assumption that adults know more and are wiser than the immature, they guide the latter through their training and growth. This involves the selection of the materials which come into their hands at an age appropriate to their understanding. Pornographic books, for instance, designed for prurient stimulation and devoid of literary excellence, have no place in a high school library. Such restrictions would seem reasonable. They prevent abuses or punish them. In no way do they curtail the fullest possible freedom of discussion for the purposes for which it is meant—namely, the advancement of knowledge and enrichment of the intellect.

But there are other cases which are less clear and arouse more disagreement. They concern the aims and methods of those who are expressing opinions, the subject-matter of the opinions, and the environment in which these are voiced. Consider the differences between propaganda, on the one hand, and the procedures of a courtroom or a classroom, on the other. The propagandist attempts to persuade people to think as he does and to remain of that persuasion. It is furthest from his intentions to present all sides of a question. The last thing he wants is an open mind. His goal is to open them just enough to receive what he has to say and then to leave them tightly shut. Truth is irrelevant to his objectives. As the whip does violence to the body, his words do violence to the mind.

Contrast with this the processes and purposes of the courtroom and the classroom. The function of a court is to serve justice by discovering the truth about a particular case and then applying the law to the facts. The key to this consists in the different, but complementary, roles performed by a trio of persons. A pair of lawyers represent the opposite sides, while an impartial judge sits in the chair. Each lawyer is an advocate. His pleading is one-sided. But the public confrontation of the two, under procedures enforced by a judge, is the best means that can be devised to elicit the whole truth. A classroom has this goal, to learn the truth, in common with a court. But it has other purposes which do not fall under this heading, and its structure takes a special form. The task of a teacher is to train his students to think freely for themselves. His aim is to make himself super-fluous. He does this by imparting information on what is already known, indicating areas of uncertainty and doubt, analyzing the pros and cons of disputed questions, and generally exciting the student's curiosity to learn more. If he succeeds in both informing and stimulating, he will end up by leaving the student with the capacity and the interest to think on his own and formulate his own opinions, which may, of course, involve rejecting those of his teacher. The propagandist seeks to induce a parrot-like dependence. The judicial system is designed for discovering the truth. Education is meant to train adult citizens who are informed, creative, and independent.

How do these distinctions apply to the problem of free discussion of opinion? Society is broader than a court or classroom. It does not acknowledge—at least, in the democratic civilization—a single judge or teacher. Totalitarian regimes with a police state will have their Big Brother who is Lord High Everything,[12] but the community which values freedom does not. Where there are many advocates and teachers, and there is no constituted judge, Everyman is a juror in the court of public opinion—be he tolerant or prejudiced, ignorant or wise. *Magna est veritas*, it has been said, *et praevalebit*. Truth is great and will prevail. So too thought Milton. "And though all the winds of doctrine were let loose to play upon the earth, so Truth be in the field, we do injuriously, by licensing and prohibiting, to misdoubt her strength. Let her and Falsehood grapple; who ever knew Truth put to the worse, in a free and open encounter?" Unfor-

12. If George Orwell can be mixed with W. S. Gilbert.

tunately we know it all too well. Men are frequently more swayed by their passions than influenced by their reason. Their ears may hear the truth. But they may not recognize it for what it is, or emotions may obstruct the receipt of the message. Nevertheless, the optimist will console himself with the hope of later victory. It is the future tense of *praevalebit* that is significant. We shall win, we tell ourselves, in the long run, which is very comforting when we remember, with Keynes, that in the long run we shall all be dead. But even in the short run some of us may not survive. Hitler and Stalin murdered millions inside a bare decade. For a mouthpiece, the Ogpu and Gestapo used the services of the propagandist.

Ethical Values and Scientific Truth

The blessings of freedom are, at the same time, its perils. What is used will on occasion be abused. You take the evil with the good, but you try to limit the former's worst effects. These can, as a matter of practice, be reduced to harmless proportions if there really is a free and open encounter on matters where the difference between truth and error can be demonstrated and proven. Both Milton and Mill obscure their case by the meaning they attach to truth and the rhetoric associated with the term. In a scientific field, it is possible to distinguish between knowledge and hypothesis. Truth can be separated from error by evidence and verification. Where the evidence is unavailable, the scientist is supposed to suspend judgment until it is forthcoming. But there are other spheres of speculation where truth and falsehood are not the only categories with which we deal. Mill and Milton confuse an ethical judgment with a scientific proposition. Galileo was forced by the Church to recant. But since the scientific evidence was on his side, his was the ultimate victory. A discussion of the principles appropriate to human society, however, involves judgments of value. Since political philosophy reposes on moral concepts, the criteria of good and bad are more relevant than those of truth and error. The latter will apply to our knowledge of factual data about society. The former will govern the interpretation we place upon them. A political goal can be characterized as good or bad. It cannot be called true or false. Take the commandment: "Thou shalt not kill." Or consider the declaration: "All men are created equal." These are not susceptible to the same method of proof as the proposition that the Earth moves. What you can say is this: If you permit people to kill, or encourage them to kill certain kinds of people, or if you divide humanity into superiors and inferiors, you can demonstrate from history that such and such consequences have followed and you can predict the same or similar results in the future. Then you proceed to an ethical judgment that the observed and probable results are either good or bad, and hence you approve or disapprove the principle.

Mill's method of defending absolute freedom of discussion misses the point in this respect because he, like Milton before him, is thinking of a market place of ideas where, if free competition genuinely occurs, the truth drives out the error. One is mindful, however, of Gresham's Law pertaining to currency that the bad money drives out the good, and it can happen in politics that the good doctrine succumbs to the bad. In the world of *Realpolitik*, virtue does not always triumph.

Even if this correction is introduced into Mill's argument, however, his basic contention on behalf of absolutely free discussion would remain un-affected. It must still be held that, where opinions involve social values and the evidence is to be appraised by the criteria of good or bad, not true or false, only the complete liberty of inquiry and debate affords the guarantee of a wise judgment. John Dewey was right in rejecting the maxim *de gustibus non est disputandum*[13] with the retort: What else is there more important to argue about? Indeed, one might say that just because it is impossible to prove a value true or false and because controversies arise over whether it is good or bad, there is every need for continuous re-evaluation in the light of experiment and experience. The community which encourages the fullest freedom of rational inquiry is the more likely to arrive at a greater degree of certainty.

But in the mass culture of the mid twentieth century rational inquiry has its pitfalls. If every adult were well-informed, highly educated, and en-lightened, liberty of discussion would function at its best and presumably would bring beneficial results. A community that was composed prepon-derantly of John Stuart Mills might so behave. But even then one cannot be sure. A university professor who is accustomed to the discussions and decisions of an academic faculty can testify that these are not always guided by pure reason, dispassionate open-mindedness, and gentle tol-erance. Shall we then expect better of the Great Society? The fact is that, even in the most advanced of countries, secondary education for three or four years was not available to everybody until a generation ago. In the electorate of a modern democracy, the majority of people have by now received enough education to understand the popular press, read an occa-sional novel, and absorb the entertainment of the motion-picture and television screens. Yet this is the milieu in which we are conducting the vast and noble experiment of governing through discussion, persuasion,

13. There is no disputing about tastes.

and consent. It is not surprising that we make some mistakes. It is surprising that we make so few.

No matter how highly we value reason and trust its potency, we cannot overlook the emotional factors which surround the process of rational inquiry. The Man of Good Will, whom democratic theory postulates, is an ideal type. He is not synonymous with the Man in the Street. Scholars may applaud the dictum of Voltaire: "I disagree profoundly with what you say, but I would defend with my life your right to say it." But such tolerance is seldom widely spread. In the workaday world, we coexist as best we may by achieving a cross-cancellation of rival prejudices. It is easy enough, of course, to be tolerant of free discussion in matters which do not concern the fundamentals of our social and political order. But people at large do not accord a generous reception to those who would re-examine vested interests, accepted dogmas, and conventional mores. Burke was terrified by the spirit of rational inquiry, unleashed in the French Revolution, because it cast doubt on everything and searched the title deeds of established institutions. Bentham's test was similarly destructive of tradition since he dared to pluck apart the threads of the inherited fabric and ask of each: What is its use? Matters of a secondary level may be fearlessly probed because they do not arouse the deeper emotions. But a community cannot fail to be disturbed when its foundations are ransacked, and rebellious spirits ask awkward questions about the four cornerstones—religion, sex, property, and government. Atheists, homosexuals, communists, and anarchists are not normally the recipients of popularity prizes. Yet, if Mill's logic be accepted, these are valuable people whose views should be most freely debated, since our truth is all the clearer for its confrontation by their error.

Are There Limits to Tolerance?

Not all change is synonymous with progress. Innovation is not always improvement. A community ought ideally to tolerate full freedom of inquiry and discussion so that it may have a rational understanding of its purposes and processes instead of merely taking them for granted. But there is a case for order as well as for liberty. It has been said that my freedom to swing my arm ends where the other person's nose begins. Likewise, my freedom to speak my mind depends on the assurance that I will be answered with words and not with a blow. A civic order is required to maintain and keep open the channels through which the streams of free inquiry may pour. Freedom of the intellect depends on attitudes of tolerance. The latter have to be spontaneous. They cannot be enforced by the state. But the state may and must intervene to outlaw overt manifestations of intolerance. As the agent of the organized community, it has the duty in a free society of seeing that the right to speak, criticize, and answer criticism, is continuously maintained. Liberty itself imposes a responsibility on those who exercise it, for it will not last if the proper conditions are not fulfilled. There exists a broad zone, without a definable dividing line, in which advocacy shades off into incitement, attacks degenerate into defamation, and opposition is transformed into sedition. People had this in mind in an earlier age when they distinguished liberty from license. In our century the need to draw a distinction somewhere has become imperative because of movements at both extremes of the political spectrum which would so take advantage of the freedom a democracy affords as to destroy it from within.

Should the tolerant tolerate the intolerant? Must a principle be applied in a manner so absolute as to facilitate its own destruction? As I to be tolerant of him who, if he had the chance, would not be tolerant of me? There is no intellectual reason why I should, since the consistency of a principle does not require its suicide. Nor can I see a moral obligation to give to another what he has no right to claim or any moral fault in denying to another what he would not give. Morality is a function of the mutual rights and duties which are created within a social framework, and political ethics are founded on the reciprocity of the *quid pro quo*. Do to others what you would have others do to you. But do not ask of others what you would not do to them.

As a constituted regime, democracy has the right to preserve itself. Liberty can be protected against abuses committed in its name. The German Nazis, Italian Fascists, and Czechoslovak Communists demonstrated in this century the possibility of undermining from within the authority which safeguards freedom. But the defense which is necessary against such dangers also involves a risk. Although all liberties depend on maintaining some order, too many orders mean sacrificing too much liberty. Hence questions of degree arise which statesmanship must settle by prudence in particular circumstances. The formula of Justice Holmes, that the state may act to forestall "a clear and present danger," is not satisfactory. Dangers are seldom clear until they are present; when they are present, resistance may be too late. On the other hand, to authorize their prevention at too early a stage can lead to the kind of censorship and curbs on public assembly which go too far in the opposite direction. When you fight fire with fire, you have to take care not to burn down the house you are trying to save. Sidney Hook has argued that we should distinguish heresy from conspiracy.[14] Heresy is an intellectual activity and is justified because it involves the expression and examination of ideas, no matter how unpopular and unconventional they may be. Conspiracy is political because it signifies not only organization, but the deliberate attempt to go outside the law and overthrow a system. A community which tolerates freedom of discussion and whose constitution allows for peaceful, orderly change has the moral right to prohibit conspiracy and the political duty to do so.

What are the implications of this argument? Some will criticize it on the ground that it concedes the entry of the thin end of the wedge and that some brutal force may then drive deeper cracks into the pillars of freedom. I grant that possibility. But what is the alternative? Either you affirm that freedom of communication is an absolute, that its definition is all-inclusive, and that its abuses may be neither punished nor prevented by authority; or you assert that, like other freedoms, it is relative, that it is exercised socially and produces consequences for others, and that it must, therefore, operate within a framework of order if its beneficial results are to be shared by all. There is an element of risk in either position. The former leaves the road clear for propaganda, demagoguery, conspiracy, and eventually intolerance. The latter employs the restraints of law and police power, which can admittedly be carried to excess against unpopular minorities whenever public fear or anger demands a scapegoat. In politics there are no automatic safety devices. Whatever policy is followed escapes one set of difficulties, but introduces another. My own opinion on this problem concurs with the view that liberty is a social conception. There should be no limits whatsoever on its exercise in the intellectual domain of discovering truth and assessing values, since the work of the mind cannot otherwise be fruitfully conducted. Social action, however, calls for organization. A *fortiori*, therefore, political action must be permitted to the fullest extent that is consistent with the like action by others. In this sphere, we surrender a portion of the sum-total of liberties in order to ensure the equal distribution of the remainder.

That last sentence, I suggest, leads to the essence of the notion of freedom. When freedom is conceived in individualistic terms and generalized as a single abstraction, there is a tendency for it to be posited as an absolute. But when the social aspect is stressed, and freedom is analyzed into its component freedoms, its relative character becomes clear. This is especially so when the concept of liberty is applied to the particular cases of its use in politics, economics, and other phases of our social life. The freedoms which men claim in these spheres are also manifestations of equality.

14. *Heresy, Yes—Conspiracy, No!* (John Day Co.: New York, 1953).

If I demand a specific freedom for myself, the democratic state is obligated to reply that I am entitled to it on the condition that others may exercise it in the same way. Hence, what is liberty when seen from the standpoint of the individual citizen becomes equality when viewed through the vision of the whole society. When the right to vote was progressively extended, liberty was broadened. Each section of the community, as it was enfranchised, acquired a freedom in the political sphere which it formerly lacked. But what should we call the result at the end, when all adult citizens were qualified to vote? Is it Liberty? Or Equality? Or is it both— equalized liberties, if you will?

Here, of course, I have used an example where the exercise of a right does not lead to any infringement of its similar exercise by everybody else. But there are other political freedoms whose use results in competition and conflict and must, in the nature of the case, terminate in someone's gain and someone's loss. A citizen has a right to participate in government. He is free to seek public employment or contest an election. But he has no right to be elected or appointed. Somebody has to be the loser. All are free to apply or to run, and, being free, they are also equal. But the outcome is unequal. The winner in a presidential race lives in the White House where he signs the official papers. His defeated opponent reads about him in the daily papers.

The same argument can be extended to other social activities. Freedom of religion is a case in point. When intolerance prevailed, as it still does in many countries, different creeds were treated unequally as a matter of official policy. Wherever there is a state religion, or one which the constitution recognizes as the "true" faith, it is accorded advantages and privileges which are denied to others. The latter are assigned an unequal status, and to the extent of that inequality, are not free. The demand for religious freedom was an assertion of equality. The same could also be called political neutrality in theological matters, or perhaps indifference. But the alternative policy results in social differences which can be seen most plainly. Look at the contemporary position of Protestants and Jews in Spain, or of Christians and Jews in Saudi Arabia. These are instances of the fanatical and intransigent, where the consequences are clearly visible. Such communities lack freedom, as they lack equality. And it is underscoring the obvious to say that they lack democracy. Religious dogmatism was never compatible with the democratic spirit. Where tolerance exists today, it was forced down the ecclesiastical throat by science and the liberal-minded secular state.

The economic developments of the modern era have similarly generated situations which bear directly on this problem of the meanings of

freedom. As was noted earlier, the use of private capital for industrial production was accompanied by a philosophy of freedom from state intervention. The results have indeed been spectacular. As consumers, all of us
have gained. But this philosophy, with its overemphasis on the negative
aspects of freedom, overlooked the side-effects upon equality. Inequalities
there were before the Industrial Revolution began. The latter did not remove them, but continued them in another form. In some instances, in
fact, as Marx observed, the rich grew richer in a relative sense and the
poor poorer. Freedom, unregulated, can accentuate inequality. Or more
precisely, the positive use of specific freedoms allows the strong to take
advantage of the weak. The latter are unfree to the extent that, and in
the same proportion as, they are unequal. Hereupon, the community reacted, employing the political weapons which democracy placed in the
hands of the underprivileged poor, to improve their material condition.
The head-on economic confrontation took place on both battlefronts,
industrial and political. But how are the process and its consequences to be
described? Shall they be subsumed under the category of freedom, or that
of equality, or do they belong in part to each? The employer has seen
certain of his liberties, and power, diminished. By the same act, the power
and certain liberties of his employees are increased. This reapportionment
of freedoms is a process of greater equalization. Is freedom then, when
socially conceived, equality under another name?

At this point, it is appropriate to shift the orientation of the argument.
The inquiry into liberty has led directly into the subject of equality. Let
us therefore make another start. Suppose we begin with equality and see in
what direction its analysis proceeds. Freedom turns out, upon examination, to be a jewel of many facets, not all of them equally lustrous. Perhaps
equality too contains implications which are contradictory.

Equality: Identical or Proportional

One of the earliest discussions of the concept is still, from this standpoint,
one of the best. Aristotle had much to say about equality in the *Politics*.
He recognized the importance of the topic and came back to it several
times.[15] Applying elementary mathematics to social practice, he offered a
simple, yet basic, distinction. Equality has two senses, the identical and

15. For example: Book III, Chap. 12, 1282b-1283a; Book V, Chap. 1, 1301b; Book
VI, Chap. 2, 1317b–Chap. 3, 1318a. He discusses equality particularly when he is
talking about justice, or when he is contrasting democracy and oligarchy.

the proportional.[16] In the former sense, two persons may be called equals if their position and treatment are exactly the same. In the latter, they are equal if both are measurable by some standard to which their position and treatment are then scaled. Usage supplies many instances of the two types. We insist that all children have an equal right to an education. This equality is uniform. But we add that each individual should be educated to the level of his or her intellectual capacities. Moreover, every teacher, who has to judge the performance and progress of a group of students, knows that they are not identical. Grading is in fact employed to classify their differences. Equality here becomes proportional.

When a political system is dedicated to the proposition that all men are created equal, it must proceed to determine what species of equality is suitable for different situations. Social policy involves not only a choice between alternative values, but also a preference for one interpretation of a particular value over another. Let us pick at random some actual examples which are politically relevant because a government has to decide what policy to follow. The owner of an automobile in the United States must pay an annual registration fee to the State in which he resides. In some States, everybody pays exactly the same amount *per annum* for the privilege of operating a car. But in others, the amount is proportioned to the estimated market-value and is reduced in successive years. Thus the owner of the latest model Cadillac pays considerably more than the driver of an ancient jalopy. Which meaning of equality is pertinent here? The same choice, between uniformity or proportionalism, must be made in the field of taxes on income. You could argue that every citizen ought to pay a fixed amount to defray the costs of government, and that all should contribute exactly the same. Second, all might pay the same, but those earning below a certain minimum would be exempt. Third, everybody might pay the same percentage of his earnings, i.e., the rate should be uniform while the amounts which are paid would vary. Fourth, one can decide in favor of graduating the rates, so that the richer pay a higher percentage than the poorer. Which of these systems is the equal one?

Similar considerations have been debated in the field of voting. Uniform equality can be obtained by following Bentham's formula that everybody should count for one and nobody for more than one. In this case each person would have one vote. But even when that is provided, the effects of each person voting once only are not necessarily identical. If I reside in a district with ten thousand voters and you in a district of twenty thousand, my vote has twice the influence of yours on the outcome. Hence, by logi-

16. Aristotle is thinking of the difference between an arithmetical and a geometrical progression.

cal extension equal voting rights can be held to require an equality of apportionment. This has been defended as "one vote, one value." Alternatively, the right to vote can be rationed. It can be given to some and denied to others. Or again, some may be able to vote several times—e.g., when the ownership of property of a certain amount is a qualification for voting and there are those who possess sufficient multiples of that amount. Double-voting, it will be remembered, was allowed under British law until 1949. A farmer's vote in New Zealand was purposely weighted by law at 28 per cent more than an urban vote until 1945. Today in an American presidential election a citizen voting in Alaska has considerably more power to affect the result than a voter in California.

What does democracy mean then by the equality it endorses? Which is the type of equality to be used in which circumstances? When should people be treated identically; and when proportionately? And how are we to determine when the ration card is more appropriate, and when the grading system?

Some clues to the answers emerge from the nature of the question. In the case of equality it is apparent, as it was with liberty, that the abstraction comprises a bundle of equalities of particular kinds. Also it would seem that the criteria for selecting these are different in various situations. But there is an aspect to these questions which was not so evident in the discussion of freedom. When equality is in issue, the prescription we should follow will be influenced by our answer to the further question: What is just? Equality and justice are interrelated concepts. Analyze one, and you arrive at a notion of the other.

Status, Rewards, and Quality

The initial queries, then, to raise are these: Equality of what? Or, equality in what respect? For this purpose, one may distinguish between equality at the beginning of a process, and at the end. The former is a matter of opportunity, which depends on status. An individual's standing or position in the community—the very words have static connotations—delimit first of all the place from which one can move. But movement is possible only if avenues are open. Where human beings are ranked in superimposed strata, as in a feudal system or any society arranged in horizontal classes, opportunities are a function of status. Different doors are open or closed at different levels in the hierarchy. Naturally, the French revolutionaries demanded égalité since they were opposed to the surviving remnants of a feudal order. An achievement of the Revolution was to inaugurate equality of opportunity, *la carrière ouverte aux talents*, wherein the individual's ability, not his family's status, would determine where he could move and how far he could go. The egalitarian notion of democracy, therefore, seeks to abolish distinctions of status in so far as they circumscribe an individual's scope of action by the bounds of the class to which he belongs. Long before Marx and Marxism, it was democracy's advocates who propounded the ideal of the classless society. A community should accord a common status to all its members as their individual right.

In this reasoning, the interrelation between liberty and equality is obvious. Differentiations of status produce differences in liberties. Some are freer; others, less free. Such differences in respect to liberties are also inequalities. Create equality of opportunity, and liberties are equalized. Abolish a hierarchy of statuses, and you both diminish the free range of action enjoyed by those at the top and enlarge the freedoms of those at the bottom. Thus a strictly quantitative calculation would indicate that the sum total of freedom increases in the whole society as the specific freedoms of all individuals are equalized.

But there is more to it than this. Not only must quantitative factors be appraised in qualitative terms, but we should consider the application of equality to the results of the process, as well as in the beginning. If the latter calls for identical equality, does the same hold true at the other end? Without overdoing the metaphor of the race of life, we may properly ask whether those who must start equal should finish so. Equality of opportunity will result in the display of unequal abilities. When the latter are recognized, how should they be treated? All of us enjoy equal rights to express our opinions. But it does not follow that all opinions are equally right. In fact, we discriminate between the accurate and the incorrect, between good taste and vulgarity, and between wisdom, common sense, and nonsense. These are qualitative judgments. They classify in unequal categories the consequences of equal freedom.

It is the same with other manifestations of social activity. Suppose one could assume a hypothetical community where all individuals actually began the race of life with the same chance, where family connections, parental influence, and wealth, had no bearing on one's education and later advancement, and where all freedoms were perfectly equalized. In such an imaginary society, the different abilities of the individual would still assert themselves. Those with better minds, stronger bodies, more forceful personalities, would show their superiority and thrust ahead. How then should they be rewarded for the merits they demonstrate as individuals? It is not fair, and does not seem just, that those who work harder, or have more original ideas, or serve their fellowmen more conscientiously, should be treated the same as those who are their inferiors in these respects. If it is unjust to deny any child an education, it is no less unjust to deprive a superior child of a superior education. A worker who produces more through his energy and skill deserves to receive more.

These propositions are elementary to state, but not on that account easy or simple to apply. The concept of equality, after all, can be approached from two sides. It can imply both leveling up and leveling down. Conversely, it can be carried to excess in both directions. There is an exaggerated egalitarianism which, if projected without check, would bring everybody to the same level at dead center. Though socially indefensible, this egalomania is an understandable psychological reaction on the part of underprivileged people who have collectively suffered inferior treatment without regard to their individual merits. Proportional equality is as necessary, however, in certain spheres as identical equality in others. The main difficulty with proportionalism lies in deciding how and where to apply it. With uniformity there is a rough and ready rule. Everybody is treated the same, as if they were identical units. But proportionalism requires a scale or standard, and this gives rise to a host of knotty problems. The standard has to be selected and, in a democratically governed society, it has to be accepted as just. Then, each individual must be assigned his notch on a scale.

Controversies and doubts will inevitably arise because the criteria for classification cannot be wholly objective. A teacher sorts out his students into groups which he labels A, B, C, D, and Fail. What he attempts to rank is their knowledge and the quality of their minds. Subjective factors necessarily enter into such a judgment. The student can be protected from arbitrariness in two ways: by the professional integrity of those who grade them and, as a safeguard against any lapse or prejudice, by ensuring that each person is also independently graded by others. In administering an income tax, one assigns numbers—i.e., rates and amounts—to data which are quantified and therefore measurable as units of currency. But the principles which lie behind the numbers involve a concept of distributive justice. Taxation is judged by its incidence, by the way it falls on the persons liable to pay, and the scale begins with a minimum and ends at a maximum.

With taxes, wages, or grades, it is possible to employ proportionalism, though there will always be some who feel they are unfairly treated. In the larger sense of evaluating human worth, justice may require that every man be treated as he deserves. But how are we properly to judge another man's deserts? There are some qualities which no quantity can measure. The virtuoso, the genius, the saint, are beyond the scale. How do you reward them? Philosophies of aristocracy or elitism go so far that, in extolling the best, they downgrade most of the human race. Nevertheless, a philosophy which upgrades the Common Man and raises his rewards must face the contrary problem and accord recognition to exceptional talent. Tocqueville and Mill were jointly aware of the danger that rare abilities might be stifled by the pressures of mass mediocrity. Society, as well as the state, could demand conformity and punish the deviant. The latter might be a criminal; he might merely be eccentric. But occasionally he might be a creative genius.

The potential conflict between quality and equality is an old one. Nor is it ended yet. Our democratic societies have assuredly made immense strides in the direction of equality during the last hundred years. The leveling up has been truly phenomenal, and amounts to an impressive gain in social justice. For justice depends on establishing the minimum below which no human being should be allowed to fall; while the criterion of our progress in civilization is continuously to raise that minimum. But what is happening to the maximum? A simultaneous process of leveling down is also in evidence. In some spheres this is deliberate and planned. We tax great fortunes, for instance, and redistribute the proceeds in the form of armaments or welfare, in military security or social security. In others, the process occurs haphazardly through the encouragement of conformity. A search for a standard can end in standardization. Ideas and tastes and conduct can flow toward a norm where individuality is drowned in the collective ocean, and the independent thinker is unwelcome because his brainstorms disturb the collective calm. I have no doubt that the contemporary Swiss, unlike their ancestors, would politely tolerate some latter-day Rousseau, were he suddenly to blaze forth in their midst.[17] If nothing else, that constitutes an improvement in political and intellectual manners. But it would be surprising if he were received with any enthusiasm.

Both types of equality—identical and proportional—conform to certain aspects of our sense of justice. It is just that in some matters all of us should be treated exactly for what we are—namely, equally human. Humanity is a category which admits neither degrees nor classes nor rates. Hence in everything which is fundamental to the dignity of a human being and the respect for his individuality, treatment should be uniform and the political system should be imbued with this principle. A democratic government subscribes to it by providing for equal participation. This means that every adult citizen is entitled to vote, to seek public

17. *Emile* and the *Contrat Social* were published just over two hundred years ago, in 1762. Soon after, the author's house was stoned.

office, and receive impartial administration of justice. But the equality, needless to say, should be one of substance, not merely of form. If, for example, the law allows all citizens to register as voters, but requires that they pay a tax as a condition of registering, this bears unequally on the poor, many of whom are effectively disqualified. Hence the requirement of a poll tax for voting violates a fundamental civic right. Similarly, the law may insist that all citizens must have attained a certain degree of literacy before they can register to vote. The effects of this rule will be unjust and anti-democratic if the government of the state in question then neglects to educate its citizens up to the level required. Equality is a mockery when it is only an empty form. As Anatole France observed in *Le Lys Rouge:* "In France we are both soldiers and citizens. To be a citizen —that is another ground for pride. For the poor, it means to maintain and preserve the wealthy in their power and idleness. They must toil for that in the face of the law whose majestic equality forbids rich and poor alike to sleep under the bridges, beg in the streets, and steal for bread."[18]

But while identical equality, both in substance and form, is necessary in fundamentals, elsewhere proportionalism should be the rule. It is a fact of nature that, as humans, we are all equal. It is no less a fact of nature that, as individuals, we all differ. Justice demands the recognition of both facts alike. Individual differences, therefore, should be treated proportionately, for this too is equality. Energy, work, skill, creativity—these, when used for socially beneficial purposes, should be differently rewarded, not only to stimulate incentive but also for the respect that is due to merit.

How is equality, of both kinds, to be attained? Can it be planned and directed? Or must it come spontaneously if it is to come at all? These are questions which touch immediately on the role and responsibilities of government. Let us consider what the alternatives imply.

Government as an Equalizer

There seems little doubt that neither species of equality can be produced except by positive action from some authoritative source. Proportionalism involves accepting a standard as just and applying it to groups and individuals. This cannot be done without the authority of an agent of the public. Likewise, the provision and enforcement of identical rights depends on governmental power. To affirm that all men are created equal, or that none shall be denied the equal protection of the laws, is not

18. Chapter 7. In the Calmann-Lévy edition, pp. 117-18.

enough. These principles become realities in practice when they are acted upon by a Supreme Court, a President, a Congress, the police—and in some cases, regrettably but necessarily, by armed soldiers. Unlike the quality of mercy, the nature of equality does impose constraint. Rousseau was writing rhetoric when he said that men must be forced to be free. But it is true of some men that they must be forced to be equal. The inequalities of the privileged are seldom surrendered without a struggle.

It follows from this argument that to attain equality strong government is needed. Observable exceptions to this generalization are indeed rare and are due to quite unusual circumstances. One such exception was the situation in the United States as Tocqueville observed it in the 1830's. Egalitarianism was what he diagnosed as the chief characteristic of American democracy, and this he attributed to the equality of social conditions. Assuredly, the state had relatively little to do with it, since at that time the functions of government, at all three levels of the federal union, were circumscribed. But the social conditions of that period were exceptional. A poor man who had energy and courage and wished, as the phrase goes, to "better himself," could move west where land was for the taking and a fortune for the making. Naturally the frontier spirit was leveling and individualistic. Rugged characters infused into the state the equality which they had won for themselves. It was not the state which made them equal. But those were special circumstances, which cannot be repeated. Normally, equality is the result of positive action by a strong state in the social sphere and the political. During the twentieth century, at any rate, that has been the rule.

Liberty Multiplied by Equality

The wheel has thus turned full circle. As the analysis of freedom arrived at the point where equality was the topic of discussion, so the examination of equality brings us back to liberty. What happens in the relation between the two is a continuous interplay of contrary tendencies which check one another and countercheck to maintain a rough sort of equilibrium. The two senses of freedom, negative and positive, are at variance with themselves, as are proportional and identical equality. By the same logic, liberty and equality become contradictory if projected to the point where they eliminate one another. Begin with negative freedom, the absence of restraints, and positive freedoms will follow. The consequent actions, if unchecked, result in inequalities. Since the latter bring advantages to some individuals, their freedom is increased. Correspondingly, the freedom of those who are at a disadvantage is diminished—which means that they are subject to restraint. But this argument can also be applied in reverse. Begin with inequality, and take measures to promote greater equalization by leveling both down and up. In the course of this process, certain individuals are losing some freedoms, while others are gaining. Liberties are then being equalized all around. To bring about this state of affairs and maintain it, strong regulation is necessary. The danger now arises that the power which is needed to produce equality may terminate in subjecting everybody to itself. "The passion for equality," lamented Acton, "made vain the hope for freedom."[19] Shakespeare put these words in the gardener's mouth in *Richard the Second:*

> "Go thou, and like an executioner,
> Cut off the heads of too fast growing sprays,
> That look too lofty in our commonwealth:
> All must be even in our government."[20]

Or, as George Orwell wrote of Stalin's Russia: "All men are equal; but some are more equal than others."[21]

In logic there is no escaping these contradictions. Nor is there in political practice either. Any tendency, unchecked, in thought or action negates another. Can they be rendered compatible? I think they can if certain points are borne in mind. Every political philosophy is concerned to provide a rationale for the functions of government and justify the effects they have on relations between individuals. What we refer to as liberty and equality is a pair of abstractions which generalize about many such relationships. Their difference is primarily one of starting point and emphasis. Liberty begins with the individual as the unit and thence proceeds to the group. Equality commences with the group for the unit and arrives at the individual members. Both concepts are the connected sides of the same problem. Both contain potentialities which thought can extrapolate but statesmen must inhibit. For each can be envisaged as filling an intermediate zone on a scale which extends between undesirable extremes. Liberty is opposed to despotism at one end, to anarchy at the other. Equality rejects the privilege which treats people unequally without regard for their merits, as it repudiates the absolute uniformity which would treat them in all respects alike. Phrased as a philosophical equation, democracy equals liberty multiplied by equality. This, be it noted, is multi-

19. *The History of Freedom, and Other Essays* (Macmillan: London, 1909), p. 57.
20. Act III, scene IV, ll. 33-36.
21. *Animal Farm.*

plication, not addition. Equality and liberty are fused together and inter-penetrate one another. The following diagram may help to illustrate what I have in mind.

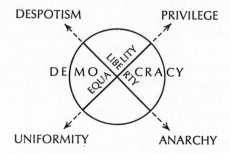

What relation does this produce between equality and freedom? Initially, the ideal which signifies their union is equality of opportunity. This does not involve the removal of all restraints. It means removing those which impose an unfair handicap, while retaining any which ensure that everybody stands an equal chance. When all are equal in fundamentals, they should be differently rewarded for individual merit. It is just that each should get his deserts, since the object of equal opportunities is to permit the development of unequal abilities. But when the latter are evaluated, the citizen's freedom from arbitrary judgment must be safeguarded. Proportional equality requires an authoritative standard, but political liberty opposes an authoritarian administration. Here is where the basic freedoms to discuss, assemble, and vote, are so crucial. Every individual may of right, and should as a duty, participate in formulating the values which prevail in the community, in organizing groups to promote common interests, in choosing the persons who will be entrusted with public office and approving the outlines of their program. The duty of government in a democracy is to undertake this truly creative task of continuously harmonizing the relations between individuals in a dynamic complex of equalized freedoms.

Plato considered justice the supreme virtue of the ideal state. What has been sketched out here might be considered the justice of the democratic state.

17

Majority Rule, Minority Rights, and the Public Good

All government embodies the phenomenon of persons in authority making and applying rules and of citizens who normally obey them. Hence arises a classic question of political philosophy: Why ought I to obey what the state commands? The answers express the different characters of the various philosophies. Perhaps the commonest is to assert that citizens should obey when the authority which issues the orders is legitimate. That reply, however, still gives rise to considerable argument over what it is that legitimizes authority. Another kind of answer goes beyond the authority which sanctions the rule to include the substance which that rule contains. In this case, the citizen would feel bound to obey for two reasons: one, that the public officials are rightfully entitled to act, and, second, that what they are requiring him to do is right.

An Ethical Source for Governmental Power

Democracy is distinguished as a political system by the importance it attaches to ethics, and the ideals which democrats espouse have a strongly ethical tinge. Every democratic philosophy is concerned, almost obsessed, with the need to rest the authority of government on moral foundations. But while there is agreement on the need, opinions differ about the source which generates that morality. Again in this respect, as in those discussed in the preceding chapter, the contradictions are patent. People who are equally good democrats believe in principles all of which cannot be equally correct because they negate one another.

The political foundation of a democracy is the supremacy of the people. Their freedom and equality are guaranteed when the ultimate power in the state is lodged in their hands. One part of the community can enslave another part; a whole people cannot enslave itself. These, however, are theoretical propositions, with a Rousseauian flavor. They have to be applied nowadays to states whose populations total up to eight or nine digits. Although a whole people cannot enslave itself, neither can it govern itself. In practice a small segment does the governing—in the name, of course, of the whole. How is that justified according to democratic doctrine? What makes it right? The concept traditionally employed to impregnate political power with morality is that of consent.[22] Democracy is the type of government which insists that the people, *en masse*, elect their highest officials and approve, in broad outline, the program they are to follow. The manner whereby this is done is based on an accepted constitution, which prescribes the procedures and establishes the institutions for the people to use. Consequently when the government of a democracy acts, it does so with the consent of those it governs, and the powers thus derived, in Jefferson's phrase, are just.

The reason why the consent of the governed confers on governmental acts a morality they would otherwise lack can be simply stated. The power employed in governing embraces the element of force. People obey their government from a variety of motives, one of which is their awareness that, if they do not, they can be coerced. But force, as such, is devoid of moral quality. It consists in a violence which is purely physical and is gauged solely in terms of strength. Something else is required in a community of civilized men to convert one's attitude toward the state from passive submission to active volition. This can be nothing else than a spontaneous manifestation of the citizen's will. If I agree, freely and uncoerced, to a set of principles, institutions, and procedures, then anything done in conformity with them is authoritative for me because authorized by me. By this reasoning, if I was consulted and have consented, I am the author of the acts of which the public official is the agent. Indeed, my authorship is his authority. Thus, when I obey the state, I do not bow to an external will, but express my own.

This argument for resting the morality of democratic government on consent is subtler than it sounds. It contains some implications which require exploring and possibly some ambiguities. It is a melange to which

22. See Chapter 10, p. 298.

Locke, Rousseau and Jefferson, have all contributed. But mingled with their voices one detects some disquieting echoes of Hobbes and Hegel, whose use or abuse of a similar line of logic led directly to authoritarian rule. That would in any case be a paradoxical result because the analysis of consent in the preceding paragraph terminates in a doctrine of freedom. The democratic philosophy takes the old question, "Why should I obey the State?," and answers it by reversing the relationship, thus signifying that the question was wrongly put. "It is not I who am obeying the state," is the gist of the democrat's reply. "Rather it is the state which is obeying me. I give the state its powers."

The Virtue of Consent

Let us look more closely at this notion of consent. If we are saying that the people's consent makes a government moral, we must further ask who is consenting and to what. As to the former point, in the normal course of events some consent and others disagree. If popular consent is the underwriter of a government's morality, then the latter's acts, by definition, are immoral for those who dissent. Thus, the doctrine of consent can be saved only if there is unanimity. But since it is unrealistic to expect this in practice, consent has to be rescued by other devices, some of which are plain subterfuges. Hegel, for instance, distinguished between the real and the apparent wills. Your consent is for the former, which embodies your true interest. Ignorance, however, may blind you, so that you fail to recognize it. Hence you should obey those who know better than you. That doctrine does not justify a democratic authority, but calls for surrender to authoritarianism. All manner of hocus-pocus can be defended if once you convince people that they do not really want what they believe and say they want.

Another solution to the problem was the one which Locke advanced. He assumes a unanimous agreement, initially, to form a civil society. Subsequently, as the young grow up and come of age, their continued residence in the community and acceptance of its obligations can be taken as proof that they tacitly support its institutions. Anyway, those who disagree are free to leave, so that, if people remain in the group, their consent is implied. This way of pretending that the unanimity is kept intact had more meaning in Locke's day than it does in ours. At that time there were areas of the world which were sparsely settled. Locke, of course, was thinking of the emigration of English colonists to America, and his principles were not entirely devoid of a factual foundation. Nowadays, however, the right to depart is not matched by the opportunity to enter. It is a fairy-tale to suggest that a citizen, who fundamentally dissents from his regime, can readily find another country which will admit him and to which he can voluntarily adhere.

As a third possibility, it can be argued that the political process involves a series of decisions at different levels of importance. At each level, alternatives are offered; but when a choice is made, it narrows the field of selection that ensues. Thus, a constitution is adopted after discussions which survey the widest possible range. When it has gone into effect, elections are held and laws enacted under the procedures it prescribes. Once those choices are made, the men in public office decide their policies within such areas of discretion as the laws permit. Because these levels vary in importance, the degree of consent may reasonably vary. It is sufficient if unanimity prevails at the original, or broadest, stage. Everybody must accept the constitution and loyally observe its basic principles. Of course—and it would be admirable if that did happen. But a community is never composed of people so likeminded that they agree unanimously, even on fundamentals. The Constitution of the United States was ratified by votes which were far from being unanimous. Even now, when its provisions have been operating for nearly two centuries, there is still bitter disagreement about its meaning in the sphere of race relations. If its present text, with all amendments included, were today submitted to the American people for ratification, I am confident that the result would be affirmative, but it certainly would not be unanimous. The dissenter is the constant negation of the doctrine of consent.

What are we left with then? Presumably we are thrust back from utopian idealism to practical necessity. Principles must take cognizance of facts, and the facts show that, when men are consulted about their preferences, they normally subdivide into many groups.[23] If, however, the choices are reduced to two alternatives, there will be a majority facing a minority. Government, therefore, must be conducted by one or other of these. Since democracy cannot concede the right of the few to prevail over the many, the only possibility that remains is majority rule. This is the conclusion that is reached, with his customary logical precision, by Abraham Lincoln: "Unanimity is impossible; the rule of a minority, as a permanent arrangement, is wholly inadmissible; so that, rejecting the majority principle, anarchy or despotism in some form is all that is left."[24]

23. A skillful analysis of the problems in applying the majority principle to actual situations is presented by Robert A. Dahl, A Preface to Democratic Theory (University of Chicago Press: Chicago, 1956), Chap. 2.
24. From the First Inaugural Address, March 4, 1861.

The philosophers of democracy travel by many routes. But no matter which they take, they generally arrive at the same conclusion. Democratic government consists, in practice, of rule by the majority.

Justifying Majority Rule

Can majority rule, however, be morally justified? When the people have voted, are the majority entitled, as of right, to demand of the minority that they submit? The criterion which distinguishes the majority from the minority is simply one of quantity. The majority has more members. Nothing could be plainer. But ethics requires some qualitative criterion. What is it that gives the larger number a moral right to prevail over the smaller? Does "more" signify "better"? Does "many" mean "right"? The difficulty which these questions pose is clearly visible in the works of the greatest masters of democratic thought. They faced this problem, as they had to. But they were unable to resolve it consistently with their own basic principles. There are many differences between the philosophies of Locke and Rousseau. They concur, however, in the initial premise that the government of an organized society must originate in the voluntary adherence of freely consenting individuals. That agreement, moreover, has to be unanimous. Yet in subsequent matters the majority makes the decision. How then do Locke and Rousseau achieve the transition from unanimity to majority? And is there an ethical justification for the latter?

Locke discusses this in Chapter VIII of the *Second Treatise of Civil Government*. He starts with the affirmation that a community is created by the voluntary agreement of its members who consent to belong. He then asserts: "When any number of men have so consented to make one community or government, they are thereby presently incorporated, and make one body politic, wherein the majority have a right to act and conclude the rest."[25] How does the majority acquire this right, and why? Locke's answer is set out in the passage immediately following, which is quoted here in full:[26] "For, when any number of men have, by the consent of every individual, made a community, they have thereby made that community one body, with a power to act as one body, which is only by the will and determination of the majority. For that which acts any community, being only the consent of the individuals of it, and it being one body, must move one way, *it is necessary the body should move that way whither the greater force carries it, which is the consent of the majority,*

25. *Loc. cit.*, sec. 95.
26. *Loc. cit.*, sec. 96. My italics.

or else it is impossible it should act or continue one body, one community, which the consent of every individual that united into it agreed that it should; and so every one is bound by that consent to be concluded by the majority. And therefore we see that in assemblies empowered to act by positive laws where no number is set by that positive law which empowers them, the act of the majority passes for the act of the whole, and of course determines as having, by the law of Nature and reason, the power of the whole." The core of the argument consists in the two clauses which are printed above in italics. The steps in the reasoning are unambiguous: unanimous consent . . . creates unified community . . . which has one body . . . must move one way . . . carried by the greater force . . . consent of the majority. So where does this bring us? The key terms are "one," "necessary," and "force," and especially the last of these. Within one body the greater force of necessity controls. The majority constitutes that force. Therefore, its will, i.e., its consent, determines the whole. Nothing could be clearer. But, what has happened to morality? Locke begins with the ethics of consent and concludes with the necessity of force. The superior strength which resides in the majority makes its will prevail. Is that anything else than a reassertion of the politics of force, awkwardly disguised in an ethical cloak?

Compare Rousseau's treatment of the same topic. He accepts the rule of the majority, emphasizing that, the bigger it is, the closer its approximation to the general will.[27] The obligation of the minority to submit to the majority is derived, not from nature, but convention, i.e., by agreement. Hence the original unanimous contract under which men form their association must include a provision for the majority to rule thereafter.[28] "There is only one law which, by its nature, requires unanimous consent: namely, the social contract. For civil association is the most voluntary act in the world. . . . Apart from this primary covenant, the voice of the larger number is always binding on everybody else. This follows from the contract itself."[29] In other words, Rousseau realized that the only way to endow majority rule with an ethical character was to include it among the hypothetical origins of civic association. Such logic holds together, as logic. But what sense does it make to put a moral coloration on the facts by inventing fictions? It is a fact of democratic political life

27. *Social Contract.* Bk. IV, Chap. 2, on "Voting."
28. "In fact, if there were no prior agreement, where, unless the election was unanimous, would be the obligation for the few to submit to the will of the many? . . . The law of majority voting is itself founded on convention and presupposes unanimity at least once." *Ibid.*, Bk. I, Chap. 5.
29. *Ibid.*, Bk. IV, Chap. 2.

that, under ordinary conditions, majorities govern. Why explain this in terms of something wholly imaginary? We cannot justify the majority's powers by basing them on an agreement that never was.

Both Locke and Rousseau are emphatic in wanting their politics to be founded on ethics. Consequently the links in the chain which would connect unanimous consent with majority rule are crucial to their thinking. If the chain breaks, it is not for lack of trying, but for another reason. The latter is merely that what they were attempting is an impossibility. They created a problem for themselves, then looked for a way out by seeking to solve something which, in the nature of the case, was insoluble. It is like squaring the circle. If the morality of a democratic regime has to be derived from the consent of the governed, this cannot be reconciled with the rule of the majority. The dissenting minority exists. It cannot be explained away. If consent justifies a government's power, the inference follows that for those who withhold consent such powers are unjustified. That is, they are immoral. A majority is a quantity. Ethics consists of a quality. A quantity cannot yield a quality.

The Rightness of the Larger Number

A case, however, can be made for majority rule. But it is not an ethical argument and should never be so presented. There is no right inherent in a majority, as such. A majority is superior in one respect only: its power. This should be faced and stated, frankly.[30] Any other defense of the majority is specious. If the majority rules in a democracy, this is because ordinarily it has the power to make its will prevail. If the minority is told to submit, this is because ordinarily resistance is pointless. All the familiar clichés which are reiterated on behalf of majority rule are variations on the same theme. "We count heads," we are told, "in order to avoid breaking them." But the implication is obvious that the side with the bigger headcount would inflict the greater damage if the two parties fought it out. "We use ballots instead of bullets." True, and this still assumes the inarticulate premise that the same hands which marked more papers could,

30. It is quite frankly implied in the passage where Dickens describes the famous election at Eatanswill. " 'Slumkey for ever!' roared the honest and independent. 'Slumkey for ever!' echoed Mr. Pickwick. . . . 'Who is Slumkey?' whispered Mr. Tupman. 'I don't know,' replied Mr. Pickwick in the same tone. 'Hush. Don't ask any questions. It's always best on these occasions to do what the mob do.' 'But suppose there are two mobs?' suggested Mr. Snodgrass. 'Shout with the largest,' replied Mr. Pickwick." *Pickwick Papers*, Chapter XIII.

if they found it necessary, do more shooting.[31] When you reduce them to the essentials, therefore, majority rule is a dictate of power; minority submission, a tactic of prudence. But even that logic, shifting democracy from a foundation of morality to one of power, cannot give solid guarantees that democracy will always prevail. Suppose that the minority is better organized and better supplied than the majority. An exchange of bullets would then work out to the advantage of the few. Actually in modern times, weapons being what they are, a disciplined band ruthlessly led can subdue a multitude with tanks and machine guns—and, for good measure, some airplanes. If majority rule is the cornerstone of democracy, and mere power is the virtue of the majority, the same argument will justify both Stalin and Hitler.

What is called the wisdom of experience is often elementary. But at times it is elemental. There is no need for elaborate argument, or repetition of cases, to prove the point that majorities do err. What the majority decides is not, *ipso facto*, right. Its opinion is not always the wiser. Its standards of justice are not necessarily higher. Hence it is impossible to accept the view of democracy which relegates its meaning to procedures and insists that, so long as the procedural requirements are satisfied, democracy is neutral as regards the result. Proper procedures are important for securing justice. But justice is more than due process. It is also substance. An incident occurred a few years ago in a suburb of San Francisco which provides a good illustration. A tract of land was subdivided and new houses were constructed and sold. The original purchasers, without exception, were white. Subsequently one family decided to move and placed its house on the market. A Chinese made an offer to purchase, which the owner accepted. When the news became known, but before the transaction was completed, the realtors, who had developed the tract and had retained an interest, canvassed the residents, stirring up opposition to the sale. They employed the usual argument that property values would decline if a family of a minority race moved into the area. In this particular case there was no other possible ground than race for objecting to the would-be owner. He was a young man who had emigrated from Nationalist China. He had taken his university education in the United States, was professionally qualified, and was steadily employed at an adequate salary. He was married and had two young children. All in all, as human beings, this family met every reasonable standard for desirable neighbors. How-

31. The transition from one technique to the other is illustrated in the anecdotes of some Latin American revolutions. An insurgent general tells the government how many soldiers he has. The government counts the number that stayed "loyal." Then the side with fewer men surrenders.

ever, when the realtors instigated opposition, a meeting of the residents was called to discuss the matter. The prospective purchaser attended so that people could see and hear him. He announced that he believed in democracy, that he and his family did not intend to settle among neighbors who did not want them, and that he would accept the verdict of the majority. When the vote was held, the majority was negative.[32]

A case such as this can be multiplied a hundred times. What are its implications for democracy? Here is a situation where the democratic procedures were faithfully observed. Proponents freely confronted opponents. Arguments were debated pro and con. Individuals discussed the matter, took sides, formed groups, and voted. The count was taken. The majority won. Procedurally, everything was perfect. But what should we say of the result? Did democracy triumph? Yes, it did—if democracy consists only in discussion, free association of individuals, and voting. No, it did not—if democracy also consists of certain values to which a community must subscribe. The methods were fair, but the outcome was unfair. This is a perennial dilemma of the democratic system. We criticize authoritarian regimes which plead that the end justifies their means. They are entitled, they assert, to take some rough-and-ready short cuts because of the "good" they intend to accomplish. But it can happen under the procedures we call democratic that our means stultify the end. If so, we too may be tempted to have recourse to authoritarianism—of the benevolent type, no doubt. We will then go ramming the "good" down people's throats and force them to swallow it, which was exactly what Mill feared.

In the case of the Chinese family, no one can cavil at the procedures employed. By these procedures, two viewpoints fought it out, and two sets of values were opposed. In the end, more persons preferred the values which, in my judgment, are inferior. But I would go further than that and say that the values which prevailed were not only inferior, but also undemocratic—in short, that democratic means were used to arrive at an undemocratic end. The majority who opposed the sale of a house in an all-white district to a Chinese took the view that they had the right to exclude a family from the neighborhood because of its race.[33] They succeeded in imposing their doctrine on the dissenting minority and on the outsider who wished to join the group. They acted as if the admission of

32. This incident was fully reported in the papers, all of which supported the Chinese, and attracted some national attention. Many homes in other parts of San Francisco were immediately offered to this family.

33. I do not ignore the economic argument—that property values might decline if the area became racially mixed. This might indeed happen. But there would be no such economic change if there were no racial prejudice. It is the latter which is fundamental.

this newcomer, owing to his racial difference, would lead to social disharmony. They therefore forced him into a position of inferiority by denying him equal access to a market economy which prides itself on being free. This is the result which I call undemocratic. In the conflict between property interests and human rights, between majority power and the worth of the individual, the wrong side won.

The Rights of Minorities

Let us pursue this point further, but approach it from another angle. Suppose one did accept the notion that democracy means majority rule pure and simple, that it must be so because unanimity is unattainable and oligarchy unacceptable. Does it not then follow that whatever the majority decrees must always be obeyed? If you assert that the majority has the right to rule, do you not conclude that what the majority says is right? But in that case we run into direct conflict with another argument which also is good democratic doctrine and has the backing of a long tradition. Democracy, we tell ourselves repeatedly, is a superior system not only because the majority rules, but also because minorities are protected. We recognize that a minority has rights, and these we feel it our duty to respect. In fact, we think these rights so important that we shelter them with all manner of legal, institutional, and procedural safeguards. As a sign of wisdom, believing as we do in moderation and tolerance, we ask the majority not to press its power to the limit. When it shows this forbearance, we applaud the virtues of compromise.

Now what does all this signify? Presumably, two things: an underlying doubt that the majority can always be trusted, and an emphatic belief that minorities have rights which governments must protect as surely as those of the majority. As to that doubt, we may not like the facts, but there is no disputing them. Majorities, too, are composed of fallible mortals. They can and do make mistakes. The revolutions which supplanted other systems and introduced democracy did not eliminate from politics the phenomenon of power. Democracy needs power as do all governments. What the democratic revolution did was to shift its location, taking it out of the hands of a ruling class and placing it in the mass of the people. Power was not abolished; it was simply transferred. And after the transfer, it was exercised in a manner which is not at all simple, but involves numerous complications. One of the latter consists in providing safeguards against its wrongful use, for even in democratic hands power can still be abused.

Nor is it only the minority which must be protected. Democratic governments have insisted historically that they respect the rights of that smallest possible minority, the single individual. They acknowledge a duty to defend each and every person in their midst, no matter how weak or humble or unpopular. Everybody knows the story of Frederick the Great who wanted to tear down a mill which looked unsightly in the view from his palace. Repeatedly, he offered to buy it; but the farmer who owned it was courageous and would not yield his property, even to the King. Frederick, an efficient autocrat, happened to believe in the *Rechtstaat*. So he reluctantly conceded the rights of his stubborn subject. In that incident, our admiration goes out to both men—to the king who had the power, but respected the right; and the farmer who had the right and stood up to the power. Shall a democracy be less worthy than the monarch? There have been notable cases in the history of democratic politics when an individual has been unjustly victimized by some act of authority and has sought redress of wrongs. Once officialdom has decided, it is not easy to obtain a reversal. Human beings do not ordinarily like to admit they were wrong or negligent or unfair. All the vast apparatus of the state, all the power of established institutional interests, will be brought to bear in favor of the principle of *stare decisis*. Those who seek to reopen a case or appeal to other courts and to higher authority will be told that they risk injuring the prestige and sanctity of a system in order to assert the rights of just one person. When certain officers of the French Ministry of War decided that it was Dreyfus who had passed on military secrets to the Germans, to prove his innocence was to impugn the honor of the Army and thus to weaken the Republic. Let a man rot in disgrace on Devil's Island rather than lessen public confidence in the organization which guarantees the security of the state. "For Order, against Justice and Truth," exclaimed one of the anti-Dreyfusards.[34] Similarly in the United Kingdom when a young naval cadet was wrongly accused and then expelled for forging a signature on a money order, it took years of protracted effort to vindicate him. The bureaucracy of the Admiralty did not readily hearken to public criticism of its procedures or welcome a judicial inquiry by an independent tribunal. The Navy's reputation must be protected, come hell or high water. Better to keep the organization immune from scrutiny than rehabilitate the reputation of a boy unjustly judged.

The case of Archer-Shee, though it became notable in British politics, did not shake society to its foundations as *l'affaire Dreyfus* did in France.

34. *Pour l'ordre, contra la justice et la vérité*. The author of the statement was the writer, Paul Léautaud. See François, Goguel, *La Politique des Partis sous la Troisième République*, p. 102.

But while more trivial circumstances were involved in the one case than the other,[35] the same issue was at stake and it was of supreme importance. When the public were told that they had a choice between upholding the honor of an institution as vital as the Army was to France or the Navy to Britain or upholding the honor of a single human being, the alternatives were wrongly stated. Such a choice may exist in the calculation of *Realpolitik*. In morality, no such choice exists, for if the individual were sacrificed to the system, the latter would lose its *raison d'être*. If politics is to be founded on ethics, right must triumph. The entire system is, in principle, designed to preserve the individual and protect him. A Jewish officer on the French General Staff or a schoolboy from a middle-class family in a naval academy possessed inherent worth and dignity as an individual human being. The state existed for him, not he for the state. Rather rectify an injustice and reform the guilty institutions than let the innocent suffer. Moreover, in both cases it was due to the politics of democracy and its constitutional arrangements that justice was finally done. In both countries, there was a press that was free to publish and criticize; there was a legislature where members could ask questions and demand answers of ministers; there were civilian heads of departments accountable to the public; there were independent courts to which appeals could be taken. Such institutions and procedures made it possible to right a wrong. But it was the ethical conception of the status of the individual and a political philosophy making his protection a supreme value for the society which finally subordinated power to justice. If democracy does not live up to and practice its supporting morality, all the machinery is worthless. Governments are means to ethical ends, and democratic institutions must be judged by how they promote democratic values.

We are brought then to an impasse of principles whose contradictions seem hard to resolve. A democracy acquiesces in the rule of the majority for reasons of prudence. Those with the greater power shall decide. Nevertheless, even the majority cannot be completely trusted. It may make honest mistakes or be intolerant or tyrannical. Whenever that happens, the minority is entitled to protect itself. Down to the very last individual, its members have certain rights on which nobody can trample; and institutions have to be organized for their safeguard. Hence we build into the structure of government a system of checks and balances to ensure the minority a protection beyond the strength of its numbers. But once that is achieved, another possibility arises. The minority may now divert the safeguards devised for its protection to purposes of obstruction. Thereby

35. The fraudulent cashing of a postal order for a few shillings is a less serious offense than giving secret technical information to a potential enemy of one's country.

it can thwart the will of the majority. All the stratagems of legislative maneuver, committee procrastination, "the law's delays," can be used by a little band of willful men to produce paralysis. Any country you pick can supply examples, although in some the harvest of frustration is more bountiful than in others.

Ideals in Conflict

What does democratic theory have to say about this? Majorities have the power of performance; minorities, the opportunity for protest. But that is not enough. If there are no limits to the power of the majority, minorities could disappear. Somewhere a limit must be set on what a majority can do. Otherwise, it can ride roughshod over all opposition. When the minority is adequately protected, however, it may be able to prevent the majority from accomplishing anything positive. The calculation of needs and risks seems to go around in circles, like a dog chasing its tail. And of course, the reason for this is perfectly obvious. We are trying to correlate two pairs of factors which have no necessary, or even contingent, relation. In talking about a majority and a minority, the terms are purely numerical. When we speak of right and wrong, just and unjust, the concept is ethical. Democratic theory is perennially hung on the two horns of this dilemma. It switches in discussion from numbers to rightness and goes back and forth. Yet, as is evident, neither a majority nor a minority, *per se*, is either right or wrong. Both are sometimes correct, sometimes in error. There are frequent occasions when the majority's view is correct or better, and it should then prevail. At other times, the minority's position is superior and should be upheld. Accepting the arbitrament of numbers gives us a convenient device for running a government under ordinary conditions, especially those which do not touch a person's basic interests. But how is the majority to know when it ought to disregard the expressed views of the minority and proceed in defiance of their wishes? How is the minority to decide when to be content with registering its protest and when it is justified in resisting to the utmost? Democracy needs some formulation of principle to help decide these questions. By what criterion do we limit a majority's power to work its will and a minority's right to oppose? In this democratic dialectic, where majorities form a thesis and minorities the antithesis, is there some higher plane of synthesis where both combine?

The Search for a Synthesis

The classic philosophies of democracy, although they do not put the question in this way, contain the essentials of an answer. Or rather, they provide two answers which envisage a solution along different lines. Broadly speaking, we can refer to these as the Lockean and Rousseauian. The contrast between them derives from their initial assumption, which is individualist in the former and collectivist in the latter. Both arguments, in various guises, are implicit in the democratic theories which pass current today.

(1) *The Natural Rights Theory*

The Lockean philosophy,[36] which fails to deduce majority rule from the ethics of unanimous consent, does succeed in sidestepping the awkward dilemma of the relation between the majority and the minority and their correlation with the just or unjust. This it accomplishes by the concept of natural rights. Positing that these antedate the founding of the state and are grounded in a higher morality than that of legal convention, it offers a standard by which to judge all public conduct, that of representatives and officials, of majorities or minorities. Since human beings retain their natural rights in civil society, they are morally justified both in enforcing them as a majority and defending them as a minority. Indeed, to act thus is more than their right. It is their duty. The wrongdoers are those who would infringe a natural right. Whether they be few or many is irrelevant.

Besides their historical importance because of the part they played in the English, American, and French Revolutions, these doctrines retain a permanent significance. To gauge their usefulness, one must of course disentangle and remove the surrounding layers of seventeenth-century metaphysics. Formulating these notions in the categories of natural rights is pointless for our purposes. The concept of nature, introduced in this connection, raises more troubles than it is worth. It implies a whole host of distinctions between natural and social which confuse the issue more than they clarify. To appeal against convention to nature does not help to decide concrete cases, for the oracle has many priests and speaks in many voices. The natural law philosophy, presupposed in a theory of natural rights, always reverts to a divine source. Probe the laws of nature, and you

36. In this passage, I am including under this term such offshoots as the doctrines of the two Thomases, Paine and Jefferson.

are brought eventually to nature's God.[37] Then the theologians take over, and they ask that their tenets be accepted on faith since they have no evidence susceptible of rational proof.

"To each, his own taste" goes the proverb. Similarly, one may say, to every age its own philosophical fashion. Although one may be unconvinced by the notion of a law and of rights inhering in nature, these assumptions were the fruit of a serious and significant effort to attack a genuine problem. How do you discover a standard of rightness by which to test the actual performance of governments? Can there be such a standard with universal validity, in the sense that it applies to all humanity and lies outside and above the relativism of a particular system established in its special time and place? The natural rights doctrine was well conceived to fill this need since it measured every government by a common moral purpose. Constitutions, institutions, machinery and procedures, although important, were secondary. They were good if they left men secure in the possession and exercise of their natural rights; bad, if they did not. The value of political freedom, of representative assemblies and so on, consisted in a common sense realism. Rights are more likely to remain inviolate if men have the chance to stand up for themselves and if government is organized with this end in view. It is less probable that a succession of benevolent autocrats can be counted on to emerge whose goodness will respect the rights of their fellow men.[38]

The solution of this problem by the invention of natural rights not only introduced the metaphysical complication of defining nature, but was also deficient in two other respects. The doctrine was strong in its emphasis on rights, weak in its attention to duties. What the individual owed to others, what the community collectively owed to each of its members, was insufficiently stressed. Besides that, the rights which were most prominently stated were the political and juridical. These included the opportunity to influence policy by direct participation or by representatives, and the protection of personal liberty against arbitrary power. While these rights continue to be primary, the advent of the industrial society has clarified their interdependence with economic factors. Consequently, all

37. The reasoning is as follows: Rights are founded on a law. Natural rights, therefore, presuppose a natural law. But the law assumes a law-giver. Nature being an abstraction, its creator is personified as God.

38. Gibbon published the first volume of his *Decline and Fall of the Roman Empire* in the same year as the *Declaration of Independence*, Bentham's *Fragment on Government*, and Adam Smith's *Wealth of Nations*. He expressed the opinion that humanity collectively were generally happier in the period when Marcus Aurelius and Antoninus Pius were Emperors than at any time before or since. But as his history and those of Tacitus demonstrate, such rulers were rare exceptions.

modern attempts at drafting lists of rights have accorded a new emphasis to the economic conditions without which men are neither free nor equal nor able to function as citizens.

Let us keep in mind the essential aim of the natural rights theory. It was to prescribe, in matters fundamental to human dignity, what treatment all persons were entitled to receive and all governments obligated to respect. A right was an opportunity which was the product of a status. The latter spelled equality; the former, liberty. Now translate these conceptions from the metaphysics and language of Locke and Jefferson to the underlying philosophy of democratic governments in the twentieth century. What we are attempting is a broader, expanded, version of the same, couched in humanitarian terms. The aim of the mature democracies is to create and guarantee for everybody the minimal conditions necessary for civilized existence. This is considered a duty of society for which it is responsible through the instrumentality of the state. The conditions are far-reaching in scope. They embrace the basic political freedoms, racial equality, religious tolerance and intellectual liberty, cultural enrichment, equal opportunities in employment and careers, and security against physical and social hazards. By a variety of methods, and in various degrees, the modern democratic states have increased their responsibilities in all these spheres. Serving as the public agent of the whole people, the government established the minima below which no person within its jurisdiction may sink and above which everyone may rise by work, luck, and skill.

This seems to be a fair way of summarizing the essential purposes of democratic government as their ideals are revealed in their functions. The latter are of many species. There are police functions which maintain a system of order and enforce the indispensable rules of an organized community. There is the military need to guard against external threats to the internal peace. There is the creative development of resources, human and material—mass education, production of atomic energy, for instance—which are appropriately undertaken by the state because of their comprehensiveness or expense and because they concern everyone. There are the common services on which everybody relies—water supply, public health, heating, transportation, etc.—and which the state must either operate or regulate. There is the general management of the economy to keep production and employment high. There are the young and the aged to help, the weak and the handicapped to protect. Does not all this amount to a picture of the state performing within society many of the central activities which contribute directly to human civilization?

Democratic governments in the twentieth century do not tell their citizens: "We will exercise only those limited powers you entrusted to us with the object of preserving intact the larger rights which you properly retained." Instead, they say in effect: "You have rights and duties, which are developed within society and sanctioned by it. Our responsibility, subject to your control, is to exercise on behalf of each the collective powers of the whole and expand the realization of those values which make all of us civilized." The two formulations have this in common: they recognize that the political art is dedicated to the ethical purpose of promoting human well-being and stipulate that governments are to be judged by how they move to this goal or back away from it. But the differences are no less profound. To begin with, the two formulas hold opposite views of the composition of society and the place of individuals therein. The eighteenth century individualized society, whereas the twentieth has socialized the individual. Furthermore, the modern notion disagrees with the earlier in the range of responsibilities it entrusts to the state. This has generally[39] come to be accepted as the indispensable institution performing a creative role in the dynamics of social change. In addition, the contemporary formulation has the distinction, and the complexity, of being all-inclusive. Its rights and obligations are applied equally to everyone. What was only a theoretical ideal for Locke and Jefferson has become the practical politics of our own age.

Finally there is the supreme merit of the contemporary doctrine that it admits indefinite expansion. No bounds or limits are set to the concept of civilization. The original values which it incorporates can be increased by the addition of new ones. The government of a particular country at a particular time will set its minimum at a level which is realistic in the light of its resources and capacity. But once that level is reached, the community can set its sights higher, and then higher, and still higher. To take but one example, from the sphere of education: only a minority of the population was literate one hundred and fifty years ago. Eventually, public primary schools were instituted for everyone. Then the opportunities for public secondary education were expanded and the school-leaving age was gradually raised. The coping stone of the structure was to throw open the doors of higher learning to all who were intellectually qualified. Here the state had to supplement and complete a university system designed under private auspices to cater to a handful. Undeniably the expansion in quantity resulted at first in some lowering of quality. When something is made available to everybody on the same terms, the veneer will be spread thin. The initial resources of revenue, trained teachers, buildings, books, are

39. Not universally, however. We still have in our midst some survivors of the mentality of earlier centuries—just as we have those who represent the potential outlook of the twenty-first.

limited. But later the supply increases and, if there is the public will to
have it, the quality rises. If this process and similar developments in other
spheres of policy are not gains in civilization, what are they then?

(2) *The Quest for the General Will*

To obtain these results through a democracy, however, as contrasted with
an enlightened autocrat, the proviso just mentioned must be fulfilled. The
public has to want them. If a democratic government is one that is subordinated to popular control, and if its *raison d'être* is to do what people
want, no government is justified in acting as it deems right unless its citizens have indicated that this is what they wish. You cannot do good to
people against their will; so the argument runs. If they do not will it, presumably they do not think it good—in which case, any government which
proceeds contrary to their will is imposing its own conception of the good
on others who disagree.

This brings us back to Rousseau's solution for the problem propounded
earlier: how do you justify the majority's power, yet ensure the minority's
protection? When is the former justified in having its way? When is the
latter right to resist? Rousseau has an answer for these questions in his notion of the general will. Some aspects of this subtle concept were analyzed
earlier,[40] but it has additional implications which are relevant here. The
doctrine assumes that all who belong to an association share a common
interest, and this is the same for all the members. Since people want what
is good for them and have a common interest in the common good, they
can be relied on to will this when they discern what it is. The will depends
on the knowledge. Government consists, therefore, in a process of creative
discovery. It is a search, through knowledge, for the general interest, which
is applied, through power, when the people see it and will it.

There is a profundity in this conception which excites one's admiration.
Rousseau possibly penetrated deeper to the fundamentals of political
association than any other thinker has done. But the difficulties in his
formulation are evident. What he posits is an ideal. How does one apply
this in a particular situation? Is there some objective reality, the public
interest, which is subjectively knowable and can therefore be willed? Rousseau stated that the citizen's duty is to will the general interest. Yet he
cannot perform his duty unless he has the capacity to recognize that interest for what it is. Even if the citizen is honest, he will err in judgment from
time to time. While desiring whatever promotes the general good, he will

40. In Chapter 3, pp. 54-56.

sometimes be mistaken in judging it. How can democracy both satisfy the desire and be safeguarded against the consequences of error?

The short answer to this is that it cannot be done. We have no fool-proof procedures; no criteria can yield certitude; no one person, nor a few, nor even a whole populace, can attain omniscience. The philosophies which found their politics on knowing the right thing to do and giving to those in authority the power to do it have to conclude with a system which is undemocratic. For such knowledge assumes an absolute good, and belief in an absolute good will justify absolute power. Rousseau's paradox[41] may indeed be turned against his own argument. If there were a people of gods, it would be governed on authoritarian principles. So infallible a regime is unfit for mere mortals. Not for nothing do Plato and Hegel arrive at a similar conclusion. The former sets his ideal republic in heaven.[42] The latter views the ideal state as "the march of God in the world."[43]

The Wisdom of the Fallible

But there is another objection to the Platonists and Hegelians, which is based on the historical evidence. One of the oldest and most persistent criticisms of democracy accuses it of subordinating knowledge to igno-rance. Wisdom is supposed to be an attribute of the few, and in a democ-racy it is the many who control. The effective response to this charge is to look at the record of non-democratic regimes in which power has clearly belonged to an elite. Assuredly they too have had their full share of errors. Their governments have frequently miscalculated the forces with which they had to deal. They have produced effects the opposite of what they sought. It is a gratuitous prejudice to overlook the stupidities of the few and exaggerate those of the mass. If one predicates the right to govern on knowledge *per se*, no species of oligarchy yet devised can show any better claim to rule than that of democracy. Reflect on the political history of the first six decades of this century and note, along with the triumphs, the catalogue of blunders and disasters. No system has been exempt from the latter. But this can be said for democracy that its record of mistakes has

41. Quoted in Chapter 2, p. 44.
42. The *Republic*, Bk. IX, sec. 592b.
43. "The state is the march of God in the world; its ground or cause is the power of reason realizing itself as will. When thinking of the idea of the state, we must not have in our mind any particular state, or particular institution, but must rather con-template the idea, this actual God, by itself." *Philosophy of Right*, trans. S. W. Dyde, (Bell: London, 1896), p. 247.

been less ruinous to itself, and far less destructive to others, than those of any alternative system.

We cannot know an absolute. Any form of government we support, therefore, must admit to fallibility. In that case, the best form possible is one which organizes and uses such imperfect knowledge as we have, admits freely to errors when proven, and takes precautions to avoid their repetition. The authoritarian regimes do not in fact avoid error. They merely try to escape the reputation for it by smothering the truth. Democracy may at times appear to make more mistakes than other systems, or contain more corruption, and so on, simply because its principles require that its faults be honestly exposed. A government may deceive the people, and will salvage its own position by so doing. But a people cannot deceive itself, for that would gain it nothing. If we are truthful with ourselves and are not self-deluded by propaganda or prejudice, we recognize that the work of government is ceaseless experimentation. The advantage of a democracy is that it permits a greater freedom to experiment and assess the results. In real political life, we do not proceed by planned programing from a complete body of calculated data to a predetermined goal. There is much more in government of gambling, trusting to luck, playing hunches, and the like, than rationalists care to admit. The one resemblance between the democratic process and the scientific method is their common reliance on trial and error. The alternative is the appeal to Superman, in one of his several guises—strong man, dictator, hero, god-king—who demands obedience and suppresses the dissident on the ground that he knows best. Trial and error is always preferable to trials and terror.

But we must be wary in political argument that in reacting against one extreme we embrace another. We deny that it is possible to construct a political system around the possession of knowledge that affords us certainty. Nevertheless, all the knowledge we are capable of acquiring should be utilized to the fullest possible extent in the service of government. There is no aspect of policy which does not depend on technical information, the culling of experience, the accumulation of comparative data, the calculation of alternatives. Objective studies conducted by experts will not always lead to the "right" solution, since there may be no particular course of action among the many possibilities which is demonstrably the correct one. Such studies, however, do contribute to the avoidance of policies which are definitely known to work badly and they contribute to a higher probability that whatever is decided may work out well. In this sense the persons who compose a government—both elected representatives and civil servants—become professionals in a field of competence where the rest of us are amateurs. By thorough study of the available facts and judicious weighing of pros and cons, a government that does its homework is normally better prepared to make a sensible decision than any random sample of average citizens. What ought its leaders to do then if they honestly believe that a certain policy is the right one to adopt, but the prevailing public opinion runs contrary to theirs?

The ordinary answer to that question is that the government must carry out the wishes of the people. Should it fail or refuse, it is not behaving democratically. But there are more complexities to the problem than are covered by so simple a response. In reality, we do not confront a clear-cut division between government on one side and people on the other. Any government has the support of some of the people. Normally in a democracy when a new government takes office, it is backed by a majority; normally, when it leaves office, the majority oppose it. In between, it will be supported sometimes by a majority and sometimes by a minority. Also there will be occasions when no clear majority exists. The people will then be subdivided into a cluster of minorities—one of which may contain a large number of persons who have no view to express. If public opinion becomes sufficiently clear and coherent so as to give a lead, it is the duty of a democratic government to follow. Often, however, it is the government which has to lead—that is, in any case, its responsibility!—and public opinion crystallizes after, and because of, the *fait accompli*. I would therefore conclude that a government should carry out the policies for which a clear majority of the public have expressed a mandate. In the absence of this, a government should always do what its members believe, after careful study, will best promote the public interest. Then they will have to trust that the outcome will justify their judgment and increase the public confidence in their stewardship.

At this point, let us pick up the several threads of the discussion in the preceding chapter and this one, and see whether they unite in any meaningful pattern. Is democratic philosophy a medley of contradictions or a self-consistent whole? Even if the latter were logically possible, would this be politically desirable?

Why Democratic Ideals Are Self-Contradictory

There can be no question that, when the several ideals to which democracy subscribes are considered separately in abstract form and when each is extended to its logical limit, they are mutually irreconcilable. The two meanings of liberty, negative and positive, are in conflict, as are the two senses of equality, proportional and identical; and equality and liberty on either definition will collide. The majority must rule, the minority may resist; but if either the resistance or the rule is overdone, the other vanishes. The individual is sacrosanct, but the government of a community should prosecute the public interest. We seek consensus, yet tolerate dissent. The list of antitheses is long. What does it signify?

An initial suggestion is not to be surprised or concerned at what may sound like double-talk. If our principles are opposed, it does not necessarily follow that the values of democracy end in self-negation. The contradictions cannot be explained away, save by sophistry and word-juggling. Therefore, they may have a reason. The conduct of politics, and philosophizing about it, are not the same activity. They are two different activities which have a relationship. The imperatives of logic are not the conditions of life. There is a salutary reminder in Burke's reflective comment: "But I cannot stand forward, and give praise or blame to anything which relates to human actions, and human concerns, on a simple view of the object, as it stands stripped of every relation, in all the nakedness and solitude of metaphysical abstraction. Circumstances . . . give in reality to every political principle its distinguishing colour and discriminating effect. . . . Abstractedly speaking, government, as well as liberty, is good."[44] For any single principle, taken by itself, an argument can be presented which will meet a logical test of self-consistency. But in actual politics, many principles are incorporated because the characteristics of each society, as well as the different characteristics of different societies, present a medley of needs which government has to satisfy. In the life we share with our fellow men, to coexist we compromise.

So it is with the theoretical underpinnings of democracy. The ideals which have been discussed are varied, because there are different needs to be served, and contradictory, because those needs conflict. Earlier I mentioned that all political philosophies, of whatever kind, must somehow interpret the same subject matter. They formulate, in ideal terms, a rationale of the place of each individual inside a group and of their relations both with one another and with their government. There are two sides, therefore, to this equation, both of which correspond to an aspect of the reality we are trying to explain and the values we are hoping to achieve. Some philosophies give priority to the individual and his uniqueness; others, to the community and its government. Others again attempt to juxtapose these seemingly contrary factors in balanced equilibrium or fuse them in creative synthesis. The theories of democracy differ, not because

44. *Reflections on the Revolution in France* (Everyman's Library, Dutton & Co.: New York), p. 6. See also pp. 58-9.

the men who propounded them were more democratic or less, but because the circumstances for which they sought solutions were not alike and they were guided to their conception of future goals by their points of departure in the historical present. When a philosopher points to the way ahead, he begins with a stress on correctives for existing deficiencies. Where the government had been authoritarian and coercive, he insisted on bringing its agents under popular control. But once that was done, the people's representatives had to receive enough authority so that they could govern. Whereas kings, dictators, and theocrats pretended their power was absolute, democracy demanded its limitation. Yet when the limits were imposed, they had to be extended again if the state was to come to the help of the majority. Since traditional institutions had left too little scope to individuality, the test of good government was now its willingness to leave people alone. But when the community lost in social justice what it gained in individual freedom, the general welfare and the public interest had to be reasserted.

It is not surprising, therefore, that the democratic philosophies exhibit opposite tendencies and that their several ideals conflict. There have, in fact, been two main streams of democratic thought. One begins with a conception of the unified community and judges the state by its contributions to the common good. It assumes that the greatest happiness is served when the greatest number is satisfied; that the majority will approximates most nearly to the general will and should therefore prevail. The other stream consists of beliefs in the primacy of the individual whose separate strivings accumulate in social progress. The works of government are justified if they enlarge his sphere of independent action and protect minorities from the kind of majority domination in which they would drown. The former philosophy elevates the value of the general welfare or public interest, stresses the importance of equality, and hopes for a society of sufficiently like-minded people so that the majority of the moment may voice the consensus of all. The latter philosophy puts individuals first, maximizes their liberty, and jealously guards their right to differ and to disagree. Aristotle listed democracy among the perversions because he saw it function as a continuation of class rule with the many monopolizing the advantages. Rousseau concluded that only a people of gods could govern itself democratically because, in a system where all must participate in acts of sovereignty, only in heaven would knowledge combine with virtue to direct the exercise of power. Individualists who fear the state are distrustful of even a democratic state since the power of the government to coerce may exceed the power of the citizens to control. Conversely, collectivists who fear that private interests may block the public good are critical of structures and procedures which can be manipulated into paralysis when they should be mobilized for action.

Thus the divergence in the ideals of democracy corresponds to demands which are logically antithetical yet politically authentic. Democracy must consent to the creation of power with the certainty that this will sometimes be abused. Consequently, it must establish safeguards which will detect and curb the infraction without obstructing the legitimate. The decisions of the majority should prevail because no alternative arrangement is superior. But when those decisions work unsatisfactorily, it should be possible to form a new majority in order to reverse them. Since the aim of government is to raise the level of civilization, all humanity is entitled to equal treatment and the same protection in everything which is fundamental. Resistance, therefore, is the indefeasible right of the oppressed, be they many or few. And as the conditions of our social existence alter, and political trends reflect the change of circumstance, we pick and choose within our treasury of ideals whatever is needed to fill deficiencies, correct mistakes, expand human welfare, and open new opportunities. How an ideal is then applied to reality depends on its practicality and contemporary relevance. The principles of democratic philosophy can never be reconciled with the rigor of metaphysical consistency. But in their many-sidedness they express and summarize the logic of historical experience and political need.

18

Conclusions

Democracy has been interpreted in this book as a political system which seeks to steer the movement of society toward its concept of civilization. It is a way of harmonizing our relationships and groupings so that increasingly these may embody the ideals of freedom, equality, and justice. Where successfully practiced, democracy can be called that government of the people which is conducted by representatives of their choosing on their behalf and under their ultimate control. Through these institutions it aspires to become a state of humanity, directed by humanists for the realization of the humaner values. When Wilson spoke of making the world safe for democracy, he had in mind the need to cultivate an environment favorable for the fruits of this civilization to ripen.

The Social Conditions of Democracy

The set of conditions which tends to foster such a result is not easily or often realized. It was not by intent or design, but by accident and chance that one leading *Polis* among many in ancient Greece developed the structure and beliefs of a democratic regime and thereby demonstrated, however tentatively and imperfectly, an operating model for future generations to reconstruct and improve. Again it was by chance that a series of trends, combining by historical juxtaposition in the seventeenth and eighteenth centuries, upset and recast the traditional modes of western Europe, and by mutual interaction provided the context for a new experiment in popular control over the agents and agencies of governmental power. Nobody, looking ahead in the early seventeenth century, could have expected or predicted that extraordinary conjunction of events, now seen in retrospect, which ushered in the democratic revolutions and permitted their later evolution in a limited number of communities. A review of the historical record would warrant some such observation as the following: Because opposition developed to the temporal corruption of the Church; because scientific experiment and rational inquiry led to the questioning of all dogma, whether theological, physical, moral, or political; because new economic opportunities generated new wealth and called for the construction of a new type of state; because the stronger kings took advantage of the discords among the feudal nobility to build a centralized government whose excesses in turn provoked rebellion; because inventions in firearms and navigation opened all oceans and continents to communication or conquest; and because certain personalities emerged in certain places at certain times—because of all these factors, some of which acted directly and some indirectly, the circle of political participants was enlarged. Accordingly, in four or five countries institutions were devised through which more people could bring a more regular influence to bear on shaping the policies of their governments.

But that account is incomplete. If that list of factors be thought a circle or chain of causation, some links are evidently missing. Before inserting them, I propose to refer back to Part II of this book, in which certain traits of the democratic society were analyzed. Let us now summarize the principal findings which emerged.

The historical approach (Chapter 4) pointed out that the successful democracies began with revolution but developed by evolution, that a fully mature democracy is a recent phenomenon, and that it always was and still is something of a rarity.

The sociological inquiry into race, religion, and language (Chapters 5 and 6) showed how a community whose population is divided in any of these respects has obstacles to overcome in practicing tolerance and equality, and that, where such diversities exist, a democratic regime is possible only if dissimilars are either treated as equals or permitted to assimilate voluntarily.

The geopolitical discussion in Chapter 7 traced a firm correlation between the compatibility of democracy with sea power and its incompatibility with large-scale land power.

The economic factors, examined in Chapters 8 and 9, revealed that when due attention is paid to chronology and comparisons, various broad generalizations must be treated with caution. Democracy has been able to flourish in agrarian no less than industrial societies; in areas where usable resources are scarce, and in others blessed with abundance; in conjunction with either a low or high volume of state activity. Two aspects of the economy are crucial to democracy—namely, the internal distribution of whatever wealth there is and the subordination of economic power to a political conception of the public interest.

Is it permissible then to argue that this complex of conditions suffices to explain the genesis and growth of democracy in modern times? Is the system we have been studying correctly conceived as a political response to the stimuli of this group of causes?

Obviously not. The analysis of democracy attempted in this book has indicated additional weights to be placed on the scales. It is these, which, while they immensely complicate the problem of understanding, heighten our eventual insight into what is significant.

In the first place, to confine the explanation of democracy to a hypothesis of social causation would omit the crucial relevance of politics itself. Ibn Khaldun has remarked that "the State is as the Form whose condition follows that of its matter, Society."[1] But to view their relation in those terms is not quite correct. The form of the state follows the materials of society only in the sense that the contents of many problems requiring governmental action arise from the social matrix. But, whatever form the state may introduce and whatever goals it pursues will take their character from political conceptions. The latter are not solely a set of consequences which society causes. In the complex of factors which make a democracy possible or likely, politics is an independent, not a dependent, variable. Though connected with the other factors, politics is not determined by them.

The Influences of Philosophy

This brings us back to the role of a philosophy of politics, a topic peculiarly relevant to the democratic state which appeals both to our intelligence as rational beings and to our sense of right as moral creatures. The ideals to which democracy subscribes grew out of specific abuses for which correctives were sought. The function of the philosophers was to universalize the ideals and formulate them as abstractions—liberty, for instance, or equality, the rights of Man or popular sovereignty. It was then possible to apply such formulas to a variety of situations, many of which were not contemplated in the original conception. When these values gradually acquired a vogue and public bodies officially endorsed them, people could demand that certain things be done on the ground that this was what the

1. *An Arab Philosophy of History*, Charles Issawi, ed. (Murray: London, 1950), p. 84.

accepted ideals required. In other words, after certain values have come to be considered desirable, the choice of these—and, by the same logic, the rejection of their opposites—has its effect on political actions. For the ideals which men profess to serve become a feature of the reality in which they live.

Originally the values of democracy took shape in reaction to particular conditions, both social and political. But the later practices of the mature democracies are explicable in part as efforts to give more substance and concreteness to symbols and abstractions. Hence, of all the conditions which produced a democracy, or which can be said to have caused it, none is more important than the subjective factor—namely, the conscious determination that society should incorporate the values of the democratic ideal. Where this feeling was sufficiently widespread that people organized themselves and took concerted action, the result was an operative system of a democratic type. In this sense, Rousseau was correct to stress the General Will as the focal principle of political association. For a democracy to be realized in practice, a will must prevail in favor of the democratic values. Unless it does, all other conditions one might specify—constitutional safeguards, high living standards, freedom of speech, and so on—are like supporting pillars with no foundation on which to rest.

Thus the goals of philosophy exert their influence at two different positions in the circle of causation. They may be conceived as the ends which will be attained after a process of change has been started and completed. But for the very reason that the desire to attain them impels men into action, the objectives belong among the initial stimuli which prompt those changes to begin. The desired conception of a yet-to-be-realized ideal is also the springboard for the forward leap in its direction.

It is in this way that I have sought to interpret the spirit of democracy. So complex a phenomenon embraces the factors which pervade one's society, since politics cannot be successfully or for long conducted on the basis of principles which the social patterns contradict. At the same time, these principles constitute a central feature of the democratic state, and the values they embody give its quality to the democratic civilization. In a democratic milieu the power which the government must wield is not simply to be understood, in behavioral terms, as a process of certain determinate persons reaching specific decision on particular subjects. For that power is what the community has sanctioned through competition between alternative parties and policies, and allows to be used in order to alter existing realities in the hope for something better. Power must therefore be understood in relation to the conditions which create it and the purposes to which it is directed.

The Mediating Role of Politics

With this in mind, let us review Part III (Chapters 10–15) and note the interplay of social forces with philosophical influences in the conduct of politics and the structure of democratic government.

Because democracy insists on popular sovereignty, and because the government of a modern democracy is run by the people's representatives, the crucial act of a citizen is his vote at a national election. The right to vote and the use of that right were discussed in Chapter 10. The democratic conception of citizenship is a universal one. It has to be. Otherwise, the doctrines of individual liberty and basic equality for all would be meaningless. Consequently, wherever these notions prevailed, traditional practices in society and government were revolutionized. The principle of universal adult suffrage had to overcome all discriminatory barriers raised by religious orthodoxy, linguistic exclusiveness, educational separatism, inequality of property, race prejudice, and class snobbery—which it has generally succeeded in doing. Here was an example of an idea, whose content was essentially ethical because it affirmed a faith in the dignity of Man, acquiring political strength as people believed it and thus breaking the time-encrusted monopoly of political power by social oligarchies.

But since an electorate numbering millions has need of sub-groups to supply coherence and a choice, the modern democratic state consists in government by parties which must learn to alternate between office and opposition.[2] In Chapters 11 and 12, where parties were analyzed, I placed considerable stress on the historical and social factors which shape the system in general and the parties individually. Such influence is a proper function of their representative character. Parties are groups of citizen-voters organized to elect their political representatives. Naturally, therefore, the parties incorporate and reproduce the various ingredients and interests of society. But the function of the parties does not end there, nor do all traits of their character issue from this source. It is the purpose of the democratic process to offer the people a choice, both of personnel and programs, for without this, there is no freedom. In this sense, the principle of competition, of which so much use is made in classical economics, becomes central to the politics of democracy. But this competition, to be meaningful, must be more than a rivalry between claimants for power. In a democracy, power must commend itself to men's reason and their sense of social justice. It is because of this need—a need arising immediately

2. This is the modern version of Aristotle's definition of a citizen as one who shares in ruling and being ruled. For "citizen" substitute "party."

from the circumstances of democratic government—that parties formulate their philosophies. Beyond the specific contents of the programs they endorse, they stand for a set of values in whose image they propose that the community be fashioned. Liberalism, conservatism, socialism, individualism, capitalism, clericalism, rationalism—doctrines or sentiments such as these ignite the fuel of party combat.

Thus in the most direct and realistic manner, the party systems of the democracies illustrate the thesis advanced in this book. Parties derive their content—that is, their membership and programs—from society. This they fashion and mold within the political framework. Because of the compulsions of competition, however, they must combine the smaller groups and broaden the special interests to make a unified appeal. Here philosophy enters the arena in the guise of ideology. Therewith the parties offer the voters a choice of directions, proposing goals to which the community should strive. Nor are these ideals the vain hopes of the visionary. They manifest themselves in the *Realpolitik* of intensely practical men who must bid for support by professing their adherence to certain values and inviting others to join them. Thus it is that in democratic politics the crude elements of society are restructured through the medium of government and fused, if possible, into notions of general welfare and the public interest.

The political arena, we have seen, is an area for combat; but democracy conducts its combat under rules. These rules are prescribed in a constitution. As was stressed in Chapter 13, a constitution derives its legal force from its correspondence with social and political realities. Hence it is an embodiment of existing interests which it is designed to protect. But if it is to last, a constitution is more than that. It has to be a vehicle for forward movement, a channel for the unrealized aspirations of a changing community. Thus the constitution establishes a structure of government, but takes care that this may be utilized in turn for preservation or for progress. It arranges for a subdivision of jurisdictions to each of which the appropriate powers are assigned. But the general power to govern, which men win or lose by political means, is harnessed with a system which regulates its exercise and regularizes its transfer. Democracy transformed the constitutions, which made citizens of the Few and subjects of the Many, by enshrining the supremacy of the whole people. It converted the phenomenon of power from a divine right or an ancestral privilege, from an adjunct of property or of social status, into a trust which was delegated for the purposes of service. Then to be sure that such power would not be abused—or, if abused, that any abuse would be detected—democracy made opposition official, criticism continuous, and publicity paramount. A constitution, therefore, is a junction of ideal principles and social components within an institutional framework.

None of those institutions is more characteristic of democracy than the legislature. This branch of the government, explored in Chapter 14, has provided the instrument by which millions of enfranchised citizens could acquire a representation in the central machinery of a large state. The legislature is an image of society reflected in a political mirror. Whether the glass distorts is an arguable question. Sometimes it certainly does, and by intention, but this does not have to be the case. Much depends on the mechanics—and mathematics—of the electoral system. In general, one can say that the legislature seeks to include a typical cross section of the community it represents. Then for purposes of government, the parties attempt to inject a principle and a rationale. But their results are not always successful, and legislatures have become the targets for frequent criticism. The crux of the difficulty is to produce the public good from an aggregate of special interests and local pressures, and to discover the common welfare through the rivalry of competing parties. All too often we fail; and when we do, the weaknesses of democracy are seen at their worst. One cannot justify government by discussion if it ends in deadlock or the sovereignty of the ballot if it degenerates into bickering.

To counteract these faults, leadership is required. Hence democracy has designed the necessary institutions (analyzed in Chapter 15) through which the supreme responsibility for acts, or omissions, of government can be focused on one person, a President or Premier, or a small group, a Cabinet or Council. The power which is concentrated in these offices is needed to energize the functions of the state, which is why it is tolerated. Yet it can become a source of danger to the public at large if it should fall into the wrong hands. Consequently, the democratic vehicle has its controls uniquely distributed. There is a driver to hold the wheel and press the accelerator. But a back seat driver, official and recognized, is in charge of the brake. Normally the passengers arrive safely at their destination, even if they suffer a jerk or two. This conception is strictly political in character. It is not directly a product of society, nor is it clearly aimed at some ethical good. The case for leadership follows from the needs of organization in a mass society. The limitations on its scope are a counsel of prudence based on long experience.

The United States and Great Britain

Besides helping to interpret the over-all character of democracy, the method of analysis attempted here can be applied in another way. I have suggested that democracy consists in a mixture of the appropriate social conditions and philosophical ideals accomplished through the creative activity of government. A general summary tends naturally to focus on the common features. But the differences must also be considered. Democracies are not uniform in character. Indeed, they vary, and the reasons are due to the special traits of each country and the diversities which follow from a commitment to the principle of liberty. Suppose then we select a few democracies and review their salient features.

The United States, being nowadays the largest[3] and most powerful of the democratic states, is crucial to the evaluation of democracy. Sheer size, both of area and population, has presented this country with complexities from the beginning. So, too, in the most recent decades has the military strength which accrued from wealth and industrial power. A tension arises in American politics because some of the original ideals no longer correspond with a society which has undergone such extraordinary changes. The institutions of government constructed in 1787-89 were well adapted to a community which was starting its development and needed the freedom to grow and the flexibility to move. Because of the dissimilar regions, races, and interests, the Constitution did not seek to embody the rule of the majority, pure and simple. Instead, it erected safeguards for significant minorities. The requirement of larger majorities (e.g., two-thirds) in matters of fundamental importance has the reverse effect of ensuring a minority veto, a point which Calhoun's doctrine of concurrent majorities merely carried to its logical conclusion. The individualism which has exerted so profound an influence on American life and thinking came naturally to people who had broken through "the cake of custom" in emigrating and had found a continent for their energies to develop.

In its origins, the Constitution was established amid a political climate which did not permit the mass of the population to participate in government. But it did provide the framework within which that could happen later. Through the steady evolution of nearly two centuries, this republic has become a democracy. The country which Jefferson once called "the world's best hope" is precisely that today, and possibly in a deeper sense than even he envisioned. American democracy has met a series of challenges which are part of this nation's success story, but which have also brought problems to surmount. I am referring particularly to the assimilation of millions of people drawn from varied ethnic backgrounds to a common citizenship and culture, the acquisition of wealth and the power

3. I am not prejudging the notable experiment in India. Another generation, at least, must come and go before one can speak with sureness about the success or failure of democracy in India.

which accompanies it, and the contemporary exercise of military and diplomatic leadership in a turbulent world. Judged in human terms, the welcome which America extended to immigrants until World War I and their absorption into the mainstream of American life is the noblest of this country's political and social achievements. The spread of citizenship unified the nation, while the grant of the suffrage created a mass democracy.[4] At the same time, an inventive community turned its wits to technology and used its opportunities to organize an economy of abundance.

The development of industrial power on a massive scale, however, transformed the environment in which the notions of liberty and equality had to function. Even when Tocqueville was stressing the equality of social conditions, the distribution of property was far from equal—especially in the areas of older settlement along the Atlantic seaboard. By the end of the nineteenth century, the inequality of wealth sharply contradicted the political and juridical equality on which democracy insisted. It has taken some six decades of this twentieth century, not to close the gap, but to modify the extremes and enlarge the middle, and the result was accomplished in the main by political means through the power of the mass electorate. In the senses of leveling up, of educational opportunity, of the lack of stratified hereditary classes, the United States has achieved more equality for more individuals in more spheres than any society known to history.

The doctrine of liberty has undergone a corresponding modification. Personal liberty continues to be an impressive characteristic of American life. Most individuals are free to move their place of residence and to live wherever they can afford to buy or rent. The great majority can obtain the education to equip them for a useful career and can choose from a variety of occupations. But certain freedoms have definitely diminished or disappeared, especially within the economy, because monster corporations and mammoth unions generated a power in private hands which had to be subjected to public control through the state. Meanwhile, the sheer congestion and interdependence of contemporary society has spawned rules and regulations on all manner of subjects. The result is an increase in everyone's security, accompanied inevitably by greater rigidity throughout the system. Notwithstanding such transformations, the advent of new facts does not always produce a new mentality. Thus in the standardized living rooms of suburbia one still may hear the myths and shibboleths of the vanished frontier, as in some union locals and college campuses attitudes may prevail which had more relevance for the early 1930's.

4. The record will not be complete, however, until discrimination against Negroes is ended.

As for freedom of speech and the intellectual liberties in general, the basic principles of American democracy are sound, but their application is sometimes at fault. Tocqueville detected the danger of conformism in a mass culture, and there is evidence today to substantiate his warning. It is not infrequent for local communities to give short shrift to the dissenting individual with the unorthodox opinion. Nor am I alluding here to those whose primary loyalties belong to a foreign government, or to those super-patriots who would subvert our constitutional system while they profess themselves its defenders, but rather to eccentrics whose unconventional opinions can be as intellectually stimulating as they are socially inoffensive, and who serve as valuable irritants because they dare to protest what others do not care to question. In general, the United States has suffered in the last two decades, not from too much freedom of discussion, but from too little. The tone of debate, both public and private, is too bland; and written commentary, like over-refined foods, has lost much in pungency and flavor. I base this judgment on what seems to me, in general, the insipid character which prevails in press reporting and editorials, in the majority of articles in the magazines of opinion and the literary and artistic reviews, the dreariness and banality of most programs on radio and television, and the dying art of vigorous conversation. The perils in this trend concern the future even more than the present. When controversy over values is muted, a culture becomes engulfed in the morasses of technique. The re-examination of goals must then submit to the elaboration of "know-how." After that, it takes but a generation for the springs which invigorate the life of the mind to drain out in the sands of the organization men. We have not yet, I emphasize, arrived at that point, and I am well aware of exceptions, as with civil rights, to the strictures stated above. But the danger must be mentioned, because the possibility exists of a much more serious deterioration if some of our present faults are not corrected.

As a preventive, what sometimes appears an embarrassing and onerous obligation may turn out a blessing in disguise. The international responsibilities which the United States now manfully shoulders, because ours is the strongest of the democratic states, have made this country the object of attention and curiosity, of envy and attack, from many quarters. The shortcomings of the potent and the prominent are more observed and remarked than are those of the weak and insignificant. Consequently, in the act of confrontation with competing political systems, the United States is compelled to be forever searching its own conscience and to be responsive to the criticism of allies and the calumnies of antagonists. Thus the conflicts of our divided world are translating the processes of democratic inquiry to the level of relations between governments and exchanges between peoples.

The British version of democracy provides some instructive contrasts with the American. The structural forms of the two governments are dissimilar, as are the political environments in which they function. Whereas the United States leaves much scope to minorities, British institutions are simplified and streamlined for majority rule. In America one often wonders how a majority can manifest itself and make its way through the complicated machinery which the Constitution established. In Britain, one wonders how any minority can survive, so formidably is power consolidated and centralized there. The reason the British developed a machinery which a majority could so easily run is their political homogeneity as a people. Living together for centuries on an island, they arrived eventually at that inner solidarity which has been the source of Britain's strength. Hence the security which this feeling affords enables them to treat heterodoxy with equanimity and dissent with tolerance. The public attitude insists on fair play between rivals; and every majority is well aware that it would forfeit respect, and thus lose support, by riding roughshod over its opponents. As a consequence, public discussion in Britain is vigorous and sometimes strident. Freedom of speech, freedom of the press, freedom of publication, are employed, like the cut and thrust of parliamentary debate, with a forcefulness which has few parallels elsewhere.

The centralization and consolidation of power to which I referred was achieved, of course, during the pre-democratic period when an oligarchy controlled the government and the nobility gave society its leaders. Later on, the structure which they had established was adapted to the purposes of democracy by expanding the electorate which chose the Members of the House of Commons. But the tone and quality which an aristocracy imparted to the nation has outlived the period of their political and economic hegemony. In the sphere of liberty, British democracy has a notable record of accomplishment. But it has not advanced nearly so far in the direction of equality. The stratification of the British into social classes is still a stubborn fact despite great changes which have occurred. The extremes at either end of the socio-economic scale are no longer as widely separated as they used to be. The material standard of living among industrial and clerical workers has risen dramatically, and educational opportunities continue to expand.

Nevertheless, the aristocratic legacy remains, with several of its vices and virtues intact. Of the latter, the finest is the ideal of an elite of quality leading by virtue of its acts of service. Of the vices, by far the worst is the confusion of hereditary status with personal worth. In a class-oriented community people become habitually accustomed to looking up or down —not sideways at their equals. Under these circumstances it is not equality which is the ideal most highly esteemed. Although contemporary Britain has evolved beyond what it was like in the 1920's, an essential similarity remains in spite of the differences. Political democracy has been achieved; social democracy has not. The country is run by an elite, to join whose ranks is the hope and ambition of able men. Nowadays, the members of that elite are recruited far more broadly than heretofore. This is an improvement, unquestionably. But if the politics of democracy require an accompaniment of social egalitarianism, one will not find it in Britain. For that one must look to Scandinavia, or to the older countries of the Commonwealth, or to the United States.

Switzerland, Denmark, Canada, and New Zealand

Among the smaller democracies, I shall mention two in Europe and a pair in the Commonwealth, exhibiting some distinctive features which merit comparison.

The Swiss put together their democracy in the way they constructed their Confederation, piecemeal and slowly. Because of the pressure of population growth on a small usable area, they are forced to work hard and are therefore prone to penny-pinching both in private matters and in public. Their surroundings require their neutrality, and their diversity imposes the need of tolerance. Tenacious of what they have inherited, they are conservative by temperament; whatever they build, they build—as the Romans did—slowly. One should respect such a people, even if their qualities are not the most exciting. Nor can one fail to admire a democracy which is the product, not so much of ideas, as of character. Add to localism an ingrained suspicion of officialdom; mix prosperity with tradition, peace with humanitarianism, and thrift with cleanliness. The results are thoroughly wholesome, and, though the scenery is more dramatic than its inhabitants, one could wish that more of the world were Swiss. From them one can learn some valuable lessons: that high living standards depend more on ingenuity, work, and trustworthiness than on abundant resources, that common people using their common sense can build a decent society and an efficient government without the benefit of Heroes, Supermen, and Dictators, that political stability can coexist with social pluralism, and that a people can maintain its dignity and give itself a civic education by constantly participating in affairs of state.

A second democracy on the continent which merits respect and imitation is Denmark. As the mountains have molded the form and spirit of Switzerland, so has the sea left its tang on the Danes. For these are the descendants of farmers and sailors who live on a group of islands and a promontory jutting out from the mainland. Their ancestry includes the Vikings, and for centuries the naval strength of Denmark was a force with which to reckon. But, lucky is the nation which has done its deeds of military glory in the past, and nowadays, without false illusion or vain ambition, can concentrate its talents on the arts of peace. Democracy, as we have seen, came late to the Danes when their power in continental politics had already declined. After vainly attempting to halt the march of Prussia, Denmark withdrew inward on itself; and, when it re-emerged, it had turned into a democracy—social, economic, and political. Today there is no country on the European continent more truly democratic, no community more deeply involved with social justice, no people more highly civilized. Alike in their farmlands and villages, in the thorough-fares of Copenhagen, in the design of their arts and crafts, and in the programs of their welfare state, the Danes exemplify a quality of good taste which can raise the commonplace to a level of superior sophistica-tion. Democracy and humanism have found here the formula for the right blend.

Of the democracies in the Commonwealth, Canada has certain re-semblances to Switzerland, while New Zealand has a partial affinity to Denmark. Canada and Switzerland are alike in containing an important minority whose ancestral culture is French. In both countries, social heterogeneity makes itself felt through the constitutional system and in political practice. Since both states are federal unions, the cantons or provinces have the function of guarding the diversity of language and religion; and the unity which overrides the internal divisions comes in part from a centripetal reaction to external influences. Two such con-trasted institutions as the Swiss Federal Council and the Canadian Cab-inet have been similarly used to represent the cultural varieties of the people. But there the similarity ends, since the Council is always a multi-party coalition, whereas the Cabinet draws its members from the dom-inant party only.

Where separate communities must somehow coexist within the struc-ture of a single government, majority rule, while prevailing in principle, is much modified in practice. Where the division between a majority and a minority coincides closely with the boundaries of culture, it is not always politically prudent, from the standpoint of maintaining national unity, for the larger number to press its power and have its way. The attendant risks are even greater in Canada than in Switzerland because in the former country the lives of religious and linguistic cleavage largely coincide, whereas in the latter they do not. Consequently, the arts of statesmanship and the theoretical doctrine of democracy, to the extent that Canadians have formulated it explicitly, are prone to stress the virtues of balance, moderation, and compromise more than the crude power of the majority to dominate. On that subject, it should be noted that English-speaking Canadians, when they were the minority, opposed the right of the majority to do as it pleased; when the numerical ratio between the cultures was reversed, the French Canadians favored this same position.

Democracy in New Zealand confronts a different set of circumstances and therefore produces yet another version. Except for the Maoris, whose numbers are few and who have not been a threat to the Europeans since the 1860's, the New Zealanders do not have a minority problem of any significance. Not only were their origins overwhelmingly British, but even within the British isles they were drawn primarily from the Protestants of the working and lower middle classes. Cultural homogeneity, therefore, is the country's dominant trait, and it manifests itself to such an excessive degree that it produces some harm. Since people differ in occupations and income, the economy affords some intelligible basis for a division between majorities and minorities. But even so, the spread is not very wide. Accordingly, New Zealand conducts its politics within a context of similarities which leaves little room for maneuver or for major disagreement. There is not much flexibility in policy, or great variety in the programs from which the public can choose. Hence the parliamentary debates in that country are notoriously dull; so, too, usually, are the general elections.

Where society exhibits such over-all sameness, majoritarianism reigns without check. Everything in New Zealand is concentrated and streamlined. The government of the Dominion has no difficulty in dominating a chaotic complex of local bodies which collectively are too numerous for efficiency and severally too small and weak for their functions. At the center, the Parliament nowadays is unicameral, the Cabinet controls it, and the majority party mans the Cabinet. The press speaks out in a united conservative monotone, so that Labor must obtain its hearing on the radio.

Connected with the same factors is the passion in New Zealand for equality. In the South Pacific, the emphasis of democracy is not libertarian, but egalitarian. People must be treated the same. If there is something good, it must be distributed to as many recipients as possible in what necessarily become increasingly smaller amounts. Consequently, because the brand of equality which appeals to New Zealanders is the uniform rather than the proportional, they succeed admirably in leveling up and are genuine zealots for social justice. At the same time, though, they exhibit the defects of these virtues. Their leveling down has pervaded all branches of society, with results which are particularly serious within the educational system. Indeed, where a homogeneous society combines majority rule with the uniform species of egalitarianism, to be unorthodox is to be unpopular, and to dissent is dangerous. From the standpoint of civil liberties, the record of New Zealand during the depression of the early 1930's and the two World Wars was none too creditable, particularly in view of the fact that the handful of individuals who were punished for deviant ideas or behavior were in no sense a danger to the general security.

Two Categories of Democracy

If one projects the characteristics of these six democracies, their tendencies exhibit some discernible patterns. For the ideals they emphasize and the institutions they employ fall in two categories. One species of democracy is primarily libertarian in tone and individualistic in temper. Zealous in protecting minorities, it devises political institutions to hedge in the rule of the majority. This is the democracy which occurs typically in the pluralistic societies, where, with equal appropriateness, the form of government is federal. The bias in favor of the individual and the privacy of his freedom has been construed here as limiting the sphere of the state. Three countries which belong generally in this group are the United States, Canada, and Switzerland.

The other species has a predilection for equality. Here the outlook is more collectivist; the philosophy more socially oriented. This kind of democracy concentrates the powers of government and centralizes its machinery. The majority dominates; if it moderates its exercise of power, this is by grace more than from necessity. Such democracies make the state truly potent. Its activities must indeed be far-reaching, because, where equality is prized, the state emerges as the equalizer *par excellence*. The function of politics is then to decide upon the ration and allot the grades. Such a democracy is well suited to the homogeneous communities. Examples of it are found in New Zealand and Denmark. Great Britain does not belong exclusively to either category. While resembling Denmark and New Zealand in many particulars, it differs from them sharply because of its social classes. British democracy is not egalitarian, but elitist.

In one important respect, however, Great Britain has made a contribution to democracy which bears closely on this general analysis. By the way they are constituted and behave, all democracies incorporate a set of principles and values. In many countries, these remain implicit, and are seldom consciously formulated and discussed. The British, despite their curious reputation for aversion to theory and addiction to practice, have actually indulged in more varied philosophizing about the democratic values than any other people—save possibly the French. In the United States, there were significant debates concerning first principles in the two periods when fundamental issues had to be faced, namely between 1770 and 1790 and again from 1840 to 1860. Apart from the seminal thinking which occurred at those times, the American contribution to democratic ideals has consisted in the construction of the consequential institutions and the subtle elaboration by the Supreme Court of the vaguer phrases in the Constitution. The Canadians, except for Henri Bourassa who served Quebec as Calhoun did the South, have functioned democratically without theorizing about democracy. Geneva gave the world a Rousseau, but his influence on politics was far greater in France than in his native land, and the style of Swiss democracy has always been more pragmatic than speculative. The Danes at a critical moment in their history drew inspiration from the ideas of the imaginative Grundtvig. Beyond his work, however, the principles which they follow must be discovered in their programs, not their writings. As for the New Zealanders, they are perhaps the most unphilosophical people in the world. In all aspects—economic, social, and political—their democracy follows from possessing a sense of justice while avoiding the analysis of its concept.

The absence of systematic philosophies, however, does not imply a lack of commitment to values either in the political order or in its social surroundings. For whether these are explicitly formulated or not, ideal ends are always implict in our acts and institutions. By observing an operating democracy, one may infer the values which people esteem from the priorities they assert and the programs they choose or reject. Nor has it been true in the evolution of democracy that theorizing occurred at the close and fulfillment of historical events, or, as Hegel expressed it, that the owl of Minerva took its flight when the shades of night were gathering. At the hour of our dawning, not of our dusk, the *rara avis* of democratic philosophy was on the wing. The doctrines—yes, and the dogmas—formulated from the mid seventeenth to the mid nineteenth century have provided the rationale and justification for the hundred years down to our time in which the modern democracies attained maturity.

What Follows Maturity?

But this leads us to ask: What is it that accompanies maturity, and what will follow it? What tendencies are visible in the democracy of today? What shapes can we discern of democracy tomorrow?

When Tocqueville crossed the Atlantic to study democracy in America, he was convinced that he was seeing the wave of the future. When Mill analyzed its character and problems, he noted that the world thus far had experience of democracy only in its militant stage. Around the turn of the century, the devotees of democracy proclaimed its triumph an accomplished fact, and considered its universal extension an ultimate certainty. Since the end of World War II, we have become more sceptical. We are troubled with doubts. We are less sure of ourselves. Unwilling to change our system for another—since none that we know appears as good, let alone superior—we nevertheless feel a gnawing anxiety lest the wave of the future become an ebbing tide. Did we vanquish the Fascists, we ask ourselves, to lose the world to the Communists? Can we expect our institutions and beliefs to be adopted in Asia and Africa, when thus far they are virtually excluded from eastern Europe, have meager support in Latin America, and even in western Europe do not prevail in all countries?

Two separate, although related, points are involved in these questions. First, in the mature democracies is the system already so fully developed that further evolution is impossible? Second, what are the prospects for democracy to function successfully in the far different societies of Asia and Africa?

Although some possible rejoinders to the former question are debatable, the crux of the answer, I think, is beyond dispute. Compare the democracies of 1964 with those of 1914, and it will be conceded that most of the primary tasks which then were only partly under way have since been completed. The economic and social issues, over which parties were embattled as late as 1939, are largely settled—at least in their general outlines. So too is the political issue of the full democratization of the structure of government. Granted that the United States has yet to accept the Negro within the circle of equality, and that the United Kingdom has still to subordinate its social elitism to political democracy. But changes in these directions are already under way in both countries, and, although their broad effects will not be felt for at least another generation, the eventual transformation will doubtless be profound.

Meanwhile, some immediate effects which accompany the maturity of democracy can be traced in the altered tone of domestic politics. For several decades prior to 1940 the majority of Democrats and the majority of Republicans were poles apart in policy and philosophy. But in the quarter of a century since the Roosevelt-Willkie contest, their differences have been reduced by many degrees. The same applies to Conservatives and Labour in Britain, to Social Democrats and their Venstre-Conservative opponents in Denmark, and similarly in many other countries. In some, this trend has led to the installation in office of long-surviving coalitions, which extend over an increasingly wider arc of the political spectrum. The Swiss have been past masters at this, and recently their neighbors, the Austrians, have tried to copy them. The political consequences for democracy there amount to a balance of gain and loss. One acquires an even stability, but misses the criticism of opposition and a choice between meaningful alternatives. If this tendency were to continue indefinitely and if the major parties in most democracies should grow still more alike, truly the democratic dialectic would have reached an unprecedented, and perhaps an unwelcome, synthesis.

But what shall we say of that possible outcome? Were such a level of social harmony ever realized and for long sustained, would this be the peace of perfection or the peace of death? Some contemporary observers lean to a pessimistic view. They believe they already detect a decline in democratic politics which could be the prelude to the end. They foresee the progressive replacement of multi-party diversity and two-party alternation by permanent coalitions and their possible consolidation into one-party regimes. I do not expect this eventuality, nor do I think it warranted to predict the passage of democracy into the limbo of political systems. What is happening is that its evolution has entered a new phase, which exhibits new problems. The problems, however, are those deriving from success more than from failure, and there is a whole new world awaiting capture.

These points can be substantiated by referring to a mood which is widespread in various democracies today, more especially the smaller ones, and speculating on the reasons which brought it about. As was previously noted, the internal problems which used to excite people because they were fundamental have generally ceased to be live subjects for political debate. The present generation can take for granted solutions and conditions which once evoked the bitterest struggles. Political life is therefore more placid; its content more technical. With this, the work of government becomes prosaic and dull. The public is no longer so actively interested. Boredom ensues, and ends in apathy. These are generalizations which could be documented by citing aspects of public affairs in Scandinavia, in Switzerland, and the democracies of the South Pacific.[5] The parties which once were crusading movements, fired with indignation at social injustice, turn into aging bureaucracies supported by hereditary

5. The inner complexity and external responsibilities of the larger democracies leave them with more problems still to be solved—which injects more stimulus into political controversy.

voters. The unions which fought the big corporations become their partners in a mixed and managed economy on whose benefits they batten. The
co-operatives which challenged the monopolies expand themselves into
large-scale businesses. And business itself, one generation or two removed
from the era of cut-throat competition, is staffed with nameless organization men and sugar-coated with public relations. I am exaggerating, of
course. But the element of truth is too large to be ignored. When you
have succeeded in erasing the worst evils from your social system, what
do you do next? And if nothing major is left to be accomplished, will a
dry rot set in? One suffers ennui in heaven, stagnation in paradise, tedium
in utopia. It is debilitating to be successful. You are then left without a
goal, save that of conserving the accomplished good. For the elderly
this can suffice. For the young the prospect is stifling.

Fresh Fields for Democracy

Fortunately, however, we are not yet reduced to the nirvana of triumphal
retirement. The dangers to which I have just referred are attributable to
two basic reasons, of which the success of democracy in achieving many
of its primary objectives is only one. The second reason is not originally
related to the phenomenon of democracy, but is the product of another
political trend which carries large implications for democracy in the future. What I have in mind is the contemporary obsolescence, not of democracy, but of the unit of government, the nation-state, which was
created some four centuries ago along the Atlantic seaboard of western
Europe. This unit has provided the outer framework within which our
politics—whether of the democratic sort or the authoritarian—has been
conducted. But the shell has cracked and is now breaking up, and the contents are spilling out over wider areas. There are major subjects today,
those of general economic concern and of military security, which no
single state is capable of handling.[6] Their regulation and settlement call
for decisions through negotiation between governments at the level of
interstate diplomacy.

These current tendencies suggest a principal reason for the changing
character of democratic politics. Problems whose solution used to fall
within the domestic competence have now been lifted to the plane of external agreement. But these novel political dimensions in which we must
learn to function, while they restrict the range of customary choice in

6. In the majority of American presidential elections since 1940, international relations
have provided some of the major issues.

one area, open up new vistas in another. There is no compelling reason why the democratic values and our inherited institutions cannot be adapted to the goals and process of creating larger political units—regional at first and then global—and there are many reasons why they can be. If people in the mature democracies grow bored with their politics, they should apply their energies anew and translate their ideals to the emerging suprastates. It is not true that democracy has begun to decline. What is declining is the nation-state. To organize its successor is the next challenge for democracy, which henceforth must raise its sights beyond the outmoded politics of the nation and introduce its civilization to the international jungle.

Indeed, for this task the democratic system possesses a powerful asset. The rich diversity of institutions and values which the democracies incorporate can serve as a storehouse of useful experience from which solutions relevant to the new conditions may be found. For an example, consider the two broad types of democracy sketched earlier in this chapter, each of which appeared appropriate to its own combination of circumstances. When states which were formerly separate voluntarily merge themselves into a larger aggregate, they will naturally carry their old characteristics into their new-found union. Initially, therefore, they will insist on constructing a framework in which their former particularity is not too quickly submerged. Hence, if their union is built on a democratic foundation, the design which they will most likely favor is the libertarian, with its accent on safeguarding minorities and limiting the functions of the central government. Later, if their union endures, they will develop into a unity. At that stage, one species of democracy will give way to the other. Egalitarianism will become more prevalent, and with it the acceptance of majority rule in a state more strongly centralized.

Apart from this development of larger units of government, the other potential field for an expansion of democracy can be found in those regions of Asia and Africa which have become independent of control by an outside power. At present, it is difficult to strike a proper balance between judgments which are overly optimistic or pessimistic. In many new states the constitutional arrangements which were the legacy of the departing imperial rulers have been speedily disregarded or discarded. Military officers or revolutionary leaders have established autocratic[7] regimes, offering by rough-and-ready methods to bring the millennium faster. Such a brand of politics, however much one wishes it otherwise, is not in itself a loss to democracy, since such countries did not really start

7. Or despotic, in some instances; e.g., Ghana.

out with a democracy to lose. Whether they will later evolve along democratic lines is a question about which prediction would be rash because
evidence is lacking to justify a conclusion. If one or two elections do not
create a democracy, neither do one or two *coups d'état* confirm the opposite. What should always be remembered is that every people has to win
its own democracy for itself. This is not what anybody can grant to someone else. Moreover, in the past record of the most stable democracies of
today, there were long centuries of authoritarian and oligarchical rule. If
the West needed several generations for the present to grow and ripen,
why should one expect it to mature speedily in other cultures? Impatient
people will not like this counsel, but I suggest that two generations must
come and go before the new states of Africa and Asia will have acquired a
determinable political character. In the meantime, it is wise to wait and
watch, to help if asked, and to avoid a final judgment.

But the judgment, which is premature for states whose independence is
of recent date, is permissible in the case of peoples where democracy is
firmly rooted and has a long indigenous tradition. The conclusion of this
book must, therefore, attempt to sum up and evaluate. From the welter
of arguments, pro and con, I shall focus on the ones which go to the heart
of the matter.

The Negative Summing-up

There are three principal objections to the democratic form of government:
that it invites the tyranny of the majority, that it constitutes the enthronement of ignorance, that it puts up a false front behind which an oligarchy
really rules. Let us consider these points in turn.

The force of the first criticism depends, in the main, on what meaning
one attaches to "tyranny." In this context, I take it to imply a ruthless
treatment of a smaller number by a larger who deny them what they consider their rights. The essence of tyranny is the notion of unjust domination. It is an act of power, judged to be wrongfully exercised. Can this happen under a democracy, and does it? I think the possibility, and, sometimes,
the actuality, has to be conceded. Every type of government requires the
consolidation and use of power, which on occasion will be abused. Since
democracies ordinarily entrust power to the majority, the chance that it
may be used tyrannically cannot be denied, ignored, or explained away. The
danger is built-in with the system. It is an element of risk which accompanies the advantages; and, when a majority becomes oppressive, it can
admittedly be cruel.

Are there safeguards against this happening? Yes, there are some kinds of defense. But we would be deluding ourselves if we pretended that they are foolproof. One protection is to build the machinery of state in so complicated a manner that minorities find numerous ways of resisting. But this, when overdone, leads to the opposite evil—that no decisions can be taken, that government is powerless, and that the majority is forever thwarted. The better safeguard is that which relies, not on institutions working at cross purposes, but on the interplay of political forces opposing one another within a context of freedom. I am thinking especially of the party system, the existence of an organized and legitimate opposition, and open channels of opinion through which injustice, if it exists, can be exposed for what it is. In a democracy which remains alert, and which contains enough of the sort of people who respond to stirrings of conscience, such political conditions, while they may not prevent all abuses by a majority behaving tyrannically, may serve to mitigate the effects and evoke a counter action. This may sound like a statement of faith. But it is a reasoned faith, since the oppressive majority has in fact been known to encounter courageous opposition.

The second objection, that democracy places the ignorant in power, is a variant of the first. It is founded on an elitist conception of human nature and the government appropriate thereto. If you argue that ruling is an art which calls for knowledge and specialized skills, you may conclude that few are competent and qualified to govern wisely. On the same reasoning, the mass of men are considered too stupid and too ill-informed to reach the right decisions. Hence, when the untutored majority is supreme, knowledge is subordinate to ignorance. In this argument one must distinguish the assertions which are valid from the inferences which are not. It is true that good government requires a great store of technical information, together with accumulated experience. Those who possess such knowledge are experts, and they are few. But it is no less true that such expertise, while it provides the intelligent basis for policy, does not necessarily indicate what the policies should be. All kinds of factors—ethical, social, and political—may be relevant to the ultimate choice. On that plane, the expert is no different from any other citizen. A professional in his specialty, he is an amateur elsewhere.

Nor can it be demonstrated from history—which, after all, is the only reliable teacher—that the alternative political systems, which consciously enshrined the domination of the supposedly superior few, have been notably wiser and have committed fewer mistakes. One can readily think of tenacious oligarchies in the past, such as the senatorial families of the Roman Republic or the Venetian commercial plutocracy, which brought power and prosperity to the state they governed and within it preserved their own privileges. But one could equally compile a long catalogue of their errors and misdeeds. In modern times, the Nazi self-styled supermen despised the ordinary run of mankind and thought to enslave the world by determination and brute force. But mistake upon mistake brought them to the day of reckoning. Similarly, the Communist parties, whose dogma persuades them that everything can be calculated and planned by a disciplined few, have as many failures on their record as successes. How else does one explain their recurrent shifts in policy? Organizing the relation of knowledge to governmental power is a very tricky affair for which no guaranteed formula will ever be found. Democracy, to be sure, has its full quota of stupidities, but not more so that in other systems; and it is certainly exempt from the bloodier excesses of treachery and cruelty.

The third of the objections rests on quite a different premise. It cuts away the ground from under the democrat's philosophy by asserting that he is the victim of an illusion and that his creed is a sham. Popular sovereignty, on this view, is a fairy tale; the common man, a dupe or a fool. The people never rules in fact—even the majority does not govern—because in simple truth it cannot. Whatever the theory may be, all government is oligarchical in character. Realistically seen, ruling is a function performed by a few. Only they can wield the power. Democracy should drop its pretensions and abandon the disguise.

This criticism, like the others, has been with us for a long time, or at least for two centuries. Rousseau mentions in the *Social Contract* that it is contrary to nature that many should govern and only a few be governed. Late in the nineteenth century when the electorate was still expanding and parties were multiplying, writers like Mosca, Ostrogorski, and Michels pointed out that the institutions which serve a democracy were not exempt from the tendencies to oligarchy in big organizations. In recent decades, a school of behaviorists and quantifiers has been busy detecting elites and mapping the social landscape with pyramids of power. The equation of politics with *Who Gets What, When, and How*[8] supplies the proof that the few get the most by skill and guile.

Where does this leave democracy? Are we foredoomed to futility by living in a dream and posing an unattainable ideal? Again let us seek to separate authentic fact from unwarranted inference. No one can deny what any statistical computation will show, that wealth, social status, and influence are unequally distributed in every society and that a small percentage of persons on the distribution curve enjoys a disproportionate

8. The title of the book by Harold D. Lasswell.

share. Nor can we refute the evident truth that our increasingly complex society is managed by ever larger organizations whose structure becomes both hierarchical and bureaucratic. But let us not forget the insight in Acton's comment that modern democracy was derived neither from the medieval state nor from the medieval church, but from the conflict between the two. The exigencies of competition even between organizations which are controlled from the top contributes to the goals of democracy. For the atmosphere of publicity which surrounds their operations, and the criticisms which they must expect from rivals, compel the heads of those organizations ultimately to be answerable, not merely to their own members, but to the community at large.

When there is an alternative to which people may have recourse, an organization cannot, in monopoly fashion, bend them to its will. Instead, it must bid for their support. This holds true whether the institution in question is a church, a corporation, a trade union, or a political party. However, since the state bears the responsibility over all of promoting the public interest, the crucial competition is that which occurs within the political order. Hence, as I emphasized earlier, the indispensable political requirement for a democracy is always to have at least two major parties between which the voters can periodically choose. Nor can the discipline within these parties ever be made so tight that splits and revolts are impossible. Nor is the people a crowd of mere spectators who applaud or jeer the contesting teams, but otherwise are passive and take no part in the proceedings. Their function is more like that of a jury which hears the evidence as it is marshalled by professionals and then on election day delivers its verdict.

The Positive Evaluation

Finally, there are the arguments in favor of democracy. Three will suffice, because these are the points which really matter. The democratic form of government has a claim on our allegiance for the reasons that it enhances human dignity, it supplies a continuing civic education, and thereby in the broadest sense it helps humanity in becoming more civilized.

Respect for the dignity of its citizens is the cornerstone of democratic government. A democracy insists that the state and its personnel exist to serve the public. To enforce that principle, machinery is provided for changing the institutions and the officials. The whole body of the people discharges at stated periods the supreme responsibility of choosing the men and women who will direct the government and of approving the general policy they will pursue. Under this system, all have some share in the common enterprise. Therefore, everybody counts for something.

That is a statement of the ideal. It expresses the intent of the democratic man, the goal he sets before himself, the standard by which he judges his government and is prepared to be judged. Hence, it is true of actual democracies only to the extent that they are true to their own principles. Actual democracies vary in their degrees of approximation to what they aspire or profess to be. But this commitment to ideals serves as a regulator of practice. Certain things are done or avoided in a democracy because the democratic values demand or deny them. At rock bottom, all of this depends on the manner in which the citizens assert themselves. They can be pushed around or hoodwinked only if they allow themselves to be so treated. The processes and institutions of democracy afford to every man and woman more scope for participation and influence than any other system. How they use their opportunity depends on the character of the people. Their dignity is what they make of it.

Because they do count for something and are expected to participate, the people of a democratic community enjoy the benefit of a continuing civic education. Public affairs are constantly engaging their attention. They are consulted and canvassed, polled and propagandized, because they have votes which they will one day cast. The debate over issues of common concern goes on without respite, and those who read and listen, learn. They also learn by doing. The work of the myriad associations which citizens form among themselves helps to knit the community and to train its members in the exercise of responsibility. The political system which places a premium on the voluntary activity of its members grows stronger as their experience augments their education. It is in this sense that Pericles was correct in stressing the educative value of the democratic process.

For this reason also, although the people will err periodically, and will sometimes be the victims of deception, the system includes the means of discovering the errors, unmasking the frauds, and exposing the charlatans. Lincoln expressed this vividly in his remark that you can fool some of the people all of the time and all of the people some of the time, but not all of the people all of the time. It is this certainty which saves democracy from the worst effects of its own misjudgment or misplaced trust. With freedom will come mistakes, but our education, individual and civic, consists in learning not to repeat them and in striving to improve on past performance.

Therein, finally, lies democracy's greatest contribution to humanity. Open inquiry, criticism, and searching are stimuli to achievement and appraisal. By the laws of its being, democracy is dedicated to a concern for the general welfare. The rhythm of parties alternating in office encourages each to vie with others and promotes, along with exposure of faults, a constructive balance between experience and experiment. The ideals of democracy are dynamic because their contents admit of progressive redefinition. Hence, as a community advances, not only in knowledge and techniques but also in the level of its ethical aspirations, the politics of the democratic state enables its government by positive measures to translate the increment into policy and program. This is what I have meant throughout this book by calling my subject *The Democratic Civilization*. The state which responds to the citizens' awareness of their needs will help them to raise the standard of the good life, as their education equips them to envision it, and because its powers are derived from all, its civilizing benefits are distributed among all.

Democracy, its critics reiterate, is not a government by the best and wisest. But of all forms of government known and tried, democracy is the wisest and the best.

Bibliography

This selection touches on various aspects of democracy, pro and con. The arrangement is broadly chronological, corresponding to three periods: the preparation for democracy, its evolution during the nineteenth century, and its maturity in the twentieth. For older works, which either are out of print or have been reprinted more than once, I have usually not named a particular edition or publisher.

1. The Older Classics

HERODOTUS, *History of the Persian Wars*.
THUCYDIDES, *History of the Peloponnesian War*.
PLATO, *Republic, Laws*.
ARISTOTLE, *Politics, Constitution of Athens*.
TACITUS, *Annals, Histories, On Germany*.
NICCOLÒ MACHIAVELLI, *Prince, Discourses*.
JOHN MILTON, *Areopagitica*.
THOMAS HOBBES, *Leviathan*.
JOHN LOCKE, *Second Treatise of Civil Government, A Letter Concerning Toleration*.
CHARLES LOUIS SECONDAT, BARON DE LA BRÈDE ET DE MONTESQUIEU, *Spirit of the Laws*.
JEAN JACQUES ROUSSEAU, *Social Contract, Letters written from the Mountain*.
THOMAS PAINE, *The Rights of Man*.
ALEXANDER HAMILTON, JOHN JAY, and JAMES MADISON, *The Federalist Papers*.
EDMUND BURKE, *Reflections on the French Revolution*.
THOMAS JEFFERSON, *Papers*, edited by Julian P. Boyd (Princeton: Princeton University Press).

2. From 1815 to 1914

THOMAS CARLYLE, *Past and Present*.

JOHN GEORGE LAMBTON, EARL OF DURHAM, *Report on Affairs of British North America, 1839*, edited by C. P. Lucas, 3 vols. (Oxford: Clarendon Press, 1912).

ALEXIS DE TOCQUEVILLE, *Democracy in America, The Old Regime*.

GEORGE GROTE, *History of Greece, Seven Letters Concerning the Politics of Switzerland* (London: Murray, 1876).

JOHN C. CALHOUN, *Disquisition on Government*.

FRANÇOIS DE GUIZOT, *Democracy in France* (Paris: Masson, 1849).

KARL MARX, *The Communist Manifesto*.

JOHN STUART MILL, *Principles of Political Economy, Essay on Liberty, Considerations of Representative Government*.

ABRAHAM LINCOLN, *Speeches and Letters*.

WALTER BAGEHOT, *The English Constitution*, with introductory essay by Lord Balfour (Oxford University Press: World's Classics edition, 1928).

HERBERT SPENCER, *Man versus the State*.

F. W. NIETZSCHE, *Thus Spake Zarathustra*.

WOODROW WILSON, *Congressional Government*.

JAMES BRYCE, *The American Commonwealth* (London and New York: Macmillan, 1888).

A. V. DICEY, *Introduction to the Study of the Law of the Constitution* (London: Macmillan, 1st ed., 1885); *Lectures on the Relation Between Law and Public Opinion in England during the Nineteenth Century* (London: Macmillan, 1905).

GAETANO MOSCA, *The Ruling Class*.

A. LAWRENCE LOWELL, *Governments and Parties of Continental Europe* (Boston: Houghton Mifflin, 1896).

T. H. GREEN, *Lectures on Political Obligation*.

JOHN MORLEY, *On Compromise* (London: Macmillan, 1898).

W. E. H. LECKY, *Democracy and Liberty* (New York: Longman's Green, 1896).

LORD ACTON, *History of Freedom and Other Essays*.

ROBERT MICHELS, *Political Parties*.

JAKOB BURCKHARDT, *Force and Freedom* (New York: Pantheon Books, 1943).

J. B. BURY, *History of the Freedom of Thought* (London: Thornton Butterworth, 1913).

3. Since 1918

ERNEST BARKER, *Reflections on Government* (London: Oxford University Press, 1942).

ALEXANDER BRADY, *Democracy in the Dominions* (Toronto: University of Toronto Press, 2nd ed., 1952).

JAMES BRYCE, *Modern Democracies* (New York: Macmillan, 1921).

C. A. R. CROSLAND, *The Future of Socialism* (New York: Macmillan, 1957).

ROBERT A. DAHL, *A Preface to Democratic Theory* (Chicago: University of Chicago Press, 1956).

JOHN DEWEY, *The Public and Its Problems* (New York: Holt, 1927); *Freedom and Culture* (New York: Putnam's, 1939).

MAURICE DUVERGER, *Political Parties* (New York: Wiley, 1959).

HERMAN FINER, *Theory and Practice of Modern Government* (New York: Dial Press, 1932).

CARL J. FRIEDRICH, *Constitutional Government and Democracy* (Boston: Ginn & Co., 1950).

J. K. GALBRAITH, *The Affluent Society* (Boston: Houghton Mifflin, 1958).

FRANÇOIS N. GOGUEL, *La Politique des Partis sous la troisième République* (Paris: Editions du Seuil, 1946).

F. A. HAYEK, *The Constitution of Liberty* (Chicago: University of Chicago Press, 1960).

SIDNEY HOOK, *Heresy, Yes—Conspiracy, No!* (New York: Day, 1953).

IVOR JENNINGS, *Party Politics*, 3 vols. (Cambridge: Cambridge University Press, 1960-62).

V. O. KEY, *Southern Politics in State and Nation* (New York: Knopf, 1949).

ADRIENNE KOCH, *Power, Morals and the Founding Fathers* (Ithaca: Cornell University Press, 1961).

HAROLD J. LASKI, *Liberty in the Modern State* (New York: Harper's, 1930); *The Rise of European Liberalism* (London: Allen & Unwin, 1936).

G. E. LAVAU, *Partis Politiques et Réalités Sociales* (Paris: A. Colin, 1953).

A. D. LINDSAY, *The Essentials of Democracy* (Philadelphia: University of Pennsylvania Press, 1929); *The Modern Democratic State* (London: Oxford University Press, 1943).

SEYMOUR M. LIPSET, *Political Man* (New York: Doubleday, 1960).

LESLIE LIPSON, *The Politics of Equality* (Chicago: University of Chicago Press, 1948); *The Great Issues of Politics* (New York: Prentice-Hall, 2nd ed., 1960).

ROBERT M. MAC IVER, *The Web of Government* (New York: Macmillan, 1947).

SALVADOR DE MADARIAGA, *Spain* (New York: Scribner's, 1930).

HOWARD LEE MC BAIN, *The Living Constitution* (New York: Macmillan, 1927).

CHARLES H. MC ILWAIN, *Constitutionalism, Ancient and Modern* (Ithaca: Cornell University Press, 1940).

ALEXANDER MEIKLEJOHN, *Free Speech and Its Relation to Self-Government* (New York: Harper's, 1948).

RAMSAY MUIR, *How Britain Is Governed* (London: Constable, 1930).

BENITO MUSSOLINI, *The Political and Social Doctrine of Fascism.*

GUNNAR MYRDAL, *The American Dilemma* (New York: Harper's, 1944).

FRANZ NEUMANN, *The Democratic and the Authoritarian State* (Glencoe: Free Press, 1957).

SIGMUND NEUMANN, ed., *Modern Political Parties* (Chicago: University of Chicago Press, 1956).

PETER H. ODEGARD and E. ALLEN HELMS, *American Politics* (New York: Harper's, 1947).

JOSÉ ORTEGA Y GASSET, *The Revolt of the Masses.*

J. ROLAND PENNOCK, *Liberal Democracy* (New York: Rinehart, 1950).

A. F. POLLARD, *The Evolution of Parliament* (London: Longman's Green, 1920).

WILLIAM E. RAPPARD, *La Constitution Fédérale de la Suisse* (Neuchâtel: à la Baconnière, 1948).

ALF ROSS, *Why Democracy?* (Harvard University Press, 1952).

BERTRAND RUSSELL, *Authority and the Individual* (New York: Simon and Schuster, 1949).

JOSEPH A. SCHUMPETER, *Capitalism, Socialism and Democracy* (New York: Harper, 1942).

ERNEST D. SIMON, *The Smaller Democracies* (London: Gollancy, 1939).

J. L. TALMON, *The Origins of Totalitarian Democracy* (New York: Praeger, 1960).

R. H. TAWNEY, *Religion and the Rise of Capitalism* (New York: Harcourt Brace, 1920); *Equality* (New York: Harcourt Brace, 1931).

DAVID THOMSON, *Democracy in France* (London: Oxford University Press, 4th ed., 1964).

ARNOLD J. TOYNBEE, *A Study of History* (Oxford University Press, 11 vols., 1954-59).

G. M. TREVELYAN, *British History in the Nineteenth Century* (London: Longman's Green, 1923).

LEON TROTSKY, *History of the Russian Revolution.*

JOSEPH TUSSMAN, *Obligation and the Body Politic* (New York: Oxford University Press, 1960).

MAX WEBER, *The Protestant Ethic and the Spirit of Capitalism.*

Index

599